The Dai

HONEST JOHN'S
**MOTORING
YEARBOOK**
2001–2002

The Daily Telegraph

Honest John's

MOTORING YEARBOOK

2001–2002

ROBINSON

London

Constable & Robinson Ltd
3 The Lanchesters
162 Fulham Palace Road
London W6 9ER

www.constablerobinson.com

First published by Robinson Publishing Ltd 1997
This edition published by Robinson,
an imprint of Constable & Robinson Ltd 2001

A copy of the British Library Cataloguing in Publication Data is
available from the British Library

ISBN 1–84119–416–6

Designed and typeset by WordSpace, Lewes, East Sussex

Printed and bound in the EU

10 9 8 7 6 5 4 3 2 1

Contents

About me

I don't have time to do much buying and selling any more. But I keep my BCA account running just in case. And I still get down to the auctions at least once a week to check what the market is doing for the website news.

My first contact with the motor trade was in 1959 when I started cleaning cars for Ron at Sports Motors on Orpington High Street. Ron's stock included a 1926 AC roadster at £225, a 1930 Austin Nippy at £90, a 1932 Lagonda 2-litre two-seat special at £225, a 1938 Jaguar SS 100 at £275. (Multiply by 100–250 to find out just what an investment some of this older stuff has been.) Ron also had comparatively modern cars, such as a pair of 1949 Riley two-seat Roadsters, MGAs, TR2s, a Buckler, a Berkeley and a gigantic Buick. Sports Motors folded in 1960 but Pete the Painter's murals remain to this day, hidden behind the dry-lined walls of the carpet shop that replaced it.

I bought my first car in 1964, and did my first deal the year after when I sold it. The car was a 1959 BMW Isetta 300, spotted rocking gently on the roof of a fabric-bodied Alvis 12/50 saloon in Shire Ted's scrapyard. The car duly arrived on the end of a rope behind a 1938 Oldsmobile and, being the canny man he was, Ted gave me £2 back from my £20. Reconstruction began, test runs were undertaken round the go-kart track in a rich neighbour's garden. A year later I sold it for £60.

Further gains (and losses) were made on a 1959 Riley 1.5 bought for £250, a 1942 Ford Jeep, bought for £20, a Thames Camper bought for £175, a modified Minivan bought for £125, a 1949 Rover P3 bought for £40, a Wolseley Hornet, and plenty of other tackle, including a rear-engined Renault and a two-stroke Saab. Then, starting by writing the ads for a Rolls Royce dealer, I got into advertising.

Four years of this was spent conveniently close to London's

About Me

Warren Street, where I shared bank, pubs and caffs with the street's car traders and did a few deals on Simcas, Minis, VW Beetles, 2CVs, Fiats and Alfas. Apart from a pair of D&AD pencils, I have to admit I never really made it in adland. The recession didn't help. Then, deep in the midst of the Gulf War, I had a brainwave. I would start a completely new type of car magazine about nothing but used cars. The aim was simply to flog it for £10,000 and carry on in the ad game, but instead I got hooked into freelancing features for car magazines. Since this involved reporting on car auctions, watching wasn't enough. Before long, I was back to buying cars and turning them round – retail, trade or on commission – to supplement the mag money into enough to live on.

For four months I commuted between London, Amsterdam and Nice, working on pan-European launches for the Mazda Xedos 6 and RX7. Then it was back to buying and selling, a column in *Car Week*, and an auction column in *Telegraph Motoring*. Life was moving along quite nicely. Then, at a contributor's Christmas party in a room above a pub in Soho, my editor Eric Bailey had an idea.

I'd arrived fresh from an auction where I'd spent £17,250 on three Vauxhalls in the space of twenty minutes, then put them each out at a mere £250 earn. Eric thought, '£250 a car. He's far too honest for that game', and 'Honest John' was born.

In the ancient tradition of all agony columns, the first questions were made up and ran on the back cover of *Telegraph Motoring* on 21 January 1995. The response was phenomenal. Within months I was answering up to 150 real letters a week. By year three, it sometimes hit 500. By year four, I'd even got myself onto the television. And at the time of writing this short personal history, the total number of letters and e-mails has risen to more than 40,000.

Honest John

Frequently Asked Questions

Honest John's mailbag contains hundreds of letters and emails each week, but the vast majority of them ask the same questions. The most popular ones are reproduced below.

In addition, Honest John's Scratchpad, on p. 36, contains a collection of useful addresses and internet links.

Here is an index of the twenty-nine most Frequently Asked Questions.

1 Cheapest places to buy

"Where are the cheapest places to buy new and nearly-new cars in the UK?"

Motorpoint, Chartwell Drive, West Meadows, Derby; tel: 01332 347357, website: www.motorpoint.co.uk.

Trade Sales of Slough, 353–357 Bath Road, Slough, Berks SL1 6JA; tel: 01753 773763; website: www.trade-sales.co.uk.

Motorhouse 2000, Wryly Brook Retail Park, Walkmill lane, Cannock WS11 3XE; tel: 01543 462300; website: www.motorhouse2000ltd.co.uk.

The Car People; tel: 01924 887654; website: www.thecarpeople.co.uk.

CP Motor Company; tel: 01443 218400; website: www.cpmotors.co.uk.

The Great Trade Centre, Hythe Road (off Scrubbs Lane: continuation of Wood Lane), White City, London NW10 6JR; tel: 020 8969 5511; website: www.greattradecentre.co.uk.

Fords of Winsford, Wharton Retail Park, Weaver Valley Road, Winsford, Cheshire; tel: 0845 345 1016; website: www.fow.co.uk.

2 Import specialists and car supermarkets

"Can you provide me with a list of specialists who supply cars at prices which more closely reflect mainland European prices?"

On-line import specialists with supersites

Motorpoint, Chartwell Drive, West Meadows, Derby; tel: 0870 1209611; website: www.motorpoint.co.uk.

Trade Sales of Slough, 353–357 Bath Road, Slough, Berks SL1 6JA; tel: 0870 127 3763; website: www.trade-sales.co.uk.

Motorhouse 2000, Wryly Brook Retail Park, Walkmill lane, Cannock WS11 3XE; tel: 01543 462300; website: www.motorhouse2000ltd.co.uk.

The Car People; tel: 01924 887654; website: www.thecarpeople.co.uk.

CP Motor Company; tel: 01443 218400; website: www.cpmotors.co.uk.

On-line import and discount UK-supplied specialists

(Note that NONE of these are checked out. This is merely information. You use it entirely at your own risk.)

www.showroom4cars.com
www.broker4cars.com
www.autoaalbersonline.com or **www.autoaalbers.co.uk**

www.broadspeed.com
www.carbusters.com
www.virgincars.com
www.alliancecarimports.co.uk
www.cancelledorders.com
www.oneswoop.com (£10 search fee)
www.autohit.com
www.carpricecheck.com (compares a basket of prices, not all)
www.paragon-euro.com
www.jamjar.com
www.eurekar.com
www.tins.co.uk
www.carimportsuk.com
www.micronetshowroom.com
www.wundercars.co.uk
www.carfaxinternational.com
www.marketvehicles.com
www.brownsnw.com
www.bobgerard.co.uk
www.newcarimportservices.com
www.pentagoncars.com
www.carpartnership.com
www.ford-calais.com

Nearly new and used car buying supersites

Motorpoint, Chartwell Drive, West Meadows, Derby; tel: 0870 1209611; website: www.motorpoint.co.uk.

Trade Sales of Slough, 353–357 Bath Road, Slough, Berks SL1 6JA; tel: 0870 127 3763; website: www.trade-sales.co.uk.

Motorhouse 2000, Wryly Brook Retail Park, Walkmill lane, Cannock WS11 3XE; tel: 0845 345 6777; website: www.motorhouse2000ltd.co.uk.

The Great Trade Centre, Hythe Road (off Scrubbs Lane: continuation of Wood Lane), White City, London NW10 6JR; tel: 020 8969 5511; website: www.greattradecentre.co.uk.

Fords of Winsford, Wharton Retail Park, Weaver Valley Road, Winsford, Cheshire; tel: 0845 345 1016; website: www.fow.co.uk.

Stephen Rayns Ltd, Leicester; tel: 0116 261 2200.

Fleetlease Direct, Union House, Kennetside Industrial Estate (off Bone Lane), Newbury, Berks RG14 5PX; tel: 0800 294 1948; website: www.fleetleasedirect.co.uk.

Used car buying websites
www.autotrader.co.uk
www.ixM.co.uk
www.CarChase.co.uk
www.fish4cars.co.uk
www.autohit.com
www.autolocate.co.uk
www.used-car-buyer.co.uk

Independent import warranties
www.carimportwarranty.com

Independent import finance
www.carfinance4less.com
www.currencies4less.com
a-plan; tel: 0845 071 1234

3 Personal imports

"I want to personally import a car from Europe. What do I need to know?"

a Get the relevant Government booklets and forms. First phone the DVLA on 01792 772134 and ask for the pack on personal imports. This includes: the booklet 'How to Import a Vehicle Permanently into Great Britain'; Form V100, which explains registering and licensing procedures and gives a list of Vehicle Registration Offices; and Form V55/5, which is an application form to license a vehicle in the UK for the first time. (Alternatively, phone the DETR on 0207

676 2094, write to DETR VSE1, Zone 2/01, Great Minster House, 76 Marsham Street, London SW1 4DR, or visit the DETR website at: www.roads.detr.gov.uk). Then phone your local VAT enquiry line, listed under 'Customs & Excise' in the telephone directory, and ask for the 'VAT Notice 728 Pack' which includes form VAT 415, 'New Means of Transport – Notification of Acquisition'. (Please don't phone Customs & Excise on either 020 7864 3000 or 01304 224372, as these lines have become overwhelmed with enquiries.)

b Decide which makes and models you are interested in and obtain the UK brochures for these cars. Then phone the manufacturers' UK customer helpline, asking for a current list of continental service dealers.
c Choose the car and specification you want, then start phoning. When you find a receptive dealer, fax the exact specification of car you want and ask for a quote, to include temporary registration and export plates. The best countries to buy in are likely to be Holland, Belgium, Germany and France. Remember, if you buy in Europe, you will be buying a Europe-spec. car with RHD as an extra. Other things, such as a radio, tinted glass, alarm/immobiliser (and seven seats in an MPV), may be extras too.

d Order your car from the dealer offering the best combination of price and delivery date. Delivery could easily be 6 to 8 months for a car such as a VW, Mercedes Benz or Alfa Romeo. You will be asked to pay a deposit of between 10 and 30 per cent on receipt of order, either by credit card, Switch or by international bank credit transfer. Make sure the dealer faxes, e-mails or posts you a receipt for this and a confirmation of your order.

e Decide on whether you are going to gamble on Sterling rising or falling against the currency in which you will be buying the car. If you gamble on Sterling rising, leave your funds in a high-interest Sterling account. If you gamble on Sterling falling, open a Foreign Currency Call Account at your bank. This is a deposit account in a foreign currency offering interest based on the much lower base rates for the foreign currency.

f Keep in touch with the dealer by phone, fax or e-mail to make sure your order is being processed. Within two months of the delivery date, start asking for a scheduled build date for your car.

g Once the dealer gives you a delivery date, ask him to arrange temporary insurance for you to drive the car back (this insurance will be Third Party only). A new EU rule now requires you to insure the car in the country of purchase. But if you want to arrange additional comprehensive insurance on the Vehicle Identification Number (VIN) from the point of purchase back to the UK, speak to Footman James on 0121 561 4196. Then organise your flight out and ferry back, and arrange for a bank draft to pay for the car.

h When you go to collect the car, inspect it carefully to make sure it complies with the specification you have ordered. Make sure the dealer gives you: a Certificate of Conformity to European Type Approval (a 'C of C'); a Registration Certificate naming you as the keeper; an insurance document to prove the car was insured in the country of origin (often combined with the temporary registra-

9

tion); and, of course, the dealer's invoice. Make sure you buy some petrol in the country of origin and keep the receipt. Keep any hotel and restaurant receipts. And keep the ferry ticket.

i As soon as possible (this must be within seven days of arriving back in the UK with your new car), fill in the form 'New Means of Transport – Notification of Acquisition' (Appendix 'D') which came with VAT 728, and take it, together with completed form C55/5, the dealer's invoice, foreign registration document, the Certificate of Type Approval Conformity, your petrol receipts and any other foreign receipts to prove you have driven the car abroad, your ferry ticket and your UK insurance certificate based on the VIN number, to your nearest Vehicle Registration Office. On payment of a £25 first registration fee, and either six months' or twelve months' VED, the VRO will issue you with a registration number and a VED disc. The date of first registration will now be the date the car was first registered in the UK, provided this is within 14 days of the purchase date, or within 30 days of the purchase date if this immediately precedes a registration letter change. Your V5 registration document will then be sent to you from Swansea.

j The VRO will send form NMT – Notification of Acquisition – on to Customs & Excise, who will then send you invoice VAT 413 for UK VAT at 17.5 per cent of the cost of the car, which you have 30 days to settle. Once settled, you will receive a receipted VAT 413.

k Order a set of plates. Phone the manufacturer's customer helpline to put the car on the manufacturer's UK data bank for warranty purposes and in case of any recalls. Though Customs & Excise only insist you keep the purchase invoice and the receipted VAT for 6 years as proof that VAT has been paid, it's advisable to keep all the documentation, including petrol receipts and ferry tickets, in a safe place with them to pass on to the new owner when you sell the car.

Imports from outside the EU
On 1 August 2000 the Government announced that it was to relax SVA quotas, which had previously restricted trade imports of non-

EU Type Approved vehicles to a total of 50 a year for any one make and model. These quota restrictions were lifted as from 18 August 2000. By January 2001, personal import rules were tightened up so that only people who have lived overseas for more than a year and owned the car overseas for more than six months can bring it to the UK as a personal import which, if it is more than 3 years old, is not subject to a Single Vehicle Approval test. All other imports up to ten years old will be subject to the SVA test.

4 Advertising privately

"Which are the best websites at which to advertise a car I want to sell?"

www.autotrader.co.uk (£7.50 for a fortnight)
www.ixM.co.uk
www.loot.com
www.classic-car-mart.co.uk (for classic and collectors' cars)
www.fish4cars.co.uk
www.CarChase.co.uk
www.autohit.com
www.autolocate.co.uk
www.used-car-buyer.co.uk

If you are not connected, then buy a copy of your local *Autotrader* oe *Exchange & Mart* for appropriate advertising rates and forms, use your local newspaper, and don't neglect postcards in newsagents' windows.

5 Manufacturers' websites

"Do you have a list of car manufacturers' websites and brochure lines?"

It follows, in alphabetical order.

AC CAR GROUP LTD www.accars.co.uk; Brochure-line: 01932 336033.

AIXAM LTD Brochure-line 01926 886100.

ALFA ROMEO (GB) LTD www.alfaromeo.co.uk; Brochure-line: 0800 718000.

ASTON MARTIN LAGONDA LTD www.astonmartin.co.uk; Brochure-line: 01908 610620.

AUDI UK www.audi.co.uk (Used cars: www.audi.co.uk/usedcars) Brochure-line: 0345 699777.

BENTLEY www.rolls-royceandbentley.co.uk; Tel: 01270 255155.

BMW (GB) LTD www.bmw.co.uk; Brochure-line: 0800 325600.

BRISTOL CARS www.bristolcars.co.uk; HQ tel: 020 7603 5554.

CADILLAC www.cadillaceurope.com; UK HQ tel: 01582 721122.

CATERHAM www.caterham.co.uk; Brochure-line: 07000 00 0077.

CHEVROLET www.chevroleteurope.com; UK HQ tel: 01582 721122.

CHRYSLER JEEP IMPORTS UK www.chryslerjeep.co.uk (Used cars: www.genuinejeep.co.uk); Brochure-line: 0800 616159.

CITROËN (UK) LTD www.citroen.co.uk; Brochure-line: 0800 262262.

DAEWOO CARS LTD www.daewoo-cars.co.uk; Brochure-line: 0800 666222.

DAIHATSU (UK) LTD www.daihatsu.co.uk; Brochure-line 0800 521700.

FERRARI www.ferrari.co.uk; Tel: 01784 436222.

FIAT AUTO (UK) LTD www.fiat.co.uk; Brochure-line: 0800 717000.

FORD MOTOR CO. LTD www.ford.co.uk (Used cars: www.forddirect. co.uk); Brochure-line: 0345 111888.

HONDA (UK) LTD www.honda.co.uk; Brochure-line: 0345 159159.

HYUNDAI CAR (UK) LTD www.hyundai-car.co.uk; Brochure-line: 0800 981981.

ISUZU (UK) LTD www.isuzu.co.uk; Brochure-line: 0990 100586.

JAGUAR CARS LTD www.jaguar.co.uk; Brochure-line: 0800 708060.

KIA (UK) LTD www.kia.co.uk; Brochure-line: 0800 775777.

LAMBORGHINI www.lamborghini.co.uk; Tel: 0118 925 2870.

LAND ROVER LTD www.landrover.co.uk; Brochure-line: 0800 110110.

LEXUS c/o Toyota GB www.lexus.co.uk; Brochure-line: 0800 343434.

LIGIER c/o Reliant Cars Ltd www.reliant-motors.co.uk; Brochure-line: 01543 459222.

LOTUS CARS LTD www.lotuscars.co.uk; HQ tel: 01953 608000.

MASERATI www.maserati.co.uk; Brochure-line: 01784 436222.

MAZDA CARS (UK) LTD www.mazda.co.uk; Brochure-line: 0345 484848.

MCC SMART www.thesmart.co.uk; Brochure-line: 0800 037 9966.

MERCEDES-BENZ www.mercedes-benz.co.uk and www.mercedesretail.co.uk (Used cars: www.directmercedes.co.uk) Brochure-line: 020 7536 3540.

MG CARS www.mg-cars.com; Brochure-line: 0800 620820.

MICROCAR UK HQ tel: 01789 730095.

MINI www.mini.co.uk.

MITSUBISHI www.mitsubishi-cars.co.uk; Brochure-line; 0845 0702000.

MORGAN MOTOR CAR CO www.morgan-motor.co.uk; Brochure-line: 01684 573104.

NISSAN MOTOR LTD www.nissan.co.uk; Brochure-line: 0345 669966.

PERODUA UK LTD Tel: 020 8961 1255.

PEUGEOT MOTOR CO PLC www.peugeot.co.uk; Brochure-line: 0345 565556.

PORSCHE CARS (GB) LTD www.porsche.co.uk; Brochure-line: 08457 911911.

PROTON CARS (UK) LTD www.proton.co.uk; Brochure-line: 0800 0521 521.

RELIANT www.reliant-motors.co.uk; Brochure-line: 01543 459222.

RENAULT (UK) LTD www.renault.co.uk; Brochure-line: 0800 525150.

ROLLS-ROYCE www.rolls-royceandbentley.co.uk; Tel: 01270 255155.

ROVER CARS www.rovergroup.co.uk; Brochure-line: 0800 620820.

SAAB (GB) LTD www.saab.co.uk; Brochure-line: 0800 626556.

SEAT UK www.seat-cars.co.uk (Used cars: www.seat-cars.co.uk/usedcars) Brochure-line: 0500 222222.

SKODA UK www.skoda.co.uk (Used cars: www.skoda.co.uk/usedcars) Brochure-line: 0845 774 5745.

SUBARU (UK) LTD www.subaru.co.uk; Brochure-line: 0990 100568.

SUZUKI GB PLC www.suzuki.co.uk; Brochure-line: 01892 100568.

TATA www.tata-telco.com; Brochure-line: 01262 402200.

TOYOTA GB LTD www.toyota.co.uk; Brochure-line: 0800 777555.

TVR ENGINEERING LTD www.tvr-eng.co.uk; Brochure-line: 01253 509055.

VAUXHALL MOTORS LTD www.vauxhall.co.uk (Used cars: www.networkq.co.uk) Brochure-line: 0345 400800.

VOLKSWAGEN www.volkswagen.co.uk (Used cars: www.volkswagen.co.uk/usedcars) Brochure-line: 0800 333666.

VOLVO CAR UK LTD www.volvocars.co.uk; Brochure-line: 0800 400430.

WESTFIELD www.westfield-sportscars.co.uk; Brochure-line 01384 400077.

6 A replacement for four-star

"I have an older car designed to run on four-star leaded petrol. What should I be using now?"

If your car is post-1990 it should be capable of running on unleaded petrol of the correct octane without any additives. Nearly all

1980s Japanese cars or 1980s cars with Japanese engines are designed to run on unleaded. Many cars with aluminium cylinder heads have been fitted with hard exhaust valve seat inserts made of chrome steel rather than cast iron.

The oil companies have agreed that all UK Lead Replacement Petrol (LRP) will contain potassium instead of lead, now dosed at 10 to 12 mg per litre (which may still not be enough to properly protect the exhaust valve seats). If your car has a compression ratio of 9:1 or higher, you may find it both cheaper and safer to run your car on premium unleaded (always the same brand), octane-boosted with exactly the correct quantity of either Castrol Valvemaster Plus (phosphorus-based, from Halfords) or Millers VSP Plus or Carplan Nitrox 4-Lead (both manganese-based – the favoured additive in Canada).

If your car has a compression ratio of less than 9:1, you can use 95Ron unleaded petrol (preferably Shell or Texaco) dosed with a wider choice of additives which include: standard Valvemaster (phosphorus-based), Millers VSP Plus (manganese-based), Superblend Zero Lead 2000 (potassium-based), Nitrox 4-Star (potassium-based), Redline (sodium-based) or Wynns (sodium-based). (**Please note** Sodium can damage turbochargers. Never mix petrol containing one LRP additive with petrol containing another, and never overdose it. Never mix manganese-based Nitrox 4-Lead with potassium-based Nitrox 4-Star.)

If your engine has hard exhaust valve seats but is unhappy on 95Ron or even 97Ron petrol, you can boost the octane from 95 to 97+ and from 97 to 98+ by using Millers Octane +. This costs around £3.00 for enough to boost 40 to 50 litres of petrol.

Castrol (Valvemaster): 01793 452222
Superblend: 0116 291 1700
Redline: 01732 866885
Millers: 0800 281 053
Carplan Nitrox: 0161 764 5981.

All the additives mentioned have been extensively lab-tested and approved by the FBHVC at the Motor Industry Research Association.

7 Four-star availability

"Where can I still find four star leaded petrol?"

You will find a full list at www.bayfordthrust.co.uk. and in every issue of *Classic Car Weekly* magazine.

8 Conversion to LPG

"Where can I get my car converted to run on LPG?"

UK LPG (Liquified Petroleum Gas) is wellhead gas, rather than refined from crude oil, and current estimates are that there is enough under the North Sea to last 40 to 60 years.

There is now a standard conversion of the Perkins 180 diesel engine for buses and trucks, enabling them to run on LPG at the increased consumption rate of 25 to 50 per cent, but using a fuel which is less than half the price of diesel. Typical conversion costs for cars and vans can be found at (www.est-powershift.org.uk). New Citroën Xantias, Ford Mondeos, Vauxhall Vectras and Volvos with LPG conversions all qualify. The LP Gas Association (tel: 01425 461612; website: www.lpga.co.uk) can recommend LPGA-accredited converters whose conversions on new cars qualify for the Powershift grant. Without the benefit of the grant, conversions for older vehicles cost between £850 and £2,000. Tanks are available to fit the car's spare wheel well.

LPG Conversion specialists include: Autogas 2000 of Thirsk, tel: 01845 523213; Autogas Conversion Co. of Hythe, Kent, tel: 01303 840901/07970 919092, email: gasman@autogas.fsnet.co.uk; Hendy Lennox Ltd of Chandlers Ford, tel: 02380 363301; Key Autogas of Leicester, tel: 0116 2608813; Marine Ecopower Ltd of Lymington, tel: 01590 688444; Autogas Northwest Ltd of Frodsham, Warrington, tel: 01928 787110; Millennium Autogas of Basingstoke, tel: 07771 993459; and LPG Auto Power UK of Bradford, tel: 01274 729425.

The Natural Gas Vehicle Association, tel: 020 7388 7598, can supply a list of CNG (Compressed Natural Gas) 'Gas Stations'. The phone number for British Gas for vehicles is: 01784 646030. The Autogas Installers and Retailers Association (01663 732030) claims to supply 'the only completely accurate and up-to-date list of outlets'.

9 Microcars: what's the story?

"I have seen some tiny cars in France and Spain, which must surely represent the answer to reducing urban pollution for those who only need or want to travel short distances. Can you tell us more?"

Reliant is now importing Ligier microcars from France. They are right-hand-drive, UK and Euro Type Approved, have 505cc 2-cylinder Lombardini petrol or diesel engines and open-belt Variomatic transmission. In de-restricted UK specification, they should have a top speed of 55 to 65mph and give 65 to 85mpg. They should also qualify for an extremely low CO_2-based rate of VED from October. And, after changes in licence regulations in 1996, they can also be driven on the same motorcycle licence as a Reliant three-wheeler. Price from £6,495. More details from Reliant Cars Ltd, Cannock Road, Chase Terrace, Burntwood, Staffs WS7 8GB, tel: 01543 459222; fax: 01543 459444. Reliant is also importing Piaggio Ape micro pick-up trucks and vans and will probably take on the cheaper Ligier Due Microcar in the near future. A second microcar contender is Aixam Ltd, Units 2 & 3, Tachbrook Link, Tachbrook Park Drive, Royal Leamington Spa, Warwick, tel: 01926 886100. Aixam has been building microcars since 1975 and offers a range of convertibles and two- and four-seater hatchbacks with diesel engines from 276cc to 479cc. The UK range is all RHD and is powered by the 479cc Kubota diesel engine which gives up to 55mph and up to 90mpg. Prices start at £6,530 on the road with a year's VED for the 2-seater Utility, or £6,630 OTR for the 4-seater Economy, rising to £8,050 for the 4-seater Super. Ex-Reliant Boss Jonathan Heynes is importing a range of right-hand-drive fibreglass monocoque models called Microcar Virgo. These are available with two seats, 505cc petrol or diesel Lombardini engines giving up to 68mph and up to 80mpg, and cost from £5,995 on the road, including a 3-year warranty: Microcar UK, Park House, The Grange, Wolverton, Stratford-on-Avon CV37 0HD, tel: 01789 730094. Other microcar makers include JRD and Erad, who will be watching the UK market to see how sales go. We shouldn't forget the LHD 599cc 6-speed 87mph MCC SMART car, now also available as a 799cc common rail direct-injected diesel or a convertible, from MB UK, at prices from £5,995, tel: 0800 037 9966; or from KSB MotorGroup, website: www.ksb.co.uk. New on the scene is the American 'Sparrow', a single-seater three-wheeler electric microcar capable of up to 70mph, but costing £8,750. Finally, the incredible two-seater 50cc three-wheeler and 350cc four-wheeler Fun Tech buggies seen at the Barcelona Motor Show can now be obtained in the UK from SMC Scooters of Torquay, tel 01803 200670 or Fun Tech UK on 01803 666610, website: www.fun-tech.co.uk; prices £2,995 and £3,995.

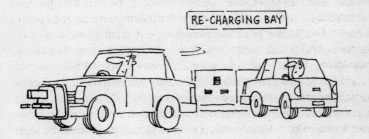

RE-CHARGING BAY

10 Electric cars

"Have any of the car manufacturers cracked the electric car nut yet? Our two cars cover around 5,000 miles each a year, almost exclusively on three miles of country lanes to and from work. As you keep saying, a vehicle with an internal combustion engine is entirely unsuitable for this sort of use."

Ford's contribution to the urban environment, first seen at 1999 Frankfurt Motor Show, is the Think City. A small, two-seater plastic-bodied car less than 3 metres long, the Think reaches 30mph in 7 seconds and has a top speed of 56mph. Power is from 19 NiCd batteries and the car's range is 53 miles. More information is available at these websites:: www.thinkmobility.com and www.think-aboutlondon.co.uk.

Alternative Vehicles Technology (AVT) has written to say that it offers 'affordable electric cars'. Unfortunately, 'affordable' is only relative, because its 'lowest-cost complete conversion' works out at £5,500 including batteries and charger but excluding the cost of the car to be converted – either a Mini or the old-model, sump-gearbox Metro, now at least nine years old. However, kits are available for home conversions from £2,995, excluding charger and batteries. The company also offers a conversion of the later and better Rover Metro or Rover 100, and of micro-vans, including the Bedford Rascal, Daihatsu Hijet and Suzuki Supercarry. AVT is in the process of developing its own AVT 100E electric car, but quotes prices from £16,995 to £19,995, plus batteries which cost from £1,481 to £2,070, including VAT. AVT claims top speeds from 56mph for its £16,995 plus battery PM2 model, to 'over 120mph' for its £17,996 plus battery S192 model. The theory of electric cars is spot-on for people who use their cars for short journeys only, a job for which internal combustion engines are particularly unsuited. Unfortunately, as yet, AVT's complete vehicle prices are still too high to attract the levels of interest that the vehicles themselves should justify. AVT can be contacted at Blue Lias House, Station Road, Hatch Beauchamp, Somerset TA3 6SQ, tel: 01823 480196, website: www.avt.uk.com. The Electric Car Association also operates from the same offices. There have been unfavourable reports on Varta semi-traction batteries, and you would be advised to source batteries from a British supplier instead. For more advice on electric vehicles, contact The Electric Vehicle Society on 01933 276618, website: www.evn.co.uk, and the Battery Vehicle Society on 01258 455470.

11 Reversing aids

"I am trying to locate an electronic car reversing aid which warns a driver of unseen obstacles in the path of a reversing car. I am told such products exist, but no motoring store appears to stock them. How reliable are these devices and where can they be obtained?"

Auto Express magazine tested a range of these devices in issue 646. The one they rated best value was the Quanan 2030 at £89.50 including post and packing, from Cleargate Ltd, tel: 0870 729 3949. Next, scoring four stars, came last year's winner: Autosonics' Backminder at a price of £160 for the DIY kit, including P&P, VAT

and a drill bit, tel: 01259 217004 (website: www.autosonics.co.uk). Next, also scoring four stars, was Safety Eye at £83.98 including p&p, from APS Marketing on 01341 450690. Next, scoring three stars, the C-Back at around £150 from Dutch Company CPL at 0031 621 532 726 (website: www.c-back.com). Next, with three stars, Ultrapark at an expensive £339.57 from Laver Technology, tel: 01279 436080. Next, with three stars, the Cobra ParkMaster 0166 at £170, including installation, from Ital Audio, tel: 01923 240525. Next, also with three stars, the Meta SR2C at £249 including installation, from Metasystem UK, tel 01905 791700. Next, the VTD MB4 at £293.75 installed from Toad VTD, tel 01928 570500 (website: www.toadplc.com). Finally, the Meta SR2C Targa at £249 installed, from Metasystem UK, tel: 01905 791700.

Another product which uses coloured lights as well as 'beeps' was originally designed for reversing caravans. It is made by Brigade Electronics, is called the 'Backscan RI-OS', costs around £200 installed and worked well when fitted as an optional extra to a Ford Scorpio I tried. Brigade Electronics can be contacted on 020 8852 3261.

12 Running in

"I have just bought a new car. What is your advice about running it in and changing the oil for the first time?"

To run a car engine in, it is vital to vary engine speeds during the first 1,000 to 4,000 miles. If you are cruising on a motorway, vary your cruising speed by 10 to 20 mph every 15 minutes or so. Don't over-rev the engine, but don't under-rev it either. Never labour the engine by driving in too high a gear. Unless it is a super-high-performance car, current thinking is to leave the factory filled oil in the engine for the first 12 months or 10,000 miles in order to promote some wear and enable the piston rings and bores to bed themselves in. After that, change the engine oil and filter and consider switching from the semi-synthetic oil the car came with to fully synthetic. Also, have the manual gearbox oil changed to get rid of any swarf thrown off while the box was bedding itself in before the swarf grinds itself into minute particles which get into the bearings and shorten their lives.

13 Fluid and cambelt change intervals

"Nowadays some car manufacturers are specifying oil changes at 12,500-mile or two-year intervals, and give no indication of when things like timing belts should be changed. What is your advice?"

After the first year or 10,000 miles, whichever comes first, I recommend using either a good semi-synthetic oil such as Texaco Havoline 5w/30 (Ford dealer 'bulk' oil), or a fully-synthetic such as Mobil 1, and changing it every 5,000 miles or every six months, whichever comes first. If you are a higher-mileage driver doing 15,000 miles a year or more, consider stretching your oil changes to 6,000 miles. If you do 25,000 miles or more and use fully-synthetic oil, consider stretching to 7,500 miles but no further. Always change the filter as well. Change the manual gearbox oil once after the first 12 to 18 months, or 10,000 to 15,000 miles. Change the coolant every 3 years if it is an MEG coolant, or every 4 years if it is an MPG coolant. Change the brake fluid every 2 years unless it is Dot 5 silicon brake fluid (unlikely on a mass-produced car). If the engine has a timing belt, change that every 3 to 4 years or every 40,000 miles, whichever comes first, unless the engine has no history of premature timing belt failures. (Ford Zetec E and Zetec S engine timing belts generally exceed their design life of 80,000 miles, so can be changed at 5 years or 80,000 miles, whichever comes first.) Change the timing belt tensioner and any weeping camshaft or jackshaft oil seals at 80,000 miles (every second timing belt change for non-Ford Zetecs).

14 Aircon maintenance

"Does my car's air-conditioning system last forever, or does it need servicing?"

You should leave the a/c on all the time, even if not using it to cool the car. You should also turn the system to full cold for ten minutes once a week – even through the winter if you can – in order to circulate refrigerant which contains lubricants for the system and its seals. Then switch to full heat through the same pipes to thoroughly dry them out. This also blows out any moisture in the ventilation passages where mould and bacteria might be accumulating.

Opinions are divided on servicing. Aircon specialists looking for business will tell you it needs servicing, preferably by a visit to an air-conditioning system specialist, every year. That way they can keep a record of how much gas is being lost from the system. But the only way to test the gas is to draw some off and lab-test it.

Re-gassing a typical air-conditioning system costs around £80 + VAT. A service and a new accumulator/dryer costs around £150 + VAT. Some a/c specialists argue that this needs to be done otherwise the silica gel dessicant in the dryer could break up and circulate through the system, severely damaging it. Refrigeration engineer Keith Wood believes that replacing the accumulator is not necessary and could be responsible for introducing harmful dirt or dust to the system. It

should only be replaced if the system has lost gas and needs to be re-gassed. In his opinion the only regular checks should be for leaks. A pool of water under the car is, of course, not the result of a leak but of condensation dripping off the condenser and is entirely normal.

The two main causes of failure are lack of gas and component breakdown. Low refrigerant means low lubricant, which is contained in the refrigerant, and this can lead to seals drying out, thus losing even more refrigerant and leading to failure of the compressor. Properly repairing a failed system is a four-figure job.

For more information, link to www.autoair.co.uk.

Air conditioning specialists include:
Coolair UK Ltd (guarantees its work), head office: Kingsley Road, Lincolnfields, Lincoln LN6 3TA, tel: 01522 682288, and ask for Emma Hayward or Nikki Miller to put you onto your local branch.

David Norton, Kingsfold Garage, Dorking Road, Kingsfold, West Sussex RH12 3SB, tel: 01403 750202.

Motor Climate, tel: 0121 766 5006.

Alpinair, 174 Honey Pot Lane, Stanmore, Middlesex, tel: 020 8204 9633.

Vehicle Air Conditioning Services, Service Centre: Unit 8, Wintersells Road, Byfleet, Weybridge, Surrey KT14 7LF; Parts: Unit A, 120 Oyster Lane, Byfleet, Surrey, tel: 01932 355825.

Vehvac Ltd, Fircroft Way, Edenbridge, Kent TN8 6AJ, tel: 01732 868080.

Halfords Garages (see local Yellow Pages for numbers).

Autoclimate, Battlefield Enterprise Park, March Way, Harlescott, Shrewsbury, SY1 3TE, tel: 01743 445566, website: www. autoclimate.com.

15 Making the change to automatic

"I am 80 years old and feel that I now need a car with automatic transmission. What do you advise?"

I think you may have left it too late to safely make the change. The problem with automatic transmission is that, unless the driver drives 'two footed', he or she has far less control over the car than over a manual – which is why we read of around 20 deaths a year caused by 'out of control' automatics. What usually happens is that during the engine's warm-up phase, or if the engine has been over-fuelling, the electronic control unit raises engine revs to above the point at which drive is taken up in the transmission, and the car starts to move. The driver may then panic, attempt to brake heavily, but hit the accelerator instead of the brake, and the car either crashes or runs someone over. (The phenomenon even has a name: 'Sudden Acceleration Syndrome'.) You cannot predict precisely when the car's ECU will increase revs independently, so my advice is to only buy an automatic if you can teach yourself to brake with your left foot at least while manoeuvring, which keeps the car fully under control. Skilled drivers left-foot-brake automatics – and even manuals – all the time, but not everyone can get their heads around the technique for everyday driving, especially if they switch between the two types of transmission.

16 Autobox specialists

"Could you recommend any automatic gearbox specialists prepared to service and rebuild automatic boxes rather than simply replace them?"

King Automatics, The Chalk Pit, College Road, Epsom, Surrey, tel: 01372 728769.

Automatic Transmissions (Tattersall), Tattersall Bridge, nr Coningsby, Lincoln, tel: 01526 342956.

17 ECU specialists

"Where can I have the Engine Control Unit of my car re-mapped or 'chipped' to give better performance? And where can I have my existing ECU tested for faults, and repaired rather than simply replaced?"

'Chipping' is the generic term for re-programming an engine's electronic management system for increased performance, different performance characteristics, better fuel economy, or to run on a lower grade of fuel. This can be done internally, by dismantling the engine ECU and either replacing or re-programming the chips inside, or externally, by altering the signals from the ECU to the fuel injection system and ignition igniter. Both petrol and turbo-diesel engines can be 'chipped'. Prices start at around £100, but are more usually in the £300 to £400 bracket. Practitioners include BBR of Brackley (petrol and diesel Starchips), tel: 01280 700800 (website: www.bbr.gti.demon.co.uk); Superchips of Buckingham (petrol and diesel), tel: 01280 816781 (website: www.superchips.co.uk); Milford Microsystems of Kidlington (system developments), tel: 01865 331552;

AMD, Oxon, tel: 01865 331226; Tim Styles Racing, Somerset, tel: 01278 453036; Siegerland (UK), tel: 0191 4286226 (website: www.tuningbox.com), Prima Racing, tel 0115 949 1903; Van Aaken Developments of Crowthorne, tel: 01344 777553 (website: www.vanaaken.com); Jetex of Stratford-upon-Avon, tel: 01789 298989 (website: www.jetexlimited.freeserve.co.uk); Webcon of Sunbury (Diesel Torqmaster), tel: 01932 788630 (Website: www.webcon.co.uk); Darley Specialist Services (Diesel Powerchip), tel 01332 553143.

ATP's Network 500 offers a nationwide ECU testing service, tel: 01543 467466. But remember, apparent ECU faults are often simply due to a poor contact in the multipin plug.

Carelect (website: www.carelect.demon.co.uk) offer a repair service for injection ECUs.

(**Please note** If you alter the specification of your car in any way you must inform your insurer or your insurance could be void.)

18 Speciality hire

"Where can I hire something special? A Ferrari, or a car which is completely out of the ordinary?"

The Classic Car Club is a sort of 'classic car timeshare', which costs £500 to join and then £1,750 a year. This gives access to around 40 days' hire of a range of 50 classic cars, from Fiats to Ferraris, according to the number of points per day required for each car. Tel: 020 7713 7313, fax: 020 7713 7316. A good classic car rental company is Bespokes on 020 8421 8686, fax: 020 8421 8588. Its fleet includes E-Types, older 911s, Aston Martins and Ferraris, at prices from £350 a day. It also does long-term contract hire. Modena offers Lotus, Ferrari and Porsche; tel: 01676 535596. Northern Sportscar Hire has a TVR Tuscan Speed Six, among others; tel: 01977 668068. Express Vehicle Rentals has Mercedes, BMW, Porsche, Lexus, Land Rover, Jeep, Jaguar and Audi; tel: 020 7383 3440, website: www.expressrentacar.co.uk. Eurostyle has Ferraris, TVRs, Porsche 996s, Porsche Boxters, Mercs and

BMWs, tel: 020 7624 1313, website: www.eurostyle.uk.com. Miles & Miles Prestige Car Rental offers new BMWs, Jaguars and Mercedes; tel: 020 7591 0555. Carriages Vehicle Agency offers a wide variety of 'classic' vehicles, from a 1920s Dennis bus, through 1930s Rolls Royces, to a 1970s VW Beetle cabriolet; tel: 01737 353926. Ray Tomkinson offers a range of 'classic taxis' from 1930s Austin Landaulettes to late 70s Checker Cabs; tel: 01204 533447. Hanwells of London W7 have a late-model RR and Bentley rental fleet; tel: 020 8567 9729, website: www.hanwells.com. Budget Rent-a-Car (now owned by Team Rental) aims to offer anything from a Harley Davidson motorcycle to a Jaguar XK8 convertible (see Yellow Pages). Euro Style in London offers TVRs, Boxters, SLKs, Range Rover 4.6HSEs and even a Bentley Azure; tel: 020 7624 1313. Tangerine (0800 975 7299) offers every kind of track day and off-road driving experience you can think of; tel: 0800 975 7299, website: www.tangerineuk.com.

(**Warning** If hiring a car for road use and paying a substantial deposit, inspect the car with a fine-tooth comb before taking delivery, so you cannot be charged for damage you did not do.)

19 Spare parts

"Which are the best sources for second-hand spare parts for cars?"

Find a Part One Call, tel: 0891 662706.

National Parts Locator, tel: 0800 525 030.

Premier Spares, tel: 0800 092 6700.

1st Choice Spares, tel: 0906 910 8400.

Universal Salvage, website: www.universal-salvage.com. Prices below trade, finance at 5.75 per cent flat, and option of warranty.

National Salvage, website: www.nsg.ltd.uk.

20 Changes to VED

"Please can you summarise the Vehicle Excise Duty (Road Tax) changes as from March 2001?"

The CO_2-based VED tax bands for new cars first registered on or after 1 March 2001 are as follows: up to 150g/km CO_2 the owner will pay £90 for a gas-fuelled car, £100 for a petrol-fuelled car or £110 for a diesel. Up to 165g/km the rates will be £110 for gas, £120 for petrol and £130 for diesel. Up to 185g/km the rates will be £130 for gas, £140 for petrol and £150 for diesel; and over 185g/km (anything from a Nissan Primera 1.6 at 186g/km to an Aston Martin V8 Vantage at 511g/km) the rates will be £150 for gas, £155 for petrol and £160 for diesel. From July 2001 all cars under 1,549cc qualify for the reduced £105 VED rate and this was backdated with rebates to November 2000. There is a website where you can find out how much tax will be due for your particular car at www.dvla.gov.uk/newved.htm, or you can obtain a leaflet by telephoning 0845 605 2222.

21 Benefit in kind tax on company cars

"Please can you summarise the changes to company car benefit in kind (BIK) tax from April 2002?"

This is the tax drivers of company cars pay for the benefit of their private use of the car. The system for calculating this tax will change from 6 April 2002 and there will no longer be any discount for high business mileage. Instead, drivers will be taxed on 15 per cent of the car's 'list price', with the tax base increasing by 1 per cent for each 5g/km CO_2 the car emits over and above 165g/km. For tax year 2003–2004, the base CO_2 will be 155g/km, and for tax year 2004–2005 the base CO_2 will be 145g/km. So, effectively, the tax base for a £15,000 car emitting 185g/km CO_2 will rise from 19 per cent (or £2,850) in 2002–2003 to 23 per cent (or £3,450) in 2004–2005. Because they emit less CO_2, diesels will be hit with a 3 per cent surcharge (though a diesel whose engine meets Euro-4 standards will be exempt from the surcharge), and no driver will be taxed on a base of more than 35 per cent of the car's list price. So, as with VED, there is no benefit to be had from driving a company car with an ultra-low CO_2 rating, even though the tax is supposed to be CO_2-based. Instead it has become a complicated banding exercise – though it does have the environmental benefit of abolishing discounts for high business miles. List prices and CO_2 tables and can be found in *What Car?* and *Diesel Car* magazines, but drivers will need to subtract registration tax and VED to arrive at the taxable 'list price'.

22 Car licensing system by area

Please can you summarise the new system of car licensing by area?

From 1 September 2001, vehicle registrations begin with one letter denoting the region, followed by one letter denoting the vehicle registration office (each VRO has 5 to 25 letters available, depending on how many of them there are in each region). This will be followed by two numbers giving the period of registration. In turn this will be followed by three random letters. So 'AA 51 ABC' will mean that the car was registered in the Anglia region at the Norwich VRO between 1 September 2001 and 28 February 2002, and is the only 'AA 51'-registered car with the random letters 'ABC'. Because of the twice-yearly registration change, the year figures get a bit complicated. 02 will mean 1 March 2002 to 31 August 2002; 52 will mean 1 September 2002 to 28 February 2003; 03 will mean 1 March 2003 to 31 August 2003; 53 will mean 1 September 2003 to 29 February 2004; and so on. The regional letters will be **A**: Anglia; **B**: Birmingham; **C**: Cymru; **D**: Deeside to Shrewsbury; **E**: Essex; **F**: Forest and Fens; **G**: Garden of England; **H**: Hampshire and Dorset; **K**: Luton; **L**: London; **M**: Manchester; **N**: North; **O**: Oxford; **P**: Preston; **R**: Reading; **S**: Scotland; **V**: Severn Valley; **W**: West Country; **Y**: Yorkshire.

23 Dent removal

"Where can I have minor damage to my car economically repaired?"

For minor dents of the supermarket carpark variety, call 'Dentmaster' (0800 433687), Paint Technik PDR (0800 298 5455) or 'Dent Devils' (0870 241 5679; website www.dentdevils.co.uk) who will put you onto their nearest operator. You might also check out S.M.A.R.T. Repair's website, www.smartrepair.com. DENTS 2 GO!!! is a mobile dent and light scratch removal service in South Wales and the South West. The repair needs no filling or painting. Call 07977 069149 or 01495 756985, or email leeburston@dents-2-go.co.uk (website: www.dents-2-go.co.uk).

For stone chips and upholstery repairs, try 'Chips Away' on 01562 755678. (Paint Technik also 'invisibly' repairs minor paint damage.)

For repairs to cracked or scratched plastic bumpers, call Plastic Technik on 01296 682105. For plastic trim and upholstery repairs call 'Magic Mend' on 0800 901 902 or Trimline Systems on 01202

480 881. For repairs and renovation of leather upholstery call Patrick Russell Leather on 0181 878 3976. And for chipped or scratched windscreens, call Glas Weld Systems on 0800 243 274 or 01372 362362 in Surrey; or Laminex Windscreen Repair (tel: 01895 675174; mobile: 07850 400826) in the Heathrow area. On modern cars with bonded windscreens this is better than having the entire screen replaced because removing the old one can damage the car body leading to leaks and rust. (Autoglass and Auto Windscreens and many others offer a similar service.)

For repairs to damaged alloy wheels, try Paint Technik (0800 298 5455); A1 Wheel renovations of 345 Bilston Road, Wolverhampton (01902 871422); 'Spit & Polish' of Tonbridge, Kent (01732 367771); or 'Wheelbrite' of London (0171 431 9015). The cost is likely to be £30–£50 per wheel. For an in-house service combining bumper repairs, glass repairs, paintless dent removal, interior and exterior plastic and vinyl repairs, leather upholstery and trim repairs and Connolising, velour upholstery and trim repairs, alloy wheel refurbishment, wheel trim refurbishment, and general valeting, visit the Smart Car Centres at Bircholt Road, Maidstone, Kent ME15 9YP, tel: 01622 609 360 and at 1 Lea Valley Road, Chingford, London. Smart Car Centres freephone: 0800 298 54 55; website: www.smart-car-centres.com.

24 Pedal extenders

"My legs are not long enough to allow me to sit a safe minimum of 10" from the steering wheel of my car and reach the foot pedals. Where can I buy pedal extenders to enable me to sit further back?"

Eze Drive Limited of 169 London Road, Leicester LE2 1EG, tel: 07970 571407; e-mail: EzeDrive@aol.com. Alternatively, a range of adjustable, removable and permanent pedal extenders is available from Roland Kerr Ltd, P.O. Box 8896, London SW15 3ZA, tel: 020 8546 8125; fax: 020 8546 7145.

25 Buying and selling cherished regs

"Is there a website offering a cheap way to buy and sell cherished registrations?"

Yes, http://registrationXchange.com. Those unconnected to the internet should refer to the advertisements in *Telegraph Motoring*.

26 Rear seatbelts

"Which cars have three lap/diagonal three-point belts in the back seat?"

At the time of writing, the list included:

Alfa 156 (£97.53 option); Alfa 166; Audi A3 5-door; Audi A4 from 2001 MY; Audi A6; Audi A8; BMW 5-Series; Chrysler PT Cruiser; Citroën Berlingo Multispace Forte 5-door; Citroën Xsara from 2001 MY; Citroën Xantia Estate; Citroën Picasso; Citroën C5; Fiat Punto from 2000 MY (standard in HLX and above; £75 option in base models); Fiat Doblo Combi ELX model; Fiat Multipla; Fiat Stilo; Ford Fiesta (2002 model); Ford Focus; Ford Mondeo from 1997 MY; Honda Accord from 1999 MY; Hyundai Santa Fe; KIA Magentis; Land Rover Freelander 5-door; Land Rover Discovery from 1999 MY; Mazda 626 from July 1997; MB C Class estate; new MB C Class from Mid 2000; MB E Class estate from May 1996; MB E Class from June 1998; Mitsubishi Galant from 1998 MY; Mitsubishi Space Star; Nissan Almera 4-door; Nissan Almera Tino; new Nissan Primera SLX; Nissan Maxima QX; Peugeot Partner Combi; Peugeot 306 Sedan; Peugeot 307; Peugeot 406; Peugeot 607; Proton Impian; Renault new Clio from May 1998 (not base models); Renault Kangoo Combi RXE model; Renault Megane and Scenic; Renault Laguna from 95M; new Rover 200; Rover 25; Rover 45; Rover 600 from 1997 MY; Rover 75; Rover 800 4-door from 94M; SAAB 900 from 94L; SAAB 9-3; SAAB 9-5 (saloon and estate); SEAT Leon; New SEAT Toledo (from 1999 MY); New SEAT Alhambra (from August 2000); Toyota Avensis Verso; Toyota

Avensis; Toyota Corolla from July 1997; Toyota Camry from 1997 MY; Vauxhall Corsa from 2001 MY; Vauxhall Astra from April 1998 (not Zafira); Vauxhall Vectra from 1997 MY; Vauxhall Omega; 1998 VW Golf IV and Bora (£100 optional extra, but standard on Golf V5 Estate); new VW Passat (£100 optional extra); VW Sharan from 2001 MY; Volvo S40; Volvo V40; Volvo S60; Volvo S70; Volvo V70; new Volvo V70; Volvo 850; Volvo S80; Volvo 940; Volvo 960; Volvo S90; Volvo V90.

27 HJ's gadgets

"Where can I buy the tyre pressure gauge and battery charger that Honest John keeps mentioning?"

The Accu-Gauge S60X circular-dial tyre pressure gauge, 0-60psi, costs £13.25, plus £2.95 for a protective rubber cover, and plus carriage. Buy online from www.international-tool.com, or telephone 01604 646433.

The Airflow Battery Conditioner costs £40 from Airflow Products, tel: 01635 569569. The advantage is it trickle charges so gently up to 13.5 volts (then recharges as and when necessary) that it can be left attached more or less permanently without the need to disconnect the battery or remove the vent plugs, even if the car has an alarm/immobiliser unit.

28 Crashworthiness

"Where can I obtain information about the crashworthiness of vehicles?"

Online, by going to http://www.crashtest.com. Alternatively, refer to the Car By Car Breakdown in this book.

29 Soft top maintenance

"What are the best products for reconditioning the canvas hood of a convertible and for restoring transparency to a plastic rear screen?"

I reckon Renovo, which offers a range of products for reconditioning and re-proofing soft-tops. These include a new-formula Ultra Proofer at £11.95 for 500ml or £19.95 for a litre, a Soft Top Dry Cleaner at £11.95 for 300ml (canvas or mohair hoods only), and a Plastic Window Polish at £4.99 for 30ml (tel: 01444 443277 or visit www.renovointernational.com).

Autocar magazine's favourite is Autoglym's Cabriolet Hood Cleaner and Protector Kit, which comes as two 500ml spray bottles for £19.95 and an abrasive sponge (tel: 01462 677766 if not stocked by your local accessory shop).

Halfords also sells its own brand Soft Top Renovation Kit, which consists of 500ml of cleaner, 400ml of Fabric Guard, a small brush and a sponge for £15.99 (neither is suitable for mohair cloth hoods). Halfords also sells an own-brand plastic window cleaning cream. Available at all branches of Halfords.

Honest John's Scratchpad

Useful addresses and internet sites

How Stuff Works www.howstuffworks.com. Best guide on the web to how anything works

API 01926 614333 Replacement Japanese engines

BBR/GTI Brackley, Northants. Tel: 01280 700800 Tuning

Micheldever Tyres Micheldever, Hants. Tel: 01962 774437, website www.micheldever.co.uk

Protech 01275 859955, website www.protech-uk.co.uk Preparation for the SVA test

Insurance Ombudsman Bureau 020 7928 4488

National Vehicle Security helpline: 0990 502 006

Association of British Insurers 020 7600 3333

Wheelbase Garage Hersham, Surrey. Tel: 01932 252515

Motorhoods of Colchester 0800 163725, website www.option7.co.uk 7-seater estate car conversions

King Automatics Epsom, Surrey. Tel: 01372 728769

Millers Oils Stockists helpline: 0800 281 053 DieselPower Plus

MER Worldwide Marketing Tel: 020 8763 2480 for polish and windscreen cleaner

London Stainless Steel Exhaust Centre 020 7622 2120

Cheesman Exhaust Centre Woking 01483 765799 Stainless exhausts with individual fabrication for special, vintage, and unusual cars

Ivor Searle 01353 720531, website: www.ivor-searle.co.uk Re-conditioned manual gearboxes

Seatbak Gorman Design Ltd. Tel: 0700 222 5732, e-mail: sales@jygorman.co.uk Seat adapter to support the pelvis, £45.50

Back Friend MEDesign, Southport. Tel: 01704 542373 Conventional seat adapter

Reap Automotive Design 0208 863 2305 For speedometer faces in mph

New Car Assessment Programme www.euroncap.com For car crash safety

Vehicle Inspectorate www.via.gov.uk Safety recalls and latest SVA information

Autobaza www.autobaza.pl A Polish website where you can check your car's place and date of manufacture by its VIN

Frequently Asked Questions

Car storage companies

Carbank Limited www.carbank.co.uk

Classic Car Storage Ltd www.classiccarstorage.co.uk

Secure Classic Car Storage www.classic-reserve.co.uk

Northern Car Storage www.northerncarstorage.co.uk

Autostore (Cambridge) 01223 872879

De-mystified Motors

All too often, car people sound like they're talking out of their exhaust pipes. Have you ever wondered what their technical terms, car jargon and dealer slang really mean? De-mystified Motors gives you the plain English anwers so you need never feel baffled again.

What's a 'warranty'?

Most second-hand cars sold by dealers come with a 'warranty' which is either part of the deal or an option at extra cost. Unless this 'warranty' is the balance of the original manufacturer's or importer's 12-month, 24-month or 36-month warranty, it is not what most of us understand as a 'guarantee'. Instead, it is a

Mechanical Breakdown Insurance (MBI), underwritten and administered by an insurance company. The cover provided by MBIs varies hugely, from 'bumper to bumper', which includes some wearing items (as is the case with Warranty Holdings warranties negotiated by Trade Sales of Slough), down to 'major components only' , with cover up to £100 per claim. A vital term of the warranty contract is that you must get any replacements or repairs approved by the warranty insurer beforehand, or your claim may be turned down. Before paying for an MBI warranty, ask to see a sample warranty booklet or document and read it thoroughly so you fully understand exactly what is covered and on exactly what terms. Warranties are sold on commission, so the last thing you want to do is buy a £300 warranty of which £250 is commission and only £50 actually pays for the mechanical breakdown insurance itself.

What's a 'Personal Contract Purchase'?

PCPs were an idea dreamed up in the USA and imported to the UK as a means of extracting full list prices for new cars from private punters. How they work is that the punter pays a deposit (which may be in the form of a part-exchange) and signs a contract to pay the difference between the list price and what the car will be worth in two or three years time, plus interest, in easy monthly instalments. This 'future value' is put on the car up front, and when the contract comes to an end the punter has three choices: pay the 'future value' as a lump sum and keep the car, use any difference between the 'future value' and the car's true trade value to part-finance the deposit on another PCP, or walk away with nothing. The trouble is, PCPs were launched at a time when used car values were high, and since then values have collapsed. So, unless the dealer puts a falsely high value on the car at the end of its contract, most Personal Contract Purchasers are left with no equity to finance the deposit on their next PCP. If the dealer does put a falsely high value on the returned car, he has to finance it by over-pricing the replacement car. You can't win.

'Screamers' and 'Dreamers'

Some car trade argot is based on Cockney rhyming slang, such as 'Nelsons', 'Billies', 'Sausaged', etc. Other terms are just a bit of fun, made up on the spot, including 'crocodiled', 'bidet' and 'camel'. 'Nelsons' is derived from '30s crooner Nelson Eddy, whose surname just happens to rhyme with 'readies'. A 'Billy Bunter' is a punter. 'Sausaged' comes from 'sausage and mash' which, of course, rhymes with 'crash'. 'Crocodiled' is a highly technical term used to describe car upholstery which has been eaten by a pet dog. A 'bidet' is exactly what you'd expect: a rear wash/wipe. And a 'camel' is, of course, a car with an odd and undesirable specification. Getting a bit more personal, a 'Screamer' is not a high-revving engine. It is a revved-up customer with a penchant for complaining. 'Dreamers' are punters who don't have the money or the credit rating. 'Tyre Kickers' are experts who don't know the first thing about cars but have heard somewhere that it's the done thing to kick the car's tyres. A 'score' is £20, a 'pony' is £25, a 'nifty' is £50, a 'ton' is £100, a 'monkey' is £500 and a 'gripper' is £1,000. 'Spinning for it' is the means auction ringers use to divide up the spoils after a sale. This causes serious 'grief' to the auctioneers, who then have to re-invoice the cars to different account customers than the ones who made the successful bids.

'Classic' conundrums

Readers have asked what is meant by the terms 'classic car', 'historic vehicle' and 'VED exempt'. Defining what is and is not a 'classic car' is guaranteed to start a protracted argument. So I'll say it's any car which a significant number of people regard as 'classic', because of either its age or its aesthetics or both. The Schlump brothers, who amassed a vast collection of Bugattis, would hardly regard a 1963 Ford Consul Classic as a 'classic'. But the man who lovingly polishes his immaculate Consul Classic every Sunday would, and there's even a club for them (see the Car Clubs directory starting on page 133). 'Historic vehicle' has now come to have a technical meaning in the eyes of the DVLA (Driver and Vehicle Licensing Authority). It is any vehicle built (not necessarily first registered) *before* 1 January 1973. These vehicles are 'VED exempt' which means that the owners are exempted from paying vehicle excise duty, but they must still display a zero-duty-paid tax disc on the windscreen. To get this they have to show a current MOT and insurance certificate and proof of the car's date of first registration or build date.

Fuel consumption

We buy our fuel in litres. So why do we persist in using 'miles per gallon' as a basis for comparing economy? The answer is that most of us simply would not understand or relate to the metric method of measuring fuel consumption. When excited engineers refer to 'the three-litre car' they're not talking about the cubic capacity of its engine. Instead, they mean that the car will require just three litres of fuel to travel 100 kilometres. 'Litres per 100 km' is how fuel consumption is measured throughout Europe. But it's not too hard for us to start measuring this way as well.

For a start, your till receipt shows how many litres you have bought, not how many gallons. Mark your mileage on the receipt after you have filled your tank to the brim. Then brim it again next time you fill up and mark the mileage on that receipt. Subtract the first mileage from the second mileage and multiply the answer by 0.0161. Then divide the litres you have used by the answer and you get your fuel consumption in terms of litres per 100 kilometres. For example, I recently travelled 391 miles on 32.94 litres of diesel fuel in a SEAT Toledo TDI 110. Multiply 391 by 0.0161 and you get 6.295. Divide 32.94 by 6.295 and you get 5.23 litres per 100kms.

For simplicity's sake, 8 litres per 100kms = 35.31mpg; 5 litres per 100kms = 56.5mpg; and 3 litres per 100kms = 94.16mpg. To convert mpg to litres per 100km, a booklet from Citroën tells us to divide 282.5 by the mpg achieved, and to convert litres per 100km to mpg divide 282.5 by the number of litres used.

'Multivalve' engines

These days, you can buy a four-cylinder engine with eight, twelve, sixteen or twenty valves. Many readers have asked why the added complexity? And what effect do 'multivalves' have on an engine's performance? Obviously, the bigger the throats that can be opened by the valves, the better the engine will inhale air and fuel and exhale burned gases. There is a limit to how big two circular valve heads can be in a combustion chamber, so the best way to increase the total size of the valve throats is to increase the number of valves serving each cylinder. Morris Minor engines have two. Audi A3 1.8 engines have five. Unless an engine with more than three valves per cylinder also has variable valve timing or variable intake ducting deliberately set to develop its power and torque low down, the engine will tend to peak quite high in the rev range. This is particularly true of most six-cylinder engines below 2.5 litres and most four-cylinder engines below 2.0 litres, and makes them less than ideal when combined with torque converter automatic transmissions which can 'bog down' at low revs.

'Understeer' and 'Oversteer'

Readers have offered at least a dozen different definitions of these two characteristics. Leaving wit at the roadside, the simplest is what the car does in relation to what you ask it to do with the steering wheel. If the car turns less than you ask it to, it 'understeers'. If it turns more, it 'oversteers'. Depending on how fast it is asked to take a corner, every car will do one or the other at some point and might even switch from one to the other. The faster it can take corners without either, the more 'neutral' the handling is deemed to be. Skilled drivers usually hate understeer and prefer a car to handle neutrally, then gradually oversteer at the limits of adhesion. One of the best in this respect was the Porsche 968 Club Sport. But because oversteer can be dangerous in the hands of unskilled drivers, manufacturers have collectively taken the decision to design it out of the handling of most cars. Legendary Swedish rally driver Eric Carlsson told me that the Vauxhall Vectra-based SAAB 9–5 is designed to understeer consistently (like the Vectra) and demonstrated how hard it is to provoke any sort of oversteer from this car. A 'Legends' racing car, on the other hand, with its locked and off-set solid back axle, oversteers luridly at the earliest opportunity and takes a lot of getting used to.

Understanding car auctions: (i) The fake 'sale'

When punters first start attending auctions regularly and see the same car seemingly sold week after week they begin to wonder what is going on. It's really very simple. On the one side, you have vendors who may be car manufacturers, fleet owners, finance companies, dealers, traders or, rarely, private individuals. They are represented by the auctioneer. On the other side you have buyers who may be dealers, traders or members of the public. The vendor sets a 'reserve' price for the car, which is the minimum he says he is prepared to accept. Trade buyers buying for stock know what they can sell the cars for, so naturally they try to bid as low as possible in order to maximise their profit. When times are hard, like now, they may want to pay a lot less than the vendors want for their cars. And this is why, at some sales, cars will be 'knocked down' (apparently sold) when they haven't been, in order to stimulate some action. Auctioneers can be extremely cunning at this. I have seen cars about to be 'knocked down' to a light fitting, then out-bid at the last second by a waste bin. Don't believe everything you see. Keep an eye on the screens at BCA auctions to find which provisional bids really have been accepted. And you'll gradually start to get the feel of the place.

Understanding car auctions: (ii) 'Trotting'

In part (i) I discussed auctioneers taking bids from light fittings and waste paper baskets in order to give the impression that cars were selling when they weren't. They may also do this against genuine bids when cars have not reached anywhere near their reserve price. This means that, though you think you are bidding against a fellow bidder, what you are really engaged in is a psychological battle of wits with the auctioneer. He will 'run you', or 'trot up' your bids, to precisely the point where you will stop bidding. One auctioneer I know is so good at this, I sometimes wonder if he has telepathic powers. Other unscrupulous auctioneers may overdo it, take a high bid 'off the wall', then, finding you do not respond, ask the ficti-tious 'high bidder' if he really made a bid or was waving to a friend. As the 'under bidder' it is then up to you to decide whether to let your bid stick or not. If you want the car, fine. But if you smell a rat, don't be bullied. Everyone knows what was really going on and the auctioneer probably won't press you if you want to back out.

What's a 'grey' import?

With unofficial car imports now soaring towards the 200,000 a year mark, the word 'grey' is being used to denigrate more imports than it should. If you go to Europe and buy a 'UK spec', RHD, European Type-Approved car from an EU franchised dealer, it is not a 'grey' import. It is a 'parallel' import. There is little or no difference between your car and one of the same make and model imported by the official importer. A 'grey' import, on the other hand, is a car built for a non-EU market which does not conform to EU Type-Approval regulations. The vast majority of these are 'Jap Scrap': cars which were headed for Japanese breakers' yards but which have been more lucratively exported to poorer countries such as the UK. Unless they are genuine personal imports, between 3 and 10 years old, all such cars less than 10 years old are subject to a Single Vehicle Approval (SVA) inspection, which they must pass before they can be registered. But before the rules were tightened up, large numbers of 'Jap Scrap' over 3 years of age were 'personally imported' by dealers, MOT tested and sold on to unsuspecting members of the public. These cars may have been modified to run properly on lower-grade UK petrol, but very few will have been rust-proofed to UK market standards, which is why it is quite common to see 'grey imports' as young as 5 years old already in an advanced state of decay. The AA Experian car data checks now covers a check on whether the car you are about to buy is registered as a 'grey' import with the DVLA; tel: 0800 234999 (have your credit card handy).

What's a 'froster'?

Thanks to the RAC Foundation we have a new vocabulary for the various easy means by which cars or their contents can be stolen. 'Jacking' is the term for hijacking an unlocked car by force at traffic lights, either kidnapping the driver in the process or leaving him or her at the roadside. The same thieves also target handbags and mobile phones left on nearside passenger seats, so always keep your doors locked in town. 'Frosting' is stealing a car while the owner has left it idling to de-frost outside his or her house (leaving a car idling from cold also damages the car and causes severe local pollution). 'Sneaking' is the term for stealing the ignition keys of a car from the owner's house. Far too many people simply leave them hanging on a hook by the door. 'Hooking' is using a stiff piece of wire through the letter box to hook car keys off a hook or a table.

'Gifting' is stealing gifts from cars. Far too many people use their cars as carpark warehouses for the first batch of shopping while they go out to buy the next. If anything of value is left visible in the car, it's an open invitation to steal it.

What's a 'chameleon'?

This is a car of many colours, or, more likely, many shades of the same colour. Some colours, especially solid, non-metallic reds such as VAG's old 'Tornado Red', are notoriously difficult to match because they start oxidising as soon as the car is parked in bright sunlight. I had a racing red Alfa once which I bought cheaply because it had been vandalised. The damage was patch-painted. Then someone reversed into the front of the car while it was parked, necessitating another 'hot job' (quick part-respray). It looked alright in the daylight, but under sodium streetlights it resembled a patchwork quilt. The trick with damage is to repaint the whole of the surrounding area up to a natural break. For example, if you scrape the bottom of a door and there is a rubbing strip along the side of the car, have the whole of the side under the rubbing strip repainted. A minor mis-match will then be much harder to spot than if you only had the one half-door re-painted. If you smash a door above the waistline, you may need to have the whole side of the car repainted (front wing, both doors, and rear panel from the roof to the back bumper). A pro will spot this straight away (and check by peeling back the rubber trim strips). But it will make paint mis-matches harder for the average private punter to spot. If you are a damage-prone driver, the best colour to match is and always has been solid dark blue, known in the trade as 'doom blue' because it's one of the hardest colours to sell.

What's 'bowler hatting'?

In the good old days, when a trader sold a car to another trader and it turned out to be a dud, there was an understanding he would take it back. Less scrupulous traders, stuck with a bad car, developed the technique of 'bowler hatting'. What they would do was visit a dealer well away from their patch who didn't know them, pretend to be the last owner listed in the log book, and either plead poverty and sell the car to the dealer, or swap it for something different of the same value. One lad, nicknamed 'Spider' because he lived by the quotation, 'Oh what a tangled web we weave when first we practise to deceive', came unstuck when a BMW 5-Series he'd bowler-hatted turned out to have a cracked cylinder head and burned out autobox. The receiving dealer figured who he really was and sent a professional leg-breaker by the name of 'Frankie the Criminal' after him. Fortunately Spider's garage was right out in the sticks, and when he drove up behind a car with a pair of shoulders completely filling the back window, he realised that returning to base wasn't an option. As is to be expected, Spider's business methods and his severe aversion to paying tax paved the way towards his current status of land-owning multi-millionaire.

What's 'car cloning'?

Very simply, it's running more than one car on the same registration. Photocopies of V5 registration documents are made while cars are 'in the trade'. I won't go into the various ways in which duplicate or 'change of keeper' V5s can then be obtained from the DVLA. But, once they are, a near identical car is stolen to order, its Vehicle Identification Number (VIN) and registration number are changed to match the car it has been cloned from, and it is then re-sold with a genuine V5. A pre-purchase check with the data registers rarely helps unless a detail mistake has been made. Alternatively, a trader importing cars less than ten years old that are not UK Type-Approved may clone successive cars to one which has a pukka SVA and V5. But by far the most common form of cloning is the simple 'registration swap' to avoid prosecution for speeding and traffic light offences caught on camera. All the dodgy owner has to do is spot a car the same model, colour and year as his own, write down its registration, and have a set of its plates made up to fit on his car. Obviously, there is an element of risk attached. He can't park anywhere patrolled by parking wardens who may spot the discrepancy between plates and tax disc. And he can't afford to get stopped by a police patrol car. But if, say, he already has nine points on his licence and needs it to earn his living, he might consider the risk worth taking. So next time you receive a 'Fixed Penalty Notice' for a speeding offence you definitely did not commit, you'll know why.

What's 'lean burn'?

Lean burn is a generic term for engines which are capable of running on a considerably higher proportion of air to fuel than the stoichiometric level 14.7:1 (known as Lambda 1). Honda V-Tech E engines, Toyota Carina E and Avensis 1.6 litre and 1.8 litre engines, and Mitsubishi's 1.8 litre and 2.4 litre GDIs, are all capable of running with air-to-fuel ratios of up to 40:1. The obvious benefits are reduced fuel consumption and reduced emissions through more complete burning of the fuel. Unfortunately, in Europe, lean burn engines have been legislated against in favour of catalytic converters, the testing of which requires all engines to be capable of running at very close to Lambda 1 in a specified rev band between 2,000 and 3,200 rpm, and this has compromised the effectiveness of lean burn. Driving a lean burn engine requires a different technique from normal economy driving: comparatively high revs with small throttle openings rather than low revs with early upchanges. The reason why so many Carina Es and Avensises tend to need very expensive Lambda sensor replacements early in their lives could be the failure of their owners to drive them as instructed by Toyota, instead adopting time-honoured economy driving techniques which are harmful to the extra-sensitive lambda sensor.

What's a 'chip shop'?

'Chipping' is the generic term for re-programming a car engine's electronic management system for increased performance, different performance characteristics, better fuel economy, or to run on a lower grade of fuel. This can be done internally, by dismantling the engine ECU and either replacing or re-programming the chips inside, or externally, by altering the signals from the ECU to the fuel injection system and ignition igniter. Both petrol and turbo-diesel engines can be 'chipped'. Prices start at £100, but are more usually in the £300–£400 bracket. Practitioners of the art include BBR of Brackley (petrol and diesel Starchips), tel: 01280 700800 (website: www.bbr.gti.demon.co.uk); Superchips of Buckingham (petrol and diesel), tel: 01280 816781 (website: www.superchips.co.uk); Milford Microsystems of Kidlington (system developments), tel: 01865 331552; AMD, Oxon, tel: 01865 331226; Tim Styles Racing, Somerset, tel: 01278 453036; Siegerland (UK), tel: 0191 4286226 (website: www.tuningbox.com); Prima Racing, tel 0115 949 1903; Van Aaken Developments of Crowthorne, tel: 01344 777553 (website: www.vanaaken.com); Jetex of Stratford upon Avon, tel: 01789 298989 (website: www.jetexlimited.freeserve.co.uk); Webcon of Sunbury (Diesel Torqmaster), tel: 01932 788630 (website: www.webcon.co.uk); and Darley Specialist Services (Diesel

Powerchip), tel: 01332 553143. Please note that if you alter the specification of your car in any way you must inform your insurer or your insurance could be void.

How do I read my tyres?

Modern tyres are covered in hieroglyphics. Where the main ones read something like '195/60 R 15 87V', '195' is the tyre width in millimetres; '/60' is the ratio of tyre height to width expressed as a percentage (the lower the figure, the less cushion in the tyre and the harder the car's ride will be); 'R 15' signifies that the tyre has a radial ply and is meant for a 15-inch wheel rim; '87' is the carrying load index; and 'V' is the speed rating. A speed rating of 'R' is up to a maximum of 105 mph; 'S' up to 113 mph; 'T' up to 118 mph; 'U' up to 124 mph; 'H' up to 130 mph; 'V' up to 150 mph; 'W' up to 169 mph; 'Y' up to 175 mph; and 'ZR' 150 mph plus with no upper limit. (Some of these ratings are now obsolete and no longer apply to new tyres.) Obviously we don't all drive at these speeds, but if a car comes with 'V'-rated tyres, any replacement tyres should be also be 'V'-rated. Though these are the main symbols, a tyre may be sold anywhere in the world, from Swindon to San Francisco, and markings applicable to other markets also appear. In the USA, for example, tyres are tested for tread wear, so a wear rating may be included. (Many thanks to Brian at Micheldever Tyres for his help with this.)

How do I rate an engine oil?

Readers keep asking me, and, thanks to Adrian at Castrol's Technical Department, this should provide all the answers. Eighty per cent of an oil is the base oil, which may be mineral, synthetic or a mixture called 'semi-synthetic' (the other 20 per cent is comprised of additives). Undesirable compounds cannot be completely refined out of mineral oil, so the purest base oil is fully synthetic. The Society of Automobile Engineers (SAE) ratings (0W/40, 20W/50, etc.) refer to the oil's viscosity (or resistance to flow) at minus 20 degrees centigrade compared with its viscosity at 100 degrees centigrade. A low cold viscosity oil (e.g. 0W) has its viscosity at high temperature increased by viscosity improving additives, which is how 0W/40 or 5W/40 is achieved. Matters have been complicated by new ratings systems devised by the American Petroleum Institute (API) and the Association de Constructeurs Europeans d'Automobiles (ACEA). These are arrived at by testing the oils in engines. For oils for petrol engines, the API rating of SG corresponds with the ACEA A1, SH with A2 and SJ with A3. For oils for diesel engines the API CD rating corresponds with ACEA B1, CE with B2 and CF with B3. The telephone numbers of Castrol's Technical Help Desk are 01793 452222 (for modern cars) or 01954 231668 (for older cars).

When is a 'write-off' not written off?

The answer is, when it's a Category C or Category D insurance 'write-off'. An insurance assessor will 'write a car off' when it is stolen and not recovered, or when the cost of repairing any damage to it exceeds 60 per cent of the car's trade value. The insured owner is then paid the car's private sale value, while the car is registered on the national 'Vehicle Condition Alert Register' and becomes the property of the insurer. If the assessor has deemed it a Category A write-off, that's the end of it and the remains of the car must be crushed. If it's deemed a Category B, it cannot be put back on the road, but it can be used as a donor car to yield spare parts for other vehicles. Category C means 'damaged, but repairable', so the car can be sold with a V5 for repair. Depending on the car's value, a professional repairer may then have his repair checked by an alignment specialist such as Autolign (01604 859424) or Popplewells (01992 561571), and a 'pass' will be entered on the VCAR register. Category D is where damage is confined to windows, locks and, possibly, a few bent panels, but the car remains roadworthy. This is often the state in which stolen cars are recovered after the insurer has paid out. These cars are the easiest to fix. HPI Equifax (01722 422422) and AA Experian (0800 234999) each offer history checks on vehicles which include their VCAR status (have a credit card handy when you phone).

What's the difference between diesels?

These days you can buy a diesel car with one of at least nine different types of injection system. The first is indirect injection (IDI), where diesel fuel is pumped to the injectors by a distribution pump, then fed through to the combustion chamber via a pre-combustion antichamber. IDI engines can be made more efficient by compressing the air fed into the combustion chamber with a turbocharger. And a turbocharged diesel engine can be made still more efficient by cooling the turbocharged air with an intercooler. This explains badges such as D, TD and TDi on the backs of cars. But badging has been complicated by the advent of direct injected diesel engines, first built for cars by Perkins, where the fuel is fed directly into the combustion chamber. Direct injected diesels may also be turbocharged and charge-cooled, and may be badged SD, DI, DT, DTI or TDI. VAG has taken direct injection a big step further by introducing 'pumpe duse' injector pumps where each individual injector contains a pump to increase the pressure at which it is pumped into the combustion chamber, enabling the dosage to be more finely controlled.

The other method of achieving this at slightly lower pressure is 'Common Rail Direct Injection', the route favoured by BMW, Mercedes Benz, Fiat and PSA. Instead of distributing the fuel charge to each injector, the pump feeds a 'common rail' of fuel from which each injector is fed at high pressure and the dosage fed into each combustion chamber is finely controlled. The air supply to common rail direct injected engines is invariably turbocharged, and for more efficient, more powerful versions it is turbocharged and intercooled. CD tends to mean common rail direct injected. CDI usually means intercooled as well.

What's the difference between an automatic gearbox and a CVT?

A lot of readers are still confused about the difference between conventional automatic transmissions and continuously variable transmissions (CVT). I'll try to explain. Instead of a clutch, a conventional automatic box uses a 'torque converter'. In very simplified terms, oil is thrown by one turbine wheel onto another, creating a flexible drive which becomes more positive as engine speed increases. This allows sequential gearchanges up or down two, three, four or five ratios according to road speed, the extent to which the accelerator is pressed, an electronic programme, or a manual override. The advantage is reliability. The disadvantages are a fixed set of ratios, a sometimes sluggish response, and overheating when the car is heavily laden or towing. Instead of a torque converter, most current-generation transaxle CVT boxes use a pair of multi-plate clutches or an electromagnetic clutch to take up drive from standstill much more positively than a conventional autobox. Instead of having fixed gear ratios, a steel belt runs between two pulleys which expand and contract in diameter, theoretically giving continuously variable ratios between the lowest and highest. However, the latest CVTs have six or seven lockable ratios, so upshifts and downshifts can be manually controlled if the driver desires. Confusing matters further, for the latest 'Hypertronic CVT M6' transmission fitted to some Primeras, Nissan has adopted a torque converter instead of an electromagnetic clutch. The new 'Torotrak' CVT does away with belts, feeding drive directly from an input cone to an output cone.

What do the flags mean at a motor race?

Once the F1 season gets under way, wives and children groan while blokes up and down the country are glued to their goggle-boxes every Sunday afternoon. You might find the procession a bit more interesting if you know what the marshals' flag signals mean. A blue flag held out in front of a driver means he must let a faster car overtake. A waved blue flag means do it now. A yellow flag held out means there is a hazard ahead and drivers must not overtake. A waved yellow flag means the hazard is imminent and drivers must be prepared to stop. A black flag held out with a driver's number means he has committed an infringement and must pull into his pit either to suffer a stop/go penalty or to be disqualified. A red flag means that the race has been stopped. We all know what a chequered flag means, but there are several other flags which may be used. A yellow and red flag signifies oil on the track ahead (when waved, immediately ahead). A white flag signifies a much slower car is ahead (when waved, immediately ahead). A black and white flag is used to warn a driver of unsporting driving. A green flag indicates the end of a danger area previously signified by a yellow flag. Red flags waved by people in the crowds mean they're Ferrari fans.

What makes a cheap tyre expensive?

The answer to this one came from Justin Edgington of Michelin, after I raised the matter of the safety of cheap replacement tyres fitted to some fleet cars. He explained that the main reason why budget tyres wear comparatively quickly is insufficient support of the tread by the steel bracing. On a high-quality radial ply tyre, the bracing extends into the shoulders but requires an expensive flexible compound or cracking will occur there. To prevent cracking on a hard compound budget tyre, the bracing stops short of the shoulder and the result is abnormal wear on the tyre shoulders. (The reason for this is often mis-diagnosed as under-inflation.) Another effect is poor water dispersal via the 'sipes' (small channels cut in the edges of the tread pattern) which either close up or get worn away. The most dangerous road surfaces, especially for motorcyclists, are where rainwater has dried up, leaving a film of oil and road grime on the surface. If the tyre's sipes cannot cut through it, these are the conditions in which the tyres can 'viscoplane', which is actually far more dangerous than 'aquaplaning' on a cushion of water.

What's a 'small child' in the eyes of the law?

A reader from Stratford-upon-Avon asked if I could clarify the law concerning small children riding in the front seats of cars. Sections 15(2) and 15(4) of The Road Traffic Act 1988 state that it is an offence for any person without reasonable excuse to drive a motor vehicle on a road unless any children under 14 in the front or rear seats of the vehicle are wearing seat belts which conform to the regulations. A child under 1 year old can travel in the front in a carry-cot restrained by straps. Children under 3 years old can travel in the front seats if they are wearing approved child restraints. A small child', defined as aged 3–12 and less than 1.5 metres tall (4' 11"), can travel in the front or rear using an adult belt if no approved child restraint is available. If there are no belts in the back and the front passenger seat is unoccupied, the 'small child' must travel belted in the front. There are further exceptions for disabled children and children holding medical certificates. There are more exceptions for motor vehicles first registered before 1 January 1965, if the vehicle has no rear seats, or if no seats apart from the driver's are fitted with seat belts appropriate for a child. And, of course, there are yet more exceptions for buses, vans, trucks, etc. Rear belts must be fitted to all cars first registered on or after 1 April 1987. Many thanks to the 'Hughes Guide to Road Traffic Law for the Enforcement Officer', copies of which can be obtained from Motorvation Consultants on 01908 639233 in file form or on CD Rom.

What's 'fuel tax'?

'Fuel tax' is the fixed amount of tax you pay per litre of fuel before the cost of the fuel itself is added and VAT is imposed on both the fuel tax and the petrol. The current rates are: ultra-low-sulphur unleaded ('city' petrol): 47.82p per litre; premium unleaded 48.82p per litre; superunleaded and LRP 50.89p per litre; and unleaded low-sulphur diesel 48.82p per litre. If you pay a pump price of 79.9p a litre for premium unleaded, 19.18p pays for the petrol, 48.82p is the fuel tax and 11.9p is the VAT, so 76 per cent of the cost of the petrol is tax and the actual tax rate on the petrol works out at 316.58 per cent. The SMMT has provided CO_2-based VED tax bands for new cars as from 1 March 2001. Up to 150g/km CO_2, the owner will pay £90 for a gas-fuelled car, £100 for a petrol-fuelled car or £110 for a diesel. Up to 165g/km CO_2 the rates will be £110 for gas, £120 for petrol and £130 for diesel. Up to 185g/km CO_2 the rates will be £130 for gas, £140 for petrol and £150 for diesel; and over 185g/km (anything from a Nissan Primera 1.6 at 186g/km to an Aston Martin V8 Vantage at 511g/km) the rates will be £150 for gas, £155 for petrol and £160 for diesel. So the owner of a low-CO_2 'Y' prefix car, such as a VW Polo 1.4 TDI which puts out 119g/km, will only benefit financially by 29 per cent compared to the owner of a 'Y' prefix Aston Martin V8 Vantage, despite the fact that the Aston puts out 329 per cent more CO_2 than the Polo. The chancellor has, however, brought all older cars under 1,549cc into the same £105-a-year tax band.

What are 'regional registrations'?

From 1 September 2001, new vehicle registrations have started with one letter denoting the region, followed by one letter denoting the vehicle registration office (each VRO will have 5 to 25 letters, depending on how many of them there are in each region). This will be followed by two numbers giving the period of registration. And this will be followed by three random letters. So 'AA 51 ABC' will mean that the car was registered in the Anglia region at the Norwich VRO between 1 September 2001 and 28 February 2002 and is the only 'AA 51' registered car with the random letters 'ABC'. Because of the twice-yearly registration change, the year figures get a bit complicated. 02 will mean 1 March 2002 to 31 August 2002; 52 will mean 1 September 2002 to February 28 2003; 03 will mean 1 March 2003 to 31 August 2003; 53 will mean 1 September 2003 to 29 February 2004 – and so on. The regional letters will be A: Anglia; B: Birmingham; C: Cymru; D: Deeside to Shrewsbury; E: Essex; F: Forest and Fens; G; Garden of England; H: Hampshire and Dorset; K: Luton; L: London; M: Manchester; N: North; O: Oxford; P: Preston; R: Reading; S: Scotland; V: Severn Valley; W: West Country; Y: Yorkshire.

What are 'residuals'?

The phrase 'residual value' appears quite a lot these days and salesmen dealing in prestige cars often stress the importance of a 'high residual value'. Unfortunately, 'residuals' quoted as percentages of car list prices can be a misleading basis on which to buy. Let's say the 'list price' of the car is £20,000, but metallic paint, a stereo upgrade and a few other knick-knacks add a further £2,500, against which you get a discount of £1,000. The car has cost you £21,500. But if you are quoted a high residual value of 50 per cent in three years time, it will be based on the list price of £20,000 and the assumption that the average prestige car is fitted with a bundle of extras. So, when you come to avail yourself of that residual value, you will get £10,000 and will have therefore lost £11,500. If, on the other hand, you buy a heavily discounted mass-market car listed at £15,000, but actually sold to you for £11,000, which has a three-year residual of 30 per cent of list, the figures pan out very differently. The car may only be worth £4,500 but, instead of losing

£11,500 on it, you will have lost a mere £6,500 (and incidentally will have had the benefit of the interest on an extra £10,500 which you did not spend in the first place).

What's a 'Top Car auction'?

Most auction houses hold themed sales. For example, Russell, Baldwin & Bright of Leominster hold some of the country's biggest auctions of 4x4 vehicles, twice a month (tel: 01568 611166); and West Oxfordshire Motor Auctions hold twice-monthly sales of retired police cars (tel: 01993 774413). But the first and best-known theme sales are BCA's 'Top Car' auctions. These are held on alternate Mondays at its Blackbushe auction centre (tel: 01252 878555) and once a month at Brighouse (01484 401555), Edinburgh (0131 333 2151), Measham (01530 270322) and Nottingham (0115 987 3311). The great advantage is that a large number of classy cars are conveniently offered in one auction hall on the same day. The obvious disadvantage to bidders is that this attracts large numbers of specialist dealers and private buyers competing for the same cars, so prices tend to be slightly higher than at general fleet auctions where a mixture of cars are offered.

What is 'SPECS'?

This is a sinister new system being used to curtail the movement of people around the country by creating such severe traffic congestion on motorways that many travel plans will be abandoned. Motorways are our safest roads by a long way and were previously speed camera enforcement-free zones. But Home Office Type Approval has now been given to a new generation of 'SVDD' (Speed Violation Detection Deterrent) equipment to be installed on motorway bridges which will be invisible to drivers until their photos are taken by digital cameras. The new system is known as 'SPECS' (Speed Police Enforcement Camera System) and works by pairs of digital cameras with time and average speed computers automatically calculating the speeds of vehicles passing between them, then taking digital colour images of vehicles going faster than a pre-set speed and recording them together with speeds, times, dates and locations on large-capacity CDs. Fines are being increased to £60 to pay for the new equipment but, as drivers slow down, thus creating and getting stuck in more traffic jams, returns from the fines will diminish. So speed limits and tolerance limits will have to be reduced in order to keep the systems profitable, putting yet more people dependent on the motor industry and free travel out of work. Many thanks to the Association of British Drivers for the information on SVDD and SPECS. To join, visit www.abd.org.uk or telephone 07000 781 544.

What is a 'three litre car'?

In mainland Europe the standard for vehicle fuel consumption is obviously not 'miles per gallon'. But it's not 'kilometres per litre' either. Instead, fuel consumption is measured in terms of 'litres per 100 kilometres'. Taking a reader from Oakhampton's formula, it is relatively easy to translate 'mpg' into 'l/100km' by dividing the figure 282.5 by the mpg achieved. Thus 30 miles per gallon translates to 9.4 litres per 100 kilometres; 40 mpg translates to 7.05 l/100km and 94mpg translates to 3.0 l/100km. This is the target figure set by VAG engineers for a new generation of super-economical diesel cars such as the VW Lupo 1.2TDI. It's actually quite easy for us to start thinking in terms of litres per 100kms rather than mpg, and obviously a lot more relevant than some halfway-house figure such as 'miles per litre'. All we have to do is make sure we brim our tanks on every fill-up and note the odometer mileage on our till receipts. Subtract the previous mileage from the mileage on the latest receipt; either divide by 5 and multiply by 8 (to convert miles to kilometres) or, more accurately, multiply by 1.60934; divide the result by 100; then divide that into the litres shown on the till receipt. Thus, on a recent series of 'brim-to-brim' fills while travelling through France, Belgium and Holland, my 836 miles translated to 1,345 kilometres, which, on 97.39 litres of Shell Premium Unleaded, worked out at 7.24 litres per 100 kilometres, or 38.95 miles per gallon. To convert mpg to litres/100 kms, divide 282.481 by the mpg; to convert litres/100 kms to mpg divide 282.481 by the litres/100kms.

What is 'Benefit In Kind' tax?

This is the tax drivers of company cars pay for the benefit of their private use of the car. The system for calculating this tax will change from 6 April 2002 and there will no longer be any discount for a high business mileage. Instead, drivers will be taxed on 15 per cent of the car's 'list price', with the tax base increasing by 1 per cent for each 5g/km CO_2 the car emits over and above 165g/km. For tax year 2003–2004, the base CO_2 will be 155g/km, and for tax year 2004–2005 the base CO_2 will be 145g/km. So, effectively, the tax base for a £15,000 car emitting 185g/km will rise from 19 per cent (or £2,850) in 2002–2003 to 23 per cent (or £3,450) in

2004–2005. Because they emit less CO_2, diesels will be hit with a 3 per cent surcharge, and no driver will be taxed on a base of more than 35 per cent of the car's list price. So, as with VED, there is no benefit to be had from driving a company car with an ultra-low CO_2 rating, which is extraordinarily hypocritical for a tax which is supposed to be CO_2-based. Instead it has merely become an over-complicated banding exercise but with the environmental benefit of abolishing discounts for high business miles. List prices and CO_2 tables can be found in *What Car?* and *Diesel Car* magazines, but drivers will need to subtract registration tax and VED to arrive at the taxable 'list price'.

What's 'GEODESY'?

Everyone has heard of radar and laser speed trap detectors, which may soon be outlawed. But GEODESY is an entirely different dash-top system which relies on Global Positioning System (GPS) technology to alert a driver that he or she is approaching the location of a known electronically mapped speed trap. If a user spots a speed trap which the GEODESY has not alerted them to, a press of a button will store its location in the unit's memory. The user then plugs the GEODESY into a self-dialling land-line interface to both upload the latest speed trap location data into the GEODESY and download the locations of any new ones into the data bank (every confirmed new location earns the user £50). Of course, GEODESY cannot identify which speed traps are active but, assuming the traps have been set up in known accident black spots, it will encourage users to take extra care when approaching them and thus makes a valuable contribution to road safety. Obviously, if the speed trap is simply there to earn revenue, then the GEODESY helps prevent it from doing so. GEODESY costs £380 including VAT, next-day delivery and a 12-month warranty. For more information, contact Morpheous Ltd, tel: 0870 2401701, website: www.morpheous.co.uk; e-mail: info@morpheous.co.uk; product test on www.speed-trap.co.uk; product description on www.speed-trap.co.uk/geodesy.doc.

What's a 'roadster'?

This is guaranteed to promote argument. In the old days, the word 'roadster' usually described an open two-seater with cutaway doors, side-screens and a rudimentary canvas top which the driver had to assemble. More luxurious open two-seaters with folding hoods and wind-up windows were called 'drop-head coupes'. Possibly the best examples of the difference were Jaguar's XK series Roadsters and DHCs. The Roadsters were two-seaters with no space behind the seats, rudimentary frame-and-canvas tops and, until the arrival of the XK150 Roadster, side-screens rather than wind-up windows. XK DHCs, on the other hand, all had folding hoods, vestigial rear seats (or space for them) and wind-up windows. By this definition, Triumph TR2s, TR3s and TR3As were all 'roadsters' even though there was a bit of space behind the seats. But TR4s had wind-up windows and later versions had folding hoods so they became true DHCs. All MGA roadsters were true 'roadsters' but, like TR4s, MGBs soon switched from frame and canvas tops to proper folding hoods. So how do we define a 'roadster' these days? The Lotus Elise has a canvas top supported by side members which have to be removed and stored in special compartments. The Audi TT Roadster has an electrically folding hood with a glass rear window and electric side windows. Same goes for the Honda S2000, which has a plastic rather than glass rear window. Same for the Toyota MR2 and Mazda MX5 which have glass rear windows but no electric assistance to the hood mechanism. The hood of the MGF folds by hand and has a plastic rear window. Today these are all considered 'roadsters', but I have to draw the line at the Mercedes SLK which, as everyone knows, has a fiendishly clever electrically folding hard top. Even though the new SLK 320 six-speed goes like stink, it's definitely a drop-head coupe.

What a 'vis-à-vis'?

'Vis-à-vis' and 'dos-à-dos' are exactly what you would expect, providing you paid attention in your French class at school. In a turn-

of-the-century 'dos-à-dos', two rows of passengers sat back-to-back, while in a 'vis-à-vis' they sat face-to-face, which was hardly conducive to safe driving. A 'brougham' and 'sedanca de ville' are large chauffeur-driven cars in the style of an early taxi, where the driver sits out in the elements while the passengers are carried in a snug closed compartment. A 'sedanca' is a two-door coupe on which the rear seats are covered by a fixed roof but the front pair are either open or covered by a removable top. A 'landaulette', on the other hand, usually has a roofed driver's compartment and roofed centre section with a folding top over the rearmost pair of seats. A 'limousine' is a stretched closed car with a glass window between passengers and driver and, usually, seating for four or more in the passenger compartment. 'Saloons' and 'sedans' are closed cars with two rows of seats and a 'B' pillar between the front and rear doors. (Without 'B' pillars they're described as 'hardtops'.) 'Estate cars', 'shooting brakes' and 'station wagons' are saloons with folding rear seats where the roof continues horizontally over the load area which can be accessed by a door at the back. Cruder versions of estate cars are sometimes described as 'utilities', except in Australia where a 'ute' is a car-based truck.

What's a 'tourer'?

What's the difference between a 1930s–50s 'tourer' and a full-blown convertible? To me, when applied to a car, the word 'tourer' conjures up a picture of a low-slung open four-seater car with two or four doors, the front pair being cut away to give infinite elbow room. The top will usually have a fully folding frame mechanism, but the only glass will be in the front and possibly the rear windows. Canvas and transparent plastic side screens are the order of the day. An 'all-weather tourer', a 'convertible' or a 'cabrio', on the other hand, denote an altogether heavier and drier conveyance, with wind-up glass front and rear side windows. BMW Bauer cabrios had solid removable roof panels between their roll bars and the top screen rail, and a folding hood behind. These should be not confused with a 'targa', which has an integral roll-over bar, usually supporting two solid pieces of roof between it and the top rail of the windscreen, but a fixed roof and rear screen behind.

What's a 'pendulum turn'?

WARNING: DON'T TRY THIS ON PUBLIC ROADS
Former touring car champion Ian Flux showed me the technique in, of all things, a Daewoo Espero, and put quite a bit of space between us and Tiff Needell in the car behind us. Approaching a 180° right-hand bend, what he did was brake hard while simultaneously turning the steering wheel left. This de-stabilised the back of the car, making it easier to throw right into a long oversteering drift, after which the car exited the bend pointing in exactly the right direction. Handbrake turns and 'J' turns may be a little more familiar. Handbrake turns are best done on a loose or damp surface, in a front-wheel-drive or four-wheel-drive car in which the handbrake works on the back wheels. You dip the clutch, turn the steering

wheel hard right or left, whack on the handbrake to bring the back round, select first gear, then engage the clutch to pull away in the direction you have just come from. A 'J' turn is similar, but starting in reverse, and using the footbrake rather than the handbrake to swing the front of the car round to face in the opposite direction.

What's a 'cant-rail'?

It's a coachbuilder's term. The 'cant-rail' is the longitudinal frame member above the door. The 'belt-rail', or 'garnish-rail', is the horizontal bar of a body frame at the bottom of the windows. The 'scuttle' is the part of the bodywork between the engine compartment and the windscreen. A 'cycle wing' is a mudguard over a front wheel which closely follows the curvature of the wheel itself and may even steer with the wheel. A 'helmet wing' is a fixed cycle wing but with an extended rear edge, like a Roman legionnaire's helmet. 'Lights' are side windows, so a 'four-light' saloon has two side windows each side, while a 'six-light' saloon has three. 'Pillars' are vertical frame members separating windows: from front to back, the 'A' pillars or scuttle pillars frame the windscreen; the 'B' pillars separate the front and rear doors; the 'C' pillars separate the rear doors from any side window behind them and the 'D' pillars surround the rear screen. 'Hardtop' and 'pillarless' saloons have no 'B' pillars. Thanks to the excellent *A–Z of British Coachbuilders 1919–1960* by Nick Walker (Bay View Books, price £24.95, ISBN 1-870979-93-1).

What's 'Gasoline Direct Injection'?

You have probably heard of 'diesel direct injection'. By injecting the diesel fuel directly into the combustion chamber rather than an adjacent chamber in the cylinder head, these engines are much more efficient and more economical on fuel. Then Mitsubishi introduced 'Gasoline Direct Injection', and now Peugeot Citroën has followed with its new 'HPi' engine in the C5. Fuel is pumped into the engine at much higher pressure than a conventional injected engine, so that what happens to it in the combustion chamber can be more precisely controlled. This enables the engine to run on a much leaner fuel–air mix at light throttle openings giving it the potential to be more economical and more environmentally friendly in stop/start traffic conditions. At wider throttle openings it reverts to a 'stoichiometric' air–fuel mixture of 14.6:1 and develops its full power. However, while this system is suited to a wide variety of vehicles in Japan from 1.1 litres to 4.5 litres, to give its best it needs high-octane petrol such as the 101Ron petrol available in Japan and the 99Ron Shell Optimax available in Germany. On standard UK 95Ron and 97Ron petrol, the engines need special catalytic converters capable of converting increased amounts of nitrous oxide into harmless nitrogen and oxygen. That's why the benefits of Mitsubishi's GDIs are not as great in versions sold in the UK, why grey-imported GDIs do not meet UK emissions regulations, and why Mitsubishi itself only imports a limited range of its GDI engines.

What's 'Transport 2000'?

'Transport 2000' is a small but well linked pressure group that favours punitive anti-motoring measures such as high petrol taxes, high vehicle taxes, inefficient vehicle speed restrictions and draconian speed limit enforcement. Yet time and time again, its spokespeople are fronted on radio and television news programmes as the voices of reason. Fortunately, with the price of a litre of unleaded approaching 89.9p and Tony Blair telling us he needs 70 per cent of that to pay for our hospitals and schools, the public has finally woken up and turned against anti-car campaigners. So what organisations can honestly be said to truly represent the average road user, each of whom is forced to contribute 10p towards our hospitals and schools for every mile he or she drives? The Association of British Drivers is one, even though a name change to The Association of Road Users might give it greater stature. The ABD has a very helpful website at www.abd.org.uk and, for those who don't have internet connection membership enquires can be phoned through to 0700 781 544. Fellow columnist Mike Rutherford founded The Motorists Association, PO Box 325, Longfield DA3 7JU. The AA joined the fight against petrol tax while it was still 80 per cent of the pump price, while the RAC has the very able Edmund King speaking up for the motorist at every chance he gets.

What is 'cost per mile'?

Various organisations, including the AA and *Glass's Guide*, publish figures estimating vehicle cost per mile. While these are extremely useful to fleet managers and to drivers who cover average mileages, they aren't so much help to readers who are interested in the cost per mile of running a small 1,200cc car for a small annual mileage so as to compare it with taxi fares. Assuming the car is two years old and under 1,200cc, the biggest annual cost from March 2001–February 2002 will be depreciation of around £1,250. Loss of interest on capital of £5,000 will be about £400. With petrol at £4.50 a gallon and assuming 35 mpg, each mile will cost 12.86p, so 2,000 miles of petrol will come to £257. Insurance will probably be about £250. The car will need at least an annual service which, with running repairs, will probably work out at around £200 a year. At the new rate for cars under 1,200cc, VED will be £105 a year. And a low-cost breakdown insurance such as that offered by the Guild of Experienced Motorists (GEM) will be around £50. So, as a basis of comparison with taxi fares, the car will cost roughly £2,500 a year, or £1.25 a mile.

What is 'Multitronic'?

This is Audi's interpretation of the CVT (Continuously Variable Transmission). Despite the good sense of dispensing with the need for a conventional set of separate gear ratios, CVTs have acquired an unenviable reputation for unreliability. Part of it comes from sensor failure in those which employ an electromagnetic clutch between the engine and the gearbox itself. Part of it arises from band failure, though the old composite bands are now mostly replaced by steel bands. And part of it is due to transmission fluid leaks, to which CVTs are particularly sensitive. To overcome all this, and to develop a CVT suitable for relatively large, high-torque engines, Audi's transmission engineering team under Reinhard Gesenhaus developed a new type of CVT. Instead of an electromagnetic clutch, Audi's Multitronic has a multi-plate wet clutch which engages automatically as engine revs rise and does not suffer the power sapping of, for example, Nissan's torque converter CVT. And instead of composite or steel bands, Audi has come up with a 'link-plate' chain, similar to the timing chain of Ford's Duratec V6, but much wider. This rides on two very special pulleys which fit over each other and the hydraulically controlled relative movement between them gives a spread of gearing ratios of over 6.1, compared to under 5.0 for a conventional five-speed automatic. The result is an extremely flexible and responsive drive which is completely jerk and jolt free, and is actually faster than the same car fitted with a five-speed Tiptronic or manual transmission. Multitronic transmissions, with steering wheel push button-selectable ratios, are now available on the new Audi A4 and A6 models.

What's an 'over'?

An 'over' is a term possibly coined by Tom Harley, the man who can get you any new car you want at the going rate. How he does this is to offer a considerable premium 'over' the car's list price to its owner, to which he adds his smaller cut. He's the best there is, never rips anyone off whether buyer or seller, and everyone from lottery winners to presidents beat a path to his wrought iron gates, appropriately in Overseal, Staffs (tel: 01283 762762; website: www.tomhartley.com).

But Tom didn't invent 'overs'. In Geoff Owen's fascinating book *Turning Back the Clock*, the author lists *Glass's Guide* used car prices for thirty models in July 1950, during the 'export or die days' when new cars were virtually unobtainable by private punters in the UK. Then you could have had a £329 Ford Anglia for £545, a £761 Austin A70

Countryman for £929 or a £799 Humber Hawk with a sunroof for £1,150. Sadly, this huge surplus of demand over supply hardly encouraged the UK motor industry to come up with better, more reliable cars, or better industrial relations. Instead it became swallowed by arrogant complacency and ended up blackmailing us to 'buy British' or lose our car industry. We chose the latter. It's one thing, like Tom Hartley's customers, to want the latest Ferrari and to want it now. It was quite another to have spent your hard-earned money on a brand new Mini, Austin 1300, Austin Maxi or Triumph TR7 and be forced to grovel to a jumped-up service manager in yet another failed attempt to get the damn thing to even run properly.

What's the 'p/x punt'?

This is an accounting procedure that can leave both new and used car buyers extremely confused about what they actually paid for their newer car. Say the newer car you want is stickered at a nice even £9,999 and you enter negotiations on that basis. Instead of thinking 'what's the bottom line?', most punters either get side-tracked or side-track themselves into complicated negotiations over the value of their part-exchange. All the salesman wants to do is make a sale, and he knows what the bottom line is. So when the punter names a price for his p/x, the salesman does some rapid mental arithmetic (or uses his calculator) to work out how much he can afford to give based on the profit margin he has in the newer car. Giving the punter what seems to be a high price for his p/x distracts the punter's attention from the fact that the sticker price might be a little on the high side, and he usually makes the sale. It isn't until the punter gets his invoice that he sees that his p/x has been written in at a much lower figure and the price of the new car has been reduced by a similar amount. So if he'd been offered £5,000 for his p/x against £9,999 for the newer car, he might find that the invoice reads £4,000 for the p/x against £8,999 for the new car, even though the bottom line is the same £4,999. The reason for this is that the p/x was never worth £5,000 and the salesman knows he can only trade it out for between £4,000 and £4,500. VAT is due as a proportion of the difference between the price a dealer pays to buy a car and the price he sells it at, but is not reclaimable on a loss. Had the punter asked for a £500 discount on the newer car, the p/x allowance would have been similarly reduced. It is extremely rare for a car to be sold to a private buyer for less than the dealer paid to buy it in.

What's a 'plug'?

You have probably wondered why traffic on a motorway often slows to a crawl or even a standstill, then, within five to ten miles, gets back up to speed with no obvious reason for the slowdown. What caused it is a 'plug'. When a motorway is very busy with traffic in the outer two lanes cruising at 70–85mph, all that is needed to create a blockage is one plodder in lane two driving at 50mph and refusing to move over into lane one. Traffic in lane one, typically travelling at the 58mph governed limit of an HGV truck, will pass the plodder's tailback on the nearside, as The Highway Code allows. But faster traffic using lane two will find itself in a bottleneck. It can either stay in lane two or move to lane three – only to find that because other lane two traffic ahead is doing the same thing, lane three slows to a lower speed than lane two. Because traffic immediately behind the plug is effectively being forced to lose 10–15mph, it ceases to clear enough space on the motorway for following traffic still piling at 70–85mph into the back of the congestion caused by the 'plug'. At the very least, the knock-on effect is to cause traffic at the back to slow down or stop. At most it can cause nose-to-tail accidents, which then create an even worse plug than the original plodder. One answer is thought to be variable speed limits which can control the rate at which traffic encounters the end of the tailback. But the effect is still to increase the time vehicles spend on the road and to increase journey times. The real answer is a fixed penalty for any driver driving in lane two or three at 60mph or less when there is space beside him to drive in lane one.

What's a 'Ronda'?

A Ronda is found on a two-lane, 60mph-restricted A road or B road. It is a snake-like procession of between five and twenty vehicles all following an 'M' to 'V' registered Honda Civic 1.5 VTEC-E, or the similarly shaped Rover 400 or 45, which is travelling at 40–45 mph. The drivers of the three cars immediately behind the Ronda are insufficiently confident to overtake but, instead of leaving adequate space between them and the car in front for a car to overtake them, they all squeeze up into what becomes a mobile roadblock. Should the driver of a much faster car take it upon himself to overtake and squeeze between two of these cars, much gesticulating, tooting of horns, flashing of lights and writing down of registrations may ensue. But who is in the wrong here? Many will argue that a driver has a perfect right to pootle along at 40–45 mph and that the real fault is with the three cars behind the pootler which squeeze up and fail to overtake. Others will argue that the faster drivers should be more patient. But since the situation described is one that leads to a significant number of fatal crashes on A and B roads, perhaps a driver who wishes to travel no faster than 45mph should pay attention to his mirrors and when he realises he is causing a hold-up should pull into the next available space at the side of the road to let the tailback past. This is what 'driving with due consideration for other road users' is all about.

What's an 'ESVA'?

Single Vehicle Approval is a means of testing and certificating imported vehicles up to ten years old which are not already European Type Approved. It was imposed by Gavin Strang as from July 1998 to provide a means of quality control over imports, mainly from Japan and the USA, but it was also used to impose quantity restrictions by restricting trade imports to no more than fifty a year of any one make and model of vehicle. Traders instantly got round this by 'personally importing' cars 3–10 years old, thus absolving them from the trade restrictions and tests, and the entire system became an unsatisfactory mess. However, on 1 August 2000 the DETR issued a press release announcing that, as from 18 August 2000, the 50-car-a-year trade quota would be lifted. From 1 February 2001 the rules about what constitutes a 'personal import' were tightened and, to qualify, the importer must have resided in the country he is exporting from for more than a year and owned the vehicle there for more than six months. As from 1 September 2001, the SVA test itself has been 'enhanced' (Enhanced SVA: ESVA) to cover safety, anti-theft security and tougher emissions standards, and to extend the full test to commercial vehicles previously subject to an abbreviated SVA. All vehicles purchased in other EU countries will normally be EU Type Approved and exempt from ESVA. ESVA public enquiry tel no: 020 7944 3000; website: www.via.gov.uk.

What's a 'jump-start'?

Almost everyone knows the answer to this. But not everyone knows the correct way to use a set of jump leads to start a car with a flat battery. What most garages and yard men at the auctions do is as follows. First connect the positive terminal (+) of the good battery to the positive terminal (+) of the flat battery. Then connect the negative terminal (–) of the good battery to a metal (negative earth) engine part of the car with the flat battery. If instead they are connected negative to negative directly, or worse still positive to negative, they could feed too much current into the Engine Control Unit and burn it out. To try and make the whole process of jump-starting a lot safer than it otherwise might be, Airflow products has developed a fool-proof jump lead kit called the Kangoo, with LED lights that tell you if you have done the job correctly at each stage. They come in a circular plastic container from Airflow, the people who market my recommended Battery Trickle Charger/Conditioner; tel: 01635 569569.

Why should I worry about Freon?

Freon is the CFC refrigerant also known as R12, which the DETR has banned from sale since 1 October 2000. While this would seem to be all very well and good for the environment, it poses two rather serious problems. The first is that most owners of air-conditioned cars built before the end of 1993 will have R12 systems. And, while it was originally thought that the R12 in their systems could simply be replaced by CFC-free R134a refrigerant, this cannot be done easily due to the incompatibility of the lubricating oils contained in R12 and R134a. Blends of R134a with the older type of lubricating oil have been tried on a trial-and-error basis, with mixed success, often leading to leaking seals and loss of refrigerant. Worse still, R12 systems refilled with R134a or with one of the blends have not necessarily been marked with what they contain. On top of all of this, R12 refrigerant removed from a system needs to be properly disposed of or its disposal creates, rather than solves, an environmental problem. Many thanks to Dave Norton of Auto Air for this. More at www.honestjohn.co.uk (Honest John's FAQs) and at www.autoair.com.

What's an 'Alteza'?

It may not melt in the mouth, but it is certainly a mouth-watering, Japanese-market incarnation of what we know as the Lexus IS200. Instead of the UK-market 2.0 litre 150bhp straight six, criticised by more than a few for its lack of grunt, you can opt for a 210bhp 'BEAMS' VVTi variable valve timing four. Pop that through the standard six-speed box, add the best steering Toyota has ever fitted to a four-door car, and you have quite a motor. Another strangely named Toyota is the Harrier. This has now reached the UK badged as a Lexus RX300 and has turned out to be the nicest Sports Utility Vehicle of the lot (I prefer it to the 3.0 litre BMW X5). We got the 2,995cc 220bhp V6 automatic 4x4 version, though two-wheel-drive and a smaller 2,164cc 140bhp engine are available in Japan. Other different Toyota names include the Aristo, which we know as the Lexus GS300, the Soarer, which has been sold in the USA for years as a Lexus coupe, the Lucida Emina, which is a slimmed-down embodiment of the old shape Previa, and the Townace which is a poshed up Lite Ace van turned into 7-seater MPV. For specialist dealers, check out the excellent *Car Import Guide* magazine or its website at www.car-import-guide.com.

What is a 'timing belt tensioner'?

A reader's letter confirms that even some dealers remain ignorant of the danger to engines posed by plastic timing belt tensioner pulleys. These pulleys run on sealed bearings at up to 15,000 revs per minute. If the pulley is made of steel or cast iron, the heat generated by the bearing is dissipated throughout the pulley itself, so the bearing runs much cooler than does the bearing in the centre of a plastic pulley. Normally it should therefore have a much longer life. When the bearing of a steel or cast iron pulley starts to reach the end of its life it shrieks, giving the owner plenty of warning that something is amiss and that he should stop before the thing seizes up, throwing off the belt. But when the bearing of a plastic timing belt tensioner pulley nears the end of its life, the additional heat this creates before it starts shrieking cannot be dissipated into the plastic so, without warning, the plastic cracks and shatters, throwing off the timing belt with disastrous consequences. That is why plastic timing belt tensioner pulleys should be replaced when the belt is replaced, at 40,000-mile or four-year intervals, whichever comes first.

What is 'Torotrak'?

This is a tough new type of Infinitely Variable Transmission which dispenses with the need for a clutch or torque converter and the drive belts used in CVTs. Instead, it relies on a system of cones and wheels to deliver a continuous range of drive ratios from full reverse through to high overdrive. As a result, the vehicle is always in the right gear ratio for the circumstances rather than a compromise ratio, as is the case even with a six-speed manual gearbox. The huge benefit of this is a fuel saving of more than 17 per cent compared to a manual transmission. Torotrak was first developed for trans-verse-engined cars and has been extensively road-tested, first in 2.0 litre Rovers and later in the 2.0 litre Ford Mondeo. Now a third-generation Torotrak has been developed specifically for rear-drive and four-wheel-drive Sports Utility Vehicles such as the Ford Explorer, Ford Expedition, Ford F-Series, Chevrolet Suburban, Chevrolet CK Series and Dodge Ram. Transmission manufacturers throughout the world have Torotrak systems on test. For more information contact Torotrak (Development) Ltd, tel: 01772 900900, website: www.torotrak.com.

What's an 'A Class' car?

Different car makers used different jargon to describe the sizes of cars they make. Though they have become a bit blurred at the edges, they start with 'Sub A', or mini, which includes the old Mini, Matiz, Amica, Ford Ka, SEAT Arosa, VW Lupo, etc. Next is the 'A' or 'supermini' class which includes the new MINI, Fiesta, 106, 206, Mercedes A Class, Micra, Yaris, Ibiza, Corsa, Polo, etc., and which, confusingly, is dubbed 'basse' or 'B Class' in France. Next, the 'B', 'small family' or 'lower medium' class of Xsara, Focus, 323, Almera, 306, Corolla, Astra, Golf, etc., known in France as 'M1'. Next, our 'C', 'large family' or 'upper medium' class of Audi A4, Xantia, Mondeo, 626, Mercedes C Class, Primera, Laguna, Avensis, Vectra, Passat, etc., known in France as 'M2'. Then comes our 'D' or 'Executive' class of Audi A6, BMW 5-Series, Mercedes E Class, Volvo S80, etc. And finally our 'E' or 'Luxury' class of Audi A8, BMW 7 Series, Mercedes S Class, etc., known collectively with the D Class in France as 'Classe H' for 'haut de game'. It's all so confusing, with cars like the Rover 25, Rover 75, BMW 3 Series and Mitsubishi Galant difficult to pin-hole. This is one piece of industry jargon best forgotten.

What's an 'Agreed Value'?

Once a car gets past 15 years old, and if it is in any way considered 'classic', then the only way to insure it is comprehensively on a classic car insurance policy. These work on an agreed-value basis. The owner has the car valued by the appropriate owners' club (which it would be wise to join anyway), and agrees to restrict his or her annual mileage to a given figure. If you don't do this, if your cherished old car is stolen you could find your ordinary car insurer values it at buttons. Specialist classic car insurers include Footman James on 0121 561 4196, Firebond on 07000 347326, Classic Direct on 01480 484827, Lynbrook Insurance on 01704 822661, Classic Club Direct on 0800 298 2754 and Heritage on 0121 246 6060. See my directory of more than 500 car clubs starting on page 133 (and updated regularly at www.honestjohn.co.uk).

What's the difference between 'MEG' and 'MPG'?

It's always a wise precaution to get the strength of your engine coolant anti-freeze checked before winter. (Vauxhall dealers offer cut-price 'Winter Check Ups'.) However, because engines are inevitably made of different metals in close proximity to each other they are what is known as 'corrosion batteries'. To prevent internal engine corrosion and the sludge this causes blocking water galleries, coolant also contains corrosion inhibitors. In normal Mono Ethylene Glycol (MEG) coolant, the inhibitors last two to three years before they are too degraded to work and internal engine corrosion beings to set in. However, around six years ago a different type of coolant, Mono Propylene Glycol (MPG) became widely available. The brand name for the additive package is 'Trigard', the corrosion inhibitors last at least four years, the coolant is best bought pre-mixed with purified water and, because it is environmentally friendly, old coolant can be safely flushed down a storm drain. Some brand names for pre-mixed MPG Trigard coolants are Comma Coldstream, Esso Ready Mixed, Quantum (VW/Audi) Ready Mixed Coolant, Bluecol Protex Anti Freeze, Unipart Super Plus Anti Freeze, Batoyle Masterfrost and Silkolene Iceguard. 'Forlife' pre-mix from Toyota dealers (£13.61 + VAT) for 5 litres is also recommended by readers.

What's a 'default test'?

Ever since August 1992 most petrol engined cars have had to undergo an 'advanced emissions test' as part of their annual MOT. But not *all* petrol engined cars. For various reasons such as unsold stocks, lack of manufacturer test data or the sheer impossibility of getting certain cars through an advanced emissions test, exemptions were allowed right up to the end of July 1995. But that's when the Vehicle Inspectorate finally drew a line and determined that any petrol engined cars first sold as new in the UK after that date would have to meet a fixed emissions requirement with the engine running between certain fixed parameters. This is known as the emissions 'default test'. At the engine's natural idle speed it must not emit more than 0.5 per cent by volume CO. And in an engine speed range of between 2,500 and 3,000 rpm, the engine must not emit more than 0.3 per cent by volume CO or more than 0.02 per cent by volume (200 parts per million)

Hydrocarbons, while the fuel/air mixture in the exhaust emissions must not vary by more than 0.03 of Lambda (which is an air/fuel ratio of 14.7:1).

What's 'multiplex' wiring?

Multiplex is a new, neater system of wiring a car's electrics introduced by Citroën in the Xsara Picasso and now also applied to the Berlingo Multispace. Multiplex enables the manufacturer to offer a number of extra features such as speed-sensitive intermittent wipers, automatic activation of the rear wiper when reversing in the rain, user friendly interior lights and 'guide you home' headlights which stay on for 60 seconds after switching off to enable you to see your way to your front door. Additionally the digital multiplexing of the Xsara Picasso means that, on the intermittent setting, the windscreen wipers will automatically adjust their speed to complement the speed of the car, while the speed-indexed stereo adjusts its volume to suit the speed and road noise of the vehicle. Other features of the Picasso enabled by Multiplex are a 'black panel' function of the digital instrument display allowing you to switch off all instruments apart from the speedometer, a digital maintenance indicator and an on-board computer by which you can set a 'speed exceeded' warning standard across the Xsara Picasso range. Multiplexing also allows a reduction in electrical connections and wires, reducing weight and greatly improving the reliability of the car's electrics.

What's 'Powershift'?

Powershift is a government-backed initiative run by the Energy Saving Trust to provide grants to buyers on new 'clean fuel' vehicles such as the Honda Insight and Toyota Prius hybrids and the LPG- or CNG-converted cars being offered by Citroën, Ford, Vauxhall and Volvo, among others. Powershift has written to tell us that it now has a website, www.est-powershift.org.uk, which contains a map showing all UK LPG refuelling stations, a buyer's guide to new clean fuel vehicles, a directory of approved gas conversion specialists, links to other relevant sites' and answers to Frequently Asked Questions about LPG and CNG conversions. For those not yet with access to the Internet, there is also a telephone hotline: 0845 602 1425. I should add that anyone considering an LPG or CNG conversion should first check with the car manufacturer that the engine is suitable for conversion. From the experience of one reader we know that Honda VTEC engines, and high performance engines generally, definitely are not.

What's 'Pass Plus'?

With insurance rates for young drivers as much as ten times the price of their old bangers, any kid with a brain wants to know how he or she can get a better deal. The answer is 'Pass Plus', a post-driving-test instruction course backed by the Driving Standards

Agency and designed to prepare young drivers for the reality of driving in all weathers, in and out of town, on motorways and at night. There's no test to get cold sweats about. Simply, once the instructor is satisfied, he or she issues a pass certificate which is not just a lifesaver in itself, it can entitle youngsters to reductions of up to 25 per cent on their insurance premiums. Over four years this could easily add up to a £1,000 saving. Insurers which offer discounts to Pass Plus certificate holders include Churchill, CGNU, Direct Line, Norwich Union and Ecclesiastical Direct (young women only). The Pass Plus hotline is 0115 901 2633; website: www.passplus.org.uk.

What's a 'car parc'?

'Car parc' is the expression used to describe the total number of cars in use in a country. In 1999, according to the SMMT, Britain's 'car parc' comprised 27,010,437 cars, plus 3,304,889 commercial vehi-

81

cles, plus 90,417 buses and coaches: a grand total of 30,405,743 – one for every two members of the population and almost all of which must be owned by someone of voting age, Government ministers please take note. For the same year, the 'car parc' in Germany was 42,423,254 (total vehicle parc 45,793,265); France: 27,480,000 (33,089,000); Italy: 32,000,000 (35,485,500); Spain: 16,847,397 (20,636,125); Japan: 51,164,204 (71,722,762); and the USA: 133,000,000 (214,302,000). It's interesting that Holland and Australia have similar sized populations of around 18,000,000 but widely differing car and vehicle parcs, a difference that is probably due to the huge difference in size of the two countries and the fact that Holland is flat (bicycle friendly) and has excellent public transport. Australia has 9,750,000 cars and a total vehicle parc of 12,132,000, while Holland has just 6,120,000 cars and a total vehicle parc of 6,894,000.

How does 'kW' relate to 'bhp?

All Continental European manufacturers now express power outputs in kW and torque in Nm. I have been criticised for converting these to the more understandable bhp and lb ft. However, the future will be metric, so a list of conversion factors makes sense.

Inches to millimetres: multiply by 25.4. mm to inches: multiply by 0.0394.
Mph to kph: multiply by 1.6093. kph to mph: multiply by 0.6214.
Gallons to litres: multiply by 4.546. litres to gallons: multiply by 0.22.
Bhp to PS: multiply by 1.0139. PS to bhp: multiply by 0.9863.
PS to kW: multiply by 0.7355. kW to PS: multiply by 1.3596.
Lb ft to Nm: multiply by 1.3558. Nm to lb ft: multiply by 0.7376.
Mpg to litres/100km = 282.481 divided by the mpg figure.
Litres/100km to mpg = 282.481 divided by the litres/100km figure.

Many thanks to Citroën UK for these figures.

What's a 'hot rod'?

We're not talking here of the Spanish 'polla caliente', which means something very rude indeed. We're talking about a generic term for boring old cars which have been made a bit more exciting. According to a wonderful 1994 book, *Authentic Hot Rods*, by Don Montgomory (ISBN 0-9626454-4-3), the foundations of hot rodding lay in speed trials on Muroc Dry Lake in 1932. Most of the cars were fenderless Ford V8s and hopped-up earlier 4-cylinder Model 'A's. By 1938 the Southern California Timing Association (SCTA) had been set up, but by 1941 its activities were curtailed by the war. But in the years 1946–49 the sport of time trials on the dry lakes blossomed. In 1949 the sport took an alternative direction in the form of drag racing. What's particularly interesting is a craze which grew in the UK about ten years ago to recreate late 1940s and early 1950s hot rods as authentically as possible, then set up a meet and race them on an old airfield. 'Hot Rod' racing, on the other hand, is the quick category of UK stock car racing and bears little relation to the origins of hot rodding.

What's a 'fender'?

A tired old cliché asserts that Britain and the USA are separated by a common language. But in the automotive (motor) industry, there are more linguistic differences than most people realise. In alphabetical order (with the British version in brackets), here are some of the more common ones: top (hood); hood (bonnet); trunk (boot); engine displacement (engine capacity); motor (engine); rumble seat (dickey seat); fender (mudguard or wing); nerf bar (bumper); station wagon (estate car or shooting brake); transmission (gearbox); gasoline (petrol); sedan (saloon); trailer (caravan); windshield (windscreen); tire (tyre); muffler (silencer); kerosene (paraffin); hard top (pillarless coupe); phaeton (tourer); stocker (touring car racer); rig (articulated truck); clunker (banger); top fuel (runs on nitro methane).

What is 'horsepower'?

Horsepower was a very strange measurement adopted by the British for the purpose of motor vehicle taxation. Many believe it was deliberately developed to penalise cheap, large-engined cars such as the Model T Ford in favour of smaller engined vehicles of British manufacture. The RAC formula for calculating horsepower is the square of the cylinder bore in millimetres multiplied by the number of cylinders in the engine, divided by 1613. This meant that a Model T Ford with a swept engine capacity of 2,890cc, a bore of 95mm and a stroke of 101.5mm was classed as a 22.4HP car and taxed accordingly. On the other hand, a Morris Cowley with a swept engine capacity of 1,548cc, a bore of 69.5mm and a stroke of 120mm was classed as an 11.9HP car, with the obvious tax benefit this brought. In Britain's strangely protected market, small-capacity, narrow-bore, long-stroke engines became the order of the day and Herbert Austin was able to get away with selling us the miniature 747cc 7.7HP Austin Seven for much the same price as Henry Ford had been charging for twice as much motor car. It was hardly surprising that, on the developing world markets of the 1920s and 1930s, the tough, large-engined, short-stroke American cars were much preferred to the fragile, small-engined, long-stroke British cars.

What is 'electronic ignition'?

These days, most cars are fitted with some form of electronic ignition or 'ignition igniter' in place of the old-fashioned distributor and points system. The disadvantage of a distributor is that the rotor arm contact and the points in the distributor are inevitably subject to wear. So what an electronic ignition system kit does is replace them with an optical switch which feeds firing information through to a power module without any physical contact. Basically, an infra red light beam is detected by a silicon photo-transistor and this beam is interrupted by a revolving chopper with wings for each cylinder replacing the rotor arm on the distributor shaft. The opti-

cal switch is fitted to the same base plate as the points were, so that speed and vacuum advance are unchanged. The earthed power module (or amplifier) receives the electronic pulses from the optical switch and charges the coil. These systems rarely go wrong, but when they do the fault tends to be either in the distributor shaft or its bearing or, more commonly, in the ignition amplifier which can malfunction intermittently.

What's a 'Hamburger Junction'?

The Transport Research Laboratory has been experimenting with various alternatives to roundabouts, some of which it has now introduced to real road situations. A 'Hamburger Junction' is where a major road crosses a minor road and a roundabout formerly dealt with traffic flow. Instead of having to drive round the roundabout, cars on the main road drive straight across it. Then, when traffic starts to build up on the minor roads into the roundabout or on the major road from traffic wishing to turn right, lights stop the through traffic to allow the other vehicles on their way. A 'Hot Cross Bun junction' takes this a stage further, allowing traffic at a crossroads between two major roads to treat the junction either as a roundabout or as a crossroads with slip roads for traffic wishing to turn left or right. A 'Signabout' does away with the roundabout altogether, dividing traffic entering the junction which wishes to turn right from traffic intending to go straight ahead or turn left. Instead of driving round the backs of each other, vehicles making turns pass left-side to left-side. Unfortunately, the new schemes seem to be causing enormous confusion, nowhere more so than at the former dosser's palace Waterloo roundabout, where, to the great surprise of many drivers, roundabout traffic suddenly became two-way with one side blocked off so there was no longer any possibility of correcting a directional error – the great boon of every roundabout.

What's a 'Christmas Tree'?

To launch the company's 8.2 litre, 1,183bhp, supercharged drag racing PT 'Bruiser', Chrysler has kindly supplied a list of drag racing jargon. A 'drag race' is a race between two cars, usually down a quarter-mile drag-strip. The first car to pass the finish line wins. A 'Christmas tree' is the stack of lights used to tell the drivers when to start their race. A 'dragster' or 'rail' is a long, low drag-racing car with an engine usually developing well over 1,000bhp; a 'blower' is a supercharger; a 'burnout' is spinning the tyres on the line prior to the race to get them as hot and sticky as possible for maximum traction off the line; an 'ET' is the elapsed time the car takes to cover the quarter mile strip; a 'bump spot' is the lowest qualifying elapsed time; a 'funny car' is a short wheelbase dragster with a plastic body resembling that of a current car; a 'holeshot' is when one racer leaves the startline before his opponent; a 'red light' is a disqualification for leaving the line before the green light on the Christmas tree; a 'pro stock' is a category for steel-bodied race cars like the PT Bruiser.

What's a 'DR10'?

This is the driving licence endorsement code for Driving with Excess Alcohol. It remains valid for three years from the date of conviction and must remain on the driver's licence for 11 years from conviction. The same applies to a DR20 (Driving unfit through drink), a DR30 (Failing to supply a specimen when suspected of drink driving) and a DR80 (Driving unfit through drugs). Other alcohol/drug driving offence codes must remain on the licence for four years from conviction. These include DR40 (In charge of a vehicle when unfit through excess alcohol), DR60 (Failing to supply a specimen when suspected of being drunk in charge of a vehicle but not driving it), and DR90 (In charge of a vehicle while unfit through drugs).

What's a 'CD10'?

This is the driving licence endorsement code for driving without due care. A CD20 signifies a conviction for driving without reasonable consideration for other persons using the road (for example, motorway lane hogging); a CD30 signifies driving without due care and reasonable consideration for other persons using the road; a CD40 is causing death by careless driving; and a CD70 is causing death by careless driving and failing to supply a specimen. All these remain valid for three years and must stay on the licence for four years except the CD40 and CD70, which must stay on the licence for 11 years. DD30 signifies a conviction for reckless driving; DD40 for dangerous driving; DD60 for manslaughter; DD70 for causing death by reckless driving and DD80 for causing death by dangerous driving. A DD30 must remain on the licence for four years; DD40, DD60, DD70 and DD80 for 11 years.

What's an 'AC10'?

This is the driving licence endorsement code for failing to stop after an accident. AC20 signifies a conviction for failing to report an accident, and an AC30 is used for other miscellaneous accident offences. A BA10 signifies a conviction for driving after a court imposed ban (usually also punished by 6 months imprisonment, especially after a Drink Driving ban); a BA20 is for driving when under age; and a BA 30 is for attempting to drive while disqualified. A CU10 is for driving a vehicle with defective brakes; a CU20 for driving a vehicle in a dangerous condition; a CU30 for driving a vehicle with defective tyres; a CU 40 for driving a vehicle with defective steering; a CU50 for driving a vehicle carrying a dangerous load; and a CU60 is for miscellaneous construction and use offences. All AC, BA and CU-coded endorsements apply for three years and must remain on the licence for four years.

What's an 'SP10'?

This is the driving licence endorsement code for driving at excess speed for the type of goods vehicle. An SP20 is for driving at excess speed for the type of non-goods passenger carrying vehicle. And an SP30 is the general endorsement code for driving at excess speed; an SP40 is for driving at excess speed for the type of passenger vehicle; an SP50 is for driving at excess speed on a motorway; and an SP60 is used for miscellaneous speeding offences. An IN10 signifies conviction for the offence of driving uninsured; an LC10 for driving without a licence; an LC20 for driving otherwise than in accordance with the licence held; an LC30 is for making a false declaration about fitness to drive; an LC40 is for failure to notify a disability; and an LC50 is for driving after one's licence has been revoked on medical grounds. All CU and SP coded offences remain valid for three years and must remain on the licence for four years.

What's a 'pre-heater'

Diesel fuel has a high 'wax' content which can crystallise at low temperatures and clog the fuel filter. Although winter-grade diesel now

has additives to help prevent 'waxing' down to around minus 20 degrees Celsius, most diesel cars are fitted with a fuel pre-heater in the fuel line before the fuel filter. It is thermostatically controlled to switch on whenever the temperature drops to just above zero. Other types of pre-heater, such as VAG's, are incorporated into the fuel pump. In cold weather, indirect injected diesel engines also require pre-heating of the combustion chambers because the heat created by the initial ignition of the fuel is soaked away through the cold engine cylinder walls. This is achieved by means of 'glow plugs' which introduce a heated element into the combustion chamber. The high compression of an IDI diesel engine and the need to heat glow plugs helps explain why they need a high-capacity battery and why the life of that battery can be short if the vehicle does lots of short runs from cold. Though direct injected diesels don't usually need pre-heaters, some do have glow plugs, but these are smaller, heat up more quickly and take less out of the battery.

What's an 'alternator'

This is the piece of engine-driven kit which generates a car's electricity supply. The 'stator' is a circular laminated iron core on which three separate lengths of wire are wound, and which remains static in the casing. The 'rotor' is a coil of wire wound on an iron core pressed onto a shaft. When current from the battery is passed through the rotor a magnetic field is created and, as it rotates inside the stator, an AC current is produced. This is converted to the DC current required by the car using six diodes which allow current to flow in only one rather than two directions. The advantage of an alternator over a dynamo is that it can be geared up to be driven at higher speeds than the engine, enabling the car battery to be re-charged more quickly at low engine speeds. Typical alternators produce useful current at around 1,500rpm up to a maximum of about 7,000rpm, and most are driven at about twice the engine speed.

What's a 'MacPherson Strut'

With a few exceptions, car suspension is composed of coil or leaf springs, damper units to absorb bounce, and various arms, links and bushes to hold the system together. The idea of the MacPherson Strut was to eliminate as many separate components as possible, particularly in the front suspension of a car – though MacPherson Struts can also be used at the rear. Very simply, strut suspension combines a coil spring, a telescopic damper and a vertical suspension arm in one. When used at the front of a car the spring and damper fit into a bearing set into a strengthened section of the top inner wing of the car. This allows it and the hub it is attached to at the bottom to rotate, so the car can be steered. A single arm containing a lower bearing for the strut provides up and down movement and is held in place by a leading or trailing arm running at right angles to it. One of the first British cars to have MacPherson Strut front suspension was the 1950 Ford Consul.

What is 'smoke opacity'

This is the density of the exhaust emissions of a diesel-fuelled engine. For all diesel-fuelled cars and light commercial vehicles first used on or after 1 August 1979, it is tested annually as part of the MOT test by a probe which measures absorption coefficient per metre and is placed in the vehicle's exhaust tailpipe. Controversy still surrounds the actual method of testing. First the engine must be brought up to its running temperature, measured by a probe placed down the oil dipstick tube. Engine revs are then very gradually increased until they reach a governed maximum. If the fuel pump governor is not working then the test will be abandoned. The engine is then revved to its maximum governed revs three times and three measurements of its exhaust smoke opacity are taken. The maximum permitted is an absorption coefficient of 3.0 per metre for a turbocharged diesel and 2.5 per metre for a non-turbo diesel. If the average of the three tests is below the permitted figures, the engine passes the test. If not, further tests take place up to a maximum of six accelerations until the average of the last three tests is below the permitted figures. If it isn't, the engine fails its MOT 'smoke opacity' test.

What's a 'SNOC6'?

This is a nasty form from the DVLA offering vehicle keepers who have failed to file a Statutory Off Road Notification an out-of-court settlement of £25, increasing to £45 if the money is not received within 14 days, instead of being summoned to court and facing a fine of up to £1,000. The trouble is, even if a car owner does comply with the law and sends the DVLA a SORN declaring his car to be off the road and therefore not subject to VED, it is up to the owner to ensure not only that it is delivered to the DVLA but also that the DVLA does not lose it, otherwise he will be subject to the fine. If a car is kept off the road unlicensed for some time, the SORN must be repeated every 12 months or the keeper will also be subject to a fine of up to £1,000. The same applies if you sell a car, complete the appropriate section of the V5 then send it to the DVLA and the DVLA either does not receive it or loses it and the subsequent owner does not tax the car. To avoid these grossly unfair penalties, anyone posting a SORN or change of keeper notification to the DVLA should do so by Recorded Delivery.

What's in a name?

We all know the simple ones, like MG which are the initials of Morris Garages, William Morris's original retail and repair garages in Oxford, and GM which stands for General Motors. Amilcar was named after the financiers Joseph Lamy and Emile Akar; BMW are the initials of Bayerische Motoren Werke; DKW: Dampf Kraft Wagen (steam car); FIAT: Fabbrica Italiana Automobili Torino; SAAB: Svenska Aeroplan Aktiebolaget; SEAT: Sociedad Espanola de Automoviles de Turismo; and SIMCA: Societe Industrielle de Mecanique et de Construction Automobile. Mercedes was named after Emile Jellinek's 11-year-old daughter. Volvo is derived from the Latin verb meaning, 'I roll' (but Nova is not a translation of the Spanish for 'doesn't go'!) Daimler allegedly named its Conquest model after its price of £1,066. The Ford GT40 was so called because it was 40 inches high. And, though 'Volkswagen' translates to 'people's car', it was originally named by the initials KdF which stood for 'Kraft durch Freude' or 'Strength through Joy'.

What's an 'MOT Refusal to Test'?

This is where an MOT examiner can refuse to examine a vehicle submitted for testing on one or more of the following grounds: the V5 registration document is not provided to prove the date of first registration if this is necessary for testing purposes (usually when the vehicle has a non-dating cherished registration); the vehicle is presented in such a dirty condition that examination would be unreasonably difficult; the vehicle cannot be driven, or has insufficient fuel or oil to enable the test to be completed; an authorised examiner considers that an insecure load or other items would prevent a proper test being carried out; the vehicle is of a size or weight that cannot properly be tested at the testing station; the vehicle emits substantial quantities of avoidable smoke; a proper examination cannot be carried out because a door, tailgate, boot lid, engine cover, fuel cap or other device designed to be readily opened cannot be; the condition of the vehicle is such that, in the opinion of the examiner, a proper examination would involve danger of injury to any person or damage to the vehicle or other property.

What are the rules about registration plates?

A number of readers enquired about the exact rules regarding the size, spacing and typeface of the characters on car registration plates. The MOT test only checks that they are of equal width along their entire length and that the gap between the groups is at least twice that of the gap between characters. Road Vehicles (Registration and Licensing) Regulations 1971 gives the exact sizes; these are: 79mm high; 57mm wide (except no 1); 14mm thick; 11mm apart; with 33mm between groups. The digits must not be confused by retaining bolts, or obscured by dirt or a towing hook. But the MOT manual does allow for the digits to be sloped or of a non-standard typeface as long as their thickness remains uniform and the letters and numbers can be clearly read. Script-face registration plates would therefore be rejected. And all reflective registration plates must comply with British Standard BS AU 145a. Obviously, foreign-registered vehicles are exempt.

What's an MOT 'screen test'?

This is the procedure an MOT inspector uses to check a windscreen as part of a car's annual test. He will first look at the area swept by the wipers in a 290mm vertical band centred on the centre of the steering wheel. Reasons for MOT failure are: damage not contained within a 10mm diameter circle; a windscreen sticker or other obstruction encroaching more than 10mm; or a combination of minor damage areas which seriously restricts the driver's view. He will then look at the entire area of the screen swept by the wipers and will fail the car if there is any damage not contained within a 40mm circle, or a windscreen sticker or other obstruction encroaching more than 40mm. Remember, it is far better to repair a windscreen if at all possible, or simply leave the damage if the car will still pass the MOT. Removing and replacing bonded screens often damages paintwork and enables rust to take hold with a vengeance.

What's an MOT 'brake test'?

Readers may be wondering exactly what sort of MOT examination the hydraulic 'foot brake' system on their car is put to. First the examiner looks for leaks in the system and checks that rigid brake and flexible pipes are securely held and are not corroded, fouled, kinked, chafed, twisted or damaged in any way. He then checks the individual brake discs and drums for corrosion and fluid leaks, and makes sure the callipers and back plates are securely fitted. He makes sure that the master cylinder is securely mounted, is free of corrosion, has an adequate fluid level, is capped and is not leaking. He then checks the servo and associated pipework. After that, on most cars, he performs a Roller Brake Test, but cars with more than one driven axle permanently engaged, with a limited slip differential or with a belt-driven transmission cannot be tested on a roller. The test includes both retardation performance and any imbalance in the braking system. Cars which cannot be tested in this way must be tested with a decelerometer on a road. For most cars, the foot brake (service brake) must have a minimum brake efficiency of 50 per cent and the hand brake (parking brake) 25 per cent.

What's a 'Trade Licence'?

These are what the public usually refer to as 'trade plates' and are subject to some surprisingly draconian restrictions. Essentially they allow unregistered or untaxed vehicles to be driven on public roads for the purposes of delivery, demonstration or testing. They do not allow the holder to make any personal journeys in a vehicle on trade plates, and traders dropping their kids off at school on their way to an auction have been fined for this. Currently the design of trade plates is under consultation. It is proposed to change them from pressed metal plates with a pointy bit on top to carry the tax triangle to simple oblong shapes with the tax disc incorporated. Consultees are being asked if they would prefer the plates to be plastic, to be designed to be clipped or fastened over existing registration plates, or to be fitted inside the windows of the vehicles using suckers.

What's 'CO$_2$ Benefit Tax'?

This is the tax drivers of company cars will pay for the benefit of their private use of the car as from 6 April 2002. Many company drivers remain unaware of the new regime and will be in for a shock. There will no longer be any discount for a high business mileage. Instead, drivers will be taxed on 15 per cent of the car's 'list price', with the tax base increasing by 1 per cent for each 5g/km CO_2 the car emits over and above 165g/km. For tax year 2003–2004, the base CO_2 will be 155g/km and for tax year 2004–2005 the base CO_2 will be 145g/km. So, effectively, the tax base for a £15,000 car emitting 185g/km will rise from 19 per cent (or £2,850) in 2002–2003 to 23 per cent (or £3,450) in 2004–2005. Because they emit less CO_2, diesels will be hit with a three per cent surcharge, and no driver will be taxed on a base of more than 35 per cent of the car's list price. So, as with CO_2-based VED, there is no benefit to be had from driving a company car with an ultra-low CO_2 rating. Automatics emit around 10 per cent more CO_2 than manuals. List prices, VED bands and CO_2 tables can be found in *What Car?* magazine.

What's a three-point belt?

This is a quicker way of describing a lap and diagonal safety belt. Over the years more and more cars have been fitted with three three-point belts across the back seat. These include: Alfa 156 (£97.53 option) Alfa 147, BMW 5-Series, Chrysler PT Cruiser, Citroën Berlingo Multispace Forte 5-door; Citroën Xantia Estate, Citroën C5, Citroën Picasso, Fiat Punto from 2000 MY (standard in HLX and above; £75 option in base models), Fiat Multipla, Ford Mondeo from 1997 MY, Honda Accord from 1999 MY; Hyundai Santa Fe, Jaguar S Type, Jaguar X Type, KIA Magentis, Land Rover Freelander 5-door; Land Rover Discovery from 1999 MY, Mazda 626 from July 1997, MB C Class estate; all new MB C Class; MB E Class estate from May 1996; MB E Class from June 1998; MB S Class; Mitsubishi Galant from 1998 MY, Mitsubishi Space Star, Nissan Almera 4-door; Nissan Almera Tino; new Nissan Primera SLX, Peugeot 306 Sedan, Peugeot 307; Peugeot 406, Proton Impian, Renault new Clio from May 1998 (not base models), Renault Kangoo Combi RXE model, Renault Megane and Scenic, Renault Laguna from 95M, Renault Espace from 1997 MY, new Rover 200, Rover 25, Rover 45, Rover 600 from

1997 MY, Rover 75, Rover 800 4-door from 94M, SAAB 900 from 94L, SAAB 9-3, SAAB 9-5 (saloon and estate), SEAT Leon, new SEAT Toledo (from 1999 MY), new SEAT Alhambra (from August 2000), Toyota Corolla from July 1997, Toyota Avensis, Toyota Camry from 1997 MY, Vauxhall Corsa from 2001 MY, Vauxhall Astra from April 1998 (not Zafira), Vauxhall Vectra from 1997 MY, Vauxhall Omega, 1998 VW Golf IV and Bora (£100 optional extra, but standard on Golf V5 Estate), VW Passat (£100 optional extra), VW Sharan from 2001 MY, Volvo S40, Volvo V40, Volvo S60, Volvo S70, Volvo V70, Volvo 850, Volvo S80, Volvo 940, Volvo 960, Volvo S90, Volvo V90.

What's an 'Italian tune-up'?

Pretty obvious to most of us. But not to the owners of cars which need it most. I get a lot of letters from readers who can't understand why their cars need chemical assistance and a hard ten-mile drive to get them through the MOT emissions test. Gently-driven diesels need it most because this sort of use is likely to lead to coked-up injectors and an exhaust system full of soot. If a diesel is only ever revved to 3,000 rpm in daily use, yet the test requires it to be revved to the governed limit, then this will dislodge accumulated soot and the car will fail its smoke test. Some friendly MOT testing stations routinely add Forte fuel system cleaner prior to testing. The best also advise customers to use something similar in the car's fuel tank and take it for a long, hard drive at high revs prior to submitting it for the test. The same applies to catalysed petrol engines to a lesser extent. With these, the difference between pass and fail is a very fine line, so anything that gets the engine running at its peak has to be good for it, including a healthy dose of fuel system cleaner and lending the car to a lead-footed driver. Do this at night and you'll see the sparks of burned-off carbon trailing the car for miles.

What's an 'RDS-TMC'?

This is a new system which will finally make satellite navigation and traffic jam pre-warning kit worth having in a car. Up until now, all satellite navigation could do was give you its ideal route from A to B, and all Trafficmaster could do was pre-warn you of a traffic jam. If the satnav route from A to B contained the jam, you were on your own. RDS-TMC will provide a direct feed of information to the driver, to his or her satnav system, or to both, enabling the satnav system to find the ideal diversion around the roads known to be blocked. The receivers will be comparatively inexpensive at under £100, but no mention has yet been made of subscription charges. The two main vendors will be the AA, which already sells Trafficmaster, and a company called ITIS Holdings. The AA should already be providing RDS-TMC coverage in London by the time you read this.

What's 'Motormilk'?

This is what the Society of Motor Manufacturers and Traders has calculated is being extracted from car owners by the government.

In a calculation tracing all costs from the purchase of a new £8,000 car in 1992 to its scrappage after 110,000 miles in 2000, the SMMT calculates that the car will have generated no less than £11,712 in tax revenue. This sum includes VAT on the original sale and re-sale of the car, Vehicle Excise Duty, Fuel Tax and VAT on fuel and Fuel Tax, Insurance Premium Tax and VAT on service, parts and repair costs. This means that out of a total of £50,984 generated within the economy by the car over its eight-year life, 22.97 per cent was tax. Apart from booze and fags, which are allegedly heavily taxed because of the health risk, nothing else is taxed as heavily and nothing else generates a tax income for the government of 146 per cent of its original purchase price.

What is a 'corrosion battery'?

On a section of steel car body, this is an electrolytic reaction which occurs when the metal is wet and there is a difference in the oxygen replenishment at the metal surface beneath the wetted area. If the moisture takes the form of a droplet, this sits on the surface in the shape of a hemisphere. The perimeter of the droplet allows easy oxygen replenishment to the metal surface but the central area under the droplet is relatively depleted in oxygen. The anode of the corrosion battery is the central point under the droplet. The cathode is a band around the circumference of the droplet. If you imagine a droplet collecting around a speck of road salt adhered to the car body, then, if the salts break through the metal's paintwork protection, a corrosion battery is created between the central anode and the surrounding cathode. Anodic corrosion will begin to occur directly under the speck of dirt due to the comparative lack of oxygen reaching that area compared to the easy oxygen replenishment around the circumference of the droplet. Translate droplet on the car body to a crevice where moisture collects and where the paint protection has not penetrated into the depths of the crevice, then electrolytic corrosion will occur in the wet area inside the crevice which is comparatively starved of oxygen compared to the entrance of the crevice.

Why motor vehicle bodies corrode and how to claim on motor 'no perforation' warranties is explained in full in *Motor Vehicle Corrosion Prediction and Prevention on Vehicles* by Dr Hugh McArthur. This is available directly from the author, priced £10 including post and packaging (cheques to Hugh McArthur), address: 18 Rawlins Close, Woodhouse Eaves, nr Loughborough, LE12 8SD.

What is 'engine icing'?

This has been covered in the column, but an anonymous reader sent me an aviation safety leaflet which explains the problem in more detail. There are three main types of engine icing. Carburettor icing is caused by the sudden temperature drop due to fuel vaporisation and pressure reduction at the carburettor venturi. A drop of 20°C to 30°C results in atmospheric moisture turning to ice, which upsets the fuel/air ratio causing loss of power and slowly strangling the engine. Once the engine has been stopped for a few minutes, residual heat melts the ice and the engine runs normally again. (It's a bit like stabbing someone with an icicle. The murder weapon will never be found.) Fuel icing can occur where condensation water held in suspension in the fuel precipitates and freezes in elbows in the induction piping, restricting the flow of fuel. In sub-zero conditions, impact ice can build up on air intakes and filters and this can affect fuel injected engines as well as carburettor engines. To prevent this sort of icing in a car, always set the intake trunking to its winter warm air position during cold weather.

What is 'satisfactory quality'?

This is the definition used in The Sale and Supply of Goods Act 1994 as the legitimate reason for a purchaser to reject goods sold to him by a supplier. The 1994 Act modified the Sale of Goods Act 1979 which defined the reason for rejection as not being of 'merchantable quality'. The later Act should have made life a lot easier for all of us but, of course, Britain being Britain and lawyers being lawyers, it didn't. We are forced to rely on case law precedents as to what constitutes 'satisfactory quality' and what doesn't. Even where a precedent is set, it can be over-ruled by a higher court, so every court case involving The Sale and Supply of Goods Act 1994 involves legal argument on the technicalities as to whether a previous judgement sets a precedent for the case being heard. Very broadly, you probably won't be able to reject a car you have owned for more than six months, you won't be able to reject it for a trivial reason and, most importantly, the only way to start the proceedings is to return the car to the supplier. You cannot reject a car while still remaining in possession of it.

What is 'endurance racing'?

June's 24 hours at Le Mans is one of the last of the world's great endurance races where man and machine battle against fatigue as well as each other. But it's by no means the longest race in history. That honour belongs to the 1948 "Las Caracas" over nearly 6,000 miles from Buenos Aires to Caracas. The official winner was Domingo Marinon driving a Chevrolet (European cars didn't tend to last the distance). Oscar Galvez in his Ford had been in the lead by two and a half hours, but lost his engine 150 miles from the finish. So an enthusiastic bystander then used his car to push Galvez all the way to the finish and he got third place. Not content with that, Galvez had his engine fixed then almost immediately moved on to Lima, Peru, to start another 3,200-mile road race back across the Andes to Buenos Aires, which he won. They don't make them like they used to. Drivers and cars.

What is 'Automobilia'?

These are all the interesting bits and pieces that go with cars and celebrate cars but don't have four wheels and an engine. Typical Automobilia (in fact, the index from 'Automobilia' by Gordon Gardiner and Alistair Morris ISBN 1-85149-293-3) includes:

Accessories, Badges, Car Cigarette Cards, Clocks, Dashboard Instruments, Documents, Enamel and Painted Signs, Event Programmes, Fuel Pump Globes, Guides, Horns, Lamps, Manufacturer's Publicity Material, Maps, Mascots, Mirrors, Motoring Clothing, Motoring Novelties, Old Books and Periodicals, Old Catalogues, Pedal Cars, Postcards, Spares, Tools, Toy Cars, Trophies. The best places to see all this stuff are autojumbles at motoring events held throughout the summer. Two such are the National Silverstone Historic Festival held in August, tel: 01327 850204; and Beaulieu Autojumble at the National Motor Museum, held in September, tel: 01590 612345.

What's a 'can-cam'?

This is what has happened in the Canadian states of Ontario and British Columbia where enlightened legislators have canned the whole idea of speed cameras. Their entirely logical grounds are that the use of speed cameras is motivated by revenue, has no safety benefits, must be propped up by a well funded spin machine to survive, is heavy-handed and arbitrary, undermines public respect for the law and for law enforcement, and invades privacy as a 'big brother' type of device. British Columbia watched the result of Ontario canning its cameras for six years, saw there had been no detrimental effect on road safety and, in the words of BC's Attorney General, Geoff Plant, concluded that 'From the day speed cameras started they undermined public confidence in the rule of law and law enforcement.' Unfortunately, the British are suckers for being conned: over the way the City has used the sanctity of Sterling to turn Britain into one of the most expensive countries in the World in which to live, and over the way most middle-class Britons believe that the law is to be respected even if it is merely there to create wealth for other people and make them poorer.

What is 'doom blue'?

This is a trade term I first heard used to describe the deadly dull 'Balliol' blue chosen by Ford as a poverty spec colour for the Fiesta, Escort and Mondeo. Ford's much brighter 'Rimini' blue was equally blighted, as was the creamy dark blue 'Ontario' which succeeded Balliol at the back of the used car lot. The colour of a car is a very serious issue for buyers because it doesn't just make a few hundred pounds difference to re-sale value, it may determine whether you can get anyone to buy the car at all. Though 'Fridge White' looks good on sports cars and convertibles it's another bad colour for saloons and hatchbacks because it reeks of stripped-out, base-spec police panda cars. Green can be dodgy in parts of London where it is believed to harbour bad luck. Brown is to be avoided at all costs unless it's the very special Royal browny green seen on ex-Royal Family Range Rovers. Solid black is a total no-no because it's impossible to keep clean and presentable. Banana Yellow is always a risk. If you want to stay safe, by far your best choice is silver, particularly if the car happens to be an Audi, BMW,

What are 'Whole Life Costs'?

These are the total costs of running a car for a given mileage and period. They are used by fleet managers for comparing the true costs of providing various different cars for a company's employees. Parkfield Leasing and Fleet Services uses the following criteria: Depreciation (the difference between invoice price at a single vehicle purchase discount and likely residual value on disposal); VED for the entire period; Interest charges on the cash flow effect of depreciation to the estimated residual value; Fuel (at current pump prices, increased by inflation year on year); Insurance on the basis of actual average costs paid by fleets; Relief Vehicles when the car is in for service or repair (excluding accident repair); Service Costs, based on Glass's Guide ICME rates; and Repair Costs (likely out-of-warranty repairs and replacements, such as clutches, brake parts and tyres). What Car? magazine and website (www.whatcar.com)

provide estimated costs per mile, excluding insurance, which are a useful basis of comparison for private buyers.

What is 'Congestion Charging'?

This is a means by which city councils hope to limit the number of vehicles entering their cities and thus reduce vehicle congestion on city streets. The intention is to create a central zone with limited numbers of streets leading into it, and controlled by cameras. Vehicle drivers have to obtain electronic permits costing, for example, £5 per day to enter this central zone, otherwise the registered keeper of the vehicle will be subject to, for example, an £80 fine. Objectors to congestion charging point out that the areas immediately outside the central zone will become even more congested with parked vehicles and confused drivers; that city centre public transport will be unable to transport the extra passengers created by the schemes; that the movement of goods and packages within the central zone will become more expensive; that business people who need flexible transport at all hours will either be hard hit or will simply pass the charges on to their customers; and that, instead of travelling into the central zone by public transport, many potential visitors will simply avoid it and take their money elsewhere.

Good Garage Guide

In the summer of 1996 the 'Motoring' section of the *Daily Telegraph* ran a reader's story about the differences between big garages in Britain and small garages in France. I felt that the contrast was more likely to be between bad garages and good garages generally, so I asked for readers' recommendations. The list continues to grow, and the most recent version is published here.

Remember, the list is based purely on readers' recommendations, and inclusion is no guarantee of quality, competence or good value. Nevertheless, many of the testimonials were fulsome in their praise, so if you are looking for good service from your garage, this list may be the right place to start.

105

The London Area

Bromley

Ted and Neil Craker, The Vehicle Test Centre, 107 Southlands Road, Bromley, Kent BR2 9QT, tel: 020 8460 6666. (Very well equipped and sensibly priced servicing workshop/MOT test centre, with two 'rolling road' brake testers and full diagnostic equipment.)

Catford

Gilbert's Motors, 304–312 Sangley Road, London SE6 2JX, tel: 020 8698 7067. (Honda agent prepared to repair expensive components rather than replace them.)

Enfield

Stephen James, Clock Parade, London Road, Enfield EN2 6JG, tel: 020 8367 2626. (Friendly BMW agent with sensibly priced servicing.)

London N4

Nick Sandamas, G & N Garages Ltd, 54/58 Wightman Road, Harringay, London N4 1RU, tel: 020 8340 3311. (Independent SAAB specialist.)

London SE6

Gonella Brothers, 9–13 Catford Hill, Catford, London SE6 4NU, tel: 0208 690 0060. (Alfa, Fiat and Lancia specialists.)

London SW2
Hearn Bros Ltd, The Hill Garage, 94 Brixton Hill, London SW2, tel: 0208 674 2888.

London SW17
Carpenters Garage, 69–71 Bickersteth Road, Tooting, London SW17 9SH, tel: 0208 672 4891. (Small, family run independent garage and MOT testing station.)

London W8
ACE Cars of Kensington, 18–23 Radley Mews, London W8 6JP, tel: 0207 938 4333. (Subaru dealer specialising in the SVX. Also specialises in older Saabs: 900, 99, 96. Very well thought of.)

London W12
AC Automotive, 247–251 Goldhawk Road, London W12, tel: 0208 741 9993. (American car parts and servicing.)

Perivale
AC Delco, Unit 14, 19 Wadsworth Road, Perivale, Middx., tel: 020 8810 4595. (American car parts and servicing.)

South of the Thames

Alton
Neil Carpenter, Froxfield Service Centre, Farringdon Industrial Centre, Alton, Hants, tel: 01420 587 403.

Andover
Martin Dix, Intech GB Ltd, Unit 12B, Thruxton Industrial Estate, Thruxton Circuit, near Andover, Hants, tel: 01264 773888. (Service and repair specialists for Japanese 'grey' imports, from Honda Beat to Lexus 'Soarer' Coupe.)

Bexhill-On-Sea
Peter Johnson Motor Engineer, Unit 3, de la Warr Mews, Station Road, Bexhill-on-Sea, East Sussex TN40 1RD, tel: 01424 224169.

Good Garages South of the Thames

Billinghurst
Geoffrey Sizzy (Automobiles) Ltd, Wisborough Green, Nr Billinghurst, West Sussex RH14 0AH, tel: 01403 700661. (Independent Peugeot specialist – sales, service, very good after-sales service.)

Bognor Regis
Middleton Garage, 169 Middleton Road, Middleton on Sea, Bognor Regis, West Sussex PO22 6DF, tel: 01243 582767. (Very helpful Fiat franchise.)

Bournemouth
Horizon Motors, 113 Charminster Road, Bournemouth, Dorset BH8 8UE, tel: 01202 294341. (Honda agents.)

Canterbury
Ashford Road Service Station, Chilham, Canterbury, Kent CT4 8EE, tel: 01227 730223.

Cardiff
Continental Cars (Cardiff) Ltd, Pentwyn Road, Pentwyn, Cardiff CF23 7XH, tel: 029 2054 2400. (Mercedes franchise, treats elderly drivers with extra consideration.)

Chertsey
Speedtest, Unit A, Gogmore Lane, Chertsey, Surrey KT16 9AP, tel: 01932 568921. (Non-rip-off servicing and MOT centre. Good with Citroëns and Renaults.)

Chessington
Mole Valley TVR, Chessington, Surrey KT9 2NN, tel: 020 8394 1114. (Good TVR dealer.)

Chislehurst
Paul and Tony at PDQ, 1a Albany Road, Chislehurst, Kent BR7 6BG, tel: 020 8295 0121. (BMW and Jaguar specialists.)

Croydon
The Silver Wing Garage, 25 Horatius Way, Silverwing Industrial Estate, Stafford Road, Croydon, Surrey CR0 4RU, tel: 020 8680 6959. (Much-praised independent garage operating a National Auto Service franchise.)

Parker Bros (Croydon) Ltd, 9–11 Bywood Avenue, Shirley, Croydon CR8 3DB, tel: 0208 654 1923. (General repairs and servicing, in business for over 70 years. Will do jobs in the most economic way possible.)

Crowborough
John Cottenham, Care's Garage, School Lane, St Johns, Crowborough, Sussex TN6 1SE, tel: 01892 653519.

Dorking
Steve Bradstock, The Carriage House, Horsham Road, Beare Green, Dorking, Surrey RH5 4RU, tel: 01306 713424.

Dover
Elms Vale Garage, Elms Vale Road, Dover, tel: 01304 201077. (Good small independent local garage.)

Eastbourne
Visick Cars Ltd, Birch Close, Lottbridge Drove, Eastbourne BN23 6PE, tel: 01323 722244.

Emsworth
Lillywhite Bros Ltd, 40 Queen Street, Emsworth, Hants PO10 7BL, tel: 01243 372336.

Epsom
King Automatic Gearboxes, 'The Chalk Pit', College Road, Epsom, Surrey KT17 4JA, tel: 01372 728769. (Automatic transmissions of all types, including CVTs).

Kwik-Fit, 166 East Street, Epsom, Surrey KT17 1EY, tel: 01372 739955.

Erith
Erith Garage Services, Maypole Crescent, Darent Industrial Park, Erith, Kent DA8 2JZ, tel: 01322 331150. (Good independent garage which also carries out restorations.)

Ferring
John Cooper Garages, 50 Ferring Street, Ferring, Worthing, West Sussex BN12 5JP, tel: 01903 504455. (Very helpful Honda franchise.)

Finchampstead
Cresswells, 427 Finchampstead Road, Finchampstead, Berks RG46 3RJ, tel: 0118 973 2201.

Guildford
A.H. Autos, Unit 11, Foundation Units, Westfield Road, Slyfield Industrial Estate, Guildford, Surrey GU1 1RR, tel: 01483 303942. (VW/Audi specialists.)

Hersham
Colin Marshall or Keith Rhoods, Wheelbase Garage, 43 Queen's Road, Hersham, Surrey, tel: 01932 242881. (VW/Audi specialists.)

Sunbury Coachworks, Unit R3, Lyon Road, Hersham Industrial estate, Hersham, Surrey, tel: 01932 254057. (Good bodyshop offering excellent Autocolor paint finish at reasonable prices.)

East Horsley
Philip Stonely, The Body Workshop, Forest Road Garage, Forest Road, Effingham Junction, Surrey KT24 5HE, tel: 01483 284805.

Hythe
Autopat, 3 Hardley Industrial Estate, Hardley, Nr Hythe, Hants SO45 3NQ, tel: 023 8080 40163.

Isle of Wight
Harwoods, Lushington Hill, IOW, tel: 01983 885500. (Very helpful Renault agent, not averse to imports.)

Leatherhead
Kingscraft Volvo, Leatherhead, Surrey KT22 7DL, tel: 01372 371900. (Helpful Volvo dealer which has picked up the pieces left by other Volvo franchises.)

Lewes
Morris Road Garage, Western Road, Lewes, East Sussex BN7 1RR, tel: 01273 472434. (Independent Bosch fuel injection specialists.)

Lymington
Dory's Garage Ltd, Sway Park, Station Road, Sway, Hants PO41 6BA, tel: 01590 683432. (Citroën specialists.)

Maidenhead
Delta Motors, Grenfell Road, Maidenhead, Berks SL6 1ES, tel: 01628 675064. Jerry Houdret, sales; Roger Towers, parts. (Efficient Renault agents.)

Merstham
John Witty, Witmun Engineering, 67 Nutfield Road, Merstham, Surrey RH1 3ER, tel: 01737 644828. (Citroën specialists.)

New Romney
Dave Alstin, Marsh Citroën Repairs, Unit 15A, Mountfield Road, New Romney, Kent TN28 8LH, tel: 01797 361234. (Dave is a fount of knowledge who gives excellent service at sensible prices.)

Orpington
Chelsfield Motor Works, Court Lodge Farm, Warren Road, Orpington, Kent BR6 6ER, tel: 01689 823200.

Good Garages South of the Thames

Poole

Connellys, 472–476 Ashley Road, Upper Parkstone, Poole, Dorset BH14 0AD, tel: 01202 738700.

Seward Vauxhall, 400 Poole Road, Poole, Dorset BH12 1DD, tel: 01202 763361/545700. (Good Vauxhall agent.)

Ripley

Colborne Garages Ltd, Portsmouth Road (old A3), Ripley, Surrey GU23 6HP, tel: 01483 224361. (Oldest-established UK VW agent, still good.)

Sanderstead

Steven Pengelly, Vorne Motorsport, 145 Limpsfield Road, Sanderstead, Surrey CR2 9LG, tel: 020 8651 5344.

Sevenoaks

Antwis Engineering, Rye Lane, Dunton Green, Sevenoaks, Kent TN14 5HD, tel: 01732 450386. (Very good with BMWs.)

Southampton

E. & J. Jarvis, Motor Engineers, Onslow Road, Southampton SO14 0JN, tel: 023 8022 9297.

Hilton Motors, Bond Road Garage, Bitterne Park, Southampton SO18 1LH, tel: 023 8055 5600. (General service, repair, sales garage and automatic transmission specialist.)

Southsea

John Skerratt, Owl Motor Services, Richmond Road, Southsea, Hants PO5 2LN, tel: 023 9273 6393.

Tankerton

Tankerton Garage, Tankerton Road, Whitstable, Kent, CT5 2AJ, tel: 01227 771108. (Owner Simon does an excellent job at exceptional prices, often well into the evenings and at weekends.)

West Malling

B. Butler, The SAAB Sanctuary, 'Almandene', Woodgate Road, Ryarsh, West Malling, Kent ME19 5LH, tel: 01732 872722. (65–86 SAABs only, and spares.)

Weybridge

S.S. Motors. 16c Hamm Moor Lane, Weybridge Business Park, Weybridge, Surrey KT15 2SD, tel: 01932 821555. (Mercedes specialist run by Mercedes-trained ex-franchise service manager.)

Dagenham Motors (Weybridge), Wintersalls Road, Byfleet, Surrey, tel: 01932 332933. (Good official Ford service agent.)

Windsor

New and Tarrant, West End Service Station, Dedworth Road, Windsor, Berks SL4 4LH, tel: 01753 862078/851685.

Woking

Colbourne Garages Ltd, 76 Maybury Road, Woking, Surrey GU21 5JD, tel: 01483 722415. (Oldest-established UK VW agent, still good.)

Worcester Park

Glen Brown, GB Autos, 16a Cheam Common, Worcester Park, Surrey KT4 8RW, tel: 020 8330 6090. (Independent Volvo and air conditioning servicing specialists.)

Worthing

Rod Waller, Denton Motors, 1–3 Park Road, Worthing, W. Sussex BN11 2AS, tel: 01903 233790.

North of the Thames

Amersham

T and F Motors, White Lion Road, Amersham, Bucks HP7 9JB, tel: 01494 765286.

Aylesbury

Ivor Miles, Churchway Garage, Churchway, Haddenham, Aylesbury, Bucks HP17 8HA, tel: 01844 291263.

Lodge Garage (Aylesbury Mazda) Ltd, Bicester Road, Kingswood, Aylesbury, Bucks HP18 0QJ, tel: 01296 770245.

C.D. Bramall (Aylesbury Toyota – formerly BMG Aylesbury), 156 Wendover Road, Stoke Mandeville, Aylesbury, Bucks HP22 5TE, tel: 01296 615656.

Bishops Stortford

Maltings Garage, Station Road, Sawbridgeworth, Herts CM21 9JX, tel: 01279 723671; fax: 01279 725555. (General servicing, repairs and MOTs. Long-standing customers.)

Franklins Garage Ltd., Stansted Road, Bishop's Stortford CM23 2BT, tel: 01279 757220. (Renault main dealer who, though extremely busy, fixed an overheated Renault miles from its home and charged a tiny £3.15.)

Gravenhurst

Chris Case, Town Farm Garage, Campton Road, Gravenhurst, Beds MK45 4JB, tel: 01462 711017.

Harlington

Exchange Gearboxes, 228, Manor Parade, High St, Harlington, Hayes, Middlesex UB3 5DS, tel: 020 8897 0601.

Hemel Hempstead

V.P. Autos, 559 London Road, Hemel Hempstead, Herts , tel: 01442 268163.

Henlow

Henlow Car Centre, Bedford Road, Lower Standen, Henlow, Beds SG16 6DZ, tel: 01462 814668.

Hounslow

Franco Motors, 29 Vine Place, Hounslow TW3 3UE, tel: 020 8570 3798.

Lower Basildon

Les Allum, Allum Auto Services, Reading Road, Lower Basildon, Berks RG8 9NL, tel: 01491 671726.

St Albans

Godfrey Davis (St Albans), 105 Ashley Road, St Albans, Herts AL1 5GD, tel: 01727 791300. (Good Ford servicing facility capable of correctly diagnosing problems.)

Wraysbury

George Williams, Lakeside Garage, 48 Welley Road, Wraysbury, Middx TW19 5DJ, tel: 01784 482158.

Eastern England

Barton

Wallis and Son, Cavendish House, Cambridge Road, Barton, Cambs CB3 7AR, Tel: 01223 263911, website: www.wallisandson.co.uk. (Independent garage, excellent service at reasonable prices.)

Boston

Mick Barsley, Barsley Motor Engineers, Park Sidings, High Street, Boston, Lincs, tel: 01205 355396.

Chelmsford

Mr & Mrs John Plumb and their son Steve, Central Garage, Latchingdon, nr Chelmsford, Essex CM3 6HB, tel: 01621 740284.

Grantham

TMS Garages, Spittlegate Level, Grantham, Lincs NG31 7UH, tel: 01476 564114. (Volvo specialist.)

Hull

Jordans of Hull, 45–52 Witham, Hull HU9 1BS, tel: 01482 222500. (Various dealerships including Mazda. Sensible service policy.)

Langworth

Paul Schmitt, Langworth Service Station, Station Road, Langworth, Lincs LN3 5BB, tel: 01522 754291. (Paul is an excellent and helpful mechanic with longstanding customers.)

Lincoln

Riccardo Emiliani, 21 Rugby Road, Lincoln ON2 4PB, tel: 01522 531735. (Helpful Honda agent.)

Needham Market

Richard Robinson, Robinson's Motor Engineers, Unit 21, Maitland Road, Lion Barn Industrial Estate, Needham Market, Suffolk IP6 8NS, tel: 01449 722240.

Norwich

Peter Whitley Motor Services, 7 Low Road, Drayton, Norwich NR8 6AA, tel: 01603 860154.

Duff Morgan, Earlham Road, Norwich NR2 3RB, tel: 01603 621393. (Citroën dealer offering sensibly priced servicing and tyres.)

Oulton Broad

John Pope, Pope Brothers, Station Garage, Bridge Road, Oulton Broad, Lowestoft, Norfolk NR32 3LP, tel: 01502 573797.

Peterborough

Frank Lofthouse, 'The Complete Automobilist', 35–37 Main Street, Baston, Peterborough PE6 9NX, tel: 01778 560444.

Soham

Crown Garage Ltd, 1–5 High Street, Soham, Cambridgeshire, CB7 5HB, tel: 01353 720779, fax: 01353 723392, website: www.crowngarage. co.uk (Rover dealership giving outstanding, efficient and very polite and courteous service.)

Stebbing

R A Rains, Drakeswell Garage, Bran End, Stebbing, Essex, 01371 856391.

Wroxham

Stewart Tubby, SMT Motors, Station Road, Hoveton, Wroxham, Norfolk NR12 8UR, tel: 01603 783966. (Always helpful and always honest, many a holidaymaker has reason to be grateful to Stewart.)

Central England

Abberley

Alan Hole, P. Owen & Sons Ltd, Motor & Agricultural Engineers, The Abberley Garage, Abberley, Worcestershire, WR6 6AY, tel: 01299 896209.

Ashbourne

Hulland Ward Garage, Main Street, Hulland Ward, Nr Ashbourne, Derbyshire DE6 3EF, tel: 01335 370209.

Ashton-under-Lyne

Quicks Ltd, Manchester Road, Ashton-under-Lyne OL7 0DG, tel: 0161 330 0121. (Ford Agent with loyal customers of long standing.)

Birmingham

R. Newman Motor Engineers, Alcester Road (rear of J.H. Hancox Ltd), Portway, Birmingham B48 7JA, tel: 01564 824996.

G. & B. Clements, Baldwins Lane Service Station, Baldwins Lane, Hall Green, Birmingham B28 0XB, tel: 0121 744 5453.

Ken Hunt Auto Services, 536 Hobmoor Road, Yardley, Birmingham B25 8TN, tel: 0121 789 7273.

Good Garages in Central England

Broadway

Alan Aston Motor Engineers, Broadway Road, Childswickham (nr Broadway), Worcs WR12 7HD, tel: 01386 852311. From autumn 2001: Alan Aston Motor Engineers, Eastwick Garage, Eastwick Drive, Evesham, Worcs WR11 6LG.

Burton-on-Trent

Peter Sharp, European Car Specialists, Unit 3, APS Industrial Park, Wetmore Road, Burton-on-Trent, Staffs DE14 1QL, tel: 01283 540414.

Chesterfield

Bridgegate Ltd, Pottery Lane, West Chesterfield, Derbys S41 9BN, tel: 01246 208681. (Very helpful BMW agent, notwithstanding age of car.)

Coalville

Mick Rolfe and Ian Whattom, Scotlands Garage, Scotlands Industrial Estate, London Road, Coalville, Leicestershire, tel: 01530 817277. (Ian is the bodywork/paint specialist, Mick the repairs/ servicing specialist. An excellent service at reasonable rates.)

Daventry

Dave Carvell Cars, Badby Lane, Staverton, Nr Daventry, Northants NN11 6DE, tel: 01327 300739.

Derby

Citronome Derby Ltd, Great Northern Road, Derby DE1 1LT, tel: 01332 345869. (Citroën specialists.)

Evesham

Evesham Volkswagen/Audi, Unit 15, St. Richard's Road, Evesham, Worcestershire WR11 6XJ, tel: 01386 48195. (Contact: Kevin.)

Leamington Spa

Midland Autocar Co., 8–16 Russell Street, Leamington Spa, Warks CV32 5QB, tel 01926 421171. (General repairs and service.)

Bull Ring Garage, Church Terrace, Harbury, Leamington Spa, Warks CN33 9HL, tel: 01926 612275. (Excellent local garage.)

Lichfield

Central Garage (Lichfield) Ltd, Queen Street, Lichfield, Staffs, WS13 6QD, tel: 01543 262826.

Mansfield Woodhouse

Leeming Car Centre, Edge Hill Service Station, Warsop Road, Mansfield Woodhouse, Notts NG19 9LF, tel: 01623 635735. (Independent garage, but specialises in Toyota Corolla GTi models and can offer reduced-cost repairs to these cars.)

Nottingham

John Harrison (Lowdham) Ltd, Southwell Road, Lowdham, Nottingham NG14 7DS, tel: 0115 966 4112. (Helpful, straight Peugeot franchise.)

Oxford

North Oxford Garage Ltd, 280 Banbury Road, Oxford, OX2 7EB, tel: 01865 319000. (Helpful BMW franchise.)

Motor World Mitsubishi, New Barclay House, 234 Botley Road, Oxford OX2 0HP, tel: 01865 722444. (Mitsubishi agent offering excellent after-sales service).

Sutton Coldfield

G. Chamberlain & Sons, Four Oaks Garage, Lichfield Road, Four Oaks, Sutton Coldfield, W. Midlands B74 2UH, tel: 0121 308 0309.

Dave Buckland, D.J. Buckland (Motor Engineer), (rear of) 162 Birmingham Road, Wylde Green, Sutton Coldfield, W. Midlands B72 4JP, tel: 0121 355 7634 (out of hours tel: 0121 350 6881).

Wantage

Paul Rivers, Hillcrest Garage, Reading Road, West Hendred (nr Wantage), Oxon OX12 8RH, tel: 01235 833363.

T.A. Collins Motor Engineers, Grove Technology Park, Grove, Wantage, Oxon OX12 9TA, tel: 01235 768321. (Volvo specialist.)

West Bromwich

The Sun Garage Company, Sandwell Road, West Bromwich, West Midlands B70 8TG, tel: 0121 553 0296.

Wolverhampton
Roger Williams, Oxley Service Station, Fordhouse Road, Bushbury, Wolverhampton, W. Midlands WV10 9EY, tel: 01902 787386.

The South West

Bath
Grants of Bath, London Road West, Bath BA1 7DP, tel 01225 858 147. (Small and outwardly rather chaotic private garage, but always knowledgeable, helpful and very reasonably priced. Ask for Nigel.)

Bridgwater
TSR Performance, 1 Stockmoor Park, Taunton Road, Bridgwater, Somerset TA6 6LD, tel: 01278 453036. (VW/Audi performance modifications at reasonable prices and labour rates.)

Stogursey Motors, High Street, Stogursey, Somerset TA5 1TB (8 miles from Bridgwater near Hinkley Point power station), tel: 01278 732237. (Car, van and motorcycle repairs and MOTs.)

Bristol
All Audi Used Part Stores, Units 26/27, Hanham Business Park, Memorial Road, Hanham, Bristol BS15 3JE, tel: 0117 949 4136; mobile: 0860 259567. (Good source of parts for obsolete Audis.)

R.J. Auto Engineers, Whitehouse Lane, Bedminster, Bristol BS3 4DN, tel: 01179 632029. (SAAB and Alfa specialists.)

Cotswold Sports Cars, Grovesend Garage, Gloucester Road (A38), Grovesend, Thornbury, Bristol BS35 3TO, tel: 01454 412413. (General maintenance and repairs.)

Castle Carey
Moff Motors, Castle Carey, Somerset (near Castle Carey station on Shepton Mallet road), tel: 01963 350310. (Independent dealers with good after-sales service.)

Crewkerne
Misterton Garage, Misterton, Crewkerne, Somerset TA18 8LY, tel: 01460 72997. (Ford retail dealer, good for servicing and repairs, reasonable prices.)

Dorchester
Loders, The Grove, Dorchester, Dorset, tel: 01305 267881. (Good franchised Audi dealer service.)

Exeter
Volkswagen Services, 11 Coombe Street, Exeter, Devon EX1 1DB, tel: 01392 493737.

Carrs of Exeter, tel: 01392 823988. (Good Mercedes and Porsche service.)

Paul Stephens, Snow and Stephens, King Edward Street, Exeter, tel: 01392 256552.

Rockbeare Motor Services, Rockbeare, Exeter EX5 2DZ, tel: 01404 822410.

Best Tyres, Verney Street, Exeter EX1 2AW, tel: 01392 411100. (Low prices, good service and excellent for suspension alignment.)

Exmouth
Karl Brigham, KHB Auto Services and Repairs, Victoria Way, Exmouth, Devon EX8 2PN, tel: 01395 223330.

Bentleys Garage, Chapel Hill (High Street), Exmouth, Devon EX8 1NN, tel: 01395 272048.

Frenchay
Frenchay Garage, Frenchay Common, Frenchay, Bristol BS16 1NB, tel: 0117 956 7303.

Frome
Marston MOT Centre, Whitworth Road, Marston Trading Estate, Frome, Somerset BA11 4BY, tel: 01373 452352. (Proprietor Stewart Herridge. Very reasonably priced local independent garage.)

Good Garages in the South West

Langport

J.A. Scott, Langport Motor Co., Westover Trading Estate, Langport, Somerset TA10 9RB, tel: 01458 251100. (Citroën specialist.)

Liskeard

Ken Rowe, Rowe's Garage Ltd, Dobwalls, Liskeard, Cornwall PL14 6JA, tel: 01579 320218. (Citroën franchise, but will gladly help owners of other makes in trouble.)

Newton Abbot

K. Tapper, Decoy Motors, Unit 10, Silverhills Road, Decoy Trading Estate, Newton Abbot TQ12 5LZ, tel: 01626 68701.

Plymouth

Simon Rouse, Peverell Garage, Weston Park Road, Peverell, Plymouth, Devon PL3 4NS, tel: 01752 266099.

South Molton

Andrew Geen, Geen's Garage, South Molton, North Devon EX36 3LJ, tel: 01769 572395.

Taunton

Paul Lyall, Fairwater Garage, Priorswood Road, Taunton, Somerset TA2 8DN, tel: 01823 277268.

Wadebridge

John Smith, Old Forge Garage, St Miniver, Wadebridge, Cornwall PL27 6QJ, tel: 01208 863323.

Wellington

Grants Repairs, Mantle Street, Wellington, Somerset TA21 8AU, tel: 01823 662067. (Independent BMW specialist – chief mechanic Trevor Klimpke.)

Weston-Super-Mare

Howards Citroën (tel: 01934 644644) and Howards Rover (tel: 01934 643434) both of Hildersheim Bridge, Weston-Super-Mare BS23 3PT.

Howards Peugeot (tel: 01934 636049), Searle Crescent, Weston-Super-Mare BS23 3YX.

Howards Nissan (tel: 01934 416454), Herluin Way, Weston-Super-Mare BS23 3YN. (Howards are franchised agents for Citroën, Rover, Peugeot and Nissan – all, very unusually, in the same town.)

Yeovil

Eastside Garage, Unit 4, Limber Road, Yeovil, Somerset BA22 8RR, tel: 01935 431412. (Citroën specialist.)

Auto Wizard, Penmill Trading Estate, Yeovil, Somerset BA21 5HZ, tel: 01935 410532.

Philip Sargent Vehicle Services, Goldcroft, Yeovil, Somerset BA21 4DH, tel: 01935 427554. ('Ready to go the 'extra mile' when you are in a fix.')

Wales and The West

Abergavenny

Abergavenny Autos, Monmouth Road, Abergavenny, Monmouthshire NP7 5HF, tel: 01873 852712. (Reliable Renault franchise.)

Aberystwyth

Anthony Motors Ltd, Llanbadarn Road, Aberystwyth SY23 3QP, tel: 01970 624444. (Good Mazda agents.)

Bridgnorth

Faintree Garage, Ludlow Road, Faintree, Bridgnorth WV16 6RQ, tel: 01746 789275. (Friendly Skoda agents, for whom nothing is ever too much trouble.)

Caerleon

Autotech, Panthir Road, Caerleon, Gwent NP18 3NY, tel: 01633 423717. (One of semi-official Autotech chain of independent BMW specialists.)

Chester

Crane Bank Garage, New Crane Street, Chester CH1 4JE, tel: 01244 317191. (One of three general garages: Winners of *Daily Telegraph* Customer Service Award 2001.)

Manor Garage, Lightfoot Street, Hoole, Chester CH2 3AL, tel: 01244 346886. (One of three general garages: Winners of *Daily Telegraph* Customer Service Award 2001.)

Newgate Motors, Countess Way, Chester CH1 4DU, tel: 01244 374473. (Expensive but fair Mercedes agent. Labour charges £58.75 an hour.)

Colwyn Bay
Meredith and Kirkham, 394 Abergely Road, Colwyn Bay, tel: 01492 515292. (Rover agent with longstanding loyal customers.)

Cwmcarn
Bijou Motor Services, rear of 99–101 Newport Road, Cwmcarn, Gwent NP1 7LZ, tel: 01495 271033. (Citroën specialists, offering enhanced servicing for this manufacturer.)

Eastham
Mitchell Mitsubishi, New Chester Road, Eastham, Wirral, Cheshire CH62 8HJ, tel: 0151 328 5555/0151 625 4555.

Holt
Eddy Lynton, Academy Garage, Castle Street, Holt, Clwyd LL13 9YL, tel: 01829 270781.

Ledbury
R. & J. Mathews, Blacklands Garage, Canon Frome (near Ledbury), Hereford & Worcester HR8 2TB, tel: 01531 670440.

Llangollen
Kenrick's Garage, Market Street, Llangollen, North Wales LL20 8RA, tel: 01978 861382. (Friendly local garage with excellent and reasonably priced 'rescue' service.)

Minsterley
Minsterley Garage, Station Road, Minsterley, Shropshire SY5 0BE, tel: 01743 790000. (Refit specialists. Reasonably priced, extremely good and efficient service.)

Moreton-in-Marsh
N.E. Repairs, Hospital Road, Moreton-in-Marsh, Gloucs GL56 0BN, tel: 01608 650405.

Penarth
Bernard Cody Motor Engineers, Station Approach, Penarth, Mid-Glamorgan CF64 3EE, tel: 029 20704293.

Penrhyndeudraeth
Dafydd Williams, Garreg Lwyd, Penrhyndeudraeth, Gwynedd, LL48 6AW, tel: 01766 770203. (Second-hand Twingos, servicing, advice and 'hard to get' parts.)

Pewsey
Stevens Cars, Nicol's Yard (rear of Post Office), Pewsey SN9 5EF, tel: 01672 563330.

Porthcawl
John Rogers, Station Hill Garage, Porthcawl, Mid-Glamorgan CF36 5DL, tel: 01656 786705.

Portmadoc
The Glanaber Garage, Borth-y-Gest, Portmadoc, Gwynedd LL49 9TP, tel: 01766 512364.

Swindon
Fish Bros, Addington Drive, Swindon, Wilts SN5 7SB, tel: 01793 512685. (Several recommendations: Fiat, Alfas Romeo and Mitsubishi franchise – good at diagnosing faults on Alfa Romeos. Also Skoda, Nissan and Renault.)

Dick Lovett Specialist Cars, Rushey Park, Swindon SN5 8WO, tel: 01793 615999. (Honest and decent BMW franchise.)

Greenmeadow Service Station, Thames Avenue, Greenmeadow, Swindon, tel: 01793 534501. (Long-standing and well recommended.)

Weobley
John Simpson, Whitehill Garage, Weobley, Hereford HR4 8QZ, tel: 01544 318268.

Wirral

Crane Bank Garage, Poulton Road, Wallasey, Wirral CH44 4BZ, tel: 0151 638 1469. (One of three general garages: Winners of *Daily Telegraph* Customer Service Award 2001.)

Durley Garage, Units 12–14, Badger Way, North Cheshire Trading Estate, Prenton, Wirral CH43 3HQ, tel: 0151 608 0788.

Wrexham

Brian Jones Garage Services Ltd, Queensway, Wrexham, LL13 8UN, tel: 01978 352077. (General garage. Happy to save a customer money wherever possible.)

The North

Bedale

John Gill Ltd, Aiskew Garage, Aiskew, Bedale, N. Yorks DL8 1DD, tel: 01677 423124. (Daihatsu dealer and general repairs.)

Blackburn

Slater Motors, Brunswick Street Garage, Appleby Street, Blackburn, Lancs, tel: 01254 57934. (Mercedes-Benz-trained independent MB specialist.)

Carnforth

The Mountain family, Lune View Garage, Melling, Carnforth, Lancs LA6 2RB, tel: 015242 21457.

Castleford

Castleford VW Spares, Methley Road, Castleford, W. Yorks, tel: 01977 518254. (VW/Audi servicing and parts.)

Durham

Volksparts, Langley Moor, nr Durham DH7 8LZ, tel: 0191 378 0284. (German car specialists: Audi, BMW, Mercedes, VW.)

Garstang

H. & J. Kitching, Hornby's Garage, Lydiate Lane, Claughton on Brock, Garstang, Preston, Lancs PR3 0QL, tel: 01995 640229.

Harrogate

Mr Greenwood, Western Garage, 54 Valley Mount, Harrogate, N. Yorks H62 0JG, tel: 01423 502902.

Nidd Vale Motors, Westmoreland Street, Harrogate, N. Yorks HG1 5AS, tel: 01423 500005. (Vauxhall agents.)

Hexham

Fred Almond, Haugh Lane Garage, Haugh Lane, Hexham, Northumberland NE46 3PT, tel: 01434 604163.

Holmfirth

M & M Engineering Services, Clarence Mills, Holmbridge, Holmfirth HD9 2NE, tel: 01484 687706.

Jarrow

David Ellis, Jarrow Coachworks, Curlew Road, Jarrow, Tyne and Wear NE32 2DX, tel: 0191 4892715; mobile: 0776 417 8390.

Good Garages in the North

Leeds
IVC (Independent VW Audi Centre), Globe Road, off Water Lane, Leeds LS11 5QS, tel: 0113 242 0875.

Leek
Andy Jackson of A&C Vehicle Services, The Yard, Ball Haye Road, Leek, Staffs ST13 6AF, tel: 01538 398227.

Littleborough
J. Stanton, Stanton's Motor Garage, Brookfield Mill, Canal Street, Littleborough, nr Rochdale, Lancs OL15 0HA, tel: 01706 370166.

Liverpool
Philip Walker, Dudlow Motor Company, Menlove Gardens West, Liverpool L18 2ET, tel: 0151 722 2396.

Manchester
Derek Boardman, Units 12/15, Morton Street Industrial Estate, Failsworth, Manchester M35 0BN, tel: 0161 681 0456.

Middlesbrough
Dave Stott Motors, Charlotte Street, Middlesbrough TS2 1DT, tel: 01642 224805. (Independent Citroën specialists.)

Preston
J.C. and M. Davis, Garstang Road Garage, Garstang Road, Pilling, Preston PR3 6AQ, tel: 01253 790322. (General repairs, but good with diesels and Citroëns.)

I.J. Woodburn, Unit 4 Garage, Langley Lane, Goosnargh (Nr Preston), Lancs PR3 2JP, tel: 01772 861126. (Reliable independent BMW specialist.)

Saddleworth
Greenfield Service Station, Chew Valley Road, Greenfield, Saddleworth, nr Oldham, Lancs OL3 7DB, tel: 01457 873700.

Salford
Leyden Bros. Ltd., Chapel Street, Salford, Lancs. M3 7AA, tel: 0161 832 3838. (Reasonable and fair prices.)

Sheffield

Bridgco Garage, 160 Broad Oaks, Sheffield 9, tel: 0114 2441775.

Cemetery Road Motors, Cemetery Road, Sheffield S11 8FT, tel: 0114 266 6500. (Specialists in high-mileage Mercedes sales and service.)

Stockport

Chris or Ben, Tenby Garage, Lavenders Brow, Churchgate, Stockport, Cheshire SK1 1YW, tel: 0161 480 5075.

The Dave Arnitt Citroën Repair Centre, Arthur Street, Reddish, Stockport SK6 1PE, tel: 0161 432 0636. (Citroën specialist.)

General Motor Co. Ltd, Cooke Street, Hazel Grove, Stockport SK7 4EG, tel: 0161 483 3883. (Independent Audi/VW specialists.)

Ryland Honda, 35 Buxton Road, Stockport SK2 6LZ, tel: 0161 480 4244. (Very helpful and efficient, even in sourcing parts for grey-imported Hondas.)

Stockton

Shearborne Engineering, 1a Norton Avenue, Norton, Stockton-on-Tees, Cleveland TS20 2JH, tel: 01642 860080. (Independent Jaguar specialists.)

Wallsend

Priory Cars, The Silverlink, Wallsend, Tyne and Wear NE28 9ND, tel: 0191 295 1295; fax: 0191 295 1123; e-mail: priory.bmw@dial.pipex.com. (BMW franchise.)

Warrington

Stan Woods, Horseshoe Garage, Hollow Lane, Kingsley, Frodsham, Cheshire WA6 8ET, tel: 01928 787323. (Well-equipped independent, capable of servicing anything from a Mini to a BMW 7-Series, labour rate just £25 an hour.)

David Roundell Services, Milner Street, Warrington, Cheshire WA5 1AD, tel: 01925 635958.

Whitley Bay

John Gallagher, Collingwood Garage, Rockcliffe Street, Whitley Bay, Tyne and Wear NE26 2NW, tel: 0191 252 2244.

Widnes

Widnes Car Centre, Moor Lane, Widnes, Cheshire WA8 7AL, tel: 0151 420 2000. (Independently owned Nissan agent.)

D & M Motors, Waterloo Road, Widnes, Cheshire WA8 0PY, tel: 0151 420 2646.

Wigan

K. Brown & Partner Motor Engineers, 131 Upholland Road, Billinge, nr Wigan WN5 7EG, tel: 01942 519522. (Independent garage, experienced in VWs.)

Windermere

Keith Donnelly, Oldfield Road Garage, Oldfield Road, Windermere, Cumbria LA23 2BY, tel: 015 394 46710.

York

John Galley Motors, Pocklington Industrial Estate, Pocklington, York, tel: 01759 303716. (VW/Audi.)

Dixon MG and Rover, Jockey Lane, Monk's Cross, York YO32 9XX, tel: 01904 667300, fax: 01904 667316 (parts, tel: 01904 636666). (Credited with 'absolutely first-class service, every time'.)

Scotland

Ballater

J. Pringle, Victoria Garage, Ballater, Grampian AB35 5QQ, tel: 013397 55525.

Drumndrochit

J.E. Menzies & Son Ltd, Lewiston Garage, Drumndrochit, Inverness, tel: 01456 450212.

Elvanfoot

Car and Truck Services, Elvanfoot, Lanarkshire MH2 6KF(adjacent to A74M), tel: 01864 502236. (General repairs and service, bodywork, breakdown and recovery.)

Forres
Pedigreed Cars, Bogton Place, Forres, Morayshire IV6 1EP, tel: 01309 672555.

Kirkwall
A.T.S., Junction Road, Kirkwall, Orkney KW15 1AX, tel 01856 872361. (Tyre specialists and general servicing.)

Largs
Waterside Motors, 24 Waterside Street, Largs, Ayrshire, KA30 9LN, tel: 01475 675020. (Excellent service and superb customer relations.)

Loanhead
McLennan Garage, 16 Park Avenue, Loanhead, Midlothian EH20 9AZ, tel: 0131 440 0597.

Skye
Ewan MacRae, Dunvegan Road, Portree, Isle of Skye IV51 9HD, tel: 01478 612554.

Northern Ireland

Bushmills, Co. Antrim
James Wylie Auto Repairs, 48A Ballyclogh Road, Bushmills, Co. Antrim BT57 8UZ, tel: 028207 32096. (Citroën specialist, as well as other makes.)

Car Clubs Directory

We're crazy about our cars in the UK. What's more, we love to share our mania with others. There are hundreds of Car Clubs across the country, celebrating both current and long-lost (but never forgotten) marques, and some even dedicated to a single model.

This list is classified in alphabetical order of manufacturer, from AC to Zil (OK, to Wolseley). A final section lists specialist clubs not allied to a specific manufacturer.

AC

AC Owners Club Ltd, Eric Gates, 8 Netherway, Upper Poppleton, York YO2 6JQ, tel: 01904 793563.

AEC

AEC Society, c/o L. Harris, 32 Kingscroft Road, Hucclecote, Glos GL3 3RG.

AJS

AJS 9 Car Club, c/o Peter Hubbard, The Chestnuts, Chequers Road, Tharston, Norwich NR15 2YA, tel: 01508 530072; website: www.ajscar.freeserve.co.uk.

Alfa Romeo

Alfa Romeo Owners Club, 9 Green Lane, Wootton, Northants NN4 6LH, tel: 01604 761813; website: www.aroc-uk.com.

Allard

Allard Owners Club, c/o Michelle Wilson, 10 Brooklyn Court, Woking, Surrey GU22 7TQ, tel: 01483 773428.

Alvis

Alvis Owners Club, c/o Charles Mackonochie, 2 Sunny Bank Cottage, Colts Hill, Capel, Tonbridge, Kent TN12 6SW, tel: 01892 832118; website: www.alvisoc.org.

The Alvis Register, c/o John Willis, The Vinery, Wanborough Hill, Guildford, Surrey GU3 2JB, tel: 01483 810308.

Armstrong Siddeley

Armstrong Siddeley Owners Club Ltd, c/o Peter Sheppard, 57 Berberry Close, Birmingham B30 1TB, tel: 0121 459 0742 (eve); website: www.siddeley.com.

Aston Martin

Aston Martin Owners Club Ltd, c/o Secretary, John Burslem, Drayton, St Leonard, Wallingford, Oxon OX10 7BJ, tel: 01865 400400; website: www.amoc.org.

Austin

The Vintage Austin Register Ltd, c/o Frank Smith, The Briars, Four Lane Ends, Oakerthorpe, Nr Alfreton, Derbyshire DE55 7LH, tel: 01773 831646.

Austin 7 Owners Club (London), c/o Yvonne King (Membership Secretary), PO Box 77, Esher, Surrey KT10 8WZ, tel: 01372 466134; e-mail: king_yvonne@hotmail.com, website: www.austinsevenownersclub.co.uk.

The Pre-War Austin Seven Club Ltd, c/o Steve Jones, 1 The Fold, Doncaster Road, Whiteley, nr Goole, East Yorks DN14 0JF, tel: 01977 662828.

Midlands Austin 7 Club, c/o John Roberts, 18 Oaktree Lane, Cookhill, Alcester, Warks B49 5LH, tel: 01789 765349 (before 9pm).

South Wales Austin Seven Club, c/o H. and G. Morgan, 90 Ammanford Road, Llandybie, Ammanford, Carmarthenshire SA18 2JY, tel: 01269 850528.

Austin Swallow Register, School House, Rectory Road, Gt. Haseley, Oxford OX44 7JP.

Austin Big 7 Register, c/o R. Taylor, 101 Derby Road, Chellaston, Derby DE73 1SB, tel: 01332 700629.

The Austin Eight Register, c/o Ian Pinniger, 3 La Grange Martin, St Martin, Jersey, Channel Islands JE3 6JB, e-mail: mail@pinniger.fsnet.co.uk

Austin Ten Drivers Club Ltd (Pre-War 10s, 12s, 14s, 16s, 18s, 20s), c/o Ian Dean, PO Box 12, Chichester, West Sussex PO20 7PH, tel: 01243 641284.

British Austin Society, c/o Barry Martin, Park Gate Oast, Cranbrook Road, Tenterden, Kent TN30 6UP. Membership £14 a year. Caters mainly for pre-war 7s, 10s and 12s but all Austin owners welcome.

North East Club for Pre-War Austins (NECPWA), contact George Halliday, 67 Balliol Avenue, Westmoor, Newcastle-upon-Tyne NE12 0PN, or the membership secretary, Tom Gatenby, e-mail: PG9882@aol.com; website: www.necpwa.demon.co.uk

Austin J40 Car Club, Marcia Blake, 9 Spades Bourne Road, Lickey End, Bromsgrove, West Midlands B60 1JW, tel: 01527 876152.

Austin Counties Car Club, c/o Ian Coombes, 44 Vermeer Crescent, Shoeburyness, Essex SS3 9JT, tel: 01702 295385; website: www.austincounties.org.uk. Includes the Austin Atlantic Owners Club.

Austin Sheerline and Princess Owners Register, c/o Ian Coombes, 44 Vermeer Crescent, Shoeburyness, Essex SS3 9JT, tel: 01702 295385.

Austin Healey Club, c/o Colleen Holmes, 4 Saxby Street, Leicester LE2 0ND.

Austin Gipsy Register, c/o Miles Gilbert, 24 Green Close, Rixon, Sturminster Newton, Dorset DT10 1BJ, tel: 01258 472680.

Cambridge/Oxford Farina Owners Club (1959-1971), c/o Malcolm Padbury, 32 Reservoir Road, Southgate, London N14 4BG; e-mail: coocmem@padburym.freeserve.co.uk.

Austin Cambridge/Westminster Car Club, c/o Mr J. Curtis, 4 Russell Close, East Budleigh, Budleigh Salterton, Devon EX9 7EX, tel: 01395 446210.

Austin A40 Farina Club, 75 Tennal Toad, Harborne, Birmingham B32 2JB.

1100 Club (all 1100 and 1300 variants), c/o Andrew Morton, 18 Ullswater Close, North Anston, Sheffield S25 4GH.

Austin Maxi Club, Send SAE to Ms C. Jackson, 27 Queen Street, Bardney, Lincs LN3 5XF.

Landcrab Owners Club International, c/o Bill Fraser, 10 Eastcott Road, Welling, Kent DA16 2SX.

Allegro Club International, 20 Stoneleigh Crescent, Stoneleigh, Epsom, Surrey KT19 0RP, website: www.uk-classic-cars.com/allegro.htm.

Princess and Ambassador Owners Club, c/o Peter Maycroft, 26 Castlehall, Glascote, Tamworth, Staffs B77 2EJ, website: www.princessandambassador.btinternet.co.uk.

Austin Maestro Owners Club (includes Montego), Jonathan Sellars, 6 Grailands Close, Fernhurst, Haslemere, Surrey GU27 3HU, tel: 07932 997770; websites: www.maestro.org.uk; e-mail: jpsellars@ maestro.org.uk.

Autocycle and Cyclemotor
National Autocycle and Cyclemotor Club: membership secretary: David Freeman, 81 High Road, Trimley, Felixstowe, Suffolk IP11 0TA.

Autovia
Autovia Car Club, c/o Gordon Thomas, Club Secretary, 43 Tilbury Road, Tilbury Juxta Clare, Halstead, Essex CO9 4JJ, tel: 01787 237676.

Bedford
Bedford Owners Club, c/o Ron Ruggins, 27 Northville Drive, Westcliff-on-Sea, Essex SS0 0QA.

Bedford CA UK, c/o P. Oakham, 2 Banmore Avenue, Higher Openshaw, Manchester M11 1BS.

Belsize
Useful contact for Belsize information: Rodney Fowler, Tithe House, Chelford Road, Knutsford, Cheshire WA16 8LY, tel: 01565 651051; fax: 01565 754204.

Bentley
Bentley Drivers Club Ltd, c/o Patricia Gee, Secretary, 16 Chearsley Road, Long Crendon, Aylesbury, Bucks HP18 9AW, tel: 01844 208233; website: www.bdcl.co.uk.

Bitter
Bitter Owners Club, c/o P. Griffith, Medina Garden Centre, Staplers Road, Wootton, Isle of Wight PO33 4RW, tel: 01983 883430; website: www.uk-classic-cars.com/bitter.htm.

BMC

BMC Farina 3000 Drivers Club (all variants), c/o Terry Burgess, 58 Fiskerton Road, Reepham, Lincoln LN3 4EF.

Scottish BMC Car Club, c/o Euan Smith, 111 Stewart Avenue, Bo'ness, EH51 9NN, website: www.geocities.com/motorcity/speedway5705.

BMC J2/150 Register, c/o Matt and Joanne Traxton, 10 Sunnyside Cottages, Woodford, Kettering, Northants NN14 4HX, tel: 01832 734441; website: www.brmmbrmm.com/bmcj2152; e-mail: matt.traxton@tesco.net.

BMC JU 250 Register, c/o Stuart Cook, 34 Thorncliffe Drive, Darwen, Lancs BB3 3QA, tel: 01254 772372.

BMC LD Register, 86 Manica Crescent, Fazakerley, Liverpool L10 9NA, tel: 0151 525 3907.

BMW

BMW Car Club (GB) Ltd, Andrew Dale, Club Secretary, PO Box 328, Melksham, Wilts, tel: 01225 709009, fax: 01225703885, email: enquiries@bmwccgb.org website: www.bmwcarclub.co.uk.

BMW Car Club Historic Section, c/o Mark Garfitt, 126 Llantarnam Road, Cwmbran, Gwent NO44 3BD, tel: 01633 871704.

BMW Drivers Club International, c/o Samantha Easton, 41 Norwich Street, Dereham, Norfolk NR19 1AD, tel: 01362 691144.

Bond

Bond Owners Club, c/o Stan Cormack, 42 Beaufort Avenue, Hodge Hill, Birmingham B34 6AE, tel: 0121 784 4626; website: www.bondownersclub.co.uk.

Borgward

Borgward Drivers Club, c/o The Secretary, Derek Farr, 19 Highfield Road, Kettering, Northants NN15 6HR, tel: 01536 510771; website: www.borgward.org.uk; e-mail: borgward@bigfoot.com.

Bristol

Bristol Owners Club, c/o John Emery, Vesutor Ltd, Marringdean Road, Billingshurst, West Sussex RH14 9EH, tel: 01403 784028, website: www.boc.net/bristol.

BSA

BSA Front Wheel Drive Club, c/o Barry Baker, 164 Cottimore Lane, Walton-on-Thames, Surrey KT12 2BL, tel: 01932 225270; website: members.aol.com/bsafwdc/home.htm.

Buckler

Buckler Car Register, c/o Stanley Hibberd, 42 Stepping Road, Long Lawford, Rugby CV23 9SG, tel: 01788 573319.

Bugatti

Bugatti Owners Club Ltd, c/o Sue Ward, Prescott Hill, Gotherington, Cheltenham, Glos GL52 4RD.

Cadillac

Cadillac Owners Club of Great Britain, c/o Bill Greenwood, 'Dunvegan', Lynn Road, King's Lynn, Norfolk PE33 0HG.

Calcott

Calcott Register, c/o Anthony Wilson, 'Willerby', 61 Ridgewood Drive, RD1 New Plymouth, New Zealand, fax: 00 64 67537461.

Chevrolet

Classic Chevrolet Club, c/o Chris Richards, Secretary, PO Box 2222, Braintree, Essex CM7 9TW, tel: 020 8244 4893.

Classic Corvette Club (UK) Ltd, c/o Andy Greenfield, 8 New England Crescent, Great Wakering, Essex SS3 0DU, tel: 01702 217075, website: www.corvetteclub.org.uk.

Citroën

For all things Citroën: www.citroenet.org.uk (an amenity website for Citroën enthusiasts).

Citroën Traction Owners Club, c/o Peter Riggs, 2 Appleby Gardens, Dunstable, Beds LU6 3DB.

Citroën Traction Enthusiasts Club, c/o Robin Rother, Preston House Studio, Preston, Canterbury, Kent CT3 1DZ.

Citroën Car Club, c/o Derek Pearson, PO Box 348, Bromley, Kent BR2 8QT, tel: 0700 0248258, website: www.citroencarclub.org.uk.

2CV GB, PO Box 602, Crick, Northampton NN6 7UW, tel: 07770 228602, email: enquiries@2cvgb.co.uk, website: www.2cvgb.co.uk.

Citroën XM 2.1TD Group, c/o John Cownley, fax: 01635 202643.

Clan

Clan Owners Club, c/o Fred Brooks, 19 Greenacres, South Cornelly, Mid-Glamorgan CF33 4SE, tel: 01656 744741, email: clanclubmembership@tesco.net

Clyno

Clyno Register, c/o R. Surman, Swallow Cottage, Langton Farm, Burbage Common Road, Elmesthorpe, Leicester LE9 7SE, tel: 01455 842178; fax: 01455 850584.

Commer

CommerCAR (Commer Archive and Register) c/o Peter Daniels (archivist), Fairway View, Netherhampton, Salisbury, Wilts SP2 8PX, tel: 01722 744766; fax: 01722 744767; e-mail: commercar@ active.uk.com.

Cougar

Cougar Club of America, c/o Barrie Dixon, 11 Dean Close, Partington, Manchester M31 4BI, tel: 0161 775 0820.

Crossley

Crossley Register, c/o Malcolm Jenner, Willow Cottage, Lexham Road, Great Dunham, Kings Lynn, Norfolk PE32 2LS, tel: 01328 701240.

Crossley Climax Register, c/o M. Sims, 10 Longbridge Road, Bramley, Hampshire RG26 5AN.

DAF

DAF Owners Club, c/o Steve Bidwell, 56 Ridgedale Road, Bolsover, Chesterfield, Derbyshire S44 6TX, email: dafownersclub@ bolsover.co.uk, website: www.dafownersclub.co.uk.

Daimler/Lanchester (*see also Jaguar*)

Daimler Enthusiasts Club, c/o Greville Taverner, Beech House, Northwell Pool Road, Swaffham, Norfolk PE37 7HW, tel/fax: 01760 721685, email: GTaverner@onetel.net.uk.

Daimler and Lanchester Owners Club, PO Box 276, Sittingbourne, Kent ME9 7GA, tel/fax 07000 356285; e-mail: DaimlerUK@aol.com.

Daimler SP250 Owners Club 1998, c/o G. Frost, 15 Broom Mead, Bexleyheath, Kent DA6 7NZ, tel: 01322 522958, email: grahamfrost@gmfltd.freeserve.co.uk.

Datsun

Datsun Owners Club, c/o Jon Rodwell, Secretary, 26 Langton Road, Wraughton, Wilts SN4 0QN, tel: 01793 845271, website: www. datsunworld.com.

Datsun Z Club, c/o Steve Kemp, Membership Secretary, 12 Palmerston Way, Biddulph, Stoke-on-Trent ST8 7SX, tel: 01782 518992; website: www.jwa.co.uk/zclub.

Classic Z Register, c/o J. Newlyn, 11 Lawday Link, Upper Hale, Farnham, Surrey GU9 0BS, tel: 01252 711297.

DB/David Brown

David Brown Owners Club, Secretary: Martin George, Champney Hill Farm, Silkstone Common, Barnsley S75 4PH. Chairman: Daryl Clegg, Hays Barn, The Hays, Helm, Huddersfield HD7 3RN.

Davrian

Davrian Register, c/o J. Rawlins, 4 Browns Lane, Uckfield, East Sussex TN22 1RS, tel: 01825 763638.

Delage

Delage Section of the VSCC, c/o Peter Jacobs, 'Clouds Reach', The Scop, Almondsbury, Bristol BS32 4DU, tel: 01454 612434, website: www.delage-world.co.uk.

Delahaye

Delahaye Club (GB) The club has ceased to exist, but Peter Jacobs is acting as a helpful contact, e-mail: peter@cloudsreach. freeserve.co.uk.

Dellow

Dellow Register, c/o John Temple, 4 Roumelia Lane, Bournemouth, Dorset BH5 1ET; tel   01202 304641; fax 01202 392170; email dellow@douglastemple.co.uk.

DeLorean

DeLorean Owners Club (GB), c/o Chris Parnham, 14 Quarndon heights, Allestree, Derby DE22 2XN, tel: 01332 230823, website: www.delorean.co.uk.

De Tomaso

De Tomaso Drivers Club, c/o Roger Brotton, Stoney Croft, Moor Lane, Birdwell, Barnsley, South Yorkshire S70 5TZ, tel 01226 292601, email: detomaso.dcuk@virgin.net.

DKW

DKW Owners Club, c/o David Simon, 'Aurelia', Garlogie, Skene, Westhill, Aberdeenshire AB32 6RX, tel: 01224 743429.

Dormobile

Dormobile Owners Club, c/o Allan Horne, 23 Fairmile, Aylesbury, Bucks HP21 7JS, tel: 01296 428580.

Dutton

Dutton Owners Club. c/o Mark Young, 6 Binyon Close, Badsey, Evesham, Worcs WR11 5EY.

Elva

Elva Owners Club, c/o Roger Dunbar, 8 Liverpool Terrace, Worthing, West Sussex BN11 1TA, tel: 01903 823710; website: www.elva.com.

Facel Vega

Facel Vega Owners Club, c/o Roy Scandrett, 'Windrush', 16 Paddock Gardens, East Grinstead, Sussex RH19 4AE, tel: 01342 326655, email: www.linscan@aol.com.

Fairthorpe

Fairthorpe Sports Car Club, c/o Tony Hill, 9 Lyndhurst Crescent, Hillingdon, Middlesex UB10 9EH, tel: 01895 256799.

Ferrari

Ferrari Owners Club, c/o Peter Everingham, 35 Market Place, Snettisham, Kings Lynn PE31 7LR, tel: 01485 544500, website: www.ferrariownersclub.co.uk.

Ferrari Dino Register, c/o B. Boxall, 43 Mayswood Road, Solihull, West Midlands.

Fiat

Fiat 500 Club, c/o Janet Westcott, 33 Lionel Avenue, Wendover, Bucks HP22 6LP, tel: 01296 622880 website: www.fiat500club.org.

500 Owners Association, c/o David Docherty, 68 Upton Park, Upton-by-Chester, Cheshire CH2 1DQ, tel: 01244 382789.

Fiat Barchetta Club. Contact Geoff Bowles on geoff@bowles.force9. co.uk for further details (website: www.fiatbarchetta.com/club/uk). Or write to 39 New Road, Great Kingshill, High Wycombe, Bucks, HP15 6DR.

Fiat Motor Club (GB), c/o Sally Robins (membership secretary), 118 Brookland Road, Langport, Somerset TA10 9TH, tel: 01458 250116; Peter Jones (chairman), tel: 020 8372 4028.

Fiat X1/9 Owners Club, c/o Lyn Robertson, Membership Secretary, Bwthyn Penygroes, Penisarwaun, Caernarfon, Gwynedd LL56 3PP, tel: 016640822395; website: www.x1-9ownersclub.org.uk.

Fiat Dino Register, 59 Sandown Park, Tunbridge Wells, Kent TN2 4RY.

Fiat Osca Register, c/o Mr Elliott, 36 Maypole Drive, Chigwell, Essex.

Foden
The Foden Society, c/o Graham Donaldson, 13 Dudfleet Lane, Horbury, Wakefield, West Yorks WF4 5EX, tel: 01924 275544, website: www.thefodensociety.co.uk.

Ford
Model T Ford Register of Great Britain, c/o Julia Armer, 3 Riverside, Strong Close, Keighley, West Yorks BD21 4JP, tel: 01535 607978, website: www.t-ford.co.uk.

Model A Ford Club of Great Britain, c/o Mike Cobell, 10–14 Newland Street, Coleford, Forest of Dean, Glos GL16 8AN, tel: 01594 834321; fax: 01594 835456.

Ford Y and C Model Register, c/o Bob Wilkinson, 9 Brambleside, Thrapston, Northants NN14 4PY, tel: 01832 734463, email: bob@bwilkinson.49fsnet.uk, website: members.pipemedia.net/ford-model-register/index.htm.

Early Ford V8 Club of America, c/o S. Wade, 'Forge Stones', Heath Road, Boughton, Monchelsea, Maidstone, Kent ME17 4HS.

Ford 400E Owners Club, c/o Sandy Glen, 1 Maltings Cottage, Witham Road, White Notley, Witham, Essex CM8 1SE, email: sandy@thames400e.freeserve.co.uk.

Ford Sidevalve Owners Club, c/o Mike Crouch, 30 Earls Close, Bishop-stoke, Eastleigh, Hants SO50 8HY, e-mail: menear@easynet.co.uk.

Pre-67 Ford Owners Club, c/o Alastair Cuninghame, Membership Secretary, 13 Drum Brae Gardens, Edinburgh EH12 8SY, tel: 0131 339 1179.

Ford Anglia 105E Owners Club, c/o M. Lewis, 81 Compton Road, North End, Portsmouth, Hants PO2 0SR.

The Sporting Escort Owners Club (all RWD cars), c/o Peter Ridgewell, Chairman, 30 Rowan Way, Thursdon, Bury St. Edmunds, Suffolk IP31 3PU, tel: 01359 231384.

Ford Classic and Capri Owners Club, c/o Ray Brandon, 1 Verney Close, Covingham, Swindon, Wilts SN3 5EF.

Capri Club International, 18 Arden Business Centre, Arden Road, Alcester B49 6HW, tel: 01789 400455; website: www.cci.planet-capri.net.

Capri II Register, c/o Kevin Hickling. 14 Beechfield Road, Welwyn Garden City, Herts AL7 3RF, tel: 07949 949297, email: capri2reg@hotmail.com.

Capri Drivers Association, c/o Moira Farelly, 9 Lyndhurst Road, Coulsdon, Surrey CR5 3HU.

Ford Capri Enthusiasts Register, c/o Glyn Watson, 7 Louis Avenue, Bury, Lancs BL9 5EQ, tel: 0161 762 9952.

Capri Club Scotland, c/o P. Lewis, 7 Logan Lea Crescent, Addlewell, West Lothian EH55 8HP.

Capri 280 Register: for details send SAE to Mark Smith, Capri 280 Register, Manchester Capri Club, Box No 5, Manchester M28 7HB, tel: 0161 790 4726 (day) 0860 568188 (eve) email: bob@bwilkinson.49fsnet.uk, website: www.geocities.com/fastfordcar/capri280register.htm.

Ford Corsair Owners Club, c/o Liz Checkley, 7 Barnfield, New Malden, Surrey KT3 5RH, tel: 020 8395 4089, website: members.aol.com/fcoc/index.htm.

Ford Cortina Owners Club, c/o Ken Wylson, 56 Barrowfield Road, Woodhouse Park, Manchester M22 1RT, tel: 0161 028 600647 (after 6pm).

Mk I Cortina Owners Club, c/o Karen Clarke, 6 Hobson's Acre, Gunthorpe, Nottingham NG14 7FF, tel: 0115 966 3995; e-mail: 106553.456@compuserve.com.

Ford Cortina Mk II Owners Club, c/o L. Willis, 7 Underdown Road, Herne Bay, Kent.

Ford Cortina 1600E Owners Club, c/o D. Johnson, 16 Woodlands Close, Sarisbury Green, Southampton SO31 7AQ, tel: 01489 602576; website: www.uk-classic-cars.com/fordcortina1600E.htm.

Ford Cortina Mk III Owners Club, c/o Steve Brookes, 146 Tudor Road, Hinckley, Leics LE10 0EH, tel: 01455 619905.

Ford Cortina Mk III Owners Register, c/o Keith Macey, 4 Fron Dirion, Brion Eeyn, Nebo, Caernarfon, Gwynedd LL54 6EN, tel: 01286 881424.

Mk I Consul, Zephyr and Zodiac Owners Club, c/o V. Pell, 180 Gipsy Road, Welling, Kent DA16 1JQ.

Mk II Consul/Zephyr/Zodiac Owners Club, c/o Del Rawlins, tel: 01286 831291.

Ford Mk II Independent Owners Club International, c/o J. Enticknap, 173 Sparrow Farm Drive, Feltham, Middlesex TW14 0DG, tel: 020 8890 3741.

Ford Mk III Zephyr and Zodiac Owners Club, c/o Dave Barnes, 27 Shurley Grove, Edmonton, London N9 8ES, tel: 020 8443 2648.

Zephyr and Zodiac Mk IV Owners Club, c/o John Glaysher, 94 Claremont Road, Rugby CV21 3LU, tel: 01788 574884.

Ford Executive Owners Register, c/o George Young, 31 Brian Road, Chadwell Heath, Romford, Essex EM6 5DA.

Ford Granada Mk I Owners Club, c/o Paul Stones, 10 Wayland Road, Grove, Wantage, Oxon OX12 0BQ, tel: 01235 768399.

Ford Granada Mk I and Mk II Drivers Guild, General Secretary: Maureen Kennedy, 26 Brent Road, Bourne End, Bucks SL8 5LU; tel: 01628 530784; website: www.ford-granadaguild.co.uk; e-mail: martin@ford-granadaguild.co.uk.

Ford Granada Mk II Owners Club, c/o P. Farrer, 58 Jevington Way, Lee, London SE12 9NQ, tel: 020 8857 4356.

Granada Mk II Collection, c/o Rod Bamford, 11 Tolton Road, Stocking Farm, Leicester LE4 2HG, tel: 0116 299 7409.

Ford Granada Mk I, Mk II and Mk III Club, c/o Cliff Robinson, 29 Rowlands Close, Cheshunt, Herts EN8 9NW.

Ford Granada Enthusiasts Club, c/o Philip Snow, 116 Whitmore Road, Hanchurch Crossroads, Newcastle, Staffs ST5 4DG, tel: 01782 657697; website: www.granada-enthusiasts.co.uk.

Mustang Owners Club of Great Britain, c/o A. Keighley, 21 Raleigh Close, Eaton Socon, Cambs PE19 3NN, tel: 01480 477254; website: www.geocities.com/MotorCity/3380/index.html.

Ford RS Owners Club, PO Box 4044, Pangbourne, Reading, Berks RG8 7XL, tel: 01189 841583 website: www.rsownersclub.co.uk.

Ford XR Owners Club, PO Box 47, Loughborough, Leics LE11 1XS; tel: Les Gent 01509 881015.

Ford Fiesta Club of GB, c/o Mrs S. Church, 145 Chapel Lane, Farnborough, Hants GU14 9BN, tel: 01276 35422; website: fiestaclubgb.co.uk.

Ford Drivers Register, c/o Neil Jones, 86 Muncaster Gardens, East Hunsbury, Northampton NN4 0XR, tel: 01604 768909.

Frisky

Frisky Register, c/o J. Meadows, Graces Cottage, Tregagle, Monmouth, Gwent NP5 4RZ, tel: 01600 860420.

FSO/Polski Fiat

FSO Owners Club (including Polski Fiat register), c/o Simon McDonald-Elliott, Cottage Workshops, The Graig, Water-Trough Lane, Llanwenarth Citra, Abergavanny NP7 7EN, tel: 01873 810517, email: fsofriends@smartgroup.com.

Gentry

Gentry Register, c/o Barbera Reynolds, Barn Close Cottage, Cromford Road, Woodlinkin, Notts NG16 4HD, tel: 01773 719874, website: www.gentry-owners.co.uk.

Gilbern

Gilbern Owners Club, c/o Peter Daye, Membership Secretary, Castlebrook, Compton Dundon, Somerton, Somerset TA11 6PR, tel: 01458 442025, e-mail: pvdaye@netscapeonline.co.uk.

Gordon Keeble

Gordon Keeble Owners Club, 26 Burford Park Road, Birmingham B38 8PB, tel: 0121 459 9587, website: www.gordonkeeble.com.

Gwynne and Albert

Gwynne and Albert Register, c/o Ian Walker, 8 Baines Lane, Knebworth, Herts SG3 6RA, tel: 01438 812041.

Haflinger

Haflinger Club, e-mail: Tony@seis.com.au; website: ftp.ccc. nottingham.ac.uk/~ppzcad/haf.html.

Healey

Association of Healey Owners, c/o John Humphreys, 2 Kingsbury's Lane, Ringwood, Hants BH24 1EL, tel: 01425 480243.

Heinkel/Trojan

Heinkel Trojan Club Ltd., c/o Peter Jones, 37 Brinklow Close, Matchborough West, Redditch, Worcs B98 0HB, tel: 01527 501318, website: homepages.tesco.net/~heinkeljb/HTCltd/main.htm.

Hillman

Hillman Register 1907–1932, c/o Clive Baker, Waterloo Mill, School Road, Wotton-under-Edge, Glos GL12 7JN, tel: 01453 843438.

Hillman Owners Club, c/o Christine Gore, 6 Askham Grove, Upton, Pontefract WF9 1LT.

Avenger and Sunbeam Owners Club, c/o Malcolm Wood, 40 Stanbeck Meadows, Workington, Cumbria. e-mail: Marcus@avenger72.freeserve.co.uk.

Imp Cruising Club, 28 Marrion Crescent, Orpington, Kent BR5 5DD.

Hillman Minx and Hunters Galore, c/o Mrs Janet Thorpe, 3 The Pinfold, Newton Burgoland, Coalville, Leicester LE67 2SQ, tel: 01530 273511, e-mail: althorpe@aol.com (Chairman and Magazine: c/o Gerald Bostock, 17 Fennel Drive, The Fallows, Stafford ST17 7HA, tel: 01785 255586.)

Holden

Holden UK Register, c/o Guy Hardy, Membership Secretary, Cawdron House, 111 Charles Street, Milfrod Haven, Pembrokeshire SA73 2HW, tel: 01646 692254, e-mail: holdenuk@ndirect.co.uk; website: www.geocities.com/ikiloh.

Honda

Honda Beat Club, c/o Stephen Finegan, 4 Leeson Walk, Harborne, Birmingham B17 0LU.

Hotchkiss
British Hotchkiss Society, c/o Michael Edwards, Yew Cottage, Old Boars Hill, Oxford OX1 5JJ, tel: 01865 735180; fax: 01865 730698. President: Paul Hickson, 20 Eldon Road, Reading, Berks RG1 4DL, tel: 0118 957 6193.

Humber
Humber Register (1896–1932), c/o Richard Arman, Northbrook Cottage, 175 York Road, Broadstone, Dorset BH18 8ES, tel: 01202 695937.

Post-Vintage Humber Car Club, c/o Harvey Cooke, 1 Hilbery Rise, Northampton NN3 5ER, tel: 01604 404363, website: www.pvhcc. fsnet.co.uk.

Invicta
Invicta Car Club, Stanley Hall, Selsey, Stroud, Gloucs GL5 5LJ, fax: 01453 791363, e-mail: renall@selseyswinternet.co.uk.

Isetta
Isetta Owners Club of Great Britain, c/o Mick and Kay West, 137 Prebendal Avenue, Aylesbury, Bucks HP21 8LD.

Jaguar/Daimler (*see also Daimler/Lanchester*)
Jaguar Car Club, c/o Jeff Holman, Membership Secretary, Barbary, Chobham Road, Woking, Surrey GU21 4AS, tel: 01483 763811, website: www.geocities.com/ikiloh.

Jaguar Drivers Club Ltd., Mrs Kathy Beech, Company Secretary, Jaguar House, 18 Stuart Street, Luton, Beds LU1 2SL, tel: 01582 419332; website: www.jaguardriver.co.uk.

Jaguar Enthusiasts Club, The Old Library, 113A Gloucester Road North, Filton, Bristol BS34 7PU, tel: 0117 969 8186; website: www.jec.org.uk.

Jensen

Jensen Owners Club, c/o Keith Andrews, 2 Westgate, Fulshaw Park, Wilmslow, Cheshire SK9 1QQ, tel: 01625 525699.

Jensen Club, PO Box 334, Aylesbury, Bucks HP22 5GL, tel: 01296 614072, e-mail: jensenclub@btinternet.com, website: www. jensenclub.com.

Jowett

Jowett Car Club, Membership Secretary: Pauline Winteringham, 33 Woodlands Road, Gomersal, West Yorks BD19 4SF, tel: 01274 873959.

Jupiter

Jupiter Owners Automobile Club, c/o Geoff Butterwick, Cowlishaw Cottage, Yarmouth Road, Melton,Woodbridge, Suffolk IP12 1QF, tel: 01394 385709, website: www.jowettjupiter.co.uk, e-mail: ed@jowettjupiter.co.uk.

Lada

Lada Owners Club of Great Britain, c/o Heather Rogers, Secretary, 10 Carnaby Close, Godmanchester, Huntingdon, Cambs PE29 2EE, tel: 01480 391343, email: p.rogers@lada-owners-club.co.uk.

Lagonda

Lagonda Club, c/o Colin Bugler, Wintney House, London Road, Hartley Wintney, Hants RG27 8RN, tel: 01252 845451, website: www.lagonda-club.com.

Lagonda Rapier Register, c/o Mrs J. Williams, The Smithy, Tregynon, Newtown, Powys SY16 3EH, tel: 01686 650396.

The Lanchester Register 1895–1931, c/o Chris Clark, The Lanches, Ledbury Road, Dymock, Gloucestershire GL18 2AG, tel: 01531 890204.

Lancia

Lancia Motor Club, PO Box 51, Wrexham LL11 5ZE, website: www.lanciamotorclub.co.uk.

Land Rover

Land Rover 1947–1951 Register, c/o Frank Mall, 10 Rowan Mount, Wheatley Hills, Doncaster, South Yorkshire DN2 5PJ, tel: 01302 367349.

Land Rover Series One Club, c/o Tim Webb, Secretary, Overmeade, Arches Farm, Malmesbury, Wiltshire SN16 0EJ, tel: 01666 823449.

Lea Francis

Lea Francis Owners Club, c/o Robin Sawers, 'French's', Long Wittenham, Abingdon, Oxon OX14 4QQ, tel: 01865 407515.

Lincoln

Lincoln Zephyr Owners Club, c/o Colin Spong, 22 New North Road, Hainault, Ilford, Essex IG6 2XG.

Lotus

The Official Lotus Club, c/o Deborah Marsh, Club Coordinator, Lotus Cars Ltd, Potash Lane, Hethel, Norwich NR14 8EZ, tel: 01953 608149, website: www.lotuscars.co.uk.

Lotus Drivers Club, PO Box 387, St. Albans, Herts AL4 9BJ.

Club Lotus, PO Box 8, Dereham, Norfolk NR19 1AD, tel: 01362 694459.

Historic Lotus Register, c/o Graham Capel, Nyes Place, Newdigate, Surrey RH5 5BX, tel: 01293 871541.

Lotus Cortina Register, c/o Andy Morrell, 64 The Queen's Drive, Chorleywood, Rickmansworth, Herts WD3 2LT, tel: 01923 836520 (day); 01923 776219 (eve).

Sunbeam Lotus Owners Club, c/o The Secretary, 7 Church Road, Maulden, Bedford MK45 2AU, tel: 01525 840331, website: www. sunbeamlotus.com.

Marcos

Marcos Owners Club, 51 London Road, Bromley, Kent BR1 4HB, tel: 020 8460 3511, e-mail: ABS.Labs@dial.pipex.com.

Mini Marcos Owners Club, c/o Roger Garland, 28 Meadow Road, Claines, Worcester WR3 7PP, tel: 01905 458533, website: www.argonet.co.uk/minimarcos.

Club Marcos International, c/o Isobel Chivers, The Spinney, Littleworth Lane, Whitley, Melksham, Wilts SN12 8RE, tel: 01225 707815.

Marendaz

Marendaz Special Car Register, c/o Mrs J. Shaw, 107 Old Bath Road, Cheltenham GL54 7DA, tel: 01242 526310.

Marlin

Marlin Owners Club, c/o J. Neeld, Sewdish Bungalow, School Lane, Wheaton Ashton, Staffs ST19 9NH, tel: 01785 841439.

Maserati

Maserati Club, c/o Michael Miles, The Paddock, Abbotts Ann, Andover, Hants SP11 7NT.

Matra

Matra Enthusiasts Club, c/o Greg Dalgleish, The Hollies, Crowborough Hill, Crowborough, East Sussex TN6 2HH, tel: 01892 652964, website: www.matra-club.co.uk.

Mazda

MX5 Owners Club UK. Mike Hayward, Membership Secretary, 17 Knights Close, Bishop's Stortford, Hertfordshire, CM23 4BZ, tel (before 10pm): 01279 656914, fax: 07715 700747, e-mail: mx5.mike@virgin.net, website: www.mx5oc.co.uk.

Mazda RX7 Owners Club, c/o M. Hocknull, 65 Coyne Road, West Bromwich, W. Mids B70 7HJ, tel: 07071 797797, website: www.rx7club.co.uk.

Mercedes-Benz

Mercedes-Benz Club Ltd., c/o Paddy Long, Whitefriars, Ashton Keynes SN6 6QR, website: www.mercedes-benzownersclub.co.uk.

Mercedes-Benz Owners Association, Merceded House, Langton Road, Langton Green, Tunbridge Wells, Kent TN3 0EG, tel: 01892 860922, fax: 01892 861363, e-mail: Join@mercedesclub.org.uk.

Messerschmitt

Messerschmitt Owners Club, c/o Eileen Hallam, Membership Secretary, Birches, Ashmores Lane, Rusper, W. Sussex RH12 4PS, tel: 01293 871417, website: www.messerschmitt.co.uk.

Metropolitan

Metropolitan Owners Club, c/o Nick Savage, The Old Pump House, Nutbourne Common, Pulborough, West Sussex RH20 2HB, tel: 01798 813713, email: metclubuk@aol.com, website: www.stevvia.demon.co.uk/metro.htm.

MG

MG Car Club, PO Box 251, Kimber House, Cemetery Road, Abingdon, Oxon OX14 1FF, tel: 01235 555552, website: www.mgcars.org.uk.

MGA Register of the MG Car Club, c/o David De Saxe, Ivy Cottage, Axford, Marlborough, Wilts SN8 2HA.

MG Owners Club, Freepost, Swavesey, Cambridge CB4 5QZ, tel: 01954 231125, fax: 01954 232106, e-mail: mginfo@mgownersclub.co.uk.

MG Octagon Car Club, Unit 1–2 Parchfields Enterprise Park, Parchfields Farm, Colton Road, Trent Valley, Rugeley, Staffs WS15 3HB, tel: +44 (0)1889 574666, fax: +44 (0)1889 574555, website: www.mgoctagoncarclub.com, e-mail: info@mgoctagoncarclub.com.

MG 'Y' Type Register, c/o J. Lawson, 12 Nithsdale Road, Liverpool L15 5AX.

Midget and Sprite Club, c/o Nigel Williams, 15 Foxcote, Kingswood, Bristol BS15 2TX, tel: 0117 961 2759.

Mini

British Mini Club, c/o David Hollis, The Mini House, 18 Aldgate Drive, Brierley Hill, West Midlands DY5 3NT, tel: 01384 897779, e-mail: british.miniclub@lineone.net, website: www.britishminiclub.co.uk.

National Mini Owners Club, c/o C. Cheal, 15 Birchwood Road, Lichfield, Staffs WS14 9UN, tel: 01543 257956, website: www.miniownersclub.co.uk.

Club Mini Classics, c/o Phil Kershaw, 15 Macclesfield Road, Wilmslow, Cheshire SK9 1BZ, tel: 01625 532969. Club magazine: 'Sliding Window'. (NB: the club promotes originality.)

Mini Cooper Club, c/o Mary Fowler, 59 Giraud Street, Poplar, London E14 6EE, tel: 020 7515 7173.

Mini Cooper Register, c/o Clive Ludden, The Spirals, Barton Road, Farndon, Chester CH3 6NL, website: www.minicooper.org.

Mini Moke Club, c/o Philip Mitchell, 53 Yarmouth Road, Ellingham, Bungay, Suffolk NR35 2PN, tel: 01508 518265, website: www.mokeclub.org.uk.

Mini Seven Racing Club, c/o Mike Jackson, Membership Secretary, 345 Clay Lane, S. Yardley, Birmingham B26 1ES, tel: 0121 707 5881, website: www.mini7.co.uk.

Mini Special Register, c/o Adrian Boyns, 30 Dalton Lane, Barrow in Furness, Cumbria LA14 4LE.

Mitsubishi

Mitsubishi Motors Owners Club, c/o Lesley Jensen, The Colt Car Company Ltd., Watermoor, Cirencester, Gloucestershire GL7 1LF, tel: 01481 850348.

Mitsubishi Sapporo Register (1974–84), c/o Graham Haswell, The Old Winchester Street, Botley, Southampton SO30 2AA, tel: 01489 785293.

Morgan

Morgan Sports Car Club, c/o Mrs Carol Kennett, Secretary, Old Ford Lodge, Ogston, Highham, Alfreton, Derbyshire DE55 6EL, tel: 01773 830281, fax: 01773 521816, website: www.itmc.net/mscc.

Morgan Three Wheeler Club Ltd., c/o E. Eyes, 280 Commonwealth Way, Abbey Wood, London SE2 0LD, tel: 020 8311 7282.

Morris

Bullnose Morris Club, c/o Richard Harris, PO Box 383, Hove, East Sussex BN3 4FX.

Morris Register (MoClub Ltd.) for Morris vehicles designed before 1940, registered office: 32 Brownleaf Road, Woodingdean, Brighton BN2 6LB. Historian and Archivist: Harry Edwards, Wellwood Farm, Lower Stock Road, West Hanningfield, nr Chelmsford, Essex CM2 8UY, tel: 01277 840697, fax: 01277 841185.

Morris Commercial Club, c/o Gordon Payley, 32 Daniell Way, Great Boughton, Cheshire CH3 5XH. (All types of Morris Commercial and BMC-built commercial vehicles 1924-1973, from 10cwt J type to 7 tons, but excluding Minors and car-derived vans. Membership £10).

Morris Cowley and Oxford Club, c/o Derek Andrews, 202 Chantry Gardens, Southwick, Trowbridge, Wilts BA14 9QX, tel: 07971 071 0292.

Morris J-Type Register, c/o Harvey Pircher, 31 Queenswood Road, Moseley, Birmingham B13 3AU.

Morris Minor Owners Club, PO Box 1098, Derby DE23 8ZX, tel: 01332 291675, fax: 01332 290661, website: www.MorrisMinorOC. co.uk

Morris Minor LCV Register, c/o D. Thomas, 61 Zeals Rise, Warminster, Wilts BA12 6PL, tel: 01747 840990, e-mail: LCVReg@ aol.com

Morris Marina Owners Club and Ital Register, 39 Portley Road, Dawley, Telford, Shropshire TF4 3JW, tel: 01952 504900, e-mail: ajmmarina@aol.com

Marina and Ital Drivers Club, c/o John Lawson, 12 Nithsdale Road, Liverpool LS15 5AX (35 members).

Morris Marina Enthusiasts Club, 45 Oak Drive, Acton Vale, Acton, London W3 7LD, e-mail: alan@mmec.freeserve.co.uk, website: www.mmec.freeserve.co.uk/mmec.htm

Morris Oxford MO and Wolseley 6/80 Club, c/o D. Gould, 2 Barleyfield Close, Heighington, Lincs LN4 1TX, fax: 01522 793994, e-mail: sixeightymo@tesco.net.

Napier

Napier Power Heritage Trust (NPHT), Hon. Secretary Alan Vessey, 188 London Road, Aston Clinton, Aylesbury, Bucks HP22 5LE.

Naylor

Naylor Car Club, c/o Freda Taylor, Naylor and Hutson Register, 21 Anglesey Place, Great Barton, Bury St. Edmunds, Suffolk IP31 2TW, tel: 01284 787539, email: freda.naylorcarclub@btinternet.com, website: www.naylorcarclub.org.uk. (Naylor Parts: Airedale Garage, Hollins Hill, Shipley, W. Yorkshire BD17 7QN.)

Nobel

Nobel Register, c/o K. Wagstaff, Keepers Cottage, The Green, Kelling, Holt, Norfolk NR25 7EN.

NSU

NSU Ro80 Club GB, Membership Secretary Mr E. Strong, Round Barn, Blackburn Road, Entwistle, Turton, Lancashire BL7 0QB, tel: 01204 852425, website: www.ro80club.freeserve.co.uk.

Oakland (*see also Pontiac*)

International Oakland Register, 105 Summers Road, Farncombe, Godalming, Surrey GU7 3BE, tel: 01483 861177, e-mail: oakland@dial.pipes.com.

Ogle

Ogle Register, c/o Chris Gow, The Stack Yard, Malt House Lane, Burgess Hill, West Sussex RH15 9HA, tel: 01444 248439.

Opel

Opel Monza: Autobahnstormers: David Waddington, 19 Olivers Drive, Witham, Essex CM8 1QJ, tel: 01376 516034, e-mail: dwgsi24v@aol.com

Opel Group, c/o Andrew Lee, 93 Bradgate Road, Barwell, Leics LE9 8FB.

Opel Manta Owners Club, c/o Richard Miller, 186 Norman Place Road, Coundon, Coventry CV6 2BU.

Packard

Packard Automobile Club of Great Britain, c/o John Bath, 16 Ruskin Drive, Worcester Park, Surrey KT4 8LG, tel: 020 7398 9000/ 020 8330 0013, e-mail: andrewb@clara.net; and Stuart Broatch, Guy Cottage, Chicklade, Hindon, Salisbury SP3 5SU, tel: 01747 820545.

Panhard et Levassor

Les Amis de Panhard et Levassor GB, 'La Dyna', 11 Arterial Avenue, Rainham, Essex RM13 9PD, tel: 01708 524425.

Panther

Panther Car Club, Secretary Fraser Robertson, Plas Yn Coed, Llandegla, Wrexham LL11 3AL, website: www.panthercarclub.com.

Panther Car Club UK, c/o George Newell, 91 Fleet Road, Farnborough, Hants GU14 9RE, tel: 01252 540217.

Paramount

Paramount Equipe Etrange, 4 Wool Road, Wimbledon, London SW20 0HW.

Peugeot

Club Peugeot UK, c/o Peter Beale, 49 Upper Green, Tewin, Welwyn, Herts AL6 0LX, tel: 01778 422274.

Piper

Piper Sports and Racing Car Club, c/o Clive Davis, Pipers Oak, Lopham Road, East Harling, Norfolk, tel: 01953 717813.

Pontiac (*see also Oakland*)

Pontiac and Oakland Club International, 105 Summers Road, Farncombe, Godalming, Surrey GU7 3BE, tel: 01483 861177, e-mail: davidjones@dial.pipes.com.

Porsche

Porsche Club of Great Britain, Cornbury House, Cotswold Business Village, Moreton-in-Marsh, Glos GL56 0JQ, tel: 01608 652911.

The Independent Porsche Enthusiasts Club, Manora, 31 The Grove, Hartlepool TS26 9LZ, tel: 07000 924 968 911.

Radford

Radford Register, c/o Chris Gow, 108 Potters Lane, Burgess Hill, West Sussex, tel: 01444 248439.

Railton

Railton Owners Club, c/o Barrie Mckenzie, Fairmiles, Barnes Hall Road, Buncross, Sheffield S35 1RF, tel: 0114 246 8357. Club Mag Editor: Mike Stenhouse, 17 Pease Hill Close, Rowdon, Leeds LS19 6EF.

Reliant/Raleigh

Raleigh Safety Seven and early Reliant Owners Club, c/o Mick Sleap, 17 Courtland Avenue, Chingford, London E4 6DU.

Reliant Owners Club, c/o Graham Chappell, 19 Smithey Close, High Green, Sheffield S30 4FQ, tel: 0114 284 8138.

Reliant Kitten Register, c/o Brian Marshall, 16 Glendee Gardens, Renfrew PA4 0AL, tel (after 6pm): 0141 886 6117, website: www.uk-classic-cars.com/kitten.htm.

Reliant Scimitar Drivers Club International, c/o Steven Lloyd, 74 Bradley Avenue, Winterbourne, Bristol BS17 1HR, tel: 01454 775282, website: www.scimitardriver.co.uk.

Reliant Sabre and Scimitar Owners Club, PO Box 67, Teddington, Middx TW11 8QR, tel: 020 8977 6625, website: www.scimweb.com.

Renault

Renault Frères Club for pre-1940 Renaults, c/o Mrs Pam Mills, 54 High Street, Durrington, Salisbury, Wilts PS4 8AQ.

Renault Owners Club, c/o J. Cowgill, 89 Queen Elizabeth Drive, Beccles, Suffolk NR34 9LA.

Club Alpine Renault, c/o Peter Whitehouse, I Bloomfield Close, Wombourne, Wolverhampton WV5 8HQ, tel (after 7pm): 01902 895590.

Rear Engine Renault Club. Advice from Kevin Gould, 2 Barleyfield Close, Heighington, Lincoln LN4 1TX, tel/fax 01522 874990, website: www.rerc.co.uk.

Riley

Riley Motor Club Ltd., c/o J.S. Hall, 'Treelands', 127 Penn Road, Wolverhampton WV3 0DU, tel: 01902 773197.

Riley Register, c/o Jim Clarke, 56 Cheltenham Road, Bishop's Cleve, Cheltenham, Glos GL52 4LY, tel: 01242 673598, website: www. rileyregister.com.

Scottish Riley Register, c/o Eric Stewart, 27 Rockfield Street, Dundee, Tayside DD2 3LD.

Riley RM Club 1946–1955, c/o Jacque Morris, Y Fachell, Ruthin Road, Gwernymynydd, Flintshire CH7 5LQ, tel: 01352 700427, website: www.rileyrmclub.org.uk.

Rochdale

Rochdale Owners Club, c/o Alaric Spendlove, 7 Whiteleigh Avenue, Crownhill, Plymouth PL5 3BQ, tel: 01752 791409, website: www. rochdale-owners-club.com.

Rolls Royce

Rolls Royce Enthusiasts Club, c/o Captain Peter Baines, The Hunt House, Paulerspury, Towcester, Northants NN12 7NA, tel: 01327 811788, email: admin@rrec.co.uk, website: www.rrec.co.uk.

Rover

Rover Sports Register, c/o C. Evans, 8 Hilary Close, Great Broughton, Chester CH3 5QP.

Rover Owners Club, c/o Ian Derby, 20 Heathbank Drive, Huntington, Staffs WS12 4NY, tel: 01543 468103.

Rover P4 Drivers Guild, c/o Colin Blowers, 32 Arundel Road, Luton, Beds LU4 8DY, tel: 01582 572499, website: www.roverp4.com.

Rover P5 Owners Club, c/o G. Moorshead, 13 Glen Avenue, Ashford, Middx TW15 2JE, tel: 01784 258166.

Rover P5 Alive Owners Club, c/o Rikki Woolf, 1 Bank Street, Faversham, Kent ME12 8PR.

Rover P6 Owners Club, c/o Brenda Griffin, Secretary, PO Box 120, Feltham, Middlesex TW13 4JN, tel (evenings only): 020 8890 9094.

Rover P6 Drivers Club, PO Box 1477, Walsall WS5 3XY, fax: 01922 648133, emails: membership@p6club.com, or secretary@p6club.com, website: www.p6club.com. Membership of 900 plus.

Rover SD1 Club, PO Box 255, Woking, Surrey GU21 1GJ, tel: 01483 888432.

Rover SD1 Mania, c/o Tom Willis, 59 Third Avenue, Enfield, Middx EN1 1BU, tel: 020 8482 7387, website: www.roversd1mania.co.uk.

SAAB

SAAB Enthusiasts Club, c/o William Glander, 4 Rochdale Avenue, Calne, Wilts SN11 9AX, tel (evenings): 01249 815792, e-mail: enthusiasts@saabenthusiasts.co.uk, website: www.saabenthusiasts.co.uk.

SAAB Owners Club of Great Britain Ltd., c/o John Wood, PO Box 900, Durham DH1 2GF, tel: 070 7 171 9000, e-mail: membership@saabclub.co.uk, website: www.saabclub.co.uk.

Salmson

British Salmson Owners Club, c/o D. Cannings, 61 Holyrood Gardens, Edgware, Middlesex HA8 5LS.

Tickford Owners Club, c/o Neville Clark, 5 The Elms Paddock, Clifton upon Dunsmore, Rugby CV23 0TD, tel: 01788 537695, email: mark.richardson@btclick.com. (Includes Salmson Tickford from 1820s.)

Scott

Scott Owners Club, c/o Brian Marshall, PR Officer, Walnut Cottage, Abbey Lane, Aslockton, Nottingham NG13 9AE, website: home.clara.net/g.harland/soc.htm.

Simca

Simca Club UK, c/o David Chapman, 18 Cavendish Gardens, Redhill, Surrey RH1 4AQ, tel: 01737 765331.

Singer

Singer Owners Club. c/o Martin Wray, 11 Ermine Riase, great Casterton, Stamford, Lincs PE9 4EJ, tel (evenings): 01780 762740, email: martin@singeroc.free-online.co.uk, website: www.singeroc.free-online.co.uk.

Association of Singer Car Owners, c/o Anne Page, 39 Oakfield, Rickmansworth, Herts WD3 2LR, tel: 01923 778575, website: www.uk-classic-cars.com/singer.htm.

Skoda

Skoda Owners Club of Great Britain, c/o B. Challis, 12 Millfields, Stansted, Essex CM24 8AS, tel: 01279 815183, e-mail: skodaclubgb@dial.pipex.com, website: www.skoda-owners-club. co.uk. Technical and Publishing Officer, Simon McDonal-Elliott, email: techoffice@llanwenarth.com.

Smart

MCC Smart Club: c/o Al Young: www.thesmartclub.co.uk (also Rob Eatwell, 9 Honeysuckle Court, 43 Grove Road, Sutton, Surrey SM1 2AW; e-mail rob@thesmartclub.co.uk).

Smart Owners Club UK, c/o Andrew Moss, 265-267 Burnley Road, Colne, Lancs BB8 8JD, tel: 01282 868806, website: smartownersclubuk.com (offers a driver's manual in English at £19.95).

Spartan

Spartan Owners Club, c/o Steve Andrews, 28 Ashford Drive, Ravenhead, Notts NG15 9DE, tel: 01623 409351, website: www.spartan-oc.demon.co.uk.

Standard

Standard Register (1903–1930), c/o Leonard Barr, 30 The Walled Garden, West Way, Cirencester, Gloucs GL7 1JA, e-mail: Standardregist@aol.com.

Standard Motor Club, c/o Tony Pingriff, 57 Main Road, Meriden, Coventry CV7 7LP, tel: 01676 522181, e-mail: pingriff@cwcom.net, website: www.standardmotorclub.org.uk.

Standard Vanguard Owners Club, c/o Ken Holstead, 7 Priory Close, Wilton, Salisbury, Wilts SP2 0LD.

Vanguard 3 Owners Club, c/o Martin Holstead, PO Box 1581, Marlborough, Wiltshire SN8 2UA, tel: 01672 520154; website: www.the-vanguard-ph3-owners-club.co.uk.

Star, Starling, Stuart and Briton

Star, Starling, Stuart and Briton Register, c/o D. Evans, 2A Hyperion Road, Stourton, Stourbridge DY7 6SB, tel: 01384 374329.

Studebaker

Studebaker Owners Club UK, c/o Doug Priston, 5 Kingsway Manor Lodge Road, Rowlands Castle, PO9 6AZ.

Stutz

The Stutz Club, c/o Norman C. Barrs, 54 Canonbury Road, London NW, tel: 020 7226 8483, fax: 020 7359 6812.

Sunbeam/Darracq

Sunbeam Talbot Darracq Register, c/o J. Donovan, Membership Secretary, Blackwell House, 21 Stubbs Wood, Chesham Bois, Amersham HP6 6EY, tel: 01494 721972; or Mrs Gill Brett, Secretary, 9 Hallet's Close, Stubbington, Fareham, Hants PO14 2JS, tel: 01329 663809.

Sunbeam Register, c/o Bruce Dowell, The Maples. Badger's Cross, Somerton TA11 7JD, tel: 01458 274700, fax: 01458 274600.

Sunbeam Rapier Owners Club, Mike Kingston, Chairman, tel (evenings): 01928 788583.

Sunbeam Alpine Owners Club, c/o Sarah Jarrett, 25 Willow Drive, Hutton, Weston-super-Mare, Avon BS24 9TJ.

Sunbeam Talbot Alpine Register, c/o Derek Cook, 47 Crescent Wood Road, Sydenham, London SE26 6SA, tel: 020 8693 1045.

Sunbeam Tiger Owners Club, c/o Brian Postle, Beechwood, 8 Villa Real Estate, Consett, County Durham DH8 6BJ, tel: 01207 508296.

Suzuki

Suzuki SC100 Enthusiasts Club, c/o Tim Smith, 57 Wordsworth Mead, Redhill, Surrey RH1 1AH, tel: 01737 766263.

Suzuki Cappucino Owners Register, c/o Alex Clouter, 6 Blenheim Fields, Riverside, Forest Row, East Sussex RH18 5EW, tel (7pm–9pm): 01342 823951, website: www.score.org.uk.

The Swift Club (1901–31), c/o John Harrison, 70 Eastwick Drive, Great Bookham, Leatherhead, Surrey KT23 3NX, tel: 01372 452120, email: john-harrison@bookham36.freeserve.co.uk.

Talbot
79-86 Talbot Owners Register, c/o David Chapman, 18 Cavendish Gardens, Redhill, Surrey RH1 4AQ, tel: 01737 765331.

Tatra
Tatra Register UK, c/o Derrick Moores, The Manse, Stratford Road, Watford, Herts WD17 4QG, tel 01923 225863, website: www.tatra-register.co.uk.

Tornado
Tornado Register, c/o Dave Malins, 48 St Monica's Avenue, Luton, Beds LU3 1PN, tel: 01582 737641, email: tornado_register@aol.com, website: www.astruc.s.easynet.co.uk/ tornado_register.

Torcars
Torcars Sun-Tor Register c/o Jim Matthews, 28 Woodfield Road, Gainsborough, Lincs DN21 1RF, tel: 01427 614128.

Toyota
Toyota Enthusiasts Club, c/o Billy Wells, 28 Park Road, Feltham, Middlesex TW13 6PW, tel: 020 8898 0740.

Toyota MR2 Mk 1 Register, 35 Alma Street, Luton, Beds LU1 2PL, tel: 01582 454971, website: www.welcome.to/mr2mk1.register.

Toyota MR2 Drivers Club, c/o Kew Kinnersley MBE, PO Box 999, Huntingdon PE17 2PX, tel: 01487 710010.

Toyota Sera UK Register, c/o Andrew Cliffe, 31, Dalbier Close, Norwich, Norfolk NR7 0RP, tel: 07798 651441, website: www.toyotasera.co.uk, e-mail: andrew@omicron.co.uk.

Toyota Landcruiser 4x4 Club, c/o J. Boatwright, 61 Graham Street, Swindon, Wilts SN1 2HA, tel: 07831 201596.

Trident
Trident Car Club, c/o Dave Rowlinson, 23 Matlock Crescent, Cheam, Sutton, Surrey SM3 9SS, tel: 020 8644 9029.

Triumph
Pre-1940 Triumph Owners Club, Mem Sec: Jon Quiney, 2 Duncroft Close, Reigate, Surrey RH2 9DE, tel: 01737 247218.

Triumph Razoredge Owners Club, c/o David Wickens, 12 Cornwall Close, Camberley, Surrey GU15 3UA, tel: 01276 65958.

Triumph Roadster Club, c/o John Cattaway, Membership Secretary, 59 Cowdray Park Road, Little Common, Bexhill-on-Sea, East Sussex TN39 4EZ, tel: 01424 844608.

Triumph Mayflower Club, c/o John Oaker, 19 Broadway North, Walsall, West Midlands WS1 2QG, tel: 01922 633042, website: www.mayflower99.freeserve.co.uk.

Triumph Dolomite Club (1970s Dolomites only), 39 Mill Lane, Arncott, Bicester, Oxon OX6 0PB, tel: 01869 242847, e-mail: info@triumphdolomiteclub.co.uk.

Triumph Sporting Owners Club, c/o P. Utratny, 57 Rothiemey Road, Flixton, Urmston, Manchester M41 6JY, tel: 0161 747 3618.

Club Triumph, Membership Secretary, FREEPOST (SWB20389), Christchurch BH23 4ZZ, tel/fax: 01425 274193, e-mail: club.triumph@btinternet.com, website: club.triumph.org.uk.

Triumph Spitfire Club, c/o Corwin van Heteren, Waltersingel 34a, 7314 NT Apeldoorn, The Netherlands.

Triumph Sports Six Club Ltd (for all Herald-based Triumphs from Herald to GT6), Main Street, Lubbenham, Market Harborough, Leics LE16 9TF, tel: 01858 434424, e-mail: tssc@tssc.uk.com, website: www.tssc.uk.com.

Stag Owners Club, The Old Rectory, Aslacton, Norfolk NR15 2JN, tel: 01379 677362, fax: 01379 677735, e-mail: stagmemsec@compuserve.com

Triumph Stag Owners Club, website: www.stag.org.uk, e-mail: martin@ford-granadaguild.co.uk.

Triumph Stag Register, c/o Mike Wattam, 18 Hazel Close, Highcliffe, Dorset BH23 4PS, tel: 01425 274638, website: www.tristagreg.org.

TR Drivers Club, c/o Jeff Black, 3 Blackberry Close, Abbeymead, Gloucester GL4 7BS, tel: 01452 614234.

TR Register, 1B Hawksworth, Southmead Industrial Park, Didcot, Oxon OX11 7HR, tel: 01235 818866, e-mail: TR.Register@onlyxnet.co.uk

Triumph 2000, 2500, 2.5 Register, c/o A. Crussell, 10 Gables Close, Chalfont St. Peter, Bucks SL9 0PR, tel: 01494 582673/873264, website: www.kvaleberg.com/t2000.html.

Triumph 2000 and 2500 Owners Club, c/o Jim Barry, 164 Polwell Lane, Barton Seagrave, Kettering, Northants NN15 6UB, tel: 01536 724512.

Turner

Turner Register. c/o Tony Hill, 9 Lyndhurst Crescent, Hillingdon, Middx UB10 9EF, tel: 01895 256799.

TVR

TVR Car Club, c/o Carol Folkard, PO Box 36, Telford TF6 6WF, tel: 01952 770635, website: www.tvrcc.com.

Vanden Plas

Vanden Plas Owners Club, c/o Brian Peebles, Vice Chairman/Membership Secretary, Cherrytrees, Llandyfaelog, Kidwelly, Carmarthenshire SA17 5PS, email: bryanpeebles@aol.com, website: www.vpoc.org.

Vauxhall

Vauxhall Owners Club, c/o Roy Childers, 31 Greenbanks, Melbourne, nr Royston, Cambridge SG8 6AS, tel: 01763 220179.

Vauxhall Convertible Car Club, c/o Phil Homer, 42 The Ridgeway, St. Albans, Herts AL4 9NR, tel: 01727 868405, e-mail: homerp@btsales.bt.com.

Vauxhall Cavette Club (Mk 1 Cavaliers and Chevettes), c/o Peter Norrish, Membership Secretary, 67 Riley Lane, Bradshaw, Halifax HX2 9QE, tel: 01422 245124, email: norrish@cavetteclub.org.uk, website: www.cavetteclub.org.uk.

Vauxhall Opel Drivers Club, c/o Peter and Sue Hicks, PO Box 65, Dereham, Norfolk NR19 1UD, tel/fax: 01362 692020, email: vodriversclub@bigfoot.com.

Vauxhall Cresta PA, PB, PC, E Owners Club, c/o Steve Chapman, 333 Eastcote Lane, South Harrow, Middx HA2 8RY, tel: 020 8423 2440.

Droop Snoot Group, c/o John Smerdon, 17 Priors Road, Tadley, Herts RG26 4QJ, tel: 01189 815238.

Vauxhall Royale Opel Monza Owners Club International, c/o Martin Yardley, 71 Polmear Parc, Par, Cornwall PL24 2AU, tel: 01726 815749, e-mail: cgodfrey4@aol.com.

Vauxhall Senator: Autobahnstormers, c/o David Waddington, 19 Olivers Drive, Witham, Essex CM8 1QJ, tel: 01376 516034, e-mail: dwgsi24v@aol.com.

Vauxhall Viva Owners Club, c/o Adrian Miller, 'The Thatches', Snetterton North End, Snetterton, Norwich NR16 2LD, tel: 01953 498818.

Viva Outlaw Club, c/o Keith Laxton, 92 Churchill Crescent, Thame, Oxon OX9 3JP, tel: 01844 217928, e-mail: eddv6@klaxton. freeserve.co.uk.

Vauxhall VX 4/90 Drivers Club, c/o Jason Callear, 1 Milverton Drive, Uttoxeter ST14 7RE.

Vauxhall Victor 101 Club. c/o Joan Caldwell, 43 Princess Street, Widnes, Cheshire WA8 6NT, tel: 0151 510 0251.

Vincent-HRD

Vincent-HRD Owners Club. Membership secretary: Mary Bagley, 9 Whitworth Close, Gosport, Hants PO12 3PF, tel: 023 9242 2320; Registrar: Gordon Powell, 7 Church Street, Upwey, Weymouth, Dorset DT3 5QB, tel: 01305 812303, e-mail: gopow@ globalnet.co.uk.

VW

Volkswagen Owners Club of Great Britain, PO Box 7, Burntwood, Walsall, Staffs WS7 8SB.

Volkswagen Type 2 Owners Club, a club for 'Vans with Fans' and 'Fans with Vans'. Club Secretary, Phil Shaw, 57 Humphrey Avenue, Charford, Bromsgrove, Worcestershire, tel: 01527 872194, email: PhilShawVW@cs.com, website: www.vwt2oc.org.uk).

Historic Volkswagen Club, c/o Rod Sleigh, 28 Lognor Road, Brooklands, Telford, Shropshire TF1 3NY, tel: 01952 242167.

Association of British Volkswagen Clubs, c/o J. Daniel, 66 Pinewood Green, Iver Heath, Bucks, tel: 01753 651538, website: www.uk-classic-cars.com/abvwc.htm.

Split Screen Van Club, c/o Robert Neekings, Membership Secretary, 21 Nabwood Road, Shipley, Yorkshire BD18 4AG, tel: 01274 596564, website: www.ssvc.org.uk. (VW vans, 1950–1967.)

VW Type 3 and 4 Club, c/o Jim Bourne, 'Brookside', Hamsey Road, Barcombe, Lewes, East Sussex BN8 5TG, tel: 01273 400463.

Club GTi: Alan Bell, Membership Secretary, PO Box 6506, Sutton-in-Ashfield, Nottinghamshire NG17 1NG, tel: 01454 626118, website: www.clubgti.com.

VW Corrado Club of Great Britain, c/o Andy Brookes, PO Box 620, Berkhamsted, Hertfordshire HP4 2SA, tel: 07801 061731.

Essex Vee Dubbers Volkswagen Club. Open to owners of all models of VW. Brian Walker, 53 Louise Gardens, Rainham, Essex RM13 8LH, tel: 01708 520669.

Volvo

Volvo Enthusiasts Club, c/o Kevin Price, 4 Goonbell, St Agnes, Cornwall TR5 0PH, tel: 01872 553740.

Volvo Owners Club, c/o John Smith, 18 McCaulay Avenue, Portsmouth, Hants PO6 4NY, tel: 023 9238 1494, email: voc@dircon.co.uk, website: www.volvoclub.org.uk.

Wolseley

Wolseley Register, c/o Mike Schilling, 46 Mansewood Road, Glasgow G43 1TN, website: www.wolseley.dircon.co.uk, e-mail: mschilling@46mansewood.freeserve.co.uk or SisEightyMO@ btinternet.com.

Wolseley Hornet Special Club 1930–35, c/o Chris Hyde, 'Kyelmor', Crown Gardens, Fleet, Hants GU51 3LT, tel: 01252 622411, e-mail: whsc.sec@btinternet.com, website: www.whsc.co.uk.

Wolseley 680/Morris Oxford Club, c/o Dave Robinson, 6 Kings Drive, Wigston, leicester LE8 1AG, tel: 0116 212 9972.

Specialist Clubs

American Automobile Club (UK), Freepost (MID00017), Tamworth, Staffs SY13 3DL. Contact: David Sword, tel: 01827 284538, website: www.uk-classic-cars.com/americanauto.htm.

Anglo American Classic Car Club, c/o Steve Seeby, 12 Davy's Close, Wheathampstead, Herts, tel: 01582629667. (This is a very small club.)

Association of Old Vehicle Clubs of Northern Ireland, c/o T. Mitchell, 38 Ballymacconnell Road, Bangor, County Down BT20 5PS, tel: 02891 467886, website: www.aovc.co.uk.

Battery Vehicle Society, c/o Mr McPhee, Secretary, 29 Armour Road, Tilehurst, Reading, Surrey RG31 6HA, tel: 0118 941 4873.

British Ambulance Society, c/o Roger Leonard, 21 Victoria Road, Horley, Surrey RH6 9BN, tel: 01293 776636.

Checker Cars. Advice from A. Pritchard, 1 Curbar Road, Great Bar, Birmingham B42 2AT, tel: 0121 608 2737.

Cirencester Car Club, c/o John Knott, Safflower House, London Road, Stroud GL5 2AT, tel: 01453 763737; website: www.cirencestercarclub.co.uk.

Classic & Historic Motor Club Ltd, Celia Sheppard, tel: 01749 676330.

Classic Camper Club, Secretary: M. Smith, PO Box 3, Amlwch, Anglesey LL68 9ZE, e-mail: ClassicCamperClub@btinternet.com; website: www.ClassicCamperClub.co.uk.

Classic Crossbred Club, 7 Wills Hill, Stanford-le-Hope, Essex, tel: 01375 679943.

Classic Hearse Register, c/o Mark Josey, 58 Winchester Street, Overton, Basingstoke, Hants RG25 3HY, tel: 01256 771158.

Classic Motor Sports Club, c/o Stephanie Taylor, 37D Heathfield Road, Wandsworth Common, London SW18 2PH.

Classic Saloon Car Club, 15 Biddenham Turn, Garston, Herts WD2 6PU.

Club of Ancient Automobiles and Rallies, c/o Nigel Woodyer, 152 Ware Road, Hoddesdon, Herts EN11 9EX, tel : 01992 444502, e-mail: caargb@btinternet.com, website: www.caeargb.com.

Commercial Vehicle and Road Transport Club, c/o Steve Wimbush, 8 Tachbrook Road, Uxbridge, Middx UB8 2QS.

Enfield & District Veteran Vehicle Society, c/o S. Clinton, Whitewebbs Museum, White Webbs Road, Enfield, Middlesex EN2 9HW, tel: 020 8367 1898.

Federation of British Historic Vehicle Clubs, c/o Mike Holt-Chasteauneuf, PO Box 2506, Henfield, W. Sussex BN5 9QW, tel: 01273 495051.

Fire Service Preservation Group, c/o Andrew Scott, 50 Old Slade Lane, Iver, Bucks SL0 9DR, tel: 01753 652207.

Friends of the British Commercial Vehicle Museum, King Street, Leyland, Preston PR5 1LE.

Friends of the National Motor Museum, Beaulieu, Brokenhurst, Hants SO42 7ZN, tel: 01590 614650, email: nmmt@beaulieu.co.uk, website: www.beaulieu.co.uk.

Historic Rally Car Register Ltd., c/o Tony Bardon, 113 Locke Road, Spondon, Derby DE21 7AP, tel: 01332 372533.

Historic Sports Car Club, c/o Philip Parfitt, HSCC, Silverstone Circuit, Silverstone, Towcester, Northants NN12 8TN, tel: 01327 858400, website: www.hscc.org.uk.

Italian Car Club (UK), The Brackens, Vicarage Court, Vicarage Drive, Kinver, West Midlands DY7 6HJ.

London Bus Preservation Trust, c/o Mike Nash, 43 Stroudwater Park, Weybridge, Surrey KT13 0DT, tel: 01932 856810.

London Vintage Taxi Association, c/o Steve Dimmock, 51 Ferndale Crescent, Cowley, Uxbridge UB8 2AY.

Mechanical Horse Club, c/o Dan Madeley, 2 The Poplars, Horsham, West Sussex RH13 5RH, tel: 01483 269051.

Micro Maniacs, c/o Roger Bentley, 3 Pine Tree Lane, Hillam, Leeds LS25 5HY.

Midlands Classic Car Club, c/o John Langham, Abbey Business Centre, Keats Lane, Earl Shilton, Leicestershire LE9 7JL, tel: 01455 444450, fax: 01455 444451, email: midclass@btinternet.com, website: www.midlandsclassic.com.

Military Vehicle Trust, c/o Nigel Godfrey, PO Box 6, Fleet, Hants GU13 9PE, tel: 01264 392951, fax: 01257 515211, website: www.mvt.org.uk.

Motorvatin' USA American Car Club, c/o Trevor Lynn, PO Box 2222, Braintree, Essex CM7 6TW, tel: 01376 552478, website: www.motorvatinusa.org.

National 39/45 Military Vehicle Group, c/o Adrian Hardgrave, 9 Cordelia Way, Rugby, Warks CV22 6JU, tel: 01788 812250.

Pedal Car Collector's Club, 4/4a Chapel Terrace Mews, Kemp Town, Brighton, East Sussex BN2 1HJ, tel: 01273 601960, website: www. brmmbrmm.com/pedalcars.

Period and Classic Caravan Club, 128 Fulbourn, Old Drift, Cherry Hinton, Cambs CB1 9LR, tel: 01223 248187.

Period Motorcaravan Guild, c/o Mrs J. Lund, House 3, Connaught Court, St Oswalds Road, Fulford, York YO1 4QA, tel: 01904 651526, e-mail: mjjl@btinternet.com; website: www.brmmbrmm.com/periodmcg.

Police Vehicle Enthusiasts Club, c/o John Oliver, 42 Walkers Way, South Bretton, Peterborough, Cambs PE3 9AX.

Post Office Vehicle Club, c/o John Targett, 7 Bignal Rand Drive, Wells, Somerset BA5 2EU, tel: 01749 675168.

Post-War Thoroughbred Car Club, 87 London Street, Chertsey, Surrey KT16 8AN, tel: 01932 562933.

Pre-1950 American Automobile Club and Ford V8 Register, c/o C. Nolson, 23 High Street, Twyford, Berks RG10 9AB.

Preston and District Vintage Car Club, c/o Mark Hindle, 4 Glendene Park, Wilpshire, Blackburn BB1 9JQ, tel: 01254 245245.

Register of Unusual Microcars, c/o Jean Hammond, School House Farm, Hawkenbury, Staplehurst, Kent, tel: 01580 891377.

Road Roller Association, D A Rayner, Vice Chairman and Archivist, Invicta, 9 Beagle Ridge Drive, Acomb, York YO24 3JH, tel: 01904 781519.

Scootacar Register, c/o Stephen Boyd, 18 Holman Close, Aylesham, Norfolk NR11 6DD, tel: 01263 733861.

Scottish Rally Car Register, c/o A Johnstone, The Clachan, Main Street, St Boswells, Melrose TD6 0BG, tel: 01835 822266.

Sprite Motorhome Owners Club, c/o Bert Raspin, 156 Farebrother Street, Grimsby, Lincs DN32 0JR.

Surrey Vintage Vehicle Society, website: www.restored-classics.com/surrey.

750 Motor Club Ltd, c/o Neil Carr-Jones, Lewes Enterprise Centre, 112 Malling Street, Lews, East Sussex BN7 2RJ, tel 01273 488750, website: www.750mc.co.uk.

Teesside Yesteryear Motor Club, c/o Graham Armstrong, 3 Tewesbury Avenue, Marton, Middlesbrough, Teesside TS7 8NB, tel: 01642 320999.

The Steam Car Club of Great Britiain, c/o Diana Goddard, 29 Nins Heath, Montford Bridge, Shrewsbury SY4 1HL, tel: 01939 260595.

United States Army Vehicle Club, c/o Simon Johnson, 7 Carter Fold, Mellor, Lancs BB2 7ER, tel: 01254 812894.

Unloved Soviet and Socialist Register, c/o Julian Nowill, Earlsland House, Bradninch, Exeter, Devon EX5 4QP, tel: 01392 881748.

Veteran Car Club of Great Britain, c/o Margaret Golding, Jassamine Court, 15 High Street, Ashwell. Herts SG7 5NL, tel: 01462 742818, fax: 01462 742997.

Vintage Motor Cycle Club, c/o Dr Derek Foxton, 4 Helensdale Close, Hereford HR1 1DP, tel: 01432 357315.

Vintage Sports Car Club of Calgary, c/o Colin Martindale, 90 Canova Road SW, Calgary, Alberta, Canada T2W 2A7, website: www.cadvision.com/vintage.

Vintage Sports Car Club, c/o Neil Murray, The Old Post Office, West Street, Chipping Norton, Oxon OX7 5EL, tel: 01608 644777, fax: 01608 644888.

How to Buy and Sell Cars

In this chapter Honest John tells you everything you need to know about the new and used car market. Topics covered include: finance; buying a new car abroad and importing it yourself; buying second-hand from a dealer, at auction or through a private ad; how to check out a prospective purchase; how to advertise a car for sale; and how to prepare your car for an auction.

Buying new
Beating the system

Though the real gap between continental car prices and UK car prices is closing, it's still possible to save thousands of pounds on a new car purchase.

One way is by buying a car imported from mainland Europe, either by yourself or by a specialist. The best deals from around 20 different sources are regularly compared at www.carpricecheck.com. Sometimes UK dealers can actually offer a better price than an import, with the added benefit of a three-year UK dealer warranty.

Always look for deals: www.honestjohn.co.uk features news of new car deals on a day-to-day basis.

You can buy 'pre-registered' cars from franchised dealers. These are cars registered by the dealer to earn a monthly or quarterly volume bonus. Depending on how old the cars are at the time of sale, savings can be as much as 20%. However, your choice will be strictly limited to oversupplied cars. There would be no chance of obtaining a much-desired new model, such as an E46 BMW 3-Series, in this way.

Alternatively, forget new, and buy 'nearly new', either at auction or from a car supermarket such as The Great Trade Centre or Fords of Winsford. This way you can obtain a 6–12 month-old car with 5,000–15,000 miles on the clock at a saving of between 20% and 50% of the new car list price.

Other methods save you less money, but involve less risk, less hassle, and usually give you a greater degree of choice.

Buying from a franchised dealer

If you are a good negotiator, during comparatively slack months such as December you might get 10%–12% off 'list price'. The best way to achieve this is to know precisely what the 'on-the-road' price of the car should be, take off the cost of Vehicle Excise Duty and the £25 First Registration tax, then subtract 15% from the remainder. On the premise that 3%–5% profit is better than no profit at all, many dealers will play ball, particularly towards the end of the month.

On the other hand, where they have more customers than cars, they won't play this game. You are unlikely to get more than 4% or 5% off a car you have to order then wait several months for.

The part-exchange trick

If you have a car you want to part-exchange for a new one, it's no good getting a decent discount then giving it all back by accepting too little for your trade-in.

Be very well aware of what your existing car is worth. Compare it with similar models of similar age and mileage which the dealer has up for sale, and don't accept an offer which is more than £1,000 or 10% (whichever is the greater) below the sticker price on these cars. This £1,000 or 10% may sound a lot, but remember the dealer will usually have to negotiate downwards from sticker prices when selling his used stock.

Also remember, what you get for your part-exchange is not the most important factor. The 'cost to switch' is. Always compare the total financial outlay involved in one deal compared to another.

For example, dealer 'A' has a new Mondeo which lists at £15,000. He offers you £4,000 for your part exchange, but no discount on the Mondeo, so the cost to switch is £11,000.

Dealer 'B' has a Laguna which lists at £15,000. He offers you £3,500 for your part exchange, plus £1,000 off the price of the Laguna. The cost to switch is therefore £10,500, so the Laguna is £500 cheaper than the Mondeo even though you get less for your part exchange.

Is the Mondeo worth £500 more than the Laguna? Or can you use the Laguna deal to chip £500 or more off the price of the Mondeo?

This is the way you should be thinking. It's not hard, is it?

Importing

Importing a car yourself

It is against European Community Law for any manufacturer to place any impediment between any EU citizen buying any car at the pre-tax price in any other European country.

EC Regulation No. 1475/95 states: 'The consumer's freedom to buy anywhere in the Common Market is one of the fundamental achievements of the European Community and the Regulation reinforces this right.'

But it goes on to state: 'The consumer's right is not accompanied by an obligation imposed on dealers to sell since it is normally in a dealer's interest to maximise its profits.'

Where a model of car is in short supply, a continental dealer may take the view that he will generate more profit from selling the car to a local who will probably insure, finance and service the car through the dealer and even part-exchange it in a few years time.

But where the model is freely available and the dealer simply wants to maximise turnover, he will usually be happy to play ball.

You will find a lists of the cheapest sources of cars in the UK in the FAQ answers in this book and at www.honestjohn.co.uk

You will also find a 'step-by-step guide to importing a car from Europe' in the FAQ answers in this book and at the website.

Where to shop for an import

Order the relevant car magazines from an international newsagent, or pick them up at the airport when you land: *DAZ, Motor Markt, Auto Motorrad Freizeit* and *Auto Motor und Sport* for Germany, *Auto Week* for Holland, *Coche Actual, Autopista* or *Top Auto* for Spain, *Irish Auto Trader* for Eire; and start phoning dealers with the intention of buying a car already in stock, either pre-tax or with the forms to reclaim the local taxes. (One very good reason for choosing Dutch or Irish dealers, of course, is that they all speak English.) Once you have located a car, send your deposit by telegraphic transfer (which takes three days). Send the rest of the money by telegraphic transfer (once more, allow three working days), take a flight to the relevant country, get the dealer to fix you up with 'export plates' and third party insurance, and make sure that the car comes with an EU Type Approval 'Certificate of Conformity' or you won't be able to register it in the UK. Then simply drive to the nearest ferry and follow the rest of the 'step-by-step' guide.

If you have bought an LHD it's a relatively simple matter to change over the lights and foglamp, get the speedo altered to mph by Reap Automotive Design (020 8863 2305), have the car inspected and have it registered via your local VRO. With Europe-wide

Type Approval for European cars from January 1998, there is no need for an SVA for a new European car, but you must make sure you get a 'Certificate of Conformity' with it, otherwise it will be subject to Single Vehicle Approval (SVA).

If you order a car from a mainland Europe dealer, the biggest worry you are likely to face is that he may demand a substantial deposit – up to 30%. If his franchise is pulled or he goes bust before you take delivery of your car, the situation is the same as it would be in the UK. Your deposit becomes one of the assets of the company, and you will be way down the list of creditors and thus unlikely to get it back.

If a continental dealer tells you he would like to sell you an RHD car but is being pressurised by the manufacturer not to, report the matter to: Mario Monti, Competition Commissioner, DG IV, European Commission, 200 Rue de la Loi, 1049 Brussels, Belgium.

Warranty claims with Euro-imports

As long as you have registered your car with the UK manufacturer or official UK importer, it will be subject to the same pan-European warranty that applies in the country of origin and which must be for at least 12 months.

It will not be subject to a UK three-year warranty unless a three-year warranty applies in the country of origin. (For example, a Nissan from Eire is covered by a three-year warranty as long as Nissan GB can be furnished with a copy of the original invoice.)

The catch is, if you buy the car in the UK, the warranty will only date from when it was first registered in the country it was exported to the UK from. So you could buy a 'new' car with no more than a 7-month pan-Euro warranty.

If a car bought in Europe proves to be seriously faulty, it is not covered by the UK's 'Sale and Supply of Goods Act 1994' which, subject to case law, allows you to reject it. The car will only be covered by consumer protection law in the country of origin. If this allows for rejection, then the car must be returned to the supplying dealer in that country.

However, if you buy your car directly from an independent import supplier in the UK, and the car is first registered in the UK, rather than collected by you from mainland Europe, then you can invoke the UK's 'Sale and Supply of Goods Act 1994' and reject the car by returning it to the UK importer.

Over the next year the EC might introduce new pan-European consumer protection laws, but there was no Directive to this effect at the time of writing.

Japanese and American imports

In 1997 and 1998 the strong pound made new RHD imports from Japan very attractive – especially super-quick Mitsubishi and Subaru four-wheel-drive saloons. But the rising Yen has been making Japanese imports progressively more expensive. There is also a possibility that the new 'Enhanced Single Vehicle Approval' test, in force from September 2001, will be so onerous and expensive it will not be worth importing from Japan and the USA.

A useful website covering all aspects of importing from Japan is http://www.importedvehicles.co.uk.

Import agents' deposits
Agents usually ask for a deposit of at least 10% and sometimes as much as 30%. You can protect this deposit against the agent going bust or doing a runner by paying it by credit card (credit card, not charge card) or by insisting it is paid into a UK 'escrow' account where the agent cannot touch it until the deal is done and it does not form part of his assets if he goes bust.

Buying used
Buying used privately
The first rule is, use your common sense. For instance, if you are buying a car from someone you know, how well do you know this person, and how well do you know the car? What are your motives for buying it? Are you trying to help this person financially, or are you after a good, known car at a sensible price?

Finding and pricing the car
Websites are an excellent means of finding out how sellers are pricing the car you want. So, in addition to buying 'Parker's Guide' and the *'What Car?* Used Car Price Guide', check the asking prices for the make and model you're after on www.autotrader.co.uk. This incorporates its own search engine and lists the model by asking prices at progressively greater distances from your postcode.

If you're buying from an advertisement, you need to establish the status of who you are buying from. If he is a trader, he is required by law to put a 'T' or the word 'trade' in his ad. This gives you rights you do not have against a private seller – in fact the very same rights you have when buying from a car showroom.

Some 'home traders' try to hide the fact that that is what they are. So when you call a number in the advertisement which does not contain a 'T' or the word 'trade', say you are calling about 'the car'. A trader who has more than one car will have to ask you 'which car?'

Assuming from now on we are dealing with a genuine private seller rather than a trader, you need to establish some more facts about the car. First, concentrate on the content of the advertisement:

By 'P reg', does he mean 1996P or 1997P? Which 'model year' is the car? For example, a 1996-model 'P' reg Mondeo was the ugly pre-facelift model, but a 1997-model Mondeo was the much more attractive facelifted version.

Ask how many previous keepers are listed on the V5, and add that number to the vendor for the true figure. Ask if the advertised mileage is genuine, and if the answer is 'yes' ask how does he know?

By now, you'll be starting to feel the measure of the person you are dealing with and your instincts will be starting to work. Trust these instincts. They are what you were born with and what you have developed through your life to protect yourself against danger.

If you're happy about the car and the person selling it, make an appointment to view. Unless the car is something rare and special, don't be rushed into a hasty twilight or nocturnal encounter. You want broad daylight and you don't want rain. Rain is the most effective disguise for a chameleon colour scheme and a host of other defects.

You may be given the opportunity to buy your 'company car'. If it's the company's own car, the company may have a policy of offering cars to employees at favourable prices as a perk. But if the car is leased, you can expect the first price the leasing company quotes you to be close to retail. They want to make money and you're a captive market. So be very sure of your ground. You know your car better than they do. Is it so good that you want to lay out your own money on it? It may have been reliable during your tenure over three years and maybe sixty thousand miles. But over the next forty thousand miles it could need tyres, exhaust, clutch, water pump and all the other things that fail just after fleets get rid of their cars.

Buying from a dealer

Most franchised dealers now offer used car schemes supported by manufacturers, such as Ford's 'Ford Direct', Vauxhall's 'Network Q' and Volkswagen's Retailer Approved. Where the warranty is backed by the manufacturer (Ford Direct) rather than simply an insured warranty, these give peace of mind but can come at a fairly high price.

Once you've shopped around a bit and got the feel of prices in the car supersites, it's worth paying the franchised dealers a visit. They have been known to beat supersite prices, and if their prices, inclusive of a cast iron warranty, are only a few hundred more than the supersites, you may be better off with the franchised dealer.

Most manufacturers support their franchised dealers with website stock locators which enable you to find cars and compare prices within the dealer chains. You'll find the internet addresses for these in the FAQ answer in this book (page 11), and through direct links at www.honestjohn.co.uk.

When you want to part-exchange your old car, franchised dealers almost always give better part-exchange allowances than the supersites. But here you need to compare the total 'cost to switch', not merely the part-exchange allowance offered.

Non-franchised specialist dealers specialise in a particular type of car, usually sports cars, prestige cars or 4x4s, but you also find '7-seater Centres', 'Mini Centres', 'Cavalier Centres' and so on.

To maintain attractive stock levels, they usually have to pay more for their cars, especially at auction, and this is likely to be reflected in the prices they ask.

You have to weigh up the convenience and time-saving they offer you against these slightly higher prices. And if they have any sports or prestige cars on offer which are less than three years old, you should question the wisdom of buying from them rather than from a franchised dealer.

The best specialists are keen enthusiasts of a marque, such as Porsche, BMW or Volkswagen, with workshops on the premises.

Independent dealers are your old-school car dealers as seen by the hundred on London's Romford Road and stretches of the A24 through Tooting, Balham and Clapham.

Some of them are really nice people. Some of them are right old rogues.

History checks

Several organisations will check the car's history for you to make sure it is not on any registers as having been an insurance damage write-off, a finance bad debt, or stolen. All you need is the car's make, model and registration number, so this is something you can do before you even make a trip to view the car.

The checks are provided over the phone for a fee, payable by credit card, of around £30. A printed report is then sent to you in the post. HPI on 01722 422422 charges £31 for a full check, plus £3.00 for a check that the MOT is not stolen, and guarantees its information. Alternatively, for £12.50 you can visit www.hpicheck.com and obtain a basic check on up to three registrations. For £15 you can then phone HPI to upgrade one of the checks to a full check with the name of the finance house if finance is outstanding and an information guarantee.

AA/Experian Car Check on 0800 234999 offers a full check for £29.99 for AA members and £31.99 for non-members. Or you can obtain an internet check via www.theaa.com which costs £27.99 for AA members and £29.99 for non-members.

Others are ABS on 0800 3895169 and *What Car?* History Check on 0845 601 0804.

The best advice is to treat all odometer readings as suspicious and

to get in touch with previous owners listed on the car's V5. If you are buying from the first owner of the car and he is a man of the cloth, then the mileage is probably correct. If you are buying from a small businessman who has used the car to travel extensively on business then, if the mileage is low, it is probably not correct.

For what to look for in individual models, see the Car by Car Breakdown in this book, starting on page 233 (and updated daily at www.honestjohn.co.uk).

Checking the car out

When you first see the car, what do your instincts tell you? Do you get a funny feeling in the pit of your stomach, or do you feel happy and excited?

Trust these feelings because they are your natural defence mechanisms at work. All too often we ignore our instincts and think ourselves into making a bad decision.

Even if you're not mechanically minded, it makes sense to carry out some preliminary checks before you go to the expense of an independent inspection.

First, does the paint match? If every panel is a different shade of red, for example, the car has been in several accidents. If the paint is fresh and new and all the same colour, the car has been in a big accident and been rebuilt. If just part of the car has fresh paint, for example the bonnet, it may merely have had a minor scrape or been repainted because it was badly stone-chipped.

Check the tyres. Uneven wear may be due to incorrect alignment settings, or it may be due to bent suspension components from kerbs, pot holes or road humps. So be particularly wary of uneven front tyre wear. Check the nearside front wheel for rim damage. Has it got a new wheeltrim?

Look at the interior and use your nose. Dirt cleans off but tears in the seats and broken bits of trim are notoriously difficult and expensive to put right. One fag burn can be invisibly repaired using new techniques, but a lot of fag burns will cost you £50 each and the repairs won't be invisible. If the entire interior stinks of tobacco smoke you'll be up against it to get rid of the lingering odour. Has there been a dog in the car? Has it scratched the paint? Has it left a smell?

Open the bonnet and check all the fluids. Look at the oil on the end of the dipstick. Is it up to the mark? What colour is it? Castor oil yellow is excellent; light brown is good; dark brown is okay; a tar-like black in a petrol engine spells disaster, though lubricating oil in all but the latest HDI diesel engines will always be black.

If there is a deposit of whitish or creamy-grey 'mayonnaise' under the oil filler cap, it means one of two things. Either the car has led a life of very short runs from cold starts, has rarely warmed up properly and the condensation this has created has mixed with the oil. Engines run like this have less than a quarter of the life of engines run properly. Or mayonnaise can symptomise a blown cylinder head gasket. It may be straightforward to replace this, or the head may need to be skimmed because it has warped.

Have a look at the condition of the power steering fluid. It should be red, not black. Same goes for the automatic transmission fluid (most autoboxes have a dipstick). With CVT transmissions it is vital that the ATF level is kept up to the mark.

190

Look under the car for leaks. Is there oil on the vendor's driveway? A leak from a cam-cover gasket is common and no big deal, but a bad oil leak from a cylinder head gasket means the head has to come off and, if it does, manifold studs may break and stretch bolts will have to be replaced. A leak from the timing belt cover is bad news because it means that the camshaft end seal has gone or a jackshaft seal has gone, contaminating the timing belt – so you won't just need a new seal, you'll need a new belt. If the gearbox/ final drive is leaking from an output shaft seal, the lack of oil in the transmission may have led to premature wear.

Now ask to see the service history. Not a book full of stamps – the actual bills for all the work on the car which the owner has paid for, or, if a fleet car, a computer print-out of its service history. If, from this, you find that the car has been 'overserviced' (had its oil and filter changed every 4–6 months), then be willing to pay more for it than the guides suggest. If, on the other hand, it has been 'underserviced' (with gaps of more than a year), then pay substantially less than guide price. If the car has a timing belt rather than a chain, in general this needs to be replaced every 35,000–40,000 miles or every 3–4 years. On some cars, such as Ford Zetecs, the replacement cycle can be pushed to up to 5 years or 80,000 miles whichever comes first, but no longer. If the service bills don't show a timing belt change, then budget £60 to £200 to have it done. Automatic transmission fluid should have been changed every two years; brake and power steering fluid every two years or three years at a push, but every year if the car is fitted with ABS. If the car has a manual gearbox and the oil in that was changed within its first 18 months on the road, this is a valuable plus point worth paying more for.

You have now made a number of checks which will have provided you with a lot of information without having to pay anyone.

Testing the car

If you own and insure a car yourself, your policy will usually cover you to drive another insured car third party only. But this means you will be personally liable for any damage you do to the car.

Switch on the ignition and look at the check lights. If there is an ABS light, make sure it goes off within seconds of starting the engine. The engine should start instantly and, when it does, are there any rattles? In an engine with hydraulic tappets you may hear a brief rattle before the tappets pump up, but this is nothing to worry about unless it persists.

If the gearbox is manual, where does the clutch take up? If near the top of the pedal travel, there will be less than 10,000 miles of life left in the clutch. If you can get it to slip, reckon on less than 2,000 miles.

If the car is front-wheel-drive, do a full-lock reverse turn in both directions. This will tell you more about the condition of the clutch, but if you also hear clonking, there is wear in the driveshaft universal joints and these are expensive to replace.

Does the car accelerate smoothly? If it's an automatic, do the gears change smoothly? But don't expect all automatics to change into fourth or even third at town speeds. If it's a manual, do the gears change easily with no graunching, and can you change down smoothly, particularly from third to second, without having to double de-clutch? Is there any gearbox whine or whirring noises? A lot of gearboxes do whine slightly and, though it's an irritant, it may be nothing to worry about. Similarly, a bit of diff lash may be terminal, or the diff may soldier on for years. But the likelihood of a transmission repair should be budgeted for and the price you pay for the car chipped down unless it already accounts for this.

Do the brakes stop the car straight and true? If you feel juddering, the discs may be warped. If retardation is slow, the discs, pads, drums, linings may be worn or grooved. Do the brakes lock up front or back during an emergency stop? If so, the rear brake compensator may be u/s.

Finally, check all the electrics: wipers, sunroof, windows, everything. If the car has a trip computer, get the owner to run through its functions. (But, obviously, if the car is cheap, you don't worry about a non-functioning trip computer.)

Having the car inspected

The four main used-car inspection organisations are: AA (0345 500610); ABS (0345 419926); Green Flag/National Breakdown (01254 355606); RAC (0800 333660). Others are: AAA Motor Vehicle Inspections (London area only: 0705 0158123); Autocheck GB Ltd (020 8678 7060); D.S. Crawford (Central Scotland only: 0131 453 4393). ABS also offers a Helpline on 01625 576441. (ABS are best for 'grey imported' Japanese cars because they know what to look for.)

Inspections tend to cost between £50 and £150 for the average car, the inspectors 'come to the car', and you are provided with a written report afterwards. Some, such as D.S. Crawford in Scotland, include an HPI status check in their very reasonable price of £55. The RAC has charged up to £250 for inspecting personally imported cars. Alternatively, phone the Institute of Automotive Assessors on 01543 251346 to get the number of your local Assessor. They use a standard 171-point checklist, supply a next-day telephone appraisal and a five-page report within 48 hours, for around half the cost of the motoring organisations.

A new service operating in Edinburgh but hoping to roll out nationwide is Carscan, at 81 Dundee Street (0131 228 2882). This offers a sophisticated performance and condition check at its premises, which includes a wheels-off visual inspection on a hoist and a proper rolling road performance analysis, and even a wheel geometry check for a very reasonable £33 + VAT. A full HPI check can also be incorporated for an additional charge.

Sports and high-performance cars need specialist inspections by experts in the particular make and model. An AA or RAC inspection of a Porsche, for example, simply isn't enough. Best to get a written report from a Porsche dealer or independent Porsche specialist and to pay the extra for a compression test on all six cylinders.

The problem is, no vendor with any sense will give you right of first refusal on a car subject to inspection at a later date unless you pay them a non-refundable deposit. If you can't cut a deal like this with the vendor, they will simply sell the car to the first buyer who comes up with the right money, and you could end up forking out an inspection fee for a 'sold' car.

Agreeing a price

Most private used car sellers will have checked the value of their car as a 'private sale' in one of the consumer car price guides available from newsagents and are likely to have built an amount into the price for negotiation.

The simplest way to check out their bottom line is to ask, 'OK, I know the advertised price, but what's the lowest you're prepared to take for the car?' Remember, though, that even when you get to what they have told themselves is their 'bottom line', it might not be as low as they are prepared to go. Much will depend on circumstances, such as the urgency of the sale, how long the car has been on the market, and/or how few people have come to see it. So think like a detective. If the bloke's bags are already packed, his furniture gone and his curtains down, he's probably leaving for Australia that afternoon. If he's already bought a replacement car, he may need to sell the older one urgently. Just chatting to the fellow may elicit little hints that tell you the true circumstances.

Having the car warranted

Motor Warranty Direct offers private used car warranties. Tel: 0800 731 7001; website: www.warrantydirect.co.uk.

Buying at auction

Auctions can be the best places to source a car. After all, unless its a 'classic car auction' aimed at the public, the cars there should sell for the trade prices the market puts on them on the day.

Auctions, especially 'classic car auctions', are also a lion's den for the naïve and unwary. Remember, from a seller's point of view, auctions provide quick sales with no comebacks. There is a directory of auction sites across the UK in this book, starting on page 211. (Classic car auctions are not included; for a list of these, see the News page at www.mysterymotors.com.)

Different types of car auction

There are many different types of car auction and some are a lot safer for the private buyer than others.

Manufacturer Sales of nearly new ex-rental and ex-demonstration fleet cars can be a good bet. The cars are clean, usually have some warranty left, and you know where they're coming from. However, such sales are increasingly aimed at the private buyer as well as the trade, and it can be difficult for obvious private buyers to actually buy at true trade money. Either rival trade bidders or the auctioneer may 'run up' your bids, and if the auctioneer runs you past your limit, the car will simply be re-entered in a subsequent auction.

True trade money for a car changes through the course of the sale and self-tracks to a variation of no more than £100 for a given make, model and mileage in a similarly desirable colour. If you write down all the prices paid you will be able to see this for yourself.

With manufacturer sales, listen carefully to the auctioneer (what he says is taped) because some of the cars may be faulty and returned to the manufacturer for a refund, either under a special scheme or simply under the Sale and Supply of Goods Act 1994.

Dedicated Fleet Sales can be good, too. These are where a section of the sale is given over to cars from a single named fleet source. MFL (Motability Finance Ltd) has the largest fleet in Europe and, for obvious reasons, its cars tend to be low-mileage, less than three years old, with a good sprinkling of power-steered automatics.

West Oxfordshire Motor Auctions (01993 774413) holds ex-police vehicle evening sales twice a month. Blue lights, sirens,

radios, 'jam sandwich' fillings, all will have been removed, so there's no chance of impersonating a police officer on the drive home. And the specification of all but 'undercover' cars tends to be a bit basic (no sun roofs, for example). But it's a great way to pick up a high-mileage, well maintained ex-Panda Escort or Astra, or even a full-blown 3-litre Omega, BMW 325TDS or Volvo T5. Well worth a visit. (They also do Britain's best auction house bacon rolls, with optional chilli sauce.)

Fleet/Finance Sales may offer a mix of cars from named and unnamed fleets and repossessed cars from finance houses. A dedicated Finance House Sale can be an excellent source, particularly where it includes pre-registered, zero-mileage dealer stock which had not been sold before the dealer's creditors pulled the plug and did a midnight swoop on his premises.

Theme sales, such as 'Diesel Cars', 'MPV & 4x4', 'Japanese', 'Late-year low-mileage', are designed to help the trade shift metal and can catch private buyers out. Most of these vehicles will be traders' cars, spiffed up for the occasion, on which the trader hopes to make his living. He may even be there on the floor bidding against you. It need not be catastrophic for a private bidder to buy such a car from a trader, especially at one of the bigger auction houses which don't tolerate 'low-lifes'. But be extra attentive to the auctioneer's description, make sure the mileage is 'warranted' and that the car comes with its V5 listing previous owners so you can check the mileage yourself within the auction house warranty time limits.

For General Sales, the same applies. But these sales often also include 'wrong make' part-exchanges, such as Mazdas from Renault dealers and vice-versa. If you happen to make the top provisional bid for a car that's already been through the halls 'over reserved' several times, the chances are the vendor will instruct the auction house to 'get it gone' and you'll lay your hands on a bargain.

Dedicated part-exchange sales to shift generally older excess stock taken in by larger groups such as Inchcape and Hartwell can be good sources. Inchcape rarely warrants any mileages, but 'gut-feel' and some broad hints from the auctioneer should tell you which cars are right and which are wrong. If, for instance, the auctioneer reads out the car's entire service history you don't usually have to worry that the mileage is not warranted.

'Classic & Historic' are another form of general sale aimed principally at the public. About half the cars will be entered by traders or restorers. But the others will be genuine private and executors' entries. Pick of the bunch are often late entries on the supplementary list rather than in the catalogue. Classics are rarely sold with warranted mileages, due to the impossibility of checking back, and it really is up to the buyer to satisfy him or herself of the car's true condition prior to bidding. Remember also that the public is easily hoodwinked by shiny paintwork and glittering chrome. It can be well worth a trader's while to fill a rusty old classic with 'pudding', give it a respray and try to get bids of £3,000 to £5,000 more than he paid. So classic auctions are one type of sale to which it's still worth taking a magnet.

Auction buying hints and tips

Keep a low profile. Noisy family groups carrying *Parkers Guide* or the *'What Car?* Price Guide' are a dead giveaway. So don't wave your

newsagent price guide around. Look up prices on the sly, and keep the guide hidden when bidding.

Give the cars you're interested in a good once-over in the auctioneer's marshalling yard. Look for obvious signs of a repaint (spray dust, over-bright paint, rubbing compound, tide marks under rubber trim strips). Check for matching shut-lines, especially between the bonnet and wings and the front wings and doors. Crouch down in front of the car and look along the sides for ripples. Check the condition of the tyres for uneven wear. (And if it's a Renault, Citroën or Peugeot, feel under the back to make sure it still has a spare wheel.)

When the yard boy comes to start it up, look for excessive smoke from the exhaust, and ask how much clutch it has left. As it moves into a different light, you may spot faults you missed before. But don't be 'all over' the car as it drives into the auction hall.

Find a spot where the auctioneer can see you very clearly, but where most rival bidders can't see you. Let the bidding start and wait until it slows down or shifts from £100s to £50s or £25s before making your bid. Do this by waving your catalogue to catch the auctioneer's eye. Then, once he knows you are in the bidding, a simple nod will suffice for each increment. If you want to get out, shake your head as soon as he looks at you for a next bid. The more you appear like a trader from out of the area, the less chance you have of being 'run up' next time you get into the bidding.

Bidding at auction for the first time can be both nerve-wracking and addictively exciting. Remember, though, you're there to buy a car as cheaply as possible, not to get high on the adrenaline rush.

Auction warranties

Auction houses usually charge a 'buyer's premium', which is higher for the public than for the trade. If the car is described as 'with warranty', this will include limited cover warranting title to the car, described condition, and mileage if the vendor has warranted this. If the car is described as 'without warranty' or 'as seen', the only guarantees are your title to the car.

These 'buyer's premiums' have risen over the past few years and, for a £20,000 car, could be as much as £500, so check this carefully before starting to bid.

Hiring an auction buyer

If you're nervous of buying at auction, at least three organisations offer to source the car for you.

Julian Trim & Co. charges the auction hammer price plus 6%, tel: 01747 838888.

Douglas Coker's Cars For Customers will source the car either directly from a fleet or from auction, with full service histories if requested, tel: 020 8351 7976.

Yet another car sourcing specialist is Sam Davies of Autobarn Direct, tel: 020 8367 1647.

Used car imports

Different pre-tax pricing to compensate for heavier taxation in other countries does not help the second-hand buyer in the same way as it helps the new car buyer. Used cars are generally little cheaper in countries such as Holland than they are in the UK. So for the used buyer there are no tax killings to be made.

What will help is any comparative strength of Sterling and a differently structured market.

Used German imports

With Sterling at around Dm3.0/£1, Germany has been a good source of extremely well cared-for high performance cars. But a quick glance through a magazine such as *Motor Markt* soon shows you that, without the heavy supply of ex-fleet cars on its used car market, most bread and butter used cars aren't particularly cheap. But sports and high performance cars can be, and LHD is no hardship if your main reason for buying a used Porsche is to enjoy yourself at race circuit trackdays.

One problem can be certification. Every car sold in most European countries since January 1998 comes with a 'Certificate of Conformity' to pan-European Type Approval. Before that date most European countries recognised most other other European countries' National Type Approval, so make sure your get that certificate.

Used Japanese imports

New cars in Japan sell for between half and two-thirds of the UK list price. But Japan also has a tough government testing regime designed to encourage Japanese owners to buy new every three, five or seven years. As a result, the already low prices of Japanese cars drop sharply once they are three years old and once they are seven years old they are of little more than scrap value on the home market.

Until the Yen recovered, this made second-hand imports from Japan spectacularly cheap.

Unfortunately the potential fortunes to be made were spotted many years ago. So as well as the rising Yen, the export factor has increased values of used Japanese cars and they are not the bargains they once were. The second factor is the condition of these cars. Most Japanese cars spend most of their driving lives stuck in traffic jams. After 20,000 miles of this sort of treatment, the diesel engine in a Shogun, for example, can be ruined. The third factor is that because they don't keep their cars for long, a significant proportion of Japanese owners simply don't bother to service them. The fourth factor is that Japanese cars are set up to run on different petrol at different speeds than in the UK. The maximum speed in Japan is 55 mph, so tyres may not be suitable for the UK, suspension may be too soft, steering too light and so on.

There is an auction of used Japanese imports every month in Dublin (Windsor Car Auctions, Bewlgard Road, Dublin, tel: 00 351 1 4599 300).

You can also try using specialists who buy cars for you at Japanese auctions. These include Spectrum on 0081-48-833-0665, website: http://www.trade.co.jp, e-mail: spectrum@trade.co.jp; and Japan Car Direct on 0081-339 280-935, website: http://www.isibike.com/isicar/, e-mail: isik@crisscross.com.

Specialists know how to get most Japanese cars through the SVA test for imports. The more complex the car, the more complex the modifications. The most experienced people are Protech, tel: 0117 986 1611, website: www.protech-uk.co.uk; and another useful website on importing from Japan is http://www.importedvehicles.co.uk.

But, and it's a big BUT, the rules about SVA are set to change from 1 November 2001 (see 'Single Vehicle Approval' on page 202).

Shipping
No problem from Europe, of course. But some tips may help if wishing to import from Japan or the USA. Be warned that when importing from Japan, car space on the huge Wallenius Lines 'RO-RO' ships may be limited and may be booked up months in advance.

A good shipper is Mann Motor Ships (tel: 023 8023 7711) which ships from Jacksonville, Charleston, Baltimore, New York and Halifax to Southampton and Liverpool, using Wallenius Lines. Mann only uses RO-RO ships, but you can have a car shipped as deck cargo or fully containerised. Expect to pay between $495 and $625 to ship a 'one-off' average car sized between 351 and 500 cubic feet. You'll also have to pay US wharfage of $75–$85 and UK wharfage of about £30. Insurance has to be negotiated with a Stateside broker.

Two other shippers are: Prestige Shipping Services Ltd, tel: 020 8462 0292; and N.S.E.W., tel: 01394 674455.

Import duties from USA and Japan

There is 10% European import duty to pay on the invoice price of the vehicle plus the shipping costs, then a further 17.5% UK VAT to pay. The appropriate two leaflets are: 'How to Permanently Import your Vehicle into Great Britain' (Department of Transport leaflet P12, printed December 1996) and 'The Single Vehicle Approval Scheme'. Both are available from the Department of Transport VSE1, Zone 2/01, Great Minster House, 76 Marsham Street, London SW1 4DR. Public Enquiries can be directed to tel: 020 7271 4800.

Single Vehicle Approval (SVA)

The rules about SVA changed on 1 February 2001 and will change again on 1 November 2001.

Essentially, any car which was not first registered in Europe and which does not carry a European Certificate of Type Approval ('C-of-C') is required to pass a Single Vehicle Approval test at a government HGV testing centre.

The only exceptions are cars more than 10 years old and cars 3–10 years old which have been owned abroad by the importer for at least six months in a country where the importer has lived for at least 12 months.

Further changes from 1 November 2001 to an 'Enhanced Single Vehicle Approval Test' seem likely to make compliance so expensive that importing used cars from outside the EU will no longer be viable.

Since there is no sense in a system so restrictive that it prevents the importation of used cars from outside the EU, we have to hope that this prediction is unduly alarmist. But until the exact position is known all I can do is issue a warning that, if you intend making a 'grey import', make sure you time it so the car can be SVA-tested before November 2001.

The relevant SVA and ESVA booklets can be obtained from the Vehicle Certification Agency, tel: 0117 951 5151, or check the website: www.via.gov.uk You also can buy a copy of the 'Single Vehicle Approval' Inspection Manual, priced £25, from the Vehicle Inspectorate, PO Box 12, Swansea SA1 1BP.

Importing a used car from Europe

1 Get the relevant Government booklets and forms. First phone the DVLA on 01792 772134 and ask for the pack on personal imports. This includes: a booklet, 'How to Import a Vehicle Permanently into Great Britain'; Form V100 which explains registering and licensing procedures and gives a list of Vehicle Registration Offices; and Form V55/5, which is an application form to license a vehicle in the UK for the first time. (Alternatively, phone the DETR on 020 7676 2094, write to DETR VSE1, Zone 2/01, Great Minster House, 76 Marsham Street, London SW1 4DR, or visit the DETR website at: www.roads.detr.gov.uk/vehicle/vse1/index.htm.) Then phone your local VAT enquiry line, listed under 'Customs & Excise' in the telephone directory, and ask for the 'VAT Notice 728 Pack' which includes a form, Appendix D 'New Means of Transport – Notification of Acquisition'. (Please don't phone C&E at either 020 7864 3000 or 01304 224372, as these lines have become overwhelmed with enquiries.)

2 Make sure the car comes with a Certificate of Conformity to European Type Approval ('C-of-C'), an invoice showing that VAT has been paid in the country of purchase, and, of course, the dealer's invoice.

3 As soon as possible, fill in the form 'New Means of Transport – Notification of Acquisition' (Appendix D) which came with VAT 728 and take it, together with completed form C55/5, the dealer's invoice, foreign registration document and the C-of-C, an MOT if the car is more than three years old (photos of a lit offside rear foglight and speedo face in mph if less than three years old) to your nearest Vehicle Registration Office. On payment of a £25 first registration fee, they will issue you with a registration number. You than have to obtain an insurance certificate containing that registration number before you can tax the car at a Post Office using form V62. Your V5 registration document will then be sent to you from Swansea.

4 Order a set of plates.

Selling used
How to prepare the car for sale
The public are suckers for clean-looking cars. So, whatever old rubbish the car may be, if it can be made to look good, someone will invariably buy it.

Making a car look good is a matter of thoroughly cleaning it inside and out, thoroughly polishing it – paying particular attention to the windows – treating the plastic with a restorative, touching up or 'blocking in' as many paint chips as you reasonably can, and blacking the tyres to make the whole show look new. An upholstery spray such as 'Apple Fresh' also goes down well. Whatever you do, don't spray the plastic around the dashboard with shiny glop. This looks and feels hideous and will make the public suspicious.

If you are selling the car privately from your doorstep, consider servicing it and putting it through a fresh MOT. It doesn't need to be a big service, but it will give buyers confidence and make them feel much better-disposed towards you.

How to prepare your advertisement

If you're using a photo ad in one of the many 'Trader' publications, don't let their bloke come round and take the photograph. Especially don't let him take his snap of the car parked next to the dustbins round the back of a block of flats.

These days you get 24 prints and a replacement film, all for a fiver. Obviously it's well worth a bit of time and a fiver if a good snap is going to sell your car faster and for a lot more money.

So shoot the whole roll. Photograph the car against a variety of backgrounds. Side on, three-quarters, against a contrasting skyline, then pick the photo that both shows it off the best and is most likely to reproduce well on fairly grotty newsprint.

Describe the car accurately and simply using no superlatives. 'Nissan Primera 2.0SLX 5-door hatchback, 97R, 55,632 miles, full service history, met blue, electric sunroof and windows, power steering, good condition, £4,500' will go down a lot better with the general public than 'Beautiful Nissan Primera, two litre, top spec SLX model, R reg, 55k, FSH, stunning metallic blue, electric roof and windows, PAS, drives superb, first to see will buy £4,499'.

Where to advertise

This depends on the car and the price range.

For cars under £3,000, it's always worth putting a postcard in the local newsagent's window. Local newspapers or freesheets usually have sections for this type of car. People who buy *Loot*, the London classified newspaper, expect cars advertised in it to be cheap. *Auto Trader* magazines also offer sections for cheap cars. And if the car is a bit specialist, *Exchange & Mart* is worth a stab.

The photo ad section in *Classic Car Weekly* has become the best for 'classics' at the cheaper end. For more expensive 'classics' it may be worth going for a series ad in *Classic Car Weekly*, *Practical Classics* and *Classic Car*.

Mid-range family cars seem to go best either from the bigger local newspapers (or groups of newspapers) or from a photo ad in an *Auto Trader*. See tips about taking the photo on page 205.

For sports or specialist cars it might be worth trying *Top Marques*, which is an upmarket national version of *Auto Trader*. If you have something you think a dealer or an enthusiast might be interested in, *Autocar* is worth a try. If attempting to get a high price or an 'over' for a car the demand for which exceeds supply, then you'll do best with an ad in The *Sunday Times*, or The *Daily Telegraph* 'Motoring' which appears on Saturdays. 'Telegraph Motoring' also has a photo section, 'Forecourt', which can be particularly good for reaching a high circulation with a classic car.

But I reckon that the best place of the lot is the website, www.autotrader.co.uk, which costs you £7.50 a fortnight and gets cars gone for me when all else has failed.

How to answer the phone

Though you are a private individual, it's better to sound fairly professional. Blaring television, loud pop music or kids fighting in the background are a definite turn-off to the buyer.

Answer with a polite, upbeat, 'Hello', followed by your telephone number. This immediately confirms that the caller has phoned the right number.

There is then a 95% chance that the caller will say, 'I'm calling about the car.' This is your cue to say words to the effect of, 'Yes, the Nissan Micra' (or whatever) and confirm to the caller that you are not a 'home trader' who has a lot of different cars for sale. Quickly add, 'What can I tell you about it?'

You're honest, you've put the buyer at ease, and you are welcoming his or her questions. What more could the buyer want? You must then try to answer every question as quickly and as straightforwardly as you can, which is not always easy when they make ill-thought demands on you such as 'Does it have any marks?' (Every car has marks, so your answer to this is 'Nothing significant'.) Similarly, if they ask 'What sort of condition is it in?' you say 'Good condition, at least I think so'.

What they should be asking are questions such as, 'Are you the owner of the car?', 'How long have you owned it?', 'Why are you selling it?', 'When did you last have it serviced?', 'Can you be sure that the mileage is genuine?', 'Do you owe anything on finance for the car?', 'Is the colour Balliol Blue, Rimini Blue, Ontario Blue, Cayman Blue, Java Blue, State Blue or Petrol Blue?' (that would indicate that the caller knew his or her Mondeos).

Remember, depending on the scarcity of the car and how competitively you have priced it, the buyer may either be working through a list or you may be the only vendor he is phoning that night. If it's obvious he is working through a list, you have to hook him, and you'll do that by charm and honesty, not by a load of old flannel.

Even if the buyer does not yet want to make an appointment to view the car, be sure to get his name and phone number before you give him your address. When subsequent callers query how much interest there has been in the car you can then read out a list of names and that might make them want to come and view the car immediately. The British are a bit peculiar like that. They always seem to want something if they think everyone wants it.

Getting the name and number of all callers also helps protect you against theft from your driveway or from the street. If you are selling a highly desirable, much stolen sportscar, take all callers' phone numbers, then phone them back on that number before divulging any address details. Smart thieves can get your address from your phone number anyway, but not all of them are that smart.

How to demonstrate the car

It is illegal for anyone to drive your car if he or she is not insured to do so. Most purchasers' private car policies will cover them to drive a car they wish to purchase on third party terms if that car (your car) is insured by someone else (you). But third party means just that. If the potential purchaser wrecks your car, his insurer will pay for any damage to third parties, but not to you. Similarly, if he steals the car from you, you will get nothing back either. And if he turns out not to be insured at all, then crashes your car, both you and he could find yourselves facing criminal charges.

So be very careful indeed about allowing other people to drive your car and don't even contemplate it unless you see their insurance certificate, or have either an 'any driver' policy for your car or a trade policy.

Assuming the insurance question is satisfactorily answered, there is not much point in you driving the car with the purchaser as passenger unless that is specifically what they want.

Why not let them drive? The procedure is for the buyer to get into the driver's seat and you to get into the passenger's seat. Both of you then make yourselves comfortable, the buyer gets familiarised with the controls and you both put your safety belts on.

Then, and only then, hand him the key.

If you drive first, there are two safe ways to carry out the swapover. You climb from the driver's seat to the passenger's seat and let the buyer walk round to the driver's seat. Or you both walk round but you take the key so he doesn't get hold of it until you're both belted in.

Never, ever, take more than one male person on a test-drive unless you also take a big bloke as your own back-up.

How to do the deal

The buyer will try to chip you down on price. If you have accidentally underpriced the car (it can happen, I've done it) and the phone has hardly stopped ringing, you can be firm on your price. Simply and politely say you're sorry, but you know you have priced the car fairly and you know you will get the asking price, if not

from the buyer in front of you then from someone else.

But, of course, if the car has stuck (this has also happened to me) you will be prepared to take a bath just to get rid of the thing. Whatever you do, don't make this too glaringly obvious. Still try and do a deal. Consult 'er indoors. Fight for the last £25. Do whatever you have to. But don't let the car go cheap easily, both for your own sake and the fact that it might make the buyer have second thoughts.

How to take payment

There are only three ways to take payment for a car.

The first is a Building Society Cheque issued by the Building Society itself, in which case you need to see the buyer's pass book to check the amount has in fact been withdrawn so you can satisfy yourself that the cheque is genuine.

The second is a Bank Draft, which you must only take during banking hours so you can phone the bank that issued it and check it is genuine.

The third, in Mike Brewer parlance, is 'Nelsons' (Nelson Eddies =

Readies). The best advice when taking cash is to swap the V5 and keys for the cash in a bank so you can bank it safely straight away. Take cash on your doorstep and you won't be the first to receive a 'cash relieving' visit shortly afterwards by big, nasty men you wouldn't want to argue with or to threaten your children.

UK Car Auction Sites

Want to buy a car at auction? Honest John's comprehensive list of auction sites is separated into 14 regions covering all of the UK.

Classic car auctions are not included here. For a list of these, see the News page at www.mysterymotors.com.

The dates and times of auction sales continually change, so to avoid misleading you with out-of-date information we are no longer listing these details. You should check with your chosen auction centre for specific sale dates. Many auctions will now take Switch or Delta/Link card payments (not credit card payments). Again, check this before leaving for the auction, and make sure you have sufficient funds in your account.

For more advice on buying at auction, go to 'Buying used' (page 185) in the chapter on How to Buy and Sell Cars.

Car Auction Sites in the London Area

The London Area

British Car Auctions, Enfield 620 Gt Cambridge Road (A10), Enfield (M25: J25), Middlesex EN1 3RL, tel: 020 8366 1144, fax: 020 83671009, website: www.bca-group.com. Catalogue DIAL-A-FAX National Directory: 0336 411411, updated daily.

Dingwall Motor Auctions, Croydon Sidney House, Beddington Farm Road, Croydon, Surrey CR0 4XB, tel: 020 8684 0138.

General Motor Auctions, Wandsworth 63–65 Garratt Lane, Wandsworth, London SW18 4AA, tel: 020 8870 3909.

Manheim Auctions, Wimbledon Waterside Way, off Plough Lane (opposite greyhound stadium, beside Wickes), Wimbledon, London SW17 7AB, tel: 0870 444 0415. Catalogue Fax-U-Back: 09003 416079 for Fleet and Low Mileage; 09003 416008 for Budget Cars.

Thames-Side Motor Auctions, Fulham Wandsworth Bridge Road North, Fulham, London SW6 2TY, tel: 020 7736 0086, 020 7736 0087.

South of the Thames

Hobbs Parker Car Auctions, Ashford The New Ashford Market, Monument Way, Orbital Park, Ashford, Kent TN24 0HB, tel: 01233 502 222.

British Car Auctions, Camberley Blackbushe Auction Centre, Blackbushe Airport, Blackwater, Camberley (M3: J4a, west of airport on A30), Surrey GU17 9LG, tel: 01252 878555, fax: 01252 879559, website: www.bca-group.com. Catalogue DIAL-A-FAX National Directory: 0336 411411, updated daily.

British Car Auctions, Paddock Wood Eldon Way, Paddock Wood (M20: J2), Kent TN12 6BE, tel: 01892 836611, fax: 01892 832965, website: www.bca-group.com. Catalogue DIAL-A-FAX National Directory: 0336 411411, updated daily.

Eastbourne Car Auctions Arkwright Road, Lottbridge Drive, Drove Trading Estate, Eastbourne, East Sussex BN22 9PB, tel: 01323 520295, fax: 01323 520330. Auction catalogue Fax-U-Back: 09003 406088.

Shoreham Car Auctions Lancing Business Park, Lancing, West Sussex BN15 8TU, tel: 01903 851200, fax: 01903 851100, website: www.sv-auctions.co.uk.

South Western Vehicle Auctions, Poole 61 Ringwood Road, Parkstone, Poole, Dorset BH14 0RG, tel: 01202 745466, fax: 01202 732036 website: www.swva.co.uk. Catalogue Fax-Back: 09003 416239.

Southampton Vehicle Auctions Ltd Southern Road (next to Dock Gate 10), Southampton, Hampshire SO15 1DH, tel: 023 806 31631, fax: 023 806 31632.

North of the Thames

British Car Auctions, Bedford Mile Road, Bedford (M1: J13), Bedfordshire MK42 9TB, tel: 01234 218161, fax: 01234 355707, website: www.bca-group.com. Catalogue DIAL-A-FAX National Directory: 0336 411411, updated daily.

Milton Keynes Stadium Motor Auctions H9 Groveway Stadium, Groveway, Ashland, near Bletchley, Milton Keynes, Buckinghamshire MK8 4AA, tel: 01908 666835.

West Oxfordshire Motor Auctions, Witney Bromag Industrial Estate, Witney, Oxfordshire OX29 0SR, tel: 01993 774413, email: buy@woma.demon.uk.

Essex and East Anglia

Anglia Car Auction, Kings Lynn The Cattle Market, Beveridge Way, Kings Lynn, Norfolk PE30 4NB, tel: 01553 771881.

British Car Auctions, Peterborough Boongate, Peterborough, Cambridgeshire PE1 5AH, tel: 01733 568881, fax: 01733 588297, website: www.bca-group.com. Catalogue DIAL-A-FAX National Directory: 0336 411411, updated daily.

Chelmsford Car Auction Drovers Way, Chelmsford, Essex CM2 5PP, tel: 01245 450700, fax: 01245 460695, website: www.chelmsfordca. co.uk.

County Car Auctions, Bourne Eastgate Industrial Estate, Eastgate, Bourne, Lincolnshire TE10 9JY, tel: 01778 424201.

East Anglian Motor Auctions, Norwich 261 Aylsham Road, Norwich, Norfolk NR3 2RE, tel: 01603 409824.

Eastern Car Auctions, Norwich South Norwich Business Park, Bessemer Road, Norwich, Norfolk, tel: 01603 666500.

Manheim Auctions, Colchester Frating, Colchester, Essex CO7 7DX, tel: 0870 4440403. Auction catalogue Fax-U-Back 09003 416006 (Tuesday sale); 09003 416013 (Wednesday sale); 09003 416009 (Thursday sale); 09003 416005 (Manufacturer sales).

The South West

British Car Auctions, Bridgwater Bristol Road (A38), Bridgwater (M5: J23), Somerset TA6 4TN, tel: 01278 685511, fax: 01278 685353, website: www.bca-group.com. Catalogue DIAL-A-FAX National Directory: 0336 411411, updated daily.

British Car Auctions, Tewkesbury Newtown Industrial Estate, Northway Lane, Tewkesbury (M5: J9), Gloucestershire GL20 8JG, tel: 01684 292307, fax: 01684 294246, website: www.bca-group.com. Catalogue DIAL-A-FAX National Directory: 0336 411411, updated daily.

Cornwall Motor Auctions Limited Falmouth Station Road, Penryn, Falmouth, Cornwall TR10 8HF, tel: 01326 372955.

Exeter Car Auctions Husseys, The Auction Centre, Matford Park Road, Marsh Barton, Exeter, Devon EX2 8FD, tel: 01392 425481.

Manheim Auctions, Bristol Ashton Vale Road, Ashton Vale, Bristol, Avon BS3 2AX, tel: 0870 444 0402. Catalogue Fax-U-Back 09003 416084.

Manheim Auctions, Dursley Berkeley Road, Cam, Dursley, Gloucestershire GL11 5JB, tel: 0870 444 0405. Catalogue Fax-U-Back (call after 6pm day before sale) 09003 416052 (cars); 09003 415666 (LCVs).

Saltash Car Auctions Burton Road, Parkway Industrial Estate, Saltash, Cornwall PL12 6LF, tel: 01752 841444.

Westbury Motor Auctions Brook Lane, Westbury, Wiltshire BA13 4EN, tel: 01373 827777, fax: 01373 864286, website: www.westburyma.co.uk.

Wales

British Car Auctions, Newport Meadows Road, Queensway, Meadows Industrial Estate, Newport, Gwent NP9 0YR, South Wales, tel: 01633 270222, fax: 01633 270444, website: www.bca-group.com. Catalogue DIAL-A-FAX National Directory: 0336 411411, updated daily.

Clwyd Car Auctions, Ewloe Hollywell Road, Ewloe, Deeside CH5 3BT, tel: 01244 532821.

Merthyr Motor Auctions Pant Road, Dowlais, Merthyr Tydfil, Mid Glamorgan CS48 3SH, tel: 01685 377818, website: www.auctioneers.co.uk.

Newport Auctions Limited Dockland Distributor Road, Newport, Gwent NP20 2BW, tel: 01633 262626.

TMA Motor Auctions, Queensferry Station Road, Queensferry, Deeside CH5 2TD, tel: 01244 812811.

South West Midlands

Brightwells Country Vehicle Auctions, Leominster 38 South Street, Leominster, Herefordshire HR6 8JG, tel: 01568 611166, fax: 01568 611802, website: www.brightwells.com, email: vehicles@brightwells.com.

Leominster Car Auctions Kingsland, Leominster, Herefordshire HR6 9RL, tel: 01568 708561.

West Midlands

Arrow Motor Auctions, Redditch Bartleet Road, Washford, Redditch, Worcestershire B98 0DG, tel: 01527 510923.

Birmingham Car Auctions 302–312 Moseley Road, Birmingham B12 0BS, tel: 0121 4464000.

British Car Auctions, Walsall Green Lane, Walsall, West Midlands WS2 7BP, tel: 01922 721555, fax: 01922 613188, website: www.bca-group.com. Catalogue DIAL-A-FAX National Directory: 0336 411411, updated daily.

British Car Auctions, Langley Drive Hayward Industrial Estate, Langley Drive (M6: J5 or 6), Birmingham B35 7AD, tel: 0121 7491331, fax: 0121 7472481, website: www.bca-group.com. Catalogue DIAL-A-FAX National Directory: 0336 411411, updated daily.

British Car Auctions, Swadlincote Tamworth Road, Measham, Swadlincote (M42: J11), Derbyshire DE12 7DY, tel: 01530 270322, fax: 01530 273595, website: www.bca-group.com. Catalogue DIAL-A-FAX National Directory: 0336 411411, updated daily.

Manheim Auctions, Coventry Rowley Drive, Coventry, West Midlands CV3 4FG, tel: 0870 4440404. Catalogue Fax-U-Back: 09003 416026.

Manheim Auctions, Darlaston Whitworth Close, Heath Road, Darlaston, West Midlands WS10 8LJ, tel: 0870 4440401. Catalogue Fax-U-Back 09003 416081 (cars); 09003 416086 (light commercial vehicles).

Newcastle Motor Auctions Silverdale Road, Newcastle-under-Lyme, Staffordshire ST5 2TA, tel: 01782 617930.

Portway Motor Centre Car Auctions Alcester Road, Portway (500 yards from M42, J3 on A435 Redditch Road), Birmingham B48 7HX, tel: 01564 822877.

Prees Heath Motor Auction, Whitchurch Heath Road, Prees Heath, Whitchurch, Shropshire SY13 2AR, tel: 01948 663166/663177, fax: 01948 665318.

Stafford Motor Auctions Browning Street, Stafford, Staffordshire ST16 3AT, tel: 01785 243470.

Telford Auctions Rookery Road, St Georges, Telford, Shropshire TF2 9BW, tel: 01952 610033.

Telford Motor Auctions Trench Lock 2, Telford, Shropshire TF1 5YL, tel: 01952 257751.

East Midlands

British Car Auctions, Derby Raynesway, Derby, Derbyshire DE21 7WA, tel: 01332 666111, fax: 01332 660186, website: www.bca-group.com. Catalogue DIAL-A-FAX National Directory: 0336 411411, updated daily.

British Car Auctions, Nottingham Victoria Business Park, Netherfield, Nottingham (M1: J24 or 26), Nottinghamshire NG4 2PE, tel: 0115 9873311, fax: 0115 9617296, website: www.bca-group.com. Catalogue DIAL-A-FAX National Directory: 0336 411411, updated daily.

Chesterfield Car Auction Lockford Lane, Chesterfield, Derbyshire S41 7JB, tel: 01246 277999.

Newark Motor Auctions The Showground, Winthorpe, Newark, Nottinghamshire NG24 2NY, tel: 01636 671167.

Leicester Car Auctions, Leicester 8 Commercial Square, Freemans Common, Leicester, Leicestershire LE2 7SR, tel: 0116 2556606.

Manheim Auctions, Shepshed Charnwood Road, Shepshed (M1: J23), Leicestershire LE12 9NN, tel: 0870 4440408. Auction catalogue Fax-U-Back: 09003 416080.

Manheim Auctions, Sutton-in-Ashfield Mansfield Fulwood Industrial Estate, Common Road, Huthwaite, Sutton-in-Ashfield, Nottinghamshire NG17 6AD, tel: 0870 444 0410. Catalogue Fax-U-Back: 09003 416076 (cars); 09003 416078 (commercials).

Manheim Auctions, Northampton The Auction Hall, Salthouse Road, Brackmills Industrial Estate, Northampton, Northamptonshire NN4 7EX, tel: 0870 4440412. Catalogue Fax-U-Back 09003 415667.

Yorkshire, Lincolnshire

Adwick Motor Auctions Church Lane, Adwick-Le-Street, Doncaster, South Yorkshire DN6 7AJ, tel: 01302 722251.

Bawtry Motor Auction Corner Garage, Bawtry, Doncaster, South Yorkshire DN10 6JL, tel: 01302 710333.

Beverley Motor Auctions Tokenspire Business Park, Woodmansey, Beverley, Yorkshire HU17 0EB, tel: 01482 887555 and 01482 888111.

Bradford Motor Auctions Midland Road, Bradford, West Yorkshire BD1 3EQ, tel: 01274 774444.

Bridlington Motor Auctions Pinfold Lane, Bridlington, East Yorkshire YO16 5XS, tel: 01262 674044.

British Car Auctions, Brighouse Armytage Road, Brighouse (M62: J25), West Yorkshire HD6 1XE, tel: 01484 401555, fax: 01484 406686, website: www.bca-group.com. Catalogue DIAL-A-FAX National Directory: 0336 411411, updated daily.

Leeds Limited Motor Auctions Hillidge Road, Leeds (M1: J46), West Yorkshire LS10 1DE, tel: 0113 2726800.

Manheim Auctions, Leeds Leeds Road, Rothwell, Leeds, West Yorkshire LS26 0JE, tel: 0870 4440407. Catalogue Fax-U-Back: 09003 416054.

Manheim Auctions, Rotherham Canklow Meadows Industrial Estate, West Bawtry Road, Rotherham, South Yorkshire S60 2XL, tel: 0870 4440413. Catalogue Fax-U-Back 09003 424593.

Manheim Auctions (formerly A1 Motor Auctions) Tadcaster Road, Brotherton, Knottingly, Yorkshire AL2 1DG, tel: 0870 4440416

Premier Motor Auctions Cross Green Industrial Park, Pontefract Lane, Leeds, West Yorkshire LS9 0PS, tel: 0113 2941111.

West Riding Motor Auctions Bruntcliffe Lane, Morley, Leeds, West Yorkshire LS27 9LR, tel: 0113 2521046.

The North West

British Car Auctions, Belle Vue Belle Vue Auction Centre, Belle Vue, Manchester M12 4RX, tel: 0161 2306000, fax: 0161 220 8065, website: www.bca-group.com. Catalogue DIAL-A-FAX National Directory: 0336 411411, updated daily.

British Car Auctions, Preston Reedfield Place, Walton Summit, Preston (M6: J29; or M61: J9), Lancashire PR5A 8AA, tel: 01772 324666, fax: 01772 334838/628621, website: www.bca-group.com. Catalogue DIAL-A-FAX National Directory: 0336 411411, updated daily.

Burnley Auctions Liverpool Road, Rosegrove, Burnley, Lancashire BB12 6HH, tel: 01282 427231.

Chorley Motor Auction Cottam Street, Chorley, Lancashire PR7 2DT, tel: 01257 262091.

Direct Motor Auctions, Chester 9 Hartford Way, Sealand Trading Estate, Chester, Cheshire CH1 4NT, tel: 01244 383789.

East Lancashire Motor Auctions, Blackburn Highfield Road (off Bolton Road), Blackburn, Lancashire BB2 3RE, tel: 01254 670190.

Ellesmere Port Motor Auction Rossfield Road, Rossmore Industrial Estate, Ellesmere Port, South Wirral CH65 3BS, tel: 0151 3572040.

Liverpool Motor Auctions Dorset House, West Derby Road, Liverpool, Merseyside L6 4BR, tel: 0151 2637351.

Manheim Auctions, Trafford Park Richmond Road, Trafford Park, Manchester M17 1RE, tel: 0870 4440409. Catalogue Fax-U-Back: 09003 416053.

National Car Auctions, St Helens Yewtree Trading Estate, Kilbuck Lane, Haydock, St Helens, Lancashire WA11 9SZ, tel: 0870 4440406. Catalogue Fax-U-Back: 0336 416074.

Preston Olympia Motor Auctions London Road, Preston, Lancashire PR2 5AN, tel: 01772 252428 and 01772 253230.

Radcliffe and District Motor Auctions Unit 10, Globe Industrial Estate, Spring Lane, Radcliffe, Manchester M26 2TA, tel: 0161 7240805.

St Helens Motor Auctions East Lancashire Road, Carr Mill, St Helens, Lancashire WA11 9LG, tel: 01744 22513.

Stoodley Vehicle Auctions, Belle Vue Hyde Road, Belle Vue, Manchester M12 4SA, tel: 0161 2233882.

West Coast Motor Auctions, Blackpool Poulton Industrial Estate, Garstang Road East, Poulton-le-Fylde, Blackpool, Lancashire FY6 8JF, tel: 01253 892488.

The North East

British Car Auctions, Newcastle-upon-Tyne Whitley Road, Longbenton, Newcastle-upon-Tyne, Tyne and Wear NE12 9SQ, tel: 0191 2700077, fax: 0191 2668786, website: www.bca-group.com. Catalogue DIAL-A-FAX National Directory: 0336 411411, updated daily.

Durham County Motor Auctions Mainsforth Industrial Estate, Ferryhill, County Durham DL17 9DE, tel: 01740 650065.

Manheim Auctions, Maltby Low Road, Maltby, Middlesborough TS8 0BW, tel: 0870 4440411. Catalogue Fax-U-Back: 09003 424594.

Manheim Auctions, Washington District 15, Pattinson Road, Washington, Tyne and Wear NE38 8LB, tel: 0870 4440414. Catalogue Fax-U-Back: Cars Wednesday and Thursday: 09003 416024; Cars Friday: 09003 416027; HGVs and Plant: 09003 416059.

Scottish Motor Auction Group, Birtley Portobello Industrial Estate, Birtley, County Durham DH3 2SA, tel: 0191 4104243.

Tyne Tees Motor Auction, Newcastle-upon-Tyne Coast Road Retail Park, Coast Road (A1058), North Shields, Tyne and Wear NE29 7UG, tel: 0191 2962020.

Scotland

British Car Auctions, Ingliston Edinburgh Exhibition and Trade Centre, Ingliston (A8 at M8/M9), Edinburgh EH28 8NB, tel: 0131 3332151, fax: 0131 3334608, website: www.bca-group.com. Catalogue DIAL-A-FAX National Directory: 0336 411411, updated daily.

British Car Auctions, Provanmill 999 Royston Road, Provanmill, Glasgow G21 2AA, tel: 0141 7709661, fax: 0141 7709592, website: www.bca-group.com. Catalogue DIAL-A-FAX National Directory: 0336 411411, updated daily.

British Car Auctions, Wishaw Main Street, Newmains, Wishaw, Strathclyde ML2 9PT, tel: 01698 383737, fax: 01698 383189, website: www.bca-group.com. Catalogue DIAL-A-FAX National Directory: 0336 411411, updated daily.

Intercity Motor Auctions, Glasgow 77 Melbourne Street, Glasgow G31 1BQ, tel: 0141 5563333.

Intercity Motor Auctions, Perth Perth Agricultural Centre, East Huntingtower, Perth (A85), Perthshire TH1 3JJ, tel: 01738 623333, fax: 01738 621000.

Scottish Motor Auction Group, Aberdeen 11 St Machar Road, Aberdeen AB24 2UU, tel: 01224 487000.

Scottish Motor Auction Group, Longstone 1 Murrayburn Road, Longstone, Edinburgh EH14 2TF, tel: 0131 4437163.

Scottish Motor Auction Group, Glasgow 199 Siemens St, Blochairn, Glasgow G21 2BU, tel: 0141 5534747.

Scottish Motor Auction Group, Kinross Bridgend, Kinross, Perth & Kinross KY13 7EN, tel: 01577 862564.

Shotts Motor Auctions Stane Road, Shotts (M8: J5), Lanarkshire ML7 5NH, tel: 01501 823337, fax: 01501 823498.

Thainstone Vehicle Auctions, Inverurie Thainstone Agricultural Centre, Inverurie, Aberdeen AB51 5XZ, tel: 01467 623700.

Wilsons Auctions Limited, Glasgow 6 Kilwinning Road, Dalry, Ayrshire KA24 4LG, tel 01294 833444.

Northern Ireland

Ballyclare Motor Auction 53 Park Street, Ballyclare, County Antrim BT39 9DQ, tel: 028 9332 3819.

Carryduff Auctions 10 Comber Road, Carryduff, County Down BT8 8AN, tel: 028 9081 3775.

Omagh Auction Group 24 Gortrush Industrial Estate, Derry Road, Omagh, County Tyrone BT78 5EJ, tel: 028 8224 1514.

Wilsons Auctions Limited, Newtownabbey 22 Mallusk Road, Glengormley, Newtownabbey, County Antrim BT36 4PP, tel: 01232 342646.

Wilsons Auctions Limited, Portadown 65 Seagoe Industrial Estate, Portadown, County Amargh BT63 5QA, tel: 028 3833 6433.

Dishonest John's Guide to Service Scams

After extensive research, Dishonest John presents 26 Top Tips for dodgy service managers who prefer to put profits before punters.

WARNING: NOT FOR THE EYES OF PRIVATE MOTORISTS

1 The Keyfob Caper

Tell the punter that his remote control keyfob needs new batteries but, for it to work again, it also needs to be re-programmed at a cost of anything from £40 to £85.

2 The Bulb Blag

Phone the customer while his car is in for service to tell him that, among the additional items needing attention, a bulb has gone. He will think, 'Can't cost much', and will agree to a bulb replacement. Then charge him 15 minutes' labour at £60 an hour to change the bulb, and another 15 minutes for the fitter to obtain it from the stores.

3 The Screenwash Scam

Always automatically charge for renewing the screenwash additive. Even if it the reservoir is full when the car arrives, leave a bottle of additive in the boot and still charge for it at an outrageous rate.

4 The Multipurpose Lubricant Leglifter

Similar to the screenwash scam. Always supply a spray can of multipurpose lubricant at every service, and charge for it of course.

5 The Oil Filter Flanker

Instead of changing the oil filter at a routine service, tell the fitter to simply give it a good clean over with a rag. It will look like new, the punter won't know any difference and you'll save 15 minutes obtaining the new filter from stores and fitting it, plus, of course, the cost of the filter.

6 The Fluids Overfill

Charge the customer for a quantity of oil, coolant, ATF, gearbox oil, brake fluid, etc. over and above what the car will actually take. Very few punters ever spot this and, if they do, tell them it's a clerical error, revise the invoice and refund them the extra money. 99 times out of 100 you won't have to.

7 The Major Component Confusion

Never, ever, repair a major component. If, for example, an automatic gearbox has a problem DO NOT INVESTIGATE THE CAUSE. Instead, simply quote for fitting an entirely new automatic gearbox. The fault may be nothing more than a duff solenoid in the valve block, but don't waste time with a £200 job when there is much more profit to be gained from fitting a new autobox at £1,750 plus.

8 The Wiper Wipe-Out

Always phone to suggest to the customer that their wipers need replacing, then not only charge a 100 per cent margin on the replacement wipers, but also charge 15 minutes' labour for fitting them. One *Telegraph* reader was quoted £104 for fitting a pair of new wipers to her Alfa Spider. For a Renault Espace, it was £40 plus fitting.

9 The Seals Scam

If the engine or gearbox is suffering from a slight oil leak (or even if it isn't and you can induce one), quote the punter for expensive new gaskets or seals, preferably internal shaft end-seals. They usually fall for it, but watch out for the bloke who has a handy mate with a ramp who can spot that all that's needed is to tighten a few nuts.

10 The Brake Blag

During a routine service, 'discover' that the front brake discs are wearing thin and are in need of replacement. Punters are getting used to having to replace discs every 30,000 miles, so even if the discs are still in good condition you will probably get away with selling the parts and a nice fat labour charge.

11 The Calliper Con

Alternatively, if the brake discs really are wearing thin it may well be due to sticking or rusty pins in the callipers leading the pads to bind on. Whatever you do, don't replace or clean these pins. To maximise replacement revenue, wait until the customer comes back with another worn thin pair of discs, then tell him the callipers need replacing as well as the discs and pads.

12 The Battery Blether

If the punter complains of slow starting, that's your cue to flog him a new battery. Persuade him that a 'maintenance-free battery' cannot be topped up or re-charged, and definitely don't mention the battery plate reconditioner that can be purchased from the banner ad on the homepage of www.mysterymotors.com.

13 The Sundries Scam

Always charge a figure of between £2.50 and £5.00 + VAT for 'sundries', and if the customer asks what they are, tell him disposable wipes, disposable rubber gloves, and oils and greases used in small quantities on things like door locks and hinges.

14 The Over-the-Top Oil Earner

Even though the workshop's engine oil comes from a bulk tank at a huge discount, still charge for it per litre as if it has been supplied in individual litre bottles.

15 The Warranty Maintenance Muckaround

If the customer has a used-car warranty requiring the car to be regularly serviced at a franchised dealer, this can be a real goldmine. Be careful to find a long list of repairs and replacements, none of which are covered by the warranty, but all of which must be made for the warranty to remain intact.

16 The Drivebelt Dodge

'Check auxiliary drive belts' will usually be included on a service schedule. But no mention will be made of making any adjustments to the tension of the belt, so at least 15 minutes' labour should be charged for this.

17 The Low Sulphur Scam

If a punter shows up with a non-functioning diesel pump, tell him the reason for the malfunction is wear due to the lack of lubricity of Ultra Low Sulphur Diesel. The problem may really be no more than a chafed cable to the pump, but it's much more profitable to sell him a new pump and fix the chafed cable without telling him.

18 The Clutch Con

Sudden clutch failure may be due to the pressure fork fracturing rather than failure of the clutch itself. On many makes and models, the fork is easy to get at and replace without any serious disman-tling. But the customer probably won't know that. So, if a clutch appears to have failed, always quote for a complete new exchange clutch and, if the problem is really no more than the fork, fit that as well and charge extra for it.

19 The Hidden Faults Hoax

Find things wrong that the punter can't see and check up on, such as a broken engine mount, a duff tailgate strut, a faulty water pump, a fractured door hinge mounting, a noisy wheel bearing, a worn steering rack, etc. The scope here is as wide as your imagina-tion, but check the car's previous service sheets to make sure you haven't tried the same stunt with the same component before.

20 The Electronics Earner

If the car is not running properly, tell the customer you will perform a complete diagnostics check on it. This will usually isolate the true cause of the problem, but, instead of fixing that, replace one of the other components in the electronics or the fuel injection system. The customer will then come back and, after pleading 'trial and error', you will probably get the chance to rip him off for replacing something else which may or may not solve the problem.

21 The Loose Connector Con

Often, all that will be wrong is that a connector plug has come loose, or some moisture has got inside it. Never admit to this, especially if it's the multipoint connector to the ECU. Always diagnose that the ECU needs replacing at a cost of £500-plus.

22 The Lambda Laugh

If the diagnostic interrogator and an emissions test isolate the exhaust Lambda sensor as the source of the problem and simple cleaning would cure it, instruct your fitters to replace it. Though Halfords sell universal-fit lambda sensors for £30, some manufacturers' prices can be very high, especially for the more complex sensors in Toyota Carina E and Avensis models. Always go for the maximum obtainable revenue, never for the minimum needed to cure the problem.

23 The MOT Megablag

The most fertile area for unnecessary repairs is the MOT test, especially if your garage is an appointed MOT testing centre. Always give the car a cursory pre-test, find it needs a few bulbs replacing and phone the customer to get permission to replace them. Then, depending on the type of customer, in the test itself make sure the tester finds things like split driveshaft gaiters, worn suspension bushes, loose brake pipes, etc. But whatever you do when applying this blag, make sure the car has no genuine major fault which would lead it to fail the test. Punters will almost always be so relieved that their car has got through its MOT, they won't mind paying for £50 to £100 worth of repairs to get it through. But if the car needs major work, you won't get away with a package of minor add-ons.

24 The Indecent Incentive

Always incentivise your fitters with things like free holidays. You have to make them prizes for tax purposes, but sending a fitter and his family off to Bali for a fortnight costs a tiny percentage of what you're going to make from his ingenuity in finding lucrative non-existent faults. He'll be happy for six months working towards his holiday in Bali and you'll be raking it in without having to pay him expensive cash incentives.

25 Suggestion Box

Don't even dream of it. The only way to make cons like this work is for everything to go unsaid.

Keep This Under Your Hat

Keep this document firmly under lock and key, preferably in the safe. Never leave it lying around on a desk. Preferably, commit it to memory then destroy it. Do not let it fall into the wrong hands or your game is up. Do not discuss it with your wife or girlfriend. Remember: Careless Talk Blows Blags!

Car by Car Breakdown

Want to change your car? Avoid costly mistakes by checking out what's good, what's bad, what to watch out for and recalls for more than 555 models, new and used.

For the past five years Honest John has been building this unique database of information and know-how, drawing upon his own vast knowledge and the mountain of feedback that reaches him daily from readers of his *Daily Telegraph* Motoring Agony Column and www.honestjohn.co.uk.

Additions are made on a daily and sometimes even hourly basis, using information from manufacturers, from the Vehicle Inspectorate, from the auction floor, from traders, from reader e-mails and from The Back Room forum at www.honestjohn.co.uk. For the very latest additions and updates, see the Car by Car Breakdown at www.honestjohn.co.uk.

AC

212 S/C, Superblower, Mk IV and CRS

What's good: With 355 bhp supercharged Ford V8 putting out 385 lb ft torque, they might as well have called the Superblower the 'Mindblower'. But there's nothing to be afraid of. Take it easy, 'point and squirt' at first, and the informative chassis soon tells you that much more is possible. Original AC Cobra looks. Probably the most fun car there is. Beautiful; hand-beaten aluminium body shared by 220 bhp Mk IV now selling at around the £25,000 mark at 18–24 months old. But new £38,000 CRS polycarbonate version with non-supercharged 240 bhp Mustang engine from Summer 1999 is a great alternative to a TVR. AC's latest is the 212 S/C at £69,000, fitted with the 350bhp lightweight twin-turbo 3.5 litre V8 from the Lotus Esprit V8. Promised 0–60 is 4.0 seconds, gearbox is 6-speed and there's a chance that with the right tyres this could be the fastest car from 0–100 in the world. 212 S/C, CRS and Superblower have nice, central dashboard. Maker's website: www.accars.co.uk.

What's bad: Driver and passenger get blown about a bit at over 100 mph (on the track, of course). Nice gearchange of Superblower has a narrow gate, and first time out you may get 5th instead of 3rd. Buy new, and Mk IV and Superblower will lose money in spades. Mk IV has terrible parts-bin dashboard.

What to watch out for: Superblower and 212 S/C could blow a big hole in your finances when you come to sell. But if you live on St George's Hill, Weybridge, overlooking the factory, you can afford it.

AIXAM

MAC 500

What's good: Beach buggy version of the Aixam 500 car with 479cc two cylinder Kubota diesel engine giving 70mpg and open-belt CVT transmission. Base price just £4,550, but add £125 for VED and Registration Tax.

What's bad: Alloy wheels, a spare wheel, a hood and even doors are all extras.

What to watch out for: Too soon to say.

Micro-Cars

What's good: Tiny French two- and four-seater micro hatchbacks. Have two-cylinder 400cc and 469cc Kubota diesel engines giving 55 mph and 75–90 mpg. Simple, exposed-belt Variomatic transmission. Under the weight limit, so can be driven on a B1 motorcycle licence. Euro Type Approved. First UK RHD sale May 1999. Can also be towed unbraked behind a large motorhome. Polycarbonate body on aluminium space frame won't rust.

What's bad: Slow acceleration will take a bit of getting used to. Quite expensive for what it is. Body leaks.

What to watch out for: Wet carpets and internal condensation damage to electrics.

ALFA ROMEO

145/146 (1994–2000)

What's good: Fabulous two-litre Twin-Spark motor, superquick power steering on 2.0 litre versions, brilliant oddball styling of the 145, good but not great handling. 1.8 and 1.6 Twin-Sparks also good. 3-year warranty on all Twin-Sparks.

What's bad: The injected and catalysed flat-fours in early models are nothing like as good as the straight-four Twin-Sparks. Dashboard a bit iffy. Not much room in the back when sitting behind a long-legged driver. In June 2001 Alfa Romeo was rated by Motor Warranty Direct as Britain's worst out of 22 marques for warranty claims (www.warrantydirect.co.uk.)

What to watch out for: Accident damage, lack of service history. Check electrics carefully. Oil leaks from gearboxes of flat-fours. Starting problems with flat-fours. Make sure it has its 'Red Key'.

Recalls: (April 1997 build): Tyres may lose pressure.

147 (2001 on)

What's good: Stunning-looking replacement for 145/146 with front-end retro styling reminiscent of late 1940s Alfas. Based on 156 floorpan. 120 bhp 1.6 Twin-Spark, 150 bhp 2.0 TS and (later in the UK) 110 bhp JTD. Voted European 'Car of the Year' narrowly pipping the Ford Mondeo for the title. February 2001 launch models are the 121mph 120bhp 1.6TS in Turismo or Lusso trim and the 129bhp 150bhp 2.0TS with Alfa Romeo's Selaspeed semi automatic gearbox. All models are well equipped with air-conditioning and ABS as standard. Prices start at £12,985 for the 1.6TS Turismo, rising to £17,340 for the 2.0TS Selaspeed. Standard 3-year warranty included in price. 5 door version with 2.0TS manual gearbox offered from May 2001.

What's bad: Problems with Selaspeed gearbox actuator on 156 models and long wait for replacement parts reported by two readers. Could be repeated with 147. Paddle shift arrangement for

Selaspeed on 147 doesn't work very well. Not a great drive.
What to watch out for: Too soon to say.

155 (1992–1998)

What's good: Brilliant later engines – both Twin-Spark and 2.6 V6.
Late 'Sport' models had 'Quick-Rack' power steering. 3-year
warranty on later cars.
What's bad: Terrible fall-apart dashboards. 'Italian Ape' driving
position. Looks like yesterday's car compared to 156. Avoid early
pre-Twin-Spark models. In June 2001 Alfa Romeo was rated by
Motor Warranty Direct as Britain's worst out of 22 marques for
warranty claims (www.warrantydirect.co.uk.)
What to watch out for: Tattiness. Kerbed alloys. Accident damage.
Duff cats. Front tyre wear. Check all electrics. Sport spec well worth
having. Make sure the car does have 'Quick-Rack' (2.1 turns lock to
lock) steering. If a later model, make sure it has 'Red Key'.

156 (1998 on)

What's good: Fabulous styling. Brilliant engines. 1.8 and 2.0 litre
Twin-Sparks are great. 190 bhp 24v 2.5 V6 is a real hooligan. All
have 'Quick-Rack' steering. Pure, unadulterated handling well up
to the job with Sports packs; less good without. 3-year warranty.
2.0 litre 'Selaspeed' with thumb operated gearchange buttons on
steering wheel works very well on country roads, but is less
satisfactory in town. 'Q' system V6 is a full automatic. Gruff but
grunty 136 bhp 2.4JTD arrived in Summer 1999, offering 224 lb. ft.
torque. Sport 1 spec adds carbon fibre console, bodykit, 16in alloys
with 205/55 tyres, sports suspension and 'Blitz' cloth trim. Sport 2
spec adds Recaro front seats. Sport 3 spec adds Momo leather. New
£13,495 120 bhp 1.6TS in UK from Spring 2000. All prices cut from
same date with 1.8TS down to £15,405. No missing 'Red Key'
problems as it has a different immobiliser system. Hot 250bhp 3.2
litre V6 156 GTA, probably capable of 160mph and possibly
offered with Selaspeed option is on its way, and already seen
testing in Germany.

What's bad: 'Police Alert' spoilers optional on Sport 2 and Sport 3 spec will attract plod. Sub-20 mpg fuel consumption of V6 if you boot it. Trim quality still not quite up to BMW standards. 5-speed gearchange on 1.8 and 2.0 can feel a bit floppy. Turn-in not as sharp as Peugeot 306 GTi-6 or 406 2.0 litre Coupe. Usual Alfa build-quality problems with electrics. Fuel enrichment device may stick, leading to poor starting. Dealers are a very mixed bag. Resale values fell heavily in early 2000 even before the price cuts. V6 eats front tyres.

What to watch out for: Worn front tyres on V6. Accident damage. Kerbed alloys. Make sure aircon works properly. Feel the discs through the wheels for scoring or shouldering. Problems with 156 Selaspeed gearbox actuator and long wait for replacement parts.

Recalls: June 1999: Safety recall No 4054: Modify rear hinge mounting on all four side doors to prevent hinges splitting from doors. 2000: 156, built Nov '97–Oct '98: brake pipe connector may crack and leak.

164 (1988–1998)

What's good: Brilliant engines, none more so than full-house 3.0 litre 24 valve mega-powerful 230 bhp Cloverleaf V6, good for 150 mph.

What's bad: Old fall-apart Alfa trim, Alfa build quality and uneven quality of Alfa dealers (some brilliant and enthusiastic, others completely the opposite). In June 2001 Alfa Romeo was rated by Motor Warranty Direct as Britain's worst out of 22 marques for warranty claims (www.warrantydirect.co.uk.)

What to watch out for: Electrics. Accident damage. Driveshaft wear. Gear selector problems. Worn front suspension springs, shocks and joints. Scored or lipped discs (try to feel them through the wheels). Rear suspension bush wear. Tattiness. Make sure aircon works. Go for post-May 1993 makeover improvements. Make sure cambelt has been changed within last 35,000–40,000 miles. Make sure it has its 'Red Key' (later models only).

Recalls: 1995 (to VIN 6272929): corrosion of front suspension spring support. (Earlier TSB check of timing belt.)

166 (1999 on)

What's good: Svelte replacement for 164. 2.0 litre 155 bhp Twin-Spark, 2.5 24v 190 bhp V6 or 3.0 24v 220 bhp V6. Autoboxes optional with V6s.

What's bad: Not as charismatic as 156. V6 eats front tyres.

What to watch out for: Check front tyres for wear.

Recalls: Problem of loss of hydraulic power assistance to steering. All RHD 1,900 166s imported to UK by April 2001 recalled.

33 (1983–1994)

What's good: Zingy flat-four pre-cat engines.

What's bad: Poor substitute for Alfasud. Same rust problems. Gearboxes break. Condensation on flat-four causes poor starting. Seat trim falls apart. Gearboxes stiffen up and break. Electrics fail.

What to watch out for: Most have recycled themselves by now. Unless it's virtually being given away, this is best avoided.

GTV and Spider (1995 on)

What's good: We're talking about the latest model here, not the mid-60s Duetto that lasted into the 1990s. The good bits are fabulous looks, brilliant engines, 'Quick-Rack' steering, better rear suspension than the saloons. 3-year warranty. Latest 3.0 24v V6 6-speed is as close as you'll get to a new Ferrari under £30k; 1999 MY RHDs have 218 bhp and six-speed gearbox. Same engine and gearbox in Spider from Spring 2001, making it an unruly hooligan of a car and capable of over 150mph with the top down. Surprisingly little buffeting at this speed, even without the benefit of cockpit ait-dam.

What's bad: Spider suffers some scuttle shake and doesn't handle as well as cars like the Toyota MR2, Porsche Boxter, Audi TT Roadster, etc. Virtually no boot room at all in the coupe. 'Saw their legs off' back seats. No RHD V6 Spider. No auto options. Cylinder head gasket failed before one owner got his new car home. S and T platers 3rd from bottom in 2001 Top Gear/JD Power Customer Satisfaction Survey. In June 2001 Alfa Romeo was rated by Motor

Warranty Direct as Britain's worst out of 22 marques for warranty claims (www.warrantydirect.co.uk.)

What to watch out for: Kerbed alloys. Electrics. Porous wheel rims (symptom: soft tyres). Undeclared personal imports lacking 3-year warranty. Disguised envy damage. Hood mechanism and tears in hood (don't forget to check hood if hood is down). LHD imports from Germany won't have 3-year warranty. Make sure it has its 'Red Key'.

Recalls: 24/1/2000: Brake master-cylinder supply pipes may crack. 1,209 cars built May '98–July '99 recalled for replacement pipes. 10/3/2000: 122 GTV6 models built June '96–March '98: radiator fan cables could overheat, short-circuit and cause a fire. Cables to be checked and modified.

Old Spider (1966–1993)

What's good: Lovely 'up and down' classic Alfa gearchange. Evergreen Alfa twin-cam motors. Early 1,570cc and 1,779cc boat tail cars had the looks. 1990 facelift brought with it a decent hardtop.

What's bad: Scuttle shake. Progressively ruined over the years by ugly 'facelifts', but 1990 facelift an improvement. Early cars rusted from new. Later cars can still rust. 'B' pillar can dig you in the back when you try to get in. Ruined by catalytic converter.

What to watch out for: Tears in hood and trim. Soggy carpets. Rusty 'cornflakes under the carpet'. Rust around the fuel tank in the boot. Duff catalytic converters on later cars. Broken window-winder cables. Dripping heater matrix. Electrics. Noisy timing chain. 3,000-mile oil changes essential (I used to change mine every three months).

ASCARI

KZ1

What's good: Stunning new 200mph carbon fibre British supercar built in Blandford Forum, Dorset. Has a BMW M5 V8 bored out to 4,928cc developing 520bhp. Six speed 'H' pattern or sequential gearbox. Top speed estimated at over 200mph. 0–60 in 3.7 seconds. 5.0 litre 400bhp £96,000 Ascari Ecosse continues. Company website: www.ascari.co.uk

What's bad: £130,000 price. Gatso speed cameras. Otherwise too soon to say.

What to watch out for: Too soon to say.

ASTON MARTIN

DB7 (1994 on)

What's good: Nice compromise between handling and ride quality. Excellent 335 bhp supercharged 3,239cc six-cylinder engine with healthy 361 lb ft torque. Supplemented from Spring 1996 by convertible Volante and from Spring 1999 by 6.0 litre V-12 Vantage version offering 420 bhp, much praised by English motoring writers.

What's bad: Expensive compared to XK8 (but Vantage comparatively 'reasonable' at £92,500). Cabin spoiled by cheap and nasty 'parts bin' switchgear. Hood of convertible does not fold away. Most six-cylinder cars fitted with old-fashioned four-speed automatic gearbox which is difficult to override manually and changes gear half way round corners.

What to watch out for: For rich English people, chosen over XK8 for exclusivity of Aston Martin name. Must have top notch service history. Don't expect this car to be 100% niggle-free.

Recalls: 10/1/2000: 140 DB7 Vantage Coupes and Volantes recalled because of insufficient welds to front damper lower mounting brackets. Brackets to be replaced if not welded on all three sides. 9/10/2000: 478 DB7 Vantage models recalled for replacement of Power Train Control Module because original ignition software could result in misfires.

Vanquish (2000 on)

What's good: 6.0 litre V-12 DB7 Vantage developed to 504 bhp, launched late 2000 at £170,000 and selling for overs.

What's bad: Too soon to say.

What to watch out for: Too soon to say.

Virage and New V8

What's good: 1990 Replacement for old Aston Martin V8 which dated back to the 1960s. 5.3 litre 330bhp V8. 5-speed manual. 4 speed auto from Jan 1993. Re-named V8 in April 1996. Got 350bhp and option of 6-speed manual box. Awesome supercharged V8 Vantage had 550bhp and six-speed box. Demand picked up again and a 35,000-mile 91J auto sold for £28,000 at a BCA Top Car auction in July 2001.

What's bad: Unsuccessful. Launched during the supercar boom and went into a tailspin once the boom went bust. Auto only a 3-speeder to Jan 1993. The engine alone is an enormous piece of engineering. Potentially huge bills.

What to watch out for: Don't buy without full inspection by an Aston Martin expert.

AUDI

100 and 'Old' A6 (1988–1997)

What's good: Galvanised against rust. 2.0 litre models handle better than heavier V6 and TDI. TDI 2.5 5-cylinder powerful and economical, especially with 6-speed manual gearbox.

What's bad: Expensive dealer servicing and parts. TDI fuelling needs re-setting regularly. TDI timing belt drives water pump and if water pump fails, so does belt. Replacing timing belt is expensive because hard to get engine and pump timing exactly right. TDI is front heavy.

What to watch out for: Worn autoboxes. PAS leaks and wear. Serious front tyre wear. Suspension joints. Wheel bearing rumble. Rattling cats, especially on 2.6 V6. Ex-fleet examples may be clocked. Accident damage repaired with non-galvanised panels or with bad welds which can rust.

Recalls: 1997 (2.8 V6): rumoured recall issued in April concerning driveline. 1997 (built Feb–March 1997): check front seatbelt top mounting height adjusters. (Built '95–'96): airbag may inflate while stationary.

80 Mk 1 (1986–1991)

What's good: Electro-galvanised body shell, hot-dip galvanised underside, so very little chance of tin-worm unless accident damaged. Switchable ABS. Powerful 2.0 litre 16-valve engine. Euro Car Parts (0541 506506) supplies cheap parts.

What's bad: Getting old now. Strangely-shaped, short, deep boot. Hard to sell without a sunroof. Tornado red paint oxidises in sunlight. Audi replacement autoboxes cost the wrong side of £3,000. BBS Replica alloy wheels on Sport models chip easily, then oxidise.

What to watch out for: Duff catalytic converters, but can be 'de-catted' for £350. Accident damage repaired with non-galvanised panels. Rattly hydraulic tappets due to insufficient oil changes (sump only holds 3 litres). Worn CV joints. Rumbling wheel bearings. Don't buy early cars without PAS. Look for PAS leaks. Rear discs rust first, leading to failed MOT. Valve stem seals may need replacing at 100,000–130,000 miles – earlier if mileage clocked up slowly.

80 Mk II (1991–1995; –1999 for soft-top)

What's good: Electro-galvanised body shell, hot-dip galvanised underside, so very little chance of rust unless accident damaged. Has switchable ABS (A4's doesn't switch off). Powerful 2.0-litre 16-valve engine. Smooth and punchy 2.6 V6. Economical TDI. All had PAS, folding rear seat and better-shaped boot than previous model.

What's bad: Franchised dealer service costs. Hard to sell without a sunroof. Tornado red paint oxidises in sunlight.

What to watch out for: Duff catalytic converters. Accident damage repaired with non-galvanised panels. Coolant must be changed every two years, especially on TDI, or head gasket problems can result. Valve stem seals need replacing at 100,000–130,000 miles – earlier if mileage clocked up slowly. Make sure ABS and ABS switch work properly. Rear discs rust first, leading to failed MOT. TDI may be worn out and oil-burning at 150,000 miles.

Recalls: 1997: 50,523 cars recalled due to possibility of 'inadvertent deployment of airbags'.

A1 (2002 on)

What's good: City car on Lupo/Arosa floorpan to be available with concertina-type electrically folding hard top. Steel and plastic panel construction with overall weight around 800kg. '3 litre' (94 mph) version with 3-cylinder 1.2 litre 61 bhp TDi, or four cylinder 1.0 litre and 1.4 litre petrol engines. Due 2002.

What's bad: Will be comparatively expensive in UK, probably from £10,000.

What to watch out for: Far too soon to say.

A2 (2000 on)

What's good: High-tech aluminium space-frame constructed 12ft 4in hatchback, with low drag coefficient of 0.28, built to take on the MB A-Class. 75 bhp 1.4 petrol engine offering a Euromix of 46.31 mpg or a 3-cylinder 1.4 litre 75 bhp, 144 lb ft TDI pump-injector diesel offering a Euromix of 67 mpg and up to 81 mpg touring. Both do 108 mph and 0–60 in 12 seconds, but diesel is more fun to drive. Two-deck rear luggage compartment. Rear seats completely removable. Decent ride quality and steering. High level of grip from tyres. Very comfortable multi-adjustable seats. 1.4 to be priced from £13,500. TDI to arrive January 2001, priced slightly higher. 1.2 litre '3 litre car' which averages 94 mpg, semi-automatic gearbox and 105 bhp 1.4 16v petrol all not due in the UK until later. Deep sills provide impressive side impact protection. Gained four-Stars in NCAP crash safety tests. Very trendy among the well heeled. Three-year warranty.

What's bad: Looks like a chopped-up A6. High rear door sills and sunken footwells do not help access to the back seats for the elderly. Gearchange quality varies a lot. Pre-production gearboxes were noisy, but production RHD examples seem to be fine. 1.4 petrol engine is rorty, needs to be revved for performance and can feel sluggish on the motorway when the car is laden. Emergency spare wheel is an optional extra. Long wait for the 105 bhp 1.4 16v. Terrible MW and LW radio reception. New A2 based on Golf Mk V floorpan due 2002/3.

What to watch out for: Accident damage and parking dings to alloy body and structure will be expensive to repair, but Audi is setting up six special repair centres for A8s and A2s.

A2 (from 2002/03)

What's good: New car with family look based on the Golf Mk V floorpan. Golf V is due 2002 so A2 may well precede it. Usual family of VAG engines, plus tansverse Multitronic transmission optional.
What's bad: Too soon to say
What to watch out for: Too soon to say.

A3 (1996–2001)

What's good: Image, quality, galvanised body. 3-year warranty. 100 bhp 1.6, 125 bhp 1.8, 150 bhp 1.8 Turbo, 200 bhp S3 quattro turbo. First application of Golf Mk IV platform. Front-drive alternative to the BMW Compact. Joint top-of-the-class for secondary safety in NCAP crash testing. 3-door version handles better than Golf Mk IV. 5-door has complemented 3-door from autumn 1999. Three-year warranty.

What's bad: Not much room in back whether 3- or 5-door. First tests seemed to indicate that 5-door A3 had lost the handling edge of the 3-door over the Golf Mk IV. Expensive compared to SEAT Leon on same floorpan. Bigger splashguards to overcome wet weather braking problems mean that later S3 brakes don't cool sufficiently under hard use and are not up to the car's performance under repeated heavy braking, for example on a track day (www.sport-3.net).

What to watch out for: Demand a proper Audi dealer service history and evidence that recall work has been carried out. Sometimes bought as 'shopping cars', so be vigilant when checking the flanks for dings. Check for accident damage repaired with non-galvanised panels or with bad welds which can rust. Plastic water pump impellers on early 1.8 20v engines fail. Newer water pumps have metal impellers. Hydraulic connection to rear brake callipers can corrode due to types of metals used.

Recalls: 1997 (built Feb–March 1997): check front seatbelt top mounting height adjusters. 1998: 2,822 cars recalled due to possible cracks in rear seatbelt brackets. 2000: A3s built Jan-May 1999: front seatbelt buckles may open in a collision. Replacement buckles to be fitted (2,855 cars). A3s built Jan-Dec 1998: seatbelt pretensioner could ignite fabric trim; A3 1.8T built Dec '97–June '98: accelerator could jam.

A3 (2001 on)

What's good: Extensively revised, smoother and better looking A3 3-door and 5-door model for 2001. Engine range, from 100bhp 1.6 petrol up to 225bhp S3 quattro. Prices from £14,605 for base 1.6 3-door to £24,770 for S3 Quattro. 180bhp 1.8T Quattro Sport 5-door comes in at £21,515 and the cheapest diesel is the 3-door TDI 90 at £15,485. To be a TDI PD 130 with six-speed box. All models have Electronic Stability Programme, transponder immobilisers, ultrasonic interior protection and front and front-side airbags.

What's bad: Same engine range as before. No PD 115 or PD 130 TDIs.

What to watch out for: As previous A3.

A4 (1995–2000)

What's good: Handles well. Good looking, galvanised body. Old 150 bhp 2.6 V6 is a nice engine and easily delivers 30 mpg. TDI 90 and TDI 110 deservedly popular, delivering up to 50 mpg driven fairly carefully. TDI V6 well liked. Other engines: 100 bhp 1.6, 125 bhp 1.8 20v, 150 bhp 20v Turbo, new 165 bhp 30v 2.4 V6; 193 bhp 2.8 30v V6; 265 bhp S4 Quattro. Comprehensively re-thought in Spring 1999. Got 115 bhp 'Pumpe Duse' TDI option from late 1999.

What's bad: Takes a few days to get used to the steering, seats and over-servoed brakes. Weight of TDI V6 takes edge off handling. Limited market for 1.6s without sunroofs or aircon. Similar expensive front wishbone bush problems as A6 and Passat – eliminated late 1999. Average performance in NCAP crash tests. Heavy salted road spray may make brakes feel spongey. In Germany, deflectors are available FOC to cure this (*Auto Bild* magazine 24/11/2000) and these are coming to the UK. Poor AM radio reception. New A4 now on UK market reviewed in road test on this site. Last of the line, ultra quick RS4s suffered from 'soft' alloy wheels easily damaged by potholes.

What to watch out for: Rear discs rust first. Rattling catalytic converters (especially on 2.6, which has two costing £650 apiece). Cats also fail on 1.9 TDIs built before August 1998. Quite a few coming off the fleets, so look out for signs of clocking and inadequate maintenance. Look for accident damage repaired with non-galvanised panels or with bad welds. Plastic water pump impellers on early 1.8 20v engines fail. Newer water pumps have metal impellers. Possible oil consumption problem with 30v V6s, so have emissions checked for excessive HCs before buying. Some A4s develop a fault with the immobiliser ignition switch transmission reader coil. Some develop faults with both the reader coil and the key transponder. If the car comes with two different keys, this is why. Creaks from front suspension indicate wishbone problem: budget for £500–£700 to replace.

Recalls: 1997 (built Feb-March 1997): check front seatbelt top mounting height adjusters. (Built '95–'96): airbag may inflate while stationary. 1998: 4,574 2.4 litre V6 cars built Aug '97–Feb '98: possibility of throttle jamming. 1999: 'S' reg 2.5 V6 TDIs recalled for brake modification; 2.5 V6 TDIs recalled for major engine modifications. 2000: A4 manuals built July '94–August '95: brake pedal may become loose; A4s built March '98–August '98: steering ball joints could fail. Also Recall 13A9 vibration damper, Recall 17B4 oil pump and Recall 46C7 brake pads. March 2001: Worldwide recall of 560,000 1999 model-year A4s, A6s, A8s and VW Passats to replace steering ball joints (track rod ends). Announced *Auto Bild* 11/3/2001.

A4 B6 (from 2001)

What's good: Code name B6. Second generation A4 on new platform with classy look about it. More leg and head room. Better ride quality. Better driving environment. Engines include a new 130bhp balancer shaft 30 valve 2.0 litre; the old 150bhp 1.8T; a new 220bhp V6; an uprated 130bhp 1.9 litre TDI PD; a 155bhp 2.5 litre V6 TDI and a 180bhp V6 TDI for Quattro versions. Five- and six-speed manual gearboxes. Multitronic automatic option. Promise of a long-lived car which will still have some value left after 5–6 years. Will also be an Avant in autumn 2001, a cabrio in early 2002, and a 5-door 'coupe' in late 2002. Three-year warranty. High equipment levels thoughtout the range. All new A4s come complete with electronic climate control, ABS, EDS, ESP and alloy wheels. It's a very classy car. Excellent Four Star 30 point rating in NCAP occupant protection crash tests. On sale in UK from March 2001. A4 TDI 130PD emits 149g/km CO_2 putting it into the lowest diesel VED bracket of £110pa and also benefiting company car drivers. TDI 130PD to be combined with Multitronic CVT transmission which will make this car very quick in traffic. Range road test at www.honestjohn.co.uk.

What's bad: Prices higher than originally anticipated at from £18,640 on the road. Expensive franchised dealer servicing. Otherwise too soon to say.

What to watch out for: Too soon to say.

A6 (1997 on)

What's good: Good looking Passat-based Audi, with Audi styled body. 2.4 30-valve V6 is a nice, powerful (165 bhp) engine. Handling 'soft' but not floaty and grip is quite good. 150 bhp 2.5 V6 TDI available as Quattro. Estate versions. 230 bhp twin-turbo 2.7T and 340 bhp 4.2 V8 S6 launched autumn 1999. V6 TDI upped to 180 bhp in July 2000. Impressive new Multitronic CVT transmission available in UK on 2.4 litre V6s from late summer 2000. Three-year warranty. Re-engineered Summer 2001. Multitronic more widely available. TDI PD 130 the most tax-efficient executive company car. Road test of new range at www.honestjohn.co.uk.

What's bad: Tiptronic gearbox lever works wrong way round (forward for upshifts, backwards for downshifts). Three-Star NCAP crash test rating. Reports of heavy oil consumption of 2.4 litre V6. ADAC in Germany reported a lot of other problems with A6 generally, including fuel pump, fuel tank, air-mass meter, wheel bearings, front wishbones, air filter, instruments, heated door mirrors and timing belts. Have had reports of repeated electric window failure, driver's side. Franchised dealer servicing can be expensive.

What to watch out for: Audi dealer service history. Accident damage repaired with non-galvanised panels or with bad welds which can rust.

Recalls: A6s built March '98–August '98: steering ball joints (track rod ends) could fail. March 2001: Worldwide recall of 560,000 1999 model-year A4s, A6s, A8s and VW Passats to replace steering ball joints (track rod ends). Announced *Auto Bild* 11/3/2001.

A8 (1994 on)

What's good: Advanced all-alloy 'ASF' space frame body construction. Lots of room inside. 300 bhp 4.2 V8 is a high quality, quick, safe, luxurious car. S8 has 360 bhp and gets up to 140 mph very quickly, even when leaving the Tiptronic box to shift itself. Lesser versions are front-drive 2.8 V6 and 230 bhp 3.7 V8. 2.8 went 30-valve and got power hike from 174 bhp to 193 bhp in 1996. 3.3 litre V8 TDI due in UK in 2001. 3-year warranty. 420 bhp 6.0 litre W12-engined version launched at September 2000 Paris Motor Show. Three-year warranty.

What's bad: Body dents easily and is very expensive to repair – requiring a special jig (makes insurance expensive). Ride quality not as luxurious as expected. Hasn't sold very well against competition from Mercedes and BMW.

What to watch out for: Don't confuse a £36,000 2.8 with a £55,000 4.2 Quattro Sport or a £61,000 S8. Mark price down heavily for even the smallest dent or scratch. Quattros must have full Audi dealer servicing history, 2.8s not quite so important.

Recalls: A8s built March '98–August '98: steering ball joints could fail. March 2001: Worldwide recall of 560,000 1999 model-year A4s, A6s, A8s and VW Passats to replace steering ball joints (track rod ends). Announced *Auto Bild* 11/3/2001.

Allroad (from 2000)

What's good: A6 Avant based 4x4 with either 180 bhp 2.5 litre TDI V6 or 250 bhp twin turbo 2.7 litre petrol V6. Choice of 6-speed manual or 5-speed Tiptronic, with low-ratio box available as a factory fit extra on the 6-speed. Height-adjustable suspension lowers for the motorway or raises for the rough, giving as much ground clearance as a Range Rover for serious off-roading. Exhaust system well tucked away. Clever bush fenders on bottoms of doors. Amazingly capable both on the road and off. Not hugely more expensive than an A6 Avant. Makes a Range Rover look like a horse and cart. Definitely one for the ski set.

What's bad: Tiptronic gearbox lever works wrong way round. Still expensive at £32,550 for the TDI and £36,630 for the 2.7T.

What to watch out for: Check for off-roading damage.

TT Coupe and Roadster (1999 on)

What's good: Totally individual shape. No other car looks remotely like it and you either love them or hate them. All UK spec cars have Haldex clutched four wheel drive with either 180 bhp or 225 bhp, which is a lot from 1.8 litres. RHD Roadsters arrived early 2000, but lots of grey imports before then. Three-year warranty. 225s are very sure footed and great fun to drive on a severely twisting road. You can buy a used LHD two wheel drive German import TT 180 coupe for £14,000 from an import specialist.

What's bad: A spate of high-speed autobahn accidents led to a German recall for suspension modifications to be made, ESP system and a rear spoiler to be fitted. Some doubt as to whether these accidents were caused by the car or by lack of skill. A new hood for the Roadster costs £5,000.

What to watch out for: The car's history. Many are grey imports and it's important to know what you are paying for and pay accordingly. Some doubts as to longevity of the 225 bhp engine. Anything left on the rear parcel shelf could shatter the glass rear window of the Roadster when the hood is electrically lowered. It can't be replaced and means a new hood at £5k.

Recalls: All 2,430 official UK imports recalled to Germany for extensive modifications to be made, including the fitting of ESP stability and traction control and a rear spoiler. Work took several weeks. Owners were supplied with an A4 courtesy car. Source *Auto Express* 16/2/2000. Official recall notice issued 17/4/2000.

AUSTIN (ROVER)

Maestro (1983–1995)

What's good: Practical size, practical shape, very economical Perkins Prima DI and TDI engines. 2.0 litre MG version by far the best. MG Maestro Turbo a bit of a hooligan. Amazingly, you can still buy 'new' 1.3s, built from CKD kits originally sent to Bulgaria and assembled with RHD and catalytic converters by Ian Yarsley of Parkway Service Station, Ledbury, for a reasonable £5,300, tel: 01531 632320. (Also in LHD from Lifestyle Garages, Fuengirola, Malaga, Spain, tel: 00 345 952 580 077.)

What's bad: Tin shed construction. 'Red Robbo' build quality. Antediluvian 'A' Series 1.3 litre engine. 1.3s are surprisingly horrible to drive – worse than you would ever have imagined.

What to watch out for: Rust in body seams. Water leaks. Dodgy engine management systems. Oil leaks from all engines. Core plug problems with 1.3. Avoid the MG 1600 Maestro due to hopeless twin-carb set-up. 1600s and 2000s need regular cambelt replacement.

Metro (1980–1990)

What's good: Quite tough. Will still drag themselves along when little more than a crumbling shell. MG Metro quite well done and fun to drive. Clever separate double-folding rear seats give good luggage space. Driving position can be adapted to suit six footers. (For Rover K Series Metro, see 'Rover'.)

What's bad: Ugly (apart from MG). Parts-bin stop-gap model – more a tribute to expediency than proper all-new design. Rust badly at the front. Many began their lives with driving schools or as panda cars. Fuel splashes out of low-set filler onto rear n/s tyre. Old now, so pay no more than banger money.

What to watch out for: Rust in front bib, down front wings, in sills, in floorpan, in doors and in all body seams. Look for engine oil leaks from cylinder head gasket, water leaking from core plugs. Jumping out of second gear due to selector collar moving down rod. Clonking drive-shafts. Rattling timing chains. Leaking radiators and water pumps. Don't believe that they can do 10,000 miles between oil changes. Some were 'exported' to Jersey then re-registered in UK as a year younger than they really are. The last 1.0 and 1.3 'A' Series 3-door Metros had fuel tank filler directly over the rear wheel instead of in front.

Mini (1959–2000)

What's good: Classic 40-year-old design. Driving position can be adapted to suit six-footers. Outlived the Metro. Lots of specials about, some with Jack Knight 5-speed manual boxes which are good but very noisy. AP autobox works well if the combined engine/gearbox oil is changed every six months without fail. If oil not changed, it can be a disaster. Retro 'Mini Seven' with 1959 style seats and painted cream dashboard launched Spring 2000. Prices cut to from £8,495 on 6/10/2000.

What's bad: Hard, bouncy ride (Alex Moulton has a new mod for this). Standard cars have just four gears. sited in the engine sump. Noisy drivetrain. Feels gutless. Prone to slipping clutch. Heavy steering on wide 12in wheels. Driving position feels strange (but is actually quite comfortable). They're so low, winter road salt gets everywhere and they rust badly underneath. Bumpers far too low to be of any use. Fell foul of EU emissions and safety laws from 2001, so production finally ended in September 2000. S and T platers 7th from bottom in 2001 Top Gear/JD Power Customer Satisfaction Survey.

What to watch out for: Rust in seams was always a Mini problem. Rust also found in sills, in area in front of the doors, in rear battery box and in rear subframes which can collapse. Early 'K reg' carb plus cat didn't work (insist on a new MOT if buying one). Water leaking from core plugs of ancient 'A' Series engine. Oil leaks. Head gasket problems ('mayonnaise' under oil cap may be gone gasket, may be from short runs). Noisy timing chain. Gears jump out of second due to internal selector collar moving down rod. Clonking drive-shafts. Wear on rear trailing arm bushes. Front tie bars can bend. Never buy a Mini without a good look underneath, preferably on a garage hoist. Be careful not to get conned into paying too much.

Recalls: 14/5/99: 5,000 Minis built from August 1999 recalled for rectification of a fault in the braking system causing it to lose fluid.

Montego (1984–1995)

What's good: Very sensible, practical estates (7-seat 'Countryman' quite sought-after). Not bad to drive. Economical Perkins Prima TDI engines. LX models had decent spec, but most lacked power steering. Diesel or catalysed 2.0 litre only from 1992K. Lots of owners loved the estates and mourn their passing.

What's bad: Rust in body seams. Hit-and-miss build quality of all but the last few years' production. Saloons difficult to re-sell for more than buttons. All are getting old and tired now.

What to watch out for: Cracked plastic bumpers. Fall-apart trim. Oil/water leaks from cylinder head gaskets. Cambelts need regular replacement. Valve gear wears on 'O' Series engines (if it's particularly quiet, it's about to give way). Same engine management foibles as Maestro. Petrol Turbo may spell trouble, but may have enjoyed doting enthusiast care. The last saloons went as special orders to taxi fleets and to the MOD, long since auctioned off.

BENTLEY

Arnage (1998 on)

What's good: BMW's relatively small but powerful 350 bhp/420 lb ft twin-turbo 4,398cc V8 engine and 5-speed auto in a very British body. Optional 6,750cc Cosworth V8 from Turbo RT offers staggering 400 bhp and 619 lb ft torque with tougher GM 4-speed autobox.

What's bad: Doomed wedding between Rolls Royce and BMW before VW turned up like Dustin Hoffman in 'The Graduate' and whipped the bride away. Values drop like a spanner down a lift-shaft. Power characteristics of twin turbo BMW V8 disliked by traditionalist customers.

What to watch out for: Thinking you want one, when it probably isn't a very good idea at all.

Recalls: 1999: possible wiring fault in heated seat circuit. 22/3/2000: fuel return pipe may be routed too close to exhaust manifold which could lead to fuel igniting. Routing of pipe on 64 cars to be checked and modified if necessary.

Mulsanne and Turbo

What's good: Image. Huge performance from Turbo versions. Stiffer suspension than Rolls Royce. Best colours: metallic bottle green or ink black. Gradually improved over the years with injection and ABS in October 1986, automatic ride control in 1987, four- rather then three-speed autobox in September 1991. Cats came in during June 1990, but were initially a no-cost option. Standard Brooklands has 226 bhp and 340 lb ft torque. Continental R had 385 bhp and 553 lb ft torque. Turbo RT from 1997 has all of 400 bhp and 580 lb ft torque. Continental T has a truly awesome 420 bhp, no less than 619 lb ft torque, and handles its power and bulk very well.

What's bad: Thirst. Stink of cigar smoke clings to the headlining. The Labour Government might ban them. Resentful drivers don't let you out of side roads, particularly during recessions. Apt to get vandalised with rusty nails or keys while parked. Trim choice may be in bad taste. White or cream paint is hideous and suitable only for wedding hire.

What to watch out for: Anything over £15,000 must have a proper Rolls Royce dealer or Rolls Royce specialist history. The engine is an old fashioned pushrod V8, so you don't want to hear ticking tappets or see any blue smoke from the exhaust pipe. Make sure the suspension is not unduly wallowy. Check expensive tyres for tread depth and uneven wear. With so much weight to stop, turbos can be heavy on their brakes, so check for signs of warp on your test drive. Best to have the car inspected by a different Rolls Royce specialist from the one who's selling it.

Recalls: 1997 (Bentley Azure): 101 cars recalled due to danger of fire from a short circuit. 1997 (Rolls/Bentley general): 29 LHD cars found to have potentially defective braking system.

BMW

3-Series E30 (1983–1991)

What's good: Nice looking. 318iS, 320i, 325i and M3 still nice to drive. Some galvanised panels from 1988. American spec 325i auto only car I've ever driven with more than 1,000,000 miles on the clock and it still ran to 6,000 rpm with no trouble. 136 bhp chain cam 16v M42 powered 318iS is already achieving classic status.

What's bad: Getting old now. 316 and 318 relatively slow and over-rated. Many drivers not ready for oversteer, especially in the wet. No room in the back of two-door versions with big front seats. All models apart from 318iS and M3 had timing belts which need to be replaced every 3 years or 36,000 miles without fail.

What to watch out for: Clocking. Rust in early cars. Make sure cambelts and tensioners were recently changed. Cylinder head studs of 6-cylinder engines can shear. Heads of 6-cylinder cars can also crack. Prime candidate for fully synthetic oil (engine won't last forever without it). Check for repaired accident damage. Most convertibles have been 'customised' in questionable taste. Some nice, obviously well cared for M3s are coming over from Germany – and M3s are all LHD anyway. (It's very hard to find a genuine old 3-Series these days.)

Recalls: 1998: 170,000 E30s recalled because radiator cap pressure valve may seize up and over-pressurise cooling system, leading to coolant leak and steaming up inside car

3-Series E36 (1991–1998)

What's good: 170 bhp 323i is a strong performer also capable of delivering excellent mid-30s mpg. 6-cylinder cars have brilliant brakes. 140 bhp 318iS coupe and run-out special 318iS saloon by far the best 4-cylinder cars. Impressive build quality. Older iron block chain cam 325 twin-cam longest-lived of all. Generally reliable.

What's bad: Average performance in NCAP crash tests. 4-cylinder disc/drum set ups nothing like as good as 6-cylinder's discs (318iS

1.9s had discs all round). 316i and 318i saloons over-rated, under powered and pretty ordinary to drive. Non-M42 8-valve four-cylinder engines had timing belts up to September 1993 – chains thereafter. Some M52 6-cylinder 320is, 323is and 328is have suffered premature bore wear. Early E36s suffered poor quality trim. Later 3-year warranty requires expensive top-up to be comprehensive.

What to watch out for: Clocked mega mile ex-fleet cars (not all fleets register their mileages on disposal). Lots of early E36 3-Series suffered premature dashboard failure, so mileage on the clock may not be the mileage on the car. Earlier 4-cylinder cars still had cambelts which need changing every 3 years or 36,000 miles. Service indicator can be reset with £30 tool. Kerbed alloys may indicate front suspension damage from uncaring company driver. Lift carpets to check for result of rainwater leaks through screen seals (condensation inside windows a sure sign of this). M52-engined 320i, 323i and 328i from December 1994/April 1995 may suffer premature bore wear due to high amounts of sulphur in some UK petrol. Solved by replacement block with steel-lined bores. 328is from April 1998 and 323is from September 1998 fitted with 'EU3' steel lined bores. Front suspension lower ball joints and inner bushes wear, but are comparatively cheap to replace. A full BMW-dealer service history should tell you all recall work has been carried out. Service light indicator can easily be re-set, so a paid invoice is the only guarantee of a recent service. Check tool kit is all there.

Recalls: 1997 (E36 from January 1996): tighten stub axle bolts. 1997 (E36 built Feb '91–Dec '94: 77,000 cars): possibility of corroded steering shafts. 1997 (M3): faulty bearings in Variable Valve Timing mechanism can deposit shards of metal in engine. Official recall. 400 cars affected. 1998: E36s built before Nov '94 recalled to fit new radiator cap.

3-Series E36 Compact (1994 on)

What's good: As E36, but lighter and therefore quicker. 1.9 litre twin cam 140 bhp 318Ti quickest of all. No RHD sixes or 'M' versions in the UK so drivers less likely to be branded as status seekers. 17th from top in 'R' reg JD Power Customer Satisfaction Survey.

What's bad: As E36. Has simpler rear suspension based on E30 3-Series. Six-cylinder 323i engine available in LHD only. Later 2nd and 3rd year dealer warranty requires expensive top up to be effective.
What to watch out for: As E36.
Recalls: 1997 (E36 from January 1996): tighten stub axle bolts. 1997 (E36 – 77,000 cars): possibility of corroded steering shafts. 1998: compacts built before Nov '94 recalled to fit new radiator cap (very few cars involved, as Compact not launched until Sept '94).

3-Series E46 (1998 on)

What's good: Fairly close to perfection. More comfortable and refined than E36. Good body control. 'Cornering Brake Control' makes it very safe. Up to 193 bhp in standard range at launch, but 328i replaced by 231 bhp 330i in UK in July 2000. All have steel bore liners eliminating problems of previous Nickasil-lined all-alloy blocks. Same 2.0 litre direct injected diesel as Rover 75, with 136 bhp instead of Rover's 116 bhp. Excellent secondary safety features. 2-door version arrived in spring 1999; Touring in autumn 1999; 323i cabrio in spring 2000. Cabrio has very little 'scuttle shake'. 184 bhp 330D, rated by Stephen Sutcliffe of Autocar as 'the best 3-Series, period'; offers the best combination of performance, handlng and fuel economy in the business (top speed 143 mph, as timed by French police near Montpellier with Jenson Button driving). New 2-door M3 boasts 340 bhp and is great fun to drive with the traction control turned off. Almost as quick on a twisting road as a Mitsubishi Lancer EVO V1. Underpowered 1.9 litre engine of 318i saloon to be replaced by new British built 143bhp 2.0 litre NG4 unit as from November 2001 when the model will be facelifted.
What's bad: Lacks character, and visual impact of the Alfa 156. Performance and driving pleasure blunted compared to the best E36s. 'Cornering brake control' can take over – but does, of course, make the car safer in unskilled hands when a corner tightens up unexpectedly. Heavier, so uses more fuel than E36. Much criticism of poor-quality conversion to RHD. Have not been entirely trouble free. Side repeater indicators pop out and damage the front wings. 3-year warranty requires expensive top up to be comprehensive in

2nd and 3rd years. Reports of a thermostat problem with 318i models; replacement parts on back order as much as 7 weeks so cars were being run without thermostat cores which meant no climate control. Heater fan resistors can fail leaving fan only running at full speed but BMW aware of this and will meet cost even though not covered by 2nd and 3rd year standard dealer warranty. Steptronic auto severely increases fuel consumption of 330D by around 25%.

What to watch out for: First year's RHD production was sold out and some people paid premiums to get cars. This was not reflected in used values. 316 and 318 not powerful enough.

Recalls: 1999 (E46 from April 1998): safety recall over failure of brake pedal clip which can allow the pedal to become disconnected, and over-sensitive side airbag trigger switches. 15/12/1999: (E46 built Sept/Oct 1999): brake light switch may fail leading to brake lights flickering or failing and switch overheating. New switches to be fitted. 3/11/2000: 887 E46 models with alloy wheels built 14/9/2000 – 7/10/2000 recalled because inside rims of wheel could have been damaged when tyres were fitted.

3-Series E46 Compact (2001 on)

What's good: As E46, but lighter and therefore quicker. Will eventually get UK-built NG4 1.8 and 2.0 litre fours, a 170 bhp 2.2 litre six and the E36/E46 Z beam rear axle. Launch engines will range from 116bhp 1.8 NG (badged 316ti) with 133 lb ft torque giving EU combined economy of 40.9 mpg and 2.5 litre 192bhp '325ti' giving combined economy of 31.7mpg. 140bhp 2.0 litre NG engine (badged 318ti), 105bhp 1.6 litre and 146bhp 2.0 litre diesel due late 2001. Will eventually be a 220bhp version of the new 2.0 litre four cylinder NG engine.

What's bad: Too soon to say. UK sales put back from March 2001 to September 2001.

What to watch out for: Too soon to say.

5-Series E60 (2003 on)

What's good: First spy pictures starting to appear of the new Five. Predicted to have angled headlights, a bit like the original Mondeo and a very squared off rump.

What's bad: Far too soon to say.

What to watch out for: Far too soon to say.

5-Series E34 (1987–1996)

What's good: Replaced square rigged E28 model. Decent quality. Good looks. Good ride and handling. Later chain-cam, iron block 2.0 litre and 2.5 sixes the best engines, but powerful 535i still impresses. All twin-cam engines from 1990 have timing chains rather than belts. Touring model is a practical estate car. 3.8 litre M5 the top performer.

What's bad: Premature bore wear in 'M60' 530i and 540i V8s and M52 engined 520i. Low inertia 4-cylinder 518i OK in town, but not strong enough for heavy motorway use and can wear rapidly. Old single cam 525i, 530i and 535i engines all need cambelt replacement every 3 years or 36,000 miles. 5-speed auto not liked by autobox specialists.

What to watch out for: Electronically 'corrected' odometer/on-board computer (clockers sometimes steal one of the chips). Accident damage. Electric window problems. Faked service indicator. Whining manual gearbox can last for years but expensive to fix. Slurry autoboxes with neglected ATF and filter changes. Accident damage to M5s. Earlier model, less powerful, imported LHD M5s. Smoke from worn valve stem seals. Overheating from cracked cylinder heads. 'Problem' M60 V8s. Duff catalytic converters. Smoking 1.8s (valve stem seals). Noisy 12-valve sixes. Misfires from faulty integrated coil units on later 24v. Rear subframe rubbers (MOT failure point – £200 to put right). Damage to front suspension and steering (look for uneven tyre wear). Duff ABS. Service light indicator can easily be re-set, so a paid invoice is the only guarantee of a recent service. Check tool kit is all there.

Recalls: 1998: 5s built 1988–Nov '94 recalled to fit new radiator cap.

5-Series E39 (1996 on)

What's good: Great looks. 528i provides huge feelgood factor. Decent economy from 528i and 523i. Petrol V8s overkill, but 4,398cc M62 540i can be had with six-speed manual. Top model is 5.0 litre 32-valve 400 bhp M5. Four Star NCAP crash test rating, but worst in group for pedestrian safety. Quiet, refined, powerful 184 bhp 3.0 litre diesel automatic from Spring 1999 the best car in the range. New 163 bhp 525D arrived November 2000 along with new 2.2 litre and 192bhp 2.5 litre petrol engines, made in the UK. 18th from top in 'R' reg JD Power Customer Satisfaction Survey. S and T reg cars came 9th in 2001 Top Gear/JD Power Customer Satisfaction Survey. Not due to be replaced by new E60 5-Series until 2003.

What's bad: Have been some quibbles about build quality and paint. Dodgy door seals. Electrical niggles. Engine gasket leaks. Wipers set for LHD. Old 2.5 litre diesel not significantly more economical than petrol, so best avoided. V8s not worth the extra. 2.8iSE is as far as you need to go. Franchised dealers know how to charge. 2nd and 3rd year dealer warranty requires expensive top up to be comprehensive. Problem with combined navigation and telephone system of facelift 5-Series. The phones don't work and owners are being issued with hand mobiles until the fault can be corrected.

What to watch out for: Repaired accident damage. Excessively high franchised dealer prices for over-specified cars. 523i, 528i, 530i and 540i may suffer premature bore wear due to high amounts of sulphur in some UK petrol. Solved by replacement block with steel-lined bores on sixes, 'Alusil'-lined bores on V8s. Production from September 1998 fitted with 'EU3' steel- or Alusil-lined bores. Check tool kit is all there. Service light indicator can easily be re-set, so a paid invoice is the only guarantee of a recent service.

Recalls: 15/12/1999: (E39 built Sept/Oct 1999): brake light switch may fail leading to brake lights flickering or failing and switch overheating. New switches to be fitted.

7-Series E32 (1987–1994)

What's good: High-mileage six-cylinder 730i and 735iSE can be real bargains. Parts prices quite reasonable. Very luxurious.

What's bad: V12 750 guzzles fuel. V8s may use oil.

What to watch out for: Avoid lower spec trim unless you like cloth interiors. Aircon system problems. Bore liner degradation in aluminium V8s. Electrical glitches. Check the on-board computer carefully (see 5-Series). Make sure the heater fan works on all speeds because replacing the resistors involved removing the dash which is a TWO DAY job. Suspension sags eventually. Make sure the ABS light goes on, then off, at the right time. Try to find one with BMW service history; if not consistent specialist history. 1998: 7s built 1988–Nov '94 recalled to fit new radiator cap.

7-Series E38 (1994 on)

What's good: More 'modern' looking than predecessor. 728i capable of 28–30 mpg. Better ride. Luxurious and capable. V8s re-engined M60 2,997cc 730i V8 replaced by M62 3,498cc 735i and M60 3,982cc 740i replaced by 4,398cc M62 740i in early 1996. 15th from top in 'R' reg JD Power Customer Satisfaction Survey (but well below Jaguar XJ8). S and T reg cars came fourth in 2001 Top Gear/ JD Power Customer Satisfaction Survey.

What's bad: Not a big improvement on predecessor. Premature bore wear can be a problem on the earlier engines. Heavy tyre wear. 2nd and 3rd year dealer warranty requires expensive top up to be comprehensive. New car due end of 2001.

What to watch out for: Be very wary of M60 730i and 3,982cc 740i V8s (the engines that were dropped in 1996). Some unsold 'P' platers still had the old engines. 728i may also suffer bore liner degradation. Check all electrics, computer (see 5-Series) and aircon system carefully. Check for duff cats, condensation corroded rear silencers from chauffeured cars. Chauffeured cars also most likely to suffer premature bore wear due to long periods spent idling. Automatic transmission specialists don't like the 5-speed autobox. Solved by replacement block with steel-lined bores. UK imports from March 1998 fitted with steel- or Alusil-lined bores, but grey imports from other markets may not be. 1998: new 7s built before Nov '94 recalled to fit new radiator cap (very few cars involved, because new 7 not launched until August 1994). Electrical fault in rear tail lights causes the contact between bulb holder and bulb to erode and contact to be lost. BMW replacements from a dealer are £280 a side, fitted.

Recalls: 15/12/1999: (E38 built Sept/Oct 1999): brake light switch may fail leading to brake lights flickering or failing and switch overheating. New switches to be fitted.

7-Series (Summer 2001 on)

What's good: All new 7 Series with new 'iDrive' dashboard ergonomics which separate the cabin into a 'comfort area' and a 'driving area'. Most secondary functions are operated by a single central controller and the result is a big reduction in the number of buttons and switches. A central monitor displays the various functions and chosen settings. All the controls in the 'comfort area' of the car can be operated by either driver or front seat passenger.Gear selection of new six-speed automatic is controlled via a steering column stalk plus Steptronic buttons on the steering wheel rim. The ignition switch is controlled by a new electronic key and the engine is started and stopped by a button, like that of the Renault Laguna II. Launch choice of two V8s: a 272bhp 3.6 with 256 lb ft (360Nm) torque, or a 333bhp 4.4 with 332 lb ft (450Nm) torque. Combining VANOS variable valve timing with new Valvetronic technology and variable intake manifolding improves both power output and economy. Combined fuel consumption for the new 735i is 26.4mpg and for the 745i is 25.9mpg. Both cars are speed limited to 155mph with the 735i getting to sixty in 7.3 seconds and the 745i managing it in 6.1 seconds. Other engines to include new 3.0 straight six and top of the range 6.0 litre 400bhp V12. More at www.bmw.co.uk.

What's bad: Its looks won't be to everyone's taste at first, but will probably grow on people.

What to watch out for: Too soon to say.

X5 4x4 (2000 on)

What's good: BMW's own Range Rover with 231bhp 3.0 litre petrol or 184bhp diesel sixes and 286 bhp 4.4 litre V8 option. First reports say it is leagues ahead of all other 4x4s as a road car. Better than a Range Rover, Discovery or Mercedes ML. 4.4 came first; 3.0 petrol in Spring 2001 priced from £33,000; diesel summer 2001 similarly priced; 347bhp X5 4.6iS due in UK late 2001 will be capable of 0–60 in 6.5 seconds and 150mph, at a price of £49,950. Capable off road as well as on the road.

What's bad: 4.4 priced from a high £46,300 and not likely to be economical. 2nd and 3rd year dealer warranty requires expensive top-up to be comprehensive. On road handling of 3.0 petrol model not as good as arch rival Lexus RX300. Feels top heavy. 3.0 can use any petrol from 87Ron to German 99Ron but only develops 231bhp on 98Ron, which is no longer officially available in the UK.

What to watch out for: Too soon to say.

Z1 Roadster (1986–1991)

What's good: Classic from day one. Groovy drop down doors. Sophisticated multi-link rear suspension. Old iron block, single cam 171 bhp BMW six.

What's bad: LHD only. Many imported used from Germany so difficult to check history, and may be clocked. 'Old' single cam 325i engine needs regular cambelt changes, can suffer cracking of cylinder head. Panels hard to replace. Prices still hover around £20,000.

What to watch out for: Badly fitting panels hiding old accident damage. Make sure the door mechanisms work properly. Cambelts need replacing every 3 years or 36,000 miles.

Recalls: 1998: all Z1s recalled to fit new radiator cap.

Z3 Roadster (1997 on)

What's good: Very compact. Snug cockpit. Doesn't buffet badly up to 80 mph. 140 bhp 1.9 auto available. 190 bhp 2.8 litre six replaced by new 231 bhp 3.0 litre six in Spring 2000. 321 bhp 3.2 litre 'M' version almost too powerful. American built. New small engine range from Spring 1999, with 115 bhp 1.9 litre 'four' and 150 bhp 2.0 litre 'six'.

What's bad: 115 bhp and 140 bhp 1.9 litre fours not really enough except for cruisers. No clever roof like the SLK. Not very sporty to drive. Soft-tops can leak. Optional hardtops offer poor seal for side windows – modification kit available from early 1999. Z3 'M' coupe may be fast but is aesthetically hideous. 2nd and 3rd year dealer warranty requires expensive top up to be comprehensive.

What to watch out for: Many RHDs were personally imported to avoid long delivery dates and don't have UK 3-year dealer warranty. 2.8s imported from other markets may have vulnerable Nickasil-lined bores rather than steel-lined bores. Check fuel tank for damaged from bottoming out (very expensive to replace). Front suspension lower ball joints and inner bushes wear, but are comparatively cheap to replace. Service light indicator can easily be re-set, so a paid invoice is the only guarantee of a recent service. Check tool kit is all there.

Z8 Roadster (2000 on)

What's good: Very fast 400 bhp V8 'retro' roadster, as driven by James Bond in limited production at BMW's Dingolfing plant.

What's bad: Expensive. Likely to blow your hairpiece off.

What to watch out for: Too soon to say.

CADILLAC

Seville STS (1998 on)

What's good: Big, squat car with reasonably restrained styling. Loaded with kit. Looks best in black. Very comfortable. Powerful, low-maintenance 305 bhp 4.6 litre V8. Not bad to drive, with strong acceleration, decent steering 'feel', good handling, nicely calculated traction control and anti-skid. Brilliant Bose stereo system (possibly the best standard in-car system available). EC fuel consumption: 13.7/27.2/19.9, so 20 mpg possible. Automatic parking brake release. 3-year, 60,000-mile warranty with 24-hour assistance. Electrically folding door mirrors.

What's bad: Severe tyre roar. Looks a bit like a larger Rover 800 4-door. Variable-ratio steering loses 'feel' on very tight corners. Some trim not up to the standards of a luxurious European car. Garish chromed alloys. Indicator switch on the right of the column.

What to watch out for: Nearside suspension damage by drivers not able to judge the width. Possibility of having previously been owned by undesirable people with enemies.

CHEVROLET

Camaro (1999 on)

What's good: Relatively cheap starter price of £17,950 for 3.8 litre V6 auto. 3.8 convertibles from £21,500. But 284 bhp 6-speed 5.7 Z28 a much hunkier choice at £22,725 and can be surprisingly economical, with 23 mpg obtained by *Sunday Telegraph*'s Neil Lyndon.

What's bad: 5-speed manual box adds £1,000 to price of V6. Crude, cheapskate interiors. LHD only. Difficult to see out of and to park.

What to watch out for: Parking dings and dongs. Lack of proper servicing.

Corvette (1999 on)

What's good: Really quick and relatively cheap at prices from £36,705 on the road. (Convertible dearer at £40,605.) 345 bhp and 356 lb ft torque give over 170 mph and 0–60 in 5.3 seconds. Surprisingly economical with over 20 mpg easy to achieve. 385 bhp ZO6 model from 2000 gives 4-second 0–60.

What's bad: Six-speed manual box costs an extra £1,150. LHD only.

What to watch out for: Parking scratches and cracks in fibreglass body. Lack of proper servicing.

CHRYSLER

'New' Neon (1999 on)

What's good: Well-equipped and reasonably priced from £10,995 OTR with standard aircon, standard electrically folding door mirrors and standard 3-year warranty. 131 bhp twin cam 16v 2.0 litre engine now smoother. £13,495 LX model loaded with goodies such as leather interior trim, wood trim, cruise control (with auto), 15in alloys, ABS and Thatcham Category-2 immobiliser. Optional no-extra-cost auto.

What's bad: Autobox still had just three speeds at launch, but has had the Euro spec four speed box from 2001 model-year.

What to watch out for: See original Neon.

Jeep Cherokee (1993 on)

What's good: Powerful yet simple 4.0 litre straight six. European VM 2.5 litre turbodiesel. Fairly compact. Much lower than Discovery and Range Rover so better in multi-story carparks. Facelifted and updated in April 1997.

What's bad: 2.5 litre petrol engine noisy and far from effortless. The model was on the LHD market for many years before it came to the UK. Small luggage area, especially with spare wheel in place. Spare wheel creates a rear blind spot. Have been automatic gearbox and transfer case problems. Lots came onto the market all at once, part-exchanged for Voyagers. Headlamp self-levelling motors cost £265 + VAT a side and are an MOT requirement.

What to watch out for: Automatic transmission problems (where fitted). Old LHD imports undermining RHD values. If buying an import, make sure it had four-wheel-drive (they didn't all have). Look for oil leaks from gearbox, transfer case and axles. Check steering box mounting carefully. Check tyres for uneven wear. Check electrics such as headlamp self-levelling motors. Cylinder head problems with VM diesels up to 1997.

Recalls: 1997 (January 1993–1997 model-year RHD; 19,200 cars): check for stress fractures around steering box mounting. 1997: 567 cars built before Sept '96 recalled due to possibility of 'inadvertent deployment of airbags'. 1998: further recall over steering box mounting problem. 2/8/2000: 651 Cherokees recalled because airbag warning light and or airbags may deploy without warning. Airbag control unit to be replaced with modified type. Check coolant level and look under oil cap of diesel for mayonnaise indicating head problems.

Jeep Grand Cherokee (1994–1999)

What's good: See Cherokee. Slightly more room inside than Cherokee. First imports were 5.2 litre V8s with 212 bhp in LHD and auto only. 4.0 litre RHD straight sixes came in January 1996 followed by a 114 bhp VM-powered 2.5 diesel in February 1997. 5.7 litre 237 bhp V8 from October 1997, still LHD auto only. American 'luxury' interiors.

What's bad: Still comparatively small inside. Old LHD 'special order' 5,216cc (212 bhp) and 5,899cc (237 bhp) V8s very 'American'. Isolate the driver from what's going on. Only do 13–26 mpg. V8 values likely to fall heavily as fuel taxes increase. Lack of crumple zones means it can be severely damaged by hard impacts at speeds as low as 5 mph. Headlamp self-levelling motors cost £265 + VAT a side and are an MOT requirement.

What to watch out for: See Cherokee. Possible head problems with VW diesel.

Recalls: 1997: 2,536 cars recalled due to danger of fire from a short circuit in heated seat wiring.

Jeep Grand Cherokee (1999 on)

What's good: Restyled, re-shelled Grand Cherokee. Slightly more room inside than Cherokee. New model including RHD 4.7 litre 217 bhp V8 from spring 1999. New 5-cylinder 3.1 litre VM turbodiesel with 283 lb ft torque for Y2K.

What's bad: Still comparatively small inside. Grille looks like the frightening central heating furnace in 'Home Alone'.

What to watch out for: See Cherokee.

Jeep Wrangler (1993 on)

What's good: Powerful but simple 4.0 litre six cylinder engines, sixes usually automatic. Completely revised in May 1997, round headlights replaced square eyes; coil springs replaced leaf springs. Still a fashion accessory. Demi Moore's chosen mount in 'St Elmo's Fire' and the car in which Alicia Silverstone memorably failed her driver's test in 'Clueless'.

What's bad: 2.5 litre four cylinder petrol engine noisy, but comes with a manual shifter. On road handling not great. Older, leaf sprung examples with PAS are pretty horrible to drive. Standard weather equipment is not up to much and a fibereglass hardtop with fibreglass doors is highly advised for winter driving.

What to watch out for: Damage from off-roading. Carefully check front axle swivel joints for pitting and oil leaks.

Neon (1996–1999)

What's good: Well-equipped. Good features such as electrically folding door mirrors very helpful in multi-story carparks. ABS and aircon standard on LX. Reasonably priced by UK standards. Good paint finish, especially metallics. 3-year warranty.

What's bad: Coarse engine. Autobox has only three speeds but better suited to engine than manual. Not as fuel efficient as a Mondeo. Huge diameter rear coil 'bedsprings' intrude into boot space. Rear backrests flop down crudely onto squabs. Seating material and interior plastics a bit iffy and more suited to a £7,000 car, which the Neon is in the USA. Reports of cylinder head gasket failure at around three years old. Possible problem with the front wheel universal joints and gaiters if excessive lock has been used.

What to watch out for: Kerbing damage. Damage to the mirror mechanisms (£350+ to replace). Tears in seat trim, especially flimsy backs of front seats. Check coolant level and look under oil cap for emulsified oil indicating head gasket failure. Check front driveshaft gaiters for splits as UJs can wear out very rapidly if grease is lost.

PT Cruiser (2000 on)

What's good: Brave, retro-styled estate car from the people who brought you the Prowler and are now in league with Mercedes Benz. Based on the new Neon with better rear suspension, stronger 140 bhp engine and practical interior that can even take surf boards. A bigger success than the new Beetle in the USA. Short throw 5-speed manual or 4-speed auto. Will get excellent MB 2.2litre CDI diesel engine. Practical with big, strong, impact absorbing black bumbers, removable rear seats, three proper rear belts and plenty of luggage space. Decent ride and handling. UK prices from £14,995, but Euro sourced £15,995 Touring models discounted to £14,295. Huge fun. See road test at www.honestjohn.co.uk

What's bad: Not everyone will go for the styling. Long waiting list could be replaced by oversupply (already building 180,000 a year in Mexico and planning to build 310,000 a year once Austrian factory comes on line). Performance hampered a bit by the weight of the body and only does 28mpg. Retro styling might actually date in a few years time.

What to watch out for: Too soon to say.

Voyager (1997–2001)

What's good: Very good looking, very 'big' MPV from the company that has made more MPVs than anyone else. Rear seat rolls out on castors. 2.5 litre VM turbodiesel does 30 mpg and has plenty of torque to pull the vast Grand Voyager body along. Excellent cruise control.

What's bad: Inconvenient 2-2-3 seating arrangement with back three seats on a single bench which is heavy to remove. 2.0 litre 131 bhp Neon engine with manual box not really man enough (3.3 litre autos more suited to the job). Terrible roadholding and handling on tight turns. Poor two-star performer in NCAP crash tests (0 points front impact; 14 points side impact). More than its fair share of electrical gremlins.

What to watch out for: Damage from heavy use and uncontrolled children. School-run kerbing damage by drivers used to Cherokees.

Recalls: 1998: voluntary European recall of old (squarer shape)

model due to possible problems with rear door latches. 2000: 15,567 UK-market current-shape vehicles recalled because excessively long parking brake cable leads to cable stretch, making brake very difficult to apply. Announced Radio 5 News 3/5/2000. Wordwide recall of 3.3 litre model affecting 1,400,000 vehicles built between 1996 and 1999 to check for fuel pipes leaking in extremely hot weather which has led to a spate of vehicle fires.

Voyager (from 2001)

What's good: Revised Voyager for 2001. Voyager is 4,803mm long, 1,997mm wide and 1,749mm high. Grand Voyager is 5,094mm long and offers much more luggage space. All are more spacious than before with better handling and stronger body structures for better crash safety. New engines include a 2,499cc twin-cam petrol four with 142bhp and 167 lb ft (226Nm) torque at 4,000 rpm (manual only); a 3,301cc petrol V6 with 172bhp and 210 lb ft (285Nm) torque at 4,000 rpm (automatic only); and a 2,500cc twin-cam diesel four with 140bhp at 4,000 rpm and 230 lb ft (312Nm) torque at 1,800rpm (manual only). Prices from £18,495 on the road for the 2.4SE manual to £28,995 for the 3.3 Limited. Cheapest diesel is the 2.5CRD at £19,695. Usual three-year warranty applies.

What's bad: Too soon to say.

What to watch out for: Too soon to say.

CITROËN

2CV (to 1990)

What's good: Good fun in its day, especially on empty summer country roads and in and around holiday resorts. Easy to appreciate the design. You can still have a laugh in them. 2CV experts say that all since the early '70s are happy on unleaded.

What's bad: It's had its day. Dreadful to drive in town and to park in multi-storeys. Can suffer severe chassis rust. Body also rusts, especially around fresh-air ventilator. Jobs like brakes very expensive (drive-shafts have to come off to replace front discs). Some 'beardy' and 'girlie' owners tend to neglect servicing or do it on the cheap. So flimsy, a crash in one is a terrifying thought.

What to watch out for: Chassis rot (galvanised chassis available, but expensive). Smoking engines. Clocking (oh, yes). Loose under-bonnet heater ducts. Ripped tops (but cheap to replace). Last of the line were built in Portugal and build quality of these was poor.

AX (1987–1997)

What's good: Chirpy, light to drive, economical. Cheap to run. 1.5 litre iron block diesel engine can be very long-lived if well maintained with regular oil, coolant, injector and cambelt changes. Also delivers 55–60 mpg. Front door pockets designed to take 2-litre bottles of wine.

What's bad: Very light build, so not good in a crash (especially early ones). Offset driving position. Fall-apart interior trim. Reports of premature bore wear on 1.5 diesels could be due to worn injectors washing out the bores.

What to watch out for: Any body rot will significantly weaken fairly feeble structure. Thin body panels easily dented. Worn engines start to rattle. Oil leaks are common. Smoking usually caused by more than just valve stem oil seals. Make sure the heater is not leaking. Also check that brakes stop the car straight and true.

Berlingo Multispace (1998 on)

What's good: Originally designed as a van on the ZX/306 floorpan with Peugeot 405 estate car rear suspension. Lots of good design points. Decent ride quality. Launched in UK in summer 1998 as Multispace with full-length electric fun-roof, bright colours and 1.8 litre 8-valve engine giving 100 mph. Relaunched spring 1999 at lower prices from £10,830 OTR with 1.4i engine. Sunroof, aircon, 1.8i or 1.9D engines now all extra-cost options. Further price cut down to £8,995 in spring 2000 for the 1.9XUD 3-door due to competition from the Renault Kangoo Combi. Relaunched for third time in summer 2000 as the Multispace Forte, now with twin rear sliding side doors, three three-point rear belts, multiplex wiring and cubbyholes everywhere including the rear floor from £9,495 for the 1.4i and £9,750 for the 1.9D. Handles well for a van (though not as much fun to drive as the Polo Caddy Combi). Excellent for gardeners, people with dogs and the elderly due to ease of ingress and egress. Sensibly priced Brotherwood conversion available for transporting the disabled in dignity. Price of perky new 1.4i Forte with aircon cut to bargain £8,995 on 30/09/2000. Three-year, 60,000-mile warranty announced 24/10/2000. Very highly recommended for the non status conscious.

What's bad: It's a van-based car, not a car-based van. 1998–2000 models only had three doors. Brakes aren't as good as you would expect on a car. Clutch a bit sharp on 1.4i and gearchange positive, but a bit obstructive. Carries no status at all.

What to watch out for: Nothing so far.

Recalls: 1/2/2000 (Sept/Oct 1999 build only): brake servo valve may fail, leading to loss of servo assistance. Inspect and possibly replace brake servo valve.

BX (1983–1993)

What's good: Excellent ride and handling. Light weight. Well designed. 1.4 was under-powered, but XU-engined cars good. Excellent estate. Diesel with PAS is the obvious choice. 1.9D will do 100 mph and 50 mpg. Height-adjustable suspension allows 'stilt effect' for floods or rough going. There was a very quick 16v version. 4x4 likely to become troublesome. Plastic bonnet and boot on all but last few years' production are light and don't rust. Suspension spheres easy and cheap to replace.

What's bad: Getting old. Not all 1980s BXs had PAS. Very light build quality. Brake pipes go. Many independent servicing dealers have moved on from BXs now.

What to watch out for: Clocking (there are plenty of BX diesels around with well over 200,000 miles under their wheels). Make all standard XU engine cambelt, cambelt end seal, coolant and cylinder head gasket checks. Clutch cables can pull through bulkhead. Make sure the brake pipes have been replaced (replacements were better protected and longer lasting). Plastic ends of car can hide rust underneath. The last BXs had steel bonnets.

C2 and C3 (from 2002)

What's good: New low price 'basic' model Citroën. Entry model to have 1.4 litre common-rail turbodiesel shared with Ford. Top model to have 110 bhp 1.6 16v. First spy pictures show very attractive three door model and completely different, more rounded five door.

What's bad: Too soon to say.

What to watch out for: Far too soon to say.

C4

What's good: Radically styled new car due to replace the boring looking Xsara in 2002. Very French, like the new Renaults. Should please Citroën fans.

What's bad: Too soon to say.

What to watch out for: Too soon to say.

C5 (2001 on)

What's good: New Citroën replaced the Xantia from April 2001. Larger car with much more interior space. Price range is around £14,500 to around £21,000. Underneath it is based on PSAs new

Platform 3 and incorporates Hydractive 3, Citroën's latest version of its active hydropneumatic suspension system which automatically lowers the car at speed and requires no maintenance for the first five years. Engine range begins with 112bhp 1.8 litre and 2.0 litre 136bhp fours. There will also be a 2.0 litre 143bhp Hpi petrol engine, a 210bhp 3.0 litre V6 petrol and a powerful 2.2 litre Hdi diese1. This impressive new motor puts out 136bhp at a low 4,000 rpm coupled with 234 lb ft torque (317 Nm) at 2,000 rpm. Dimensions are: length 4,618mm (15 feet 2 inches); width 1,770mm (5 feet 10 inches); height: 1,476mm (4 feet 10 inches); luggage capacity (rear seats up): 456 litres. Galvanized body. Three-year mechanical warranty. Estate version launched at Geneva Motor Show on 27th February uses hydractive suspension to lower the rear for easier loading. Estate is by far the best C5. 3-piece bumpers cheap to replace. For more details and driving impressions of C5 hatchbacks and estates models, see the two road tests at www.honestjohn.co.uk. More at www.citroen.co.uk.

What's bad: Bland looks compared to Mondeo and Laguna. Otherwise too soon to say. New 2.2 HDI not brilliantly economical with combined figure of 44.1mpg. Not as enjoyable to drive as the Xantia.

What to watch out for: Too soon to say.

Saxo (1997 on)

What's good: Bigger, better, stronger AX. Quite refined. 1.1 is very economical. 125bhp 1.6 VTS very quick. Seem to be pretty good and relatively problem-free for a Citroën. Good value by UK standards. 1.5 diesel does 55 mpg. Autumn 1999 facelift includes galvanised panels, now with 12-year no-perforation warranty. Most now have PAS apart from 1.1 base models. SXs have switchable passenger airbags. 1.1i LPG version available in Europe. Starter prices dropped to under £5,995 in spring 2000, including driver's airbag and radio/cassette. 1.6 VTR got boost to 100bhp for 2001 and now gets to 60 in 9.4 seconds for just £8,995. Saxo First got power boost from 1.0 litre to 1.1 litres and 60bhp for same low list price of £5,995. Three-year, 60,000-mile warranty announced October 2000.

What's bad: Twisted spine from offset driving position. 3-speed 1.6 automatic replaced by 3-speed 1.4 auto. Can suffer mechanical problems and unsympathetic dealers. Only two stars in Euro NCAP crash tests. ECU problems begining to be reported. Reports of premature bore wear on iron block 1.5Ds could be due to dirty or worn injectors washing out the bores. Saxo VTS can suffer same problem of water ingress to gearbox after driving through floodwater as Xantia and Synergie. S and T platers 14th from bottom in 2001 Top Gear/JD Power Customer Satisfaction Survey. In June 2001 Citroën was rated by Motor Warranty Direct as Britain's 3rd worst out of 22 marques for warranty claims (www.warrantydirect.co.uk.) 'Free' insurance now only for 22 to 80-year-olds.

What to watch out for: Two years free insurance made them attractive to 17-year-olds who may have crashed them. See Peugeot 106 for what to watch out for on VTR and VTS.

Recalls: 1997: faulty driver's seat catch on 3-door model. 1/2/2000 (Sept/Oct 1999 build only): brake servo valve may fail, leading to loss of servo assistance. Inspect and possibly replace brake servo valve.

Synergie (1995 on)

What's good: Good, well-planned, bright walk-through interior with dash-mounted gearshift. Nice trim colours. Compact for an MPV and easy to park. Sliding doors easy to get in and out of in tight parking spaces. Excellent, economical 110 bhp HDI diesel engine from autumn 1999. Similar Peugeot 806 was a Three-Star performer in NCAP crash tests (7 points front impact; 15 points side impact). 12-year body warranty from September 1999. Three-year, 60,000 mile warranty announced October 2000.

What's bad: Doesn't handle as well as Galaxy family. No automatics. Centre rear passenger only gets a lap belt. Flood water ingress to the gearbox is a problem, causing the box to seize. In June 2001 Citroën was rated by Motor Warranty Direct as Britain's 3rd worst out of 22 marques for warranty claims (www.warrantydirect.co.uk.)

What to watch out for: Some may be ex-rental or ex-taxi. Make sure sliding side doors open smoothly and don't stick. Check for uneven front tyre wear. Look for signs of having been overloaded. May have done a few Calais beer runs.

Xantia (1993–2000)

What's good: Good looking, 'different' hatchbacks and estates with excellent front-end grip, safe handling, fine ride quality out of town plus the ability to raise themselves on their suspension to clear obstacles and to sink down to the ground if required. Good rear legroom. Estates have three lap/diagonal rear belts. Suspension never goes baggy. Suspension spheres quick, easy and cheap to replace. 'N' reg on 16 valve 1.8 and 2.0 litre engines quite sporty but can use a bit of oil in valve stem lubrication. Facelift Feb '98 with 3-piece bumpers. Turbo-diesel automatic from Spring '98 a good cruiser. New HDI diesel engine from October 1998 best fuel miser in class. 12-year body warranty from September 1999.

What's bad: Hydraulic pumps can still go. ABS computers fail. Parts of more complex VSX and Activa suspension can stick. Average performance in NCAP crash tests. TD auto a bit high geared for town work (lingers in 2nd or 3rd). If clutch cable comes off at the pedal end, it's a long, tedious and expensive job to put right. Rate of depreciation can take you by surprise. Hatchbacks of Xantia estates apt to leak through wiper spindle seal. Early 'K' and 'L' reg Xantias fetching less than £1,000 at auction. New model due soon. Very heavy depreciation and difficult to sell. Flood water ingress to the gearbox is a problem, causing the box to seize.

What to watch out for: LX non-ABS models are the best used buy because there's less to go wrong. ABS computers are a common problem. Check spare wheel is in its underboot cradle and not nicked. Look for smoke from diesels – may be curable with a dose of injector cleaner and a new air filter. 1.6s likely to wear out first. If fitted with aircon, make sure it blows cold. If 2.0 litre petrol engine knocks, don't buy the car (see XM for reason).

Recalls: 1994 (May 1993–Oct 1994): parking brake mod.

XM (1990–2000)

What's good: Excellent ride and handling once you get to 'feel through' the steering to the front wheels. 2.1TD can be very economical and give quick journey times at 40 mpg. 2.5TD altogether more powerful, less economical. 1994 Mk II brought much higher-quality electrics. Best petrol engine is the 150 bhp 8 valve 2.0 litre turbo. Estates are very spacious and comfortable.

What's bad: Riddled with niggly problems and rattles prior to 'M' reg. Mark IIs from 'M' reg much better. Mk I V6 24v fast but not a success. Horrible American-style foot-operated parking brake. In June 2001 Citroën was rated by Motor Warranty Direct as Britain's 3rd worst out of 22 marques for warranty claims (www.warrantydirect.co.uk.)

What to watch out for: Where to start? Clutch problems (best replaced at a CitroÎn dealer), slurry automatics due to neglected ATF changes, dodgy electrics mainly due to poor contacts (solved on Mk II), ABS computer can give up, ABS pump will rust up inside if hydraulic fluid not changed frequently. Uneven tyre wear can mean serious chassis problems. Hard ride and excessive roll means suspension links have seized up. Brakes eat pads and discs will eventually wear. Make sure aircon blows cold. Listen for knocking from engines of 2.0 litre models (both 8v and 16v) due to design of piston skirts. If fault developed early, pistons were replaced FOC, but only when knocking became excessive.

Xsara (1997 on)

What's good: Bigger, more refined ZX. Much improved safety features. Ingenious (patented) side-impact protection. 3-Star above-average performance in NCAP crash testing. Good 1.8 litre 16-valve engine. Excellent ride quality and bump absorption. Sharp turn-in with enhanced rear steer effect (very little understeer). 2.0 litre 167 bhp coupe seriously quick and a fine, safe handler. Estates better than 5-door hatchbacks, with lots of room, better handling and no sacrifice in ride quality. Evergreen XUTD still good. New HDI diesel from early 1999 engine should be best in class. Three-piece bumpers cheap to replace. 12-year body warranty from September 1999. Major facelift in autumn 2000 made it much better looking, but slightly reminiscent of defunct Ford Scorpio. New 110 bhp 1.6 litre engine replaces old 1.6s and 1.8. SX with a/c and abs costs £11,995 after £1,000 cashback. Three-year 60,000-mile mechanical warranty announced 24/10/2000. New 137bhp 2.0 litre 16 valve engine available in coupe, 5-door and estate car bodies. Still a family car that offers good handling and driving pleasure. HDI 110 with 10.3 second 0–60, 54mpg and £110pa VED launched in May 2001 at £12,350 for the hatchback and £13,150 for the estate. Automatic gearbox option available on both at an extra £1,020.

What's bad: Nondescript looks of 5-door and coupe. Instrument bezel can reflect in screen. Only two three-point rear seatbelts. Model for model, lacks the equipment of equivalent Astras. Depreciates more quickly than class average. Fairly steep depreciation curve. ECU problems starting to be reported. In June 2001 Citroën was rated by Motor Warranty Direct as Britain's 3rd worst out of 22 marques for warranty claims (www.warrantydirect.co.uk.) Xsara to be replaced by radical new C4 in 2002.

What to watch out for: Check spare wheel is in its underboot cradle and not nicked.

Recalls: 1998: 14,000 owners of cars registered Sep '97–Feb '98 notified that may be a delay in airbag inflating in an accident. Also possibility of faulty seatbelt pretensioner. 2000: 1.8i models built April '97–May '98: possibility of underbonnet fuel leak. 1/2/2000 (Sept/Oct 1999 build only): brake servo valve may fail, leading to loss of servo assistance. Inspect and possibly replace brake servo valve. 12/6/2000: VIN VF7N*****367694 to VF7N*****367779626: passenger airbag 'off' switch may not de-activate airbag. If switch defective, to be replaced. 25/9/2000: 3,648 Xsaras built 7/2000 – 9/2000 recalled because front suspension ball joint clamp bolt hold may have been incorrectly machined leading to disengagement of the ball joint. Pivots replaced of necessary. 20/11/2000: 1,314 Xsara diesels built in 1999/2000 recalled due to possibility of failure of brake vacuum pump dog drive leading to loss of power assistance to brakes. Drive dog to be replaced on all Xsara diesels fitted with Magneti Marelli vacuum pumps.

Xsara Picasso (2000 on)

What's good: Xsara-based and by far the best looking of the new 5-seater MPVs. Also the best handling and most car-like to drive, with very little roll understeer. Excellent ride quality. Really pleasant to drive. Electro-galvanised body with 12-year warranty. Three full sized rear seats, each with its own lap/diagonal safety belt. 90 bhp 1.6i petrol, 115 bhp 1.8i 16v petrol, or 90 bhp 2.0 litre HDI. 1.8i will do over 60 mph in 2nd gear, but relaxed HDI engine suits the car best and can manage 50 mpg. 'Walk through' cabin allowing the driver to get out kerb-side or attend to a child in the rear seat. Huge boot. Optional full-length electric canvas sunroof. Galvanized body with 12-year warranty. Three-year, 60,000-mile dealer warranty announced 24/10/2000. Launch prices from £13,600 petrol and from £15,000 diesel, but 1.6LX on offer at Citroën dealers such as Lovekyn of Kingston-upon-Thames for £8,995 in late 2000. Very good four star NCAP crash safety rating announced 28/3/2001.

What's bad: Front window pillars can slightly obscure front three-quarter vision. Aircon £650 extra on base-spec LX models. A really tricky road will show up its handling limits, but still impressive for a mini MPV.

What to watch out for: Too soon to say.

Recalls: 25/9/2000: 3,648 Xsaras and Picassos built 7/2000 – 9/2000 recalled because front suspension ball joint clamp bolt hold may have been incorrectly machined leading to disengagement of the ball joint. Pivots replaced of necessity.

ZX (1992–1998)

What's good: Excellent ride and handling combination, second only to Peugeot 306. Comfortable and absorbs bumps well. Low used prices. 1.8 Furios can be spectacular bargains. 1.4 TU engines and diesels are the best buys. All capable of 150,000 miles plus if properly looked after. Non-turbo XUD capable of 50 mpg. Turbo XUD surprisingly quick. Sensible nearside-only electric door mirror.

What's bad: 1.6 is a bit of a camel, 1.8 less so. Turbo XUD not that economical – can drop to as little as 36 mpg. Boot not much bigger than Peugeot 205. Early front brake problems cured by modified callipers. Brake warning light very sensitive to low brake fluid level. If this happens with a diesel, which has a brake vacuum pump, disappearing brake fluid could leave you with no brakes. Brake master cylinders themselves also fail. Cambelts and camshaft end seals must be changed every 3 years and 36,000 miles. Coolant must be changed every two years to avoid cylinder head gasket problems. (Coolant is difficult to change without getting air-locks.) Radiators apt to fail every 3 years or so. Petrol models may have cat converter MOT test problems. Always difficult to sell and becoming increasingly so. In June 2001 Citroën was rated by Motor Warranty Direct as Britain's 3rd worst out of 22 marques for warranty claims (www.warrantydirect.co.uk).

What to watch out for: See above. 'J' reg ZXs could suffer front brake calliper problems cured by fitting later callipers (this will have been done to most of them). Some reports of sticking handbrakes, easily checked by seeing how easy the car is to push. Early Avantage diesels lacked power steering, as did early Avantage diesel estates which came out long after the hatch got PAS. 16v noisy, not really that quick and best avoided. Upholstery tears easily and is difficult to repair. Make sure all the electrics work. Insist on new MOT, especially if car is post-August 1992 and fitted with a cat. Check spare wheel is in its underboot cradle and not nicked. Look for engine oil leaks, gearbox oil leaks, coolant leaks from radiator and heater matrix, brake fluid leaks from rear brakes.

Recalls: 1994 (mostly Volcane, May 1992–Oct 1992, and 16v 1992–1994): Brake pipe chafing. 1996 ('facelift' model from June 1994): faulty seatbelt pretensioners and, on cars so fitted, faulty airbag sensors.

DAEWOO

Espero (1995–1997)

What's good: Lots and lots of car for the money. Even better used value than the Nexia and much better looking. 1.8 CDi has standard aircon which will always make it a good summertime seller. Makes a perfect replacement for those who mourn the passing of the Montego saloon. May have some of its original 3-year warranty left. Not my cup of tea, but cheap.

What's bad: Infra dig at first, but now accepted. Interior trim not as good as exterior of car. May suffer premature front tyre wear. Not great at fuel economy. Aircon has been known to pack up. Not worth much once 3-year warranties and service contracts have ended. P reg cars down to £1,000 to £1,500 at auction by mid 2001.

What to watch out for: Why bother with base spec 90 bhp 1.5GLXi when 95 bhp 1.8CDi is only a few hundred pounds more? Esperos struggled to sell at first, many went onto rental fleets where they could have suffered damage to front suspension. As a second-hand buy they have been popular as minicabs, so watch out for clocking when buying third-hand. If it hasn't been serviced on time, why not? (The first three years' routine services were included in the price.) Make sure the ABS works properly as this is expensive to replace. Check under oil filler cap for emulsion as expansion tank pipe has been known to blow off leading to overheating and warped cylinder head. Bonnet catches break, so you have to ask yourself how long it has been broken and how long it is since anyone looked underneath. Central locking can play up. Make sure aircon blows cold.

Recalls: 3/7/2000: all 22,266 Esperos sold 1995–1997 recalled to replace seatbelt buckles.

Lanos (1997 on)

What's good: Rover 200-sized. Lots of standard features, including power steering, twin airbags, three years routine servicing included in price. Better value than a Rover 200. Decent colours and paint.

Doesn't look naff and cheapskate. 74 bhp 1.4 or 105 bhp 1.6. £10,700 1.6 comes with standard ABS, aircon, electric mirrors and electric windows. Has sold well to private market. Average performance in NCAP crash tests.

What's bad: A bit nondescript. Not particularly nice to drive. Interiors not great. Smaller than Nexia, so less space for rear passengers and luggage. Trim rattles, wind noise, poor mpg. R reg 1.6s down to £1,500 at auction by mid 2001 due to doubt about company's future.

What to watch out for: A reasonable new-car buy for a certain type of owner. Questionable used-car buy because why would anyone sell it before they had used up the three-year deal? Used Lanos at Daewoo 'Motor Shows' likely to be ex-rental.

Leganza (1997 on)

What's good: Bigger than the Espero and almost in the Galant/Passat size category, but much cheaper and in UK terms a 'new car bargain'. Loaded with kit, including ABS, aircon, electric windows, height-adjustable seats. £13,800 SX better value than £15,000 CDX. Smooth 2.0 litre engines. New car Daewoo Deal includes three-year warranty and servicing. Daewoo's best car so far. Smooth engines praised.

What's bad: Not the world's greatest driver's car, but how you judge it depends on what you're used to. Came bottom of the list in USA Insurance Industry crash tests. Doubts about company's future.

What to watch out for: Sensible new car buy for people who want a biggish motor.

Matiz (1998 on)

What's good: Styled by Giugiaro from scratch and much better looking than Move, Wagon R or ATOZ. Sensible, eco-friendly city car or suburban runabout. Excellent for the school run. Not bad value with full Daewoo 3-year servicing and warranty package. Handles well enough given its obvious limitations. More powerful version was on the way, seen testing at over 100 mph in 2000. Tiny size makes it easy to park. Outsells Fiat Seicento in Italy. Reasonable Three-Star rating in Euro NCAP crash tests. Facelifted inside and out for 2001. Hold their value very well. Price cut to £5,995 summer 2001.

What's bad: 796cc 50 bhp engine not quite up to motorway travel. Rolled over on high-speed reverse-turn by *Autocar* magazine. Trim quality not brilliant. Terrible Neil Lyndon road test report in *Sunday Telegraph* on 4/10/98. The company itself has been in trouble for some time.

What to watch out for: Proper Daewoo/Halfords service history.

Recalls: 18/7/2000: 4,837 Matiz models recalled due to possibility of corrosion in fuel filter which could lead to a fuel leak. Fuel filter to be replaced with modified type.

Nexia (1995–1997)

What's good: Based on the old (pre–1991) Astra with 1.5 litre 75 bhp and 90 bhp engines. Lots of kit as standard, including power steering and ABS on even the most basic cars. Aircon was a buyer-tempting standard fit from May 1996. 4-speed auto optional from October 1995. Used models very sensibly priced for the age and specification.

What's bad: New cars priced to include the Daewoo Deal, so initially lost value very quickly (bounced back up once the public realised what value they were). Poor ride and handling by late 1990s standards. ABS is a desirable feature, but a very expensive MOT failure when it goes wrong. The booted version looks hideous. Poor build quality. Can suffer electrical problems. Heavy tyre wear. Sudden failure of plastic timing belt tensioner pulleys. Reports of bulkhead failure. The company itself has been in trouble for some time. Under a grand at auction.

What to watch out for: Needs frequent brake fluid changes to prevent damage to ABS. Watch out for kerbing damage. Expect trim troubles, particularly driver's door seal. Creaks and rattles are normal from ageing design. May have been bought by elderly people with no previous experience of PAS. Popular with Motability lessees, so may be holes where cars have been adapted.

Recalls: 1997 (to May '95): check engine bay wiring harness routing (helpline: 0800 060606). 3/7/2000: all cars built from 1995 to 1997 recalled to check seatbelt buckles and replace if necessary.

Nubira (1997 on)

What's good: Second generation Daewoo, sized between old Nexia and Espero. British designed. Usual Daewoo Deal benefits. 1.6 litre twin-cam 90 bhp engine or 2.0 litre twin-cam 132 bhp quite powerful for car's size. Useful, reasonable looking estate. Standard ABS and aircon across the range. Sensibly priced by UK standards when Daewoo Deal is taken into consideration. Sold well in UK. Bigger headlight facelift in Spring 1999. Decent ICE.

What's bad: Engines a bit coarse. Estate car load area suffers from rear suspension intrusion. Wind noise. Reports of bulkhead failure. The company itself has been in trouble for some time.

What to watch out for: Not a bad new car buy for those not seeking the ultimate in refinement and handling. Used Nubiras at Daewoo 'Motor Shows' likely to be ex-rental, so check carefully for careless driver or accident damage. Watch out for uneven front tyre wear from kerbed and bent front suspension.

Recalls: 19–6–2001: 3000 Nubira CDX models recalled due to possible fault with the fuel filter. 30 minutes work required to be carried out 'while you wait'. Freefone helpline 0800 060606.

Tacuma (2000 on)

What's good: Daweoo's Scenic-sized mini MPV. 1.8 litre or 2.0 litre petrol engines. Standard c/a, aircon, ABS. Driver's seat has height adjustment and lumbar support. Front passenger seat swivels. Plenty of room inside. 4-speed auto option on 2.0CDX. Underseat drawers and picnic tables in the front seat backs. Rides and handles quite well. Quality better than previous Daewoos.

What's bad: High rear load sill. Not cheap with 1.8SE listed at Daewoo Deal price of £12,495 and 2.0CDX at £13,495. Parcel shelf cannot be removed without first folding the rear seats forward. Centre rear belt just a lap belt. Not the best looking small MPV and that's putting it mildly.

What to watch out for: Too soon to say.

DAIHATSU

Applause (1992–1996)

What's good: Looks like a 3-box saloon, but is really a hatchback. Can be reliable, efficient and good value but has no image whatsoever. People may wonder what it is, but won't bother to ask. All had 1.6 litre engines: 91 bhp with carb; 105 bhp with injection. PAS always standard.

What's bad: Old before its time. Very light 'feel-free' power steering, soggy ride, uninspiring plastic trim. Body parts likely to become hard to get.

What to watch out for: Worn steering and tyres and kerbed front suspension due to lightness of steering. Needs new timing belt every 3 years. 2nd gear can get noisy. Emulsified oil from short runs leads to premature camshaft, cam follower wear. Injected models have rear discs which may be rusty from lack of use.

Charade (1987–1993)

What's good: Good looking. 993cc three-cylinder 99 bhp GTti very quick and lots of fun to drive. 52 bhp Charade 1.0 CXs decent enough pre-cat superminis. PAS was available from September 1990 in CX Special and 2-speed autos. 1.3 litre 16v four-cylinder 75 bhp pre-cat engines were more robust. 89 bhp 'cat' engine launched July 1991. 1.3s had 3-speed rather than 2-speed auto. Ultra-economical 3-cylinder 993cc 46 bhp turbodiesel.

What's bad: Light build now that the cars are getting old. Two-speed auto struggles. Plasticky interior and not great to drive. Ride and handling of all but GTti not quite up to the mark. Most diesels kicked off their lives with driving schools.

What to watch out for: GTti very likely to have been thrashed. All models likely to be showing their age by now, could have some rust which will weaken an already light structure. GTti needs expert servicing – can't be done by the bloke with the lock-up round the corner. Only buy GTti from enthusiastic owners who have changed the oil every 3,000 miles. Timing belts need replacing every 3 years. Watch out for uneven tyre wear on all models and excessive tyre scrub on GTti.

Charade (1993 on)

What's good: Much more highly rated than previous model. Grew up with base engine now an 84 bhp 1.3 litre catalysed four. Also an 88 bhp 1.5, a 105 bhp 1.6 and, from February 1997, a 97 bhp 1.3 GTi with lowered suspension, ABS and alloys. All light and easy to drive. All got driver's airbags from January 1988.

What's bad: Not much boot space and still has poor ride quality.

What to watch out for: Lasts quite well. But check carefully for short-run syndrome ('mayonnaise' under the oil filler and a rusty rear silencer). GTis need regular brake fluid changes. Airbag may have gone off for no reason and the steering wheel trim panel simply stuck back on.

Cuore (1997 on)

What's good: Replaced Mira. Little screamer of an engine. Prices start at £5,995 for three-door 'Start' model, rise to £9,750 for turbocharged all-wheel-drive 660cc Cuore Avanzato TR-XX R4. Standard model useful for school run. Reliable and frugal on fuel. Easy to steer and park. Slow depreciator in both percentage terms and money terms.

What's bad: Handling and drivability OK, but nothing special. Manual transmission whines. Fared badly in German TUV/Auto Bild front offset crash tests.

What to watch out for: Front suspension damage and excessive tyre wear. Make sure brake servo is assisting the brakes. Uneven tyre wear on souped-up Avanzato. Supermarket carpark dings and dents. Emulsified oil under the oil filler cap a sure sign of short-run syndrome. Check for tears and damage to trim.

Fourtrak (1985 on)

What's good: The Yorkshire farmer's favourite. Tough as old boots. Very good at towing. Independent model from July 1993 by far the best. 2.0 litre 87–90 bhp engine lasted from Jan '89 to July '93, otherwise all diesel. Slow 72 bhp non-turbo 2.8 from Jan '89–July '93; 90 bhp turbo from Jan '90–July '93; 101 bhp turbo 2.8 TDS from July '93 also has automatically freewheeling front hubs. Power then cut to 97 bhp from March '96 to meet new emissions regs. Lots of special editions include 'Timberline', 'Anjou' and 'Riviera'. Discovery-style side-facing jump seats in back okay for short trips.

What's bad: Since it's a farmer's car, it has probably seen some hard use by farmers. Pre-'Independent' models have harsh ride from two solid axles. Disadvantage of only three doors makes getting into the mid-row seats difficult.

What to watch out for: What's it been towing? If it has a tow hook, check transmission carefully. Give it a really thorough 4x4 check. Expect bodywork, suspension, axle, steering, exhaust and general underside damage, as these cars are rarely bought by townies. Look for oil smoke from worn turbo bearings, burned-out turbo oil seals.

Grand Move (1997 on)

What's good: Charade-based tall estate car (not really an MPV). Grand Move+ well equipped with standard aircon, and relatively well priced by UK standards. Lots of armrests and cupholders. Optional 4-speed auto. 1.5 litre 88 bhp engine. All seats recline flat to form double bed. 'Secret' compartment for valuables. A niche model appealing to an elderly niche market which wants upright seats, cupholders and reclining seats for Sunday outings. Facelifted in October 1998.

What's bad: Not inspiring to drive.

What to watch out for: See Charade (1993 on).

Mira (1993–1995)

What's good: Cheap, updated Domino a useful school-run special. Reliable and frugal on fuel.

What's bad: Not happy on motorways. Very light build.

What to watch out for: High mileage would be quite unusual. Kerbing could damage structure as well as front suspension. Look for dings and dents and especially rust, as this will seriously weaken an already weak structure. Emulsified oil under the oil filler cap a sure sign of short-run syndrome. As long as exhaust not smoking white, this should be curable with a flush and oil change. Oil is best changed every six months, but make sure it hasn't been left to more than a year. Timing belt needs changing every 3 years.

Move (1997 on)

What's good: Low centre of gravity means it handled surprisingly well in the *Daily Telegraph* 'slalom' test. Little screamer of an engine. More fun to drive than bigger Suzuki Wagon R. Restyled for 1999 model-year.

What's bad: Costs less than £4,000 in Japan. Looks like a phone box on wheels. Feels like it's made out of Bacofoil (don't have an accident in one). Not much room inside. Large glass area and lots of bare metal means it suffers severe condensation in winter. Though road wheels are tiny, still has a 'space saver' spare.

What to watch out for: Any damage likely to be obvious, but a kerbing or serious potholing could damage the structure as well as the suspension. Has a timing belt which will need to be changed every 3 years or so.

Naked

What's good: Curious retro basic hatchback may come to the UK at a very low price.

What's bad: Too soon to say.

What to watch out for: Too soon to say.

Sirion (1998 on)

What's good: Cheap, well-built, small 5-door hatchback with three-year warranty. Lots of safety kit and reasonable three star rating in

Euro NCAP crash tests (but see TUV test results). Optional four-speed autobox. Revised range from October 2000 priced from £7,495 for 1.0E and now including quick 102bhp 1.3 litre versions from £8,995 (F Speed auto £9,995). Drive with a light foot and 1.0E can be very economical.

What's bad: Peculiar looking. 3-cylinder 989cc 54 bhp engine needs working hard to deliver acceptable performance. Did not do well in German TUV/*Auto Bild* front offset crash tests.

What to watch out for: Complaints about original model from *Telegraph* readers include coolant leaks, poor panel alignment, clutch cable failures, frequent failure of front nearside suspension strut and rust on the tailgate around the chrome handle. Make sure the car has proper franchise service history.

Recalls: 17/1/2000 (April/May 1998 build: 902 cars): horn and head-lights could fail due to bad connection. Connectors to be replaced.

Sportrak (1989–1998)

What's good: Cheap, niche, short wheelbase 4x4 with 94 bhp 1.6 litre petrol engines. Hood, hardtop or both, depending on model. Cheap.

What's bad: Not much room in the back. Hard top components hard to store and quite a job to remove. Not really strong enough for serious off-roading. Some of the trim is a bit flimsy. Very hard ride, not very stable at speed and a bit slow on the road.

What to watch out for: Probably has seen some off-road use, most likely launching sailing dinghies. Do all the usual 4x4 checks and have a good look for rust from salt water.

Taruna

What's good: Smart-looking grown-up Terios with two-wheel-drive and seats for seven by virtue of two jump seats facing each other in the extreme rear. So far seems to be Indonesian market only.

What's bad: Not available in UK.

What to watch out for: Any imports likely to be tough to get through SVA as will lack UK safety belts, heating and de-misting system, etc.

Terios (1998 on)

What's good: Titchy but tall and narrow 4x4. 82 bhp 1,296cc engine, 5-speed gearbox and 4-speed auto option. Terios+ has alloys, aircon, passenger airbag and electric front windows. Very capable off road and one of the lightest 4x4s you can buy, which helps enormously in snow. Starting prices under £10,000. Late models have same 1,298cc Toyota Yaris engine as YRV.

What's bad: Some people might think it looks a bit silly.

What to watch out for: Unlikely to have seen hard off-road use, but sold by same dealers who sell Fourtrak so could have gone to a farmer's kids.

YRV

What's good: Attractively styled small five door hatchback from March 2001. Standard engine is a 1,298cc twin cam four developing 86bhp and 88.5 lb ft torque, as in the updated Sirion. Daihatsu's F-Speed automatic transmission also available. Emissions are 145g/km CO_2 for the manual and 156g/km for the auto, qualifying the manual for £100pa VED. An important fitting for this type of car is ABS with electronic brake force distribution on all but the base model. UK list prices include a three-year unlimited mileage warranty. A reasonable alternative to the Toyota Yaris, but doesn't handle as well. F speed button automatic works fine as long as you remember to switch it on using the dah mounted button. Cut price, cut spec YRV Radical at £7,995 and new YRV 4-trak four wheel drive at £10,995 from July 2001, Also 5-year unlimited mileage warranty on Premium and F-Speed models. A 140bhp turbocharged version already on sale in Japan should arrive in the UK during late 2001.

What's bad: Too soon to say.

What to watch out for: Too soon to say.

ECOVEC

Merlin

What's good: Amazing single seater three wheeler coupe powered by an all new range of water-cooled V-Twin engines of between 749cc and 1,198cc. 1,200 develops 100bhp, does 60mpg and takes the car to 100mph. All-up weight is just 900lbs so can be driven on a B1 motorcycle licence. Due to arrive in the UK in 2001. Projected price £10,999. Visit the website at www.corbinmotors.com
What's bad: Only for one.
What to watch out for: Too soon to say.

Sparrow

What's good: American-built extraordinary plastic-bodied single seater electric car. Has a top speed of 70mph and a range of 40–60 miles, making it ideal for cross-city commuting. Battery charger is on board so only needs to be connected to a power supply. Takes 3 hours for a full charge costing about 50p. Price £5,999. CD player and electric windows. Visit the website at www.corbinmotors.com
What's bad: Odd, but makes sense. Otherwise too soon to say.
What to watch out for: Too soon to say.

FERRARI

456M

What's good: Big, hugely powerful 5.5 litre 442bhp four seater coupe. Awesome performance of 0–60 in under 5 seconds and top speed of 186mph. The original 437bhp 456 Gt has been around since 1993 and second hand examples can be bought for as little as £50,000. Excellent independents such as DK engineering can look after it for more affordable buckets of cash than official Ferrari dealers.

What's bad: Fuel consumption, losing your licence in the UK.

What to watch out for: Accident damage. Cars stolen from another country. Anything remotely dodgy about the car's history, stay well away.

Recalls: 17/12/98: barrel nuts of fuel hoses could be over-tightened causing fuel leaks. Hoses and barrel nuts to be replaced and tightened correctly. 9/8/99: connection from brake fluid reservoir to master cylinder may fail. Replacement connector to be fitted.

550 Maranello

What's good: Fabulous front-engined coupe with all of 485bhp from its 5.5 litre V12. 0–60 in 4.1 seconds, a top speed of 199mph. Reaches 170mph with indecent ease and easily capable of lapping the Millbrook bowl at 180. Remarkably unflustered and docile in traffic. Feels immensely strong. Probably the best supercar you can buy.

What's bad: Just two seats. Quite a big car. Gobbles fuel.

What to watch out for: Accident damage. Stolen imports. If there is anything strange or unexplained about the car, trust your gut feelings and walk away.

Recalls: 21/9/98: insufficient clamping may lead to engine compartment fuel leak and risk of fire. Fuel lines to be replaced and correctly clamped. 11/12/98: damage to inner hydraulic seals of steering rack through driver using too much lock will lead to loss of steering power assistance. Steering rack and oil cooler to be replaced.

F355 (1994–1999)

What's good: Stunning looks. Stunning performance. Stunning handling. Low depreciation. Jeremy Clarkson bought one with his own money so it must be really special. Option of sequential gearshift controlled by buttons on steering wheel.

What's bad: Brakes aren't as good as some race drivers expected. Enormously high maintenance costs whether you use the car or not. Frequent timing belt replacement essential.

What to watch out for: Repaired accident damage. Lack of maintenance (very common among little-used supercars). Flat battery. Rusted discs. Seized handbrakes. Any sign of emulsion in the engine oil. Clutch cables go (Jeremy's did). Badly worn tyres (from 'track days'). Needs new timing belts every 12,000 miles – job costs £1,000-plus.

Recalls: 23/4/96: steering rack retaining bracket may loosen. To be replaced by better quality bracket. 23/7/97: fuel line retaining bolts my split leading to duel leakage. 10/6/98: installation of hood mechanism in 355 Spider may lead to a bolt puncturing the fuel tank. To be checked and bolt re-aligned (fuel tank replaced if necessary). 27/1/98: water hose clamp may chafe on fuel line. To be re-aligned. 3/2/98 (repeat of 23/7/97 recall): fuel tank retaining nuts may split leading to fuel leakage. Fuel lined to be replaced. 30/9/98: throttle pedal pivot may snap. Pivots to be replaced. 9/8/99: connection from brake fluid reservoir to master cylinder may fail. Replacement connection to be fitted.

F360 (1999 on)

What's good: Brilliant sportscar. Even better than 355. 400 bhp at 8,000 rpm and 275 lb ft at 4,750 rpm. Top speed over 180mph. Out-pointed all other cars at *Autocar* magazine's 1999 handling day at Oulton Park. 360 Spider and Spider F1 from October 2000. F1 has sequential gearshift controlled by buttons on steering wheel.

What's bad: One of the few cars selling at a significant premium in 1999 and still very hard to get. High CO_2 at 395g/km may be more severely penalised by VED in the future.

What to watch out for: See 355.

Recalls: 10/2/2000: 115 cars built in 1999 recalled because screws retaining the airbag ECU may not be long enough. To be replaced with longer screws; 18/2/2000: 125 cars built 1999–2000 may suffer from ABS ECU problem increasing bias to rear brakes. ECU software to be upgraded. 26/4/2000: 27 cars built 1999–2000 to fit American-standard fuel tank side protection plates to make tank less vulnerable in a side impact accident. 20/10/2000: 188 360 models recalled because fixing bolts holding starter ring to clutch may fracture causing severe damage to clutch bellhousing. Ring gear and fixing bolts of affected vehicles to be replaced.

FIAT

Barchetta (1995–2000)

What's good: Cute, 1,800cc twin-cam, front-wheel-drive sportscar with some nice design touches. Drives quite well.

What's bad: Left-hand-drive only. Most will have been personally imported from Europe where they can cost as little as £10,000 new.

What to watch out for: Imports with the wrong lights and speedos being re-sold as UK-market cars at UK prices. Make sure it has its 'Red Key'.

Recalls: 1999: problem of sticking control valve for engine variable valve timing-makes engine sound like a diesel. Announced on BBC 'Watchdog' 21/1/99.

Bravo and Brava (1995–late 2001)

What's good: Bravo (3-door) styling. Brava (5-door) practicality. Particularly good, sharp steering. Easy to use dash-top radio/cassette. Excellent, fully-adjustable seats and steering wheels throughout the range (designed by Professor Mark Porter's Ergonomics Group at Loughborough University). 5-cylinder HGT is a powerful, well-balanced 'hot hatch'. Used prices came down sharply in 1998/99. Diesel Bravas particularly well priced at 6 months old with 12,000–16,000 miles. Even better range of metallic colours than Punto. 'Ink Black' and 'Juvarra Ivory' best of the lot.

What's bad: Many UK cars begin their lives on rental fleets. First thing that breaks is the cassette lid. Bravos (three-door) about £1,000 dearer than more practical (five-door) Bravas. Bravas can be affected by side winds. Two-Star below-average performance in NCAP crash tests. Small number of cars have suffered from faulty engine speed sensor leading to erratic running and cut-outs. Timing belt changes on 5-cylinder HGTs are a very expensive, engine-out job. Need frequent oil changes to avoid carbon build up in oil feed pipe to camshaft. Came joint bottom with Marea in 2001 ADAC list 2001 of cars which break down most on German autobahns. S and

299

T plate Bravo 11th from bottom in 2001 Top Gear/JD Power Customer Satisfaction Survey. To be replaced by Stilo late 2001.

What to watch out for: Cassette lid. Silly damage from careless renters and their kids. Check aircon on cars where fitted. Check operation of electric sunroof and windows where fitted. Reports of premature HT lead failure which could, in turn, spike the catalytic converter. Bonnet catches break (see Tipo). Plastic timing belt tensioner pulley can shatter without warning. Best to change timing belt and tensioner every 3 years/35,000 miles. Trim starts to creak and rattle. Check everything electrical. Make sure it has its 'Red Key'.

Recalls: 1997 (1996–97 build: 17,000 cars): petrol may contaminate brake vacuum diaphragm leading to loss of power assistance to brakes. 1998: Bravo/Brava 1.4 and 1.6 with ABS built before Oct '97: check for chafing of brake hoses.

Cinquecento (1993–1998)

What's good: Cinquecento Sporting 1.1 litre 'Fire' engine from Punto 55 is by far the best engine and the most likely to get some proper exercise.

What's bad: Polish build quality. Not as practical as the Panda. Cinquecento 900s have the old 899cc pushrod engine which can suffer premature rocker shaft wear due to insufficiently frequent oil changes. Rear window can break if you shut the hatch from one side.

What to watch out for: Lack of maintenance and 'short-run syndrome' typical of city cars. Ticking tappets. Duff cats. Signs of careless driving by inexperienced youngsters. Check trim for damage. Check for cylinder head gasket failure on 1.1 Fire engines. Make sure it has its 'Red Key'. Make sure fuel tank not rusty (see recalls). Report of metal fatigue in the clutch driven plate.

Recalls: Recall to replace rusted fuel tanks FOC, but only notified to the first owner of the car or via Fiat dealers.

Cinquecento (2002 on)

What's good: 3-door version of Ecobasic project car with same space-frame construction as Multipla. To be powered by a 60 bhp

1.2 litre diesel capable of 100 mph and 60 mpg, and to sell from around £5,500.

What's bad: Polish build quality. May not now happen due to cancellation of Ecobasic.

What to watch out for: Too soon to say.

Coupe (1995–2000)

What's good: Great-looking coupe, first with twin-cam 2.0 litre 4-cylinder 16v injected or turbo engines, then with stronger 2.0 litre 5-cylinder 20 valve injected or turbo engines from November 1996. Six-speed gearbox from 2000.

What's bad: Back seat is only suitable for dwarfs and pre-teen children. Quality/assembly problems. As with a Ferrari, timing belt changes of 5 cylinder cars are an engine-out job and can cost as much as £1,300. Dropped from range in spring 2000. S and T platers 15th from bottom in 2001 Top Gear/JD Power Customer Satisfaction Survey.

What to watch out for: Signs of being driven hard or badly. Avoid any cars with kerbed wheels. Make sure it has its 'Red Key'.

Doblo (from (2001)

What's good: Boot space floor to parcel shelf is a huge 750 litres and folding the back seats releases a cavernous 3,000 litres. That's 200 litres more than the Berlingo and Partner and 400 litres more than the Kangoo. Relatively compact at 4,160mm long, 1,710mm wide and 1,800mm high (13ft 8ins x 5ft 7ins x 5ft 10ins). Power steering with just 2.2 turns lock to lock and a tight turning circle of 10.5 metres help make manoeuvring stress free. 700mm (27.5 inch) wide sliding rear side doors and high rear seats make it easier for the elderly or disabled to get in and out. At 1,245mm (4ft 1ins) high and 1,231mm (4ft 0.5ins) wide the rear door aperture is also bigger than the Berlingo, Partner and Kangoo. The rear load sill is just 21 inches from the ground. Engine choice of a 65bhp 1,242cc petrol which delivers 75 lb ft (102Nm) torque at 3,500rpm or a 63bhp 1,910cc IDI diesel which churns out 87 lb ft (118Nm) torque at

2,500rpm. The petrol model has a top speed of 88mph, gets to sixty in 17.5 seconds, emits 183g/km CO_2 (£140pa VED) and manages a combined consumption of 36.7mpg. The diesel also does 88mph, but takes about 19.5 seconds to get to sixty, emits 191g/km CO_2 (£160pa VED) and squeezes 39.2 miles out of a gallon on the combined cycle. Air-conditioning (optional on SX, standard on ELX) increases the CO_2 output of the diesel to 204g/km. Remote central locking, height-adjustable steering wheel, height adjustable drivers seat with adjustable lumbar support, dash-mounted gear stick, two dashboard accessory power points, driver and passenger airbags are standard on all models. ELX models have five three-point seatbelts, alloy wheels and air conditioning. Air-conditioning is optional on the SX at £651, and ABS with EBD are optional extras on both models at £564. Prices are: 1.2 petrol SX: £8,694.65; 1.9D diesel SX: £8,949,65; 1.9 diesel ELX: £9,995. Independent tests say it handles well. More at www.fiat.co.uk

What's bad: Very slow.

What to watch out for: Far too soon to say.

Ecobasic

What's good: The true car of the future. Plastic panels on a space frame. 1.2 litre 61bhp direct injected diesel engine and 5 speed Selaspeed autoclutched gearbox giving up to 94mpg, 100mph and 0–60 in 13 seconds. Weighs less than 750kilos; emits just 80 g/km CO_2. Could sell for around £4,000. To form basis of the next Panda.

What's bad: Project shelved in 2001 due to EU regulations.

What to watch out for: Nothing, since it's not happening.

Marea (1997 on)

What's good: As Bravo/Brava. Replaced Tempra. Useful 'Weekend' estate. Tremendous 125 bhp diesel followed by even better 130 bhp JTD. Handles well.

What's bad: Ugly. Lousy build quality. Problems not easily put right by dealers, themselves thin on the ground. Timing belt changes on 5-cylinder cars are a very expensive, engine-out job. Came joint bottom with Bravo and Brava in 2001 ADAC list 2001 of cars which break down most on German autobahns.

What to watch out for: As Bravo/Brava. Make sure it has its 'Red Key'.

Recalls: 1998: 1.6 16v, non-ABS: check for chafing of brake hoses; 1999: 1.8, 2.0 and 1.9TDS (1993–96 build): front coil springs

Multipla (2000 on)

What's good: Bravo-based, but shorter. Six seats in two rows of three, all with proper three-point belts. Funky interior styling. Dashboard gearshift, so no obstructions in the floor. Excellent 105 bhp 1.9JTD engine pulled it to 115 mph on the Millbrook test bowl, so must be more aerodynamic than it looks. 103 bhp 1.6 16v has very good steering, handles much better than diesel and can be thrown around like a hot hatch. Twin lens mirrors make it easy to judge kerbs for parking. Bright range of colours. Has become a fashion item.

What's bad: Controversial looks. Diesel suffers roll understeer on tight bends (petrol doesn't). A long step up to the seats and down from them for the elderly or infirm (much easier from a high kerb). Petrol model is short-geared and gets noisy at around 80 mph. Lots of niggling faults, especially with alarm/immobiliser. Poor performance in TUV/Auto Bild front offset crash test. Worst mini MPV score of all of 56% in Euro NCAP 2001 crash safety tests (but FIAT now claims to have modified it to achieve a four star score). Some of the trim is a bit cheap: rubbery plastic on ashtray peels off.

What to watch out for: Make sure everything works.

Palio Weekend (2000 on)

What's good: FIAT's 'World Car' marketed in Europe at sub-Punto prices may finally come to the UK in useful RHD 103 bhp 1.6 litre estate car form at a price level of around £8,000–£8,500. Will be a lot of car for not much money.

What's bad: Design not up to new Punto standards and quality levels not brilliant.

What to watch out for: Too soon to say.

Panda (1984 on)

What's good: Simple, practical, cheap car. 999cc 'Fire' engines go on and on. 4x4 was best lightweight 4x4 of the lot (I found one that had done well over 200,000 miles). They're still being made, but, sadly, with the 899cc pushrod Seicento engine rather than the ohc 'Fire' engine. Sell for £3,500 new in Italy. Cheap to buy and cheap insurance. Part-galvanised from 1990.

What's bad: Pre-1990s Pandas rusted badly from new and even '90s models rust in the doors. 'Old' pushrod 903cc engine should be avoided. Selecta troublesome and expensive to fix. Can suffer cold-starting problems. Clutch cables snap. Wheel bearings go. Suspension bushes wear. With the Fire engine, if the engine cuts out when hot, will restart after about 10 mins, then last another couple of miles, the reason could be that the cable insulation cracks and shorts inside the distributor from the magnetic pickup to the ignition module. Results in no spark. Happens on cars from late E reg onwards. Pre mod distributors had red and green cables which never gave a problem. If the Fire engine suffers from flat performance, the vacuum advance/retard units on the distributor has failed. Units can be purchased separately from Fiat for about £12. If the Fire engine suffers from fast idle, very weak mixture the reason is Weber carbs designed in Germany. These suffer from air leaks, hence fast idle and weak mixture. Fitting repair kit risky! Best by new from FIAT (£110 + VAT). Weber charges a lot more.

What to watch out for: Rust. Fall-apart trim. Don't pay extra for low mileage. Many low mileage cars serviced once every two years or worse. Look for wear in 4x4 drivetrain. Bounce the car on its suspension to make sure shocks are still absorbing. 'Mayonnaise' under oil filler denotes life of short runs, never properly warmed up. Oil leaks common. Timing chain gets noisy on 903cc pushrod engine (not recommended). Make sure timing belt changed recently on 'Fire' engines. Check tyres for uneven wear. Any clunks selecting 'drive' on the Selecta should be avoided like the plague. Look for rust in the back corners of the non-galvanised side doors.

Punto (1994–1999)

What's good: The best-designed small car in the world and a worthy 'Car of the Year' award winner. Excellent upright seating. 4-door SX and ELX versions have height-adjustable seats and steering wheels and are the easiest cars for the elderly to get in and out of. Best of the range are basic 55 or 60 three-door models with sunroofs, 85 SX 5-doors with standard PAS. Galvanised bodies won't rust unless accident-damaged. Cheap 'nearly new' because most start their lives on rental fleets. Amazing range of bright and attractive metallic colours, best of which is 'Rialto' blue (adds £200 to the used price). 60S does over 40 mpg. Recommended.

What's bad: Choppy ride quality. Handling and roadholding not as good as the latest Fiestas. Rear brake adjusters a bit gimpy. Selecta CVT auto is excellent in both theory and practice, but can become troublesome. Diesels not brilliant. Bonnet releases break (see Uno). Hydraulic clutch slave cylinder may develop a leak. High number of cylinder head gasket failures being registered. Franchised dealers thin on the ground and not always helpful. Isolated report of front suspension wishbone collapse.

What to watch out for: Accident damage. Silly damage from careless renters and their kids. Rear suspension arm bushes wear and are expensive to replace (check for uneven rear tyre wear). If test driving a Selecta, make sure the electromagnetic clutch is 100% (there should be no jerk when you put the lever in 'drive', no jerk when you drive away, and no 'creep' at idle). Make sure it has its 'Red Key'. Check for cylinder head gasket failure. Make sure that the fuel pump is not leaking (new pump: £159 + VAT + fitting.)

Recalls: 1998 (March–Nov '97 build): faulty seatbelt pre-tensioner.

Punto II (1999 on)

What's good: FIAT improved the Punto in every area where the old model was criticised. The current car has a sharp 'designer' look that could tempt Polo buyers, and the best driving environment of any small car. New torsion beam rear suspension helps handling and comfort and eliminates the bearing wear problem of the old model. Galvanised bodies won't rust. Amazing range of bright and attractive metallic colours. All models have height-adjustable steering wheel and driver's seat with lumbar support. Plenty of headroom. Engines now: 60 bhp 1.2 8v; 80 bhp 1.2 16v; 130 bhp 1.7 16v; 60 bhp 1.9 diesel; 80 bhp 1.9 JTD common rail diesel. 6-speed manual box available with 80 bhp 1.2 in 'Sporting' model. 'Speedgear' CVT available with 7 speeds and 80 bhp 1.2 or 6 speeds and 60 bhp 1.2. Witty 'Spirito di Punto' advertising campaign. Four-Star NCAP crash safety rating. Three proper three-point rear seatbelts standard in HLX spec and above; £75 extra in base models. 'Red Key' security system abandoned, which makes buying second-hand easier.

What's bad: Interior not quite as roomy as old model, but has stowage pockets everywhere and lots of brilliant design features that bring a smile. Indicator stalk unpleasant to use and does not always self-cancel. Dual mode power steering gives electric power to column rather than rack, and in 'City' mode feels almost frighteningly light. 7-speed CVT may seem to have too many gears, and constant gearchanging slows acceleration. Doubts remain over longevity of CVT.

What to watch out for: Signs of water ingress (wet carpets). Problems with the electric power steering and steering column (the column is directly driven by an electric motor) on Puntos built between 12–2–2001 and 18–5–2001. See Recalls. If buying a 'new' or 'nearly new' Punto check with your FIAT delaer that the bearing bush has been replaced.

Recalls: 26/7/2000: 2,016 Puntos with air conditioning built 8/1999–7/2000 recalled because fuel vapour recirculation pipe might foul against a/c compressor resulting in risk of fire. Recirculation pipe to be repositioned away from compressor. 31/5/2001: faulty batch of bearing bushes fitted to the top section of powered steering columns of Puntos and Punto vans built between 12–2–2001 and 15–5–2001. Affects 7,000 UK cars. Recalls website from late June 2001: www.via.gov.uk.

Seicento (1998 on)

What's good: Replaced Cinquecento in Spring 1998. Much cuter, with optional PAS and optional citymatic autoclutch. The best older model is the SX-based 'En Suite' which has a bigger, longer-lasting 1,108cc 'Fire' engine, standard PAS and aircon. Cosmetic facelift in autumn 2000. No Red Key problems. All UK-market Seicentos powered by 54 bhp 1,108cc multipoint injected 'Fire' engine with standard electric power steering as from October 2000 facelift.

What's bad: Many used models still have 899cc version of old Fiat 903cc pushrod engine which is apt to develop rocker shaft wear. Only two stars in Euro NCAP tests. To be replaced in 2002.

What to watch out for: As Cinquecento, except they don't have Red Keys. Check for cylinder head gasket failures.

Stilo (from late 2001)

What's good: New models code named Project 192 to replace Bravo and Brava. To be built on new 'C' platform with engines from a 1.2 litre four with 80bhp to a 2.0 litre five with 155bhp. Will be much more space efficient than current cars with handling goal to rival Ford Focus. Like the Bravo and Brava the 3-door and 5-door Stilo models are very different cars from each other. The 3-door is rakish and sporty, the driver sits lower down and the appeal is generally younger. The 5-door, on the other hand, while still very fresh and stylish compared to competitors such the new Peugeot 307, is altogether more practical. Both models are 1,760mm wide, but the 3-door is 4,180mm long and 1,460mm high while the 5-door is 4,250mm long and 1,760mm high. More at www.fiat.co.uk

What's bad: Too soon to say.

What to watch out for: Too soon to say.

Tempra (1990–1996)

What's good: The saloon and estate ('Weekend') versions of the Tipo.

What's bad: See Tipo. Not as good looking or as well designed as the Tipo.

What to watch out for: See Tipo.

Tipo (1988–1995)

What's good: Brilliant, practical design, more roomy inside than any other car in its class before or since. Cheap to buy. Electro-galvanised bodies won't rust unless accident damaged and badly repaired. Evocative 'Sedicivalvole' (16-valve) version a bargain performance buy. 1.9 TD quick, economical and cheap to buy once the miles pile on. Most Tipos now selling for banger money.

What's bad: Shape and design qualities not generally appreciated. Dodgy cost-saving digital dash on early 'DGT' versions. 1.6 not much quicker than 1.4. 1.8 not a good engine. Most 1.4ies began their lives on rental fleets. Some reports of non-galvanised subframes rusting prematurely. Called the 'teapot' in the trade.

What to watch out for: Leaks between cam carrier and cylinder head of modular 1.4 and 1.6 engines. Also cylinder head gasket failure common. All need coolant changed every two years, particularly iron-block, alloy-headed diesel. Electrics develop problems. Make sure all the lights work. All-too-easy to cross the threads in the alloy head when replacing spark plugs. Bonnet catch cable release mechanism breaks, begging the question of how long it's been since anyone looked underneath.

Ulysse (1995 on)

What's good: As Citroën Synergie. Has PSA XUD diesel rather than Fiat engine. Early models now cheap for a 7 seater.

What's bad: As Citroën Synergie. S and T platers 5th from bottom in 2001 Top Gear/JD Power Customer Satisfaction Survey.

What to watch out for: As Citroën Synergie.

Uno (1983–1994)

What's good: Some panels galvanised from 1990 when all acquired plastic hatchback. 999cc 'Fire' engine good for 200,000 miles plus with proper maintenance. Good range of bright metallic colours. Uno 1.0 'Start' models were well equipped and great bargains. Low insurance and low used prices means they make good sense for youngsters. Part-galvanised from 1990 facelift which includes non-rusting plastic tailgate.

What's bad: Avoid the 903cc 'Uno 45' engine (the timing chain and valve gear rattle and it's well past its sell-by date). Unos look like refrigerators in white. Many started their UK lives on rental fleets. Privately owned Unos that are used for shopping and the school run never warm up, contaminate their oil and suffer premature engine wear. If the car suffers from crashing from rear suspension, replace rear upper shock absorber mounts. About £12 from FIAT.

What to watch out for: Rust by the bucketload in pre-1990 facelift models. Duff catalytic converters. Kerbing damage. Bonnet catch cable releases break, so you have to ask yourself how long it has been broken and how long since anyone looked underneath. Selecta best avoided due to potentially expensive problems.

FORD

Cougar (1998–2000)

What's good: Sharp-suited Mondeo coupe with Mondeo 2.0 litre and 2.5 litre engines. Good looking and different. Low wind noise. 2.5 V6 recovers lost speed extremely well. Handles and holds the road nicely without much understeer. Effective 'eyeball' vents. Sensible boot. Fold-down rear seats ideal for golf clubs. Rear-view mirror well placed for motorways and heavy traffic. Sounds a bit like an Alfa 156 2.5 V6. 30 mpg possible from 2.5 litre; 36-plus from 2.0. 4-speed auto available, but not a very good one.

What's bad: Hopeless rear headroom. Harsh, crashy ride. Quite a few rattles, even when new. Console straight out of Mondeo. 2.5 V6 lacks low-down torque and needs to be revved for maximum effect (red-line only starts at 7,000 rpm). Short-range tank only good for 300 miles at a push. Odometer under-reads by 2%. Fairly heavy tyre wear on 2.5 V6. Withdrawn from UK market due to poor sales of just 12,000 in two years (*Daily Mirror* 21/11/2000).

What to watch out for: Damaged panels and trim which may become difficult to obtain replacements for.

Recalls: Cars Built Sept-Nov '98 recalled in October 1999 to cure possible failure of door latches.

Escort (1983–1990)

What's good: Popular. Cheap. Now selling for buttons.

What's bad: Old. Rust badly underneath and fail the MOT on structural corrosion which isn't worth attempting to repair. CVH engines choke themselves to death with black sludge.

What to watch out for: Crash repaired, cloned, clocked, stolen in their thousands. An Escort bought in 1998 may have been stolen and ringed ten years ago and never been noticed. Often fail the MOT on structural rust.

Escort (1990–2000)

What's good: Popular. Bland, but not bad looking. Handling and roadholding improved through the car's model life and 'wide mouth' cars from 1995 model-year on are by far the best. Almost all of these later models from LX up have power steering. Best model is probably a post-1995 1.6iLX, and most late cars had aircon.

What's bad: Had a terrible start. Early cars were a disgrace with awful handling, terrible steering and suspect bodyshells which rotted in the bulkhead and around the rear window. Early diesels had overstrength valve springs which caused them to snap their cambelts. Early Zetec engines from 1992 suffered sticky valves (see Mondeo). Rear suspension trailing arms up to 1995 were too weak and twist when they're not supposed to. Mid-life 'oval grille' facelift looks terrible and very dated. Fuse boxes rust out. Two-Star below-average performance in 1999 NCAP secondary safety tests. Close to bottom in 'R' reg JD Power Customer Satisfaction Survey.

What to watch out for: Bodged rust repairs on early cars. Clocked mega-mile ex-fleet cars. Inadequate 'home servicing'. Poor quality aftermarket parts – especially brake parts. Check for uneven tyre wear due to suspension damage from kerbing. Electrics may play up (check for damp and/or rusting inside fusebox). Rear suspension arms flex too much and may weaken as a result (16-valves were strengthened with rear anti-roll bar). Some 1992/93 Escorts came out of the factory with misaligned front suspension which caused the insides of the front tyres to wear excessively. Diesels should have had nylon timing belt idler replaced with a steel idler. These should both have been sorted out 'in service', but if the car was maintained 'in house' by a fleet or by a private owner, it may not have been done. CVT automatic is prone to problems and is best avoided.

Recalls: 1994 (1.3 and 1.4CFi-92 VIN NE, NL, NY, NS, NT; 93 VIN PJ, PU, PM, PP, PB, PR, PA, PG, PC, PK): electrical check. 1995 (VIN: SE): brake lights may not work. 1995 (Escort diesels: VIN: SY, SS, ST): brake vacuum pump may not create enough vacuum for servo. 1995 (VIN: SE, SL): loose rear brake cylinders. 1995 (VIN: SC, SK, SD): possible damage to seatbelt webbing. 1998 Escorts with passenger airbags built Aug '96–Feb '98: passenger airbag may go off while car is stationary.

Explorer (1997–2000)

What's good: Starred along with the other dinosaurs in 'Jurassic Park'. American alternative to the Range Rover and Jeep Grand Cherokee. 4.0 litre V6 gives decent motorway cruising and adequate performance. Quite a good towcar for people with twin-wheel 20ft caravans. Under £10,000 on used market from early 2000.

What's bad: Oversized and over here. Not as well rust-proofed in body cavities as you might expect. Fuel consumption difficult to justify. Major scandal over Firestone Tyres blowing out when wrongly inflated. Suffered from jamming electronic throttle, caused by electronic interference to the cruise control giving maximum engine revs. If this happens to you, knock the selector into neutral and switch off the engine as soon as you have stopped. Once the car is out of its 3-year or 60,000-mile warranty repairs can be frequent and expensive. Common to need new front wishbone balljoints at three years old (MOT failure point) and these cost £500, so book an early first MOT that falls within the 3-year warranty. Also if the engine oil is less than perfectly clean, the oil feed to the timing chain tensioners can block leading to noise when the engine is first started each day. Eventually the tensioners break and replacement is a £2,000 engine out job. S and T platers 9th from bottom in 2001 Top Gear JD Power Customer Satisfaction Survey.

What to watch out for: More of a suburban status symbol than a serious off-roader. Look for damage due to underestimated vehicle size. Check front wishbone ball joints and listen for timing chain rattles (see above).

Recalls: Oil pump recall notice issued January 1998. Bonnet latch recall issued 2000. Explorer TSBs include curing a transmission shudder. Warning in May 1998 that accelerator may be jammed open by the driver's floormat. This turned out to be a fault with the cruise control which, while switched off, can receive an electronic signal giving maximum revs. 14/3/2000: tailgate lift cylinder brackets may weaken. Strengthening plates to be fitted. Only 5 UK imports built 1/4/93 to 17/2/95 affected. 10/8/2000 Firestone Wilderness, ATX and ATX II tyres fitted to some Explorers recalled for free replacement regardless of age and wear. 2001: Rumoured recall to check for cracking of front stabiliser bar. Many owners yet to be contacted at 18/2/2001.

Explorer (2001 on)

What's good: New Ford Explorer now with up to seven forward facing seats rearmost of which fold into the floor when not wanted. Has options of 210bhp 4.0 litre V6 with 255 lb ft (346Nm) torque at 4,000 rpm and 5-speed autobox giving a top speed of over 100mph and a 0–60 of 8.9 seconds, 5.0 V8 with 215bhp and 288 lb ft (390Nm) torque and forthcoming common rail diesel engine. Reported to drive, ride and brake much better than the old Explorer on the road. No Firestone Wilderness tyres to be fitted. Due in UK December 2001.

What's bad: Fuel consumption of 18–24mpg and see Recalls.

What to watch out for: See Recalls.

Recalls: 2001 American Recall to replace exploding back windows. 2001 second American recall to check for cuts in tyres caused during building of vehicles.

Fiesta (1977–1989)

What's good: Low insurance groups. Cheap and simple. 'Valencia' pushrod engines are long-lasting so long as the cars get driven. Spares cheap and second-hand parts plentiful. Larger 1.3 and 1.4 CVH engines best avoided apart from 1.6 CVH in XR2. CTX auto could be reliable in '84–'89 cars.

What's bad: Old and rust-prone. Too light. 'Square front' (pre-1984 model-year) very rust-prone, particularly front inner wings just above strut top mountings. A rust-weakened light car is a disaster waiting to happen, particularly with young people aboard. 'Round front' 1984–89 Fiesta has improved anti-rust treatment, but all these cars are well over ten years old and need checking carefully.

What to watch out for: Rust. 'Short-run syndrome', because many were used for shopping by elderly ladies and never got properly warmed up. A 10-year-old Fiesta with 25,000 miles will be close to needing a new engine and clutch. On the other hand a white socks

313

and back-to-front baseball cap XR2 might have been surprisingly well cared for apart from huge holes in the parcel shelf for oversize speakers.

Recalls: (None known 1994–98, but check seatbelt inertia reels.)

Fiesta (1989–1995)

What's good: A bigger, better Fiesta with more than a hint of the Peugeot 205 about it. The cheapest, most basic ones seem to be the best. Some 1.3s had power steering. Pre-cat 1.0 litre cars cheap to buy, insure and run. (Continued as Fiesta Classic to Jan 1997.)

What's bad: Roadholding and handling a far cry from 205's higher standards. Fiestas suffered badly from catalysation in 1992. 1.1s and 1.3s from this date on were almost unbelievably slow and suffer from oil emulsification problems, over-rich running, premature rocker shaft wear and a variety of other ailments. Catalysed 1.1s probably best avoided. CTX autoboxes became troublesome due to oil leak. On 1.1 and 1.3 pushrod engines spark plugs may either have corroded into the head or been over tightened (taper fit) which means head removal to drill them out. Bodies rust quite badly in places.

What to watch out for: Front suspension bushes wear and suspension likely to have been 'kerbed'. Be very wary of uneven front tyre wear. Brake discs don't last long and can start to judder after 20,000 miles. CVHs need regular timing belt changes. Timing chains of 1.1 and 1.3 pushrod engines can start to rattle. Engines suffer badly from sludging up due to short-run syndrome and insufficiently frequent oil changes. More than its fair share of recalls, so satisfy yourself that the recall work has been carried out. Make sure nylon timing belt idler gear in diesel engine has been replaced with a steel idler. 1.4CVHs with ECUs may suffer starting and running problems due to loose flywheel sensor connector. Rust can seriously weaken the base of the centre door pillar of 5-door cars. Also check for severe rust in the nearside back wing in the corner under the petrol cap and in the front valence.

Recalls: 1995 (VIN: SK, SD): Tyres may be incorrectly fitted. 1995 (VIN: SE): Brake lights may not work. 1995 (Fiesta diesels: VIN:

SIGHS, ST): Brake vacuum pump may not create enough vacuum for servo. 1996: (March 1989F-Sept 1990H build): Check for possibility of front seatbelt inertia reel locking mechanism failure.

Fiesta (1995–1999)

What's good: Zippy 1.25 Zetec 'S' engines. Nice power steering. Vastly improved chassis offering excellent ride, handling and roadholding. Good fun to drive. Came out well in NCAP crash tests. Favourable insurance ratings due to reduced damageability and improved repairability.

What's bad: 1.3 'Endura' pushrod engines starting to show their age. Cabin lower and not as roomy as Punto, Ibiza, Polo. Water ingress via ventilation system. Starting to get reports of piston ring failures on 1.4 Zetec 'S' engines. The oil burned as a result may also wreck the catalytic converter. On Endura 1.3 pushrod engines Spark plugs may either have corroded into the head or been over tightened (taper fit) which means head removal to drill them out. The pins which hold the foot pedals in place may fall out, leaving the driver unable to brake or declutch. Tend to get through front discs and pads very rapidly. Either replace front pads at 18,000–20,000 miles or expect to have to replace discs every 25,000 miles. May simply need calliper pins cleaning and lubricating.

What to watch out for: Have been a number of recalls. Double recall over front brake pipes because original recall failed to remedy the problem. Make sure these have been carried out. A wet carpet may mean failure of the bulkhead sealant. Check for high oil consumption, smokey exhaust on 1.4 Zetec S. Check front discs if you can and budget for replacement.

Recalls: 1995 (VIN SE): Brake lights may not work. 1995 diesel (VIN SY, SS, ST): Brake vacuum pump may not create enough vacuum for servo. 1996 (Fiesta and Courier van, 1996 model-year; 47,500 cars): Check for faulty piston seal in hydraulic clutch master cylinder. Check for contamination of brake fluid and incorrect front brake hose routing. 1997 (5-door models built Oct '95–May '96): may have faulty rear door latches. Also TSB 107 concerning complaints about noisy alternator drive-belt of diesel model causing battery discharge. Modified parts to be fitted (was not always done). 1998 (July 1995–June 1996 build-67,000 cars): Possibility of brake failure due to front brake pipe chafing on bracket. Modified pipe and bracket to be fitted to both front brakes. (Repeat brake pipe recall announced on radio 12/2/98). Fiestas with ABS (Mar '98–Sep '98): Brake master cylinder may fail. Fiestas with passenger airbags built Aug '96–Feb '97: passenger airbag may go off while car is stationary.

Fiesta (2000–2001)

What's good: New face to old favourite. 104 bhp Zetec S is fun and makes this a good substitute for the old Peugeot 205GTi. Drives as well as the previous version, with really sharp handling. Reasonable Three-Star rating in Euro NCAP crash tests.

What's bad: An old favourite, as basic bodyshell dates back to 1989, and will be replaced by new model in 2002. Not much more than a '2+2'. De-motivated workforce, all facing redundancy at Dagenham plant for final year's production 2000–2001. (New Fiesta to be built at Cologne.) The pins which hold the foot pedals in place may fall out, leaving the driver unable to brake or declutch. Several reports that the 1.25 engine has become much coarser in this latest version, apparently due to changes to meet the latest emissions regulations. On Endura 1.3 pushrod engines Spark plugs may either have corroded into the head or been over tightened (taper fit) which means head removal to drill them out. Further brake failures have occurred.

What to watch out for: Too soon to say.

Recalls: See Fiesta 1995–1999.

Fiesta (2001 on)

What's good: All-new Fiesta due to be lauched at September 2001 Frankfurt Motor Show. Looks very much like a slightly smaller Focus, but with a less radical rear-end treatment. Also to be offered as tall cabin mini MPV. New engines to include 1.4 litre PSA diesels of 60bhp and 110 lb ft torque or 90bhp and 145lb ft torque.

What's bad: Not to be built in the UK.

What to watch out for: Too soon to say.

Focus (1998 on)

What's good: 1998 'Car of the Year', and cars in its class come no better. Brave all-new styling. Different from the mainstream. Proper independent rear suspension. Excellent roadholding/handling and ride quality combination on optional 15in wheels fitted with 195/60 tyres. Plenty of leg and headroom inside. Good seats. Multi-adjustable steering wheel. Nice deep door pockets. Close gearbox ratios and precise shift quality (60 mph at 6,500 rpm in 2nd in a 1.6). Galvanized body with 12-year anti-perforation warranty. Joint top of the class for secondary safety in NCAP tests. Should appeal to the public as well as the fleets. 1.4 and 1.6 16-valve Zetec 'S' engines; same 1.8 litre and 2.0 litre 16-valve Zetec 'E' engines as Mondeo. You get the feeling that everything has been very carefully thought through. Three-year warranty on Focuses sold by UK Ford dealers from November 2000. New 1,753cc TDCi diesel engine available from late Spring 2001 develops 115bhp at 3,800rpm and up to 206 lb ft torque (280Nm) at 1,850rpm. Combined consumption is stated to be 51.4mpg. Until the new Mondeo, the best Ford ever built. Finally becoming popular in Germany among a population deeply cynical of Fords which is at last realising it's a far better car than the Golf Mk IV. Highly recommended. Focus 'Black' special edition launched Summer 2001. £12,495 price includes 1.6 engine, 15" alloys, mesh grille, Panther Black metallic paint, air-conditioning, black leather seats, 6000 series radio/CD and Quickclear front screen. More at www.ford.co.uk

What's bad: Sharp edges of rear hatch. Bonnet opened by key-lock in grille badge which could be vulnerable to road salt. ABS, aircon etc. all extra, bundled in £500 'extras' packs. 1.6 is overgeared at 23.35 mph/1,000 rpm (3,000 rpm = 70 mph and 6,500 rpm would equal 152 mph) which gives flat performance at motorway speeds. Estate not as good looking as hatchback. Saloon is plain ugly and depreciates more heavily than the hatch. 1.6 with Mazda 4-speed automatic proved to be a disaster due to ATF leaks between transmission and engine (see recalls about this). Now fixed and no further reports of failures. Some late 'W' and early 'X' reg 2.0 litre Focuses were fitted with Mondeo inlet manifolds and sometimes refuse to drop below 2,500 rpm. The pins which hold the foot pedals in place may fall out, leaving the driver unable to brake or declutch. Rear silencers can rot through in two years. Contacts in rear number plate light can rust up. Can suffer water leaks at rear through vertical light clusters and light contacts can rust up causing current drains.

What to watch out for: See Recalls.

Recalls: 61,000 cars built Sept '98–Mar '99 recalled in July 1999 for better waterproofing of alternators to prevent short circuits. Announced *Daily Telegraph* 16/7/99. Cars built Sept-Nov '98 recalled in October '99 to cure possible failure of door latches. 2000: rear light bulb holders rust around the bulbs. New rear light fittings are installed under a Technical Service Bulletin if a rear bulb fails. (Discovered 28/2/2000.) 101,000 Focuses recalled: 1.8 litre and 2.0 litre Zetec E-engined Focuses recalled because oil filler cap can come adrift and oil then be blown out over engine. Wiring harnesses also to be checked for correct routing. ECUs of 1.6 litre Zetec S to be re-programmed if engines suffer from intermittent loss of power. (Announced *Daily Telegraph* 18/3/2000.) TSB issued to Ford agents to replace the rear hubs of Focus models fitted with rear disc brakes when in for a service due to snapping of the wheel studs. (Announced 25/4/2000): defect in ECU of Saarlouis and Valencia cars built March 1999 could cause inadvertent deployment of airbags and seatbelt pre-tensioners. 30/5/2000: all Focus automatics recalled because excessive crankshaft end float may allow torque convertor to contact crankshaft position sensor leading engine to cut out. Revised crankshaft thrust bearing and new crankshaft position sensor to be fitted. (Unknown date) 2.0 litre Focus models recalled for brake master cylinder to be replaced. 2001: diesels checked under Ford TSB system for possible air leaks into the fuel system.

Galaxy (1995 on)

What's good: Good styling, low wind noise, decent handling, nice to drive. Up to seven proper seats. TDI 90 takes 10,000 miles to run-in, then goes quite well and delivers 38 mpg fuel economy. Similar VW Sharan was a Three-Star performer in NCAP crash tests (6 points front impact; 15 points side impact). 'New Edge' face for 2001, on sale in UK from September 2000.

What's bad: Hard to park. 2.8 VR6 okay in manual form but VR6 autos guzzle fuel. You have to open the doors to turn the GL's front seats right round. Lots of quality problems. On early models, water can enter car via ventilation, soak the underfloor and get into the ECU which controls the electric windows and alarm system. On later models, this ECU has been moved. Aircon vulnerable to front end shunts. Also shifted in later models. TDIs can blow turbos and catalytic converters. Have also been manual gearbox problems with TDIs. Came last in 'P' reg JD Power Customer Satisfaction Survey, but by 'R' reg had improved.

What to watch out for: Make sure 7-seaters are genuine 7-seaters with rearmost area heating and not just 5-seaters with two extra seats clipped in. Make sure recall work carried out.

Recalls: 1996 (April '96–July '96): check for overheating of brake system. 1996 (2-litre with air-conditioning Jan '95–Feb '96): air conditioning compressor may seize up. 1997 (built Jan '96–Apr '97): check optional child seats. 13/1/2000: 80,000 Galaxys, Alhambras and Sharans VIN TV000001 to YV509825 recalled to check for contamination of brake fluid through master cylinder vent. Brake master cylinders of older cars to be replaced.

Granada/Scorpio (1985–1998)

What's good: Big, soft, comfortable, overgrown Sierra. 2.0 litre twin-cam petrol is reasonably economical.

What's bad: Hideous facelift in 1995 and hatchback dropped from range. Dropped entirely from Ford line-up in April 1998. Autobox problems common from 60,000 miles. ECU problems common, leading to catalytic converter problems. Fuseboxes vulnerable and contacts rust. Standard ABS costs a fortune to fix. Timing chain of 24v only lasts 60,000 miles. Cracked heads and oil leaks on two litre twin-cams.

What to watch out for: Oil leaks caused by cracked head on 2.0 litre 16v. Smoking V6s. ABS failure. ECU failure. Fusebox failure. Cat failure. Alternator failure on 2.5TDs (instead of 120 amp alternators,

319

some Turbodiesel models were fitted with 75 amp alternators which are not up to the job and cost £900 to replace with 120 amp units). 24-valve needs a new timing chain and associated tensioners every 60,000 miles. Autoboxes only last 60,000–80,000 miles. Clocking rife on these cars. Avoid 4x4. Check footwells for damp because a leaking heater matrix costs £500 to replace.

Recalls: 1996 (Aug '94–Jul '96): check for sticking throttle due to corrosion by road salt. 1996 (Feb '96–March '96): rear axle mounting may loosen. 1997: TSB 21: replace 75 amp alternators with 120 amp alternators on 2.5 litre Turbodiesel models. 1998 Scorpios with passenger airbags built Aug '96–Feb '98: passenger airbag may go off while car is stationary.

Ka, Ka², Ka³ (1996 on)

What's good: Like it or lump it styling. Flexible edges good for parking bumps. Good ride comfort. Great handling. With PAS, nice to drive, easy to park. Aircon available. Promise of £12,000 1.6 Zetec 'StreetKa' roadster (see separate entry). Base model Ka now with PAS reduced to £6,495. Reasonable Three-Star rating in Euro NCAP crash tests. Ka Sun Collection from March 2001 with big electric folding canvas sunroof at a steep £8,560 on the road. 'Free' insurance offers. More at www.ford.co.uk.

What's bad: Endura E 1.3 pushrod engine very long in the tooth, apt to emulsify oil, block oilways and develop rocker shaft trouble. Not much space in the back. Doors unprotected from parking damage. Have been complaints of over-servoed brakes. May suffer engine idle flare between gearchanges (see TSB below). Due for replacement 2002. Spark plugs may either have corroded into the head or been over tightened (taper fit) which means head removal to drill them out. The pins which hold the foot pedals in place may fall out, leaving the driver unable to brake or declutch. Ka 2s and Ka 3s can suffer from corrosion of the door wiring loom connectors, leading to electric window and central locking failures. Cost of replacing the wiring can amount to £300 for parts plus up to a full day's labour. Either replace front pads at 18,000–20,000 miles or expect to have to replace discs every 25,000 miles.

What to watch out for: Flaking paint. Suspension damage from kerbing. Hidden damage underneath deformable ends. Kids sweets, etc., stuck to carpet and seats. Aircon much better than an aftermarket sunroof, but can develop problems (see Ka Sun Collection in 'What's Good'). Make sure remote central locking and electric window winders work properly (see 'What's Bad'). Beware of emulsified oil under oil filler cap.

Recalls: 1998 Kas with ABS (Mar '98–Sep '98): Brake master cylinder may fail. 2000: TSB issued to replace throttle position sensor and connector if revs fail to decrease on lift off when upchanging. TSB issued advising dealers to use copper grease on spark plugs to aid removal.

Maverick (1993–1997)

What's good: Nissan Terrano II with Ford badge. Reasonably effective off-road. LWB 5-door model has 7-seat option. High driving position. High- and low-range gears. 2.7 TD got power boost from 100 bhp to 125 bhp in July 1996 and this is the best engine to go for. Had a 3-year dealer warranty to match Nissan's for Terrano II.

What's bad: 4x4 on-road handling. Dropped from Ford line up in April 1998 along with Scorpio. 3-door very high and narrow looking, so not bought by suburbanites as a style statement.

What to watch out for: Make all usual 4x4 hard usage checks, especially if fitted with a tow hook. Tends to suffer premature wheel bearing wear. TD needs oil changes at least every 5,000 miles to protect turbo from coking up and rest of engine from burned out oil. Be very wary of blue oil smoke from burned out turbo oil seals.

Recalls: 1995 (Maverick with Michelin 215/80 R15 tyres – VIN: PM, PP, PB, PR, PA, PG, PK, PD, PE, RL, RY, RS, RT, RJ, RV, RM, RP, RB, RA): tyres may lose pressure. 19/7/2000: 4,898 Terrano IIs built 1995–1997 recalled because metal brake pipe linking front brake circuit to rear pressure regulation valve may chafe on floorpan, eventually leading to brake fluid leak. Vehicles to be inspected and pipes either repositioned or replaced if worn.

Maverick II (2001 on)

What's good: New Maverick signed off before Ford decided to buy Land Rover. More of a tarmac than an off-road 4x4. Monocoque, chassisless construction. Whereas the old Maverick was developed jointly with Nissan and built in Spain, this is an all new Ford/Mazda co-production built at Mazda's Hofu plant in Japan and a much more refined, road-friendly vehicle with a unitary body rather than separate chassis. Fully independent suspension front and rear rather than solid axles, rack and pinion steering, MacPherson strut front suspension, Control-Trac II automatic 4x4 system and ABS with Electronic Brakeforce Distribution. Already well proven, having been launched as the Ford Escape in the USA in August 2000 and selling 75,000 units in its first three months. Apart from the Lexus RX300 it's the nicest, most car-like 4x4 of all to drive. It really handles well with none of the top-heaviness of some of the opposition. More at www.ford.co.uk.

What's bad: Interior plastics criticised in first independent reports. Did badly in American IIHS and NCAP crash tests. Airbag failed to inflate in American test. Some drivers may not like the column mounted shifter of the 3.0 V6 auto (I found it no problem at all). 2.0 litre a bit underpowered, but the only way to get a manual gearbox.

What to watch out for: Too soon to say.

Mondeo (1993–2000)

What's good: Decent build, decent handling, tremendous 'feelgood factor', multi-adjustable steering (in, out, up, down). Hugely improved from 1997 model-year facelift, which made the 5-door much better looking than rather dowdy 93K-96N Mk 1s; three lap/diagonal rear belts now standard. Faults virtually all eliminated from '97 model-year and 2.0LX can offer 40 mpg economy. Very strong bodyshell at the front. Comparatively good performance in NCAP crash tests. Easy and cheap to repair body damage. 1997 MY on is sensational used value for money and highly recommended.

What's bad: Lacks spaces for oddments such as mobile phones inside cockpit. Subframe needs dismantling to change the clutch, making it a £500–£600 job. Incorrect reassembly leads to tracking problems. Sticking valves on pre-1997 1.6s, 1.8s and 2.0s run short distances on cheap petrol (most have now been cured by 'in-service' modifications which cause engine to use a bit more oil.) 2.0 litre is still a bit coarse and boomy and gear ratios are for town rather than open road use. Engine management problems on 2.5 24v V6 can burn out catalytic converters (the car has three). 1.8 diesel engine very antiquated. ST 200 has very short gears and traction problems. Question-mark over longevity of front wishbone bushes on V6 – even post-97MY version. Suspension bags out after 120,000 miles. Reports of early front coil spring failures on 'R' and 'S' reg cars, now also coming in on earlier cars. Report of £500 diesel injector pumps 'only' lasting 100,000 miles, but this could be due to the lack of lubricity of the fuel being used. Reports of driveshaft failures on the last of the old shape 'W' and 'X' reg Mondeos. Seems the driveshaft UJ boot clips were wrongly fitted, allowing water ingress to the UJs causing them to fail. Free replacement for affected cars. Chrome comes off the smart 12 spoke wheels fitted to some high spec Mondeos at the time of the 97MY facelift.

What to watch out for: Slipping clutch. Baggy suspension. A bang on a speed bump can knock out the otherwise well protected catalytic converter on 4-cylinder cars. Infamous 'pulling to the left' caused by kerbing damage, by worn track control arm bushes, by misaligned reassembly of front subframe after clutch replacement or by failure to re-track properly after replacing track control arms. Look for uneven tyre wear (outer shoulder wear normal). Early (1993) Mondeos prone to starter motor failure. If ABS fitted, make sure light goes out after 3 seconds or new pump or ECU may be needed. Shafts of front electric window winder mechanism can go: make sure both work. More than its fair share of recalls. The Mondeo is a bigger, heavier, wider car than the Sierra. May not fit your garage. If automatic, make sure shifts are smooth and check ATF which should be red, not black. Timing belts on Zetec petrol engines last 5 years or 80,000 miles, but belts on diesels only good for 3 years or 36,000 miles. Reports of shorting out of resistors to heater/ventilator fan motor. Resistors situated upper RH side of passenger footwell. If you smell an electrical fire, this is the first place to look for the source.

Recalls: 1994 (92 VIN NY, NS, NT; 93 VIN PJ, PU, PM, PP, PB, PR, PA, PG, PC, PK, PD, PE; 94 VIN RL, RY, RS, RT, RJ, RU, RM): headlamp failure. 1995 (Mondeo diesels: VIN: SY, SS, ST): brake vacuum pump may not create enough vacuum for servo. 1995: fuel pipe. 1995: (VIN: RP, RB, RR): static sparks may occur when refuelling. 1996: free recall (per *What Car?* 9/96, p. 132) to sort out problem of sticking valves – work will usually be carried out when car is in for a routine service. 1996 (1996 model-year with hydraulic clutch – excluding V6): check, replace if necessary clutch master cylinder/slave cylinder. Check front brake callipers. 1997: (24v built 1/8/94–14/6/96; 9,000 cars): free official recall to replace catalytic converter closest to exhaust manifold. 1998 Mondeos with passenger airbags built Aug '96–Feb '97: passenger airbag may go off while car is stationary. Ford Mondeo V6 with ABS (Dec '97–Jan '98): ABS system may fail. Cars built Sept-Nov 1998 recalled in October 1999 to cure possible failure of door latches. TSB issued to replace door light switches of cars built 8/96 to 11/98 as can cause current leakdown and alarm problems. 2000: Mondeos built June '95–Sept '97 recalled to check for chafing of front seatbelt webbing. 30/5/2000: 160,376 Mondeos without ABS built 2/1/96 to 7/8/98 recalled to replace rear brake pressure limiting valve which may corrode and leak. 2001 TSB to add section of damper pipe to power steering of 1999 cars to prevent clonking from steering when negotiating uneven surfaces. 2001 TSB to fit 24v V6 models with larger air intake pipe to cure tendency for engine to hunt when idling.

Mondeo (2000 on)

What's good: Slightly bigger than the already big 1993–2000 Mondeo. More roomy inside. Better handling from Focus-like 'control blade' rear suspension. 'New Edge' styling. Estate car even bigger inside than E-Class Mercedes. Engine range includes new 125 bhp 1.8 litre Duratec HE petrol, new 143 bhp 2.0 litre Duratec HE petrol; 168 bhp 2.5 litre Duratec V6 and new 113 bhp 2.0 litre 16 valve direct injected Duratorq diesel engine. The new petrol engines already meet Euro 2005 emissions limits. Smallest wheel/tyre combination is 16in with 205/55 R16 tyres, going up to 17in and 18in wheels. UK list prices: £14,595 for 1.8iLX and £15,095 for

2.0iLX both with a/c, alloy wheels, three-year warranty and 12-year anti-corrosion warranty. On your first drive of the car it immediately feels fantastic. Then it gets better. V6 Zetec S launched at £19,095 (note that 10-spoke alloys much better looking than 5-spoke). 4x4 version of estate with higher ground clearance on the way. V6 ST Concept shown at Geneva. Pips even the new VW Passat at its own game and now becoming popular in Germany. Looks best in silver or metallic grey. Highly recommended.

What's bad: Still seems to lack space for oddments inside cockpit. Stopgap diesel engine. Still waiting for all new diesel engine in Summer 2001. Otherwise, too soon to say.

What to watch out for: Too soon to say.

Recalls: 29/12/2000: 2,500 2001 model-year Mondeos recalled to have side airbag trigger electronics replaced. (Source *Daily Mirror* 29/12/2000.)

Orion (1983–1993)

What's good: As for equivalent Escort, but with a boot.

What's bad: As for equivalent Escort. Diesels more likely to have once been taxis. Orion name dropped in 1993 in favour of 'Escort 4-door' – which helped to boost 'Escort' sales figures.

What to watch out for: As for equivalent Escort.

Recalls: As for equivalent Escort.

Probe (1994–1998)

What's good: First fruit of Ford's gradual buying into Mazda. Launched in the USA in 1992. Essentially a re-styled Mazda MX6 with the same smooth and revvy quad-cam 163 bhp V6, but also offered with a 2.0 litre 128 bhp four from the 626. Only started to sell once it dropped to a sensible price on the used market and actually bounced back for a year or so.

What's bad: A model Ford would prefer to forget. Huge and variable panel gaps. Not enough rear legroom. Harsh ride. Far too expensive new. A Ford dealer even tried to pre-interest the trade with a UK 'K' registered 3,000-mile LHD 24v. Between December

1992 and January 1993 it dropped from a top 'bid' of £14,800 to £12,700, clearly showing that a list price of £19,350 was pie in the sky.

What to watch out for: Accident damage. And the sort of deterioration that results from sitting around unsold in compounds (rusty discs, rusty exhaust, flat battery, aircon shot, etc.). 2.0 litre best avoided. V6 may need a new timing belt.

Recalls: 2000: Probes built Jan '95–Oct '96: fuel vapours may escape from tank.

Puma (1997 on)

What's good: Highly rated, brilliant handling, Fiesta-based coupe. Yamaha-developed 125 bhp 1.7 litre Zetec S engine supplemented by 90 bhp 1.4 Zetec S in February 1998 and 153 bhp 'Racing' in early 2000. 'Racing' Puma offers outstanding grip and 'race car feel' for those prepared to fork out £20k-plus. Trade Sales of Slough were offering 1.7s with Lux pack (including aircon) for £10,999 in July 2001.

What's bad: Could suffer similar brake problems to Fiesta. Longterm life of special bore linings of 1.7 unknown in day-to-day use, though no problems to date. Misfiring 1.7 litre engine may be due to weeping core plugs leaking coolant onto spark plugs.

What to watch out for: Possibility of having been thrashed. Check the oil level as well as the oil colour of 1.7s. 5,000-mile oil changes far more sensible than Ford recommended 10,000-mile intervals. Don't switch to fully synthetic oil without written approval from Ford as this may affect bore liners. Kerbing will throw out critical front suspension alignment. Uneven front tyre wear should put you on your guard. Don't pay too much just to get one.

Recalls: 1998 (built Mar '98–Sep '98): 4,500 Pumas recalled to have brake master cylinder replaced.

Sierra (1982–1993)

What's good: All independently sprung successor to the Cortina, sold as 'man and machine in perfect harmony'. Early 2.0 litre versions were fast cars with 9-second 0–60 and 120 mph max. Cheap.

What's bad: Front suspension wears out and makes it terrible to drive. Sierras are one of the few cars better bought after accident repairs to the front which can make them feel new again. But make sure damage has not crumpled transmission tunnel, severely weakening the shell. All are now getting old and tired and were never supposed to last 10 years-plus.

What to watch out for: Every single trick in the book. Clockers. Cloners. Cut 'n' Shuts. Rust traps in doors. Warped front discs. Cracked heads and oil leaks on two litre twin-cams. Treat all 4x4s and Cosworths with particular suspicion. This is just the tip of the iceberg, so check everything.

StreetKa (from 2003)

What's good: Ford's £12,000 Ka based roadster due to hit the UK market in early 2003 using the 1.6 litre 103bhp Zetec S engine from the Fiesta and Focus. May also have option of 125bhp 1.7 from Puma. Very attractive and bound to sell well at this price level.

What's bad: Too soon to say

What to watch out for: Too soon to say.

Think City

What's good: Ford's contribution to the urban environment. Small, two-seater plastic bodied car 9ft 10 ins long (2,990mm) first seen at 1999 Frankfurt Motor Show. Reaches 30mph in 7 seconds and has a top speed of 56mph. Power is from 19 NiCd batteries and range is 53 miles. Fully recharging takes around 8 hours and costs 38p; 80% recharging 4–6 hours. Has a driver's airbag and aquitted itself well in US crash tests. On trial with London businesses from September 2001. Free parking in London and free recharging at special sites in Westminster. Zero rated VED. Exempt from London congestion charges. Could become the ideal London commuter car for those living within 30 miles of the centre. Websites: www.thinkmobility.com and www.thinkaboutlondon.co.uk.

What's bad: Not due on public sale in UK until mid 2002.

What to watch out for: Too soon to say.

HINDUSTAN

Ambassador

What's good: Basically an Indian built 1957 Morris Oxford with a catalysed 1.8 litre Isuzu engine. Heavy and cumbersome, but interesting to lovers of nostalgia. Some used as mini cabs in London and share driving characteristics with the FX4 taxi.

What's bad: Became a nightmare for the importer, Fullbore Motors of Fulham, and ultimately sent the firm into liquidation. What started as a good idea became entangled in European Type Approval and emissions regulations. This meant the change of engine from the old, Indian built 1,500cc 'B' Series pushrod engine to the Isuzu, the price escalated from £6,000 to £10,000; then, because the cars had to be virtually re-built before they could be sold in the UK the price rose to around £12,000 at which there were very few takers.

What to watch out for: You'll have to get your spare parts from the Morris Oxford Motor Club or from India. Will rust quite badly due to the poor quality of the welding and the steel.

HONDA

Accord (1989–1993)

What's good: Extremely well regarded, reliable Japanese-built saloon cars give ten years fault-free service as long as serviced on time. Badged Acura, have been the USA's top selling car. Healthy 135 bhp 2.0 litre catalysed down to 131 bhp from December 1991. Alternative engine was always catalysed 148 bhp 2.2. Excellent four-speed autoboxes. Beautifully built.

What's bad: Steering a bit light. Bonded windscreens very difficult to replace and this usually leads to scratches, rust and water ingress around screen area. Sheet metal not as thick as German cars. An intermittent fault which causes the engine to cut out may be nothing more than a failed ignition amplifier. A replacement part costs £50 and some RAC patrolmen actually carry them.

What to watch out for: Tend to be entirely trouble free as long as serviced on time. Check screen area for rust. Make sure aircon blows cold. Aircon may still contain environmentally unfriendly R12 refrigerant. Needs to be recharged with CFC-free 134A refrigerant and this may lead to weeping seals. Look for uneven tyre wear as a result of kerbing. Check under oil cap for emulsified oil due to short runs from cold starts – also likely to have rotted out rear silencer box.

Beat (1990–1995)

What's good: Tiny 656cc 64bhp three cylinder 'K' class sportscar from Japan, introduced in 1990 and production of which ended in 1995. Has a cult following. Revs to 8,000rpm. LCD stereo. Zebra striped seats. Available on the used grey market from around £3,500 to £9,000 for a top example.

What's bad: You need to find a specialst to look after it and they are few and far between. Because of this, some cars may not have been properly serviced.

What to watch out for: Excessive oil consumption (check exhaust gas colour carefully). Minor damage because parts can be difficult to source.

CRV (1997 on)

What's good: Very good 'supermarket' 4x4. Rear drive only cuts in when front wheels slip. The most car-like 'multi activity vehicle' to drive. Lots of useful knick-knacks. Cheaper and better than equivalent Land Rover Freelander. Honda three-year warranty. 11th from top in 'R' reg JD Power Customer Satisfaction Survey. Power increased from 125bhp to 147bhp from March 1999. In June 2001 Honda was rated by Motor Warranty Direct as Britain's 4th most claim-free used marque (www.warrantydirect.co.uk).

What's bad: Not much. You can't drive at much more than 40 mph with the centre sunroof open unless you also open a few windows or fit a Clim Air deflector. The seats are lower than in a Freelander – fine if you have a long back, but not if you're little and want to look over the tops of hedges.

What to watch out for: Signs of severe usage. Tow hooks (what's it been towing?) – can indicate wear in both front and rear clutches. But this is the most suburban-friendly 4x4 of the lot and therefore the least likely to have led a hard life.

UK CRX (1992–1995)

What's good: In 1992 the CRX became a two seater convertible rather than a 2+2 coupe. There was a 123bhp 1.6 with 5 speed manual of 4 speed automatic gearboxes, or a hot 158bhp 1.6 VTi VTEC version. Normally the roof panel has to be manually removed, but the top VTi had an electric mechanism that automatically lifted then stored the hardtop in the boot. Still very popular and a good little car.

What's bad: Not much. Honda servicing can be steep. Can go through discs and pads a bit quickly.

What to watch out for: Mainly front suspension damage from careless parking and accident damage, especially with VTis. Compression of VTi should be carefully checked because these engines rev and a previous owner may have revved the nuts off the one you're about to buy. Check condition of discs and adjust price paid if they need replacing. Make sure the ABS is functioning correctly on a VTi, because a malfunction is an MOT failure and it could cost you a furtune to put it right.

HRV (1999 on)

What's good: Be-spoilered suburban style wagon with part-time four-wheel-drive. Slightly cheaper than CRV with smaller 1.6 engine offering 104 or 123 bhp. 4x4 5-door version added from spring 2000 together with two-wheel-drive version of 3-door. Two-wheel-drive 123 bhp version is quite fast with 10.8-second 0–60. Much better than a Vitara.

What's bad: If there's a niche, Honda might as well exploit it.

What to watch out for: Nothing significant so far.

Insight (2000 on)

What's good: Aluminium-bodied two-seater aerodynamic hybrid coupe reminiscent of Le Mans Panhard DB endurance racers. 1.0 litre 3-cylinder VTEC engine offering 76 ps supplemented by 10 kW brushless DC electric motor. Very high geared, yet surprisingly quick and good to drive with 11.5-second 0–60 and 112 mph top speed. Ultra low CO_2 emissions of just 80 g/km and 83 mpg capability. Government subsidy dropped projected £17k price to £16k.

What's bad: Two seats only, plus luggage shelf and luggage cubby hole at rear. Lease only to Jan 2001. £16k from then on, but price does inclued batteries. Very high insurance premiums due to high cost of repairs.

What to watch out for: Too soon to say.

Japanese Civic (1991–1996)

What's good: 3-door hatchback with split tailgate; 4-door saloon. Impressive engines: 74 bhp 1.3; 89 bhp 1.5; 123 bhp 1.6 and 158 bhp VTi. 4-speed autos available on 89 bhp 1.5 and 123 bhp 1.6. In June 2001 Honda was rated by Motor Warranty Direct as Britain's 4th most claim-free used marque (www.warrantydirect.co.uk).

What's bad: Very small luggage area in split tailgate hatch. Saloon not as roomy inside as exterior dimensions suggest because roofline is quite low. Honda servicing is usually pricy. Ride not very smooth. Suits the small rather than the tall.

331

What to watch out for: Needs to have been regularly serviced, preferably with six-monthly oil changes. VTECs must have clean oil and are particularly vulnerable to extended service intervals.

Recalls: 1994: Honda Civic 3-door, 4-door, CRX automatics: auto gear indicator may show wrong transmission mode.

Japanese Civic (1996 on)

What's good: Restyled, slightly bigger, quieter Civics. 3-door now has conventional hatchback and more luggage space. Engine range now 90 bhp 1.4, 114 bhp 1.5, 116 bhp 1.6, 158 bhp VTi. Normal 4-speed auto or option of CVT auto in 116 bhp 1.6ES 3-door only. Two-year warranty grew to three. In June 2001 Honda was rated by Motor Warranty Direct as Britain's 4th most claim-free used marque (www.warrantydirect.co.uk).

What's bad: Average NCAP crash test results. Goggle-eyed restyle not wholly successful. 3-door side doors very long, so difficult to emerge in tight parking spaces with any dignity.

What to watch out for: Still quite new and should still be in the hands of Honda dealers for servicing. The last thing you want to see in a Honda is dirty oil on the dipstick.

Jazz (from early 2002)

What's good: Entirely new one box model on sale in Japan from June 2001. New Jazz 5 door hatchback replaces the lacklustre Logo and should arrive in the UK early in 2002, providing stiff competition for the Toyota Yaris and Daihatsu YRV. Features new 1-DSI engine technology. Dual and Sequential Ignition System comprises two spark plugs per cylinder in a compact combustion chamber where sequential ignition results in low emissions and high fuel economy. These engines are four cylinder of 1.2 and 1.4 litres capacity. Dimensions are: length: 3,830mm; width: 1,675mm; height: 1,525mm; wheelbase: 2,450mm. Offers five seats with entirely new rear seat arrangement said to offer unprecedented flexibility. Might be built at Swindon. More at www.honda.co.uk.

What's bad: Too soon to say. Launched in Europe at the Frankfurt Motor Show September 2001.
What to watch out for: Too soon to say.

Legend (1991 on)

What's good: A one-time Quentin Willson favourite – four-door saloon or plush two-door coupe. Grew up once it shook off Rover 800 association, first with 201 bhp 3.2 V6, then with 202 bhp 3.5 V6 from June 1996. In June 2001 Honda was rated by Motor Warranty Direct as Britain's 4th most claim-free used marque (www.warrantydirect.co.uk).
What's bad: Any problems tend to be expensive.
What to watch out for: Treat like a Lexus, so must have full dealer service history with frequent ATF, brake fluid, coolant, aircon refrigerant changes. Check carefully for any signs of uneven tyre wear. Look for oil leaks on ground where car has been standing. Give it some heavy braking on the test drive to check for warped discs caused by drivers holding the car on the brakes after a heavy stop.
Recalls: 2000: Legend saloons and coupes built 1996 to 1999: automatic gearbox fault leading to selector slipping into 'Park'. Cars built in 1996 and 1997: steering ball joints could separate.

Logo (2000–2001)

What's good: Worthy, perpendicular small three-door hatchback sold in Europe for more than a year finally reached UK in Y2K, to be built at Swindon. 1,343cc 64 bhp engine with 80 lb ft torque and 5-speed manual or CVT auto. Deep-section tyres give fairly good ride quality. Also manual-only diesel version in Europe. Did reasonably well in German TUV/Auto Bild front offset crash tests. Three-Star NCAP 2000 crash safety rating. ABS and aircon standard on official UK market cars. SE version replaced S version in July 2000. Additional kit includes rev counter, white-on-black dials, LCD odometer, 2-spoke sports steering wheel, black interior trim, black door mirrors and body coloured bumpers. Prices cut to £8,995 for manual and £9,895 for CVT auto in September 2000. Further price cut to £7,995 for SE manual from 5/10/2000, still including a/c.

What's bad: Styling isn't exactly inspired. Ridiculous launch list price of £9,495 and replacement SE even dearer. Criticised for 'gutless' and 'rough' 1.3 engine, 'lifeless' steering and 'too much body roll'. Already three years into its model life when launched in the UK. Quietly dropped from the UK market after all stocks were sold in January 2001. To be replaced by Jazz.

What to watch out for: Too soon to say.

NSX (1992 on)

What's good: Surprisingly civilised supercar. As easy to drive as a Honda Civic, but has storming VTEC V6 with 271 bhp that sounds wonderful. Early 5-speed models did not have standard PAS and were better for it (optional PAS was electric). Aircon standard, naturally. Auto optional. Targa came along in July '95 with standard PAS and optional F-Matic auto or six-speed manual. Engine grew to 3,179cc in Feb 1998 giving same power but more torque. Far more reliable and easy to live with on a day-to-day basis than a Ferrari. In June 2001 Honda was rated by Motor Warranty Direct as Britain's 4th most claim-free used marque (www.warrantydirect.co.uk).

What's bad: Tends to understeer quite a lot rather than catch you out with snap-oversteer. Power-steered cars lack steering feel. Eats rear tyres (6,000–8,000 miles).

What to watch out for: Must have full dealer service history with super-clean fully synthetic oil, frequent ATF, brake fluid, coolant, aircon refrigerant changes. Check carefully for any signs of uneven tyre wear. Alloy suspension is vulnerable to off road (or off track) excursions and pot hole damage.

Prelude (1992–1996)

What's good: Old Prelude turned from a glassy coupe into a more serious looking car altogether. Nice shark-nose 'mini XJS' styling. Useful range of engines include 131 bhp 2.0 litre; 158 bhp 2.3 and 183 bhp 2.2 VTEC. VTEC is the enthusiast's choice, but they're all good.

What's bad: Honda maintenance is expensive, particularly VTEC. Aircon may play up (best serviced and recharged with CFC-free 134A refrigerant by an aircon specialist who knows what he's doing). Not much room in the back seat. Paint may flake, particularly silver.

What to watch out for: Rusty or damaged exhausts and blown cats. Look for mismatched paint and check if due to flaking or accident damage. Check for kerbed alloys, uneven tyre wear, suspension damage. Has the car left the Honda dealer servicing fold? If so, who's been servicing it?

Prelude (1996–2000)

What's good: American styling not as interesting or original as predecessor. 132 bhp 2.0 litre or strong 185 bhp 2.2 VTi. 4-speed auto has 'Tiptronic'-type manual control. Motegi-kitted 132 bhp 2.0 and 183 bhp 2.2 from summer 1998. Aircon standard on all. One of the few cars the look of which is improved by lowered suspension and a factory body kit. Best colour: dark metallic blue. 13th from top in 'R' reg JD Power Customer Satisfaction Survey. In June 2001 Honda was rated by Motor Warranty Direct as Britain's 4th most claim-free used marque (www.warrantydirect.co.uk).

What's bad: Autobox manual control the wrong way round (should be back for upshifts and forward for downshifts to match laws of physics). Production ended in June 2000.

What to watch out for: Watch out for kerbing damage to big alloys and front suspension. Check for uneven tyre wear. Engine oil should be clean. Honda dealer service record should be complete.

Recalls: Cars built in 1997 and 1998: steering ball joints could separate.

S2000 (1999 on)

What's good: Two-seater roadster with astonishing 2.0 litre 237 bhp VTi engine that revs to 9,000 rpm allied to six-speed box. Has track car performance if you use the revs. Electric roof goes up and down in seconds.

What's bad: Doesn't have track car handling, so you feel a bit nervous about using the power on the road. Torque output doesn't match power output, so gears need to be used. Plastic back window.

What to watch out for: Kerb damage from over-exuberant drivers.

Recalls: 26/5/2000: June-Dec 1999 build: seatbelt webbing could become trapped between seat back and roof cover and fail to tension properly. Modified roof cover to be fitted. 24/11/2000: 1,426 S2000 models built 29/6/1999 to 21/4/2000 recalled because seat belt webbing may lock in the retracted position (same recall as May?). Locking mechanisms of both belts to be replaced.

Shuttle MPV (1997–2000)

What's good: Air conditioning standard. Excellent, obedient four-speed autobox with good column shift as standard. Powerful 2,156cc 150 bhp engine also standard (grew to 2,258cc from early 1998). Handles very well for an MPV. Called the 'Odyssey' in the USA where it is far and away the most reliable MPV of the lot. Late-model LS offered with seven seats at new low £18,000 price, sometimes discounted as low as a real bargain £15,000. Rear pair of seats fold away into the floor. Not too juicy (25–28 mpg). Looks more like a big car than a van. Top MPV and sixth from top overall in 'R' reg JD Power Customer Satisfacton Survey. In June 2001 Honda was rated by Motor Warranty Direct as Britain's 4th most claim-free used marque (www.warrantydirect.co.uk) Can be under £6,000 at auction for a high mileage 'R' reg. RECOMMENDED.

What's bad: Not as versatile as Galaxy/Alhambra/Sharan or Renault Espace. Lap belt only for centre mid-row seat. Sadly, dropped in April 2000 because new, larger Odyssey being built for USA and hugely inferior Civic based Stream for the UK.

What to watch out for: Look for a proper Honda service history. Buy on basis of current £18,000 LS model rather than previous, overpriced £24,000 six-seater ES. Aircon needs servicing and recharging every two years with CFC-free 134a refrigerant – costs around £150.

Recalls: Shuttles built in 1997 and 1998: steering ball joints could separate.

Stream (2001 on)

What's good: New 7-seater MPV based on the 2001 Honda Civic platform but with bigger engines including a 125bhp 1.7 litre VTEC and a 156bhp 2.0 litre VTEC, giving a 0–60 of 9.2 seconds and a top speed of 130mph. Same 'walk through' interior design as new Civic. 5-speed manual gearbox with dash mounted lever or new 5-speed sequential automatic. Effectively replaces the old, larger Shuttle. Road testers praise the steering, roadholding and handling as better than any other MPV.

What's bad: Rearmost row of seats unsuitable for all but small children making the car effectively a '5+2' rather than a 7-seater. These seats are also very difficult to access as the centre seats need to be slid forward. Cannot compete against the Zafira and Avensis Verso for versatility.

What to watch out for: Too soon to say.

UK Accord (1993–1998)

What's good: Accord saloons built in Swindon. Smooth Swindon built engines: 113 bhp 1.8 from March '96; 129 bhp 2.0 from May '93; 148 bhp 2.2iVTEC from March '96; 156 bhp 2.3iSR from October '93–March '96. Decent roadholding and handling, especially 2.2 and 2.3. Excellent four-speed autoboxes. Recommended. Two-year warranty grew to three. In June 2001 Honda was rated by Motor Warranty Direct as Britain's 4th most claim-free used marque (www.warrantydirect.co.uk).

What's bad: Steering a bit light. Exhaust rear silencer boxes rot out on low mileage 'short run' examples. Electric front windows have a habit of popping out of runners. New 1999 model instantly 'dates' a 98R old model.

What to watch out for: Tend to be entirely trouble-free as long as serviced on time with regular changes of coolant and brake fluid. Look for stone and screen chips on the quicker versions. Make sure electric front windows work properly and are not sluggish. Look for rust bubbling through just behind each rear wheel arch. This is a big panel in short supply, so the problem is very expensive to remedy. Check for emulsified oil under the oil cap of 2.3i engines as this could indicate a cracked cylinder head which is £2k to replace.

UK Accord (1998 on)

What's good: Re-engineered and rebodied Swindon Accord. Very well received and a good alternative to the VW Passat. 5-door hatch supplemented 4-door saloon from Summer 1999. 136 bhp 1.8 and 146 bhp 2.0 powerful enough. Fire-breathing 210 bhp Type R very fast indeed and an excellent handler with the best pedal set I've ever driven. Rover-engined diesel now dropped from line-up. Three-year warranty. Four-Star performance in NCAP crash safety tests.

What's bad: Reports of problems with manual gearboxes.

What to watch out for: Too soon to say.

Recalls: 2000: Accords built July '98–July '99: check for sticking throttle.

UK Civic (2001 on)

What's good: Radical, good looking and stylish new 5-door 'Swindon' Civic hatchback launched at September 2000 Paris Motor Show and sold in UK from January 2001. Flat floor and very spacious 'walk through' interior ideal for mothers with babies and small children. Front seats recline fully into single beds if required. Fascia-mounted gearstick. New 90 bhp 1.4 litre non-VTEC and 110 bhp 1.6 litre VTEC-II engines. Already meet Euro 2005 emissions limits. 5-speed manual or 4-speed automatic options in all but base 1.4iS. Electric power steering, ABS with electronic brake distribution and air conditioning in all models. Achieved five stars in American National Highway Traffic Safety Adminstration tests and four stars in Euro NCAP crash tests. Also got the highest pedestrian impact safety score ever recorded. 2-door coupe from April 2001 and 3-door hatch to follow in September 2001. Range will include a 200 bhp 2-door Type R. Three-year, 90,000-mile manufacturer warranty. Deservedly becoming very popular and a better car than the new Peugeot 307.

What's bad: 1.6 can be a bit noisy on the motorway due to harmonics of its flat floor (1.4 seemed to be better). Doesn't handle in the same sporty fashion as the Ford Focus. Body not electro galvanized so only has a six-year no perforation warranty. Otherwise too soon to say.

What to watch out for: Too soon to say.

Recalls: 7/6/2001: (affects 9,000 cars Worldwide): Make sure circlip on brake pedal pivot is properly positioned to hold the clevis pin in place. Make sure clip holding fuel filler pipe to tank has been tightened sufficiently.

UK Civic (to late 2000)

What's good: 'Swindon' 5-door hatchbacks and estate on floorpan shared with Rover 400. 89 bhp 1.4, 89 bhp 1.5 VTEC-E, 111 bhp 1.6 from '95–'97; 112 bhp 1.5 VTEC, 114 bhp 1.6 and rip roaring 167 bhp 1.8 VTEC from '97 on. Smooth 4-speed autos. 1.5 VTEC-E was capable of 45–50 mpg, but at a price. Very nicely built, under-bonnet looks like Honda motorcycle high tech. VTEC-E replaced by 85 bhp Rover 2.0 DI engine. Average performance in 1998 NCAP safety tests. Two-year warranty grew to three. In June 2001 Honda was rated by Motor Warranty Direct as Britain's 4th most claim-free used marque (www.warrantydirect.co.uk).

What's bad: 1.5 VTEC-E sometimes seen at head of long traffic queue as elderly driver tries to keep in economy range. 5-door range did not sell as well as Honda might have hoped as still some anti-Japanese ill-feeling and 'True Brits' go for the Rover equivalents.

What to watch out for: Quite a few 1.5 VTEC-Es were laundered into second-hand cars via the rental fleets. All 'Swindon Civics' appreciate frequent servicing and clean oil. Some complaints of poor reverse gear selection, so check this on test drive.

Recalls: 20/5/2000: 1999 and 2000 MY: 12,711 1.4s and 1.5s not fitted with ABS may suffer failure of brake proportion control valve leading to instability when braking. Part to be replaced with modifed unit. 3/11/2000: 2,327 5-door Civics built 10/3/1999 yo 10/10/2000 recalled because of possibility of breakage of rear suspension lower arm bolts. Bolts to be replaced.

UK Concerto (1989–1994)

What's good: Smooth Honda engines: Pre-cat 88 bhp 1.4; 106 bhp 1.6; 130 bhp twin cam 1.6 to August 1991. Post-cat 89 bhp 1.5; 110

bhp 1.6; 121 bhp 1.6i-16 from August 1991. Twin-cam 16-valve cars were quick. Smooth 4-speed autos. Decent UK build quality formerly from Rover, latterly from new Swindon factory. 'Blaise' run-out 1.6i 16v well liked.

What's bad: Old cars now, past their design life. Same body problems as old Rover 200. Honda engines require more maintenance than Rovers. Honda dealer labour rates can be high. Expensive ignition igniters tend to go at 50,000–60,000 miles and resulting misfire could hot-spot the cat. Relatively expensive to service and repair. The cost of a new ABS unit can be more than the car is worth.

What to watch out for: Serious rust around windscreen under rubber surround. Rusty sunroof surrounds. Frequent oil changes important – vital with twin-cam 16-valve cars. Ignition ignitor problem. High incidence of ABS pump failures when the brake fluid had not been changed regularly.

USA Accord (1994–1997)

What's good: Good-looking American built 'Aerodeck' estate cars and two-door coupes, badged Acura in the States. High specification includes aircon. 131–134 bhp 2.0 litre engine, 150 bhp 2.2 litre (same as Shuttle). Two-year warranty grew to three. In June 2001 Honda was rated by Motor Warranty Direct as Britain's 4th most claim-free used marque (www.warrantydirect.co.uk).

What's bad: Load area compromised by suspension intrusion. Honda servicing can work out expensive.

What to watch out for: Aircon needs recharging every three years with CFC-free 134A refrigerant. Must have regular servicing to remain reliable.

Recalls: 2000: Aircon wiring may chafe and short-circuit.

USA Accord Coupe (1998 on)

What's good: New American-built coupe from summer 1998 with choice of 145 bhp four-cylinder engine man/auto or 197 bhp V6 auto only. Understated good looks. Three-year warranty.

What's bad: A bit too 'American' for some European tastes.
What to watch out for: Nothing yet.

USA Civic (1994 on)

What's good: 2-door coupes, launched as 100 bhp 1.5s in February 1994 and ran through to January 1996. Then relaunched in January 1996 as LS with same goggle-eyed front as Japanese Civics with 103 bhp 1.6 or SR with 123 bhp 1.6, ABS and alloys. 4-speed auto optional. Aircon optional from June '97. Praised for much softer ride than other Civics. Reasonable rear head and legroom. In June 2001 Honda was rated by Motor Warranty Direct as Britain's 4th most claim-free used marque (www.warrantydirect.co.uk).
What's bad: Not much.
What to watch out for: Same as Japanese Civics.

HYUNDAI

Accent (1994–1999)

What's good: Replaced Pony X2 and a much better car with something akin to sporty handling. Engines include 83 bhp 1.3, 87 bhp 1.5 or, from Jan '97, a 98 bhp 1.5. PAS standard on 1.5s. 4-speed auto optional on 1.5 saloon and 5-door hatch. Quite well screwed together and generally cheap. Proper three-year warranties. Good reputation for reliability and helpful, inexpensive dealers. Came top in *Which?* Y2k reliablility survey.

What's bad: Comparatively poor 1.5-Star NCAP crash test results. Base 1.3s don't have PAS. Dumpy looks. Styling of front valance is dubious. Replaced by new Accent for 2000 model-year.

What to watch out for: Some did go onto leasing, rental and particularly Motability fleets. If less than three years old, make sure has not disqualified itself from 3-year warranty. With older cars watch out for same inadequate or incompetent kerbside home servicing as Pony. Front tyres tend to wear badly. Must have cambelt changes every 3 years or 36,000 miles.

Recalls: 1998 (built 1994–1997): possibility of road salt corrosion to front coil spring causing spring to damage tyre.

Accent (from 2000)

What's good: New model looks 'all new' and takes the car up half a class – bigger than a supermini, but smaller than a Focus/Golf. Slots into Hyundai/KIA range between KIA Pride and KIA Shuma. 3-door hatch, 5-door hatch and 4-door saloon. 1.3 manual has 55 bhp; 1.3 auto has 63 bhp; and 1.5 man/auto has 65 bhp with 97 lb ft torque. All models now have PAS. All autos 4-speed. All can do over 100 mph. Average fuel consumption: 36.22 mpg to 44.14 mpg. Good ride quality. Twin airbags. All have PAS. Owners of previous model consulted about improvements. Price competitive, from £6,799. Good dealers.

What's bad: Grille styling won't appeal to everyone. Handling is

not inspiring, but typical owners don't want it to be.
What to watch out for: Too soon to say.

Amica (2000 on)

What's good: New tall and short 5-door hatch on ATOZ platform, but radicaly different and lower priced. 55 bhp 1.0 litre 4-cylinder timing belt engine from ATOZ with 5-speed manual gearbox. First cars had 3-speed auto option; 4-speed auto introduced summer 2000. £5,999 for Si, or £7,799 for SE with PAS, a/c, electric front windows and central locking. PAS just £199 extra on base model. Auto £699 extra. Decent-sized boot. Full-sized 'spare'. Brilliant for the school run. Should share Three-Star NCAP crash safety rating of ATOZ.
What's bad: A/c heat exchanger right at the front is a bit vulnerable to road salt and stone or parking damage.
What to watch out for: Too soon to say.

ATOZ (1998–2000)

What's good: Quite good, tall, 5-door micro competed against Daewoo Matiz. Name springs from 'A to Z'. Power steering and three-year unlimited mileage warranty standard in price cut to £5,799 in May 2000. But £7,947 bought 'Plus' model with PAS, air-conditioning, driver's airbag, alloys and central locking. 3-speed auto option. Makes much more sense for the school run than a Grand Cherokee. Fits tiny parking spaces or a short, narrow, pre-war garage. 55 bhp, 90 mph and 45 mpg. Three-Star NCAP crash safety rating.
What's bad: Snobs driving their offspring to school in Grand Cherokees will look down their noses at you. Build quality a bit light. Looks like a wardrobe on castors. Cost just £4,750 in Spain. UK imports discontinued in favour of Amica in late 2000.
What to watch out for: Kerbing damage. Damage to thin body panels. Damage to trim by children.

Coupe (1996 on)

What's good: If the Lantra is 'the curvy car', then this is 'the swoopy coupe'. Good looking and a lot of coupe for the money. 112 bhp 1.6 the entry level at a reasonable £14,000. 137 bhp 2.0 litre a more serious car with standard alloys. Aircon optional on 1.6 and 2.0i; standard on 2.0iSE which also comes with leather seats. FI has big alloys and low-profile tyres. Will impress those who don't know what it is and is not a bad car in its own right. 130 mph plus. Handles nicely. Sells very well. Re-styled Y2k model has better sound-proofing and re-tuned, pleasant-sounding exhaust. Priced from £12,999 for the 1.6i.

What's bad: OTT launch advertising campaign compared the look of it to a Ferrari. Will not confer quite the same status on driver as a 3-Series, a Corrado, a Celica or even a Prelude. Year 2000 front-end restyle is not to everyone's taste.

What to watch out for: Cars that are flash for not much cash can be prime candidates for the repo man, so used examples may be without service books and some of the keys, and definitely warrant an HPI check. Still young enough to want to see full dealer service history.

Elantra (from March 2001)

What's good: The Elantra saloon and hatchback replace the Lantra model from March 2001. Engines are a 106bhp 1.6 which takes the car to 113mph and a 139bhp 2.0 which reaches 128mph and reaches 60mph in 9.1 seconds. ABS, air conditioning, three three-point rear seatbelts and and driver and passenger airbags are standard across the range, while the 2.0 litre CDX model has traction control, cruise control, climate control and leather seats. On the road prices which include a three-year warranty are: 1.6Si five-door £10,999; 1.6Gsi four or five-door £12,199; 2.0CDX four or five-door £13,999. More at www.Hyundai-car.co.uk.

What's bad: Too soon to say.

What to watch out for: Too soon to say.

Lantra (1991–1995)

What's good: Not bad Orion-sized four-door with Mitsubishi-derived power trains. 84 bhp 1.5, 112 bhp manual 1.6, 104 bhp 1.6 auto, 124 bhp 1.8. All had standard PAS. 1.6Cdi and all 1.8s had standard aircon. 1.8Cdi got standard ABS from October '93.

What's bad: Danger of being seduced by high spec of CD version. This is a reasonable car, but it's no BMW.

What to watch out for: Must have regular cambelt changes every 3 years or 36,000 miles. ABS needs frequent brake fluid changes. Aircon needs recharging with CFC-free 134A refrigerant every 3 years.

Recalls: 1996 (1991–1996): check for fracture of rear suspension bolt.

Lantra (1995–2000)

What's good: Quite nicely styled saloon or 5-door estate. Grown-up engine range of 112 bhp 1.6, 126 bhp 1.8 or 137 bhp 2.0 litre. PAS standard on all; ABS either standard or optional. Aircon standard on CDs; optional on 1.8Si and 1.6s. 16th from top in 'R' reg JD Power Customer Satisfaction Survey, just ahead of BMW 3-Series. Prices from £8,999 for 1.6i, including 3-year warranty.

What's bad: Advertised as 'the curvy car', which was an odd way to attract customers. Dealers try to sell them as more upmarket than they are.

What to watch out for: Must have regular cambelt changes every 3 years or 36,000 miles. If less than 3 years old, make sure has been regularly serviced and still qualifies for warranty.

Matrix

What's good: Smart, European-designed 5-seater MPV based on the Elantra platform to go on sale in the UK late 2001. Engine options are a 107bhp 1.6 petrol with 105 lb ft (143Nm) torque; a 133bhp 1.8 petrol with 122 lb ft (165Nm) torque; and a 76bhp 1.5 common rail direct-injected turbodiesel with 125 lb ft (170Nm) torque. The 1.6 petrol engine will be available with manual or automatic transmission; the others manual only. At an overall length of 4,025mm Hyundai states that the Matrix is the shortest mini MPV on the market. Width is 1,740mm and height, 1,625mm. Versatility is enhanced by a 60/40 split sliding and double-folding rear seat. More at www.Hyundai-car.co.uk .

What's bad: Too soon to say.

What to watch out for: Too soon to say.

Pony X2 (1990–1994)

What's good: Cheap and fairly reliable if properly serviced. 1.3 litre had 72 bhp; 1.5 had 83 bhp. 1.5 has PAS. Not overly complicated so not too much to go wrong.

What's bad: Ugly. Cheap trim. Sunroofs leak. Power outputs of both engines fell sharply when catalysed from August 1992. 'Pony and trap' is Cockney rhyming slang for 'crap'. Automatic gearboxes can start to give trouble after 6–7 years.

What to watch out for: Inadequate or incompetent kerbside home servicing. Could have sat around for a long time before being first registered. Cheap when new, so should be very cheap by now.

Santa Fe (from 2001)

What's good: Hyundai's new Sports Utility, a five door 4x4 with a choice of 143bhp 2.4 litre or 177bhp 2.7 litre V6 engines and a 115bhp 2.0 litre common rail diesel. The 2.4 has a manual five-speed gearbox, while the 2.7 has an H-tronic automatic offering manual over-ride. Equipment includes driver and passenger airbags, ABS with EBD, air conditioning, and a rear hatchback window which can be opened separately to accommodate long loads such as surfboards. The 2.7 also has leather covered seats. On the road prices, including a three-year warranty, are £15,999 for the 2.4, £16,999 for the 2.0 diesel and £17,999 for the 2.7 automatic. More at www.Hyundai-car.co.uk.

What's bad: Too soon to say.

What to watch out for: Too soon to say.

Sonata (1994–2000)

What's good: Biggish cheap car. Reliable enough. Surprise restyle in September 1996 gave it a new begrilled nose but 2.0 litre dropped in power to 123 bhp. 1994–96 2.0 litre had a reasonable 136 bhp. 5-speed manual or 4-speed auto. ABS standard on 2.0CD and 3.0 litre. CDs and V6s also have aircon, while V6 offers cruise control and leather. Revised again in June 1998 when V6 went down in size to 2,493cc, but up in power to 160 bhp. 2.0 litre fours also back up to 136 bhp. Still not the subject of any rave reviews. Y2K model 2.0GSi priced from £12,999.

What's bad: Ride and handling not up to European standards for the class. Power of 2.0 litre dropped to 122 bhp after the 1995 restyle. 3.0 litre V6 only ever had 143 bhp and a sluggish autobox.

What to watch out for: Though it may be out of warranty, you still want to see a proper dealer service history showing regular brake fluid, ATF, coolant, timing belt and aircon refrigerant changes. Don't buy an ex-taxi that's been serviced on the taxi rank.

Terracan

What's good: The Terracan is a tough, chassis-framed 4x4. Engine options are a 2.5 litre petrol, a 3.5 litre V6 petrol and a 2.9 litre common-rail turbodiesel. Standard equipment includes ABS with electronic brake force distribution, driver and passenger airbags, variable ratio steering; the option of manual or automatic transmission; and the option of either part-time four-wheel-drive with electric shift transfer or full-time four-wheel-drive. Dimensions are: length: 4,710mm; width: 1,860mm; height: 1,790mm. The Terracan is intended to meet the requirements of people who need a serious off-roader, leaving the Santa Fe for those who like the looks of a 4x4 but rarely venture off the tarmac. More at www.Hyundai-car.co.uk.

What's bad: No decision yet reached as to whether the Terracan will be marketed in the UK.

What to watch out for: Too soon to say.

Trajet MPV (2000 on)

What's good: 7-seater launched June 2000 priced from £15,500. 133 bhp 2.0 litre 4-cylinder and 167 bhp 2.7 litre V6 petrol engines (£20,000) plus a 111bhp 2.0 litre common rail direct-injected diesel with 188 lb ft (255Nm) torque from June 2001, mpg 37.2 combined, priced at £16,499. Seats in 2-3-2 pattern; all five rear seats individually removable. A/c, ABS, Electronic Brake Distribution (important on an MPV), CD and two de-powered airbags all standard. 30 mpg economy possible from 2.0 litre. Plenty of equipment including underseat trays; map, bottle and pen holders; four reading lights; luggage net, etc. 168bhp 2.7 litre V6 announced for 2001 giving top speed of 120mph and 0–60 of 11.5 seconds at an on the road price of £19,999. Towing capacity of this version is 1,950kg assuming driver only on board. 4-speed autobox no extra cost on V6.

What's bad: Rather anonymous. Yet another 7-seat MPV, curiously from the same company that builds the new KIA Sedona.

What to watch out for: Too soon to say.

XG30 (from 2000)

What's good: Hyundai's big car, slightly larger than MB E-Class and BMW 5-Series, but smaller than S-Class, with 3.0 litre 192 bhp V6 and 5-speed 'Tiptronic'-type auto offering 9.3-second 0–60, 140 mph top speed and Euromix economy of 26.4 mpg. Soft ride with very quiet cruising – two qualities much sought after by many owner-drivers. Handling is reasonable in the circumstances. ABS, aircon, alloys, lots of kit and lots of car for £20,999. Three-year warranty.

What's bad: Front-drive chassis tramps badly at the front when pushed on tight corners (though, of course, the car isn't likely to be driven in a manner that exposes this).

What to watch out for: Too soon to say.

ISUZU

Trooper (1987–1992)

What's good: Square, 'honest' and quite well-thought-of 4x4s with petrol or diesel engines and short 3-door or long 5-door bodies and the option of 7 seats in the 5-door. Engines: 2,254cc 109 bhp petrol four; 2,559cc 111 bhp petrol four; 2,238cc ohc 74 bhp diesel four to Jan 1988, then much better 2,771cc 95 bhp TD from Jan 1988. 'Duty' pack offers better kit and, from Jan 1988, a limited slip diff.

What's bad: They do rust, quite badly. Older ones are likely to have had a hard life and may well be simply worn out.

What to watch out for: Rust, signs of hard usage such as a battered floor, scrubs on bodywork, oil leaks from powertrain, inadequate servicing, broken springs, shocked out shocks, uneven tyre wear, excessive smoke from turbodiesel, crunchy gearchange. Make sure four-wheel-drive engages properly. Some reports of cracks developing in cylinder heads of petrol models. The car could easily be an older 'grey import' offering no means of checking on its past.

Trooper (1992–1998)

What's good: 3.1 litre 113 bhp TD or 3.2 litre 174 bhp petrol V6 in two wheelbases – short with 3 doors or long with 5 doors and the option of 7 seats. 3-year warranty. 'Duty' pack takes trim up one stage from basic. 'Citation' takes it up another stage.

What's bad: Brick-like styling. The last two years worth sat around for a long time waiting to be sold which delayed the UK launch of the new model. Not quite as reliable as you might expect, possibly due to long wait for a buyer. Re-incarnated (disastrously) as the Vauxhall Monterey.

What to watch out for: Rust, signs of hard usage such as a battered floor, scrubs on bodywork, oil leaks from powertrain, inadequate servicing, broken springs, shocked out shocks, uneven tyre wear, smoke from diesel's turbo, crunchy gearchange. Make sure four-wheel-drive engages properly. If it has a tow hook, what has it been towing – and where? Could have been pulling a livestock trailer over a Welsh mountain. Not quite the same 'green welly' appeal as a Discovery or a Shogun, so more likely to have been a working vehicle.

Trooper (1998 on)

What's good: New 159 bhp twin-cam 16-valve direct-injected common rail diesel engine gives stump-pulling 246 lb ft torque at just 2,000 rpm. Combined fuel consumption figure of 31.6 very good for this type of vehicle. (Also a 215 bhp 3.5 litre petrol V6.)

What's bad: Essentially, the old body with a more rounded front – and we had to wait for it while stocks of the slow-selling old model got shifted.

What to watch out for: Shouldn't be troublesome yet, but problem areas likely to be same as old model. First common rail DI in the UK, so first test of individual electronically controlled injectors.

JAGUAR

S-Type (1999 on)

What's good: New small Jaguar with design cues from 1960s Mk II. Choice of 240 bhp Duratec V6 or 280 bhp Jaguar V8 engines. Manual (V6 only) or Ford auto. CATS option of adaptive damping and 17in wheels worth having. Prices start at £26,700 OTR. Good to drive, with enough steering feel, decent handling and good ride quality. A success from day one. Six-cylinder manual model the recommended choice. See road test of £30,600 S-Type 3.0 V6 Sport manual at www.honestjohn.co.uk. S and T reg cars came a good 17th in 2001 Top Gear/JD Power Customer Satisfaction Survey, ahead of the Toyota Corolla.

What's bad: Automatic 'J' change can be sloppy and apt to drop a gear unasked when you're halfway round a corner.

What to watch out for: Too soon to say.

Recalls: 4/10/2000: 2,109 S Types built 5/2000–7/2000 recalled because part in front seatbelt buckles not to standard and may release the belt when subject to load. All buckles assemblies between production dates to be replaced. 23/11/2000: 18,062 S Types built 1/1999 to 9/2000 recalled because first thread of the ball stud in the front suspension lower ball joint could fracture leading to separation of the lower control arm from the knuckle leading to limited steering control. Ball joints to be checked and vertical links to be replaced if necessary.

X-Type (2001 on)

What's good: Engines are a 195bhp 2,495cc Duratec V6 offering 180 lb ft torque at 3,000 rpm and a 231bhp 2,968cc Duratec V6 with 210 lb ft torque at 3,000 rpm. Five-speed manual and five-speed automatic transmissions are available with both engines. Performance of the 2.5 manual is 0–60mph in 7.9 seconds, 140mph top speed, combined mpg of 29.5 and CO_2 emissions of 234g/km which puts cars registered from 1st March into the £155pa VED bracket. The 3.0 manual gets to 60 in 6.6 seconds, goes on to 146mph, delivers a combined mpg of 27.5 and emits 244g/km CO_2 which puts it in the same £155pa VED bracket. On the Road List Prices, which include a three-year warranty, are: 2.5 V6: £22,000; 2.5 V6 Sport: £24,000; 2.5 V6 SE: £24,750; 3.0 V6 Sport: £25,500; 3.0 V6 SE: £26,250. Air-Conditioning, ABS, Alloy Wheels and All-Round Airbags are standard on all models. Automatic Transmission is an extra £1,250, Dynamic Stability Control an extra £480, and Rear Parking Sensors an extra £310. 2.2 litre V6 to come later. Will give the new Audi A4, the BMW 3-Series, the Mercedes C Class and the Lexus IS200 a serious run for their money, but will also compete with Ford's Volvo S60. *Autocar* magazine scoop in issue 13/12/2000 shows 330bhp 155mph X-Type R to rival BMW M3. Softish suspension allows the car to handle really well without taking it into Mitsubishi Evo VI territory. 2.5 is smoother and sweeter than 3.0 litre but very obviously lacks the power of its bigger engined brother. Manuals much better than automatics. But this is an excellent car which is bound to be hugely successful. More at www.X-TYPE.com.

What's bad: Over-enthusiastic traction control system can temporarily lock a wheel.

What to watch out for: Too soon to say.

XJ6 and XJR (1994–1997)

What's good: 300 Series gained an impressive reputation for reliability both on the fleets and in private hands. Better even than Mercedes or BMW. Well liked by owners. 216 bhp 3.2 litre straight six; 245 bhp 4.0 straight six; 322 bhp 4.0 litre supercharged straight six. 5-speed manual or 'J-change' 4-speed ZF automatic. XJR has much better Mercedes 600 autobox. Three-year 60,000-mile warranty.

What's bad: A glut of these were p/xd for XJ8s by status seekers when the XJ8 came out and prices fell. They climbed back up once the market realised how good the sixes were.

What to watch out for: Less than pristine examples are worth a lot less – pay no more than 'Parker's Guide' Fair prices for scruffy XJs.

Also check the spec, because you don't want a standard model with cloth seats and no aircon. Still new enough to insist on a proper Jaguar dealer service record. Bodies may flex and crack windscreens. Alloys oxidise easily. Rear bumper protector falls off. Check all electrics, particularly the dashboard computer. Feel the discs for lipping or scoring and watch out for uneven braking on the test drive. Brake judder may be due to drivers sitting on the brakes after a hard stop which causes localised overheating and warps the discs. For older cars, see tips for previous model XJ 40 above.

XJ6 SIII (1979–1986)

What's good: Last of the classic 'feline'-shape XJ6 and prices of good late examples have been rising. 4.2 had 205 bhp. 5.3 V12 had 299 bhp and carried on alongside XJ40 to September 1989.

What's bad: Old cars now with old car problems. The dashboard is a mess. Rust may have set in.

What to watch out for: Buy carefully from an expert specialist such as Robert Hughes (01932 858381) to avoid pitfalls. The coolant needs to have been changed every two years without fail or the block will sludge up at the back, overheat, blow its head gasket and possibly warp its cylinder head. Rust first appears under rear valance, under the front wings behind the headlamps and along the top of the wing seam. Use a magnet. Otherwise, see XJ40 below and be very wary if the car overheats.

XJ6 XJ40 (1986–1994)

What's good: Less likely to have build faults than previous Jaguars. Quiet and quick, nice ambience inside a Sovereign. Non-cat 3.6 has 221 bhp. Catted 3.2 AJ6 has 200 bhp. Pre-cat 4.0 has 235 bhp, sinking to 205 bhp with cat. 4.0 XJR has 248 bhp. Catalysed 5.3 V12 has 264 bhp. All should take unleaded.

What's bad: Styling the most boring of any XJ. Lack of steering 'feel'. Too low for some. Not as much rear legroom as length implies. 165 bhp 2.9 litre version best avoided unless really cheap (less than £1,000).

What to watch out for: Must have leather seats (or at least leather seat facings) – a £750 trimming job. Aircon more desirable than sunroof. Make sure aircon blows cold. Good news if has been recharged with CFC-free 134A refrigerant instead of old R12 and the seals aren't leaking. Will rust – the first place is around number plate lights in the boot lid, but if there's rust in the wings, sills and inside the boot, walk away. Light reflectors also let in water and rust. Listen for timing chain rattle – a sign of age and insufficiently frequent oil changes. The coolant needs to have been changed every two years without fail or the block will sludge up at the back, overheat, blow its head gasket and possibly warp its cylinder head. If the brake fluid isn't changed every two years, the ABS pump could rust up inside, so make sure the ABS light goes on when you switch on and goes off again a few seconds after start-up. Check all electrics. Check for uneven tyre wear signifying suspension or steering damage. If tyres are worn, they're costly to replace. Listen for clonking from the rear axle on gearchanges, which should be smooth. Manuals are rare and early ones had a clutch problem, but all should have been sorted by now. If fitted with self-levelling suspension, make sure it self-levels. Try and feel the discs for scoring, lipping and wear. Brake callipers can seize and are expensive, so be very suspicious of uneven braking on test drive.

XJ8 and XJR8 (1997 on)

What's good: Same car as 300 Series with new 240 bhp 3.2 V8, new 290 bhp 4.0 V8 and stonking 370 bhp supercharged 4.0 V8. 5-speed automatic (Mercedes box on XJR8). Climate control on all models. Three-year 60,000-mile warranty. The XJR8 is one of the best £50,000 cars you can buy. A very creditable fourth from top in the 'R' reg JD Power Customer Satisfaction Survey. S and T reg cars came seventh in 2001 Top Gear/JD Power Customer Satisfaction Survey.

What's bad: Painted front bumper looks organic and is easy to scratch. No means of checking 5-speed ZF autobox oil level or refilling it. Jaguar says 'sealed for life', but no oil changes could mean a 'life' of just 10 years. No manual option.

What to watch out for: Must have a full Jaguar dealer service history (without it, you lose the 3-year warranty) and must be immaculate to command top money.

Recalls: Jaguar XJ8 (July-October 1997: 11,221 cars): may suffer sudden deceleration due to weak retention bracket on accelerator cable. Extra clip 'costing pennies' solves the problem. (Announced on radio 7/2/98.)

XJS 3.6 and 4.0 (1983–1995)

What's good: 3.6s didn't have cats and did have 225 bhp. Roll-bar cabrio from 1986–87 was stiffer than later convertible. Convertible 4.0 litre from 1992 was much better looking. Rare option of a 5-speed manual instead of 4-speed autobox.

What's bad: Early 1986–87 AJ6 3.6s don't like unleaded and had dodgy engine management systems. 4.0 litre came with a cat so, despite an extra 390cc, is down on power to 223 bhp.

What to watch out for: Fairly apt to suffer front suspension and steering damage, so check this carefully. Any signs of uneven tyre wear – either avoid the car or budget for a big bill. The coolant needs to have been changed every two years without fail or the block will sludge up at the back, overheat, blow its head gasket and possibly warp its cylinder head. Check that standard aircon blows cold. Good news if has been recharged with CFC-free 134A refrigerant instead of old R12 and seals aren't leaking. Look for rust in the flying buttresses at the back, sills and wheelarches. Otherwise, see XJ40 above.

XJS V12 (1975–1995)

What's good: Monster 5.3 litre 299 bhp lost 20 bhp to catalyser, but 6.0 litre V12 from May 1993 was back up to 308 bhp. Only a few early versions were manual. Rest automatic only and all are oilwell emptiers. 6.0 litre pre-cat XJRS from Sept '89 had 318 bhp, boosted to 333 bhp in October 1991. Can be very reliable, but see below.

What's bad: Ask yourself if you really need all this power in a soft car with overlight power steering which lacks 'feel'. I know of two

XJS single-car accidents within half a mile of each other on the same stretch of road.

What to watch out for: The rearmost pair of spark plugs are hidden by plumbing, take hours of dismantling to get at and consequently are rarely changed. Contrary to the horror stories, these big, unstressed V12s can be very reliable and trouble-free if treated and maintained with respect. This means 3,000-mile or six-month fully synthetic oil changes (no later), annual transmission oil changes, new brake fluid and coolant every two years without fail. Fairly apt to suffer front suspension and steering damage, so check this carefully. Any signs of uneven tyre wear – either avoid the car or budget for a big bill. Otherwise, see comments on XJS 3.6/40 and XJ40. If it overheats it's going to be trouble, so leave it alone.

XK8 and XKR (1996 on)

What's good: Much better looking, more 'Jaguar-like' than XJS. Tried and tested styling seen before on Aston Martin DB7. Convertible looks lovely. Says you're rich, British and proud of it. 290 bhp in standard form. Supercharged XKR has 370 bhp and 387 lb ft (525Nm) torque, plus better Mercedes gearbox – and there is an XKR convertible. 0–60 in 5.2 seconds. Three-year 60,000-mile warranty.

What's bad: May suffer from infuriating build quality problems. No easy means of checking 5-speed autobox oil level or refilling it. Jaguar says 'sealed for life', but no oil changes mean a 'life' of 10 years tops. (XKR has a stronger Mercedes box.) These cars gulp gas, of course. Rear passengers need to be legless.

What to watch out for: Vital to buy the right trim combination – the 'Classic' rather than the 'Sport' or the base model.

Recalls: 1997: rear suspension. 1998 (July-October 1997 build – 11,221 cars): may suffer sudden deceleration due to weak retention bracket on accelerator cable. Extra clip 'costing pennies' solves the problem. (Announced on radio 7/2/98.)

JENSEN

C-V8

What's good: Coupe version of S-V8, due to be launched late 2001 at prices slightly higher than the £39,650 of the Jensen S-V8. See Jensen S-V8.

What's bad: Too soon to say.

What to watch out for: Too soon to say.

S-V8 (2000 on)

What's good: Marque revived as a two-seater sports car with front end styling reminiscent of the C-V8. Powerful 32-valve 4.6 litre 316 bhp Ford engine also delivers 316 lb ft torque. 5-speed manual box. Priced at £39,650 + £675 on the road charges it's a comfortable alternative to an AC Mk IV or a TVR. Extensive list of luxurious extras. Website: www.jensen-motors.com.

What's bad: Too soon to say.

What to watch out for: Too soon to say.

KIA

Carens (2000 on)

What's good: Strangely styled multi-purpose estate car based on KIA Shuma. 110 bhp 1.8 litre engine. Five seats in two rows or six seats in three rows. Prices start at less than £10k. ABS and aircon standard on more expensive GSX. 3-year warranty.

What's bad: Just look at it. Six-seater has no boot space and rearmost seats are for children only.

What to watch out for: Too soon to say.

Clarus (2000–2001)

What's good: Mondeo-sized 4-door saloon and estate, but much cheaper. 116 bhp 1.8 litre SX priced close to new Neon at £10,995; 133 bhp 2.0 litre Executive top model with a/c, alloys, ABS and leather just £13,495, or £14,295 with 4-speed autobox. Station wagon also available with huge lights set high in rear 'D' pillars. Standard 3-year warranty.

What's bad: Zero image. Replaced by KIA Magentis in Summer 2001.

What to watch out for: Too soon to say.

Joice

What's good: 7-seater 'carlike' MPV. 2.0 litre 139 bhp engine. Standard ABS. Based on KIA Shuma. 110 bhp 1.8 litre engine. Standard 3-year warranty.

What's bad: Utilitarian external looks. May not come to UK.

What to watch out for: Too soon to say.

Magentis (mid-2001 on)

What's good: The biggest new car bargain currently available in the UK. A 166bhp 2.5 litre V6 saloon for just £12,995 on the road.

4,720mm long with an interior volume of 2,832 litres and a boot capacity of 386 litres. Standard equipment includes 4 sensor ABS with Electronic Brakeforce Distribution, air-conditioning, alloy wheels, front fog lights, CD player, remote control central locking, a useful 60/40 split folding rear seat and 5mph impact-sustaining bumpers. Sports H-Matic automatic transmission is a £1,000 option. Combined fuel consumption figure for the manual is 28.2mpg with CO2 emissions of 237g/km (£155 VED); for the automatic the figures are 25.9mpg and 257 g/km (£155 VED). Prices are £12,995 on the road for the LX as described; £13,995 for the LX automatic; and £15,995 for the more luxurious, leather trimmed SE automatic. All prices include KIA's three-year 60,000-mile warranty and three-year recovery/assistance package. Replaces the KIA Clarus. More at www.kia.co.uk.

What's bad: Too soon to say.

What to watch out for: Too soon to say.

Mentor (1996–1999)

What's good: Quite well made and quite reliable. Owners seem to like them. Available as 4-door saloon or 5-door hatch.

What's bad: Zero image, completely ordinary, fairly small 4-door saloon (slightly smaller than an Orion) or 5-door hatch. Lacks specification (sun roofs are cheap aftermarket 'pop-up' add-ons). Strange engine line-up on earlier models. 1.5 litre had 80 bhp and 88 lb ft torque; 1.6 litre had 79 bhp and 92 lb ft torque. But peak power and torque figures closer in rev range on 1.6.

What to watch out for: Hard to match damaged body panels. Likely to have been privately owned by the over-50s and frequently parked facing the sea.

Mentor (mid-2001 on)

What's good: Re-launched Mentor saloon at low prices from £8,995 in Summer 2001. At 4,510mm the new Mentor is 15mm longer than a Vauxhall Vectra saloon. Power comes from a twin cam 1,594cc 16 valve engine giving a top speed of 115mph and a 0–60 of 11.5 seconds. Combined consumprion is 35.3mpg and CO_2 enissions 190g/km (£155 VED). The automatic tops out at 109mph, gets to 60 in 13.4 seconds, does 33.6mpg on the combined cycle and emits 198 g/km CO_2 (also £155 VED). Standard kit on the £8,995 L includes twin airbags, central locking, electric front and rear windows, seatbelt pre-tensioners and 14 inch wheels. The £10,200 LX also has ABS, air-conditioning, electric mirrors and height and lumbar adjustable driver's seat. Automatic is a NO COST option on both. All prices are on the road including KIA's three-year 60,000-mile warranty and three-year recovery package. More at www.kia.co.uk.

What's bad: Too soon to say.

What to watch out for: Too soon to say.

Mentor II/Shuma (1999–2001)

What's good: New 4-door saloon and 5-door hatch, more modern and much better looking than previous model. 1.5 litre 88 bhp and 1.8 litre 110 bhp engines. Mentor II saloon has more restrained styling. Shuma 'Fastback' goes for twin headlight look. Optional 4-speed auto. Three-year mechanical and six-year body warranties. Low prices (from £8,500 OTR). Shuma hatch continues but new Mentor from Summer 2001.

What's bad: Too soon to say. Mentor II replaced in Summer 2001.

What to watch out for: Too soon to say.

Pride (1991 on)

What's good: Old Mazda 121 re-incarnated, built in South Korea. Helped KIA establish UK foothold. 1,324cc model relaunched at lower price in summer 1999 after company taken over by Hyundai. Standard 3-year warranty.

What's bad: Old design. UK never got estate car version.

What to watch out for: Uneven tyre wear signifies worn front suspension bushes. Catted versions may have problems. Treat only as a cheap buy offering decent reliability.

Rio (Summer 2001 on)

What's good: New Focus-sized 5-door 1.3 litre (74 bhp) and 1.5 litre (97 bhp) hatchback launched in Korea in December 1999, and in Europe at the 2000 Geneva Show. Coming to UK Summer 2001 at very low prices from around £7,000. Top speed of 1.5 111mph and 0–60 in 10.6 seconds (1.5 auto 96mph and 0–60 in 13.9 seconds). 3-year 60,000-mile warranty.

What's bad: First reports were not keen on the driving experience. Criticised rubbery manual gearchange. Doesn't come with USA 10-year 100,000-mile warranty.

What to watch out for: Too soon to say.

Roadster

What's good: Effectively a re-working of the much sought after front-wheel-drive Lotus Elan, now with less powerful 136 bhp 1.8 litre engine. Standard 3-year warranty.

What's bad: Not quite the car it looks to be. Top speed only 123 mph with 0–60 in 9 seconds. May not come to UK. Victim of KIA's 1998 take-over by Hyundai.

What to watch out for: Too soon to say.

Sedona (1999 on)

What's good: Big, heavy, Voyager-sized 7-seater MPV with side sliding doors and either a 126 bhp 2.9 litre 16-valve TDI diesel engine with 249 lb ft torque or a 165 bhp 3.0 litre petrol V6 with 164 lb ft torque. Top speed of manual V6 is 116 mph with 13.5-second 0–60; diesel does 105mph with 17-second 0–60 and 34.03 mpg. Autobox available with both engines but is slower. 'Slide through' driving compartment with dash-mounted gearlever. Centre row seats of LS version swivel to face rear seats. Aircon standard in LS. RS base models priced from £14,000. Not bad looking out on the road and not bad to drive. Selling very well. Standard 3-year warranty.

What's bad: Inconvenient 2-2-3 seating arrangement with back three seats on a single bench. A bit slow for the power outputs.

What to watch out for: Too soon to say.

Sportage (1995 on)

What's good: Cheap alternative to Vitara, Rav 4, Honda CRV and Land Rover Freelander. Lively enough, with 128 bhp and 88 bhp turbodiesel. Re-launched summer 1999 to include longer wheelbase version five-door and a retro-styled short-wheelbase 'Sportage classic' as well as the standard SWB three-door. Standard 3-year warranty.

What's bad: Not exactly sophisticated. Or very roomy. Not as good as any of the expensive alternatives. Can be troublesome and, when they are, the dealers may not be very good at putting them right. S and T platers 6th from bottom in 2001 Top Gear/JD Power Customer Satisfaction Survey.

What to watch out for: Evidence of off-road use. Has the upholstery been 'crocodiled' (eaten by dogs)? Better to buy a town car than a country car.

Recalls: None known 1994–98, but some cars have been riddled with faults.

LADA

Niva (1978–1995)

What's good: Lada's 4x4. Dates back to the 1970s, but quite good if your need is for a tough, basic 4x4. Usual Lada full tool kit supplied. Reasonably competent off road. Latest cars have Suzuki-like front. Some have been fitted with aftermarket PSA XUD diesel engine. Should be very cheap.

What's bad: Very noisy, slow, thirsty and dated. Quite a small cabin (looks like a Fiat 127 on stilts). Trim not up to the job. Horrible to drive on the road (swaps ends in the wet). Obstructive gearbox.

What to watch out for: Make all the usual working 4x4 checks as these aren't bought for status and are bound to have been hammered off road. Look for leaking gaskets and seals in the axles, gearbox and transfer case. Check the hub bearings and steering bushes carefully. Look for rock damage to sump and axles. Expect the seat trim to have fallen apart. Expect some rust. If there are holes on the surface panels, check the structure very carefully with an old screwdriver. Be highly suspicious of fresh underseal.

Riva (1983–1995)

What's good: Based on 1960s Fiat 124. Very tough. They gave you a full set of tools to fix it when it went wrong. Kids don't steal them for joy rides. Made infamous by Maureen and Dave Rees from 'Driving School'. Owners display their own brand of inverted snobbery. Quite a few 'catless' cars legally took advantage of extended 1993 'cat' deadline. Estate cars make the best sense. Dealers and parts specialists can be 'salt of the earth'. Should be very cheap.

What's bad: Appalling build quality. Very basic. Noisy, thirsty, dated and lumpy to drive (nothing like a real Fiat 124). Spare parts supply not guaranteed to last indefinitely. Factory infiltrated by the Russian Mafia. Post-August 1992 models fitted with cats have severe trouble passing MOT advanced emissions systems test.

What to watch out for: Where do you start? Conscientious owners look after them properly. People who buy them for £100 at an auction don't bother and simply run them into the ground. Listen for signs of big ends going. Expect some gearbox whine, but not too much. Unscrew a spark plug to see if it's burning oil. Trim may have fallen apart of its own accord under the inevitable seat covers. Electrics play up (fusebox shorts, distributor wears out). If you're paying a proper price, make sure the tools are all there.

Samara (1984–1996)

What's good: Engines and gearboxes not that bad. Body reasonably robust. Cheap.

What's bad: Usual dreadful Lada build quality. Slothful suspension. Horrible handling. Rickety ride. Terrible trim. Eccentric electrics. May not pass MOT 'advanced emission control system' test.

What to watch out for: Depends who's had it before (see Riva). Check all electrics. 'Reverse-turn test' driveshaft joints for clonks.

LANCIA

Dedra (1990–1995)

What's good: Mostly galvanised Tipo/Tempra-based Lancia saloon, so won't rust like a Beta. 165 bhp 2.0 turbo is a bit of a tyre shredder, but will give BMW 318i drivers a nasty shock. 2.0ie has 120 bhp which sank to 115 bhp with cat. SE has automatic suspension control. 1.8ie has 110 bhp – down to 107 bhp with cat; 1.6ie has 90 bhp, down to 80 bhp with cat. Good ride quality, decent handling. Alcantara trim is nice, but not everyone likes the colours. These cars are cheap and can be bargains.

What's bad: Ugly, especially from rear. Dated. Very few around. Body parts hard to source.

What to watch out for: Check for uneven and excessive front tyre wear (especially turbo) – may be suspension damage. Heater may be u/s. Look for exhaust smoke from turbo oil seals. Satisfy yourself that performance of turbo is up to the mark. Check all electrics (of course). Expect the odd oil leak, especially from gasket between two-piece head and cam carrier. Need regular 35,000–40,000 mile timing belt changes.

Delta HF and Integrale (1987–1995)

What's good: Sensational performance. 165 bhp 8v HF May–Dec '87; 185 bhp 8v Integrale Feb '88–March '89; 196 bhp 16v Sep '89–Jan '92. Special order only last-of-the-line 210 bhp Evo 2 from Jan '92 is a collector's item and if kept immaculate will hold its value. Late models had swish leather and Alcantara interiors.

What's bad: Left-hand-drive only. May be an expensive performance car, but is still based on the Delta which itself is based on the Fiat Ritmo/Strada. So will rust. Will have iffy electrics (dash, rear wash-wipe, heated rear screen, central locking, electric door mirrors). Expensive to keep in good shape.

What to watch out for: First, decide if you want a competition car for rallies or track days, or a flash road car with air and leather. A used

365

competition car will have had offs and will have suffered damage. Uneven tyre wear could be due to suspension misalignment, suspension damage or a distorted shell and is a big job to set up correctly. Timing belts must be changed every 36,000 miles or 3 years, whichever comes first. Brake fluid needs changing every year on ABS systems. Coolant needs changing every two years. Look for coolant and oil leaks. Don't buy one that smokes. Check the condition of the very expensive brake discs. You really need an Integrale specialist to go over one of these for you.

Thema (1985–1989)

What's good: Decent handling, decent performance. The 8.32 of 1988 even had a 215 bhp Ferrari V8 engine, but the 165 bhp 2.0 Turbo is probably the best performance buy. Normal 8-valve 2.0 litre 120 bhp, 2.8 V6, 150 bhp. Lots of room inside cabin. Big boot. (See Thema from 1989.)

What's bad: An old car now. Tainted by Lancia's UK reputation for unreliability and rust and not entirely immune from either.

What to watch out for: Urgently need new timing belts every 3 years or 36,000 miles. Benefits from fully synthetic oil with regular changes (particularly 8.32 and Turbo). 8.32 often low mileage and doesn't take well to sitting around. Will need expensive timing belt change before you drive it anywhere (this work could cost £1,000). Look for mayo under oil cap – usually indicates cylinder head problems. Check turbo exhaust for oil smoke. Gearbox synchromesh gets worn. Do a reverse-turn driveshaft test and listen for clonking. Check condition of discs. Check all electrics – some are bound to be u/s so use your judgement and adjust your price. Rattles and squeaks are normal. Do look for rust. If front tyre wear uneven, look carefully for signs of accident or suspension damage.

Thema (1989–1994)

What's good: Range rationalised from 1989. 2.0 litre 16-valve now has 150 bhp; turbo 185 bhp. Turbo SE best Thema ever on sale in UK, though Italians had an estate car version and a diesel. Cats from August 1992 strangely brought yet another power hike: to 155 bhp and 205 bhp. To help curb torque steer, Turbo got Viscodrive diff. Late models are a lot of car for not much money.

What's bad: Lancia's poor UK reputation robs a good car of the status it deserved. Turbo has high insurance group. Market doesn't like them. No Lancia dealers, just specialists. Increasingly hard to get parts.

What to watch out for: As '85–'89, but exclude notes about 8.32. Smoky exhaust, excessive oil consumption may be turbo, may be valve stem seals.

Y10 (1985–1992)

What's good: Fiat Panda-based upmarket mini. Range included excellent, long-lived 45 bhp 999cc 'Fire' engine, 55 bhp ohc 1,049cc Brazil engine; 85 bhp 1,049cc Turbo Brazil, 57 bhp 1,108cc 'Fire' engine and 1,301cc ohc from Strada with multipoint injection giving 78 bhp to GTie. 1,108cc 55 bhp 'Selectronic' CVT auto also available. Size always a benefit for parking. GTie best model. The first car with suede-like Alcantara trim.

What's bad: Rust, rust, rust, citycar abuse, handling abilities strictly limited.

What to watch out for: Look for oil and coolant leaks, accident damage, rust, damaged trim.

LAND ROVER

Discovery (1989–1998)

What's good: High driving position good for sightseeing. Outstandingly competent and comfortable off-road. Diesels are surprisingly economical with 30 mpg on the cards. Autobox goes well with the four-cylinder diesel. Seven-seat versatility (though the two back jump seats are not suitable for journeys).

What's bad: Build problems went from bad to worse in the transition from 200 to 300 model. Very ponderous on the road due to high centre of gravity. Dangerous to carry anything on the roof. Generally poor build quality. Post–1993 '300 Series' manual gearbox has better change but suffers severe input shaft wear (can be alleviated by high-tech gearbox lubricants). 300 TDi engines also prone to timing belt failure after 40,000 miles. Kits are available to extend timing belt life, but fitting them is a long job. V8s guzzle fuel. Avoid the underpowered 2.0 litre 16v 'MPi' model. Lack of crumple zones mean it can be expensively damaged by hard impacts at speeds as low as 5 mph. In June 2001 Land Rover was rated by Motor Warranty Direct as Britain's 2nd worst out of 22 marques for warranty claims (www.warrantydirect.co.uk).

What to watch out for: Signs of severe usage. Tow hooks (what's it been towing? It's rated to 3.4 tons). Underbody 'off-roading' damage. Leaks from axles, transmission, transfer case. Worn suspension and steering bushes. Worn and noisy gearboxes (especially post-1993 '300 Series'). Rust where steel chassis touches alloy body panels. 5-door models worth much more than 3-doors. If it's a TDi 300, has the timing belt modification been carried out? Check the trim carefully as dashboards of post-'94 models can warp.

Recalls: 1995 (VIN LJ163104–LJ172980 and LJ501920–LJ504252): check seatbelts. 1997 (April '95–July '96: 22,723 vehicles): possibility of failure of RHS front door latch. 1998: (build Jan '94–Mar '97): airbag may go off involuntarily. 1998 TSB dated 25/3/98 warned dealers of timing belt failure due to misalignment of belt and pulleys on 300TDi's up to VIN WA748935 and gave procedures for repair under warranty if warranty conditions apply.

Freelander (1997 on)

What's good: Good styling. Comfortable. Likeable. Plenty of room for four or five passengers. Kids enjoy the high back seat. Proper three-point centre belt. Useful underfloor lockable cubby-safe. The hill descent control works well. The more you drive it the more you like it. Longer 3-year warranty inclusive from spring 1998. Fairly damage-proof at the front because even the wings are plastic. 175bhp/177 lb ft 2.5 litre KV6 and 110bhp/192 lb ft 2.0 litre BMW TD4 diesel with Steptronic automatic options on both finally arrived in Autumn 2000. TD4 does 102mph and 0–60 in 13.2 seconds, a useful improvement on the slow old Rover diesel. Still depreciates less than a mass-market estate car. 2001 list prices from £15,995 for 1.8, from £17,195 for TD4 and from £21,595 for KV6. TD4 5-door recommended.

What's bad: TD4s hard to get hold of due to supply problems with BMW engines. Initial promise of high quality build not met. Lots of niggly failures. Also failures of hill descent control, driveshafts and gearboxes and blocked ventilation slots (*Sunday Times* 6/3/99). More ponderous than Honda CRV and much more expensive. Not as economical as expected, but Rover diesel can average 35 mpg at a 70 mph cruise. Become increasingly expensive with Freelander 50th 5-door diesel listed at £24,995. Several recalls. Many owners taking a hit, getting out and getting into fault-free Honda CRVs. Low profile tyres fitted to 'Millennium' model Freelanders aren't up to suburban kerb mounting, which is the main off road activity of these vehicles. S and T platers 16th from bottom in 2001 Top Gear/ JD Power Customer Satisfaction Survey. In June 2001 Land Rover was rated by Motor Warranty Direct as Britain's 2nd worst out of 22 marques for warranty claims (www.warrantydirect.co.uk).

What to watch out for: Signs of severe usage. Tow hooks (what's it been towing? Neither the 1.8 nor the diesel is really powerful enough). Underside damage. Drivetrain leaks. Make sure everything works, especially the 'hill descent control', if fitted.

Reports of accelerator of 1.8 petrol models sticking and leading to accidents. Reports of gearbox failures.

Recalls: TSBs (Technical Service Bulletins) over some part-time four-wheel-drive clutch systems failing due to fluid leaks and replaced 'in service' by Land Rover dealers. Official November 1998 recall (build dates June '97–June '98) to check welding on joints of rear suspension arms. 1999: official note to owners to reduce tyre pressures from 2.1 bar to 1.8 bar when not fully loaded, to increase tyre life.

New Discovery (1998 on)

What's good: Revised, more expensive, slightly longer model from October 1998 with new 'TD5' 5-cylinder direct injected diesel engine, up to seven forward-facing seats and much better road handling than the old model. Same high driving position good for sightseeing. Outstandingly competent and comfortable off-road. Price of entry level Discovery E TD5 cut to £21,995.

What's bad: Appalling catalogue of build problems – worse even than 300 model. Sometimes delivered with wrong spec. Hard to distinguish visually from old model, so the neighbours may not realise you've got the new one. Fuel consumption of TD5 around 17% worse than previous four-cylinder diesel.

What to watch out for: See old model.

Recalls: October 1999: all 9,296 new model Discoverys sold to date recalled because of a problem with the ABS brakes. Ten minutes' work required on car. March 2000 recall of vehicles built July-Dec 1999: Active Cornering Enhancement system could malfunction due to pipes fracturing. New pipes to be fitted. June 2000 recall of 11,000 TD5s built between September 1998 and June 1999 because flywheel of manual versions could fail. Further recall of V8s because engine idler pulley could fragment throwing drive belt off and leading to loss of cooling, power steering.

Range Rover 'Classic' (1970–1995)

What's good: 'Classic' Range Rover, warts and all. Some people still love them. 4-cylinder VM diesels the most economical, and accepted in country circles (later models had Land Rover TDI). Unrivalled cross country performance until the new model arrived. Final metallic-blue 25 individually numbered '25th Anniversary' models the most valuable.

What's bad: V-8s guzzle petrol. Misfires destroy 'cats'. Litany of quality problems which may or may not have been sorted by the previous owner. The three-door CSK (Cyril Spencer King) was an interesting aberration – not wanted at 2–3 years old, but might develop a cult classic following in years to come if kept clean. Air suspension fitted to LSE and Vogue SE can be troublesome. In June 2001 Land Rover was rated by Motor Warranty Direct as Britain's 2nd worst out of 22 marques for warranty claims (www. warrantydirect.co.uk).

What to watch out for: Signs of severe usage. Check suspension bushes for wear. Steering box may be worn. Look for oil leaks from gearbox, transfer case and axles. Make sure rear axle breather not blocked. Make sure VM diesel not suffering from cracked cylinder heads (white smoke from exhaust; mayonnaise under oil cap). Sludge on dipstick is really bad news – a walk-away fault because it means the oil has rarely been changed. Look for dog damage to leather seats and trim. Scuff marks and trim damage from shooting trips. Alloy parts of body won't rot, but steel parts and chassis do, particularly at the back, and electrolytically corrode where the steel and alloy meet. Check Boge rear suspension unit. Avoid cars with specialist, heavy duty tow bars (may have been pulling a 6-ton yacht or, worse still, a mobile hamburger stand). Try to buy town cars rather than country cars. May be reliable, but you can still expect niggling faults.

Recalls: 1998: (Jan '94–Mar '97 build): airbag may go off inadvertently.

Range Rover (1994 on)

What's good: Undeniable road presence. Far less vague on the road than the old model. 4.6HE is a powerful car. All are brilliant off the road, soak up the bumps and are the most comfortable way to travel cross-country. Slow diesel comes into its own off road.

What's bad: Apalling catalogue of build problems. Water ingress into ECU will stop the car. BMW-powered diesel version is ridiculously slow on the road – especially in automatic form. 4.6HE drinks petrol, may be hit by future 'guzzler' taxes. 4.0 V8 a bit less juicy. 4.6HE loses value fast. Heavy duty prices of £53,000 for the 4.6 Vogue, £57,500 for the 30th Anniversary (30 years ago a Range Rover was £2,000) and £64,495 for the Holland & Holland (no shotguns included). S and T platers 19th from bottom in 2001 Top Gear/JD Power Customer Satisfaction Survey. In June 2001 Land Rover was rated by Motor Warranty Direct as Britain's 2nd worst out of 22 marques for warranty claims (www.warrantydirect.co.uk). Complaints of collapsing rear air suspension on late examples.

What to watch out for: Signs of severe usage. Tow hooks (what's it been towing?). Listen for transmission noise on manual versions. Make sure all gearbox functions work (manual and automatic). Look for oil leaks from axles, gearbox and transfer case. Look for dog damage to leather seats and trim. Scuff marks and trim damage from shooting trips. Check all electrics. Make sure wheels will come off as the alloy wheels have a habit of corroding to the hubs. If paying dealer prices, make sure it comes with a full service history. See 5/12/2000 Recall notice below. This has resulted in some cooling systems becoming over-pressurised resulting in total engine failure.

Recalls: 1995 (VIN LP311035 to LP312917): ABS braking hose may fail. 1998 V8: cooling system hoses found to be failing. 2000: June '94–August '98 build: automatic gearbox fluid can seep out and spill onto hot exhaust creating fire risk. V8 models built June '98–Sept '99 may lose power steering. 5/12/2000: 15,767 Range Rover V8s recalled because of possibility of premature failure of cooling system hoses and throttle body heater gasket. Expelled coolant allowed to remain on hot engine components could result in the evaporation of the water content and leave an artificially high concentration level of anti-freeze which is both corrosive and inflammable. Affected vehicles to be recalled to replace cooling system hoses and throttle body heater gasket.

LEXUS

GS300 (1993–1998)

What's good: Beautifully built and quite good looking with plenty of road presence. Smooth, 209 bhp six-cylinder engines. Warranty lasted 3 years and 100,000 miles.

What's bad: Steering, handling, roadholding and ride quality not up to BMW standards (over-light steering and can snap into oversteer). Not as much space inside as length suggests. Will not endow drivers with the status of a Mercedes E-Class. Sport model best looking but doesn't drive as well as it looks.

What to watch out for: Full Lexus service history. Evidence of having been carelessly driven by people with business rather than driving on their minds. Suspension damage from kerbing.

Recalls: June 1999: all GS300s built July '95–July '97 recalled to replace potentially faulty suspension links.

GS300 (1998 on)

What's good: VVT engine gives more power (219 bhp); 5-speed auto helps to use it. Longer wheelbase gives more room inside. Double wishbone suspension improves handling and roadholding. Traction Control and Vehicle Stability Control help keep drivers out of trouble while they're on the phone. 3-year, 100,000-mile warranty. S and T reg cars came third in 2001 Top Gear/JD Power Customer Satisfaction Survey.

What's bad: In dubious taste. Chopping off the front and the back did not improve the looks of this car.

What to watch out for: Full Lexus service history.

GS430 (2001 on)

What's good: Smaller GS300 body with LS430 engine. 283bhp 4.3 litre engine makes this car very quick with 0–60 of just over six seconds. Priced at £36,995.

What's bad: See GS300.
What to watch out for: See GS300.

IS300 (2001 on)

What's good: Answers criticism of IS200's lack of power at low engine speeds. Has 215 bhp 3.0 litre six with either 5-speed manual or 5-speed Tiptronic automatic (engine has too much torque for 6-speeder). Standard 17in wheels with ultra-low-profile tyres.
What's bad: No six-speeder.
What to watch out for: Too soon to say.

IS200 (1999 on)

What's good: Toyota's answer to the BMW 3-Series and Audi A4. Fresh, 'clean sheet' styling. Promising 153 bhp twin-cam 24v 2.0 litre straight six. Six-speed manual gearbox has rifle-bolt precision (four speed auto optional). Rear-wheel-drive with proper rear drive handling. Interesting instruments. Big 17in alloy wheels. Much sharper steering than other Lexus models. Sport has traction control, which is a mixed blessing for keen drivers. Prices start at £20,500. Recommended. S and T reg cars came fifth in 2001 Top Gear/JD Power Customer Satisfaction Survey.
What's bad: Needs to be revved to perform, otherwise doesn't feel powerful enough. Auto can be sluggish at times.
What to watch out for: Too soon to say.

LS400 (1990–2000)

What's good: World's most refined V8. Effortless acceleration. Brilliant, fully controllable, utterly obedient 5-speed autobox from Oct '97 (4-speed before, and 3-speed before that). Unobtrusive traction and stability control system. As luxurious, reliable and trouble-free as you'd expect of an S-Class competitor built by Toyota. 3-year, 100,000-mile warranty. Quentin Willson reckons they're fantastic buys at over 100,000 miles. He has no trouble with them. Trade generally approves of quality levels, particularly trim and switchgear. Lexus servicing seems to be top notch. Pre-August 1992 cars can legally be 'de-catted' for better performance and economy (talk to BBR on 01280 702389). 241 bhp 3-speed auto Jan '90–Oct '94; 260 bhp 4-speed auto Oct '94–Oct '97; 280 bhp 5-speed auto from Oct '97. S and T reg cars came first in 2001 Top Gear/JD Power Customer Satisfaction Survey.

What's bad: Lack of steering 'feel' (even the Cadillac Seville STS is better in this respect). Pre–1995 model-year cars could suffer from engine surging. Limo 'stretchers' not happy about the thickness of the body panels. Lacquer coating on early-model alloy wheels peels off, allowing them to oxidise badly.

What to watch out for: Underservicing. Some busy company directors run these cars very hard as mobile offices, clock up 75,000 miles a year, don't always have time to get services done on time. Check 'cats' (£610 each). Buy young with high mileage rather than old with low mileage. Toyota GB says: make sure the car has a full Lexus service history, that the automatic transmission fluid and filter have been changed every year, that the shocks and suspension are okay, that the timing belts have been changed at 60,000-mile intervals and that there is no excess wear on the rear discs through misuse of the parking brake.

Recalls: 1998 (April '95–June '96 build): Risk of underbonnet fire due to faulty wiring.

LS430 (2001 on)

What's good: 'All new' large Lexus with new 4.3 litre 282bhp Variable Valve Timing V8 priced at £49,950 on the road or £53,950 for 'Premium Pack' version. Top speed 155mph; 0–60 in 6.7 seconds; combined economy figure: 23.5mpg (31.7mpg possible cruising at 75mph); CO_2 emissions: 289g/km. 5-speed automatic box. Navigation system standard. 'Premium Pack' includes self-levelling air suspension, multi-function wood and leather steering wheel, individual controls for rear compartment air-conditioning, electrically operated reclining rear seats with memory functions and, get this, 'electric vibro-massaging rear seats'.

What's bad: Ostentatious rather than a genuinely good looker,

otherwise too soon to say.
What to watch out for: Too soon to say.

RX300 (2001 on)

What's good: UK market name for the 4x4 version of the Harrier which has been around in other markets for some time now. 201 bhp, 208 lb ft torque 2,995cc 24 valve V6 engine. 4-speed autobox. 0–60 in 9 seconds; top speed 112mph; EC Urban fuel consumption 15.9mpg. A/c standard on all. List priced at £28,950 and £32,550 for SE. Reasonably compact. Handles very well indeed for a 4x4 – on a par with the new Ford Maverick – and really good to drive. Better steering than a Lexus GS or LX. Better to drive on a difficult road than a BMW X5 3.0.

What's bad: The two-wheel drive option available in other markets with a lower ride height might have made sense in the UK.

What to watch out for: Beware of paying too much for 'personally imported' Harriers, etc. posing as the genuine UK Lexus RX300. A 99V 4x4 Harrier with all the kit and negligible mileage sold for just £16,125 at auction on 1/12/2000. And if you're knowingly buying an import, check the spec very carefully. It may not even be four-wheel drive.

SC430

What's good: Luxurious new two seater from Lexus to compete with the Mercedes SL. Has an SLK-like retractable hard-top that folds up or down in a matter of seconds. Two tiny child seats in the back. Top speed from revised 278bhp LS430 engine is 150mph. Price over '£50,000'.

What's bad: Not actually due in the UK until 'Summer of 2001'. UK 2001 allocation 'sold out', as per announcement on 28/11/2000.

What to watch out for: Paying a premium to buy a 'sold out' car.

LIGIER

Ambra Micro-Car (1999 on)

What's good: Tiny French two-seater micro hatchback built at the rate of 300 a week imported by Reliant since 1999. Has two-cylinder 505cc Lombardini diesel engine developing 15bhp giving 50 mph and up to 85 mpg, or the same capacity petrol engine with 25bhp giving 70mph and up to 65mpg. Simple, exposed belt CVT transmission. Electric windows and stereo. Alloy wheels and RHD standard in UK. Under the weight limit, so can be driven on a B1 motorcycle motorcycle licence from the age of 17. Euro Type-Approved. Base models on offer at £4,995. Re-styled for 2001.

What's bad: Slow acceleration of diesel will take a bit of getting used to but petrol version is a fair bit quicker.

What to watch out for: Too soon to say.

Be Up

What's good: Bizarre two seater minimalist resort car by Giugiaro Design. Powered by 505cc 4-stroke twin-cylinder petrol engine developing 21bhp with open belt CVT transmission and can be driven on a B1 motorcycle licence from the age of 17.

What's bad: It rains in the UK.

What to watch out for: Too soon to say, but people will certainly see you coming.

377

LOTUS

Elan (1989–1992; 1994–1995)

What's good: Fine handling front-drive sports car with excellent grip. An instant 'classic' despite KIA lookalike with not quite the same dynamics. Non-turbo Isuzu engine has 130 bhp. Turbos have 165 bhp pre-cat, down to 155 bhp with twin cats when re-launched as S2 in June 1994. Engines and gearboxes tough and reliable. Holds its value well.

What's bad: Eats front tyres. Promotes heavy wear of front driveshaft joints, bushes and bearings. Fizzy electrics. Hoods leak. Hard driven, underserviced turbos will smoke. Red examples can develop a paint problem.

What to watch out for: Repaired accident damage. Smoking turbos. Kerbed alloys. Front suspension, hubs and driveshaft wear. Need to see evidence of proper servicing, in particular frequent fully-synthetic oil changes.

Elise (1996 on)

What's good: Gorgeous, mouthwatering little road racer in the mould of the Porsche RSK and Elva BMW. Brilliant, ultra-lightweight chassis design and construction. Tremendous handling and grip best checked out under instruction at a race circuit 'track day'. Facelifted with new targa top and uprated standard engine from October 2000. Last of the original shape hold their value better than new shape.

What's bad: Not enough power in standard 118 bhp form for the track, but BBR (01280 702389) does an Interceptor 2000 for better mid-range grunt. 'Sport' version's 190 bhp almost too much for the road. Minimal weather protection. Not a 'girlie townie' fashion accessory. Not for wimps. Expect roof to leak. Snap oversteer in the wet hard to predict and catch on first acquaintance, especially on slicks in the wet. 2001 facelift not nearly as attractive as original car. S and T platers 17th from bottom in 2001 Top Gear/JD Power Customer Satisfaction Survey.

What to watch out for: Typical track day 'off' damage underneath, bent suspension, crunched ends. Cat damage from misfiring off rev-limiter. Won't pass advanced emissions test at first MOT if cat has been removed.

Recalls: Lotus modified the rudimentary soft top in Spring 1998 because owners complained of leaks. Daft, really. You just don't buy an Elise as an everyday car. 10/3/2000 recall of all Elise 111S models built before 1/2/2000 to fit electromagnetic interferance shield to prevent interferance causing misfires.

Esprit SE/S4/S4S/Sport 300/V8 (1987 on)

What's good: 'James Bond' submarine car still listed. (Original Esprit launched in 1976. SE launched in 1987.) In the 'junior supercar' league, light in weight with 264 bhp (S4) or 300 bhp turbocharged engines (S4S). Excellent handling and roadholding. Sport 300 is a lightweight 300 bhp car. 3,506cc V8 has 349 bhp. At £49,950 the V8 GT is a supercar bargain with Porsche 996-beating grunt and safe yet fantastic handling.

What's bad: Four-cylinder Lotus engines stretched to the limit. Poor gearchange. 'Lie down' seats. Apt to go wrong quite a lot. Still looks like a kit car inside.

What to watch out for: This car really needs expert and frequent attention. If it hasn't been checked over at least every six months, leave it alone. You don't want to hear any rattles from the engine, especially the timing belt tensioner. Look for smoke from turbo, oil leaks, fizzy electrics, leaking heater matrix, inoperative aircon, hotspotted cats. If 1992K or later, make sure it has passed a recent advanced emissions test.

Recalls: 1998: 200 V8 models recalled for new timing belt, idler pulley bearings, new clutch and 5th gear locknut, cost to Lotus at least £1,500 per car. Also check rear alloy wheels for hairline cracks.

Excel (1985–1992)

What's good: A Lotus with four seats. Decent handling, fast, reasonably economical and quite reliable in the right hands.

What's bad: Collector's car jokes still apply (you have to collect the bits that drop off). Fiercely defended by club members. Screen surround comes adrift. Trim comes unstuck. Needs to be revved to perform (not a town car). If you don't know these cars you need to find someone local who does.

What to watch out for: Make sure no leaks from heater matrix and that air conditioning works. Needs frequent correct maintenance by experts, not the bloke under the arches (unless he is a Lotus genius). May have been 'owner serviced' so make sure it's been done properly by cross-examining the owner. Fully synthetic oil preferred.

MARCOS

Mantis and Manta Ray

What's good: 352 bhp 4.6 litre Rover Buick V8 with hefty 330 lb ft torque gives 4.1-second 0–60 capability. Well developed, safe, precise handling. At £43,995 a very serious alternative to a TVR. New Manta Ray range with engines from 2.0 litres and prices from £32,500 launched at 1998 Motor Show. Taken over by Dutch firm Eurotech in June 2000. Future parts to come from Holland but assembly still to be in UK.

What's bad: Basic shape was launched in 1964. Has a lie-down seating position, poor rearward visibility, only the pedal carrier adjusts, heavy but very tight gearchange gate.

What to watch out for: Second-hand needs an expert check.

MASERATI

3200GT

What's good: Dubbed by *Autocar* magazine Best Maserati for 20 years, it's also Maserati's best seller in the UK. 3,217cc twin turbo V8 puts out 370bhp at 6,000rpm and 352 lb ft torque at 4,500rpm. Top speed 160mph for the four-speed auto; 175mph for the six-speed manual, and very comfortable even at these speeds. Has the most wonderful engine note of any current production car. 0–60 around six seconds. Praised for excellent brakes. Decent amount of room in the back for a couple of kids, or for two adults on a short journey. Manual priced at £60,575 on the road; automatic £62,950. Best to go for the manual. Auto puts out a very high 422 CO_2/km. 3200 Assetto Corso launched June 2001 has many detail improvements to chassis and brakes at £65,950 for the six-speed manual and £67,950 for the four-speed automatic.

What's bad: Criticised by press for firm ride and old fashioned 4-speed BTR autobox. Change quality of Getrag six-speed box varies from car to car.

What to watch out for: See Recalls. If this work hasn't been done, it will be very expensive.

Recalls: 20/10/2001: 374 cars built 1999–2000 recalled because brake fluid reservoir supply hoses may contaminate the fluid causing degradation of various seals, leading to leakage of fluid and loss of braking efficiency. Reservoir supply hoses, brake master cylinder, ABS/ABR hydraulic control unit all to be replaced.

MAZDA

121 (from 1996)

What's good: 3-year warranty, otherwise see Fiesta.

What's bad: Really a Fiesta, built at Dagenham. More popular in Holland than in the UK due to Mazda's excellent advertising there.

What to watch out for: See Fiesta.

Recalls: 1996 (1996 model-year): Check for faulty piston seal in hydraulic clutch master cylinder. Check for contamination of brake fluid and incorrect front brake hose routing. 1997 (5-door models built Dec '95–May '96): may have faulty rear door latches. 1998 (Dec '95–Jun '96 Build): possibility of brake failure due to front brake pipe chafing on bracket. Modified pipe and bracket to be fitted to both front brakes.

121 Hatch (1988–1991)

What's good: Lived on as the KIA Pride. Full length electric sunroof cheered it up. All were pre-cat.

What's bad: Old now. Even though it's a Mazda, it looks like a KIA Pride. Front suspension bushes wear. Carburettor engine can give trouble.

What to watch out for: Treat only as a cheap, fairly reliable buy. Almost all will already have been scrapped in Japan.

121 Saloon (1991–1995)

What's good: Amazing headroom, fun looks. Later model specification (from April 1993) of manual gearbox, power steering and full length sun roof by far the best. 1,324cc 74 bhp engine identical to stronger-selling 323. May have scarcity value in years to come.

What's bad: Derided by motoring press and simply failed to sell in the UK. Pre-April '93 models had silly spec of automatic, but no power steering and no sun roof. So few UK sales that body spares situation is not promising in years to come.

What to watch out for: You have to ask yourself what sort of person would buy one. Look for eccentric modifications and evidence of bad driving, such as kerbing. Make sure the electric sunroof works properly and has no tears.

323 (1989–1991)

What's good: Beautifully built and attractive. Low-roofed 5-door F-Type hatchback more of a 5-door coupe. Neat 4-door saloon tends to appeal more to the elderly. Sweet engines, all 16-valve. (1,324cc 75 bhp carb; 1,598cc 87 bhp carb; 1,840cc 140 bhp twin-cam injection.) Sensationally reliable. Typically Japanese slick gearchanges. Automatic choke problems of pre-October 1989 323s was solved for this model. SE Exec models very well equipped. I owned one for 6 months and still saw a profit.

What's bad: Immensely complicated model range of 3-door hatchbacks, 5-door hatchbacks, 4-door saloons and 5-door estates. Handling and roadholding not quite to UK tastes. Very light power steering. Not immune to snapped timing belts. Excellent factory paint finish can be hard to match. Average ventilation on saloon is poor on F-Type hatchback, which is prone to misting up. Not much room in the back seat of F-Types.

What to watch out for: Make sure car has been regularly serviced, at least every 6,000 miles. Damaged trim is expensive to replace. Make sure all the electrics work. F-Types may have suffered parking damage due to poor rearward visibility.

323 (1991–1994)

What's good: All got fuel injection, as from May 1991, same bodies as before. General good points as above.

What's bad: All got catalytic converters. Power outputs now 74 bhp from 1.3, 89 bhp from 1.6, but just 129 bhp from 1.8. General bad points, as above, but no carburettor worries.

What to watch out for: Make sure car has been regularly serviced, at least every 6,000 miles. Damaged trim is expensive to replace. Make sure all the electrics work. F-Types may have suffered parking damage due to poor rearward visibility.

323 (1994–1995)

What's good: Re-styled range introduced in August 1994. F-type 5-door hatchback became even more coupe-like. Unusual, but attractive. New 1,489cc 89 bhp engine replaces 1.6. 146 bhp V6 from Xedos 6 introduced to top of the range 323F models. V6 very good looking on its bigger wheels. Service miles extended to 9,000, but still better to stick to 6,000.

What's bad: An odd period for the 323 with only a handful of new 3-door hatchbacks and very pretty 4-door saloons imported and no estates. Power output of 1.8 drops to 115 bhp.

What to watch out for: Make sure car has been regularly serviced. Damaged trim is expensive to replace. Make sure all the electrics work. Uneven tyre wear may be evidence of kerbing. Paint is hard to match and a giveaway of accident damage. Make sure the central locking works on all the doors. If you buy a 'glassback' 3-door or the pretty 4-door, be aware that body panels will probably have to come from Mazda's HQ in Brussels, and any RHD bits from Japan.

323 (1995–1998)

What's good: Range shrunk to just one body, the 323F, until 1997, when a new 1.3 hatchback and a new 1.5 saloon both appeared. Some of 3-year warranty may remain. 20th from top in 'R' reg JD Power Customer Satisfaction Survey. Mazda was rated by Motor Warranty Direct as Britain's most claim-free marque (www. warrantydirect.co.uk).

What's bad: 3-door hatchback and pretty 4-door saloon disappeared from range from 1995–1997. New model range arrived late 1998/early 1999. 'F' model dropped.

What to watch out for: As above. Some 1995 cars suffered from a faulty batch of clutches.

Recalls: 1997: 'Mystique' special edition based on 323F 1.5LXi may have loose wheel nuts on spare wheel.

323 (1998 on)

What's good: Back to just one body, but a new five-door hatchback. Initially a bit bland, still with low roofline. Looks improved enormously by dropped suspension and a range of smart alloy wheels. Flat cornering from 'Diagonal Roll Axis' suspension. Clever interior touches such as a front passenger seat that folds to become a table, and split, fully folding back seats. Engines: 1,324cc, 75 bhp; 1,498cc, 87 bhp; 1,840cc, 114 bhp-plus 118 lb ft torque. Range topping Sport introduced Spring 1999 at £16,320. Mazda was rated by Motor Warranty Direct as Britain's most claim-free marque (www.warrantydirect.co.uk).

What's bad: Needs alloy wheels to look good.

What to watch out for: Too soon to say.

626 (1992–1997)

What's good: Nicely styled 5-door, with amazing built-in rear boot spoiler. Briefly available as 'GT' (Feb '92–Dec '94) with full-on 165 bhp 2.5 litre V-6 from MX6, but not many were imported. Mazda was rated by Motor Warranty Direct as Britain's most claim-free marque (www.warrantydirect.co.uk).

What's bad: 4-door less inspiring, but still well liked. Comprex supercharged 2.0 litre diesel not a success – only lasted from May '94 to Oct '95. Body damage extremely difficult to repair, particularly to rear of 5-door hatchback. Paint quality virtually impossible to match. No estate cars except carryovers with older body.

What to watch out for: Repaired accident damage. Uneven tyre wear from kerbed suspension.

Recalls: 1997: 'Mystique' special edition based on 626 1.8LXi may have loose wheel nuts on spare wheel.

626 (1997–1999)

What's good: Same Mazda qualities of good build, excellent reliability, superb paint finish. Useful engine range of 89 bhp 1.8, 113 bhp 2.0 litre and 134 bhp 2.0 litre GSi. Aircon standard throughout. Three three-point rear seatbelts. Estate car back in range. 19th from top in 'R' reg JD Power Customer Satisfaction Survey. S and T reg cars came 13th from top in 2001 Top Gear/JD Power Customer Satisfaction Survey. Mazda was rated by Motor Warranty Direct as Britain's most claim-free used marque (www.warrantydirect.co.uk).

What's bad: Very 'ordinary'-looking 5-door hatchbacks and 4-door saloons.

What to watch out for: Make sure has full Mazda service history or warranty could be void. See Recalls, particularly timing belt tensioner recall.

Recalls: 1998 (Nov '96–May '97 build): Possibility of timing belt failure leading to total loss of engine power and power assistance to steering and brakes; 626 diesel (to May '98 build): Faulty fuel injector may stall engine. July 2000: further recall of 5,431 petrol-engined 626s built May '97–November '97 to inspect the spring of the timing belt tensioner. Inspection/replacement takes 1.6 hours. Helpline: 0800 387942. 1/8/2000: 5.431 626 models built 5/97 to 11/97 recalled because spring in timing belt tensioner may fail leading engine to suddenly lose power. Timing belt tensioners to be replaced.

626 (2000 on)

What's good: New-look 626 with corporate pentagonal grille. Engines: 100 bhp 1.8 and 122 bhp 2.0 litre petrol, plus 2.0 litre diesel. ABS standard. Likely to be very reliable. 3-year warranty. Mazda was rated by Motor Warranty Direct as Britain's most claim-free used marque (www.warrantydirect.co.uk).

What's bad: Not likely to set the roads alight.

What to watch out for: Too soon to say.

Demio (1998 on)

What's good: Neat and versatile small boxy estate, with sliding, folding and reclining rear seats that can be turned into a bed. 72 bhp 1,324 cc engine. 3-year warranty. A bit more substantial than the Move/Wagon R/ATOZ/Matiz brigade. Five carbon dioxide absorbing trees planted for every car sold to achieve first year carbon neutrality. Facelift launched at Y2K Geneva Motor Show with much improved handling, from a reasonable £9,000 in UK (a £1,500 price cut) and option of 1.5 litre 75 bhp automatic. New version quite nimble and nice to drive. Mazda was rated by Motor Warranty Direct as Britain's most claim-free used marque (www.warrantydirect.co.uk).

What's bad: Criticised for lack of things like internally adjustable door mirrors. Original version slow and stodgy to drive. Also consider the bigger £9,995 Colt Space Star.

What to watch out for: Secondhand 'school run' damage, but won't be many secondhand around for a while.

MPV (2000 on)

What's good: Third of Mazda's family of MPVs, but this one has 7 seats and is 626-based. Separately controllable front and back aircon, twin sliding side doors, comfortable, well-equipped with good luggage space behind the third row. 1,991cc engine with 121 bhp and 129 lb ft torque, plus 5-speed gearbox. Pedigree comes from ten years of Japanese/American Mazda MPVs. UK launch at 1999 London Motor Show. Price cut from £19,800 to £16,995. Mazda was rated by Motor Warranty Direct as Britain's most claim-free used marque (www.warrantydirect.co.uk).

What's bad: No auto option, no more powerful petrol engines, no torquey and economical turbodiesels. Didn't sell at original price.

What to watch out for: Too soon to say.

MX3 (1991–1998)

What's good: Very sweet 1,846cc 134 bhp 24v V6. Electric roof. Oddball but inoffensive styling. Mazda was rated by Motor Warranty Direct as Britain's most claim-free used marque (www.warrantydirect.co.uk).

What's bad: 1,598cc 88 bhp automatic much less impressive. Back seat strictly for small children. Power of V6 dropped to 128 bhp in August 1994.

What to watch out for: Don't buy at the 80,000-mile mark unless it has had a timing belt change. Look for a proper Mazda history. Don't pay a 'coupe premium' price without it. Check if it's a personal import and, if so, pay less.

Recalls: 1994: MX3 1.6 and 1.8 (build March '92–Aug '94: VIN JMZ EC13** 00100001–00113020): front suspension coil may fail and puncture tyre. 25/4/2000: front springs of 108 cars built May/June 1995 may rust and fail. Springs to be replaced.

MX5 (1990 on)

What's good: Sweet, neat, 'back to basics' sportscar. The best small, affordable sports car ever made. Twin-cam 16-valve engines, 5-speed gearboxes. Nice 'works' hard-top. Hood opens with one hand from driver's seat. Revised in spring 1998 with heated glass rear window, fixed headlights, bigger boot. 1.8 recommended. Further facelift in Japan now and in UK spring 2001. The best-selling sportscar ever. Re-facelifted in Spring 2001. Mazda was rated by Motor Warranty Direct as Britain's most claim-free used marque (www.warrantydirect.co.uk).

What's bad: Cheaper to build than a 323 but sells for a lot more money. Lots of dodgy second-hand imports about. Catalysed 1.6i engine from April 1995 not powerful enough (just 88 bhp, as against 114 bhp for previous 1.6, 130 bhp for 1.8 and 150 bhp for 1.6 BBR Turbo). Even the later 1.6 doesn't really have enough power.

What to watch out for: Uncertificated Eunos Roadsters imported by traders after May 1998 could not legally be registered, so any Eunos Roadster might be a 'clone'. MX5s are sports cars, so could have been thrashed. 'Fashion accessory' MX5s may not have been serviced properly. SVA 'kits' available to get imports through SVA, but non-SVA Japanese parts may then be put back. Check speed ratings on tyres (Japan has a 55 mph limit.) Series 1 headlight motors go. Uneven tyre wear probably signifies accident damage. Ageing MX5s can rust in the sills. Jap market Eunos Roadsters were not rustproofed from new.

Recalls: 7/12/2000: 135 Jasper Conran Limited Edition MX5s to be recalled because driver's floormat my interfer with throttle pedal causing throttle to stick open. Mat to be replaced with modified mat.

MX6 (1992–1998)

What's good: Interesting looks. Lovely 2.5 litre 24v 165 bhp V6. Decent American build quality. Automatic and aircon optional. Mazda was rated by Motor Warranty Direct as Britain's most claim-free used marque (www.warrantydirect.co.uk).

What's bad: Looks not universally liked (looks a bit like an old Opel Manta). Chassis not nearly as good as engine and gearbox.

What to watch out for: All that glass means it gets hot in summer, so aircon highly desirable. Check tyres for uneven wear – may be misadjustment or may signify suspension damage.

Premacy (2000 on)

What's good: Mini MPV based on mix of 323 and 626 components from the same mould as the Colt Space Star. Good to drive, practical and versatile. Scenic-like, separately reclinable, foldable and removable rear seats. Front passenger seat folds to form a table or support for long loads. 99 bhp and 113 bhp 1.8 litre petrol or 89 bhp 2.0 litre turbodiesel. A/c standard on all and electronic brake force distribution, which can be much needed on a short boxy car braking heavily. Starting price cut to £12,900 in spring 2000. Average three star NCAP crash safety rating announced 28/3/2001. Mazda was rated by Motor Warranty Direct as Britain's most claim-free used marque (www.warrantydirect.co.uk).

What's bad: Nothing so far.

What to watch out for: Nothing so far.

RX7 (1989–1992)

What's good: Attractive Porsche 944 lookalike with 200 bhp turbocharged rotary engine. Good looking cabriolet with well fitting power top.

What's bad: Needs specialist maintenance.

What to watch out for: Engine must idle smoothly (rough idle sure sign of rotor tip wear). Make sure no smoke. Uneven tyre wear signifies accident damage. Must see a record of specialist maintenance even if not all done by Mazda dealers.

RX7 Twin-Turbo (1992 on)

What's good: Sensational looking retro minimalist classic. Searing 'junior supercar' performance from 237 bhp engine. Quick steering. In the same league as a Porsche 911 C2 or a Porsche 968 of the same age. Better looking than either. Can be uprated to 280 bhp.

What's bad: Power had to be restricted to get through EU emissions laws. Not enough 'feel' in the quick steering. Heavy fuel consumption. Strictly a two-seater. Needs expert specialist maintenance.

What to watch out for: Evidence of proper, regular specialist maintenance, with regular changes of all fluids. Worth having an MOT cat test done even if not due, to check for excess hydrocarbons which could mean that the rotor seals are wearing out. Don't buy without getting the car properly checked by an expert in the model, even if the inspection costs you £250. There are a few dodgy grey imports about that won't pass a proper UK MOT emissions test.

Tribute SUV (2001 on)

What's good: New 'Sports Utility Vehicle' from Mazda/Ford with choice of 3.0 litre V6 or 2.0 litre four. Five-door, double opening tailgate with hinged window, 50/40 split folding rear seat, standard ABS, four wheel drive on demend and a three-year 60,000-mile warranty. On sale in UK early 2001. The same vehicle as the new Ford Maverick.

What's bad: Did badly in American IIHS and NCAP crash tests. Airbag failed to inflate in American test. Not as good looking as Maverick II.

What to watch out for: Too soon to say.

Xedos 6 (1992–1998)

What's good: Beautiful looking car. Really stunning. Could have been the prototype for a new small Jaguar – with Mazda reliability. Sensationally smooth, free-revving 2.0 litre 24-valve engine (which powered Ford's Mondeo Touring Cars). Mirror-like thick lacquer over paint has to be baked on while the car is rotating on a rotisserie. Suspension and handling much improved from 'N' reg on. Mazda was rated by Motor Warranty Direct as Britain's most claim-free used marque (www.warrantydirect.co.uk).

What's bad: Early suspension not up to the engine or the sporty looks. Really just a 626 with strut braces. Difficult to feel what's going on through the steering. Very difficult to match the original paint quality, particularly metallics, so don't think a £300 bonnet respray will work. MX5-powered 1.6 is underpowered.

What to watch out for: Early UK SEs did not have aircon, just an aircon button with a sticker over it, so make sure aircon blows cold. (Aircon standard on SE from 'N' reg on.) Look for clean oil on the dipstick and evidence it has been changed regularly. Any mayonnaise under the oil cap, leave the car alone. First jobs: change coolant and brake fluid. Check for uneven tyre wear.

Recalls: 1994 (VIN JMZ CA1***01100001–01119137): engine may stop without warning. 1997 (built March '92–Aug '94): suspension coil may break and puncture tyre.

Xedos 9 (1994 on)

What's good: Bigger Xedos 6 with MX6/626GT 168 bhp V6 engine. Loaded with kit. Aircon, sunroof, ABS, 4-speed autobox all standard. Leather and walnut trim standard from June 1996. Tasty new alloy wheels and lowered suspension from 1997 transform the car and make it an eye-catcher. Brought huge handling and roadholding benefits. Supercharged 208 bhp Miller Cycle 2.3 litre V6 from 1999 makes it an even better car offering surprising 35 mpg economy. Mazda was rated by Motor Warranty Direct as Britain's most claim-free used marque (www.warrantydirect.co.uk).

What's bad: Not the same stunning looker as the Xedos 6 – until it got those new alloys in 1997.

What to watch out for: Make sure has full Mazda service history so warranty is still valid. '97 model onward the one to go for second-hand. Be very wary of uneven tyre wear.

MCC

Smart (1998 on)

What's good: Quite powerful 599cc 45 bhp to 55 bhp petrol engines coupled to six-speed sequential autoboxes. Much faster than other microcars. And, of course, has city style which other micros lack. Euro Type-Approved. 799cc CDI diesel from autumn 1999 has 41 bhp, 74 lb ft, does 85 mph and 85 mpg – and, at 90 g/km, has ultra-low CO_2 output. Convertible version from early spring 2000. Low chassis sports roadster on the way. Four seater planned. Also mean-looking 70 bhp Brabus version for under £10,000. Did well in German TUV/Auto Bild front offside crash test. Three-Star NCAP crash safety rating. Official imports by MBUK from October 2000, tel: 0800 037 9966. website: ww.thesmart.co.uk. Official Smart Centres now at Chiswick (0870 2400 944); Piccadilly, London (0870 240 940); Brentford Service Centre (0870 2400 942); Milton Keynes (0870 2400 950); Birmingham (0870 2400 960); and Manchester (0870 2400 963). Summer 2001 facelift brought a power boost from 45bhp to 55bhp for the Smart & Pure and a boost from 55bhp to 62bhp for the Smart & Pulse plus better front suspension. Official imports of diesel due in UK in February 2001. 70bhp petrol turbo engine and RHD due early 2002.

What's bad: Gearbox and accelerator can take some getting used to. LHD only. Two seats only. Definitely doesn't handle like a hot hatch, though handling can be hugely improved by fitting wide wheels and tyres to the front. Official imports of City Cabrio disappointingly expensive at £9,360 on the road.

What to watch out for: Take care on corners, or fit wider front wheels and tyres.

Recalls: May 2000: Official recall by Daimler Chrysler via DVLA records on all 602 MCC Smarts imported in 1998 and 1999 to uprate part of the stability control system software, to check the front axle ball joints for water ingress and corrosion and to check the throttle pedal module. Any replacements free of charge wherever the car was purchased.

MERCEDES

190 Diesels (1983–1993)

What's good: The most economical 190s, if driven with economy in mind.

What's bad: Slow and dreadfully boring. None more so than 72 bhp 2.0 litre diesel automatic. 5-cylinder 90 bhp 2.5 is better. UK did not get turbodiesel engines.

What to watch out for: Clocking especially, otherwise see 190.

190/190E 1.8/2.0 (1983–1993)

What's good: Build quality, solidity, door latching system. Takes age and mileage very well indeed if properly maintained. 1989 model-year facelift brought more legroom in back. Hard, flat seats like those of W123 are longest-lasting seats I know. Good autoboxes. 190 2.0 carb engine has 90 bhp, 1.8 injection 113 bhp, 2.0 injection 122 bhp. Was a 136 bhp 2.3 injection in Europe, LHD only. Better built than C Class which followed.

What's bad: Hard, flat seats not comfortable for everyone. 'Simplex' timing chains on pre–1989 model-year cars prone to snap at around 60,000 miles. Some facelift cars (with lower body side-moulding) used up old stocks of 'Simplex' engines. Tinny boot lid. Clumsy manual gearbox.

What to watch out for: If buying an 'F' or 'G' four-cylinder 190 or 190E, open the oil filler cap and look at timing chain underneath. Single link = 'Simplex'; Double link = 'Duplex'. If buying high mileage, make sure service records show 5,000-mile oil changes. 190s more than 10 years old may have started to rust. Clonking autoboxes. Noisy rear axles. Power steering leaks. Kerb damage to front suspension (look for uneven tyre wear). Clocking of these cars is rife so a full service history with receipts and old MOTs tells you a lot more than that the car has been properly serviced. (A 93K with 140,000 miles makes £5,000 at auction. Don't pay £10,000 for the same car with a haircut.)

190E 2.3/2.5 16v (1985–1993)

What's good: The 'hot' 190 2.3 has 187 bhp; 2.5 has 197 bhp, rising to 204 bhp from September 1990. Autobox available with 2.5 16v.
What's bad: Manual gearboxes not the best.
What to watch out for: Clocking. Uneven tyre wear a particularly bad sign on this one as could have been crashed. Otherwise, see 190/190E 1.8/2.0.

190E 2.6 (1986–1993)

What's good: This simple, smooth and brawny 160 bhp chain cam engine is the best of the bunch. 130 mph performance, 28 mpg and no running out of breath when overtaking. Ideal when mated to autobox. Properly maintained, can run well over 12 years and 200,000 miles without serious engine or gearbox problems. Recommended (if you can find a good one). Still worth paying £3,000 for the best.
What's bad: Getting old now. See 190.
What to watch out for: Could have been clocked, or odometer may simply have broken at around 160,000 miles (make sure it's working on your test drive). Will need new valve stem seals at around 120,000 miles (a £120 job at a specialist, but much more at a Mercedes dealer). See 190 1.8 and 2.0 litre for other checks.

A-Class (1998 on)

What's good: Brilliant packaging. Choice of 1.4 or 1.6 litre petrol engines, 1.7 litre common-rail direct-injected diesel or 125 bhp 1.9. Manual, clutchless manual or automatic gearchanges all 5-speed. Various trim options. Interesting full-length sliding sunroof. Double-skin floor lifts passengers into safer position in side impacts. Four-Star performance in 1999 NCAP crash safety tests. Loaded with anti-skid, anti-roll-over technology. Prior to Audi A2, the most status you could buy at its length. Modifications for Spring 2001 include 'S' Class quality trim, better seats, new traction control system, a parcel shelf instead of retractable luggage cover and new 75bhp and 95bhp CDI diesels capable of combined mpg figures of up to 59mpg. 2001 models are identified by new rear door

395

handle housed in an oval-shaped flap and a new front. Stretched model seven inches longer also available from June 2001 (see A-Class LWB) 3-year mechanical warranty and 30-year Mobilo roadside assistance + anti corrosion warranty. MB was rated by Motor Warranty Direct as Britain's 2nd most claim-free used marque (www.warrantydirect.co.uk).

What's bad: Not as well built as you expect from Mercedes. Convoluted right hand wheel to left hand rack steering column robs steering of feel. Ride quality far from brilliant. Still suffers from top-heavy 'roll understeer' on tight, adversely cambered corners. Essential to pay full attention on the motorway or can swap lanes. Long step up or down from seats for elderly or infirm unless parked against a high kerb. Expensive. Lots of drivers have trouble with the keyfob immobiliser control. There have also been alarm system faults, water leaks, problems with anti roll bar links and faulty air flow sensors. Another widespread problem is fractured fuel filler pipes leading the rear of the car to fill with petrol if the tank is over-filled.

What to watch out for: Doubts beginning to emerge over clutch life of semi-automatic with 170CDI diesel engine. Two reports of slippage after 40,000 miles received within a week of each other. Anti-roll bar links on early models prone to problems and may need replacing with the modified links of later models. Also take great care to check the car's stability electronics before buying. A140 Classics will be coming off Easy Rent-a-Car fleet in large numbers.

A-Class LWB (2001 on)

What's good: Stretched A-Class launched as a mini MPV on sale in UK from June 2001. Seven inches longer, stretched from the B pillar back. Offers 1,930 litres of interior space. With rear seats removed has 1,530 litres of loadspace. Longer wheelbase means it handles better than the short wheelbase A Class, but still has some unusual handling characterisitics. For other A Class improvements from June 2001, see A Class.

What's bad: Too soon to say.

What to watch out for: Too soon to say.

C-Class (1993–2000)

What's good: Galvanised body has 30-year warranty. Extensive range of engines offer something for everyone. Start with 122 bhp C180, 136 bhp C200, 150 bhp C220 four, 148 bhp C230 four, 193 bhp C230 Kompressor, 170 bhp C240 V6, 193 bhp C280 straight six, 280 bhp C36AMG; 94 bhp C220D, 113 bhp C250D and 150 bhp C250TD. C250TD is a very good diesel – now replaced by new 125 bhp/221 lb ft C220 CDI common rail indirect injected diesel. Estates are smart and offer more status than saloons. 5-speed autos standard from 1997. Top model, 4.3 litre 40 valve 310 bhp V8 C43 lists at £47,640 and originally sold for over list, as did 218 bhp 320 CLK coupe and convertible. Progressive spec upgrades over the years. S and T reg cars came 11th in 2001 Top Gear/JD Power Customer Satisfaction Survey. MB was rated by Motor Warranty Direct as Britain's 2nd most claim-free used marque (www.warrantydirect.co.uk).

What's bad: Early build quality not up to scratch and headlamps poor (much improved later). Not as good to drive as 190E or E-Class. Steering over light and lacking in feel. C180 classic manuals without sunroofs or aircon don't hold their value in the way Mercedes owners expect. Average performance in NCAP crash tests. Huge overs paid by snobs to get hold of CLK coupes and convertibles did not feed through into used values. C180, C200 and C220 seems to be unusually prone to premature failure of the catalytic converter, leading to an £800 repair bill. Reports of cylinder head stretch bolts failing on four-cylinder engines, with replacement a 'head-off' job. Up to 1999, C180s had a low-rated battery and alternator that wasn't up to a life of short runs.

What to watch out for: Chip lots of price off if the car is scruffy (a good way to get a cheap, long-lasting car you would have damaged yourself over the years). Glut of cancelled Far East export orders hit used values hard in 1998. C180 classic manuals without sunroofs became very hard to sell. Make sure wiper mechanism works because it's prone to failure and costs £800 to replace. Cat failure also likely to set you back £800. Oil leaks from cylinder head a sign of stretch bolt problem. Beware of cancelled export order 1995–1997 C-Class sold in UK as new when they were up to 3 years old.

Recalls: 1996: Check for sticking bonnet catch and safety catch which may lead bonnet to fly open.

C-Class (2000 on)

What's good: Complete new range launched September 2000 starting with 4-door saloon and later to include 3-door hatchback and 5-door estate. Pretty 4-door saloon looks exactly like a small S-Class. Galvanised body with 30-year warranty. Engines are 129 bhp 2.0 litre four; 163 bhp 2.0 litre supercharged four; 170 bhp 2.6 V6; 218 bhp 3.2 V6; 143 bhp 2.2 CDI four-cylinder; and 170 bhp 2.7 CDI five-cylinder. Gearboxes either a six-speed manual, five-speed fully automatic or five speed Sequentronic semi-automatic. 220CDI should offer 45 mpg economy. Three lap/diagonal rear belts, a/c, driver and passenger airbags plus side bags and window bags and cruise control with 'Speedtronic' speed limiter standard throughout the range. Now has rack and pinion steering and polycarbonate headlight lenses. Decent sized boot. Electric folding door mirrors incorporate indicator repeaters. Optional 'Command' voice-activated telephone, navigation system and sound system. Later developments to include new direct-injected petrol engines from 125 bhp to 200 bhp and a CVT auto. 354bhp C32 AMG launched at Detroit Show in January 2001. Estate version and coupe from Summer 2001. Estate with punchy 170bhp 2.7 litre CDI and Sequentronic box is almost as quick as 3.2 V6 fully automatic. Excellent score of 31 points in 2001 Euro NCAP crash safety tests. See Road Test of Estate and coupe at www.honestjohn.co.uk.

What's bad: Indicator stalk on RHD models is clumsy and difficult to use. Six-speed manual box can be a bit notchy with smaller engines. Autobox quadrant markings on wrong side for RHD. Steering better than old C-Class but still over-light and lacking in road feel. Ride quality of 'Classic' base model far from brilliant. 163 bhp 200K a bit boomy. Definitely not as good to drive as equivalent 3-Series. Sold out to end of 2000, but expected to sell 22,000 units in UK in 2001.

What to watch out for: South African build quality niggles. Consumers Association members have reported minor rattles and electrical faults. Six speed manual gearbox has sometimes given trouble on other MB models fitted with it.

E-Class W123 (to 1985)

What's good: The last beautifully-built working-class Mercedes. Solid as a rock. I've seen them with 350,000 miles still looking almost like new. The seats don't sag. 230E the most popular. 240D slow, but goes on for ever. 5-cylinder 300D slightly faster, with similar longevity, less likely to have been a taxi. 280E fastest. Handsome, useful estates.

What's bad: Old cars now. They do rust and diffs do go. Don't take well to unleaded. Must have 3,000-mile oil changes and a new timing chain every 60,000 miles or 5 years whichever comes first. 1984–85 230Es tried to go unleaded and suffered premature valve guide wear. Slow changing manuals best avoided. Don't buy without a sunroof. Avoid the 250 six-cylinder engine because it's badly engineered. A new engine for a 280E is £6,000.

What to watch out for: Most of the good ones were bought up by 'private hire' and minicab operations who will have serviced them pragmatically but run up a mega mileage and don't let them go until they're knackered. If the big bumpers are damaged it means a heavy impact which may have deformed the structure. Find out when the Simplex timing chain of 4-cylinder engines was last changed. Listen for rattles and look for oil smoke signifying valve guide wear. Listen for noisy, clonky rear axle. Bounce the rear suspension to make sure shocks still absorb. Estate car rear shocks are very expensive. Look for oil leaks underneath.

E-Class W124 Estates (1985–1996)

What's good: Estate cars come no better. Strong, reliable, comfortable, well-built, safe with more floor-to-window loadspace than any Volvo. 6-cylinder 300E and 5-cylinder 300D best older engines. 280 and 320 24v best newer engines. Smaller radiator grille introduced in August 1993.

What's bad: 200s are underpowered, especially automatics. 230TE autos with aircon struggle with a full load. (See W124 saloons.) Cats from September 1990 when power dropped from 136bhp to 132bhp. 16 valve 220 engine from August 1993 had 150bhp.

What to watch out for: Very important to check the rear suspension as replacement shocks are expensive. Has it been towing? 200TEs and 230TE autos aren't really powerful enough to tow a caravan, so will be well worn if they have been trying. Engine and autobox may have overheated. The electric tailgate closer is vulnerable to failure and expensive to replace. Otherwise see W124 saloons.

Recalls: 1995: passenger Footrest. 1996: airbag may inflate on wrong side.

E-Class W124 Saloons and Coupes

What's good: Strong, reliable, comfortable, well-built, safe. Bigger, more modern car than W123. Best compromise engine in older models is the six-cylinder 12-valve 260E (not available in UK estates). Best in newer models is the 280E. 260E is rare in the UK because large numbers were exported second-hand to Malaysia, Thailand and Singapore in the mid-1990s.

What's bad: Lots of quality problems when the model was launched. Four-cylinder 200E and 230E had valve trouble running on unleaded and can still wear out their valve stems in the guides. Six-cylinder 300 12 valve and 300 24 valve engines sometimes prone to cracking of the cylinder head. 'Simplex' timing chains not replaced by 'Duplex' chains on 4-cylinder engines until 1988 (see 190). American-style foot parking brake on automatics. Manual gearchange slow and not very pleasant. Reports of cylinder head stretch bolts failing on later four-cylinder engines (200, 220) with replacement a 'head-off' job.

What to watch out for: Built to cover high mileages and many did, but may not show it. Listen for noises from top of engine, look for oil smoke in exhaust. Simplex timing chains on older 200E and 230E last only 60,000 miles and require 3,000-mile engine oil changes. No such problems with later Duplex chains or with 260E, 300E, 300E 24v, 320E 24v. Look for oil in the coolant, low coolant and emulsified oil under the oil filler cap of six-cylinder models (could signify cracked head). Check for uneven tyre wear (kerbed suspension, worn steering or merely adjustment needed). Brake hard and check for judder (front discs may be warped). Look for oil leaks underneath. Avoid 4-Matic unless you really need a large four-wheel-drive saloon car. Make sure autobox works in 'sport' (if fitted), feel for 'slip', check colour of ATF (should be dark red), listen for diff rumble. Make sure ABS light goes on and off when it should (brake fluid changes may have been missed). Ask to see a proper service history, if not by a Mercedes dealer, then by a competent specialist. Oil leaks from cylinder heads of four-cylinder engines a sign of the stretch bolt problem. Some cancelled export order W124s still being sold as new in 2000 when 5 years old.

Recalls: 1995: Passenger footrest. 1996: Airbag may inflate on wrong side.

E-Class W210 (1995–2002)

What's good: Good-looking cars with slightly better ride and handling than W124. Engines range from 2.0 litre 136 bhp four through straight sixes and V6s to 280 bhp E430 V8. Very good 177 bhp 300 Turbodiesel goes well with reasonable economy, replaced by 195 bhp 320CDI with massive 350 lb ft torque. 125 bhp 220CDI boosted to 143 bhp and 232 lb ft. Estate cars particularly elegant. Top model 5.5 litre 40-valve 354 bhp V8 E55 competes head on against Jag XJR8. 1995–99 models got Three-Star NCAP crash test rating (marked down for distortion of pedal box). 2000 models onwards were modified and achieved a Four-Star NCAP rating. 220CDI or 320CDI 5-speed auto recommended. S and T reg cars came eighth in 2001 Top Gear/JD Power Customer Satisfaction Survey. Conflicts with *Telegraph* readers' experiences, but MB was rated by Motor Warranty Direct as Britain's 2nd most claim-free used marque (www.warrantydirect.co.uk). High mileage '96–'97 E230 Elegance models with 5-speed autobox (MUST be 5-speed) sought after for export to Far East and fetching big money at auction.

What's bad: These are expensive cars. Old 5-cylinder 113 bhp E250D slow, but would be the taxi driver's choice. Standard 'Brake

Assist' caused lots of problems which took Mercedes years to sort out. Reports of cylinder head stretch bolts failing on four-cylinder engines, with replacement a 'head-off' job. 1995 and 1996 cars had a few paint problems. '96 and '97 cars have a rust problem in Germany. Replacement E-Class due 2002. May be a problem with the engine mounts of the E320CDI.

What to watch out for: Cancelled Far East export orders found their way back to the UK at mammoth discounts. Make sure any car you buy from a non-Mercedes dealer is properly certificated with either an EU Certificate of Conformity or UK SVA. Oil leaks from cylinder head a sign of the stretch bolt problem on 200s. Beware of cancelled export order 1995–97 W210 E-Class sold in UK as new when they were up to 3 years old. An 'R' reg could be a 1995 car.

Recalls: 1995: passenger Footrest. 1996: airbag may inflate on wrong side. 2000: 1997-build cars recalled to have both sills re-treated with cavity rust-proofing. 13/10/2000: 15,105 E Class VIN A000043 to A313828 built late 1994 to 1994 recalled because insufficiently tightened PAS steering damper screw could result in fluid loss. In extreme circumstances this could ignite on a hot exhaust manifold. Torque of steering damper screw to be checked and damper O ring seals to be replaced if leaking.

M-Class (1998 on)

What's good: MB's 4x4 much in evidence around places like Weybridge, Surrey (famed for 4x4s that never do any more off-roading than climbing over the kerb outside Cullens). 3,199cc six-cylinder engine or 4,256cc V8. Standard autobox. 430 model does 0–60 in under 8 seconds and runs to 130 mph, which is comfortably better than a Range Rover 4.6 and at £43,390, a lot less money. Five-cylinder 270CDI model a comparative bargain at prices starting from £29,000 for the six-speed manual or £30,500 for the more powerful auto. The only M-Class capable of 30 mpg plus. MB was rated by Motor Warranty Direct as Britain's 2nd most claim-free used marque (www.warrantydirect.co.uk). Comprehensively facelifted for Autumn 2001 with 292bhp ML 500 replacing the ML 430 and 347bhp ML 55 AMG on offer.

What's bad: American build quality not quite up to Stuttgart's. Very tall, so take care on corners. Hideous optional external rear wheel carrier that blots out rearward vision from the interior mirror. Not as good as a Range Rover off-road. Quite a few complaints from *Telegraph* readers about the inability of MB dealers to rectify faults. Isolated complaints of failures of 6-speed manual gearboxes fitted to 270CDI.

What to watch out for: Highly unlikely damage from off-roading. Highly likely damage from kerbs, but most are fitted with ultrasonic reversing aids so parking damage will be minimal.

Recalls: 4/2/2000: driver's seatbelt may unbuckle. To be replaced with modified buckle.

S-Class W126 (1986–1991)

What's good: Good looking, carved from solid Mercedes from the same box as the W123. Engines range from 185 bhp twin cam 12-valve 280 six to 300 bhp 560 V8. You can still get a good one with 10 years useful life left in it.

What's bad: 280SE and 300SE not significantly more economical than the smaller V8s. All these cars like petrol.

What to watch out for: When checking a V8, take off the top of the air filter plenum chamber and look for oil. If there's oil in there, the car needs a £12,000 new engine. Listen for timing chain rattle, signifying infrequent oil changes. Don't want to hear any coarseness from the engine, transmission, diff or rumbles from the wheel bearings. Look for uneven tyre wear – could signify suspension wear. Small dinks and donks in the bodywork cost an arm and a leg to fix properly. Remember, these cars only go on forever if frequently and expensively maintained. Cut back on the maintenance and they will break, leaving you with bills for more than the value of the car. Could have been clocked – especially if on its 2nd or 3rd owner.

S-Class W140 (1991–1999)

What's good: Sensible engine range from 190 bhp S280 through 228 bhp S300, 286 bhp S420, 308 bhp S500 and awesome 408 bhp

S600 (power on this cut back to 389 bhp in October 1992). MB was rated by Motor Warranty Direct as Britain's 2nd most claim-free used marque (www.warrantydirect.co.uk).

What's bad: All these cars are just a bit too big. European mid-90s slump left a lot of 'S'-Class unsold – sitting outside in Baltic Sea dockside compounds which won't have done them much good. Used prices go up and down like a lift in a department store. The coupes were pointless and merely told the world you're rich. All were slow sellers in the UK, particularly in 1997–98. Official sales hit by diverted Far East exports at up to £17,000 less.

What to watch out for: Can be a huge amount of car for the money if bought right. Tyres are enormous, wear heavily and are very expensive, so budget for this.

Recalls: 1997 (1995–96 build): may lose brake fluid from hose.

S-Class W220 (1999 on)

What's good: Galvanised body has 30-year warranty and car carries 30-year MB Mobilo roadside assistance. Nice looking, beautifully built, unaggressively styled big cars. Sensible engine range from S280 through To S600. Smaller 280 and 320 are V6s. Rack and pinion steering gives good road feel and makes the cars much better to drive then 140 Series without sacrificing ride comfort. Excellent 'Tipfunction' side-flick manual control over 5-speed automatic. S320 V6 is just about adequate. 430 V8 probably the best compromise. Nothing better as a quiet, refined 140 mph Autobahn cruiser. Straight-six S320CDI diesel arrived in UK in Spring 2000 with 197 bhp and 347 lb ft torque giving 143 mph or 35 mpg. V8 S400 CDI has 247 bhp and a staggering 414 lb ft giving 155mph or 30mpg. Not unreasonably priced for what you get. Could be considered 'The Best Car in the World'. Recommended. S and T reg cars came 19th in 2001 Top Gear/JD Power Customer Satisfaction Survey.

What's bad: As length and weight increases from S280 to S600L, handling qualities deteriorate. Not a lot of boot space for such a big car. Huge options list can increase new price considerably, and spec needs to be checked carefully when buying second hand. Vulgar £554 walnut/leather optional steering wheel not nice to hold. There may be a problem with the engine mounts of the S320CDI diesel and has been criticism of false alarms from dashboard oil light.

What to watch out for: Niggling build-quality problems. Make sure every electic/electronic gizmo works as it should. If it's an import you don't get the same warranty so should allow for that and lower resale values in what you pay.

Recalls: 8/8/2000: 780 new S Class built 1/2000–5/2000 recalled because a short circuit could result in the heater blower motor regulator overheating which could lead to charring and smouldering. Blower motor regulator units to be replaced.

SL (1989–2001)

What's good: Vastly better looking top people's sports roadsters. Six-cylinder cars probably the most sensible. 300 12-valve: 190 bhp; 280 12-valve 193 bhp; 300 24v 231 bhp, 320 24v also 231 bhp, pre-cat 500 V8 326 bhp, catalysed 500 from Sept '90 down to 308 bhp, then power up again to 315 bhp from May '95; 600 V12 has 389 bhp; AMG SL60 is a bored-out 5,956cc 381 bhp V8 handles better than 600SL. All these cars came with a standard, lift-off hardtop which is a two person job to remove. Just about the safest way to travel with the top down and tell everyone you've won the lottery. MB was rated by Motor Warranty Direct as Britain's 2nd most claim-free used marque (www.warrantydirect.co.uk).

What's bad: Splodgy fat car handling. Autobox apt to change gear on corners when you don't want it to. Replacement model due late 2001.

What to watch out for: Lots of iffy cars with doubtful pasts in the trade: LHD to RHD conversions. Clones. Cancelled Far East Export orders. Check carefully for repaired body damage. Look for rust near the edges of the hard top. Make sure the aircon blows cold. Don't buy with the hardtop fitted and no chance to check out the hood operation and the hood itself for mould or tears. Really need 3,000-mile fully synthetic oil changes.

SL W107 (1971–1989)

What's good: Roadsters for movie stars, nouveaux riches and pools winners, had very long model life from 1971 to 1989. Six-cylinder engines more economical and cheaper to repair than V8s. A lady in Weybridge used to drive her pet parrot around in one. It just sat there on a box in the passenger seat chattering away.

What's bad: I call these 'ribside' roadsters from the Fiat Panda-like ribbing along the sides. To some eyes, they are really ugly and look like oversized fairground dodgem cars. But other people like them and there is still some status attached to driving one around with the top down. Unlikely ever to be as 'classic' as previous model 230SL, 250SL, 280SL 'Pagoda Top' and light years behind the '50s to early '60s 300SL.

What to watch out for: Fell into the wrong hands in those middle years between being old cars and becoming 'classics'. Lots driven by rich women, some of whom bounce them off kerbs, so check for uneven tyre wear signifying suspension damage. Be very wary of 'customised' SLs with oversize alloys, vulgar body kits and white leather steering wheels. If it has aircon, make sure the aircon blows cold. Faulty ABS means a very expensive MOT failure. Make sure the power hood works properly and has no tears. Must have had 3,000-mile fully synthetic oil changes. Take the air filter top off and look for oil in the plenum chamber underneath. If you find any, walk away sharpish.

SLK (1996 on)

What's good: Beautifully engineered electrically folding hard-top. High build quality. Galvanised body has 30-year warranty. Revised for Y2K with three engine options: 163 bhp 200K, 193 bhp 230K and 218 bhp 320 V6, and either a six-speed manual of five-speed autobox. Now a much better, sportier car than the original UK 230K auto, with 200Ks more reasonably priced, from £26,390. 320 six-speed goes like a real sports car at last and gets up to 120 mph very quickly. MB was rated by Motor Warranty Direct as Britain's 2nd most claim-free used marque (www.warrantydirect.co.uk).

What's bad: Silly premiums paid for the first few years' cars on UK roads. Offset driving position. 'Kiddy car' looks from side and rear. Original official UK imports were automatic 2.3 'Kompressor' only, so more a two-seat roadster than a 'sports car'. Autobox changes gear on corners when you don't want it to (manual obviously doesn't). Some problems reported with the 5-speed autobox. Steering is old-fashioned recirculating ball. Not much boot space. Older 230K models devalued by arrival of new range. Isolated complaints of failures of 6-speed manual gearboxes.

What to watch out for: Sellers may try to base used prices on premium price paid rather than market value. LHD 2.0 litre manual 'personal imports' can be a better bet at £12,500 v/s £25,000 for RHD 2.3 auto.

SLK 32 AMG

What's good: Effectively a new high performance supercharged model of the SLK boasting all of 354bhp and 332 lb ft torque giving the car a 0–60 of 5.1 seconds, yet capable of running on 95Ron premium unleaded petrol. 17" wheels with 225 tyres on the front and 245s on the back. Will also be available with 5-speed 'Speedshift' selectable automatic transmission. More information at www.mercedes-benz.co.uk.

What's bad: Insurance premiums likely to be stiff, otherwise too soon to say.

What to watch out for: Too soon to say.

V-Class (1996 on)

What's good: Based on the smart Vito van. New 2.2 litre common rail direct-injected diesel is powerful and economical. Lap/diagonal seatbelts for everyone in 7-seater version. Most have just six big seats, all fully removable. Seats themselves lightened for 2001 model from 39kg to 28kg, making them easier to handle. List prices cut to £23,230 from £29,280. All covered by 3-year mechanical warranty and 30-year Mobilo warranty giving 30 years roadside assistance and a 30-year guarantee against perforation by corrosion.

What's bad: 'V' stands for Vito van with rear side windows, but can't really stand the move up-market and loses buckets of value over the first two years. Many only had 6 seats. Bits drop off. Sliding side door mechanism fails. Van-like to drive. S and T platers 2nd from bottom in 2001 Top Gear/JD Power Customer Satisfaction Survey.

What to watch out for: Dings and dents. Check all trim carefully inside and out. Watch for signs of hard usage. Drive-shaft boots prone to failure (MOT failure point, but worth checking or the UJs will lose their lubrication and replacement drive-shafts are expensive).

Recalls: 1999 V-Class and Vito van (1996–98 build): tread may separate from tyres.

Vaneo (2001 on)

What's good: Stretched A-Class 4.2 metres long with voluminous rear (3,000 litres) and removable kombi-style second row of seats aimed at families and small businesses and tradesmen who want one vehicle for both work and domestic use. Will have ESP. Brake Assist and the sandwich floor design of the A Class, but should be inherently more stable due to its longer wheelbase. To be launched the the Frankfurt Motor Show 13th–23rd September 2001.

What's bad: Too soon to say.

What to watch out for: Too soon to say.

MG

MG ZR

What's good: Rover 25-based ZR160 boasts the same 160bhp VVC engine as the MGF Trophy 160, with a 0–60 of 7.4 seconds and a top end of 131mph. List price is a reasonable £14,345. MG ZRs with smaller engines from £9,995.
What's bad: See Rover 25.
What to watch out for: See Rover 25.

MG ZS

What's good: Rover 45-based ZS180 has a 177bhp version of Rover's 2.5 litre KV6 to propel it to 60 in 7.3 seconds then on to a top whack of 139 for a list price of £16,395. Handling praised by *Autocar* magazine issue 11–7–2001. MG ZSs with smaller engines from £12,495.
What's bad: See Rover 45.
What to watch out for: See Rover 45.

MG ZT

What's good: Rover 75-based ZT190 has 2.5 litre KV6 boosted to 190bhp, getting the heavier car to 60 in 7.8 seconds and on to 141mph, which is easily handled by the much improved 75 chassis. ZT190 priced at £21,095. Less powerful MG ZTs from £18,595. Basic chassis of Longbridge built Rover 75 much improved over original Cowley built car.
What's bad: See Rover 75.
What to watch out for: See Rover 75.

MGF (from 1995)

What's good: The car MG enthusiasts had been clamouring for and, true to their words, they bought it in droves. 118 bhp 1.8 or 143 bhp 1.8 VVC. BBR (01280 702389) does a cheap tweak to improve mid-range performance of both engines. Works hard-top looks made for the car. Clever 'crush' boxes built into front bumpers protect the structure of the car in low-speed impacts. Excellent brakes. Plenty of boot space front and rear. Easy to get in and out through wide opening doors. Three-years warranty and servicing included from 6/10/2000. Range brightened up considerably in March 2001 with announcement of £15,500 112bhp 1.6i with standard alloys and rip-snorting £21,000 160bhp Trophy SE models. See range road test at www.honestjohn.co.uk.

What's bad: More of a modern MGB than an MGA or Midget. Fine for the over-40s and for women, but not a young man's car. Early MGFs suffered a lot of quality problems, most serious of which was a leaking top, windscreen and bootlid, but fixes were quickly found (park the wrong way on an incline, though, and the softop may still leak). Suspension and suspension subframe misalignment is more serious. Plastic back window. Started to lose value quite heavily in 1999. Steptronic auto not very good in this car and has horrible, naff and nasty plastic model kit steering wheel buttons. Possibility of camshaft sprocket coming adrift on VVC. S and T platers 10th from bottom in 2001 Top Gear/JD Power Customer Satisfaction Survey.

What to watch out for: The MGF bulletin board (www.ipl.co.uk./cgi-bin/forum/MG/sub69/cmtlist.html) is a useful means by which owners can swap information about faults. First look for uneven tyre wear which signifies misalighned suspension or suspension subframes. Then silly things, like a bent cable from the exhaust manifold lambda probe can lose its insulation on the hot pipes, short out and stop the car. British Racing Green paint chips easily on flexible front. Have a good look under the carpets for rust caused by water from leaking hoods. Look under the car for damaged coolant pipes from front radiator to mid-engine (loss of coolant will lead to head gasket problems and possible cracking or warping of the head). Stretch bolts may also stretch leading to head gasket problems and possible need for a reskimmed head and block face. Full dealer service history essential or 'in service' mods may not have been made. Flexible under-engine exhaust joint gives up (like Cavalier diesel) and rattles. It's in unit with rear silencer and the section costs £380. Gear linkages can be troublesome so check for clean changes on test drive. Hard tops are £1,450 – worth remembering if car has not got one. If buying an MGF with a hard top fitted, take it off and check the hood for damage. Immobiliser frequency can suffer interference. The clutch and brake pedals share the same mounting shaft and the clutch pedal can interfere with the brake light switch.

Recalls: Boot and windscreen seals carried out as 'in-service' modifications. No official recalls known 1995–98. 1998: 20,000 MGF's recalled to check for snagging of drivers seatbelt webbing.

X80

What's good: New high performance sports car bases on the Qvale Mangusta, to have a 4.6 litre V8 delivering up to 380bhp, manual or automatic transmissions, coupe or roadster bodies. Launch date 2002.
What's bad: Too soon to say.
What to watch out for: Too soon to say.

MICROCAR

Virgo (1999 on)

What's good: French two-seater micro hatchback. Has two-cylinder 505cc Lombardini petrol or diesel engines giving up to 68 mph and up to 78 mpg. Simple, exposed-belt Variomatic transmission. Electric windows and stereo. Fibreglass rather than polycarbonate body. Under the weight limit, so can be driven on a motorcycle licence. Euro Type-Approved. From £6,402 on the road. Three-year warranty on engine.

What's bad: Slow acceleration of diesel.

What to watch out for: Too soon to say.

MINI

MINI (2001 on)

What's good: Re-launched as the MINI brand in 2001 and shown at the 2000 Motor Show. Great to sit in with retro dials and switchgear, good seats, straight-ahead seating position, adjustable steering column. Engines are 90 bhp 8-valve 1.4 (for MINI One); 115 bhp 16v 1.6 (for MINI Cooper) and 163 bhp supercharged 1.6 (for MINI Cooper S). Cooper has 15in alloy wheels; Cooper S huge 17in wheels. Prices from £10,400 to £16,000. On sale from 7th July 2001. Very desirable. Own website www.mini.co.uk.

What's bad: Not how the original Mini was conceived, but should offer plenty of fun. Not much room in the back seat (but was there ever in a Mini?) Nasty and aggressive legal copyright action by BMW lawyers against people specialising in the old Mini. 163bhp Cooper S will not arrive until 2002.

What to watch out for: Too soon to say.

MITSUBISHI

Carisma (1995 on)

What's good: Decent engines, especially 1.8GDI which gives 40 mpg plus economy or strong acceleration from 125 bhp – but not both at the same time. Painless to drive and own. Excellent three-year unlimited mileage warranty. Designed for low servicing costs. Facelifted summer 1999 with new beak-like front. In June 2001 Mitsubishi was rated by Motor Warranty Direct as Britain's 5th most claim-free used marque (www.warrantydirect.co.uk).

What's bad: Bland Nedcar Eurobox, more Orion- than Mondeo-sized. Not great to drive. Diesel version much slower and not much more economical than petrol GDI.

What to watch out for: No known problem areas, yet. Ex-fleet cars may have been abused by drivers. Steering could have suffered damage from kerbing. If you smell petrol, it could be that the in-tank fuel pump retaining cap ring has shattered. Was a recall but did not reach all early Carisma owners.

Recalls: Unknown date: recall of early Carismas to correct a fault with the plastic in tank fuel pump cap ring which could shatter.

Challenger (1998 on)

What's good: 4x4 pick-up-based cut-price alternative to the long wheelbase Shogun, with Shogun's 'old' 2.5 diesel and 3.0 V6 petrol engines plus independent front suspension. Tough and should last well. Improved for 2000 model-year with option of INVECS II four speed autobox.

What's bad: Ride and handling not up to Shogun.

What to watch out for: Evidence of heavy off-road use or heavy towing.

Colt (1989–1992)

What's good: Pleasingly-styled along same lines as larger Galant and Lancer 4-door and 5-door. Better looking than Lancer. Engines: 1,298cc 68 bhp; 1,468cc, 74 bhp; 1,596cc, 123 bhp GTi 16v grew to 1,836cc and 134 bhp in April 1990 putting it firmly in the Golf GTI 16v league. All models run on standard premium unleaded.

What's bad: Service costs and parts prices, particularly body parts.

What to watch out for: Rust in the seams and floor pan. Skimped, independent servicing after 3-year warranty ran out.

Recalls: 1996 (1991–1994 build): check for loss of brake fluid.

Colt (1992–1996)

What's good: Quite a pretty car which became the Proton Compact when Mitsubishi restyled the Colt in 1996. 1,298cc 74 bhp; 1,597cc 111 bhp; 1,834cc twin-cam 138 bhp. Very well built. In June 2001 Mitsubishi was rated by Motor Warranty Direct as Britain's 5th most claim-free used marque (www.warrantydirect.co.uk).

What's bad: Only one small three-door body-style, more supermini-sized than Escort-sized.

What to watch out for: Skimped, independent servicing after 3-year warranty ran out. Tappety engines. Badly shifting autobox. Uneven tyre wear signifies kerb damage, possibly strained PAS rack. Could need a cambelt change.

Recalls: 1996 (1991–1994 build): check for loss of brake fluid.

Colt (1996 on)

What's good: Smooth 88 bhp 1.6 engine feels more powerful (more like the 111 bhp it used to have). Gives excellent combination of performance and up to 42 mpg. Other engine option: 74 bhp 1,298cc. Decent steering, ride and handling. Beautifully built. In June 2001 Mitsubishi was rated by Motor Warranty Direct as Britain's 5th most claim-free used marque (www.warrantydirect.co.uk)..

What's bad: Only one small three-door body-style, more supermini-sized than Escort-sized. Not very space efficient and not as neat looking as previous model. Mirage bodykit ugly and rear spoiler not car-wash proof. Not much back seat room. Shorter people find restricted rear visibility makes it difficult to reverse.

What to watch out for: Must have been dealer serviced to retain warranty. Aircon was a very expensive dealer aftermarket extra.

Recalls: 1997 (June–August 1997 build): 213 cars found to have sticking brake booster valve. 6/11/2000: 4,249 Colts built 1996 – 1999 recalled because crankshaft pulley securing bolt may not have been torqued correctly and may loosen or break leading to detachment of pulley. All engines up to YD2145 remove pulley securing bolt, increase the depth of thread in the crankshaft by 5mm, check for damage and renew if necessary. Lubricate threads, refit and tighten to specified torque. Engines from YD2146 on: remove pulley securing bolt, examine for damage and renew if necessary, lubricate threads, refit and tighten to specified torque.

FTO

What's good: Looks like a 3/4 size Aston Martin DB7 and now backed by the UK Mitsubishi service network. Front wheel drive. GS model has 1,834cc 125bhp four cylinder engine giving 0–60 in 9.2 seconds and topping out at 125mph. GR and GX have 1,999cc 170bhp V6 giving 0–60 in 7.9 seconds and 136mph. GPX and GPR have 1,999cc 200bhp MIVEC V6 giving 0–60 in 7 seconds and 142mph. Can pick one up in the UK from around £7,000. In June 2001 Mitsubishi was rated by Motor Warranty Direct as Britain's 5th most claim-free used marque (www.warrantydirect.co.uk).

What's bad: As they come off the boat from Japan numerous mods are needed for the cars to run properly on UK petrol and meet UK/EU Type Approval regs. A good outfit to sort the car out is Protech, tel: 01179 861611.

What to watch out for: Mainly watch out you're not buying a GS for GPX MIVEC money. Make sure the car is properly UK SVA certificated, or has at least been sorted by a specialist such as Protech.

Galant (1988–1993)

What's good: Quite good looking and well equipped. GLSI an early beneficiary of ABS. Much improved by Diamond Option Pack. Wood trim packs also help. Normal models very reliable.

What's bad: 4WD/4WS model too complicated to make a sound second-hand buy. Diesel engine only available briefly in 1989. Parts for major repairs are expensive.

What to watch out for: If fitted with ABS, make sure warning light goes out and that it works. Check for aircon and, if fitted, make sure it delivers cold air. Independent servicing once warranty ran out may have been skimped. Water pumps go (check expansion tank level and check under oil cap for mayonnaise indicating a cooked engine and cylinder head trouble). Power steering pump or rack may leak fluid. Engines wrecked by timing belt failure, so best changed every 36,000 miles or every three years. Uneven tyre wear on 4WD/4WS could signify suspension problems which cost a fortune to put right.

Galant (1993–1997)

What's good: Better looking, slightly bigger Galant, still in Mondeo/Vectra class. In June 2001 Mitsubishi was rated by Motor Warranty Direct as Britain's 5th most claim-free used marque (www.warrantydirect. co.uk.)

What's bad: 2.5 V6 four-wheel-drive with four-wheel steer a bit too complex to be a sensible second-hand buy.

What to watch out for: See 1989–93.

Recalls: 1994/1995 models (2,000 UK cars): possible fault with brake booster. (Announced August 2000. Owners to be contacted later.)

Galant (1997 on)

What's good: Grew from being Mercedes C-Class size to Mercedes E-Class size. (Made Sigma redundant.) Very Japanese, but very striking styling. By UK standards, quite good value. 2.5 litre V6 automatic estate is a big, heavy, luxurious car. Usual excellent three-year unlimited mileage warranty. Three three-point rear seatbelts from 1998 model-year. Amazing VR4 estate has 280 bhp, four-wheel drive, 'Tiptronic'-type auto, anti-yaw control, and is both quick and safe. In June 2001 Mitsubishi was rated by Motor Warranty Direct as Britain's 5th most claim-free used marque (www.warrantydirect. co.uk.)

What's bad: Quite hard to judge the front when parking. More suspension 'clonks' than a BMW. Don't hold their value as well as a Mercedes or BMW. Mix of officially imported and grey imported VR4s. Only pay grey price for a grey.

What to watch out for: Minor body damage could mean a major repair bill.

Recalls: Mitsubishi Galant 2.4GDI (264 cars in UK): possible fault with brake booster. August 2000 official recall. 24/8/2000: 1,921 Galants and Spacewagons built 1998–99 recalled because nipple of brake booster vacuum hose may become choked with combustion products from engine causing reducec braking efficiency. Nipple to be relocated away from source of combustion products.

Lancer (1988–1992)

What's good: Essentially a slightly stretched Colt with either a 4-door saloon or 5-door hatchback body. Looks very much like a shrunken Galant. Engines: 1,298cc 68 bhp; 1,468cc, 74 bhp; 1,596cc, 123 bhp GTi 16v grew to 1,836cc and 134 bhp in April 1990. Also, just to complicate matters, a 1,755cc 95 bhp engine for the GLXi with four-wheel drive. All models run on standard premium unleaded.

What's bad: Not much rear legroom for a four-door saloon. Looks a bit truncated. GLXi had an (unnecessary) catalytic converter. Lancers dropped from official UK line-up from 1992. Next generation Japanese Lancer became Proton Persona. Current generation very successful in international rallying. Some personal imports in UK.

What to watch out for: Rust in the seams and floor pan. Skimped, independent servicing after 3-year warranty ran out. Uneven tyre wear may signify suspension damage or misalignment on four-

417

wheel-drive model. Very hard to re-set and get right.

Recalls: 1996 (1991–1994 build): check for loss of brake fluid.

Lancer Estate (2000 on)

What's good: 1,600cc 5-door air-conditioned estate launched in UK at a bargain price of £10,995 complete with 3-year warranty. Some specialists cut the price back to an incredible £8,995.

What's bad: Too soon to say.

What to watch out for: Too soon to say.

Lancer Evo (1996 on)

What's good: Hat-trick, three wins in a row Tommi Makinen World Rally car, now officially imported by Mitsubishi Ralliart. £31,000 280 bhp EVO VI reckoned to be better than the best Imprezas, and GSR450 has 450 bhp. EVO VI does 0–60 in 5 seconds and tops out at 150 mph at 7,000 rpm in 5th. Incredible anti-yaw control means it always corners flat. In the hands of a good driver (some of which are policemen) it's probably the fastest road car for UK driving conditions. Very safe as well as enormous fun to drive. So good it flatters the driver. Apart from on a motorway or dual carriageway virtually nothing could outrun one. Cut-price stripped out EVO V1 RSX loses aircon, anti-lock brakes and anti-yaw control but sells for £25,995 OTR. New EVO VII on sale in UK from September 2001 is based on Japanese Lancer Cedia model.

What's bad: Most UK cars weren't officially imported. Older Japanese grey imports start rusting in as little as three years. Specifications of grey imports may be all over the place, so tread very carefully. Could be problems with Enhanced Single Vehicle Approval from August 2001.

What to watch out for: Accident damage and hidden suspension damage.

Recalls: Apparent suspension recall notified to owners, but by February 2001 parts to rectify had still not arrived from Japan.

Shogun (1991–1999)

What's good: Big, but not 'aggressive' looking. Better on the road than a Discovery or Range Rover. 3-year unlimited mileage warranty from new. Very good 3.0 litre 24v V6. Auto available. 5-door is a full seven-seater, but driver's rear vision badly restricted. Curious 'bitty' facelift as from autumn 1997 Motor Show. In June 2001 Mitsubishi was rated by Motor Warranty Direct as Britain's 5th most claim-free used marque (www.warrantydirect.co.uk).

What's bad: Don't buy for economy. Even the 2.8 litre diesel in the 5-door body is pushed to better 22 mpg and the 2.5 diesel is not really powerful enough. 3.0 litre V6s even more thirsty. Diesels are a bit slow. Gearboxes are the first bits to break. Timing belt of V6 drives water pump, so seizure of water pump wrecks engine.

What to watch out for: Eventually, they do rust and it's important to check all the points where the body meets the chassis. Listen for transmission whine (used replacement gear and transfer boxes are available from API, tel: 0500 830530). Make all usual 4x4 checks: underbody damage; grumbling wheel bearings; suspension alignment; if it's been towing, what has it been towing? Steering arm balljoints go, but are fairly cheap to replace and easy to get at. Quite a few 'exported' to BFPO squaddies and re-imported tax-free. Make sure it's a real UK-market Shogun and not a 'Pajero' or 'Montero' badged as one. Pay less for Pajeros and Monteros.

Recalls: 1996: (1991–94 build): check for loss of brake fluid. 27/9/2000: 278 Shoguns built in 1994 recalled because brake fluid may seep from front hoses. Hoses to be replaced.

Shogun (1999 on)

What's good: Still obviously a Shogun, but now more rounded looking with monocoque shell. New '4M41' 3.2 litre 16-valve direct injected diesel replaces underpowered old 2.8, offering 173 bhp and 282 lb ft torque. 217 bhp/257 lb ft 3.5 litre GDI V6 replaces thirsty old 24v V6. Suspension now independent both front and rear which improves on road ride comfort and handling enormously. Improved water pump on V6 to help prevent engine failures. Cut price Classic model from October 2000 with 3.2 DI-D engine and 3-door or 5-door bodies from £22,995.

What's bad: Nothing yet.

What to watch out for: Beware of grey imports and RHD Pajeros stolen in another country.

Shogun Pinin (1999 on)

What's good: Cute 'Shrunken Shogun' designed to compete with 3-door RAV 4 and Freelander. 120 bhp 1.8 litre GDI engine helps economy. 5-speed manual or 4-speed auto options. Charming to drive on road in two-wheel drive. Short overhangs, selectable four-wheel drive, high/low-range gears, centre diff lock and light weight make it very capable off-road. By far the best junior 4x4. 2.0 litre 5-door version also available from January 2001 at prices from £15,995 on the road with Mitsubishi's bulletproof 3-year warranty. ABS and EBS standard on this model. New 2.0 litre GDI engine develops 127bhp at 5,000 rpm and 140 lb ft torque at 3,500 rpm. Top speed 106mph, 0–60 10.6 seconds v/s max 104 mph and 0–60 10.0 seconds for 1.8 GDI Pinin 3-door.

What's bad: Not as quick as RAV 4 on the road. Limited interior space. Not much luggage space behind rear seats of 3-door version.

What to watch out for: Evidence of heavy off-road use.

Recalls: 18/12/2000: 1,488 Shogun Pinins built 1999–2000 recalled due to possibility that a condensor may come away from the circuit board due to a wiring breakage resulting in the engine stopping or becoming difficult to start. Silicone to be applied to the condensor to act as a vibration damper to conteract shocks transmitted from the suspension to the circuit board.

Sigma (1991–1996)

What's good: Two cars: Japanese-built high-tech 202 bhp 24-valve 3.0 litre V6 'executive' saloon or Australian-built 168 bhp 12-valve 3.0 litre V6 estate which came later in Feb '93. Both front-wheel-drive, both capable of over 130 mph and saloon capable of over 140. Engines sound wonderful. Steering a bit too light. Manual option on estate, but not saloon. Aircon standard on saloon, optional on estate. In June 2001 Mitsubishi was rated by Motor Warranty Direct as Britain's 5th most claim-free used marque (www.warrantydirect.co.uk).

What's bad: 202 bhp Sigma saloon too complicated for long-term reliability at more than three years old. Lots of geegaws to go wrong. Body parts can be hard to get.

What to watch out for: Make sure estate has aircon. Check for damage in load area from loads and dogs. If it's had a towbar, what has it been towing? Look for skimped independent servicing once warranty ran out. Especially important to look for things like body damage and cracked light lenses because replacements are hard to get.

Recalls: 1996: (1991–94 build): check for loss of brake fluid.

Space Runner (1992–1999)

What's good: Strange looking, but very practical car. Rear seat comes right out leaving large cube of space. Excellent 3-speed plus overdrive automatic gives 35 mpg. Neat handling. Good performance from 121 bhp 16-valve 1.8 litre engine. Upright driving position. Optional aircon does not hurt fuel consumption unduly. Excellent vehicle for the disabled. 3-year unlimited mileage warranty. In June 2001 Mitsubishi was rated by Motor Warranty Direct as Britain's 5th most claim-free used marque (www.warrantydirect.co.uk).

What's bad: Rear seat in one piece and heavy. Needs optional £35 rear bumper protector to avoid scuff marks. Only one (left hand side) sliding rear door. Comparatively high used prices due to usefulness and scarcity. Replaced in UK at end of 1998 by new Carisma-based Space Star. (We didn't get new Japanese market Space Runner.) Regular timing belt changes essential.

What to watch out for: Check sliding door mechanism. Timing belts need changing regularly or engines destroy themselves. Have a good sniff for lingering doggy smells. Check for damage from clumsy wheelchair ramp modifications. Servicing may have been skimped after 3-year warranty period.

Space Star (1998 on)

What's good: Carisma-based, Netherlands built 5-door mini MPV to compete against Scenic. Had 85 bhp 1.3 Colt engine or 125 bhp 1.8 GDI at launch. 3-year, unlimited mileage warranty. Versatile rear seats can be double-folded, slid forwards or reclined. Three proper three-point rear seatbelts. Prices from just £9,995 OTR. Auto option from October 2000. New 96bhp 1.6 engine gives top speed of 112mph and combined consumption of 39.2. Average three star NCAP crash safety rating announced 28/3/2001. 'Mirage' 1.6 from Summer 2001 has alloys, central locking, front electric windows, radio/cassette, driver and passenger airbags, metallic silver paint, colour coded bumpers and alloy dashboard trim all for £10,695. Mirage also available with 81bhp 1.3 engine for £9,995.

What's bad: 1.3 will tug a family of four along at a reasonable pace, but economy suffers. Not powerful enough for five adults and their luggage. For this you need the 1.6 or the 1.8GDi.

What to watch out for: Nothing yet.

Space Wagon (1992–1999)

What's good: Car-sized seven-seater. Not as high as other MPVs. More car-like to drive. 121 bhp 1.8 litre engine replaced by 131 bhp 2.0 litre in August 1992 ('K' reg onwards). In June 2001 Mitsubishi was rated by Motor Warranty Direct as Britain's 5th most claim-free used marque (www.warrantydirect.co.uk).

What's bad: Rearmost seat slopes forwards, not very comfortable for adults. Heavier, so doesn't handle as well and not as much fun to drive as Space Runner.

What to watch out for: Timing belts need changing regularly or engines destroy themselves. May have been mini-cabbed and run up huge mileage under 3-year warranty. Servicing may have been skimped after first three years. Check for uneven tyre wear. Cable gearchange of manual can become sloppy. Also quite a few grey imports knocking around, so satisfy yourself as to proper UK spec unless offered extremely cheaply.

Recalls: 24/8/2000: 1,921 Galants and Spacewagons built 1998–99 recalled because nipple of brake booster vacuum hose may become choked with combustion products from engine causing reducec braking efficiency. Nipple to be relocated away from source of combustion products.

Space Wagon (1999 on)

What's good: Bigger than its predecessor, now with 147 bhp 2.4 litre four-cylinder GDI engine and option of cheaper 2.0 litre engine. All have dash mounted gearlever and very useful 'walk through' cab design enabling the driver to get out kerbside or walk between the front seats to reach a child in the rear.

What's bad: New model only a Three-Star performer in NCAP crash tests (4 points front impact; 15 points side impact).

What to watch out for: As predecessor, but will still be under the 3-year warranty, so will have been properly dealer serviced.

Recalls: Mitsubishi Space Wagon 2.4GDI (1,657 cars in UK): possible fault with brake booster. August 2000 official recall. 24/8/2000: 1,921 Galants and Spacewagons built 1998–99 recalled because nipple of brake booster vacuum hose may become choked with combustion products from engine causing reducec braking efficiency. Nipple to be relocated away from source of combustion products. 18/5/2001: Worldwide recall of all 250,000 new shape Space Wagons to check for cracks around fuel tank mounting plates.

NISSAN

100NX (1992–1995)

What's good: Small Sunny based targa topped coupe with twin removable glass panel roof. Seats two adults and two kids. 1,597cc catalysed 16 valve engine pumps out 89bhp. 4 speed auto optional. Power increased to 101bhp from February 1993. Limited edition 'Pacific' model in June 1995. Holds its value well because much loved by its fans. Timing chain rather than timing belt engine.

What's bad: Odd looking and neither practical not sporty, but some people love them.

What to watch out for: Same twin timing chain engine as Primera, Sunny and Almera 1.6. Needs clean oil.

200SX (1994–1999)

What's good: Transformed by new body from October 1994. Squat, well-proportioned, almost Italian looks. Very tasty. 1996 facelift made it even better. 197 bhp 2.0 litre turbo four not bad either. Manual or automatic. Usually with leather and aircon. Rear drive handling. Better ride than previous version. More room inside, especially back seats.

What's bad: Not as sharp to drive as previous model. (But still inclined to swap ends in the wet.)

What to watch out for: Oddball grey imports not to proper spec with 55 mph limited Japanese tyres, and wipers that lift off the screen at 70 mph. Must have been serviced zealously, with extra oil changes to protect the turbo bearings. Synthetic oil a wise move.

300SX (1990–1994)

What's good: Very serious twin-turbo 280 bhp junior supercar, killed off by European emissions legislation. 'Full on' manuals or 'Mr Softy' autos, usually with leather and air. Very comfortable. Goes like stink and handles surprisingly well.

What's bad: Rear three-quarter vision not good. Handbrake a long way back. To drive, the manual is best, but buy an auto.

What to watch out for: Grey imports without the twin turbos and other important items of kit. Greys have less rust-proofing so tin worm is also a problem with these cars. Noisy engines. Exhaust smoke (turbo oil seals), dirty oil, lack of maintenance. Look for uneven tyre wear – may be simple misalignment, may have been 'sausaged'. Manual boxes and clutches lead a hard life and boxes are mega expensive to replace. Cars which have been sitting require a full recommission or you'll be in for all sorts of problems. Tyres may have 'flat-spotted', discs rusted, exhaust rotted (especially rear silencer boxes). Targa roof panels may leak – not easy to get new seals for them. Power steering may have sprung a leak.

Almera (1995–2000)

What's good: Tough. Strong, chain-driven twin-cam engines. Decent handling, good to drive, good ride quality, good roadholding. 143 bhp GTi (launched 1996) is a good 'hot hatch'. Four-door saloon version by far the best looking and has three three-point rear belts.

What's bad: Hopeless styling of original hatchbacks. Some 1.4 litre models have very mean equipment levels. Diesels are slow. We pay about twice as much for them as they do in Japan. Comparatively poor performance of hatchback in 1999 NCAP secondary safety crash tests.

What to watch out for: Make sure engine has clean oil and that coolant has been changed every two years (a messy, but necessary, service job, often neglected). Engines have two timing chains so if any rattles in this department, don't buy. Expect noises from multi-link suspension – often cured by spraying with WD40.

Recalls: 1998 (Dec '97–May '98 build): inertia reel seatbelts may not lock on impact.

Almera (2000 on)

What's good: New Almera from early 2000. Has more exaggerated 'beaked front' look than new Primera. 5-door hatch does away with 'D' pillar side windows and looks much better for it. 1.5 and 1.8 litre petrol engines. New 2.2 litre direct injected diesel. British built at Sunderland alongside Micra and Primera. Very good 30 point four star NCAP crash safety rating announced 28/3/2001, actually beat the Volvo S80. Much prettier saloon version from June 2001 at prices from £11,065 including air-conditioning.

What's bad: The UK taxpayer had to fork out for it to be built in Sunderland.

What to watch out for: Too soon to say.

Almera Tino (2000 on)

What's good: New, good looking Scenic-sized MPV first seen at the Barcelona Motor Show in May 1999, being built by Nissan Motor Iberica in Barcelona. Three lap/diagonal rear seatbelts. Power-trains will include reliable 2.0 litre Sunderland-built 136 bhp chain-cam 16v engine with Nissan's Japanese-made torque converter CVT. Very good four star NCAP crash safety rating announced 28/3/2001.

What's bad: Torque converter robs CVT of instant response.

What to watch out for: Problems reported by the Consumers Association include faulty exhausts, rattles from rear seats (recall for this: see below), faulty airbag warning light, stuck petrol gauge, noisy clutch.

Recalls: 1/12/2000: 761 Almera Tinos built May–Sep 2000 recalled because side airbag satellite sensor may be incorrectly programmed and side bags may not deploy during a side impact. Sensors to be re-programmed. 1,015 Tinos built May–Aug 2000 recalled because pins which locate centre rear seat hinge may not have been installed correctly which could lead to the hinge failing under load. Rear seat hinges to be replaced where found to be defective (explains Consumers Association 'rattles from rear seats'.

Bluebird 1984–1990

What's good: This is the front wheel drive Bluebird, later examples of which were UK built at Sunderland. Available as a four door saloon, a five door hatchback or a five door estate car. Introduced with 90bhp overhead cam 1,809cc engines, the same block but turbocharged to 135bhp, or a 105 bhp 1,973cc ohc unit. 3-speed auto optional on 1.8; 4-speed auto optional on turbo and 2.0. Facelift and 82bhp 1.6 introduced in March 1986, plus new 1,796cc engine with 88bhp. 1.8 turbo and 2.0 continued as before. 2.0 'Executive' introduced in October 1989 with 115bhp and ran to the end in September 1990 when the range was replaced by the Primera. Always solid and reliable. Name used on later Sunnys in Indonesia and there is a 460 strong 'Bluebird' taxi fleet on Bali.

What's bad: Old cars now. Some would say 'stolid' and reliable. Banger territory, but previously a great favourite among mini-cabbers, though almost all Bluebirds this happened to will have died. Very little underbody protection until 1985, which is why you rarely see a pre-'85 on the road any more. These cars also had dodgy carbs and are generally not recommended unless you're paying a fiver to end the car's life on a banger racing circuit. Pre-1996 Bluebirds also had poor cooling systems which were apt to silt up.

What to watch out for: Only go for a post-March 1986 Bluebird if you're planning to run it. Check brakes and suspension carefully. Look for signs it's been a family car rather than a mini cab. If you're looking at a turbo, it's getting a bit old for a performance car, so check turbo oil seals by getting someone to follow behind on your test drive looking for puffs of black smoke. Also check the discs themselves and adjust what you pay if they are lipped or scored. (But, of course, you're not going to be paying much anyway.)

Maxima QX

What's good: Nissan's all new large car designed to compete against the Omega and supply an alternative to the defunct Scorpio. V6 engines from a 2.0 litre V6 to a 200bhp 3.0 litre V6. List prices from £20,700 to £27,400. Manual option on 2.0 litre, otherwise all automatic. Loaded with goodies such as climate control. Three

proper lap/diagonal seatbelts in the back. Three-year warranty.
What's bad: Nothing has come up.
What to watch out for: No feedback.

Micra (1983–1992)

What's good: Amazingly reliable until they get old. Can be run on a shoestring. Cambelt replacement is a cheap £60 job, but best to replace camshaft end seal and water pump at the same time. API can supply good quality second-hand replacement engines for £455 plus VAT (0500 830530).

What's bad: Bodies start to rattle after 4 years. Very light build makes occupants vulnerable in a crash. Scratches rust quickly. Cambelts need to be replaced regularly and camshaft end seals at the same time. Waterpumps eventually go and either snap the cambelt or lead to severe overheating which can wreck the engine. Fuel pump diaphragms fail, leaking neat petrol into the oil sump leading to severe engine wear and possibly even an explosion. Failed engines not worth replacing now, even at API's low prices.

What to watch out for: Far too many suffer from neglected servicing and 'short run syndrome'. Elderly owners simply forget to service them. Mayonnaise under oil filler cap may be condensation, but mayonnaise under the radiator cap is a sign of a head problem. If the engine overheats on the test drive, its cylinder head is warped. Requires coolant replacement with special Nissan coolant (or Trigard) every two years or engine will corrode internally. After high mileage, will start to burn oil and need either new valve stem seals or a replacement engine. If engine has been replaced or reconditoned it may be dodgy. Any 'rumbling' from the bottom of the engine is likely to be the water pump about to fail (allow £150–£200 for new water pump, timing belt, camshaft end seal). A smell of petrol under the bonnet usually signifies fuel pump failure (allow £100 for new fuel pump plus oil and filter change).

Recalls: Early Micras from 1985–87 recalled for gearbox oil loss fault. Oil fed its way up the speedo cable and dripped onto the pedals. Many Micras did not come back for the modification.

Micra (1992 on)

What's good: Jewel-like 16-valve chain-cam engines. Broadened the market for the Micra, making it a young person's car as well as an old person's. Well built, in Sunderland. Sensible parts prices (cats are £200). Special pre-facelift 1998 run out 1.0 litre model had CVT and power steering. Restyled in 1998. 1,275cc '1.3' engine increased to 1,348cc in July 2000, with increase in power from 75 ps to 82 ps and torque from 76 lb ft to 80 lb ft at 2,800 rpm.

What's bad: Cute 'blobby' styling works for some, not for others. Most did not have power steering. Average performance in NCAP crash tests. Must have 6-monthly oil changes to avoid timing chain trouble. Japanese 'March' models look the same but many parts are not interchangeable. Can suffer from poor starting in damp conditions due to suceptibility of the spark plugs to condensation. Poor starting can also be caused by the wrong temperature sensor which leads the combustion chambers to flood and the ECU to shut down the engine to prevent spiking the catalytic converter. To be replaced by new car on same platform as new Renault Clio in late 2002.

What to watch out for: Clocking. Dirty oil. Must have clean oil. If the timing chain rattles and the car is out of warranty, leave it alone. You could be in for a £400–£500 tensioner replacement job. May have suspension damage from kerbing – most likely and most damaging on power steered cars. Clutches of early cars don't last, but most will by now have been replaced. Previously reliable CVT has started to develop the same electromechanical clutch problems as Puntos. If it thumps when you move the lever to drive, or if the lever is hard to move, leave the car alone.

Recalls: 1994 (Sep '92–June '94 VIN 000001–237783): floor may crack next to handbrake.

Prairie (1989–1992)

What's good: Replaced box-like 1983–89 Prairie, still Sunny-based, but now with up to seven seats. Much liked by mobility converters because the design allows a drop floor and slightly raised rear roof so electric wheelchairs can drive straight in. 2.0 litre Bluebird engine.

What's bad: No nicer to drive than old Prairie due to vague steering and body roll.

What to watch out for: Rust, sticking sliding side doors, suspension wear from overloading, dog-eaten upholstery, gears difficult to select, uneven tyre wear. Engine needs regular timing belt changes.

Primera (1990–1996)

What's good: Unbreakable chain-cam engines on 2.0 litre petrol but not diesel. 2.0 litre twin cam petrol engine very punchy. Decent ride/handling combination. Very good (Sunderland) build quality. Big boot. 2.0 litre petrol models are the best buy among 1990–96 upper-medium-size cars. Recommended.

What's bad: Not a great 'looker'. Steering a bit light on Mk I models. Gearbox a bit weak and won't stand abuse. Complex rear suspension develops squeaks and rattles (easily cured with a spray of WD 40). Non-turbo diesels are slow and have timing belts rather than chains. Shielding makes it very difficult to drain the block to change the coolant (best changed every 3 years to prevent internal engine corrosion). Two timing chains in 1.6 engine are one too many, but still no record of problems from them unless oil changes neglected.

What to watch out for: Clocking. Evidence of lack of oil changes (black sludge on the dipstick) and lack of coolant changes (highly likely due to difficulty of job). Uneven tyre wear will mean front suspension damage from kerbing or wear in suspension bushes. Rear silencer boxes rust out rapidly even on 25,000-mile-a-year cars. High incidence of hydraulic clutch and starter motor failure on 'N' reg Primeras. Could have been mini cabbed.

Recalls: 1995 (VIN 000001 to 472213): front brake hoses may chafe. 1997 (June '96–Feb '97 build): fuel vapour may leak from tank.

Primera (1996–1999)

What's good: Unbreakable chain-cam engines on 2.0 litre petrol but not diesel. Drivetrain feels exactly the same as previous model. But steering slightly better and roadholding from new rear suspension is astonishing. Very good build quality. Big boot. Comparatively good performance in NCAP crash tests.

What's bad: Not a great 'looker' compared to the rest of the class. Gearbox still a bit weak and won't stand abuse. Still difficult to drain the block to change the coolant (best changed every 3 years to prevent internal engine corrosion). Still two timing chains in 1.6 engine. Delays in supply of spare parts can put cars off the road for three months.

What to watch out for: Clocking. Evidence of lack of oil changes (black sludge on the dipstick). Uneven tyre wear and front suspension damage from kerbing.

Recalls: 1997 (June '96–Feb '97 build): fuel vapour may leak from tank.

Primera (1999–2002)

What's good: New sheetmetal from September 1999 turned the Primera from an excellent car let down by nondescript looks into a real polariser of tastes. New flexible 1,769cc 114 bhp engine develops 111 lb ft torque from 2,400–4,800 rpm. New 'Hypertronic' CVT transmission is the first CVT with a 2.0 litre engine. CVT also offered with six-ratio electronic manual hold. By far the best to drive is the 138 bhp 2.0i 16v Sport manual.

What's bad: Do you like the way it looks? Do your neighbours like the way it looks? Different models have different suspension set-ups, some not as good as previous model. Torque converter makes CVT slow to accelerate. Due to be replaced early 2002.

What to watch out for: Too soon to say.

Primera (from 2002)

What's good: At last, a really good looking Primera, based on the Fusion concept car seen at the Paris Motor Show in September 2000 and shown as the new Primera at the 2001 Barcelona Motor Show. Will have choice of 115bhp 1.8 petrol, 140bhp 2.0 litre petrol or 110bhp 2.2 litre turbodiesel. GT-R version planned. Prices to be from £14,000.

What's bad: Too soon to say.
What to watch out for: Too soon to say.

Serena (1993–2000)

What's good: Tall, narrow MPV, fits a normal car-size parking space. Rear-wheel drive (though specials were made with front- or four-wheel drive). 2.0 litre 126 bhp Primera engined SGX models with independent rear suspension and aircon by far the best. SLX and 'Excursion' models have standard aircon from May '97. The cheapest 7–8 seater. Reliable. Timing chains on petrol models. Three-Star performer in NCAP crash tests (5 points front impact; 16 points side impact).

What's bad: A step back from the '89–'92 Prairie. Crude, commercial van-based design, built in Spain. Unpleasant to drive. 67 bhp 2.0 litre and 75 bhp 2.3 litre diesels plain awful, with horrible droning jerky drive-train like a pre-war double decker bus. S and T platers 8th from bottom in 2001 Top Gear/JD Power Customer Satisfaction Survey.

What to watch out for: Likely to have been airport taxis and to have covered more miles than on the clock. Some had two side doors; some had only one. Check for excessive smoke from diesels (dirty injectors or air filter). With its two timing chains, 1.6 petrol needs to have had regular oil changes. Electric windows stick.

Skyline GT-R (1989 on)

What's good: Phenomenal four-wheel-drive junior supercar that looks like a tricked-up coupe. Astonishing performance and handling. Three different generations of GT-R among unofficial imports: R32 (1989–1994); R33 (1995–1998); and R34 (1999 on). Also V-Spec models. Have been chipped in Japan to more than 1,000 bhp, but standard conservatively estimated 280 bhp (more like a true 320 bhp) is plenty.

What's bad: Very limited official UK imports (and performance limited to get through SVA).

What to watch out for: Lots of grey imports about dating back to the early 1990s, so make sure you know what you're getting. New grey imports now restricted by quota so don't buy a car which isn't registered. Check for uneven tyre wear and for pulling to either side on a flat road. Extremely complex suspension and drivetrain difficult to get parts for, to repair and to set up. Make sure the car is a GT-R and not either a rear-drive-only R33 GT-S or, worse still, an ordinary Skyline which could be eleven years old.

Sunny (1987–1991)

What's good: Easy to drive. Strong engines. Can be cheap to run and home maintenance is possible.

What's bad: Hideous styling. Uninvolving to drive. Thin sheet metal will rust quickly if paint is broken. Not built to last.

What to watch out for: Skimped or incompetent home maintenance. Rust (especially structural rust underneath). Oil smoke denoting either bore wear or worn valve stem seals. Suspension damage from kerbing by elderly owners (most likely with 1.6 litre power-steered cars). Need regular timing belt changes.

Sunny (1991–1995)

What's good: Better looking than previous model. Reliable, easy to drive, reasonable build and decent equipment levels. 143 bhp 2.0e GTi is quick.

What's bad: Nondescript 'Golf clone' styling, with excessive rear overhang for a car of this type. Apart from GTi, uninvolving to drive. 'K' reg 'carb and cat' combination is troublesome.

What to watch out for: Carry out reverse turn test for driveshaft clonks. Look for oil leaks. Check for uneven front tyre wear signifying suspension misalignment or damage from kerbing by elderly owners. Never pay extra for ultra-low mileage. Look for front end damage on GTi from falling off the road. Best cars will have a full service history with oil changes every six months and coolant and brake fluid changes every two years, but most will have been serviced once a year if the owner remembered. Vital to see a recent MOT emissions check on K reg 'carb and cat' cars as they are very difficult to get through this test.

Terrano II (1993 on)

What's good: Unbreakable, simple, old fashioned 4x4. Vastly improved in July 1996, especially 2.7 litre diesel which gained intercooler and 25 more bhp. (This is the same engine as most London taxis.) 5-door LWB versions can have 7 seats. Carried on when Ford pulled the plug on the Maverick.

What's bad: Tall and narrow, so you have to be careful on corners and better not pile stuff on the roof. Jerky on-road ride – partly due to suspension, partly to driveline. Spanish build quality not 100% up to the mark, especially trim items.

What to watch out for: Quite likely to have been off-roaded, especially if registered in a country area. Farmers' cars will have seen some work, though remember farmers drive to preserve their vehicles – it's the off-road enthusiasts who break them. Look for weeping seals, noisy hubs, clonky driveshafts, driveshaft 'lash', noisy gearbox or transfer case, oil leaks from engine and drive-train. Smoke from diesel may indicate that turbo oil seals have failed.

Recalls: 1995 (with Michelin 215/80 R15 tyres: VIN 200000–242699): tyres may lose pressure.

X-Trail

What's good: New Nissan 4x4 aimed at Freelander, CRV, RAV-4 market and new Maverick. Front drive with selectable four wheel drive. Familiar 150bhp 2.0 litre twin cam Primera engine for UK. Up to 276bhp available in Japan. Due UK late 2001. Big advantage of totally flat floor with rear seats folded – ideal for dogs and as a working vehicle.

What's bad: Too soon to say.

What to watch out for: Too soon to say.

PERODUA

Kenari (2001 on)

What's good: New in the UK for 2001 and basically the old Daihatsu Move with a new, much cuter Far East retro front. Has a 989cc 3 cylinder twin-cam engine developing 55bhp and 66 lb ft (88.3 Nm) torque. So is faster than the old Move and should be an absolute riot to drive. Low CO_2 emissions at 136g/km. Combined fuel consumption figure: 50.4mpg. Priced from just £5,800 for the GX manual and £6,600 for the EZ automatic (both plus £125 VED and registration tax). Power steering standard, 2-year 24,000-mile warranty and a 6-year body warranty.

What's bad: The foot or so of air over your head helps handling but makes the Move (on which the Kenari is based) feel like a shed to drive. Very thin sheetmetal and lots of glass means lots of condensation in winter.

What to watch out for: Too soon to say.

Nippa (1997 on)

What's good: Strong Sterling exchange rates against the Malaysian Ringit has enabled the importer to offer its EX model as low as £4,495, including a two-year 24,000-mile warranty but plus £125 for VED and registration tax. For the UK, that's cheap. Has same responsive 42 bhp 850cc three-cylinder engine as Daihatsu Mira, Cuore and Move. Sells well in North East England, but brilliant for cities, shopping, suburbia and the school run.

What's bad: Very small. Very basic. Very simple little car. Very limited cornering abilities and uninspiring to drive. For £4,495 you don't get a radio (can't have everything). Called a 'Prodder' in the trade.

What to watch out for: If previously owned by an elderly person, may have suffered heavy clutch wear and over-revving when cold. Younger owners may also have revved the nuts off them trying to find some performance.

435

PEUGEOT

106 (1991–2002)

What's good: All handle well. Stronger (and actually heavier) than bigger 205. Revised and facelifted range from June 1996 includes hot 120 bhp GTi 16v generally reckoned to handle better than equivalent Saxo. 3-year warranty from January 2000. 60bhp 1.1 litre Independence model with sunroof, metallic paint and a year's insurance (for 22–80-year olds) included at a bargain at £6,495 as from June 2001.

What's bad: Twisted-spine offset driving position. Tall people just don't fit. Automatics have only 3 speeds. Reports of premature bore wear on iron block 1.5Ds could be due to dirty or worn injectors washing out the bores. Also see Citroën Saxo which is virtually the same car.

What to watch out for: Check spare wheel is in its underboot cradle and not nicked. Front suspension wear. Oil leaks. Needs frequent timing belt changes. 1.5 diesels need regular servicing and regular coolant replacement – are especially heavy on front tyres. Check for falling-off-the-road damage to GTi 16v. 16vs tend to blow their cats when run against rev limiter.

Recalls: 1997 (March–Nov '96 build: 15,821 cars): ignition switch harness may foul on steering column. 1/2/2000: possibility that brake servo valve may not operate correctly resulting in loss of servo assistance. 18,405 cars recalled for inspection and possible replacement of brake servo valve.

107 (2002 on)

What's good: New small car, same length as 106 but taller, like a cross between a 206 and a Honda Logo so has more space inside.

What's bad: Too soon to say.

What to watch out for: Too soon to say.

205 (1983–1997)

What's good: The definitive 1980s hatchback. Brilliant 'wheel in each corner' design, no space wasted anywhere and great looking. Also no rust traps. It's rare to see a rusty 205 except at the leading edge of the roof and door bottoms. Excellent ride and handling combination. GTi models very throttle sensitive with lift-off oversteer available on demand. Sold 5.3 million. Later post-1988 'TU' sub-1.4 engines better than early small engines which still had their gearboxes in the sump. Diesels capable of 50 mpg and late versions came with power steering. Clever cantilever folding front seats of three-door bodies give good access to rear seat. I've done 950 miles in a day in a 1.6 GTi without even a twinge of backache.

What's bad: Very light build, so vulnerable in accidents – especially at the back. Small front discs of early diesels lead to heavy pad wear. Single front reservoir of pre-86 cars could lead to problems with rear wash/wipe. Valve stem seals of GTis give out at around 60,000 miles. Cambelts and camshaft end seals of all XUs must be changed every 3 years and 36,000 miles. Coolant of diesels must be changed every two years to avoid cylinder head gasket problems. No underbody rust traps, but superficial rust a problem on early cars.

What to watch out for: Check spare wheel is in its underboot cradle and not nicked. Front suspension wear (205s and 306s tend to 'lean' on the front suspension and are particularly vulnerable to kerb damage). Oil burning petrol engines needing new valve stem seals (allow £120). Crash damage and rust in doors, window surrounds and brake pipes. Rusty rear discs on 1.9 GTis.

206 (1998 on)

What's good: Interesting new 3- or 5-door supermini sized between 106 and 306. 60 bhp 1.1, 75 bhp 1.4 and 90 bhp 1.6 petrol engines from 106, but new 70 bhp 1,868cc DW8 diesel based on XUD. PAS and height adjustable steering column standard. Same excellent 306 suspension. 136 bhp 2.0 litre 16v GTi, 90 bhp HDI diesel and 1.4 litre automatic all came later. More roomy inside than new Clio. 500 a day built in Coventry. Image promoted by 300 bhp WRC rally version. Well thought out inside with options such as a folding passenger seat that turns into a desk. 3-year warranty from January 2000. Price-cuts down to £8,795 for 'Look' special edition in Spring 2000 included PAS, aircon and 1 year's insurance. Very Good Four-Star rating in Euro NCAP crash tests. SLK like folding roof Coupe Cabriolet arrived October 2000, but a 2+2 rather than 4-seater. New sporty 110bhp 1.6XSi priced at £11,695 and ultra economical 63mpg 2.0HDi eco priced at £9,845 both launched February 2001. Haynes manual now available. Automatic 110bhp 1.6 litre Coupe Cabriolet from late June 2001, listed at £15,380. Estate 'urban activity vehcile' on the way.

What's bad: Not quite the style classic the 205 and 306 were (styled in-house by computer, not by Pininfarina). Mixed reactions from journalists to handling qualities, but Quentin Willson liked it and the model has been very successful. Reports of side airbags going off for no reason. Reports of water getting into electric door locking control box of late 1998/early 1999 build cars. Easy DIY replacement using Haynes manual, saves typical £55 garage labour cost (part alone £75). (Peugeot Customer Services will sometimes pay for the job.) Water gets in through bonnet vent and plenum chamber underneath is not well drained so drips are carried in through vents in the control box. Repeat of Peugeot 106 problem of sudden losses of power caused by faulty throttle position sensing potentiometer seems to re-occur on some 206 1.4s. Problems with the roof mechanism of the coupe cabriolet. If driven through floodwater, gearbox can suffer from water ingress via breather. Technical problems with automatic gearboxes on 1.4s led to many orders being cancelled in early 2001. Reports of severely rusted exhaust systems on GTis after just 12 months.

What to watch out for: Misfiring problem with 1,150cc models could lead to spiked catalytic converters (see 'Recalls'). Make sure central locking system works (see above). Reports of 1,150cc 206s still being sold with faulty ECUs and a shortage of chips to repair them in March 2001.

Recalls: 1,150 cc models only, 1,000 cars affected: TSB issued in spring 2000 to replace ignition coil pack, leads and plugs owning to misfire, but correction packs only supplied at rate of 20 a month. 1/2/2000: possibility that brake servo valve may not operate correctly resulting in loss of servo assistance. 18,405 cars recalled for inspection and possible replacement of brake servo valve. 19/9/2000: 1,415 206s fitted with side airbags recalled because they may unintentionally deploy. Side airbag control units to be replaced.

306 (1993–2001)

What's good: Excellent ride and handling combination, best in class until Focus came along. 1.6 TU best petrol engine for family car – very nicely balanced. 167 bhp 2.0 litre GTi-6 is track-car quick with roadholding and handling to match, plus a six-speed gearbox. All capable of 150,000-plus miles if properly looked after. Non-turbo XUD capable of 50 mpg. D-Turbo surprisingly quick. Three-Star 'above average' performance in NCAP crash tests. 3-year warranty from January 2000. 306 cabriolets and estate cars continued after the launch of the 307.

What's bad: High used values due to prettiness of body. 1.8 8-valve XU petrol is the worst engine and many were fitted with the wrong engine management chip leading to failed emissions tests. Autobox not recommended. Cambelts and camshaft end seals must be changed every 3 years and 36,000 miles. Coolant of diesels must be changed every two years to avoid cylinder head gasket problems. Like Citroën ZX, can have cat converter test problems. Build quality a bit 'light'. Easy to fluff 2nd to 3rd gearchange on GTi-6. Clutch cable of RHD cars is routed close to the exhaust, which dries out the lubrication and prevents the self-adjuster working properly which leads to premature clutch failure. (Thanks to Mike Brewer of Channel 4's 'Driven' for this snippet.) Contacts fail in remote keys leading to rapid discharge of batteries. Reports of failure of rear disc brake callipers. Reports of engine compartment fuse box short out on diesel almost leading to engine compartment fires (see Recalls).

What to watch out for: See above. Front suspension bush wear (205s and 306s tend to 'lean' on the front suspension and are vulnerable to kerb damage. They also suffer badly from road hump damage). Oil burning petrol engines needing new valve stem seals (allow £120). Not all diesels have PAS and all need it. Check spare wheel is in its underboot cradle and not nicked. If fitted with low profile tyres, check for tyre and rim damage. If fitted with aircon, make sure it works properly. Some reports of fuel line failure on petrol cars, cured by reinforced pipes. If car has rear discs, check calipers for fluid leaks. Check for stiff clutch, as cable may need replacing.

Recalls: 1995: Check accelerator cable. 1996 (July '93–Feb '96 build – 150,000 cars): underbonnet wiring may chafe leading to short circuit and fire. 1997: possible starter motor fault on 1996 model cars. Free replacement. 1997 (Feb–May '97 build – 2,060 cars): incorrect brake compensator fitted. 1998: (Sep '97–Oct '97 build): steering wheel hub may crack; (Nov '97–Apr '98 build): front suspension may collapse. May 1999: R reg 1.8 and 2.0 litre petrol engined models recalled for reinforced fuel lines to be fitted. 2000: 1.9TD October '98 build: front brake pipes may chafe. All March '98 build 306 models: steering rack bolts could crack if overtightened during assembly. March '99–April '99 build 306s with ABS only: possibility of air in brake fluid. 1/2/2000: possibility that brake servo valve may not operate correctly resulting in loss of servo assistance. 18,405 cars recalled for inspection and possible replacement of brake servo valve. Technical Information Circular No 1555 issued in 2000 re airbag warning light flashing then remaining on. Remove both front seats, carry out repairs to harness connectors, replace seats. 3/10/2000: 4,898 306s and Partner vans recalled because of chance of incorrect machining of front stub axles which could lead to excessive wear and possibility of lower ball joint collapsing. Vehicles to be checked and front stub axles to be replaced if necessary.

307 (2001 on)

What's good: Combines elements of 206 with mini-mpv attributes. Five basic spec levels: Style, Rapier, LX, GLX and XSi with choice of seven interiors and five ambiences which together provide around 79 different combinations of interior finish including colour co-ordinated dashboards. Engines are 1.4 litre petrol, giving 75bhp at 5,500rpm, 0–60 in 14.2 seconds and combined mpg of 42.2; a 1.6 litre 16v petrol giving 110bhp at 5,800rpm, 0–60 in 10.6 seconds and combined mpg of 39.2; a 2.0 litre 16 valve petrol giving 138bhp at 6,000rpm, 0–60 in 8.9 seconds and combined mpg of

35.8; and a 2.0 litre HDI diesel giving 90bhp at 4,000rpm, 0–60 of 12.4 seconds and combined mpg of 54.3. A new 70bhp 1.4 litre HDI diesel and a 110bhp 2.0 litre HDI diesel will be launched in late 2001. All 307s have six airbags: front, side and curtain; ABS with electronic brake force distribution and emergency brake assist; active anti-whiplash front seat head restraints; three three-point rear seatbelts; large front and rear storage bins with storage drawers under the front seats; air conditioned gloveboxes to cool drinks on most models; and a choice of 14 exterior paint finishes. Anti theft measures include reinforced lock cowlings inside the doors, an emergency door lock button on the dash and automatic locking of the boot as soon as the car exceeds 6mph after start-up. On the road prices, which include a three-year part manufacturer part dealer warranty, start at £10,860 for the three door 1.4i Style, rising to £15,560 for the 5-door 2.0Xsi. Other price examples are £12,460 for the 1.6i 16v 3-door Rapier with air-conditioning and £14,560 for the 90bhp 2.0HDI GLX 5-door with air-conditioning. More at www.peugeot.co.uk.

What's bad: Mini MPV attributes do not extend to a flat floor and no centre console as in the much better packaged Honda Civic. Doesn't shift the goalposts set by the Ford Focus.

What to watch out for: Too soon to say.

309 (1986–1993)

What's good: Not as bad as it looks. Stretched 205 floorpan gives good combination of ride and handling, plus decent-sized square-shaped boot. Old 'suitcase' pre-TU engines (they need to be unpacked before you can work on them) good for 170,000 miles. Later TU and larger XU engines good. Diesels were the best of their day. The 309GTi 1.9 outhandled the Golf GTi Mk II and many thought it a better (though flimsier) car. High back seats of 3-door GTi give back seat passengers a good view. Clever levers next to handbrake open rear windows. Rare and desirable LHD only 309 GTi 16v illustrated.

What's bad: Its looks. Truly dreadful British styling (Peugeot's only departure from Pininfarina between 1959 and 1998). Was supposed to be a successor to the awful American Chrysler Horizon. To see what good looks could do for basically the same car, read Peugeot 306. Getting to be an old car now.

What to watch out for: TU and XU cambelts and cambelt end-seals need changing every 35,000–40,000 miles whatever the handbook tells you, especially now these cars are getting older. Mk I (high boot sill) rear hatchbacks are leak-prone and this may have led to rusting of boot floor. GTis tend to start smoking at around 60,000 miles, but all they usually need are new valve stem seals.

405 (1988–1996)

What's good: Fine Pininfarina styling. All handle and ride well. Practical estate cars. Narrow enough to fit most garages. At least one diesel model has done more than 600,000 miles. Like 205, rust traps are designed out, so these cars don't rust badly.

What's bad: Light build. So any rust in seams will seriously weaken structure. Rusty brake pipes common on early examples but all should have been replaced with coated pipes by now. Not all had power steering and all need it. Aircon system on GTX models prone to problems. Early 'plip key' immobliser system was a joke because it was easy to unplug inside the centre console. Little things like failed heater thermostatic controls can cost £500 to replace which is usually more than the car is now worth. Trim does not take a hammering.

What to watch out for: Check spare wheel is in its underboot cradle and not nicked. Look for front suspension wear. Rusted brake pipes are an MOT failure point (later models had coated brake pipes). Many diesels were taxis so look for the signs. Clocking of diesels is rife. Run diesels with dipstick out to check for excessive fumes from worn engine. Check for mayonnaise under oil cap signifying head gasket problems. All 405s, petrol or diesel, need a cambelt and camshaft end seal change every 3 years and 36,000 miles. Early carburettor petrol cars suffered from fuel vaporisation. All XU engines can suffer premature bore and big end wear if the oil has not been changed regularly. Look for fluid leaks from power steering rack and pump, clonky driveshafts, seeping gearbox driveshaft oil seals, worn bushes in external gearshift mechanism. A heavy clutch could either mean the clutch is on the way out or the cable is binding.

Recalls: 1995 (1995 model-year to VIN 71339513): airbag may fail to inflate in an accident. 1996 (Sept '93–May '95 build): check for seepage of fuel from feed pipe.

406 (1996 on)

What's good: Bigger 'classier' car than the 405. Spare wheel now inside boot. Excellent ride and handling compromise. Powerful and economical 2.1TD. New class-leading HDI diesel engine from October 1998. Three lap and diagonal rear belts. 7-seater estate. Spare wheel now in boot floor well. Facelifted in March 1999. 3-year warranty from January 2000. New 2.2 litre 160 bhp SRi from July 2000. New 2.2 litre 136bhp HDI with particulate filter from March 2001 at prices from £19,390.

What's bad: Build still feels a bit light. 2.1TD is a nightmare for mechanics to work on. Average performance in NCAP crash tests. Have received a well-above-average number of complaints from owners. Spate of starter motor failures on 2.1TD model. Starting to get reports of radiators failing after 3 years. Combined rear discs and parking brake drums apt to give trouble after 3–4 years. Replacement of discs/drums, pads and parking brake shoes is a £450 job. Can suffer coolant loss from hoses or rad which can lead to damage from overheating.

What to watch out for: Small dings in sheetmetal. ECU problems not sorted out in 96N/96P reg cars. Wrong chips fitted to ECUs on first year's production may or may not have been replaced (an MOT emissions test should tell you). 'Clonking' (likely to be wear in anti-roll bar bushes). Clocking of diesels (has it been a taxi?). Oil consumption of 1.8i and 2.0i 16v petrol engines. Aircon system prone to problems. Look for leaks: coolant, power steering fluid, gearbox oil, engine oil.

Recalls: 1996 (1.8i and 2.0i petrol): Free upgrade of engine management chip if owner complains of 'rough' running, flat spots and lack of power on hills. 1997 (Nov '95–Apr '96 build: 13,412 cars): ignition switch harness may foul on steering column. 1997 (Feb '97 build: 333 cars) incorrect front subframe mountings. 1998: 'Low level recall' no XKG to replace timing belts and tensioners of 1.8litre XU7JP4 engines at 36,000 miles. 2000: check alloy wheels as damage could lead to fractures. 1/2/2000: possibility that brake servo valve may not operate correctly resulting in loss of servo assistance. 18,405 cars recalled for inspection and possible replacement of brake servo valve. 1/2/2000: 487 cars: possiblilty that brake pedal assembly nuts may work loose. Nuts to be tightened and lost nuts to be replaced.

406 Coupe (from 1997)

What's good: Impeccable Pininfarina styling. One of the best looking cars in the world – better looking than more expensive Volvo C70 and Mercedes CLK. A truly beautiful car. Plenty of room for four passengers. Big boot. Airconditioning a more sensible option than sunroof. 2.0 litre versions go and handle like a sports car – much better than 406 saloon. 3.0 litre V6 has four-pot Brembo front brake callipers. Hold their value reasonably well. 3-year warranty from January 2000. 136bhp 2.2 HDi diesel version with 235lb ft (315Nm) torque and 129mph top speed from June 2001 qualifies for 18% list price benefit in kind tax base.

What's bad: Steering and handling of 3.0 litre V6 not as sharp or as sporty as 2.0 litre 16v. Could suffer same aircon system problems as saloon and estate. Can suffer coolant loss from hoses or rad which can lead to damage from overheating.

What to watch out for: The 2.0 litre engines are easily chipped and power can be anything from standard 135 bhp up to 155 bhp. They don't have the low back pressure tubular exhaust manifold of the 167/180 bhp GTi-6, though. Oil consumption may be quite high. 3.0 autos may suffer from warped discs due to owners holding them in gear on the brakes. Look for leaks: coolant, power steering fluid, gearbox oil, engine oil.

605 (1989–1999)

What's good: Big car with the best rear legroom in its class. V6s handle very well and can be thrown about like a 205GTi. 2.1TD is economical and a relaxed long-distance cruiser. Build quality much improved after January 1995 facelift. 1990–94 SVE 24-valve had 200 bhp and was a seriously fast car. 170 bhp 12-valve V6 not a bad compromise. 150 bhp 2.0 8v turbo not a bad engine.

What's bad: Overlight power steering. Riddled with build-quality and electrical problems. The UK market never took to it. 2.1TD very hard to work on. Manual gearboxes a bit weak for V6 engines. 16-valve 2.0 litre engines had ECU problems. 2.1TD auto more suited to long distance than town work. Plummeting residual values. K reg cars going for less than £400 in Summer 2001.

What to watch out for: Most 2.1TDs covered mega mileages, so may have been taxis, may have been clocked. Check all electrics. Make sure aircon blows cold. Make sure petrol catalytic converters aren't hot spotted. (Put it through an advanced emissions test.) If manual, satisfy yourself that clutch and gearbox are in good health. ABS prone to failure and cost of repairing may be more than the car is worth.

Recalls: (None known 1994–96, but that's surprising.)

607 (from 2000)

What's good: Peugeot's new big car starting with new 2.2 litre 160 bhp 'four' at around £22,995 and rising to £31,995 for the 210 bhp 3.0 V6 SE auto. Also a new 2.2 litre HDI from £24,295, the first diesel with a particulate trap exhaust system. 3-year warranty should help put minds at rest.

What's bad: Might be doomed by the lack of success of the 605. Severe lift-off oversteer problem in 'Elk avoidance' test which delayed the launch but made sure the car is properly sorted.

What to watch out for: Too soon to say.

806 MPV (to 2001)

What's good: Same well-planned, reasonably compact MPV as the Citroën Synergie, with the same PSA engines, including new HDI

110 bhp. Three-Star performer in NCAP crash tests (7 points front impact; 15 points side impact). 3-year warranty from January 2000. Earliest 7-seaters now in £5,000 bracket.

What's bad: See Citroën Synergie.

What to watch out for: See Citroën Synergie.

Recalls: 1996 (Sept '95–Oct '95 build): Check airbag trigger. March '99–April '99 build 806s with ABS only: possibility of air in brake fluid. March '98–July '98 build: handbrake ratchet could fail.

807 MPV (2001 on)

What's good: Much better looking than box-like 806. 3-year warranty.

What's bad: See Citroën Synergie.

What to watch out for: See Citroën Synergie.

Partner Combi (from mid-2001)

What's good: Exactly the same vehicle as the excellent Citroën Berlingo Multispace Forte. Same choice of 75bhp 1.4 litre petrol engine at £9,095 on the road, or 70bhp 1.9 litre XUD diesel at £9,360 on the road. CO_2 emissions are 168g/km (£140 VED) and 181g/km (£150 VED); combined fuel consumption 40mpg and 41mpg. Standard features include two huge sliding rear side doors and a gigantic, washing machine swallowing hatchback; driver's airbag, side impact beams, seatbelt pre-tensioners, engine immobiliser, remote central door locking; three-point seatbelts for all three rear passengers; Isofix mountings for two child seats. Does nothing the Citroën Berlingo Multispace doesn't do, but if you live nearer to a Peugeot dealer than a Citroën dealer it's the obvious choice. 3-year warranty. More at www.peugeot.co.uk.

What's bad: See Citroën Berlingo Multispace.

What to watch out for: See Citroën Berlingo Multispace.

PORSCHE

911 (1983–1989)

What's good: Some say the last 'classic' 911 (I don't agree, I prefer the '89–'93 964). Galvanised body parts. Properly looked after, it will last for ever. Easier to work on and cheaper to service than '89–'93 964.

What's bad: Can be a handful in the wrong hands, particularly the 300 bhp 3.3 Turbo. Very likely to have seen a few 'track days'.

What to watch out for: Signs of accident damage (suspiciously new-looking rear wing stays); clutch slip (a new clutch is a £2,000 engine-out job); exhaust system (as expensive as a clutch); oil cooler (expensive). Feel the discs for ridges, wear and shouldering. Make sure callipers aren't sticking at the back. Find a good local independent Porsche specialist to inspect the car and give it a compression test before you buy it. Once you own the car, take it in for regular servicing at least every 6 months even if you hardly use it.

911 C2 and C4 964 (1989–1993)

What's good: More power than previous 911 (250 bhp v/s 231 bhp). A great drive with far more controllable and exploitable oversteer than bar talk would have you believe. Nothing to be scared of at all. C2 preferable to four-wheel-drive C4. 260 bhp Carrerra RS Lightweight the pick of the bunch. Recommended.

What's bad: Idiots still crash them on the road. 320 bhp Turbos are for experienced racing drivers only. Very likely to have seen a few 'track days'. More expensive to service than previous 911.

What to watch out for: If they fall off the road, C2s still tend to do it arse-first. So check the back end very carefully. New stays inside the rear wings are a sure sign of damage repairs, as are rear reflectors full of condensation (once the car has been smacked, they're difficult to seal). C4s, on the other hand, go straight on, so you need to check the fronts of these. You need to see a full and consistent service history from a Porsche dealer or respected Porsche specialist with no major gaps during which it might have been stolen or awaiting a rebuild. Proper histories also make clocking more difficult. A duff clutch is an engine-out £2,000 job to replace. Town-driven cars may wear out their oil stem seals – not easy to replace on a quad cam flat six (don't buy without a compression test). Exhaust systems and heat exchangers still expensive. Feel the brake discs for scoring and lipping through the wheels (when they're cool, of course). Make sure pop-up rear spoiler works.

Recalls: 1996 (1989–1993 build): 54,000 cars worldwide recalled (2,966 in UK) to check universal joint in steering column which may fail. Early signs are noises or free play in the system.

911 C2 and C4 993 (1993–1997)

What's good: The last incarnation of the flat six, air-cooled 911 and also the cleanest looking. 272 bhp from December '93 to October '95; 285 bhp from then on.

What's bad: Monster 408 bhp four-wheel-drive Turbo not a very nice drive. All 911s still have floor-hinged pedals. Very likely to have seen a few 'track days'.

What to watch out for: See above, and then some. Pay an expert to inspect it for you.

Recalls: 1996 (1993 build): 54,000 cars worldwide recalled (2,966 in UK) to check universal joint in steering column which may fail. Early signs are noises or free play in the system.

911 C2 and C4 996 (1997 on)

What's good: Top-hinged pedals at last. 300 bhp 3.4 litre engine. Lighter, more powerful 360 bhp GT3 with adjustable suspension by far the best. Substantial UK price cuts in May 2000. Incredible, 414bhp 190mph Turbo. C2 and C4 revised again with 3.6 litre Variocam engine developing 315bhp for September 2001. Top speed 177mph, 0–60 4.8 seconds, prices from £55,950.

What's bad: Watercooling has proven to be a mixed blessing with lots of engines mixing their oil and water and needing to be replaced. Wet-sump 996s can suffer oil starvation when driven hard round corners. Can lead to problems with road as well as race cars.

(Dry-sump GT3 and GT3-based Turbo not affected.) Surprising amount of understeer. Four-wheel-drive versions have a very noisy drivetrain. Turbo selling at substantial premiums in Summer 2001.

What to watch out for: Major Warning. Any mayonnaise-like emulsion or scum in the radiator header tank or under the oil filler cap, don't touch the car. It probably needs a new engine. Check rear brake discs carefully as they tend to rust on cars not subjected to regular hard braking.

Recalls: Porsche 911/996 Carrera (1998 MY 996 model: 540 UK cars): wrong size pulley fitted driving ancillaries drive belt which may slip affecting PAS, brakes, water pump and alternator (announced 3/6/98). Porsche 911/996 Carrera 4: 1,179 RHD Carrera 4s built between October 1998 and April 2000 recalled to correct software fault which affects fuel gauge reading (Auto Express issue 598).

928 (1977–1995)

What's good: Sporty, reliable alternative to the Jaguar XJS V12 and to a Mercedes SL. Kids' seats in the back will also take small adults for short distances. Manuals more satisfying to drive, but autobox less likely to give trouble. High quality German engineering. Original 4,474cc V8 had 240 bhp. Final incarnation had 5,399cc V8 with 340 bhp.

What's bad: A new engine will set you back £12,000. A clutch and gearbox rebuild could hit you for £6,000. Catalysed exhaust systems are also a fortune. Early 3-speed automatics aren't the iron fist in a velvet glove like the later cars. Need to inflate space saver spare tyre if you get a puncture.

What to watch out for: Don't buy unless from a Porsche dealer or after an inspection by an independent Porsche specialist. Automatics go through brake pads and discs. Feel the brake discs for scoring and lipping through the wheels (when they're cool, of course). Don't buy town-driven cruisers.

944 (1982–1993)

What's good: A grown-up 924 with a proper Porsche engine rather than the Audi engine out of a VW LT van. 2.5 had 163 bhp from

449

Jan '86 to Sept '88; 2.7 had 165 bhp from Sept '88 to June '89. 2.5S16v had 190 bhp from Sept '86 to June '88; 2.5 Turbo had 220 bhp from Jan '86 to Sept '88, then 250 bhp to May '92. 3.0 S2 had 221 bhp from Jan '89 to May '92.

What's bad: Strong acceleration likely to have been used. Many were stolen. Likely to have seen time on 'track days' and could have come off the track. Confusing engine range, but 211 bhp S2 the best overall. 165 bhp 3-speed autos are comparatively slow.

What to watch out for: Getting old now and may have fallen into the hands of abusers unable or unwilling to afford proper maintenance. This doesn't have to be Porsche dealer, but does have to be a respected Porsche specialist who knows what he's doing. (Visit the bloke who maintained it and see how many Porsches he's working on that day.) Has two timing belts (one for the balancer shaft) and periodic re-tensioning of these is critical. Needs a new chain between the two cams plus tensioner every 70,000–80,000 miles (particularly if oil changes have been pushed). If engine vibrates, the hydraulic engine mounting may have failed and needs replacing.

968 (1992–1995)

What's good: Very punchy 240 bhp 3.0 litre 4-cylinder engine more powerful than 231 bhp 1983–89 911. 6-speed manual gearbox. Near-perfect balance. Brilliant rear-wheel-drive handling. Stripped-out 'Club Sport' model for purists. Became a 'classic' as soon as it went out of production. Will do 160 mph 'on the clock'. Recommended.

What's bad: Will probably have seen a few track days on race tracks. (Club Sport models definitely will have – no point in the car otherwise). 4-speed Tiptronic cabriolet comparatively slow. Cabriolet hoods attract envy slashes.

What to watch out for: Check carefully, preferably by professionals, that it has not been thrashed and crashed. HPI or AA/Experian check will make sure it's not on VCAR, but if crashed on a circuit would not have been insured anyway. Make sure the clutch still has plenty of life left in it. Look out for damaged alloys (could be from kerbs, could have had an off.) Cat could be blown from running against rev limiter. Also as everything in this section under 944.

Boxster (1996 on)

What's good: Of the original MB SLK, BMW Z3 and Boxster, the Boxster is the best of the bunch. Some echoes of old RSK. Original 2,480cc Boxster had 204 bhp. Engine grew to 2,867cc and 220 bhp in August 1999. But 3,179cc 252 bhp Boxster S also from August 1999 stole sales from standard 911 cabrio. Substantial UK price cuts in May 2000. Facelift in 2001 and 320 bhp 2.7 Turbo set to arrive. Very good to drive with such high limits of adhesion most drivers will never find them.

What's bad: Takes a while to learn and fully exploit the car's handling, especially the more powerful Boxster S. Still selling for 'overs' in 2000. Engine is completely concealed behind difficult-to-remove panels (owner drivers aren't supposed to touch it). You check the oil and water and top them up from the boot. Standard model could do with a bit more power, which it got in the 'S' version. Even small out-of-warranty problems can be very expensive due to inaccessibility of engine.

What to watch out for: Must have fully stamped up Porsche dealer service history, preferably itemised bills as well. Any mayonnaise-like emulsion or scum in the radiator header tank or under the oil filler cap, don't touch the car. It probably needs a new engine. (Difficult to spot with a Boxster because oil and water fillers are remote and engine cover cannot easily be removed.)

Recalls: 1998: 9574 cars recalled to replace steering lock assembly because of faulty ignition switches. 2,692 Tiptronics recalled because gear selector bearing sleeves could seize up over time.

GT1, GT2, GT3

What's good: Special 911s based on current 996. GT1 has 544bhp 3.2 motor; GT2 has 456bhp; GT3 has 350bhp 3.6. Ceramic disc brakes.

What's bad: Limited editons: GT2 just 300 cars.

What to watch out for: Police speed traps. Track day damage.

PROTON

Compact (1995–2000)

What's good: The previous model Mitsubishi Colt hatchback with a Persona front. Re-named Satria. Good engines. Decent handling. Autumn 1999 cuts brought prices down to from £6,750 with alloy wheeled 1.6 litre 'Spectrum' model at £9,999, 133 bhp 1.8 coupe at £12,499 and fine handling Lotus-developed GTi at £14,524. Re-named 'Satria' from 2000. (See Satria.)

What's bad: Just a bit cramped. See Mitsubishi Colt.

What to watch out for: As Persona.

Recalls: 1996 (from October 1995 build): fuel pump can allow fuel to leak when tank is brimmed. 1997 (July–Aug '97 build: 1,797 cars): Mitsubishi sourced brake booster valve may stick. 1998 (13in wheels only Aug '97–Aug '98 build): Front tyres may lose pressure.

Impian (July 2001 on)

What's good: All new Proton designed medium saloon in UK from July 2001. Mitsubishi derived 102bhp 1.6 litre engine with 103 lb ft (140Nm) torque and later option of a twin-cam 1.8 litre Renault engine. Strong body/chassis structure. Lotus tuned suspension. ABS, traction control and four airbags all standard. Combined consumption of 1.6 is 42.2 mpg. CO_2 output is 161 g/km (£120pa VED) for the manual and 214g/km (£155pa VED) for the automatic. Top speed 110mph. 0–60 12.0 seconds. Insurance Group 10. Length: 4,465mm; width 1,740mm. ABS, traction control and three three-point rear seatbelts all standard. Price £12,000 (manual); £13,000 (automatic).

What's bad: Too soon to say.

What to watch out for: Too soon to say.

MPI (1989–1997)

What's good: Reliable with good first-owner warranty package. Very cheap. Based on an old mid-'80s Mitsubishi Lancer.

What's bad: Hideously ugly and irredeemably naff. Has some of the most ridiculous wheeltrims ever seen on a car.

What to watch out for: Rear suspension can collapse. Highly likely to have been mini-cabbed at the bottom end of the market. Old ones mostly owner-serviced or simply neglected.

Perdana

What's good: Malaysia's economic recovery has allowed the launch of its larger car with looks a bit like those of the Toyota Camry. 2.0 litre V6 with auto, a/c, leather, etc. for around £16,000.

What's bad: Criticised for restless ride and uninvolving handling at launch. Undercut in price by KIA Magentis at £12,995.

What to watch out for: Likely to depreciate quickly from list, so should be a serious bargain second-hand.

Persona (1993–2000)

What's good: Really a Mitsubishi Lancer model which never reached the UK, but which, when highly modified, was hugely successful in international rallying. Quite good to drive with perky 1,600cc engine. Light years ahead of ancient Lancer-based Proton MPI. Prices from £7,750 for 1.3LSi, rising via 2.0TDi diesel at £11,024 to 1.8 EXi at £11,524. Re-named 'Wira' from 2000.

What's bad: Slightly unfinished, undeveloped feel to gearchange and interior. Rattles.

What to watch out for: Trim doesn't wear well. Rattles become more pronounced. Cambelts need changing regularly. Could have been cabbed.

Recalls: 1997 (July–Aug '97 build: 1,797 cars): Mitsubishi sourced brake booster valve may stick. 1998 (13 wheels only Aug '97–Aug '98 build): front tyres may lose pressure.

Satria (2000 on)

What's good: New name for Compact. See Compact for range. Fine handling Lotus-developed GTi at £14,524. Satria 1.5 Sport with Gti bodykit £9,299 from July 2001.

What's bad: Detailing of GTi a bit fussy and 'boy racerish'.

What to watch out for: As Persona.

Waja

What's good: Code name 'XG'. Good looking Mondeo-sized car due in UK early 2001. Mitsubishi 1.6 litre and Renault 1.8 litre 16 valve engines. CNG version for Malaysia. Sauber-Petronas high performance 1.8 engine due later. Big boot. Well equipped. Three three-point seatbelts in the back. Suspension developed by Lotus. Re-named 'Impian' before UK launch (see Proton Impian).

What's bad: Too soon to say.

What to watch out for: Too soon to say.

Wira (2000 on)

What's good: See Persona. Prices cut to from £8,999 for 1.6Exi from October 2000. Three-year warranty and six-year powertrain guarantee continue.

What's bad: See Persona.

What to watch out for: See Persona.

RELIANT

Scimitar

What's good: Reliant name Scimitar to return soon on a very pretty modified version of the former De La Chapelle roadster. 2.0 litre Peugeot engines develop 135bhp and 167bhp. Also a PSA 3.0 V6 with 200bhp. Model with 167bhp should do 0–60 in 6 seconds and go on to 140mph.

What's bad: Too soon to say.

What to watch out for: Too soon to say.

RENAULT

19 (1988–1996)

What's good: 1.4s surprisingly trouble-free. You can reckon on 8–9 years and 90,000–100,000 miles before they start to get expensive. Even the catalytic converters can last 9 years and 90,000 miles. Diesels are rough but tough with good economy. 16-valve models are screamers and were one of the 'cars to have' in the mid-90s.

What's bad: Dull looks before the beak-like facelift. Autos can give up at around 60,000 miles. In June 2001 Renault was rated by Motor Warranty Direct as Britain's joint 4th worst out of 22 marques for used car warranty claims (www.warrantydirect.co.uk).

What to watch out for: If the paint has faded, it may come up with Mer polish. Torn seat trim difficult to do much about unless you call a local car upholsterer (Yellow Pages). Switches break. Non-PAS have heavy helms. Autobox the first bit to break. Likely to be rust under plastic window sill trims. Rear shocks eventually punch their way through their towers.

Recalls: 1994 (Renault 19 Phase II, Apr '92–Mar '94): faulty seatbelt pretensioners and bonnet catch.

21 (1986–1994)

What's good: Cheap. 175 bhp Turbo and Turbo Quadra were flyers in their day. Comfortable enough, but the market is not really interested unless the cars are seriously cheap.

What's bad: Cheap, flimsy build. Quite a few parts are hard to get, such as rear discs for turbos and TXis. 19 model tended to be much stronger, better built and more reliable. Dashboards expensive to remove to replace bulbs or heater matrix. Automatics often troublesome.

What to watch out for: Have to be cheap to be worth buying. Check all electrics carefully. Look for uneven front tyre wear. Check coolant for mayonnaise (blown head gasket). If has ABS, make sure it works. Sniff for fishy smell – a sure sign of a failed heater matrix (putting this right may cost more than the car is worth).

21 Savanna (1986–1995)

What's good: Estates have option of seven forward-facing seats with reasonable luggage space behind. Diesels are economical, but range was complicated: 67 bhp 2,068cc non-turbo from Jan-Sept 1989; 65 bhp 1,870cc non-turbo from Sept '89–Oct 95; 88 bhp 2,068cc turbo from Jan '89–Oct '90 and then again from Nov '93–Oct '95.

What's bad: Two completely different drivetrains – across the engine bay on 1.7 petrol engines and along the engine bay on anything bigger. Lousy ventilation – particularly bad for rearmost passengers on long hot summer journeys. Not cheap to repair. Dashboards expensive to remove to replace bulbs or heater matrix. Automatics can be troublesome. Mild steel retaining straps of plastic fuel tank rust through. In June 2001 Renault was rated by Motor Warranty Direct as Britain's joint 4th worst out of 22 marques for used car warranty claims (www.warrantydirect.co.uk).

What to watch out for: Repaired accident damage (high used values made them worth repairing for a while). Rust. Family and dog damage. Torn upholstery. Sagging suspension. Don't buy one that's been towing because seven occupied seats and a caravan is just too much. Sniff for the fishy smell which means the heater matrix is leaking and you are in for a stiff replacement bill. Look under the back and check that fuel tank retaining straps are not about to rust through and drop off, depositing the tank on the street with dire consequences.

25 (1984–1992)

What's good: Much loved by owners and many have clocked up 300,000-plus miles. Can be extremely cheap.

What's bad: Automatic gearbox can give trouble. Heater matrix may fail. Huge labour cost in removing dashboard to replace heater matrix, or minor failures such as warning or dash light bulbs. V6 not a specially good engine and guzzles petrol. Turbos too old to remain reliable. Automatics can be troublesome.

What to watch out for: May have covered more miles than indicated on odometer. Make sure ABS is okay (pump not as dear as some at £660, but ECU is another £460 plus VAT). Check all electrics (even the dashboard bulbs give up). Check auto especially carefully (some 25s go through three of four in a lifetime). PAS pump or rack may leak (common old Renault problem). Try to feel discs for scoring, lipping or wear. Fishy smell inside and condensation on screen usually indicates failure of heater matrix, many of which were poorly made. You could easily buy a 25 for £750 then have to spend £2,000 on it immediately. Buy only from a careful, appreciative, enthusiastic owner who's had it for years. Definitely not a backstreet buy.

Recalls: (None known 1994–98 but autobox a well known problem area.)

5 Supercinq (1984–1996)

What's good: Simple, old car, quite rightly kept in production as the 60 bhp 1.4 Campus until March 1996. Cheap.

What's bad: Shows its age. Can be very difficult to get through MOT advanced emissions test after 5–6 years. Work can cost as much as £2,000 which is more than the car is worth. In June 2001 Renault was rated by Motor Warranty Direct as Britain's joint 4th worst out of 22 marques for used car warranty claims (www.warrantydirect. co.uk.)

What to watch out for: May suffer cat converter problems. Don't buy without a recent MOT certificate and emissions pass printout.

Recalls: 1995 (Campus 1.4: VIN C4070510214892 to C4070511788781): car may pull to left when braking.

Clio (1991–1998)

What's good: Amazingly quiet at town speeds. Decent ride quality. Hot and red-hot Clio 1.8 16v and 2.0 Clio Williams. Engines start with old pushrod 49 bhp 1,108cc ohv from Renault 8 in 1992 'Night and Day' special. Rise through 60 bhp 1,171 single point injected and 1,149cc multipoint injected OHCs, 75 bhp 1,390cc OHCs, 110 bhp 1.8s to 137 bhp 1.8 16v and 150 bhp 2.0 16v Clio Williams. Also a 65 bhp 1,870cc diesel. PAS widely available from 1.4s up. 4-speed auto became 3-speed auto in 1.4s from Jan 1996.

Facelift with new grille from March 1994. Second facelift with bigger headlights and high level brake light from May 1996.

What's bad: Nicole-Papa advertising saga became boring marketing speak, despite Estelle Skiornak. Average performance in NCAP crash tests. Watch out for kerbing damage, especially on power-steered Clios. In June 2001 Renault was rated by Motor Warranty Direct as Britain's joint 4th worst out of 22 marques for used car warranty claims (www.warrantydirect.co.uk).

What to watch out for: 4-speed autobox cooling system (oil cooler within the water radiator) can cause problems. Kerbing damage to front suspension. 1998: (June '97–Nov '97 build): possibility of inadvertent deployment of airbags. 2000: may lose brake servo assistance.

Clio (1998 on)

What's good: Pleasingly 'different' with cute protruding bottom. Looks good on the streets and definitely has cred. High spec includes electro-hydraulic power steering, sunroof and driver's airbag. Famous 'Size Matters' TV campaign. 172 bhp Sport Clio launched in spring 2000 is very quick, a bundle of fun to drive and the best junior hot hatch. Very good Four-Star rating in Euro NCAP crash tests. Red-hot mid-engined Clio Renaultsport V6 24v from October 2000. Three-year, 60,000-mile warranty from October 2000. Plastic front wings deform and shrug off minor impacts. To get a 'nose job' in autumn 2001. Facelift July 2001 and new 1.5 litre diesel engine.

What's bad: Renault build quality. Complaints of seat material fraying. To be replaced with new car on same platform as new Nissan Micra in late 2002.

What to watch out for: See above and expect kerbing damage, easily spotted by damaged protruding plastic wheeltrims.

Recalls: 21/2/2000: 29,000 cars built Jan '99 to Nov '99: possibility that brake servo valve may malfunction resulting in loss of servo assistance. Valve to be inspected and replaced if necessary.

Espace (1985–1997)

What's good: Immensely practical design. Individual seat removal system much copied and only bettered by new Espace. Easy to see out of and to park. Early models up to the first (1991) facelift handled the best. Nevertheless, your best bet is the facelifted 2.1 litre turbodiesel. Clutches will last 3 years and 120,000 miles in mostly motorway use. Engines can run up to 200,000 miles with few problems.

What's bad: Strange relationship between driver's seat and accelerator pedal leads to ankle cramp. There was a recall over a wiring loom problem. Trim is a bit flimsy, not up to hard family use. Automatic transmissions have a history of problems. Be very careful driving the diesel in standing water as apt to suck it up and blow its cylinder head off. Serious reliability problems reported by ADAC (the German breakdown organisation) in its 2001 report. In June 2001 Renault was rated by Motor Warranty Direct as Britain's joint 4th worst out of 22 marques for used car warranty claims (www.warrantydirect.co.uk).

What to watch out for: Clocked ex-taxis. Dodgy electrics. Chipped or cracked windscreens (expensive to replace). Wear in front and rear suspension from carrying heavy loads. Clonking driveshafts. Wear in gearshift linkage. Clutch wear (can last up to 120,000 miles, but depends on usage). Leaking or groaning power steering. Duff cats in post-1991 facelift model. Automatics best avoided. Make sure 2.1TD has received regular oil changes. Pull the dipstick and look for clean oil in all petrol versions, especially the V6. Look for mayonnaise under the oil filler cap, signifying cylinder head problems. Family damage from baby's bottles, food, sweets, felt-tip pens, dogs, etc. Check that seat locking mechanisms aren't damaged from misunderstandings. Fishy smell inside and condensation on screen usually indicates failure of heater matrix, many of which were poorly made. Make sure the heater works on all speed settings, not just maximum (a common fault). Make sure recall work has been carried out.

Recalls: 1995 (2.1TD built 3/93–6/94). install fuse in preheater wiring circuit, re-route wiring away from main loom and install clip to keep it away from loom to prevent risk of insulation damage.

1996 (Espaces-on original tyres built March '91–Oct '92): check for separation of tyre tread.

Espace (1997–2002)

What's good: Revamp of the original design put it back at the top of the class again. No other MPV has such a versatile seating arrangement. Longer-bodied Grande Espace overcomes lack of luggage space with seven aboard. Best buys are the diesels (air intakes now in mirror assemblies). Four-Star performer and the best MPV in NCAP crash test (11 points front impact; 16 points side impact). Three-year 60,000-mile UK warranty from October 2000. New 130bhp 2.2 litre direct injected common rail dCi diesel from Laguna II became available in March 2001 from £21,350. Diesels hold their values better than most other MPVs.

What's bad: Have heard of one wiring fire, which was a recall problem on the previous model diesels. Have been problems with the older 2.2 diesel engine. Quite a lot of niggling problems. Whole dashboard needs to come out to replace a single dashboard bulb. Serious reliability problems reported by ADAC (the German breakdown organisation) in its 2001 report. In June 2001 Renault was rated by Motor Warranty Direct as Britain's joint 4th worst out of 22 marques for used car warranty claims (www.warrantydirect.co.uk).

What to watch out for: Chipped or cracked windscreens (it's a lot of glass). Family damage from baby's bottles, food, sweets, felt-tip pens, dogs, etc. Make sure the seat locking mechanisms aren't damaged.

Recalls: 2000: March '99–August '99 build: fuel could be ignited by heat from exhaust. 18/4/2000: 1,000 diesel engined cars built February to April 2000 may be fitted with defective brake vacuum pumps. 2001 TSB to replace Exhaust Gas Recirculation valves on 2000 model 2.2 litre diesel engines.

Espace (2002 on)

What's good: Radical new Espace with some styling themes from Avantime show car, to be launched in 2002. Has already been seen testing. Three-year UK warranty.

What's bad: Too soon to say.

What to watch out for: Too soon to say.

Kangoo Combi (1999 on)

What's good: Renault's answer to the Citroën Berlingo Multispace – with two more doors and a lower price. 75 bhp 1.4 litre 8-valve petrol or 65 bhp 1.9 litre non-turbo diesel. Prices from a very sensible £9,500 OTR which includes PAS and metallic paint. RXE versions (£1,000 extra) have passenger airbag, three three-point rear seatbelts and front driving lights. Extremely sensible. Brilliant doggy wagon. Three-year 60,000-mile warranty from October 2000.

What's bad: Fairly basic and certainly not for the status conscious – unless, of course, the Kangoo Combi becomes trendy. Driving experience inferior to Citroën Berlingo. Watch out for trapped fingers in those sliding rear doors. Kangoo's sliding side doors forced PSA to follow suit.

What to watch out for: Nothing significant as yet.

Recalls: 21/2/2000: 29,000 cars built Jan '99 to Nov '99: possibility that brake servo valve may malfunction resulting in loss of servo assistance. Valve to be inspected and replaced if necessary. 4/10/2000: 25,000 Kangoos, including 200 UK market Kombis fitted with Kleber tyres recalled because tyres can suddenly deflate. December 2000: 14,054 Kangoos recalled for modifications to the sensor which controls seatbelt pretensioners and airbags.

Laguna (1994–2001)

What's good: Three clever lap and diagonal rear seatbelts fitted from Jan '95 (third belt retracts into offside 'D' pillar). New 110 bhp 1.6 16v and 120 bhp 1.8 16v engines from spring 1998. 2.0 litre twin-cam 149 bhp RTi 16v also good. Roomy inside, comfortable ride, big boot. Non-turbo 2.2 12-valve diesels make good taxis – pleasant to drive in heavy traffic. But 115 bhp TD better still. All better-built than old 21. New 194 bhp 2,946cc Peugeot-powered V6 from October 1997 much better than previous Laguna V6. Estate cars have masses of loadspace, but 7-seater option is rear-facing and folds to the side rather than into the floor. Comparatively good performance in NCAP crash tests. But so many problems likely I can't recommend the Laguna 1 as a second-hand buy.

What's bad: 85 bhp 2.2 diesels sluggish on the open road. Long-backed drivers find themselves sitting too close to the top of the huge windscreen. Old 95 bhp 1.8 and 115 bhp 2.0 litre 8-valve engines outclassed. Old 170 bhp 2,963 cc V6 not a very good package. Poor quality electrics lead to all manner of irritating failures, including alternator and the auto gearbox multi-function switch. More than its fair share of recalls. Power steering failure common. Heater matrixes fail in the welds. Dashboards expensive to remove to replace bulbs or heater matrix. Automatics troublesome (front drive clutch drum splits). Timing belt of diesel drives the water pump and these have been known to seize at as little as 59,200 miles and two years old, stripping the teeth off the belt and causing £1,100 worth of engine damage. In June 2001 started to get reports of noisy front dampers on 2000W reg Lagunas. Possibility of a faulty batch. In June 2001 Renault was rated by Motor Warranty Direct as Britain's joint 4th worst out of 22 marques for used car warranty claims (www.warrantydirect.co.uk).

What to watch out for: Look for leaking power steering on all Lagunas. Check for 'clonking' from wear in front anti-roll bar bushes. 2.2 litre diesels could have been cabbed and clocked. Check tyres for uneven wear denoting crash damage, suspension damage or simple misalignment. Check automatic transmission fluid for signs of overheating (will be black instead of dark red). Need cambelt changes every 35,000–40,000 miles (ex-fleet cars may be on borrowed time). Try to feel the brake discs as these may need replacing. If aircon fitted, make sure it blows cold. Fishy smell inside and condensation on screen usually indicates failure of heater matrix, many of which were poorly made. Damp under carpets confirms this. Make sure keyfob transmitter was replaced under free recall.

Recalls: 1996 (May '94–Aug '94 build): Automatic transmission may lock up. 1996 (Jul '94–Dec '94 build): Airbag warning light may be faulty. 1996 (April '96–Aug '96 build): Fuel injection system computer may be faulty. 1997 (April-August '96 build: 12,494 cars): Engine ECU may malfunction causing exhaust manifold to overheat and set fire to bulkhead insulation. 1998: failed heater matrixes replaced FOC. 1998: 'plip' key transmitters can go out of sequence due to static or fiddling with them in the pocket. Improved 'plip' key transmitters now available free of charge to Laguna owners. (Per BBC 'Watchdog' 12/2/98) 1998: 17,000 cars recalled due to possibility of inadvertent deployment of airbags. Cambelt tensioner on diesel engines may lead to premature cambelt failure. To be checked as a TSB item at services. 2000: July 1998 buld only: driveshaft CV may fail and affect steering. All Lagunas: possible sudden failure of gear selectors. 12/1/2000: 4,422 F9Q diesel engined cars built Dec '98 to May '99: brake vacuum pump may leak allowing oil to enter the brake servo resulting in loss of servo assistance to the brakes. Magnetti Marelli brake vacuum pumps to be replaced; servos to be inspected for oil ingress and replaced if necessary. 21/2/2000: 29,000 cars built Jan '99 to Nove '99: possibility that brake servo valve may malfunction resulting in loss of servo assistance. Valve to be inspected and replaced if necessary. 18/4/2000: 1,000 diesel-engined cars built February to April 2000 may be fitted with defective brake vacuum pumps.

Laguna II (2001 on)

What's good: New Laguna launched September 2000 Paris Show to compete with new Xantia (or C5), new Mondeo and new Vectra. Very good looking. Novel 'keyless' entry and starting system easy to get used to. Engine line-up includes 110 bhp 1.6 litre 16v; 123 bhp 1.8 litre 16v; 140 bhp 2.0. litre 'IDE'; 210 bhp 3.0 litre V6; 105 bhp 1.9 litre dCi diesel; 135 bhp 2.2 litre dCi diesel. The Sport Tourer estate car is very good looking. Three-year, 60,000-mile UK warranty. Plastic front wings deform and shrug off minor impacts. Much better to drive than old Laguna. Excellent, top-of-the-class FIVE STAR NCAP crash safety rating announced 28/3/2001.

What's bad: Not quite as good as the new Mondeo, but a better cruiser at 70–80mph and has a slightly better ride. Worrying number of gimmicks. Complex spec variations led to delivery

delays of cars built to order in Spring and Summer 2001.
What to watch out for: Too soon to say.

Megane (1996 on)

What's good: Sweet, precise handling. Economical diesel. Even more economical TDI from May 1998. Joint top of the class for secondary safety in NCAP crash testing. Galvanised body has 12-year warranty. New, much better 1.6 litre 16-valve engine from Summer 1999. Booted 'Classic' saloon. Two-door coupe and 'Roadster' cabrio originally available with 90 bhp 1.6 or 150 bhp 2.0 litre 16v engines. Later 1.6 16v has 110 bhp. Three-year, 60,000-mile warranty from October 2000.

What's bad: Silly things go wrong, such as flywheel sensor cable connector failure which immobilises the car. 8-valve 1.4s and 1.6s a bit underpowered. 'Classic' saloon not the best looking car in the world. Coupe pointless except as a basis for the smart cabrio. Engine has to come out to replace the clutch. Several *Telegraph* readers reported needing a replacement engine around 8,000 miles. 1.6 8-valve engine prone to head gasket failure. Heater matrixes may also fail and cost £350 to replace if the car does not have a/c or £600 if it does. Dashboard costs a fortune to remove even just to replace a bulb. Automatics give trouble (front drive clutch drum splits). One report of digital odometer failure requiring a new instrument cluster, but Renault paid most of the cost even though the car was two years old. In June 2001 Renault was rated by Motor Warranty Direct as Britain's joint 4th worst out of 22 marques for used car warranty claims (www.warrantydirect.co.uk). Radically restyled new Megane with Vel Satis look due to be launched in Spring 2002.

What to watch out for: Kerbing damage, strange electrical faults. To check for head gasket failure on 1.6 8v look under oil cap for 'mayonnaise'. (Low-mileage cars had head gaskets replaced FOC under a Renault 'Tech Note'.) A 'fishy' smell inside the car and damp under the carpets is usually a symptom of heater matrix failure.

Recalls: 1997 (Megane and Scenic July–Sept '97 build): 7,434 cars found to have potentially defective braking system. 2000: July 1998 build only: driveshaft CV may fail and affect steering. 12/1/2000: 4,422 F9Q diesel engined cars built Dec '98 to May '99: brake vacuum pump may leak allowing oil to enter the brake servo resulting in loss of servo assistance to the brakes. Magnetti Marelli brake vacuum pumps to be replaced; servos to be inspected for oil ingress and replaced if necessary. 18/4/2000: 1,000 diesel engined cars built February to April 2000 may be fitted with defective brake vacuum pumps.

Megane Scenic (1997 on)

What's good: By far the most popular Megane. Sensible, practical, without being in the least dull. Brilliantly planned, versatile interior with lots of cubbyholes and strong, two-level rear parcel shelf. Three three-point rear belts. Huge square-shaped boot. Economical diesel. Even more economical TDI from mid-1998. Galvanised body has 12-year warranty. Refreshed from October 1999 with a new front, new 95 bhp 1.4, 110 bhp 1.6 and 140 bhp 2.0 litre engines and 35 different models. 1.6 16v reckoned to be the best of the bunch. Three-year, 60,000-mile warranty from October 2000. Facelifted model has plastic front wings which deform and shrug off minor impacts. Very good 29 point four star NCAP crash safety rating announced 28/3/2001.

What's bad: Loses out to Citroën Xsara Picasso. 1.6 8v and 1.6 16v are underpowered. Non-electric sunroofs don't slide and serve as no more than pop-up vents. Needs aircon. Clutch replacement is expensive. Don't try to carry things on the roof. Comparatively poor performance in TUV/Auto Bild offset crash test. Automatics problematic (front drive clutch drum splits). Flywheel sensor connection may fail, immobilising car. Starting to get reports of wiring loom failures due to poor insulation (an old Renault bugbear). 1.6 8v prone to head gasket failure. (Low-mileage cars had head gaskets replaced FOC under a Renault 'Tech Note'.) One report of manual gearbox mounting bolt failing on a 1.6 16v Alize. Bolt replaced by by 'a modified part'. 'Sporty' facelifted 2.0 litre 16v criticised for harsh suspension and unsporty steering. The plastic front wings of facelift models change shape, leaving gaps around the headlights. Problem of leaking sunroofs due to kinked drainage channels on facelift Scenics. In June 2001 Renault was rated by Motor Warranty Direct as Britain's joint 4th worst out of 22 marques for used car warranty claims (www.warrantydirect.co.uk).

What to watch out for: Check gearbox carefully, whether manual or auto. Renault history means PAS rack may spring a leak. To check for head gasket failure on 1.6 8v look under oil cap for 'mayonnaise'. Also look for kerbing damage, electrical faults, stained seats, unspeakable smells left by incontinent babies, 'fishy' smell denoting leaking heater matrix.

Recalls: 1997 (Megane and Scenic July-Sept '97 build): 7,434 cars found to have potentially defective braking system. 1998: (June '97–Sep '97 build): roof bars may fail under load. Replacements redesigned and sourced from a different manufacturer. 2000: July 1998 build only: driveshaft CV may fail and affect steering. 12/1/2000: 4,422 F9Q diesel-engined cars built Dec '98–May '99: brake vacuum pump may leak allowing oil to enter the brake servo resulting in loss of servo assistance to the brakes. Magnetti Marelli brake vacuum pumps to be replaced; servos to be inspected for oil ingress and replaced if necessary. 18/4/2000: 1,000 diesel-engined cars built Feb–April 2000 may be fitted with defective brake vacuum pumps.

Safrane (1992 on)

What's good: Very comfortable with cosseting ride and excellent rear legroom. Revised and facelifted in October 1996. Volvo-engined 2.5 litre 5-cylinder automatic capable of covering immense distances at high average speeds. Reasonable fuel consumption. Low used prices.

What's bad: Electronic autobox problems on pre-1996 facelift versions expensive to fix. ECU problems with pre-facelift V6. Lose value quickly. Jerky cruise control. Dashboards expensive to remove to replace bulbs or heater matrix which is prone to leaks. In June 2001 Renault was rated by Motor Warranty Direct as Britain's joint 4th worst out of 22 marques for used car warranty claims (www.warrantydirect.co.uk).

What to watch out for: Clonky autobox. Duff cats. Make sure aircon blows cold. Check all electrics. Hard ride signifies failure of top model's variable suspension. Fishy smell inside and condensation on screen usually indicates failure of heater matrix, many of which were poorly made.

Recalls: 1994 (Dec '91–Mar '94 build): heat shield required to protect fuel tank from exhaust. 1996 (May '94–Aug '94 build): automatic transmission may lock up. 1996 (Jul '94–Dec '94 build): airbag warning light may be faulty. 21/2/2000: 29,000 cars built Jan '99 to Nov '99: possibility that brake servo valve may malfunction resulting in loss of servo assistance.

Twingo (1995 on)

What's good: Great design, practical and fun. Looks like Kermit the frog. Sliding rear seat (like Citroën ZX) gives choice of bootspace or rear legroom. Transmission options of: 5-speed manual; 5-speed electric clutch 'Easy' or 3-speed 'Matic'. Electro-hydraulic PAS also became available in 1996. Latest airbagged version did reasonably well in German TUV front offset crash tests. All new 5-door 'one box' Twingo due in 2003 and will be sold with RHD in UK.

What's bad: LHD only. Never officially sold in the UK. Lots about with unconverted digital speedos and right-dipping headlamps which dazzle oncoming drivers and may fail the UK MOT. (Daffyd Williams does a speedo mod for £99 which converts the French speedos to mph, tel: 01766 770203.) In June 2001 Renault was rated by Motor Warranty Direct as Britain's joint 4th worst out of 22 marques for used car warranty claims (www.warrantydirect.co.uk).

What to watch out for: Second-generation multipoint injected 60 bhp 1,149cc engines much better than older single-point injected 1,171cc engines.

Recalls: June 2000: 14,000 2nd generation Twingo 2s recalled to correct fault which can lead to premature triggering of airbag. 18/9/2000: three Twingos recalled for same reason. Airbag computer to be replaced.

ROVER

Metro (1990–1995)

What's good: Decent new 'K' series 1.1 and 1.4 engines. End-on gearbox and up to 5-speeds at last. Front-end rust traps largely eliminated. Better built than Austin Metro and generally reliable. Simple CVT auto worked well – far less troublesome than Ford and Fiat CVTs. Comfortable. I've done 450 miles in a day in a Metro CVT. Decent fuel consumption. 1.4 TUD diesel engine comes from Citroën AX and Peugeot 106.

What's bad: Cramped cabin due to bigger, more luxurious seats. Heavy, non-power-assisted steering – the wider the tyres the heavier it is. Diesel very slow and not that economical if worked hard. Still rust-prone in seams.

What to watch out for: Oil leaks from engine. Cracked cylinder heads (look for mayo under oil cap). Head gasket leaks due to stretched or re-used stretch bolts which go all the way to the sump. Tappety noises. Abused 16-valve versions. Kerbed alloy wheels (suspect suspension damage). Many still went to driving schools. Some were built long before they were UK registered.

100 SERIES (1995–1998)

What's good: Restyled Rover Metro. CVT auto one of the best and still has a small market. Killed off in early 1998.

What's bad: Past its 'sell by' date. Poor performance in NCAP crash tests. Not much market for them. No power steering option and steering very heavy when wide tyres are fitted. 'K' Series engine inlet manifold 'O' rings tend to perish between 25,000 and 30,000 miles.

What to watch out for: As Rover Metro.

200 (1995–1999)

What's good: Compact. Good looking. Low wind noise at speed. Stainless steel kickplate 'Rover' image. All good performers for their engine size apart from 1.1 and 1.4 8-valve. Vi, fitted with MGF VVC engine tremendously quick and also very economical. Perky 1.6 CVT automatic offers instant acceleration out of side roads. 1.1 replaced Rover 100 as a sub-£10,000 offering. All have three three-point rear belts. One of the few cars offering warm air to the feet and fresh air to the face at the same time.

What's bad: Slow, over-light steering spoils all models, including Vi. Not quite out of Rover build-quality problems. CVT could be too 'instant' for some elderly drivers not used to automatics. 'K' Series engine inlet manifold 'O' rings tend to perish between 25,000 and 30,000 miles. Possibility of camshaft coming adrift on 1.8 Vi.

What to watch out for: Variable gearshift quality. Different models have different linkages, but a hollow pin wears and may drop out. No big deal since a replacement costs just 6p. 'K' Series cylinder heads have been known to become porous and their head gaskets to fail (look for mayo under oil cap). Timing belt replacement essential every 35,000–40,000 miles or every 3–4 years. Backroom advice from expert David Lacey on buying a Rover 200 diesel: 'Watch out for oil leaks from the oil pump area, coolant leaks from the thermostat housing at the front of the engine, cracked/broken/missing underbelly acoustic trays (Expensive), cambelt and fuel pump belt change at 84000 miles. Check that the radio and remote control on the steering wheel works and also check that you receive TWO sets of keys with TWO remote controls as the key will be useless to start the engine on its own without the remote. Another remote will cost about £80.'

200 and 400 (1989–1996)

What's good: Product of Honda/Rover marriage and first to use 'K' series modular engines. English 'feelgood' factor from stainless steel kick-plates, bits of wood fillet in the dash and doors. Honda 1.6 engine is the best engine, often wedded to smooth Honda autobox. From July 1997, 400 'Tourer' estate could be had with 109 bhp 1.6 'K' Series engine and CVT transmission or 143 bhp 1.8 litre VVC 'K' Series engine and manual box. (Continued as Cabrio and Tourer to 1999.)

What's bad: Diesels are pretty terrible. PSA XUD engines at their noisiest and least refined. Gearbox/clutch problems can occur relatively early. 220s seem to develop all sorts of problems. Turbos best avoided. Distributor ignition igniter of Honda 1.6 can fail at about 50,000 miles and might lead to catalytic converter damage. Rover 'K' Series modular engines not as reliable, particularly pre-'K' reg monopoint injected versions. Cylinder head problems not uncommon and stretch bolts can stretch. Rover 2.0 litre M16 engine least reliable; later T16 from 'K' reg on (badged 'ROVER' on cam cover) more reliable, but even T16 apt to coke up its valves if run on cheap petrol with inadequate detergent content. Honda-engined 216 and 416 models starting to prove very expensive to service and repair at Rover dealers. High incidence of ABS failure on cars so fitted. Another problem is a leaking gearbox input shaft oil seal. This is symptomised by oil leaks and slipping clutch (due to oil contamination). Cause: input shaft bearing of gearbox worn leading to excessive movement on the seal. Difficult to source secondhand gearbox.

What to watch out for: Premature clutch wear. Noisy gearboxes. Clonking suspension. Cooling system leaks. Hidden rust around windscreen. Visible rust at top of hatch and around hinges. Coolant leaks from corroded coolant rail at back of engine (coolant should be changed every 2–3 years). Look under oil cap for mayonnaise – sure sign of distorted or cracked cylinder head. ECU faults causing misfires. Excessive oil consumption. Diesel turbo hose can rub on front bulkhead. No power steering (if PAS, look for leaks at the pump). Make sure cambelt has been changed. Allow £160 for new distributor ignition igniter for Honda 1.6. Front anti-roll bar drop links rattle, but cheap to replace. Clonks from rear could be trailing arm bushes which are £200 a side to replace, or one of the roof support bars come unstuck. Rear silencer box rots inside out quickly. If fitted with ABS, the pump may fail if the brake fluid has not been changed often enough. A smell of petrol may indicate a rusted and leaking petrol tank – especially on 'N' reg cars. If car has ABS, make sure the warning light goes on and off as per the handbook.

400 (1995–1999)

What's good: Honda 'Swindon Civic' in drag, but mostly with Rover's own 'K' Series engines and (Rover claims) better ride and handling. Automatic retains Honda's 1.6 engine and autobox with engine in front of passenger rather than driver. Available as 5-door hatch or good-looking 4-door saloon (not many good looking saloons in this class). Falling sales led to cut prices in 1998 with a 1.4Si 16v with alloys selling for £12,000 OTR. One of the few cars offering warm air to the feet and fresh air to the face at the same time.

What's bad: If it's been owned by an elderly person, may be three years old and not yet run-in. 'K' Series engine inlet manifold 'O' rings tend to perish between 25,000 and 30,000 miles. T16 2.0 litre engine apt to coke up its valves if run on cheap petrol with inadequate detergent content.

What to watch out for: 'K' Series cylinder heads have been known to crack and their head gaskets to fail (look for mayonnaise under oil filler cap). Timing belt replacement essential every 35,000–40,000 miles or every 3–4 years. Front suspension bushes tend to wear. T16 2.0 litre engine apt to coke up its valves if run on cheap petrol with inadequate detergent content. A smell of petrol may indicate a rusted and leaking petrol tank – especially on 'N' reg cars (applies to both 'old' and 'new' 'N' reg 400s).

Recalls: 1996: driver's seat lock does not always click into place properly. May mean seat slides when car is being driven. Most likely on cars with several drivers where seat is moved to and fro.

600 (1993–1999)

What's good: The most reliable Rover (really a Honda Accord). Nice-looking car. Wood, leather and stainless steel kickplate image. 156 bhp 2.3 litre Honda engine by far the best. Chassis also greatly improved on 2.3s. All manuals have good gearchanges and 129 bhp Honda 2.0 litre engines are smooth and economical. 113 bhp 1.8 is an 1,850cc multipoint injected Honda engine, not a Rover 'K'. Automatics by Honda. Good metallic paint colours, such as 'Nightfire Red', 'Caribbean Blue'. Generally a good, cheap second-hand buy.

What's bad: Understeery handling, over-light steering on all but 2.3. Ride quality not up to luxurious image. Body mods over Honda Accord were difficult to assemble and can lead to premature rust, especially in rear inner wings. 620Ti Turbo with Rover 'T' Series engines apt to blow gaskets. Average performance in NCAP crash tests. Production ended in 1999, but still on *Glass's Guide*'s new car price lists in Summer 2000 so watch out for late registrations.

What to watch out for: Check everything electrical (windows, roof, mirrors, seats, etc.). Look for rust bubbling through just behind each rear wheel arch. This is a big panel in short supply, so the problem is very expensive to remedy. Will run to high mileages (150k plus) so might be clocked. A 50,000-miler should not have excessive paint and windscreen chips, front number plate should be original. Avoid the 'ti' petrol turbo model. Ignition igniter on Honda engines can fail and is expensive to replace. Rover direct-injected 'T' Series diesels okay, but only gain about 7 mpg on the petrol 2.0 litre. Exhaust rear boxes blow on low-mileage 'short-run' cars. A 'V' or 'W' reg will have been sitting around for months before it was registered. Check for emulsified oil under the oil filler caps of 2.3i engines as this could indicate a cracked cylinder head which is £2k to replace.

Recalls: 1996 (built between 12/94 and 12/95): check to ensure steering rack mounting bolts are secure. Symptom of problem: stiff steering.

800 (1986–1999)

What's good: Cheap big cars that don't look cheap. Wood, leather, etc. on Sterling models and decent trim levels generally. High-revving 2.0 litre 16-valve engines. Smooth Honda 2.7 litre V6s. (Early Honda 2.5 and later 2.5 KV6 less highly regarded.) T16 2.0 litre engine better regarded than earlier M16. Tough but gruff VM 2.5 litre diesel engines.

What's bad: Clonky front suspension. Cambelts of 2.0 litre M16 engines (pre-1991 facelift) need replacing every 3 years or 36,000 miles and must be correctly tensioned. Water pumps fail, leading to distorted cylinder heads. Brake callipers seize. Power steering pumps of early cars pack up. Depreciate rapidly. Even T16 apt to coke up its valves if run on cheap petrol with inadequate detergent content. Individual cylinder heads on VM diesel may crack. Production ended in April 1999, but still on *Glass's Guide* new car price lists in July 2000.

What to watch out for: Front suspension can deteriorate alarmingly. Rust in seams, sills and particularly around all windows. Iffy electrics. Head gasket problems from failure to replace antifreeze every 2–3 years. ECU problems. Duff cats in catted facelift model. Earlier M16 valves can burn out on unleaded petrol (a very quiet engine is a bad sign). Look for white exhaust, mayonnaise under oil cap signifying head failure on diesels. Pay no more than £500 for a pre-facelift 820, however good it may look. Make sure aircon blows cold if fitted. A 'V' or 'W' reg will have been sitting around for months before it was registered.

Recalls: 1994 (VIN RS 100001–117697 and RS 150000–187439): front seatbelt security. 21/1/2000: 956 825 diesels VIN RS 230976 to RS 260898 recalled because while engine is performing a pre-determined self-diagnosis the engine could stall. Modified ECU to be fitted.

25 (1999 on)

What's good: Successfully re-thought Rover 200, aimed at the younger market, now with faster, meatier steering, more sporty suspension, much more sensible pricing and, importantly, a three-year warranty. Prices cut to from £8,495 for 84bhp 1.4i with three years servicing included as from October 2000. Basic 1.1i announced from April 2001 at £7,995 on the road. New 'Steptronic' ECVT has more controlled take-off than old 200 CVT and works really well in town or out. 150bhp Gti replaces VI as top of the range at a reasonable £13,495. 103 bhp 1.4Si is now as much fun to drive as a Fiesta Zetec or Focus with an excellent set of gear ratios giving 60 mph plus in 2nd. Ventilation system allows cool face/warm feet.

What's bad: Fascia a bit old fashioned. Light-coloured dash tops reflect badly in windscreen. Irritating 'twist-stalk' for wipers and lights. Electric window switches on centre console. A/c rarely fitted. Steptronic upshift and downshift is the wrong way round. 'K' Series engine inlet manifold 'O' rings tend to perish between 25–30,000 miles. Re-named MG ZR in Summer 2001.

What to watch out for: As 200.

45 (1999–2000)

What's good: Not as well re-thought as 25 and aimed at the older market. Engine range includes a 2.0 litre KV6 mated to the 'Steptronic' CVT automatic. New three-year warranty. Prices cut to from £9,995 for 103bhp 1.4IE 5-door to £17,095 for V6 Connoisseur. Amazing, diesel-like economy. Autocar averaged 41.8 mpg in its road test 45 1.6 (issue 8/3/2000). One of the few cars offering warm air to the feet and fresh air to the face at the same time.

What's bad: Testers thought the steering too light and the ride too soft, but this may suit the market. High-revving KV6 not very well matched with Steptronic transmission. Faced the axe soon after Phoenix took over Rover and looked at the sales figures. Continued poor sales could lead to the model being dropped from the Rover line-up. 'K' Series engine inlet manifold 'O' rings tend to perish between 25,000 and 30,000 miles. Re-named MG ZS in Summer 2001.

What to watch out for: As Rover 'new' 400.

75 (1999 on)

What's good: Replaced both 600 and 800. Very good looking with styling cues from 1950s Rover P4. Looks a bit like a Rolls Seraph from the back, and sits in the market exactly where P4s did between 1955 and 1965. Nice retro-look cream oval dial instruments. 1.8 litre 120 bhp K Series four; 2.0 litre 150 bhp KV6, 2.5 litre 175 bhp KV6, or pleasant, quiet and torquey 2.0 litre 115 bhp BMW common rail direct-injected diesel. All front-wheel-drive. JATCO 5-speed automatic or Getrag 5-speed manual. Softish, cosseting ride quality. Not a sports saloon, but still handles fairly well. Good sized but fairly shallow boot. Excellent cool face/warm feet ventilation system. Prices now from £16,494 including three-year warranty. 'Tourer' estate car and shift to production at Longbridge in Spring 2001 brought across-the-range handling improvements. S and T reg cars came an excellent sixth in 2001 Top Gear/JD Power Customer Satisfaction Survey. Very good score of 30 points in Euro NCAP crash safety tests.

What's bad: The badly-timed debacles over the future of Rover which marred its launch, and the fiasco of March to May 2000. Driving position and handling at speed not in same class as Mondeo. Rear-seat passengers feel confined. Suspension clonks. Susceptible to strong side winds. Not easy to reverse. Hazard light switch hard to find. Diesel really needs the full 136 bhp power output of the same engine in the BMW 320D. Question mark over whether Longbridge can achieve same build quality levels as Cowley. MG ZT version from Summer 2001.

What to watch out for: Parking dings in easily damaged slab-side doors.

Recalls: 13/3/2000. 8,550 cars VIN RJ 001242 to RJ 127623 built between Feb '98 and Oct '99 recalled to correct crankshaft position sender fault which could cause the engine to cut out, announced Radio 4 News 10/3/2000. Sensors to be replaced with modified units

ROLLS ROYCE

Silver Seraph (1998 on)

What's good: The Rolls Royce version of the Bentley Arnage. Smoother BMW 5.3 litre V12 engine pumps out 322 bhp through five-speed auto in similar very British body.

What's bad: As Arnage.

What to watch out for: As Arnage.

Recalls: 1999: possible wiring fault in heated seat circuit.

Silver Spirit and Silver Spur (1980–1999)

What's good: Plutocrat's car. Poshest colour is a dark browny green. Gradually improved over the years with injection and ABS in October 1986, automatic ride control in 1987, four- rather than three-speed autobox in September 1991. Cats came in during June 1990, but were initially a no-cost option. Company taken over by VW in spring 1998.

What's bad: Stink of cigar smoke clings to the headlining. 9 mpg in town. Likely be hit hard by engine-size or carbon dioxide-based annual taxation. Resentful drivers don't let you out of side roads, particularly during recessions. White or cream tells the public it's a wedding hire car, or has been. Daft RR defensive habit of not giving power outputs. (1993 Silver Spur had 226 bhp and 340 ft lb torque; 1994 Flying Spur turbo had 360 bhp and 552 ft lb torque.)

What to watch out for: Must have a proper Rolls Royce dealer or Rolls Royce specialist history. The Cosworth-built engine is an old fashioned pushrod V8, so you don't want to hear ticking tappets or see any blue smoke from the exhaust pipe. Make sure the suspension is not unduly wallowy. Check expensive tyres for tread depth and uneven wear. Make sure aircon blows cold. Good Rolls Royces have a patina and aura about them. Bad ones make you feel uneasy. Best to have the car inspected by a different Rolls Royce specialist from the one who's selling it.

Recalls: 1997: 29 left-hand drive cars found to have potentially defective braking system.

477

SAAB

9-3 (1998 on)

What's good: Steering, handling and roadholding all improved over previous same-shape 900. Even better with 17in wheels and Michelin Pilot tyres. 115 bhp 2.2 litre direct injected diesel particularly good to drive – better than 2.0 litre petrol. 225 bhp 2.3 litre HOT Viggen from March 1999. Very impressive safety features include a full set of five 3-point belts, two airbags and excellent side-impact protection. Clever anti-whiplash head restraints. Rear boot sill has been lowered to make it more like the old 900 and you can use the rear bumper to sit on. 2.0 litre eco turbo engine replaced 2.3i for 1999 model-year. Four-Star NCAP crash safety rating due to excellent side impact protection but much less satisfactory front offset impact protection due to bulkhead inherited from 900. In late October 2000, power of the 2.2TiD diesel was increased to 125bhp and torque to 206lb ft at a very low 1,500 rpm, giving 0–60 in 10 seconds and combined cycle fuel economy of 45.6mpg.

What's bad: Still has bulkhead mounted steering rack like Cavalier. Scuttle-shake of popular convertible can still set your teeth rattling. Turbo a bit vicious. Diesel needs to be kept on the boil (above 1,900 rpm) so not too good for caravan towing. Some GM 2.2 litre DI diesels use a lot of engine oil.

What to watch out for: Timing chains of 4-cylinder SAAB engines need clean oil or can give problems at around 60,000 miles. (No timing chain problems yet reported on GM 2.2 litre diesel.) Clean oil also essential for turbo life. Turbos best run on fully synthetic oil once run-in.

Recalls: 2000: 9-3 models built August '97 to July '99: front seats may move during heavy braking. 2001: TSB to replace ECU on older 9-3 Viggen models free of charge.

9-5 (1997 on)

What's good: SAAB's latest 'big' car loaded with safety features. Nothing quirky about this one. 170 bhp 2.3 eco turbo, 150 bhp 2.0 eco turbo and 200 bhp 3.0V6 auto. 2.0 litre much improved compared to 9000 series. Most people find the seats very comfortable. Should both be capable of over 30 mpg. 2.3HOT Aero from September 1999 has 230 bhp. Four-Star 31 point NCAP crash test rating and best of all 'executive cars' (second only overall to new Renault Laguna). Super-safe estate version from early 1999 usurps Volvo as probably the safest estate car you can buy. Year-2000 model achieved highest ever NCAP crash safety score of 91% overall. 14th from top in 'R' reg JD Power Customer Satisfaction Survey. 'New' SAAB 9-5 from October 2001 with option of General Motors' new 3.0 litre 176bhp common rail turbodiesel V6 engine which puts out 258lb ft (350Nm) torque. Will feature 'chassis revisions to enhance driver control'. More at www.saab.co.uk.

What's bad: Vectra-based, so not a true SAAB, but now has subframe mounted steering rack. No hatchback apart from estate. Early production did not share the latest thinking on front suspension with the 9-3. Had peculiar lurch understeer. Later cars still understeer, but much more progressively. In June 2001 SAAB was rated by Motor Warranty Direct as Britain's joint 4th worst out of 22 marques for warranty claims (www.warrantydirect.co.uk). This conflicts with the JD Power survey findings above.

What to watch out for: No known problem areas yet.

900 (1993–1998)

What's good: Excellent safety features. Hatchback, with big boot and proper passenger protection against load. Five 3-point safety belts. Good side protection. Interesting clutch-free 'Sensonic' five-speed box dropped for 9-3.

What's bad: Cavalier based with bulkhead mounted steering rack, so not a true 'SAAB'. Disappointingly soggy steering, handling, roadholding and ride quality. Comes a bit more alive with turbo, but still not a car you'd ever choose for handling finesse. Bulkheads apt to crack around steering rack mounting points. In June 2001

SAAB was rated by Motor Warranty Direct as Britain's joint 4th worst out of 22 marques for used car warranty claims (www.warrantydirect.co.uk).

What to watch out for: Timing chains of 4-cylinder SAAB engines need clean oil or can give problems at around 60,000 miles. (GM V-6s have belts, best replaced at 60,000 miles.) Clean oil also essential for turbo life. Turbos best run on fully synthetic. Put the car through a £70 check at a SAAB dealers, then buy a used SAAB warranty. Average performance in NCAP crash tests. Make sure aircon blows cold if fitted. Listen for steering creaks and look for cracks around steering rack bulkhead mounting points, a £700 job to repair. Abbot Racing of Spinnels Farm, Manningtree (tel: 01255 870636) have a means of mounting the rack more rigidly, and also replacing the soft rubber suspension bushes which not only solves the problem but makes both Cavaliers and SAAB 900s steer and handle much better.

Recalls: 1994 (VIN R2000001–R2028886): delayed braking action. 1994 (5-door VIN R2000001–R2022754): cracking of driver's seat rails. 1995 (VIN R2027373–S2009903 and S7000001–S7013081): welds missing from seat frames. 1997 (1996–97 build: 21,661 cars): corrosion on the throttle housing can cause a sticking throttle. Relevant parts to be replaced with brass items which cannot corrode.

900 (to 1993)

What's good: Eccentric, 'classic' SAAB looks. Much loved by the entertainment industry and often the car of the star. Convertibles best, despite scuttle shake. 185 bhp Ruby Turbo (last of the line) is now an appreciating classic. Understeer can be overcome by judicious left-foot braking. Heavy, solid and capable of mega mileages if looked after properly. Hatchback has long, flat luggage area. Rear bumper makes a good seat for events. Nice old cars with bags of desirable character.

What's bad: Lots of understeer. Timing chains and tensioners tend to need replacing every 60,000 miles. Even non-turbos are fairly thirsty. Parking brake of pre-1988 cars worked on front discs and was never satisfactory – often an MOT failure point and expensive to fix.

What to watch out for: Rattling timing chains, dirty oil, cracked cylinder heads (check for mayonnaise under the oil cap), cracked turbo manifolding (remember, it glows red hot), can be gear-selector problems, check suspension bushes, front hubs and driveshafts carefully. Make sure turbo not 'coked' as SAAB-sourced replacements are expensive. Make sure big bumpers have not been used as buffers. Check that aircon blows cold.

Recalls: 1996 (900 convertible 1993–1995: old shape): check for loss of steering control.

9000CD (1988–1997)

What's good: Booted, better looking 9000CS, so same general comments apply. Truly enormous boot.

What's bad: As 9000CS. In June 2001 SAAB was rated by Motor Warranty Direct as Britain's joint 4th worst out of 22 marques for used car warranty claims (www.warrantydirect.co.uk).

What to watch out for: As 9000CS.

Recalls: See list under 9000CS.

9000CS (1986–1998)

What's good: Great cars, none better than the 170 bhp 2.3 eco turbo which covers the ground quickly and still returns 32 mpg. Capable of huge mileages if looked after properly. Decent 'big car' handling. Innocuous looks. Wonderful seats. Good, old-fashioned 4-speed automatic does what you want and doesn't 'hunt'. Full-on 2.3 turbo Carlsson puts out 220 bhp, which is very nearly too much.

What's bad: Ride quality a bit firm, but made up for by the excellent seats. Direct ignition module can give trouble. ABS pump needs fresh brake fluid every year. Timing chains oil-sensitive (best run on fully synthetic, particularly turbos). 2.0 eco turbo not as well suited to autobox as 2.3i or 2.3 eco. V6 best avoided. Subject to quite a lot of recalls. Automatic doesn't seem to last. Tends to fail due to a bush wearing in the pump and rebuilds cost £1,800 (new box

£3,500). In June 2001 SAAB was rated by Motor Warranty Direct as Britain's joint 4th worst out of 22 marques for used car warranty claims (www.warrantydirect.co.uk).

What to watch out for: Timing chain rattles. Smoky engines (especially turbos). Check for white smoke from blown head gasket or cracked head. Look under oil cap for mayonnaise. Huge discs are expensive to replace (feel them through the wheels). Look for wear in front suspension bushes, hubs and driveshafts. Best put though a £70 pre-check at a SAAB dealers, then purchase a comprehensive used SAAB warranty. Make sure aircon blows cold.

Recalls: 1994 (VIN N1041085–N1049024 and P1000001–P1015289): fuel leak. 1994 (9000/Turbo: VIN N1000001–N1049024, P1000001–P1042386, R1000001–R1027659): oil leak and faulty brake light switch on some models. 1995: (*manual with TCS): VIN N1000001–N1049024, *P1000001–P1042386, *R1000001–R1026535: loss of brake pressure and/or ABS. 1999: 1993/94 build (5,300 cars): possibility of moisture corrupting computer chips which control passenger airbag trigger mechanism.

SEAT

Alhambra (1996 on)

What's good: SEAT's version of Galaxy/Sharan, all built on the same line in Portugal. All had air conditioning, but otherwise fairly basic trim. VW 2.0 litre petrol and 1.9 litre TDI 90 110 or even chipped 130 engines. Also 125 bhp 1.8 20v and 150 bhp 1.8 20v Turbo. Three-year unlimited mileage warranty. More cheerful trim than Galaxy and Sharan. Similar VW Sharan was a Three-Star performer in NCAP crash tests (6 points front impact; 15 points side impact). Attractive Y2K facelift includes new 115 bhp TDI PD and 204 bhp VR6 – both with four-wheel-drive option. Six-speed VAG gearboxes now standard throughout the range. List prices cut September 2000 to start at £17k for 2.0 litre 7-seater S with 7 three-point seatbelts, a/c, ABS, driver, passenger and side airbags, roof rails, luggage cover, electric mirrors and 3-year 60,000-mile warranty.

What's bad: Trim quality and damage from family use may let the vehicle down. Below-average 'customer satisfaction'. On early models water can enter car via ventilation, soak the underfloor and get into the ECU which controls the electric windows and alarm system. On later models, this ECU has been moved. Aircon vulnerable to front end shunts. Also shifted in later models. TDIs can blow turbos and catalytic converters. Have also been manual gearbox problems with TDIs and one report of gearchange cables separating on a 1996 2.0 litre petrol model. Galaxy from same family came last in JD Power 'P' reg survey and Sharan second bottom, but by 'R' reg had improved.

What to watch out for: Lowest list prices mean most likely of Galaxy TDI 90 family to have been used as a taxi, so look for signs of clocking. Make sure servicing up to date and warranty still in place. Make sure 7-seaters have rear compartment heater. Spec was progressively improved. Later Alhambra TDI 110 has aircon and pop up picnic trays on backs of front seats. Make sure manual Ford gearbox isn't 'clonky'.

Recalls: 1997: brake pads may overheat. 13/1/2000: 80,000

Galaxys, Alhambras and Sharans VIN TV000001–YV509825 recalled to check for contamination of brake fluid through master cylinder vent. Brake master cylinders of older cars to be replaced.

Arosa (1997 on)

What's good: Cheap, well-equipped, very cheerful small cars, all with power assisted steering. Decent ride quality. Originally, numerous 'option packs' included comfort pack, safety pack and even aircon. Later restricted to base and SE spec. 1.4 litre four-speed auto one of the cheapest autos with PAS (1.4 manual introduced later at same price). Tall body good for entry and exit by the elderly. 1.7 litre SDI with unpainted bumpers the most practical city car, capable of 65 mpg. Initially built at Wolfsburg, now Barcelona. 'SE' version replaced 'Comfort Pack'. Three-year unlimited mileage warranty. Did well in German TUV front offset crash test. New 118 mph 100 bhp 1.4 16v petrol engine and 106 mph 75 bhp, 66 mpg 75 bhp 1.4 litre TDI now in UK. 1.4TDI sensibly priced at £9,995 and £8,995. Cute new SEAT corporate front for 2001. Good, friendly dealers.

What's bad: Handling not to standard set by Ford Ka, but it's okay. Clutch cables stick and may break. Door mirrors feel a bit cheap. Clutch replacement unusually expensive on 1.0 version (more than £500). Quite a few problems both from Wolfsburg and Barcelona production. UK unlikely to get 1.2 litre '3L' super economy diesel because UK diesel tax is too high to justify the cost.

What to watch out for: The 'Comfort Pack' of height-adjustable seats, parcel shelf, better trim etc. costs £245 new and is so good it's worth paying an extra £300 for second-hand. Make sure servicing up to date and warranty still in place. Have been known to misfire so make sure the cat isn't torched by having it MOT emissions checked.

Recalls: SEAT has admitted a cold weather fault with the 1.4 automatic, manifesting itself in a loud noise when changing up from 1st to 2nd gear. Replacement parts are fitted free.

Cordoba (1994 on)

What's good: Saloon version of Ibiza that also became the Polo saloon. Excellent 1.6 litre 100 bhp engine. Cordoba Vario estate is the best-looking of the range and comes with TDI 90 or TDI 110 engines. Same revisions as Ibiza from September 1999. Good, friendly dealers.

What's bad: Cordoba coupe is ugly. Cordoba saloon has a bouncy ride. Vario estate is not a true estate because it has a high load lip to give the body rigidity.

What to watch out for: VW's 'self adjusting' clutch cable that can lead to a slipping clutch. Make sure servicing up to date and warranty still in place.

Ibiza (1985–1993)

What's good: These did used to shift a bit on Spanish roads. Had 'Porsche-design' engine, VW gearbox, good handling. Not bad looking in a chunky sort of way.

What's bad: Not very well made. Rust-prone Fiat Ritmo underpinnings. The last of the pre-VW SEATs. Neglect has nearly always taken its toll on the car's looks.

What to watch out for: Rust, fall-apart trim, rattly dashboards, groaning wheel bearings, total lack of maintenance by people who buy them for next to nothing and chop them in as a '£500 minimum part-exchange'.

Recalls: 1994 (1985–1991 VIN 09045074–D119002): fuel leak.

Ibiza (1993–1999)

What's good: The development car for the current Polo, essentially the same underneath but slightly longer wheelbase. Neat shape. Sporty image from rally success. Fun 'Mediterranean' image. Ibiza TDI 90 noisy, but goes well, handles well, ideally geared for city driving, does 55 mpg even at 80 mph. Think of SEATs as 'fun' Volkswagens. Now come with three-year unlimited mileage warranties. TDI recommended. Good, friendly dealers.

What's bad: No protection strip means doors vulnerable to damage in supermarket car parks. Build not quite up to Wolfsburg standards.

What to watch out for: Lots of model variations: 1.3s, then much better 1.4s, etc. You need a *Parker's Guide* or *The Book* to find out just how much of a saving you're making. Make sure servicing up to date and warranty still in place.

Ibiza (1999–2002)

What's good: Reworking of the 1993 model, itself the first manifestation of the Polo platform, from the 'A' pillar forwards. Better handling and improved ride comfort from new 'silentblock'-mounted front suspension. Interior design and quality much improved. Range includes 156 bhp 1.8 petrol turbo which is a fantastic town car. While TDI 110 with switchable traction control gives true GTi performance plus 55 mpg economy. Remember, Seats are 'fun' Volkswages – and Ibizas are more fun to drive than Polos. 68 bhp SDI diesel from October 1999 launch at a reasonable £8,995 with PAS. New 'tax-break' 1.0 litre 16v 70 bhp engine from early Y2K. Three-year unlimited mileage warranty. TDI 110 recommended. 'Cool' models with a/c at no extra charge from spring 2000. 156 bhp Cupra model from October 2000 actually has more power, excellent brakes with Brembo calipers and costs just £12,995. Good, friendly dealers. Three Stars in Euro NCAP crash tests. 180bhp Cupra R new for 2001 giving 0–60 in 7.2 seconds and top speed over 140mph.

What's bad: Re-engineering the brake servo for RHD meant no UK 1.8 Cupra Turbo until spring 2000 and no TDI 110 at all. Steering wheel still only adjustable up and down and seats still only have old rocking adjustment of Golf Mk II GTi. May be replaced by new Ibiza on Skoda Fabia floorpan or new Salsa in 2002. Official 180bhp Cupra R very expensive at £18,900. Cupras eat front tyres.

What to watch out for: Build quality complaints include: battery earth lead bolt becoming unscrewed, windscreen wiper spindle unwinding itself and damaging bonnet, ECU unit becoming detached from its under dash mounting.

Ibiza (from 2002)

What's good: New Ibiza due 2002 or 2003 on Fabia platform. SEAT's Sitges design team under Walter de Silva and Steve Lewis offer the most design flair in the VAG group.

What's bad: Project currently on hold.

What to watch out for: Too soon to say.

Leon (1999 on)

What's good: Great looking Golf IV-based 5-door hatch, essentially a shortened Toledo, pronounced 'Lay-on'. Not unlike a latter-day Alfasud. Shares Toledo's superior road feel and handling. Galvanised body with 12-year warranty; 3-year unlimited mileage mechanical warranty. UK engine range from 75 bhp 1.4 16v to 147 mph 180 bhp 1.8 20v turbo six-speed (or the 143 mph Haldex-clutched four-wheel-drive version), and including the usual 90 bhp and 110 bhp TDIs. 4WD Haldex clutch allows use of different circumference wheels and for the car to be towed with two wheels off the ground. At £14,995 the 180 bhp 20VT Sport is a fantastic performance buy and more fun to drive than the four-wheel-drive. Its switchable traction control is also less obtrusive than ESP of 20VT Cupra. Even has Brembo front brake calipers. 204 BHP V6 four-wheel-drive Cupra 4 and 150 bhp TDI PD announced at September 2000 Paris Show but LHD only and not coming to UK. Hot new hand built front drive 210bhp Cupra R due January 2002. Cabrio version seen testing. Built in Brussels and Martorell. Good, friendly dealers. Highly recommended.

What's bad: Drain holes in door bottoms can get blocked with wax and waterproof door membranes can lift, leading to ingress of water into car. Can lead to clutch footrest lifting. May also need re-sealing between plate holding window mechanism and the door itself. Seals around rear lamp clusters can also let in water.

What to watch out for: Obviously the 180 bhp 1.8 litre engine is not going to last for ever. 100bhp per litre is a lot of power.

Marbella (1988–1995)

What's good: Cheap skate for cheapskates, especially in Spain where they sold for not much more than £3,000 new. Terra Vista combi van the best version.

What's bad: Hideous Panda re-style. Based on old SEAT Panda, not post-1988 Fiat Panda, so has old 903cc pushrod engine and old unimproved suspension. Rust-prone. Poor quality trim. Like Panda, clutch cables snap.

What to watch out for: Rust, front struts, wheel bearings, smoky and rattling engines. (The rattle is usually the timing chain tensioner.) Front suspension problems (check for uneven tyre wear). Don't touch one with a catalytic converter. Could you really live with a car this ugly that makes you look so much of a miser?

Toledo (1991–1999)

What's good: Jetta-based family hatchback with enormous boot. Had mid-life facelift in 1995. Most models very well equipped for their price bracket. TDI 90 is a good package with decent performance and economy at (for the UK anyway) a sensible price.

What's bad: Not a great looking car. SEAT built a special Taxi-spec diesel Toledo. The big hatchback did nothing for the car's structural rigidity.

What to watch out for: Toledos that began their lives as taxis. VW's 'self adjusting' clutch cable that can lead to a slipping clutch. Leaks from ill-fitting tailgate (it's big, so twists out of shape easily). Check all electrics, including lights. Make sure servicing up to date and warranty still in place.

Recalls: 1996: cooling fan motor may seize, leading to overheating in traffic or on hills.

Toledo (1999 on)

What's good: Golf IV-based family saloon. Really good looking in the manner of the Alfa 156. Much sportier than Skoda Octavia, using lessons learned on the Skoda. Better steering and handling than Golf IV and Bora due to 15in alloys with 195/65 tyres, stiffer four-door body and softer suspension settings. Good ride quality, comfortable, rattle-free, galvanised body with 12-year warranty; otherwise 3-year unlimited mileage warranty. 170bhp V5 has a perfect set of gear ratios and is a lot of car for £16,995. But 52 mpg TDI S 110 with standard aircon by far the best buy at £15,495. Good, friendly dealers. Highly recommended.

What's bad: Deep boot, but you have to post your luggage through a narrow slit. V5 gives nice, progressive power but lacks the grunt of the old VW VR6. Drain holes in door bottoms can get blocked with wax and waterproof door membranes can lift, leading to ingress of water into car.

What to watch out for: Too soon to say.

SKODA

Estelle (1977–1990)

What's good: Some people liken the oversteering handling to that of a Porsche. Engine in the back means you leave engine noise behind you. Decent-sized front boot. Pocket money cheap.

What's bad: Skoda 'skip' image dating from the days when these cars were assembled by convicts. Fall-apart trim. Becoming difficult to obtain spares (VW doesn't want to know about this model). Only buy with a long MOT and be prepared to throw the car away at the first sign of any expense.

What to watch out for: Paying more than £100 for one. Screeching gearboxes, iffy electrics (check all lights and indicators – I've seen new Estelles where the indicator cables were cross-connected). Cheapskate home maintainers will have used the cheapest oil, changed it grudgingly and never bothered to change the coolant. But buy a car from an obsessive DIYer with a Haynes manual and the chances are he'll have sorted out all the faults.

Fabia (2000 on)

What's good: First incarnation of the next VW Polo floorpan. Chunky good looks. High quality electro-galvanised construction. Height- and reach-adjustable steering wheel and height-adjustable driver's seat giving huge range of adjustment. Switchable passenger airbag. Safety 'door open' red lights in both front doors. Engines include an aluminium pushrod 68 bhp 1.4 litre petrol based on the old Favorit/Felicia 1.3; a 101 bhp 16v 1.4 from the Polo/Lupo and the 64 bhp 1.9 litre SDI diesel. New 100bhp TDI PD engine with 177 lb ft torque arrived in November 2000 priced from £11,300 to £12,000 according to trim. Will eventually get VAG's new 1.0 litre 16v 70 bhp petrol engine, VAG's 75 bhp 1.4 litre 16v; and a 120 bhp 2.0 litre ohc unit. Good ride and handling (much better than current Polo). Decent-sized boot. Full-sized 'spare'. Very easy to park and manoeuvre. Nice radio with pop-out volume knob.

Optional a/c even on 68 bhp 1.4.'Classic', 'Comfort' and 'Elegance' trim levels. Ten-year body warranty. *What Car?* Car of the Year. Prices from £7,500 for 1.0 litre. Friendly, sensibly priced dealers. Very good Four-Star rating in Euro NCAP crash tests. Kombi estate car with 100bhp TDI PD engine arrived March 2001.

What's bad: More expensive than outgoing Felicia. Slow, overlight, lifeless but very accurate steering. Lack of character. 1.4 8-valve slow and thirsty at just 30.28 mpg. 1.0 very slow. High quality but extremely dull 'parts-bin' dashboard with nowhere to put things. High rear door sills contribute to strength, but make rear seat entry/exit difficult for the elderly. High boot sill. Centre rear belt only two-point. ECU is mounted on the engine compartment scuttle and could be subject to moisture ingress. Very soft engine mountings result in occasional 'clunks' and affect the steering. Euro 4 throttle damping takes some crispness out of throttle response, especially on 1.4 16v, but there are no problems exiting junctions, etc. No auto option at UK launch. Complaints of water leaks from ventilation plenum chamber into driver's footwell, head gasket failure on 1.4 8v and misaligned auxiliary drive belt on 1.4 8v.

What to watch out for: Make sure the 1.4 8v is not losing coolant.

Recalls: Faulty relay can result in electric windows opening about one minute after doors are locked with the key. These relays are in the process of being replaced under a low priority recall.

Favorit (1989–1995)

What's good: Gave a massive boost to Skoda's image. Handles quite well. Decently engineered. A good, sound, practical low-budget car. Much better than a Lada. Very cheap.

What's bad: Memories of Skoda image die hard. Build quality still 'pre-VW'. Fall-apart trim, grotty plastic, iffy electrics (particularly lights). Soft brake pedal (like old Polos). Engines start to smoke if oil not changed regularly and decent oil not used. Starter motors fail and can chew up the starter ring.

What to watch out for: Penny-pinched home servicing using the cheapest oil. Duff cats on catalysed models. Does the owner impress you as someone who really knows how to look after a car?

Recalls: 1994 (VIN P0670305–R0916381 and P5019665–R5043486): wheel bearing failure.

Felicia (1995–2000)

What's good: Looks like a Favorit, but really a VW Polo in Skoda clothes. PAS now available with 1.6 petrol and 1.9 diesel engines. Sound, practical cars. Well built. Excellent paint quality, good shut lines. Strangely, high quality trim and plastics seem as if they're deliberately made to look cheaper than those of Polo. 1.3 versions cheap, but the engines feel it. Haynes manual available from March 1999. 3-year warranty means dealer servicing for first three years but dealers are friendly and sensibly priced. An amazing 3rd from top in 'R' reg JD Power Customer Satisfaction Survey.

What's bad: Skoda image not good for the status conscious. Old-fashioned single-plane door and ignition key up to April 1998 grille facelift, when it was replaced by twin-plane key. Diesel version a bit front heavy for standard width tyres – can lose adhesion. Very limited model range from early 2000 with most models discontinued.

What to watch out for: Owners home-servicing using the Haynes manual from March 1999 may take short cuts and will miss any rectification work carried out by Skoda dealers on TSBs.

Recalls: 1998: (models with airbags): wiring for airbag may chafe. 2001: Recall by Continental Tyres for free replacement of CT22 tyres on Felicias because they may split.

Octavia (1998 on)

What's good: Galvanised body has 10-year warranty. VW Golf Mk IV underpinnings. Excellent 1.6 litre 100 bhp, 1.8 litre 125 bhp petrol engines and 1.9TDI with 90 or 110 bhp. Very well built. Estate car much better than saloon. 2.0 litre VAG 115 bhp engine replaces non-turbo 1.8 20v from autumn 1999. 150bhp 1.8 20v Haldex clutched 4x4 estate from February 2001 priced at a reasonable £16,200. 180bhp RS front drive from April 2001 at low £15,100 OTR got a great reception from journalists. Good, friendly dealers. S and T reg cars came 12th in 2001 Top Gear/JD Power

Customer Satisfaction Survey.

What's bad: Still a Skoda in the eyes of the golf club secretary. Looks like a Passat with the back wheels in the wrong place. Early LHD examples understeered heavily and late models can still be frightening in icy conditions, especially TDI with its heavy, torquey engine. 180bhp RS has only a 5-speed, not 6-speed gearbox.

What to watch out for: Plastic water pump impellers on early 1.8 20v engines fail. Newer water pumps have metal impellers.

Recalls: 2000: LXi models built May '98–Jan '99: incorrect ABS servo fitted could lead to brakes locking up.

SPYKER

C8 Spyder

What's good: Stunning new aluminium space framed sports car from Holland that revives the old Dutch car maker's name. (Spyker was corrupted to Spijker, but Spyker is the correct original name.) The new car has a 400bhp 4,172cc Audi V8 also developing a healthy 354 lb ft torque. Top speed is estimated at 187mph and 0–60 in just over 4 seconds. Variable F1 suspension. New glass-topped Laviolette coupe version announced February 2001. Maker's website: www.spykercars.com.

What's bad: Looking for initial deposits of £2,500 to allocate a chassis number. Car will then be tailor made to customer's requirements and final price will depend on what these are. Standard C8 has no weather protection.

What to watch out for: Too soon to say.

STRYKER

SC-5A

What's good: Terrific new minimalist sportscar from the family of motoring Lord Davis Strathcarron. 125bhp 1,200cc motorcycle-derived engine and very low weight of 550kgs should give amazing performance and handling. Price £22,450 on the road. 160bhp racing version to come in January. Entry level SC-6 at £19,995 to arrive in March. Maker's website: www.strathcarron.com.

What's bad: Too soon to say.

What to watch out for: Too soon to say.

SUBARU

Forester (1997 on)

What's good: Impreza-based four-wheel-drive estate with boxier body and more ground clearance than Impreza. 175 bhp Turbo very good. 8th from top in 'R' reg JD Power Customer Satisfaction Survey. Forester S-Turbo down to £20,494 from October 2000. S and T reg cars came 14th in 2001 Top Gear/JD Power Customer Satisfaction Survey.

What's bad: Exhaust system hangs quite low and could be vulnerable on bumpy tracks. Second-hand examples quite hard to find.

What to watch out for: Check for underside damage from 'off-road' use. Check for uneven tyre wear due to damaged suspension. Feel through the wheels for scored rear discs.

Impreza (1993–2000)

What's good: Came top of Top Gear/JD Power 'N' and 'P' reg Customer Satisfaction surveys, and 2nd to Legacy in 'R' reg survey. Excellent reports from owners. Engines are 88 bhp 16v 1.6 flat four, 101 bhp 1.8 litre 16v flat four and 113 bhp 2.0 litre. Auto optional on 1.8 and 2.0. 2.0 obviously the best engine, but 1.6 much cheaper. Recommended.

What's bad: There was a 1.6 litre two-wheel-drive version from 1994 to 1996. Change of piston skirt design in 1997 led to knocking noise on start up – usually cured under warranty by replacing just one piston. Clutch wear is common because drivers do not adjust their driving technique to the requirements of a four wheel drive car.

What to watch out for: Don't bother with two-wheel-drive versions. All Subarus are prone to scoring of the rear discs. Try and feel them through the wheel when cold. Check underside with torch for rocky lane accidents. Check for uneven tyre wear. Make sure clutch not slipping.

Impreza (2000 on)

What's good: New car from late 2000 after a very long model life by Japanese standards. Same choice of 5-door semi-estate or 4-door saloon. List prices start at £13,950 for 1.6TS Sports Wagon. New six-speed gearbox for WRX turbo at £21,495 for saloon and £21,995 for Sports Wagon.

What's bad: Plain ugly. 340 bhp WRX Turbo version may not be officially imported to the UK.

What to watch out for: Too soon to say.

Impreza Turbo (1994–2000)

What's good: Good anyway with standard 208 bhp engine, improved to 215 bhp in March 1999. But special import WRX STis offer 240–280 bhp and two-door WRX has up to 300 bhp. These cars are very fast indeed. 1999 UK 'special' 236 bhp RB5 offers a terrific drive. Officially imported two-door WRX P1 with 277 bhp, 4.7 second 0–60 and 155 mph at 7,500 rpm priced at £31,495. Impreza Turbos outsell the non-turbo Impreza in the UK, with 13,000 sold. If you can find an RB5, that's the one to go for.

What's bad: Not much. In short supply so WRXs command substantial 'overs'. Impreza P1 just beaten by Mitsubishi EVO V1 in *Autocar* head-to-head test.

What to watch out for: Check for underside damage from 'off-road' rally stage excursions. Check for uneven tyre wear. Feel through the wheels for scored rear discs. Smoke from exhaust could mean burned out turbo oil seals. These cars really need 3,000-mile fully synthetic oil changes. All WRXs are non-approved grey imports, so make sure they're legal with proper SVA certificates. To avoid the SVA 50-car quota, some may have been 'cloned' (more than one car on the same registration). Be very careful not to pay official UK import price for a grey standard model Impreza Turbo.

Justy (1989–1996)

What's good: Cheap, small, reliable four-wheel-drive hatchback. Multipoint injected, catalysed 73 bhp 1,189cc 3-cylinder engine from September 1992 (3-door chassis 007401; 4-door chassis 009601) the best, but previous 67 bhp engine avoids the cat. Not great to drive, but excellent in the snow.

What's bad: CVT automatic transmissions fail and a replacement costs the wrong side of £2,000.

What to watch out for: Avoid automatics. Look for suspension, drivetrain, engine damage underneath from rocks. Be very suspicious of uneven tyre wear. Make sure drivetrain doesn't shriek or scream (expensive to fix). Have it emissions tested to make sure cat converter not smashed. Interior damage from children, dogs or farm animals should be obvious.

Justy (1996 on)

What's good: Now Suzuki Swift-based and built in Hungary, with four rather than three cylinders and no unreliable auto option.

What's bad: Hungarian build quality not the world's best. Interior trim not particularly tough.

What to watch out for: 1,298cc Suzuki Swift engine has been known to suffer from cracked cylinder head. Be suspicious of uneven tyre wear. Try to get it on a ramp for a good look underneath, or take a torch. Check for oil leaks, bent suspension, dents in underside.

L-Series (1984–1992)

What's good: A Texas bank got 600,000 miles out of one. Can represent a cheap, reliable car for those who need four-wheel-drive in the winter.

What's bad: Starting to get really old now and onto their third or fourth owners. May be impossible to check history. Suspension bushes go. Remember, Japanese cars are designed to be very reliable for up to 7 years. They aren't built to last longer than this.

What to watch out for: Avoid turbos (too old now to expect them to be reliable). Rust. Broken front subframes. Any signs of having been used by a farmer (bits of straw under the carpet, strange dents, farmyard smells). If it has seat covers, look underneath – especially the top of the back seat. If tyre wear is uneven, best to walk away unless car is sub-£300.

Legacy (1990 on)

What's good: The most sensible large country estate car you can buy. Spacious, strong and reasonably economical (25–28 mpg). Facelifted in April 1994 and October 1996. Clever 'hillholder' brake system. Low transmission range very useful for crawling along in a traffic jam. Avoid the 2.0DL or 2.0DLSE (Feb '92–April '94) which has only part-time four-wheel drive and lower rear roof line. New American-built Legacy from December 1998 has revised floorpan with less suspension intrusion into load area. Did very well in USA Insurance Industry offset crash tests. Came top in JD Power 'R' reg Customer Satisfaction Survey. Fresh price cuts October 2000 bring latest 2.0GL estate down to £15,995. 3.0 litre Outback H6-3.0 automatic expensive at £26,995, but a brilliant tow car. Recommended.

What's bad: Spartan interior. Frameless side windows. Propensity to score rear discs. Cheap, old shape 'Classic' models dropped from line-up in autumn 1999 and new models were £2,000 dearer. Used prices rose strongly after JD Power result.

What to watch out for: Have been known to sit around on dockside compounds for years before finding buyers. Always check the rear discs for scoring. If it has a tow-hook, check whether it's been pulling a single or a double horsebox. Use a torch to peer underneath just in case it's been up a rough track and suffered serious damage from a rock. Mk Is from 1989–94 are getting old now. Second or third owner may have skimped maintenance and used it for hauling animals. Have a good look under load area carpeting for dents. If the car has seat covers, take them off – a dog may have eaten the seats underneath.

Legacy Turbo (1991–1998)

What's good: Nick-named in the trade the Subaru 'Lunacy', these are very quick yet full five-seaters and the estate is a full-size estate car.

What's bad: They do get crashed.

What to watch out for: Accident damage. Twisted shell. Suspension and or steering damage from 'falling off the road'. Smoke from exhaust could mean turbo oil seals have gone.

SUZUKI

Alto 1.0GL (from 1997)

What's good: Not bad looking for a tiny car. 53 bhp 993cc four-cylinder engine. Five-speed manual or three-speed auto option.

What's bad: May be bought as a marginal retirement car. Built in India. Perodua Nippa is better value. Auto dropped in June 1999.

What to watch out for: Dings in the very thin sheetmetal. Premature rusting.

Alto FX, GL, GLA (1981–1997)

What's good: Cheap, tiny, basic car with 40 bhp 796cc 3-cylinder engine and 4-speed manual gearbox or optional 2-speed autobox. It was UK's cheapest auto at £4,000.

What's bad: Very small indeed. Noisy. Too slow for the motorway. Very light build, so rusts easily. Model dropped from UK line-up between 1992 and 1997.

What to watch out for: Rust will seriously weaken the structure. Suspension gets tired quickly. Uneven tyre wear a more-than-usually bad sign.

Baleno (1995 on)

What's good: Range of 3-door hatch, 4-door saloon, 5-door estate, all with same 1.6 litre engine. Power steering. Decent equipment levels. Owners like them. Got the 'ladies prize' at the 1996 Birmingham Motor Show.

What's bad: Comparatively poor NCAP crash test results, but not tested with standard UK spec. Driver's airbag. Bland to drive with overlight steering. No image. New model arrived August 1998.

What to watch out for: No known problem areas.

Grand Vitara (1998 on)

What's good: By UK standards, quite well priced at just over £16,195 for the 2.5 litre V6 5-door. Turbodiesel option. Seats fold flat to make double bed. £800 clip-on tent available. 2.0 Litre 126 bhp GV2000 3-door manual or 4-speed automatic launched spring 2000 to compete with Honda's much sharper HRV.

What's bad: Still not a great drive.

What to watch out for: Too soon to say.

Ignis (2001 on)

What's good: New small car aimed at same market as Toyota Yaris and priced from £6,995. 3- or 5-door hatchbacks with 88 bhp 1.3 litre 16-valve VVTi engine. All have power steering, twin airbags, split folding rear seats and oddments tray under boot floor. High and flat load deck will suit older drivers. Optional a/c, ABS, automatic transmission.

What's bad: You sit up high and this adversely affects the car's centre of gravity. Otherwise too soon to say.

What to watch out for: Too soon to say.

Jimny (1998 on)

What's good: Cute-looking with decent off-road ability. Reasonable performance (0–60 in 13.6 secs; top speed 100 mph) from 1,298cc 85 bhp engine). Separate chassis for strength. Part-time four-wheel-drive, on the road driving rear wheels only for economy. Soft-top version launched at Barcelona Show in May 1999.

What's bad: Noisy and unrefined. Poor 'on-road' manners, especially with large wheels and tyres.

What to watch out for: Too soon to say.

Liana (from July 2001)

What's good: New monobox hatchback from Suzuki, from Summer 2001. 4,230mm (13ft 9in) long; 1,690mm wide (5ft 6in), 1,550mm (5ft 1.5in) high and high hip points of 23in at the front and 24.5ins at the back make it particularly easy to get in and out of. Engine is a 1,586cc 'all alloy' twin-cam putting out a healthy 102bhp at 5,500rpm and 106 lb ft (144NM) torque at 4,000rpm. Combined fuel consumption is 39.8 mpg for the 5-speed manual and 35.8 for the 4-speed automatic. CO_2 outputs are 171g/km (£140pa VED) and 192g/km (£155pa VED). Prices are £9,995 for the GL and £11,495 for the GLX, which has ABS with EBD, air-conditioning, alloy wheels and a CD player as standard. Bodies are 80% galvanized (unusual for a Japanese car) and covered by a 12-year no perforation warranty. The mechanical warranty lasts 3 years or 60,000 miles, backed up by 24 hour roadside assistance. Undercuts new, non-galvanised Honda Civic by a wide margin. More at www.Suzuki.co.uk.

What's bad: Too soon to say.

What to watch out for: Too soon to say.

MR-Wagon concept car

What's good: Cute little town car from the same mould as the Daewoo Matiz. Good enough looking to be a hit.

What's bad: No specific plans for its future, but could be coming 2002.

What to watch out for: Too soon to say.

SJ 410/413 (1982–1995)

What's good: The smallest, cheapest off-roader you can buy in the UK. Relatively light weight helps in snow and 'soft' conditions.

What's bad: Santanas are Spanish built; SJs Japanese. Superseded by 'Jimny' late in 1998. Can suffer cracked cylinder heads after 50,000 miles (look for emulsified oil under oil filler). Not nice to drive on the road, but okay as a holiday villa runabout or as an off-road working car where small size is important.

What to watch out for: Uneven front tyre wear means the tracking's out, so has the front suspension been damaged? Has it been off-roaded (much more likely than Vitara because these are classed as a working vehicle). Check drivetrain for oil leaks. Make sure it slips easily into four-wheel-drive (transfer boxes have been known to take in water and corrode inside). Listen for gearbox rattles, especially with the clutch disengaged. Check everywhere for rust, especially the hood mechanism the joints of which can rust up and snap. Check under matting on cargo floor for rust in the seams. Take care on corners.

Swift (1985–1993)

What's good: 101 bhp GTi 16v fast and furious. Odd 1,590cc 91 bhp GLX four-wheel-drive saloon lasted from March 1990 to January 1993

What's bad: Cylinder heads of 8-valve 1.3s and 1.6s can crack.

What to watch out for: Cracked cylinder head on 8-valve 1.3. GTi 16v likely to have been thrashed – expect heavy tyre wear but look out especially for uneven wear. Country-bought GLX four-wheel-drive saloons may be damaged underneath.

Swift (1993 on)

What's good: Cheap, especially 1.0 litre GC 5-door version. GTi 16v by far the best.

What's bad: Built in Hungary. Cylinder heads of 1.3 8vs can crack. GTi 16v dropped in October 1996. Ex-rental 1.0GCs took forever to sell into the trade.

What to watch out for: Cracked cylinder head.

Recalls: 15/12/2000: 300 Swift 1.0 and 1.3 litre models recalled because fasteners of steering rack and inboard engine mounting may not have been tightened correctly. If these come undone, the driver could lose control of the car. All models to be checked and fasteners correctly tightened and torqued.

Vitara 5-Door (1993–1998)

What's good: Tall body easy to get in and out of. Will carry 4/5 and their luggage. The only 4x4 of its size. Range includes a 95 bhp 16-valve 1.6 petrol, a 70 bhp turbodiesel manual and automatic and a 134 bhp 2.0 litre 24-valve V6. All have power steering.

What's bad: Superseded by new model in spring 1998. Not a nice drive.

What to watch out for: Usual 4x4 checks: is it a town car or a country car? Has it been towing? (If so, what?) Check steering gear for play and damage from kerbing (even on town cars). Has it been rolled or turned on its side? Brake callipers can stick (need servicing, not replacing). Avoid if drivetrain unduly noisy. Back seat and backs of front seats may have been crocodiled by dogs. Drive carefully, especially round corners. Prone to cracked cylinder heads due to silting and clogging of oil and waterways (see Vitara SWB).

Recalls: 1994 (Sep 1993–Jul 1994 build): wheel bearing failure. 1997 (Jul–Dec '97 build): steering shaft could detach. 8/5/2000: Vitara V6 and diesel built June '95 to Sept '96: chance that flexing of suspension strut mounting turret may cause strut studs to shear. Reinforcement plates to be fitted to strut turrets and top mountings.

Vitara SWB (1992–1998)

What's good: 1.6 litre 8-valve engine range has four outputs: 74 bhp, 79 bhp and 80 bhp. A bit of a hairdresser's favourite (especially convertible) and these cars don't go off road.

What's bad: Spanish built. Cylinder heads can crack. Poor oil feed to rocker shaft may lead to premature wear. Not very nice to drive.

What to watch out for: Prone to cracked cylinder heads due to silting and clogging of oil and waterways, so look for low heder tank coolant level and emulsified oil under the oil filler cap. Avoid ludicrous fat-wheeled, running-boarded 'customisation' because it's like wearing a chest wig and pedestrians will laugh at you helplessly. Make sure the four-wheel-drive works. Clean oil, changed every 3,000 miles, is essential to avoid blocking oil feed. Brake callipers can stick (need servicing, not replacing). Avoid if drivetrain unduly noisy. Back seat and backs of front seats may have been crocodiled by dogs. Drive carefully, especially round corners.

Recalls: 1994 (Sep 1993–Jul 1994 build): wheel bearing failure. 1997 (July-Dec '97 build): steering shaft could detach. 1998: (Oct '91–Oct '93 build): front seatbelt stalk may fracture.

Wagon R+ (1997–2000)

What's good: Chain-cam little screamer of a 64 bhp 996cc engine revs to nearly 8,000 rpm. Light controls. Easy to drive. Holds its own on the motorway – just. Much more elbow room than Daihatsu Move. Not as small as you think it's going to be. Shopping basket, bucket hidden under passenger seat. Reasonable legroom in the back. 3-year warranty. More powerful 68 bhp 1.2 litre engine, front-end restyle and automatic option from June 1998, still qualifies for reduced-rate VED.

What's bad: Daft looking, but not as daft as the Daihatsu Move. Severe understeer. Little feel from power steering. Wouldn't like to be hit by a Toyota LandCruiser while driving one. Can have short front disc life due to corrosion of discs on lightly braked town-used cars.

What to watch out for: Make sure it's not coming apart at the joints.

Recalls: 8/11/2000: 3,490 Wagon Rs built 1/2000–8/2000 recalled because handbrake lever pawl may not rotate freely leading to handbrake slipping off after having been applied. Replacement handbrake assembly to be fitted where necessary.

Wagon R+ (2000 on)

What's good: All-new structure and built in Hungary. Similar in concept to original, but much better looking. 76 bhp chain-cam 1,298cc engine with 85 lb ft torque. 14in wheels. Basically the same as the Vauxhall Agila. To get Fiat's 60 bhp, 1.2 litre 100 mpg CDI diesel engine in 2002.

What's bad: Cars registered before 1/3/2001 don't qualify for reduced rate VED, otherwise too soon to say.

What to watch out for: Too soon to say.

Recalls: 8/11/2000: 3,490 Wagon Rs built 1/2000–8/2000 recalled because handbrake lever pawl may not rotate freely leading to handbrake slipping off after having been applied. Replacement handbrake assembly to be fitted where necessary. Further 1,542 Wagon Rs built 14/6/2000–15/9/2000 recalled because fasteners on the steering rack, rear suspension and near-side engine mounting may not have been tightened to the correct torque and could become detached. Fasteners to be tightened to correct torque.

TOYOTA

Avensis (1997 on)

What's good: A much improved Toyota Carina E. Same range of lean-burn engines. 1.8 litre the most frugal (40–45 mpg) and fitted with Michelin Energy tyres as standard. Much better looking than Carina E with all-new panels which hide its slab sides and high waist. Three proper lap and diagonal rear seatbelts. New 16v common rail direct injected 2.0 litre diesel, called 'D-4D' for 2000 MY, more economical than lean-burn petrol engine. Launch advertising campaign left impression of a high-quality car. Range includes a useful estate. Has a 3-year manufacturer warranty, and 5-year extended warranty on expensive Lambda probe. Nice unaggressive 'smiley face' cheers up other drivers. In June 2001 Toyota was rated by Motor Warranty Direct as Britain's 3rd most claim-free used marque (www.warrantydirect.co.uk).

What's bad: Still Carina E-based, so it's not going to set your pants on fire with excitement. Lean-burn engines require same economy driving style of high revs with small throttle openings – not holding high gears and labouring the engine. Pre-2000 MY diesels pointless. Lost its 'smiley face' for 2000 model-year. Some reports of premature clutch and gearbox failures. Isolated report of problems with immobiliser.

What to watch out for: Nearly-news likely to have been ex-rental. Look for minor damage from rental car carelessness. May have been kerbed, so check for uneven tyre wear and damaged hubcaps. Some problems experienced with steering column; subject to TSB and replaced FOC if owners complain. Make sure clutch still has plenty of bite and feel carefully for any gear-change problems.

Avensis Verso (from August 2001)

What's good: The new Toyota Avensis Verso on sale from 1st August 2001 offers seven seats in two-three-two layout and ample luggage space for seven, all within a length of 4,560mm (15ft 3ins). Engine choice is a 2.0-litre timing-chain VVT-i petrol engine offering

147bhp at 6,000rpm and maximum torque of 142 lb ft (192Nm) at 4,000rpm. Top speed of the manual is 119mph with a 0–60 of 11.2 seconds. (Auto 112mph and 0–60 12.0 seconds.) Fuel economy is 32.8 mpg on the EU combined cycle with a CO_2 output 202g/km for the manual and 213g/km for the automatic (both £155pa VED). Alternative engine is a 114bhp 2.0 litre D-4D common rail diesel engine stumping up 184 lb ft (250Nm) torque from 1,800 to 3,000rpm giving the Verso a top speed of 112mph and a 0–60 of 12.2 seconds. Fuel economy is 43.5mpg on the combined cycle and CO_2 output 173g/km (£150pa VED). For BIK purposes, the tax bases are 22% of list price for the petrol manual; 24% of list for the petrol automatic and 19% of list for the diesel. Clever packaging of the spare wheel under the front passenger floor helps result in a low centre of gravity and a low overall height of 1,675mm (5ft 6ins). This leaves space for an underfloor rear luggage compartment helping to give 282 litres of luggage space with all seats in place or a massive 2,422 litres with all five rear seats removed. All five rear seats can be bi-folded or removed entirely. The rear compartment length is a useful 2,104mm (6ft 11ins). Standard kit on all models includes ABS with EBD and Brake Assist, lap and diagonal seatbelts for every seat, air-conditioning and a Thatcham Category 1 alarm/immobiliser and a single CD player. In addition, GLS models have rear air-conditioning, 16-inch alloy wheels, roof rails, turn-by-turn satellite navigation, front fog lamps and leather steering wheel and gear knob. In a test by German magazine *Auto Motor und Sport*, the Avensis Verso was found to have the shortest, safest braking distances of any MPV. Passengers are not squeezed for shoulder width and three adults can sit across the second row in comfort. Interior width is 1,505mm, with shoulder width of 1,446mm, 1,456mm and 1,340mm in front, second and third row seats respectively. Headroom is equally useful at 1,048mm, 1,012mm and 911mm respectively. Drivers of all shapes and sizes can be accommodated. The driver's seat slides through 240mm and has 44mm of height adjustment. The steering column is adjustable for tilt. List prices are £17,795 for the GS VVT-I manual; £18,795 for the GS VVT-I automatic; £18,795 for the GS D-4D manual; £19,795 for the GLS VVT-I manual; £20,795 for the GLS VVT-I automatic; and

£20,795 for the GLS D-4D manual. All include a full three-year or 60,000 mile warranty and a 12-year no rust through perforation warranty. Colour choice is solid Pure White or metallic Silver Steel, Merlot Red, Island Green, Carlo Blue, Basalt Grey, Orb Gold or Teal Aqua. All are trimmed in Kirkfell Grey cloth. Highly rated by George Fowler, 'Motormouth' of the *Star*. More at www.Toyota.co.uk.

What's bad: Too soon to say.

What to watch out for: Too soon to say.

Camry (1991–1995)

What's good: Large saloons and estates with extra rear-facing bench on US-built estate, making it a 7-seater. Good 134 bhp 2.2 litre four (manual or 4-speed auto) and smooth 185 bhp 3.0 litre V6 (auto only). Spacious inside and comfortable. Very reliable for first 5–7 years. Depreciates rapidly so makes an excellent value-for-money used buy. Rear seat of 7-seater estate is vinyl so sticky sweets and other child mess wipes off. In June 2001 Toyota was rated by Motor Warranty Direct as Britain's 3rd most claim-free used marque (www.warrantydirect.co.uk).

What's bad: Estates discontinued and saloons only available to order from Sept 1995.

What to watch out for: Not much goes wrong, so look for signs of abuse, such as towing something heavy or carrying heavy loads. Make usual checks of front suspension geometry – look for signs of uneven tyre wear and reverse turn in both directions to check for driveshaft clonks.

Camry (1996 on)

What's good: Very good-looking large four-door saloon, high spec, badged as a Lexus in some markets. Three proper three-point rear seatbelts. 2.2 litre down on power slightly to 128 bhp; V6 up slightly to 188 bhp. Available in standard or 'Sport' trim (lowered, with bodykit and 17in alloys). Far better than Scorpios or Omegas, but top models getting expensive. Four-Star NCAP crash test rating among the best. S and T reg cars came 10th in 2001 Top Gear/JD

Power Customer Satisfaction Survey. In June 2001 Toyota was rated by Motor Warranty Direct as Britain's 3rd most claim-free used marque (www.warrantydirect.co.uk).

What's bad: Over-light steering not quite in the BMW league. No 'image'. Depreciates steeply over first three years.

What to watch out for: No problem areas known, but wise to buy with full Toyota service history. (If not available, why not? No history disqualifies the car from its 3-year warranty.)

Carina E (1992–1997)

What's good: Derbyshire-built upper-medium-size cars with quite powerful and particularly frugal 1.6 litre and 1.8 litre engines (40 mpg plus). Easy for anyone to drive. Useful estate cars. Decent build quality but not quite up to UK Honda and Nissan standards. Built to do a high mileage in a short time with no trouble.

What's bad: Fairly ugly slab-sided body with high waistline. Reliability and 'customer satisfaction' factor not quite up to levels set by Japanese Corolla and previous Carina II. Unresolved damping causes handling problems. Lean-burn engines require unusual economy driving style of high revs with small throttle openings – not holding high gears. Front tyre wear can be heavy: 14,000 miles or so.

What to watch out for: Check for missed services, clocked ex-fleet cars (could have had the haircut years ago). Once they're a few years old, must have six-monthly oil changes. Had its fair share of immobiliser problems, cured by new keyfob transmitter. Rear shocks can spring a leak. Expect a few behind-dash rattles. One report of timing belt failure at 39,000 miles, so change at 35,000 miles rather than the recommended 63,000 miles. 'Lean burn' lambda sensor failure quite common (£416 a pop). Toyota guarantees them for 5 years, but after that you're on your own.

Recalls: 1996: anti roll bar linkages may fail (first sign is a rattling noise). (Was covered under 3-year warranty. Only affected 2% of cars.) 1997 (Sept '93–Jan '96 build): stop lights may fail. 2000: rear axle hub may detach.

Carina II (1988–1992)

What's good: Fantastic reputation for 'high mileage, trouble-free' motoring. Easy to drive, good engines, good automatic. Available as saloon, hatch or estate.

What's bad: Bland to drive. 'Feel-free' steering. 1.6 engine sounds strained at speed. Ride quality not wonderful. Getting old now.

What to watch out for: Be very suspicious of any of these with a tow hook. Will probably have been pulling a large caravan. Starting to get a bit old for a Japanese car now, so look for rust, saggy suspension, shocked shock absorbers. Expect failures such as water pumps, oil pumps, brake cylinders, etc. and parts are expensive because in Japan cars of this age are scrapped.

Celica (1990–1994)

What's good: Weird-looking coupe. 201 bhp to 205 bhp GT-Four has warts and growths over its bonnet area. 'Carlos Sainz' GT-Four was collectable. Very quick, with excellent rally pedigree – notorious for being banned for a year for ingenious flouting of air restrictor rule. Basic front-wheel-drive models have 158 bhp, which is enough. Handle well. Good to drive.

What's bad: It really is ugly in an organic way – like something designed for 'Alien' by H. Gigor. All models have a firm ride. The interior is black as a coal mine. Reliability of front-drive models is typically Toyota, but GT-Four power train comes under strain.

What to watch out for: GT-Four is a gearbox breaker. Must have specialist service history, but even then gearbox may fail. All need six-monthly oil changes, preferably using fully synthetic oil. Watch out for used RHD imports from Japan. May not be fully up to UK spec.

Celica (1994–2000)

What's good: Very good-looking car, especially the convertible. GT-Four has 240 bhp. Front-drive GT has 173 bhp. Cut-price 1.8 much slower with just 114 bhp, but this is enough for cruiser types. Good seating position and good steering. Typical Toyota reliability. 12th from top in 'R' reg JD Power Customer Satisfaction Survey. In June 2001 Toyota was rated by Motor Warranty Direct as Britain's 3rd most claim-free used marque (www.warrantydirect.co.uk).

What's bad: Strange set of gear ratios and generally a softer car than the previous Celica. Doesn't handle or hold the road as well.

What to watch out for: GT-Four may follow in footsteps of old model and break its gearbox. Must have specialist service history (from Toyota or Japanese performance car specialists such as Intech or Protech). All need six-monthly oil changes, preferably using fully synthetic oil. Watch out for used RHD imports from Japan brought in at half the UK price. May not be fully up to UK spec. Watch out for 1.8s disguised as 2.0s. Could have been a drug dealer's car.

Celica (2000 on)

What's good: Entire car has been re-thought. Now 101 mm shorter with much better steering and handling than previous car. Six-speed manual or sequential four-speed auto. Standard 1.8 VVT-i has 140 bhp, but 1.8 litre Celica 190 has 192 bhp, and 133 lb ft, giving 0–60 in 7 seconds and a top speed of 140 mph. Best colour is dark metallic blue. List prices cut to from £16,995 for 140bhp but increased from £19,995 to £20,495 for Celica 190. The best handling front wheel drive car you can buy, and the extra 52 bhp of the 190 makes it better still. By far the best 2.0 litre coupe. Highly recommended.

What's bad: Not much leg or head room in the back.

What to watch out for: Grey imports not to UK spec.

Corolla (1992–1997)

What's good: The world's most popular car (even though Corolla can mean different cars in different markets). Blandly efficient and extremely reliable over first 5 years or so. Easy but dull to drive. 87 bhp 1.3 quite powerful, but economical. 1.6 has 113 bhp. Autos on 1.3s are 3-speed; on 1.6s are 4-speed. Full range of hatchbacks, saloons and estates. Well regarded and hold their value well. Has been top or near top in JD Power Customer Satisfaction Surveys. In

June 2001 Toyota was rated by Motor Warranty Direct as Britain's 3rd most claim-free used marque (www.warrantydirect.co.uk).

What's bad: Too bland, too dull for enthusiasts (this is not a criticism – they are deliberately made this way).

What to watch out for: Early cars had 6,000-mile service intervals and all need an oil change every 6,000 miles or every 6 months (whichever comes first) if you want to them to last. Quite likely to have been mini-cabbed and clocked, so look for excessive back seat wear and tear, worn door mechanisms, etc. Look for signs of a tow hook as may have been towing something too heavy. Estates may have had a hard life visiting cash and carrys for small businesses. Look for signs of sagging rear springs, damage to trim inside load area.

Corolla (1997 on)

What's good: The market seems to have taken to the somewhat jokey re-style. Looks by far the best as a 3-door in silver. Huge range of cars offered as 3-door or 5-door hatches, 4-door saloon, 5-door estate. Five- or six-speed manual gearboxes, or three- or four-speed automatic. GS models all have aircon. Limited range of engines – just an 85 bhp 1.3 16v, a 109 bhp 1.6, or a 71 bhp 2.0 litre diesel. Manufacturer 3-year warranty. Five lap and diagonal seatbelts. Three-Star above-average performance in NCAP crash tests. Restyled at the front for 2000 with new 95 bhp 1.4 litre and 109 bhp 1.6 litre VVT-i engines, 90 bhp 1.9 HDI diesel and six-speed gearbox for 1.6SR. List prices cut to from £8,995 still with three-year warranty as from October 2000. Seventh from top in 'R' reg JD Power Customer Satisfaction Survey, but see 'What's Bad' for latest model. S and T reg cars came not quite so good 18th in 2001 Top Gear/JD Power Customer Satisfaction Survey. Came top in this year's German ADAC reliability survey. In June 2001 Toyota was rated by Motor Warranty Direct as Britain's 3rd most claim-free used marque (www.warrantydirect.co.uk).

What's bad: 1997–1999 1.3G6 6-speed manual with ABS is a bit of an oddity. 1.3 with 3-speed auto is fairly slow and can lead to worrying moments when overtaking (no 1.4 auto in the Y2K range). Very 'Corolla'-like to drive, so expect bland efficiency rather than fun. British-built Y2K models proving to be less reliable than predecessors with reports of front wheel bearing and ECU failures. Instruments of Y2K restyle difficult to read in daylight.

What to watch out for: Repaired accident damage (a surprisingly high proportion seem to be involved in minor 'dings'). Still a new car so to remain under warranty will have needed to be serviced on time by a Toyota dealer.

Corolla (2002 on)

What's good: All new, much more attractive Corolla 5-door hatchback and estate. Will have current 1.4 litre and 1.6 litre VVT-i engines, plus a more powerful 1.8 and a new common-rail diesel.

What's bad: Japan gets it first, from Summer 2001. We have to wait.

What to watch out for: Too soon to say.

Landcruiser Amazon (1996 on)

What's good: Huge, big, restyled VX 'Landbruiser'. Power of 4.2 litre diesel rose from 165 bhp to 201 bhp with 317 lb ft torque. Still with gear-driven overhead camshaft, so no belts or chains to worry about. Official combined fuel consumption 25.4 mpg. Recommended. Also even more powerful 4.5 litre V8 version. Seven forward-facing seats. List prices cut by £3,000 in October 2000. S and T reg cars came 20th in 2001 Top Gear/JD Power Customer Satisfaction Survey. In June 2001 Toyota was rated by Motor Warranty Direct as Britain's 3rd most claim-free used marque (www.warrantydirect.co.uk).

What's bad: Too big to be safe for the school run. 202 bhp 4.5 litre V8 does just 17 mpg combined.

What to watch out for: If history is not impeccable, highly likely to have been clocked. Avoid oilwell-emptying petrol version.

Landcruiser Colorado (1996 on)

What's good: 3 litre 123 bhp 4-cylinder diesel manual or automatic, or 176 bhp 3.4 litre V6 petrol automatic with cruise control. Most have five doors. Re-styled for 2000 model-year. List prices cut by £2,500 in October 2000. New 3.0 litre common rail direct injected diesel engine from 1/2/2001. The new engine puts out 161bhp but, more importantly for a 4x4, a stonking 253 lb ft torque (343Nm) at just 1,600 rpm. Prices start at £23,795, rising to £31,695. Fuel consumption is quoted at 30.1mpg on the combined cycle and CO_2 emissions 287g/km. In June 2001 Toyota was rated by Motor Warranty Direct as Britain's 3rd most claim-free used marque (www.warrantydirect.co.uk).

What's bad: 3-door version dropped September 1998.

What to watch out for: Check history very carefully and don't buy from itinerants.

Landcruiser VX (1990–1996)

What's good: Huge, big, brutal 165 bhp 4.2 litre diesel capable of towing a Jag on a trailer at 100 mph. Has gear-driven camshaft rather than belt or chain. Seven forward-facing seats. Auto available, but manual best. In June 2001 Toyota was rated by Motor Warranty Direct as Britain's 3rd most claim-free used marque (www.warrantydirect.co.uk).

What's bad: Almost certain to have been used as a towcar, probably pulling something heavy. A lot used by people of no fixed abode to tow chrome plated caravans. Clocking is rife. Too big to be safe for the school run.

What to watch out for: If history is not impeccable, highly likely to have been clocked. Avoid oilwell-emptying petrol version.

MR2 (1985–1990)

What's good: Better-executed Fiat X19 successor, with revvy 1.6 litre twin-cam set sideways in the middle. Super handling, great fun to drive and just enough performance not to be dangerous. Good value new. Held its price extremely well. Has developed a cult following.

What's bad: So many were thrashed and crashed or rusted out that good ones are now regarded as classics and fetch top money

(*Parker's Guide* prices are usually about right.) No bootspace of any significance.

What to watch out for: They rust badly. Smart, fresh paint is likely to hide basinfuls of 'pudding'. Feel all round the edges for crumbly bits. Look inside the front boot for rust, fresh paint and signs it has been front ended. Brake balance is all-important on these cars – not enough bias to rear and the front wheels will lock up in the wet. DIY kerbside servicing can't do a proper job as they need to be up on a ramp. Driveshafts start to clonk, diffs whine, gearbox bearings get noisy, valve stem seals go, electric window and headlight motors fail. Check tyres for uneven wear – may signify crash, kerbing or simply misalignment. Check floorpan for leak damage from T-bar roof.

MR2 (1990–2000)

What's good: Bigger, much more powerful car than the original. Moved into a different league. Base model had just 119 bhp, but 'GT' had 158 bhp. Improved from March 1992 with bigger 15in alloys, better suspension, Yokohama tyres. The real improvements came in March 1994 with better suspension, ABS and power boosted to 174 bhp. Mar '94–Aug '96 is the model to have. In June 2001 Toyota was rated by Motor Warranty Direct as Britain's 3rd most claim-free used marque (www.warrantydirect.co.uk).

What's bad: A much more 'lardy' car than the original. 1990–92 models had a reputation for swapping ends, especially in the wet. 1992–94 variable rate power steering can be a liability on a mid-engined car and power catalysed down to 154 bhp. After 1994 boost, power cut back to 168 bhp from August 1996. New, cheaper lightweight replacement arrived in 1999 in spirit of MX5 and original MR2.

What to watch out for: Grey Japanese second-hand imports may not pass UK emissions tests. (Turbos are all grey imports.) Check all wheels for uneven tyre wear which could be due to accident damage, falling off the road, kerbing or may simply be misadjusted alignment. Full service history essential – either Toyota or Japanese performance car specialist. Needs 6-month services with fully synthetic oil. Make sure front brakes aren't snatching (needs new front-to-rear compensator, but may need new discs as well). Feel the state of the discs through the wheels and budget accordingly.

MR2 (from April 2000)

What's good: MR2 went back to its routes and became a sporty spyder once again. All new 1.8 litre 140 bhp VVT-i engine. 0–60 in 7.9 seconds; tops out at 130 mph. Soft top has glass rather than plastic rear window and is very easy to raise and lower. Low weight: just 975kg. Combined mpg figure 38.2 mpg. Thatcham 1 security system. Extra-cost sequential manual 5-speed sports shift works the right way round: lever back to change up; forwards to change down, but better still using press buttons on the steering wheel. This is the best version to drive because it enables you to more fully exploit the fantastic handling. A good driver in one of these can keep up with an average driver in a Mitsubishi EVO VI. Huge fun. Options include hard top, air conditioning, leather seat facings. Prices cut to from £17,995 still with three-year warranty from October 2000, but available from Trade Sales of Slough and Motorpoint of Derby at £14,999 without the extra two years warranty. Much better drive than MGF.

What's bad: Hardly any luggage space at all: just two small compartments behind the seats and barely enough for a briefcase under the bonnet. Power steering unnecessary. Small and low, so drivers need to be aware that other drivers may not see them.

What to watch out for: Too soon to say.

Picnic (1997–2001)

What's good: Scenic-sized six- or seven-seater. Seems to handle quite well. Powerful 2.0 litre 126 bhp engine same as RAV-4. Same five-speed manual or excellent four-speed auto as well. 2.2 litre IDI turbodiesel gives more mpg at expense of performance. GS is basic model with 7 seats. GLs and GXs have aircon and ABS. Four-star performer in NCAP crash tests (10 points front impact; 15 point side impact). Second-best MPV and 9th from top overall in 'R' reg

JD Power Customer Satisfaction Survey. In June 2001 Toyota was rated by Motor Warranty Direct as Britain's 3rd most claim-free used marque (www.warrantydirect.co.uk).

What's bad: No luggage space when all six or seven seats in use. Seats don't fold very cleverly, but rear pair can be removed. Clutch on diesel Picnics reported to be short-lived and troublesome.

What to watch out for: Unlikely to have been a taxi. Most likely to have been privately owned. Trim may have received 'deposits' from very young children, sticky sweets may be stuck in seams. Dogs may have crocodiled the upholstery. Check clutch of manual diesels carefully.

Previa (1990–2000)

What's good: One of the bigger MPVs with room for up to 8 and their luggage inside. 5-speed floor-change or 3-speed plus overdrive column shift auto. Good build quality. Oldest are now affordable and can be 'de-catted' if necessary to save expense. In June 2001 Toyota was rated by Motor Warranty Direct as Britain's 3rd most claim-free used marque (www.warrantydirect.co.uk).

What's bad: Only one sliding side door on the nearside. No diesel, supercharged petrol or 4x4 in UK. Only one petrol engine (but ripe for an LPG conversion). Auto holds its gears for a long time, can be frenetically noisy and a bit juicy.

What to watch out for: One sliding rear door may preclude use as a taxi under some local authority rules. Airport taxis do huge mileages they may not show. 8-seater versions best. 6 'captain's' chairs pointless. Cylinder head gaskets can go if coolant not changed every two years. Look for mayonnaise under oil filler cap and in coolant expansion tank (though, since these are remote from the engine, it may not have reached that far). White exhaust smoke also indicates head gasket problems. Rear diffs eventually whine. Interior may have been trashed by kids or 'crocodiled' by dogs. Catalytic converters go eventually. Diesel 4x4s are all Lucida Estima grey imports. Slightly narrower than Previa.

Previa (2000 on)

What's good: Huge, all-new Previa now with sliding rear doors on both sides. Still offered as a six-, seven- or eight-seater. Plenty of room for luggage, even with eight passengers aboard. Has 2.4 litre VVT-i petrol engine developing 154 bhp and 166 lb ft torque. Now front rather than rear-wheel-drive with 5-speed manual or 3-speed column shift autobox with press-button overdrive. 0–60 in around 11 seconds for either with 115 mph top speed. Official 'combined' fuel consumption 30.0 mpg manual; 26.9 mpg auto. 114bhp 2.0 litre D-4D diesel engine option offering 184 lb ft toprque (250Nm) at 1,800 rpm with 5-speed manual box from May 2001, list prices of diesels from £21,450. 191g/km CO_2. Combined mpg 39.2.

What's bad: Rear bench seat of eight-seater not completely removable. Severe roll understeer. Doesn't like two sudden changes of direction in a row.

What to watch out for: Too soon to say.

Prius (2000 on)

What's good: The first hybrid car on general sale and a proper 4/5-seater hatchback. 1,496cc 58 bhp VVT-i engine feels bigger. Combined dash-mounted automatic transmission selector and parking brake. Excess power output charges a bank of nickel-metal hydride batteries, which are also charged by regenerative braking when descending hills. These feed a 40 bhp electric motor. The engine switches itself off at rest and the car moves off on its electric motor, starting its ic engine when needed. It works remarkably well and the car even has a lively feel to it. Very low carbon dioxide emissions of 114g/km – already meets Euro 2005 emissions limits. Annual VED from March 2001 just £90. Official urban fuel consumption figure an incredible 61.4 mpg. Air conditioning and CD radio included in UK price of £16,495. First 200 sold in UK qualify for £1,000 Powershift grant bringing the price down to £15,495. Highly recommended. Dedicated website: www.prius.co.uk.

What's bad: Beaten to the UK market by the two-seater, much sportier Honda Insight, but that's all.

What to watch out for: Too soon to say.

517

RAV 4 (1994–2000)

What's good: The first fashion 4x4 that really was car-like to drive. Strong performance from 126 bhp twin cam 2.0 litre Celica engine. Manuals have a centre diff lock; autos don't. Autobox is typically excellent Toyota with good ratios and is fully controllable (does 60 in second). 5-door versions are more practical and handle better, 3-doors are faster and more fun. Nice low rear load height for dogs, etc. Reasonably economical (30 mpg). Typical Toyota reliability. In June 2001 Toyota was rated by Motor Warranty Direct as Britain's 3rd most claim-free used marque (www.warrantydirect.co.uk).

What's bad: Not great in an 'elk avoidance test'. Rear seat of 5-door slopes forwards and is situated over rear wheels, so not comfortable. Suspension wishbones hang too low for serious off-roading.

What to watch out for: Bent suspension wishbones. Uneven tyre wear. Don't buy one with silly, over-large wheels and ridiculous running boards or you'll lose a lot of money on resale.

RAV 4 (2000 on)

What's good: Freshly restyled swb 3-door and lwb 5-door. Choice of front-wheel-drive with 1.8 litre VVT-i engine and 123 bhp or four-wheel-drive with 2.0 litre VVT-i and 148 bhp. Rear seats now slide, fold, double fold or can be removed altogether. Official 'combined' fuel consumption: 1.8 is 38 mpg; 2.0 is 32 mpg; 2.0 auto is 30.36 mpg. Typical Toyota reliability. List prices reduced to £13,405 from October 2000 still with three-year warranty. D-4D common rail direct injected diesel engine option from September 2001 in both 3- and 5-door bodies. Main benefits are an EU combined fuel consumption figure of 39.8mpg and a CO_2 output of 190g/km (£160pa VED; 23% list price BIK tax base) for the three door. D-4D develops 114bhp (85kW) at 4,000rpm and offers constant torque of 184 lb ft (250Nm) across the power band from 1,800rpm to 3,000rpm giving a top speed of 106mph and a useful 0–60 of 11.9 seconds. This broad torque band is also very useful for off-roading, of course. D-4D RAV4s from £15,995 (NV 3-door) or £17,495 (NV 5-door), including a full three-year or 60,000 mile mechanical warranty. No automatic option for the D-4D. More at www.Toyota.co.uk.

What's bad: Too soon to say.
What to watch out for: Too soon to say.

Starlet (1990–1996)

What's good: Toyota's smallest car (in the UK anyway). Good little 12-valve 1.0 litre 54 bhp and 1.3 litre 74 bhp engines. 1.0 litre dropped in January 1993. Totally reliable for the first five years. 3-year warranty. In June 2001 Toyota was rated by Motor Warranty Direct as Britain's 3rd most claim-free used marque (www.warrantydirect.co.uk).
What's bad: No power steering. Not very well packaged. Limited rear seat and load area. Expensive new.
What to watch out for: Lots of 'specials' such as 'Kudos'. Tend to be owned by uninterested people who want no more than a very small, reliable car. Make sure it has been serviced regularly and that the owner hasn't 'forgotten'. Look for evidence of parking dings, behind-bumper damage. May need a cambelt change.

Starlet (1996 on)

What's good: Better styled, better value and better packaged. New 1,332cc 74 bhp engine and 3-speed automatic option. PAS standard on 5-door manual and 3-door and 5-door auto. Totally reliable for the first five years. 3-year warranty. Wider range appeals to wider range of buyers than before. S and T reg cars came 15th in 2001 Top Gear/ JD Power Customer Satisfaction Survey. In June 2001 Toyota was rated by Motor Warranty Direct as Britain's 3rd most claim-free used marque (www.warrantydirect.co.uk).
What's bad: Sporty SR version not exactly sporty.
What to watch out for: If a 3-door manual, check that optional PAS has been fitted. Must have Toyota service history for remaining warranty to apply.

Yaris (1999 on)

What's good: New small Toyota 3- and 5-door hatch replaces Starlet, initially all with same 68 bhp 1.0 litre 16v VVTi iron block engine, but 85 bhp VVTi alloy 1.3 and 4-speed auto option from October 1999. Low parts prices, good repairability, low insurance groups, combined finance and servicing package, three-year 60,000-mile warranty, slide-forward back seat, option of 'Free-Tronic' automatic clutch with 5-speed gearbox. High seats make it easy for the elderly to get in and out of. Praised by road testers for its excellent steering, good handling and the roominess of its interior (far better than a Polo in all these respects). Unusual central digital speedometer set in a tunnel is clear and easy to read. Light years ahead of the Starlet it replaces. Price competitive with alternatives on UK market. Did reasonably well in German TUV front offset crash tests. Excellent Four-Star-plus rating in Euro NCAP crash tests. European 1999 Car of the Year. Prices cut to from £6,995 from October 2000, still with three-year warranty. 1.5 T Sport launched March 2001 with sub 9 second 0–60 and 119mph top speed at a price of £11,995. Recommended range. S and T reg cars came second in 2001 Top Gear /JD Power Customer Satisfaction Survey. See also Yaris Verso mini-MPV.

What's bad: To be built in France, and quality may suffer. Bonnet is prone to paint chips.

What to watch out for: Build quality problems starting to emerge.

Recalls: 18/4/2000: 19,639 Yarises built Jan 1999–Jan 2000. Brake proportioning valve may cause car to become unstable under braking. Modified valve to be fitted.

Yaris Verso (1999 on)

What's good: Weird looking but very useful mini-MPV, ideally suited to the needs of the elderly. 85 bhp VVTi alloy 1.3 litre engine and 4-speed auto option. Supremely easy to step in and out of, with huge front-to-back grab handles to help. Rear door is side hinged on the right-hand side and sufficiently low for loading wheelchairs, etc. Removable false floor to rear enables the long-legged to be comfortably accommodated. Rear side seats fold away under this false floor, but narrower centre seat needs to be removed and stored. Easy to drive. Height-adjustable steering wheel. Handles surprisingly well with good steering and good front end grip (better than a Zafira). Automatic cruises at a relaxed 3,000 rpm at 70 mph. Very clear digital instrumentation. 3-year warranty. Discounted prices from £8,499 at Trade Sales of Slough (but don't include 3-year warranty). My recommended choice for elderly drivers and the disabled. Also see 'Toyota Yaris' above. S and T reg cars came second in 2001 Top Gear / JD Power Customer Satisfaction Survey. Best colour: solid bright red.

What's bad: To be built in France. Bonnet prone to paint chips. Quite a lot of rattles from dual height rear parcel shelf. First timers need to be careful folding the seats as fingers can be trapped. Doors feel tinny and the car doesn't have any side protector strips – which it needs. Big gap between 4th and 3rd on automatic. Accessory 'Protection Pack' includes door mats, mud flaps and door rubbing strips, but the strips fit too low to offer proper protection to the doors.

What to watch out for: Build quality problems starting to emerge.

TVR

What's good: Hairy-chested all-British sports cars we can now feel proud of. Compact new AJP8 engine is utterly brilliant. New AJP6 'Speed Six' and Tuscan are promising, with 350 bhp 4,185cc six putting out 320 lb ft torque allied to six-speed gearbox. Older models still used modified Rover/Buick pushrod V8s. S1s, S2s and S3s had Ford pushrod V6s with 187 bhp (S3C). Late cars reliable and well put together. Some owners do 25,000 miles a year in them. Buy one and you buy into a club. Tuscan racing series well worth a watch. Company run by the hands-on owner, Peter Wheeler.

What's bad: Lack of problems by no means guaranteed. Many cars have an extremely hard ride and are very noisy. Cerbera coupe with AJP8 has very little flywheel effect and revs like a racing car which can catch out the unskilled with snap oversteer. S and T plate Chimaeras 13th from bottom in 2001 Top Gear / JD Power Customer Satisfaction Survey.

What to watch out for: Only buy from true enthusiasts or from TVR specialists. Be prepared to spend a few grand to get a used car the way you want it. Use your judgement or get the car checked by a TVR expert. HPI or AA/Experian history check also well advised as the car could have been bought on the drip, after which the 'owner' hit hard times.

VAUXHALL

Agila (2000 on)

What's good: Five-door minibox based on Suzuki Wagon R. 12-year anti-perforation warranty. Same 1.0 litre 58 bhp and 1.2 litre 75 bhp engines. Upright and easy for the elderly to get in and out of. To get Fiat's 60 bhp, 1.2 litre 100 mpg CDI diesel engine in 2002. Three-year warranty from October 2000.

What's bad: See Suzuki Wagon R. Four, not five, seats.

What to watch out for: As Suzuki Wagon R. Consumers Association members have reported transmission problems, fiddly head restraints and noisy suspension.

Astra (1984–1991)

What's good: Well-liked and still good enough to form the basis of the 1994–1997 Daewoo Nexia. GTE 16v was quick in a straight line. Nicely judged end-of-the-line SX and SXE hatches and estates.

What's bad: Solid blue and solid red paint both oxidise. Lacquers on metallics peel off. Hard, jiggly ride not matched by good handling and road feel. Dodgy digital instruments on GTEs. ABS pumps very expensive to replace. Belmont saloon is hideous. Pretty convertibles suffer severe scuttle shake. Getting old now and rusting.

What to watch out for: Could have done 400,000 miles, particularly diesel estates, so look for all the signs. Clutches stick (may need a cheap new cable or may have damaged bulkhead). Suspension bushes wear. Main problem is camshaft wear, which can be terminal for the engine. Listen for thrashing noises and look for signs of oil weeping from top of engine. Fuel evaporation problem with all late injected models. Check for driveshaft wear by doing reverse-turns in both directions. Split driveshaft boots are common and an MOT failure point. Regular 3,000-mile oil changes essential. If not, engines will sludge up and rattle. Cambelts must be changed every 35,000 miles; tensioners every 70,000 miles. Always lift the boot carpet and look for signs of accident damage repairs because

523

bodyshells are very difficult to pull back into proper alignment. Check the floorpan of convertibles for rust caused by leaks.

Astra (1991–1998)

What's good: Model designation is 'F Type'. Not bad looking and with metallic paint gives impression of reasonable quality. Estate car the most practical in the class. Useful improvements for 1995 ('V' grille) model-year include power steering across the range and 'low pressure turbo' GM diesel. LPT diesel estate the best buy and deservedly the most popular. 1.6 E-Drive petrol engine slow, but very economical (45 mpg): a good choice if worried about diesel price increases. 'High torque' 60 bhp 1.4 the most popular engine, but even more short of puff than E-Drive. 16 valve 1.4 and 1.6 engines much more perky.

What's bad: Better than the Escort when it came out in 1991, but not much better. 4-door versions look hideous. Over-light power steering and severely lacklustre handling, even on 'Sport' and 'GSi' versions. 16 valve versions criticised for sticking valves – usually the owner's fault for driving short distances from cold starts on the cheapest petrol (switching to a high detergent petrol might cure the problem in a few hundred miles). On 1.4 16v, timing belt also drives the water pump, so if this fails it will lead to timing belt failure. Most likely reason for the water pump to fail is lack of water (coolant) so check this regularly. See Recalls re GF50 plastic timing belt pulleys.

What to watch out for: Sagging rear suspension on hard-used ex-fleet estates. Kerbing damage to front suspension (look for uneven tyre wear). Worn front suspension bushes and steering joints. Damaged suspension arms from jacking by them. Unpleasant clutch action (might be cured cheaply with a new cable). Electric front windows can stick. Valve gear gets noisy with mileage and ambitious 9,000-10,000-mile oil changes. Valves of 16vs may stick if run on cheap detergent free petrol. Petrol engine cambelts need changing every 35,000–40,000 miles. Floor around handbrake mounting and driver's seat mounting can crack (symptom: having to pull handbrake right up). This could be the reason why more than a few

Telegraph readers complain of being unable to release the handbrake of Astras with drum rear brakes. Ex-Vauxhall Masterhire cars on full service contracts come with very comprehensive computerised service histories, itemised down to light bulb replacements. Watch out for dodgy histories in kerbside or auction sale cars. More likely than most to be clocked.

Recalls: 1995: fuel pipe, airbag. 1995 (TD: VIN S5000001–S5241939; S2500001–S2707652 and S8000001–S8216827): chafing of wiring harness and possible fire risk. 1995: airbag may fail to inflate in an accident. 1995: static sparking during refuelling. 1997 (1993–96 1.4 and 1.6 16vs only): 1999: possibility of failure of plastic cambelt idler pulley GF50 on 16v engines 1993–96, which can snap cambelt. Changed as an 'in service mod' when cambelts are changed at 35,000–40,000-mile intervals. (Vauxhall Recall Helpline: 01189 458500 or 01582 427200.) 17/4/2000: 620,000 F-Type Astras built 1991–99 recalled to check for water contamination of brake fluid and to fit rubber grommet to underside of bonnet. Customers to be advised that brake fluid is hygroscopic and a service item that needs to be regularly replaced.

Astra Coupe (2000 on)

What's good: Debut car for Vauxhall's new family of chain cam ECOTEC petrol engines (has 2.2 litre 147 bhp version). Decent performance. Three-year warranty from October 2000. New 190bhp Turbo version launched November 2000 at £18,995 will clock up 150mph. Convertible from Spring 2001 is much prettier than the coupe.

What's bad: Ordinary coupe dull to look at and very disappointing to drive. Rattly, crashy, felt unfinished. Turbo is much better to drive, but all are utterly shamed by the Toyota Celica.

What to watch out for: Too soon to say.

Calibra (1989–1998)

What's good: Good-looking, practical four-seater coupe with a big, golf-bag-sized boot. Some good engines in the line-up. Some very fast, very powerful cars such as six-speed 4x4 turbo. Some nice trim combinations. 2.5 V6s with leather and white instruments on 'R' plates can represent a lot of coupe for the money. Usefully had a lever behind the headlights to switch from left dip to right dip for continental driving (explained in the driver's manual).

What's bad: Hard to see out of and very difficult to reverse. Based on the Cavalier and though it handles better it still suffers from the understeering limitations of the Cavalier. Front-drive Calibras will always come off the road front-first. Six-speed gearbox on 4x4 turbo fails and costs a fortune to replace. Bulkhead may crack around steering rack mountings.

What to watch out for: Ex-Vauxhall Masterhire cars previously on service contracts come with trustworthy print-out of full service history, including cambelt changes every 36,000–40,000 miles. Listen for steering creaks and look for cracks around steering rack bulkhead mounting points, a £700 job to repair. Abbot Racing of Spinnels Farm, Manningtree (tel: 01255 870636) have a means of mounting the rack more rigidly, and also replacing the soft rubber suspension bushes which not only solves the problem but makes the car steer and handle much better.

Recalls: 1999: possibility of failure of plastic cambelt idler pulley GF50 on 16v engines 1993–96, which can snap cambelt. Changed as an 'in service mod' when cambelts are changed at 35,000–40,000-mile intervals. (Vauxhall Recall Helpline: 01189 458500 or 01582 427200.) June 2000 recall of V6 models due to crankshaft fault.

Carlton (1986–1994)

What's good: Solid, German-built saloons and estates capable of mileages of 300,000 or more with little trouble. Big, comfortable, well-liked by many owners, particularly 'Strasbourg' box automatics. Strong loyalty factor. Good handling and ride. Pre-August 1992 may be pre-cat (check for fuel filler restrictor). Estate car has a huge capacity. 3.0GSi 24v is quick. Twin turbo Lotus Carlton is seriously quick. Dubbed by Jasper Carrott 'the family car for the Fittipaldis'.

What's bad: Power steering a bit vague. Can suffer from electrical glitches. Diesels are lacklustre. Obstructive manual gearboxes. Starting to look old. ECU connector block prone to hairline cracks which allow moisture in and lead to intermittent faults which could hot spot a 'cat'.

What to watch out for: Clocking, obviously, because these cars take the miles so well. Some engines require timing belt replacement every 35,000–40,000 miles. Others have chains. Vital to check special rear shock absorbers in estates as these are expensive. Want to see evidence of regular maintenance, including biannual autobox ATF and filter change. Beware of clonky or noisy manual boxes – they're expensive to rebuild. Oil breathers of four-cylinder engines sometimes get blocked. Noisy valve gear often denotes missed oil changes. If it has a tow hook or signs of one having been fitted, be extra careful. Watch out for clocked ex-taxis.

Cavalier (1988–1995)

What's good: Popular, reliable, good build quality, comfortable, cheap spares, cheap servicing, cheap and easily replaced clutch. Good, smooth, economical Japanese (Isuzu) turbodiesel engine. Cheap-to-replace ABS from 1994.

What's bad: Stodgy handling. Rust in seam on rear wheelarch. Brakes can develop judder. Combined alternator/brake vacuum pump of turbodiesels is very expensive. ABS pump of early SRis is eye-wateringly expensive (more than the cars are worth). Lost steering-wheel height adjustment when gained drivers airbag in early 1993. Six-speed gearbox on 4x4 turbo fails and costs a fortune to replace. GF50 plastic timing belt tensioners can fail on 16-valve engines built Aug '93–Jan '96. Lower front suspension arms may have been damaged by use as jacking points. Bulkhead may crack around steering rack mountings. Plastic fuel filler pipe between cap and tank can develop hairline cracks leading to petrol fumes entering the cabin when the tank pressurises. On 2.0 16v models a problem can develop with the idle adjustor control valve, necessitating the fitting of an oil separator.

What to watch out for: ABS light on early SRis (make sure it hasn't been disconnected). Signs of clocking as lots of 200,000-milers have received haircuts. Damage from being jacked up by front suspension arms. Timing belts not changed at 36,000–40,000-mile intervals. Camshaft wear on 1.6 litre 8-valve engines. Serious engine oil leaks. Track rod end wear. Shot shock absorbers. Juddery braking due to warped front discs. Non-fused wiring can rub against base of battery holder and cause a short. Alternator may short out due to ingress of water through worn rubber steering rod sleeves. Choke mechanism of 1.6 carburettor models fails: may be no more than blocked water heating passage, or may require £100 repair kit. Creaking from steering may indicate cracks in bulkhead at base of steering column – especially on V6s. It's a £700 job to repair. Abbot Racing of Spinnels Farm, Manningtree (tel: 01255 870636) have a means of mounting the rack more rigidly, and also replacing the soft rubber suspension bushes which not only solves the problem but makes both Cavaliers and SAAB 900s steer and handle much better.

Recalls: 1994: (1.7 TD Mar '92–Mar '94 VIN NV201488–R7560941): loss of braking efficiency. 1995: static sparking during refuelling. 1999: possibility of failure of plastic cambelt idler pulley GF50 on 16v and V6 engines 1993–96, which can snap cambelt. Changed as an 'in service mod' when cambelts are changed at 35,000–40,000-mile intervals. (Vauxhall Recall Helpline: 01189 458500 or 01582 427200.)

Corsa (1993–2000)

What's good: Ageing design but still a good, 'different' and practical shape for a supermini. Plenty of room in the back of the 5-door version. Doesn't make demands on the driver. Good engines, especially the ultra-economical Suzuki 1.0 litre 3-cylinder 12-valve, often badged 'Breeze'. Generally reliable, last well and cheap to run. 1999 model awarded well.

What's bad: Still based on the Nova floorpan, so stodgy and characterless to drive. 1.4s have suffered cat problems. Awarded Two-Star NCAP crash safety rating in 1997. Short runs may lead to sticking valves on 16-valve models (usually cured by switching to a high detergent petrol). See 'Recalls' about timing belt pulleys which need renewing at least every 40,000 miles. On 1.4 16v timing belt also drives the water pump, so if this fails it will lead to timing belt failure. Most likely reason for the water pump to fail is lack of water (coolant) so check this regularly.

What to watch out for: Could have been a courier's car or a driving school car ('Engineering Education Trust' on the V5 = BSM). Clutch cables can be troublesome (cheap to replace). Heavier diesel engines promote high front tyre and suspension wear. All Corsas prone to front suspension wear. Check driveshafts for clonks by reverse turns in both directions. Cracking around door hinges on 'A' pillars of 2-door models (also look for cracks in the paint on 'B' pillars – an MOT failure point). Feel front discs for grooves, 'shouldering' and wear. GTEs may have been thrashed by kids. Beware of any noises from the water pump (see 'What's Bad').

Recalls: 1995: static sparking during refuelling. 1997 (1993–96 1.4 and 1.6 16vs only – 27,000 cars): Possibility of plastic cambelt idler pulley breaking which can snap cambelt. 1998 (diesel K to N reg: 26,000 cars): live cable may rub against bonnet hinge, lose insulation and cause a fire; (1.0 12v, P to R reg: 8,000 cars): cable may touch engine inlet manifold. (Vauxhall Recall Helpline: 01582 427200.) 1998: Vauxhall Corsa diesel (K to N reg: 26,000 cars): live cable may rub against bonnet hinge, lose insulation and cause a fire. (3/6/98.) Vauxhall Corsa 1.0 12v (P to R reg: 8,000 cars): cable may touch engine inlet manifold. (3/6/98: Specific Helpline: 01189 458500.) February 2000: Safety recall to reinforce front seat rails and replace fatigued or worn front seatbelt buckles.

Corsa (2000 on)

What's good: New model due Autumn 2000, similar but prettier than before. Fully galvanised bodies with 12-year no perforation warranty, active front head restraints, 'Dynamic Safety' chassis, combined information and entertainment system. Three three-point rear seatbelts. Engines include 125 ps 1.8i 16v and 1.7 DTi. 5-speed 'Easytronic' semi-automatic on 1.2 16v similar to the system in the MCC Smart and avoids a power-sapping torque converter. Three Stars in Euro NCAP crash tests. Three-year warranty. List price examples: £7,995 for 1.0 12v Club; £9,995 for 1.2 litre 16v SX1; £11,495 for 1.4 litre 16v SRi, all inclusive of three-year warranty and first year's insurance.

What's bad: Too soon to say.

What to watch out for: Too soon to say.

Frontera (1991 on)

What's good: Not bad looking, in a chunky sort of way. Right car at the right time when launched in 1991 to feed 4x4 fashion fad. Initially well-priced as alternative to a Cavalier. Held value well until the public started to wonder why they were driving crude old-fashioned 4x4 trucks instead of proper cars. Reasonably competent off-road. 1998 'Round the World' endurance run helped improve public perception of reliability. Range revamped for 1999 with 113 bhp 2.2 direct injected diesel or 204bhp 3.2 litre V6. Sport V6 listed at £19,995 does 114mph, 0–60 in 9.5 seconds but just 15.9mpg in the EC urban cycle. Three-year warranty from October 2000.

What's bad: Really no more than a dressed-up Isuzu pick up. Legion of quality problems. Short-lived direct injected 2.8 Isuzu diesel withdrawn due to emissions problem. 2.3 and 2.2 petrol engines guzzle petrol. If you want a chunky 4x4 to use as a day to day car the Honda CRV, Toyota RAV4, Hyundai Santa Fe and Land Rover Freelander are vastly superior. Has been rock bottom in JD Power Customer Satisfaction Surveys and still second bottom in the 'R' reg survey. S and T platers 4th from bottom in 2001 Top Gear / JD Power Customer Satisfaction Survey. Some 2.2 litre DI 16v models thought to use a lot of engine oil, but oil from the 16v heads takes a long time to drain down and dipstick can give a falsely low reading. Repeated alarm system problems reported by readers. In April 2001 a shortage of rear windscreens for the 5-door model with over 400 on back order. Vauxhall dealer advice has been to try and get one from a breakers. Not recommended.

What to watch out for: Is it a townie's car (never gone off road) or is it a farmer's car? Big difference in likelihood of damage to underside and drive train. Has a towing hook been fitted at some time? If so, what has it been towing? (Anything from a one horse horsebox to a mobile catering stand, so look for saggy rear suspension, groaning rear diff., noisy wheel bearings). Look for oil leaks from engine and drive train. Check that it tracks straight. Look for wear in front suspension and steering joints. Listen for big-end rattles, noisy tappets (signs of insufficiently frequent oil changes). Check dipstick for clean oil.

Recalls: 1995: VIN NV500400–RV628644: faulty bonnet safety catch. 1996 (Sport): fit heat shield between exhaust system and petrol tank (fire risk). Replace catches for removable roof section. Spring 1999: warning issued to all known owners to take vehicles to Vauxhall dealers at 4 years or 40,000 miles for a replacement timing belt and timing belt idler wheel. 1999: all 'new' Fronteras built from June '98 to Sep '99 (6,557 vehicles) officially recalled for a check on steering components. This recall was repeated in 2001 to correct 'steering to the left'.

Monterey (1994–1999)

What's good: Badge-engineered Isuzu Trooper.
What's bad: Slow seller and lots hung around unsold in compounds for more than a year. See Isuzu Trooper.
What to watch out for: See Isuzu Trooper.
Recalls: See Isuzu Trooper.

New Astra (1998 on)

What's good: New G Type Astra vastly better than previous F Type. Steering, handling, roadholding now class-competitive. Better steering feel than four-cylinder Golf Mk IVs. Three proper three-point rear seatbelts standard across the range. Ski-hatch to boot. Useful 'head up' information display. Four stars for secondary safety in 1999 NCAP tests. Long-lived direct-injected chain-cam 16-valve small turbo 'DI' diesel works well in this car allied to excellent 4-speed autobox: gives 45 mpg. Decent build quality. Most UK cars built in UK at Ellesmere Port. Aircon often fitted. 160 bhp 2.0 litre GSi from autumn 1999. 147 bhp 2.2 litre chain cam four available from September 2000, plus uprated 125 bhp 1.8 petrol and uprated

85 bhp 1.6. Three-year warranty from October 2000. Price cuts brought Astra 1.6i Club 5-door with a/c down to £11,225.

What's bad: Nondescript, 'hamster'-like road-hugging styling. Ride quality may be too firm for some. Is regarded as 'also ran' to Golf Mk IV and Ford Focus and does not hold its value as well. (This is something for the second-hand buyer to take advantage of.) DI 16v has reputation as an oil burner. The real reason may be that oil collects in the 16v head and takes a long time to drain back to the sump. Dip within an hour of stopping and you will get a falsely low reading leading you to overfill with fresh oil which then gets burned. Diesel automatic dropped from line-up. Water leaks (see below).

What to watch out for: Nearly-new examples likely to be ex-rental, so look for signs of careless driving such as kerbing. Check front tyres for uneven tread signifying suspension misalignment. A batch of faulty sealant left some mid-1999 Astras prone to condensation inside the headlights and foglights. Make sure it does have aircon and that the aircon blows cold. A problem seems to have developed with the ECUs of early 1.4s which are being replaced FOC but are in short supply. Lift front carpets and check for water underneath. The cure is re-sealing the front bulkhead. See recalls about noisy power steering pumps.

Recalls: Depending on source of supply, some models developed noisy power steering pumps. Free-of-charge replacement programme spring 1999. 14/7/2000: 3,008 3-door models built between January 1998 and October 1998 recalled for replacement of front seat adjuster spring which can lose its tension. (Press release received 15/7/2000.)

Nova (1983–1993)

What's good: One of the better 'older' superminis. 3-door is nicest and most valuable, but also available as 5-door and 2- and 4-door saloon. Most had decent ohc engines. Easy DIY. Lots of cheerful trim combinations on updated range from 1990. GTEs 'caught on' among young *Max Power* and *Revs* readers, who spend thousands of pounds doing them up. Insurance hikes mean they do the same with 1.2s, the stereos of which may be more powerful than the engines.

What's bad: Stodgy handling and indifferent ride. 3-door not very space-efficient. Getting old now.

What to watch out for: May have been couriers' cars (especially diesels) and could have been clocked back at anything up to 12 years ago. DIY servicing may have been incompetent or skimped. Really needs an oil change every 3,000 miles or every 6 months, whichever comes first. Main problem is camshaft wear, which can be terminal for the engine. Listen for thrashing noises and look for signs of oil weeping from top of the engine. Early '80s fuel pump problems should have been rectified in service by now. Check for driveshaft clonks by reverse turning in both directions. Look for split driveshaft gaiters. Expect to have to replace some front suspension bushes. If it has an aftermarket 'pop-up' sunroof, expect water leaks and check carpets. Rust starts in area of hatchback and rear wheel arches. Always lift boot carpets (especially in saloons) to check for repaired accident damage, rust, or both. 'SR' gearboxes don't last long. Interiors weak on all but post-1990 facelift models. Dashboards fall off. If the brakes of the 1.5 litre Isuzu turbodiesel lack servo assistance, you're in for a £600 combined brake vacuum pump and alternator.

Omega (1994 on)

What's good: Well equipped, comfortable, handles well with more road feel than Senator. Both 2.5 litre and 3.0 litre V6s nice to drive. 150 mph 207 bhp 3.0 MV6 was almost good value by UK standards at list price of £24,445. Manual boxes better suited to engines than Senator manuals. Get a white, grey or otherwise dark coloured one and the cars in front will still think you are a police car. Three-Star NCAP crash test rating. Comprehensively facelifted and re-engineered in autumn 1999 with option of new 2.2 litre chain cam 146 bhp four-cylinder engine offering 151 lb ft torque. Three-year warranty from October 2000. 2.5 litre 6 cylinder BMW diesel supplemented then replaced by GM's own 2.0 and 2.2DTi four cylinder diesels from January 1998. Comprehensively facelifted in October 1999 for 2000 model-year.

What's bad: Poor paint quality on some early cars. Large number of quality problems and complaints, often over BMW powered 2.5 litre straight six diesel. The police had great difficulty getting their kit into the limited dashboard and front-of-engine space. Started looking at Volvo T5s instead. New front-wheel-drive Omega from 2002. Timing belt drives water pump, so seizure of water pump wrecks engine. Some 2.2 litre DI 16v models thought to use a lot of engine oil, but oil from the 16v heads takes a long time to drain down and dipstick can give a falsely low reading.

What to watch out for: Electrical and electronic problems (check everything works, including computer and especially ABS warning light). Ignition ignitor coils vulnerable to water ingress and condensation. BMW diesel must have had 4,500–5,000-mile oil changes (easy for busy company drivers to forget). Serious reliability problems of Opel badged version (exactly the same as the Vauxhall) reported by ADAC (the German breakdown organisation) in its 2001 report.

Recalls: 1995: static sparking during refuelling. 1995 (16v: VIN R 1000001–S1155206): fuel feed pipe may chafe. Reposition and clamp into place. 1999: possibility of failure of plastic cambelt idler pulley GF50 on 4-cylinder 16v engines 1994–98, which can snap cambelt. Changed as an 'in service mod' when cambelts are changed at 35,000–40,000-mile intervals. (Vauxhall Recall Helpline: 01189 458500 or 01582 427200.) General problem of ignition steering wheel lock failure, usually replaced FOC. June 2000 recall of V6 models due to crankshaft fault.

Senator (1987–1995)

What's good: The policeman's favourite police car. Highly successful 1987 re-style looked longer and lower than Carlton and garish 'chip-cutter' grille is just right, especially pitched against bland looking Granada. High-spec 3.0 24v CD obviously the best (not all had leather). Glovebox of air-conditioned CD can be used as a fridge or drinks cooler. Later 2.6 12v CD is okay, 3.0 12v also okay. The police liked these cars so much, they stored them and some did not come into service until 'M' reg. Enthusiastic Owners Club (see clubs directory at www.honestjohn.co.uk).

What's bad: Top spec 3.0 24v CDs with less than 75,000 miles now very rare. Lots of electrical glitches on CDs, particularly autobox electrics. Early 2.5 12v lacked essentials such as proper engine cooling. Police spec had no sunroof or aircon, wind-up windows and manual five-speed boxes. They're not that easy to drive because the engine lacks the expected low down torque. All the cheap ex-police versions have now been auctioned off. Getting old now.

What to watch out for: Re-trimmed ex-police cars. Repaired accident damage on ex-police Senators. Police cars are very well maintained, usually with new clutches and 'cats' at around the 80,000–90,000-mile mark. Check all electric windows and sunroof (if fitted). Make sure aircon blows cold (if fitted). Privately owned cars may have suffered skimped maintenance, leading to camshaft wear. Beware of Senators used for 'private hire' (i.e. taxis). Servotronic steering should have 'over centre' feel (more steering effect at extremes of lock). Check for evidence of having had a tow bar. Bounce each corner, especially the back two as springs may have sagged and left shocks in a state of shock. Try to feel the discs through the wheels and budget for replacement accordingly. Timing chain tensioners on privately-owned cars not serviced and driven to police standards tend to fail at around 90,000 miles and the timing chains themselves at 100,000–110,000 miles.

Sintra (1997–1999)

What's good: Vauxhall's large MPV. Previa-sized, with advantage of two sliding rear side doors. Powerful 201 bhp 3.0 litre petrol V6, 141 bhp 2.2 litre petrol four. 1998 introduced 2.2 litre direct Injected diesel the most sensible choice, but a bit short of low-down grunt.

What's bad: American built, so trim not up to European standards. Not especially different or particularly attractive. Blitzed in the market place by the Chrysler Voyager. Poor two-and-a-half star performer in NCAP crash tests (3 points front impact; 15 points side impact). Came rock bottom in 'R' reg JD Power Customer Satisfaction Survey and rock bottom again in 'S' and 'T' reg JD Power Customer Satisfaction Survey. NOT RECOMMENDED.

What to watch out for: Has it been an airport taxi? (Late introduction of diesel means this is unlikely.) Watch your fingers when fiddling with the seats (see recalls).

Recalls: 1998: Catches for removing rear seats may sever fingers. Covers to be fitted to seat release lever mechanism.

Tigra (1994–2000)

What's good: Cute, cleverly repackaged Corsa. 'Girly' car image. Decent pair of 1.4 litre and 1.6 litre 16v engines. Reasonably economical. Enough of a sports car for less demanding drivers. Three-year warranty from October 2000.

What's bad: All it really is underneath is a Corsa. 'Girly' car image (if you're not a girl). Glass hatchbacks leak. Can suffer from sticking valves if used for short runs on petrol lacking adequate detergent. Rear seats too small for adults. Came close to bottom in 'R' reg JD Power Customer Satisfaction Survey. Timing belts and tensioners must be changed every 35,000 miles.

What to watch out for: Must be serviced regularly (preferably every 6 months). Look for uneven tyre wear. Broken wheel trims or damaged alloys denote a kerb-prone driver, so expect suspension and steering damage. Feel front discs for grooves, 'shouldering' and wear.

Recalls: 1997 (1993–1997): possibility of GF50 plastic cambelt idler pulley breaking which can snap cambelt. (Vauxhall Recall Helpline: 01189 458500 or 01582 427200. February 2000: Safety recall to reinforce front seat rails and replace fatigued or worn front seatbelt buckles.

Vectra (1995 on)

What's good: Half a step forward from the Cavalier. Reasonable build quality, comfortable ride, cheap spares, smooth ride. Especially good on motorways. Smooth, economical Japanese (Isuzu) turbodiesel engine in early diesels. Important improvements for 1997 model-year include height-adjustable steering wheel, better seats and Trafficmaster. Standard aircon from Sept '97 in lieu of sunroof. Long-lasting chain-cam direct-injected 2.0 litre DI 16v engines in later diesels. Vastly improved SRi and GSi models from spring 1998 with steering and front suspension modifications developed jointly with SAAB. Comparatively good performance in NCAP crash tests. Major facelift in spring 1999 made it a better, but not better-looking, car. Most UK cars built at Luton. Bargain model 1.6 16v Expression with a/c launched 24/8/2000 at £10,995 OTR. 147 bhp 2.2 litre chain cam four replaces 2.0 in Vectra from 2001, plus uprated 125 bhp 2.2 DTi 16v diesel and uprated 125 bhp 1.8 petrol. 2.5 V6 grew to 2.6 litres with same power but more torque. Three-year warranty from October 2000. New prices announced on 7/11/2000 from £13,250 for 1.6i 16v Club to £20,945 for 2.6i V6 CDX estate, with 147bhp 2.2LS competing directly against 125bhp Mondeo 1.8LX at £14,595. Suspect 20,000-mile oil change regime introduced at the same time. 145mph 2.6 GSi with bigger brakes, priced at £18,595 from Spring 2001.

What's bad: Until the 1998 improvements, a whole step backwards from the Cavalier. Clutch replacement remains a five- to six-hour job involving engine removal instead of the simple half-hour job it was on the Cavalier. Earlier cars suffer stodgy handling with severe understeer, which is not entirely cured even in the latest 1999 model Vectras. Terrible driver's seat on early models with no steering wheel height adjustment (corrected from 1997 model-year). Styled door mirrors give limited view. DI 16v has undeserved reputation as an oil burner. What actually happens is that oil collects in the 16v head and takes a long time to drain back to the sump. Dip within an hour of stopping and you will get a falsely low reading leading you to overfill with fresh oil. 2001 model-year ex-fleet cars which have been subject to 20,000-mile oil changes will not be as good a second-hand buy as cars which have had their oil changed every 6 months or 7,000 miles at most. On 1.8 and 2.0 litre models a problem can develop with the idle adjustor control valve necessitating replacement and modifying by the fitting of an oil separator. Plug leads deteriorate and are ridiculously expensive to replace. Whole dash needs to come out to replace odometer bulb. Hand on heart, I cannot recommend these cars.

What to watch out for: Ex-Vauxhall Masterhire cars come with trustworthy print-out of full service history, including cambelt changes every 35,000–40,000 miles. Vectras from other fleets might have been clocked, so be sure to check mileages properly. Older SRis on Firestones may suffer premature tyre wear. Best tyres for older non-sporty Vectras are Pirelli P6000s. Best for new SRis and GSis are Yokohamas. Front suspension can wear prematurely. Make sure ABS light comes on, then goes out when it should. If engine misses, may have faulty ECU and cat may be hot spotted. Alternatively, may be camshaft sensor failure: a £150–£170 job, but a lot more if the misfire has spiked the cat. May suffer steering column rattle. May have been run on cheap petrol and suffering sticking valves as a result. Readers also report problems with air-conditioning systems and window regulators. If idle speed of 1.6, 1.8 or 2.0 petrol engine is 1200–2000 rpm the problem is the idle speed control valve. Needs cleaning with fuel system cleaner but if that doesn't work it needs replacing at £113 + VAT. Tends to happen at 60k–70k miles.

Recalls: 1996 (8/95–2/96 build: 40,000 cars): check front seatbelt mounting bolts and tighten if necessary. 1997 (1995–96 1.6 16vs only: 27,000 cars): Possibility of failure of plastic cambelt idler pulley GF50, which can snap cambelt. Changed as an 'in service mod' when cambelts are changed at 35,000–40,000-mile intervals. 1997 (Jan-May '96 build): Fuel pipe may come off at tank. 1998 (all 200,000 built before July 1998): handbrake cable subject to premature wear. Modified cable free replacement service. 1998 (automatics only): in service modification to autobox ECU mapping. 1999: possibility of failure of cambelt idler pulley on petrol engined 'P' to 'R' reg Vectras. (Vauxhall Recall Helpline: 01189 458500 or 01582 427200.) June 2000 recall of V6 models due to crankshaft fault.

Vectra II (from 2002)

What's good: Radical 'all new' Vectra, code name J3200, with more chunky styling and 12-year body warranty due in 2002. Speculated engine options to include 1.8–2.2 litre chain cam alloy block fours, 2.4 litre Fiat JTD, Isuzu 3.1 V6 diesel and a 3.2 litre petrol V6. Particularly different styling for estate models.

What's bad: Too soon to say.

What to watch out for: Too soon to say.

Viva (2003 on)

What's good: Y2k Corsa-based 6-seater mini MPV with 'flex 6' seats in 2-2-2 arrangement. All four in the back fold into the floor.
What's bad: Not due to arrive until 2003.
What to watch out for: Far too soon to say.

VX220 (2000 on)

What's good: New Elise-based Lotus-built mid-engined sports car powered by 147bhp chain-cam ECOTEC 2.2 litre engine. Three-year warranty. Comparatively low Group 16 insurance. No power steering. Massive kickback through the steering wheel. You feel and are aware of everything the car is doing. More forgiving than the Lotus Elise and with a more powerful engine. Wonderful, crude race-car feel to the gearchange. An absolute hoot to drive, and a better choice than the facelifted Elise. Recommended.
What's bad: Very limited production run, so beware of paying over the odds, otherwise too soon to say.
What to watch out for: Too soon to say.

Zafira (1999 on)

What's good: Seven seats in a body the same length as an Astra hatchback. Rearmost fold into floor. Centre seats fold and push forward, giving a completely flat load bay. 1.6 litre and 1.8 litre 16v engines on launch; long-lived chain-cam 50 mpg DI came later. Very impressive build quality with an immensely solid feel and no rattles at all even on a 10,000-miler. Galvanised body guaranteed not to rust for 12 years. Drives nicely as long as you don't push too hard. Did quite well for driver and front passenger protection in TUV/Auto Bild offset crash tests. Uprated 125 bhp 1.8 petrol from September 2000. Three-year warranty from October 2000. Option from February 2001 of 147bhp 2.2 litre engine from VX220 which puts out 150 lb ft torque and gives the Zafira a 9.0 second 0–60. £16,245 for 2.2 Comfort; £17,495 for 2.2 Elegance. Automatic option. 190bhp 138mph Zafira Turbo announced at Geneva Motor Show. Scored an impressive 12 out of 16 points for frontal impact and full marks for side impact in German ADAC crash tests. Prices cut from Spring 2001, from £12,995, but check out www.broadspeed.com for some amazing deals on imported Opel Zafiras. Recommended.

What's bad: Gearlever just a touch too far back, and flop-down driver's armrest gets in the way. Suffers usual roll understeer on tight bends and on long sweepers taken too fast. No DI automatic due to weight problems. Some DI 16v models use a lot of engine oil. 138mph 7-seater Turbo may be difficult to insure. Did badly in 2001 NCAP MPV Crash Tests achieving only a 65% mark due to 'unstable' body and pedal box intrusion (but see contradictory ADAC crash test results above). DI 16v has reputation as an oil burner. What often happens is that oil collects in the 16v head and takes a long time to drain back to the sump. Dip within an hour of stopping and you will get a falsely low reading leading you to overfill with fresh oil which then gets burned.

What to watch out for: Too soon to say.

Recalls: 25/4/2000: 268 RHD 2000 model-year DI models recalled for check on fuel line in engine compartment which could rupture in a front end crash. Fuel lines to be replaced with ones of improved specification.

VOLVO

240/260 (1978–1993)

What's good: Built like a tank. Pioneered a lot of secondary safety features. Estate cars will take fairly large items of furniture if you don't mind blotting out your rear view. Capable of Starship Enterprise mileages.

What's bad: A dinosaur to drive. Some drivers think that the safety features make them 'safe', but heaven help the rest of us. Hideous looks. Appalling steering. Horrible handling. Wallows like a hippo in a mudbath. Load platform is high and rear overhang too long which make an overloaded 240 estate doubly dangerous.

What to watch out for: Kerbed front suspension (all too easy with no steering 'feel' at all). Saggy springs. Soggy shock absorbers. Rust does eventually attack these cars.

340/360 (to 1991)

What's good: Strangley popular among Brits. Early cars were all 1.4 litre Renault pushrod powered CVT autos. Later cars mostly manual with option of 1.7 litre Renault overhead cam engine from the 11 and 19 or Volvo's own 2.0 litre in two stages of tune. Many mechanical parts cheaper from Renault dealers than from Volvo dealers. Easy to change clutches of manuals because box is a transaxle and the engine and clutch are at the front. 1.4 has a decent twin-choke Weber carb and, because it's an ancient pushrod unit, a timing chain rather than a belt.

What's bad: Getting very old hat now and being replaced by most owners with Rover 400s or Swindon built Honda Civics. Can rust badly. 1.7s susceptible to distributor problems due to ingress of damp. Cured by special Renault/Volvo plastic bag.

What to watch out for: These days '80s cars to be bought only as £50–£100 bargain bangers to use up the 'ticket and rent' (MOT and VED), but you might find a cherished 1990 or 1991 model which could be worth preserving.

440/460 (1989–1997)

What's good: Plenty of attention to secondary safety. Crude but effective Renault diesel. 1.8 CVT automatic probably the best combination. Many former 340/360 owners liked their 440s and 460s just as much and mourn the passing of this car.

What's bad: Booted 460 an aesthetic compromise. Poor Dutch build quality of early production from factory in Born. Ride quality not brilliant, especially of 460 with a laden boot. May rust prematurely.

What to watch out for: Rust, especially in body seams. Oil-consuming 2.0 litre versions may have required 'mod 2371', carried out 'in-service' by Volvo dealers. Look for at least four years' official Volvo dealer servicing to make sure 'in-service' improvements were carried out. PAS not always fitted, but can be retro-fitted for about £600. Late, facelifted 440s and 460s the best.

Recalls: 1994: 440/460 2.0 litre (440 VIN 419000–602090; 460 VIN 419001–602089; 480 VIN 586300–590058): airbag may deploy accidentally. 1996: 440/460 (1991–1995): fire risk from faulty electrical connections.

480 (1987–1995)

What's good: Coupe version of 440/460 on same floorpan from same factory in Born reached the market first. Owners seem to like them with a passion. The last of the line were the best with very comprehensive spec, including air conditioning. Galvanised, so rust not a problem.

What's bad: Poor Dutch build quality led one magazine to dub it 'the coupe from hell'. But the car was progressively improved and almost all problems will have been solved 'in service'. Seals above rear side windows start to leak.

What to watch out for: Oil-consuming 2.0 litre versions may have required 'mod 2371', carried out in-service by Volvo dealers. Look for at least four years' official Volvo dealer servicing to make sure 'in-service' improvements were carried out. Check aircon blows cold (if fitted). Make sure no water under the carpets.

Recalls: 1994: 480 2.0 litre (VIN 586300–590058): airbag may deploy accidentally. 1996: 480 (1991–1995): fire risk from faulty electrical connections.

740/760 (1984–1990)

What's good: Built like a tank. Better looking than antiquated 240 in a curious 1970s American way. 'Genteel', very middle-class, 'respectable' image (but see 'What's bad').

What's bad: Ugly looks. Horrible handling. Very mixed image: genteel and middle-class, but, on the other hand, sometimes driven by very aggressive drivers. High-intensity high-level rear brake light on automatics must be fitted with low-intensity bulb or will dazzle the driver behind in a traffic jam (technically an offence under the RVLR 1989). Duff old PSA V6 (don't buy a 760 with a 'V' engine). The market is for Volvo estates, and saloon versions are very hard to sell. Old estates that began with antiques dealers end up with painters and decorators. Saloon has very small boot due to fuel tank intrusion. All now at least 11 years old.

What to watch out for: Steering and front suspension damage from 'kerbing'. Baggy suspension on estates from carrying ludicrously heavy loads. Fluid drips near back wheels could be leaking rear shocks. Engine and exhaust system damage from 'short run syndrome'. With 3,000-mile oil changes engines will do 300,000 miles plus, but most of the other bits won't. Previous owners may have replaced alternators, water pumps and starter motors but may have offloaded the car because the gearbox or diff is about to give up. On autos check ATF: should be red, not grey-black. High risk of clocking or having run 100,000 miles 'unhooked'. Cats are £600, but can be ditched because all 740s are pre-August '92. Front crossmember can crack, leading to chafing of battery cable and possible underbonnet fire.

Recalls: 1995: VIN 37400–39877 and 16300–38007: battery short circuit leading to possible fire risk.

850/S70/V70 (1992–2000)

What's good: The first sporty, modern Volvo. Changed Volvo's image completely, especially when estates were entered for 1994 Touring Car Championship. T5s are seriously quick. T5 saloons or estates replaced Senators on many police fleets. Ex-police two-year-olds available for around £4,500 (West Oxfordshire Motor Auctions, tel: 01993 774413). TDIs not far off T5 performance and give 35 mpg economy. Rock-solid build quality. Good, predictable, safe handling. More fun to drive than any previous Volvo. Changed the image of the company. Original S70 earned Three-Star NCAP crash test rating. Late 1999 mods earned Four-Star NCAP rating. S70 was 10th from top in 'R' reg JD Power Customer Satisfaction Survey but, strangely, V70 was only 34th.

What's bad: Daytime running lights can dazzle other drivers. Estates are only commodious if you load them to the roof. Hard ride and sharper steering came as a shock to old-school, traditional Volvo owners. Front tyre wear of TDI, T5 and T5R can be severe: manuals 6,000–8,000 miles; autos 12,000–14,000 miles. TDI timing belt drives water pump and, if water pump fails, so does belt. Serious reliability problems reported by ADAC (the German breakdown organisation) in its 2001 report.

What to watch out for: Kerb-damaged front suspension and front driveshafts. Front tyre wear. Retrimmed, clocked ex-police cars.

Recalls: 1995: VIN 078000–120420 and 175000–220678: fault with jack which could allow the car to fall. 1997 (1996 and 1997 model-years): check for sticking throttle. 1997 (19,400 TDI models built 1995 and 1996): TSB to Volvo dealers worldwide warning of leak in rubber hose from brake vacuum pump to servo could cause loss of brake servo assistance. Many cars were never checked for this. 2000: S70 and V70 1997 and 1998 model-years: side airbags may inflate for no reason. Headlamps may fail. 2001: TDI brake vacuum pipe problem made subject of a safety recall in the UK affecting 1,300 UK imports.

940 (1992–1997)

What's good: Lots of 'passive' safety features. One of the first cars with a built-in rear child seat. 'Genteel', very middle-class, 'respectable' image (but see 'What's Bad').

What's bad: Boring to drive. Flabby handling. Very mixed image: middle-class, but, like 740, sometimes driven by very aggressive drivers. High-intensity high-level rear brake light on automatics must be fitted with low-intensity bulb or will dazzle the driver behind in a traffic jam (technically an offence under the RVLR 1989). The market is for Volvo estates and saloon versions are very hard to sell.

What to watch out for: Steering and front suspension damage from 'kerbing'. Engine and exhaust system damage from 'short run syndrome'. Front crossmember can crack, leading to chafing of battery cable and possible underbonnet fire.

960 and S90 (1994–2000)

What's good: The ultimate 'Q' car. Stonking 204 bhp twin-cam 3.0 litre straight six makes this old dowager really fly. Sports car drivers simply can't believe their eyes. Not over-dear once they've done a few miles. Became S90/V90 for 1997 model-year.

What's bad: Volvo image may or may not be what you want. Ridiculous damage-prone protruding alloy wheels fitted 1996 (though low-profile tyres hugely improved handling).

What to watch out for: Some 960 24vs have suffered from cracked cylinder heads. Check very carefully for water and oil leaks and for signs of water and oil mixing. Check for steering and front suspension damage from 'kerbing'. Look for engine and exhaust system damage from 'short run syndrome'.

C70 (June 2000 on)

What's good: Good-looking coupe launched June 1997 with 240 bhp 2.3 litre T5 engine. Convertible and lower powered variants followed. Smallest engine 163 bhp 2.0 litre light pressure turbo.

What's bad: Daytime running lights can dazzle other drivers. Expensive. 2.0 litre LPT not really powerful enough. Serious reliability problems reported by ADAC (the German breakdown organisation) in its 2001 report.

What to watch out for: Kerb-damaged front suspension and front driveshafts. Front tyre wear.

Recalls: 2000: C70 1997 and 1998 model-years: side airbags may inflate for no reason. Headlamps may fail.

S40/V40 (1996 on)

What's good: Top in class for secondary safety in NCAP crash tests. Turbo versions are very fast. 1.8 litre 125 bhp GDI versions economical. Always had three three-point rear belts. Plenty of places to store oddments inside. Significant, much needed suspension improvements from spring 2000. 5-speed 2.0 turbo automatic is a real flyer. LPG options from June 2001.

What's bad: Bright, quartz iodine daytime running lights can dazzle and infuriate other drivers, especially at 'traffic calming' points. If you switch to sidelights to avoid this you get no lights-on warning when you leave the car. Ride, steering, handling and roadholding not up to expectations created by good-looking body and clever marketing. Lots of early production quality problems at Dutch factory, later rectified. Not the car the image leads you to expect. Pre-spring 2000 cars had indifferent handling and overlight steering. Bottom front suspension ball joints tend to wear prematurely. Problems of valves carbing up on T4s and also on lesser injection models driven on petrol with inadequate detergent content.

What to watch out for: Minor accident damage buckles the inner-wing structure. Car may have been badly repaired to save cost. Check front suspension bottom ball joints.

Recalls: Volvo has an 'in service' cure for intermittent poor running, applied if owners complain. 2000: 2000 model-year cars: front brake callipers may crack and leak fluid.

S60 (2000 on)

What's good: Good looking new front-drive mid-range model from autumn 2000 sharing styling of S80. Impressively solid, with decent handling and roadholding. All engines turbocharged from 180bhp 2.0 litre through 200 bhp 2.4 litre to 250 bhp T5. Prices from £19,995 for 2.0T. But 200bhp 2.4T is the best all round model and even works well with the standard automatic transmission. An S60 T5 set a new record by averaging 135.1 mph for 24 hours around the Millbrook bowl on 14th October 2001, driven by the Channel 4 'Driven' team. LPG and CNG options from June 2001. Volvo's own lightweight 163bhp common rail diesel from Summer 2001 offers 251 lb ft (340Nm torque) from 1,750rpm, combined consumption of 47.1mpg, CO_2 of 158g/km and prices of £20,750 for the S or £22,950 for the SE.

What's bad: Not much legroom in the back, particularly for the centre passenger.

What to watch out for: Too soon to say.

S80 (1998 on)

What's good: Front-wheel-drive 960 replacement. Good-looking, dignified, rounded body. Same 204 bhp 2.9 litre straight six; 140 bhp 2.5 litre TDI, 144 bhp 10v and 170 bhp 20v 5-cylinder engines from S70. Flagship S80 T6 has 273 bhp 2.8 litre twin turbo and 4-speed Tiptronic auto. T6, 2.9 and TDI are all good to drive with lots of grip and nice steering. 2.4 litre is 'softer' and more vague, but still okay. All have excellent radios with knobs for volume, channel changing and function/waveband selecting. Integrated hands-free car phone system (you simply insert your SIM card into a slot in the dash). Lots of bottle, cup and can holders. Very good 29 point Four-Star 85% NCAP crash safety score. After top results in US-NCAP and Insurance Institute of Highway Safety has been nominated 'The World's Safest Car'. S and T reg cars came 16th in 2001 Top Gear/ JD Power Customer Satisfaction Survey. LPG and CNG and options from June 2001. Volvo's own lightweight 163bhp common rail diesel from Summer 2001 offers 251 lb ft (340Nm torque) from 1,750rpm, combined consumption of 46.3mpg, CO_2 of 161g/km and prices of £22,340 for the S or £24,240 for the SE.

What's bad: In the diesel, the 2.9 and the T6 you feel every ridge and draincover – not something traditional Volvo owners are used to. High first-year depreciation for a new car of 46%. Top auction bid on a 17,000-mile year-old £26,000 SE 140 was £14,150. Expensive to repair after a low-speed crash – could lead to rising insurance costs.

What to watch out for: Lots of build quality niggles. One report of an S80 having to go back to the supplying dealer 17 times.

Recalls: August 2000: 116,000 S80 models (5,500 in UK) recalled because front suspension ball joint can work loose or fail.

V70 Estate (2000 on)

What's good: A great-looking estate car. Confusingly, based on the new S80, but replaces the 'old' V70. Wide range of engines including petrol turbos up to 250 bhp, Audi's 140 bhp straight five TDI and a new TDI. Widely praised for convenience features. XC is a four-wheel-drive cross-country version on raised suspension with 200 bhp petrol turbo engine. 200 bhp V70T is a nice drive. Excellent medium wave radio reception and a really good integrated hands-free mobile phone system. All you have to do is slip in the SIM card from your pocket cellphone, key in your pin and you're in business. 250 bhp T5 model very popular with police forces, so look out for bargain high-milers in white from 2002. LPG and CNG options from June 2001. Volvo's own lightweight 163bhp common rail diesel from Summer 2001 offers 251 lb ft (340Nm torque) from 1,750rpm, combined consumption of 44.1mpg, CO_2 of 169g/km and prices of £23,960 for the S or £25,960 for the SE.

What's bad: See S80. Poor steering lock can make it difficult to swing into a parallel parking space. Bright, quartz iodine daytime running lights can dazzle and infuriate other drivers, especially at 'traffic calming' points. If you switch to sidelights to avoid this you get no 'lights on' warning when you leave the car. Serious reliability problems reported by ADAC (the German breakdown organisation) in its 2001 report.

What to watch out for: See S80, but depreciation will always be lower for an estate car.

Recalls: August 2000: V70 models recalled because front suspension ball joint can work loose or fail.

VW

A000 (from 2004)

What's good: New back to basics small car to replace Lupo and cost around £4,000. Will also be a Skoda version.

What's bad: Too soon to say.

What to watch out for: Too soon to say.

Beetle (1998 on)

What's good: Golf Mk IV-based and an instant cult car in the USA and Europe. Standard engine is updated 8-valve 2.0 litre from Golf III, which is pleasantly torquey and suits town work. TDI 90 engine available and 100 bhp 1.6 petrol. Four-Star performance in NCAP crash safety tests.

What's bad: No more than a Golf Mk IV in a beetle shell, which is nothing like as practical as that of the Golf. Very little room in the back seats. Small luggage capacity. UK prices started at £15,775 for LHD with a/c, alloys and a full spec including a bud vase. Strictly a fashion accessory 'fun' car. Difficult to park. Batch of 500 non air-conditioned 2.0 litre models dumped on UK market Summer 2001.

What to watch out for: Grey imports started arriving in the UK in 1998. Trade imports restricted to 50 by SVA, so don't buy a non-registered Beetle or you won't be able to register it. Look out for parking damage at the ends. Don't buy without a/c.

Recalls: May 1998, first 12,000 recalled in USA because wiring could become trapped by battery, overheat and catch fire.

Bora (1999 on)

What's good: Good-looking saloon version of Mk IV Golf with stiffer suspension and V5 engine available from launch. Superb set of gear ratios in V5 giving nice, linear acceleration. Big boot. Higher specs than Toledos with similar power outputs. Galvanised body has 12-year warranty. 2.8 V6 4-Motion introduced early 2001.

150bhp V5 increased to 170bhp with new cylinder head. Cut-price 2.0 litre S version, non PD TD 110 and 150bhp 1.8 petrol turbo versions launched to expand the range in May 2001. TDI PD 130 replaced TDI PD 115 in early Summer 2001 at price premium of £275. Very low CO_2 emissions of 146g/km. 5-speed Tiptronic available with PD 130.

What's bad: More expensive than SEAT Toledo and Skoda Octavia siblings. Stiffer suspension might be an advantage on open roads in the dry, but lacks 'bite' and can make the overlight steering feel a bit frightening when turning in on a wet bend. Bora estate not available in the UK.

What to watch out for: Too soon to say.

Caravelle (2002 on)

What's good: New Caravelle based on practical new T5 van.
What's bad: Too soon to say.
What to watch out for: Too soon to say.

Corrado (1989–1995)

What's good: The best application of VW's VR6, here in superb 2.9 litre 190 bhp form. Excellent front-drive handling. Best bought for sensible money LHD in Germany. VR6 recommended.

What's bad: They were part of the drug dealer's 'uniform', so don't be surprised if low lifes edge up to the car and flash money at you. Can suffer more than their fair share of niggly faults. Demand exceeds supply, so these cars are expensive. Cheaper used German imports will, of course, have been driven at 150 mph on the Autobahn and will suffer stone damage to the body and paint. Parts prices are high with very few cut-price alternatives.

What to watch out for: Pre-digital odometers easy to clock. VR6s fashionable among drug dealers 1996–97, often evidenced by 'flash' modifications. If aircon fitted, make sure it blows cold. Superchargers of G60s wear out (can be reconditioned by Jabbasport from £320, tel: 01733 571769). Check water level in expansion chamber and look for emulsified oil under oil cap as engines tend to blow head gasket at about 60,000 miles. Very hard to re-surface narrow angle V6 block and head and coolant in combustion chambers leads to burned out piston crowns.

Recalls: 1996 (4-cylinder cars 1988F–1989G): bypass valve to be inserted into heater pipe; heater matrix to be replaced if degraded. 1996 (VR6 1993–95): cooling fan motor may seize.

D1 (2002 on)

What's good: VW's rival to BMW 7 Series and Mercedes S-Class. Shown at 1999 Frankfurt Show with 'green' 5-litre V10 diesel engine producing 313 bhp, but also to be available with Audi V8 and a new V12 petrol engine. To be built alongside Passat at Dresden from early 2001.

What's bad: Not what you'd call a looker. Not endowed with MB status. Does the world need yet another big car?

What to watch out for: Too soon to say.

Golf Mk 1 GTI (1975–1983)

What's good: Giugiaro designed, the original and lightest GTI, first with Bosch injected 1.6 but the one to go for is the 112bhp 1.8 fitted for the last three months of production. A real flying machine and still exhilarating, only bettered by the Peugeot 205GTi which handled, braked and looked even better. Now a collector's piece with the best examples worth £12,000 +. Converting to 1.8 or 2.0 litre 140bhp 16v engine adds rather than reduces value. Some also running latest 1.8 20v four.

What's bad: Rust. All Mk 1 Golfs rust and though rustproofing was improved by the introduction of RHD GTIs they can still be bad. Complicated right to left brake linkage robs brakes of feel and makes action unpleasant. Notchy 'across the gate' gearshift. (The first LHD Golf GTis were 4-speeders). No power steering unless retro fitted using LHD Scirocco GTi 16v parts or a kit from TSR of Bridgwater. Old, but a classic.

What to watch out for: Accident damage, rust, and the general quality of the inevitable modifications.

Golf MK II (1983–1992)

What's good: Image. 16v the one to have. Unlikely to rust in the glued rather than welded seams. Long-life engines, exhausts, batteries, shock absorbers. Euro Car Parts (0541 506506) supplies cheap parts. The older they are, the less replacement parts they seem to need – almost as if the originals were designed to wear out.

What's bad: Rattles. Needs a cambelt change every four years or 40,000 miles and a tensioner change every 80,000 miles. Plastic door membranes go, leading to soggy carpets. Water pumps, clutches, front strut top bearings, etc. have only average life. Clutch cable self-adjusters go, leading to premature clutch wear. Hubs go in 8–12 years (80,000–120,000 miles). Underfloor fuel pump on fuel-injected cars springs a leak after 9–10 years. Water pumps last 5–10 years. Radiators last 5–10 years. Rear disc callipers on GTi can go and cost £300 each. Pneumatic central locking starts to fail on rear doors after 11 years. Steel wheels can fleck with rust after 6 years. Getting old.

What to watch out for: Make sure heater matrix bypass has been installed (major recall 1995–97). Check oil filler cap for black sludge (oil not changed regularly enough) or mayonnaise (cylinder head gasket problems). Check driveshafts by reversing car on full lock in both directions. Easily clocked so look for signs of more miles than the odo shows. Rear discs rust first, become pitted and fail MOT. Clutches last 70,000–80,000 miles on average, less with town driving. Driver's seat upholstery should last 12 years and 100,000 miles before starting to wear through. Bonnet slam panel should be matt black, not body colour. After 12 years, cam cover of all but 16v should have lost almost all its paint unless owned by someone particularly fastidious. Engines should look scruffy, not 'steam cleaned', because steam cleaning washes off rustproofing. Look for a square white sticker showing the vehicle identification number on the inside of the boot sill. No sticker is a sure sign that the car has been rear-ended. Went hydraulic tappets in 1986: cheaper to service. Rusts first on top of scuttle between screen and bonnet.

Recalls: 1995 (Golf 1.6 and 1.8 1983A to 1989G): bypass valve to be inserted into heater pipe; heater matrix to be replaced if degraded. 1996 (Golf 1.3 1983A to 1989G): bypass valve to be inserted into heater pipe; heater matrix to be replaced if degraded.

Golf MK III (1992–1997)

What's good: Strong image. High residuals. Best engines: TDI, 2.0 16v and 2.8 VR6 engines. Also 100 bhp 1.6 fitted to last Golf GLs. Euro Car Parts (0541 506506) supplies cheap parts.

What's bad: Strong image not completely justified. Three-door models flex quite badly (five-door models are better). Handling and roadholding not brilliant by '90s standards. 4-speed autobox can have problems. Since VW dealers charge £4,000 for a new one, this is best sorted by an independent specialist. Often no more than an oil control valve. Though car may remain solid and rust-free, many replacement parts will be needed over 10-year life. More than its fair share of recalls.

What to watch out for: Premature clutch wear due to faulty self-adjusting cable. Oil-burning TDI engines. Clocking. See Mk II. Also reports of wiring faults developing in electric window circuits, lights, rear window demister, so check all electrics carefully before buying (see recalls).

Recalls: 1995 (Golf GTi, 16v, VR6, Convertible: VIN 1HPW 439315–1HSW 418237 and 1ERK 000001–1ESK 025159): headlamp failures. Headlight switch on RHD models can overheat, leading to headlight failure. 28,000 cars affected. 1996: (1993–95 build): cooling fan motor may seize. 1997 (single headlight models). January 1997 recall for headlight failure. Headlight switch on RHD models can overheat, leading to headlight failure. 9,700 cars affected. 1997 (1994–97 build): September 1997 recall for headlamp modification for all cars. Total 150,000 cars affected. 1997 (1991–94 models with electric front windows: 16,000 cars): insulation on power cable may chafe and short-circuit. Needs protective shield in cable opening of door. 1997 (Aug '93–Jan '97 build): engine wiring loom may overheat.

Golf MK IV (1998 on)

What's good: Status and strong used values. Much better looking than Mk III. UK market cars have high equipment levels, including ABS. 3-year manufacturer and dealer warranty. More room, safer and better handling than Mk III. Super-efficient and quick 110 bhp TDI available for first time in UK. Later 115 bhp TDI with six-speed gearbox even quicker and 35 mph/1,000 rpm makes it even more economical at speed. 100 bhp 1.6 petrol good 'cooking' engine. 150 bhp VR5, later uprated to 170bhp, makes a wonderful noise, has a good set of gear ratios and is good basic engine. 204 BHP V6 six-speed 4 motion is the spiritual successor to the Mk III VR6, and a much better car with grippy four-wheel-drive chassis. Joint top of the class for secondary safety in NCAP crash testing after side airbags fitted from August 1998. Excellent car-like estate not the biggest in its class but feels very classy. The qualities of these cars grow on you. Galvanised body has 12-year warranty. Mk V Golf cabrio due in 2002 with folding steel top. V5 uprated in late 2000 with new 20-valve cylinder head, raising power to 170bhp and torque to 166lb ft. (NB: Like the VR6, the V5 is a narrow-angle V5 with a single cylinder head for both banks.) More price competitive in UK after December 2000 price cuts and newfound willingness of dealers to discount. PD 130 TDI replaced PD 115 TDI in early Summer 2001, but in short supply and at £275 premium. Very low CO_2 emissions of 146g/km. 5-speed Tiptronic available with PD 130.

What's bad: Steering very light. Modification to 'B' pillar delayed production. Cable gearchange on all but 1.6 and 1.4. The 1.8 20v and 1.8 20v Turbo work well but don't involve the driver. 1.8 20v replaced by old 115 bhp 2.0 litre 8 valver in 1999. Not everyone likes the relatively hard seats. The back of the car gets very dirty. Alarm sensitivity on early production corrected by unnecessary pillar-mounted sensors (all drivers had to do was shut off the air supply to inside the car). Front door lock barrels of 1998 Golf Mk IVs can be prised out with a screwdriver and the doors opened without activating the microwave alarm. (Golfs from 1999 on have ultrasonic alarms which can only be deactivated by the remote fob.) Heavy, so slower than Mk III when fitted with the same engines. Some TD 110s had a problem of stalling while coasting to a standstill from about 15 mph in neutral. The cure is to replace the ECU, but if the car is a personal import out of its 12-month pan-Euro warranty, the owner will have to pay. Glass headlamp lenses of GTI and Highline models break easily and cost £260 to replace. Best protected by £25 headlamp protectors from VW dealers. Quite a few build quality niggles emerging, such as squeaking seats, rattling window mechanisms inside doors which can fail entirely, clutch bearing failure, trim panel for sunroof falling off rails, pipe to rear washer coming off and staining ceiling trim. Also reports of complete failure of ancilliary electrics and problems with six-speed gearbox on TDI 115. Faulty power steering switch on 1.6 can cause hunting of engine and erratic idle. New Golf Mk V including 7-seater mini MPV due in 2002.

What to watch out for: RHD personal imports not to full UK spec – especially estate cars. Some TDI 110s suffered a low-speed running problem which could only be cured by a modified flywheel and inlet manifold and in some cases a re-chipped ECU. See faults list above.

Recalls: Announced *Daily Telegraph* 1/10/98: 9,500 Mk 1V Golfs from SE spec upwards fitted with volumetric alarms recalled to fit less sensitive volumetric sensors. (Not actually necessary because problem can be solved by using ventilation control to shut off outside air.) 1999: 70 early production 115 PDs recalled to replace pistons because they were not properly coated with a Teflon-like material in production.

Golf Mk V 7-seat MPV

What's good: VAG's Zafira competitor due in 2002, before Golf Mk V hatchback, to be priced from a similar £12,995 in UK. Engine line-up to start with a 1.6 and include a 130bhp 2.0 litre, and TDI PD engines of 100bhp, 115bhp and 150bhp. 170bhp 2.3 V5 may follow. Will be 4,380mm long, 1,8770mm wide. Scoop pictures in *Autocar* issue 11/4/2001.

What's bad: Too soon to say.

What to watch out for: Too soon to say.

Jetta (1983–1992)

What's good: Underrated 'Golf with a rucksack'. Stiffer body so handles better than a Golf with fewer rattles. 16v seriously quick, does 60 in 2nd gear, and gets there in 7 seconds. 'Long life' bodies, exhausts, batteries, shock absorbers. Euro Car Parts (0541 506506) supplies cheap parts.

What's bad: Dowdy image. See under Golf Mk II.

What to watch out for: See Golf Mk II.

Recalls: 1995 (1.6 and 1.8 1983A to 1989G): bypass valve to be inserted into heater pipe; heater matrix to be replaced if degraded. 1996 (1.3 1983A to 1989G): bypass valve to be inserted into heater pipe; heater matrix to be replaced if degraded.

Kombi Bully (2002 on)

What's good: Retro styling like original VW Type 2 Microbus, but with 225 bhp 3.2 litre VR6 and front-wheel/four-wheel-drive.

What's bad: Apparently to be bigger than T4 Caravelle.

What to watch out for: Too soon to say.

Lupo (1999 on)

What's good: High build quality. Same car as SEAT Arosa, built at Wolfsburg, with cute front-end styling, much nicer interior, twin airbags, height-adjustable driver's seat and steering wheel as standard. Formed basis of '3-litre car' – capable of 100kms on three litres of petrol, equal to 94 mpg. 1.4s have new twin-cam 16v engine. 1.7SDI charming, economical and not too slow – a far better bet than the 1.0 litre petrol version. 100 bhp 1.4 16v Sport from September '99. 75 bhp 1.4 direct injected diesel option. Lupo FSi with direct injected petrol engine giving 105 bhp and 56 mpg shown at 1999 Frankfurt Show. Lupo did well in German TUV/Auto Bild front offset crash test. Four-Star NCAP crash safety rating. Six speed gearbox and alloy body panels for 125bhp Lupo GTi at no extra cost from mid-2001. Now does 127mph, 0–60 in 8 seconds.

What's bad: Prices higher than SEAT Arosa. Power steering a £450 option on 1.0 litre base model. 1.0 litre horribly, painfully slow.

What to watch out for: Too soon to say.

Microbus Concept

What's good: VW concept vehicle is 4,722mm long, 1,904mm high and 1,909mm wide. (Note that its height disqualifies it for the best discounted fares on the Eurotunnel Shuttle.) Power comes from VAG's 236bhp 3.2 litre V6, as found under the bonnet of top versions of the latest Audi A4. Torque is 236lb ft and the gearbox is a five-speed Tiptronic. Interior design features include a dash mounted gearshift lever, seven TV/video plasma screens and three rows of seats the centre pair of which swivel. No decision has yet been taken as to whether the vehicle will go into production. More at www.volkswagen.co.uk.

What's bad: Too soon to say.

What to watch out for: Too soon to say.

Old Passat (1988–1997)

What's good: Estates have excellent rear legroom, are comfortable and handle well. Was a 174 bhp VR6, briefly, 1993–95. TDI 90 best compromise engine. Estates hold value well. Saloons worth £2,000 less. Aircon available in lieu of sunroof.

What's bad: Good, well-specified estates hard to find and sell for strong money. All diesel models may have been cabbed. Saloons have dowdy image.

What to watch out for: As Golf/Jetta/Vento. Make sure aircon blows cold. Make sure not cabbed. A lot began their lives on rental fleets.

Recalls: 1995 (VIN3ARE 0000001–3ASE 142536): headlamp failures. 1996 (4-cylinder Passats 1988F–1989G): bypass valve to be inserted into heater pipe; heater matrix to be replaced if degraded. 1996 (1993–95 build): Cooling fan motor may seize. VW Passat (Dec '95–Mar '98): may be airbag activator fault.

Passat (1997–2000)

What's good: The best quality car in its class; really a class above. Much more status than a Mondeo or Vectra. TDI 90 and 110 engines better than 1.8 20v, but 20v turbo will do 140 mph – and brake from 140 mph safely. Very low levels of wind and road noise.

Excellent economy from TDI 90 and 110 – most owners will better 50 mpg. Comparatively good performance in NCAP crash tests. Improved 115 bhp, 210 lb ft TDi for 2000 model-year. High spec, reasonably priced SEL trim versions lauched summer 2000 from £15,570 OTR for 1.8 20v to £17,110 OTR for TDI 115 PD. Galvanised body has 11-year warranty. Trim lasts well. Properly looked after, these cars can stay looking new for years.

What's bad: Hasn't lived up to its quality promise. Since 1997, Ford Mondeos have been far more reliable. Yet perceived quality still leads to high residuals making Passats expensive used buys until they hit high mileages. Steering a bit too light, especially on motorways. Imprecise gearshift. Alarming number of build-quality faults and problems, such as leaks from screen area, under-dash rattles, seatbelts failing to free-reel, rear shock absorbers failing, whining 4-speed automatics when mated to 1.8 litre 20v engine (1.6 auto, diesel auto and 5-speed Tiptronic OK). Front door lock barrels of 1997–1998 Passats can be prised out with a screwdriver and the doors opened without activating the microwave alarm. (Passats from 1999 on have ultrasonic alarms which can only be deactivated by the remote fob.) Cats fail on TDIs built before August 1998. Came lower than Mondeo and Freelander in 'R' reg JD Power Customer Satisfaction Survey. Heavy salted road spray may make front brakes feel spongey. In Germany, deflectors are available FOC to cure this (*Auto Bild* magazine 24/11/2000). Poor AM radio reception. Reports of corroded rear brake seals and failing front suspension wishbones at around four years old. Wishbone replacement is a £500–£700 job.

What to watch out for: Needs to be the right colour (not white, solid green or solid blue). Check very carefully for signs of water leaks (feel footwell carpets for damp). May be a structural leak, or may be because the a/c condenser drain pipe is blocked leading to water being dumped into the footwell. Listen for rattles. Check front tyre wear. Blue exhaust smoke from diesel indicates faulty turbo oil seals. Plastic water pump impellers on early 1.8 20v engines fail (newer water pumps have metal impellers). If dash warning light stays on permanently, it's usually because a wrong button has been pressed on the VAG 1552 electronic interrogator when the car was in for a service.

Recalls: 1998: 11,450 cars built May–Nov 1997 recalled due to potential fault affecting front seatbelts. Involves replacing complete belt units. 1998: Passat Synchro (Dec '97–Apr '98 build): throttle and brake hose problems; 11,450 Passats built between May and Nov 1997 recalled due to potential fault affecting front seatbelts. Involves replacing complete belt units. 2000: Mar–Aug '98-built Passats recalled because steering track rod ends could work loose. £500 factory accessory removable towbar has been recalled twice. March 2001: Worldwide recall of 560,000 1999 model-year A4s, A6s, A8s and VW Passats to replace steering ball joints (track rod ends). Announced *Auto Bild* 11/3/2001.

Passat (2001 on)

What's good: New Passat looks more classy and hides very comprehensive improvements under the skin. Now with a 12-year body warranty. Steering gives slightly better road feel. Sloppy gearchange improved. New engine range begins with 2.0 litre 8-valve 115bhp shared with Golf Mk IV GTi, but at a low price of £14,495 which includes ABS, climate control, Thatcham 1 alarm immobiliser and much more. TDI 130 S is an excellent car for company drivers because it combines a low CO_2 output of 154 g/km with a low on the road price of £16,310. Has no less than 228 lb ft torque and goes like a steam train. Range also includes a 100bhp TDI PD, a 150bhp 1.8 petrol turbo, a 150bhp V6 TDI, a 170bhp V5 and a 193bhp V6 4Motion four wheel drive. 6-speed manual gearbox on TDI PD 130 Sport and TDI V6 Sport. Others have 5-speed manual, 5-speed Tiptronic auto or 4-speed auto. Will be a 280bhp W8 4Motion capable of 0–60 in 6 seconds and 150mph top speed for less than £30,000 by the end of 2001. TDI PD 130 voted *Diesel Car* magazine Car of the Year. Full road test and comprehensive range and spec description in the road tests at www.honestjohn.co.uk. 150bhp petrol turbo S versions of saloon and estate introduced May 2001 with 5-speed Tiptronic auto option. Acheved 4-star Euro NCAP crash safety score.

What's bad: Gearchange still not as good as cars like the Mondeo and a lot worse than the very precise cable shifter in Chrysler's PT Cruiser.

What to watch out for: Too soon to say.

Old Polo (1981–1994)

What's good: Reasonable build quality whether put together in Germany or Spain. Steel 'factory' sunroof a desirable extra, adds £200 to price. Euro Car Parts (0541 506506) supplies cheap parts.

What's bad: Weak front suspension. Not very roomy. Tiny boot. Surprisingly heavy steering. No brake servo prior to 1991 facelift. If water pump seizes, will usually snap cambelt. Catalysed and just 45 bhp from 1.0 litre version from 1991 model-year.

What to watch out for: Piston-slapping tiny mileage shopping cars, serviced 'every two years whether they needed it or not'. (They need an oil change every six months.) Pre-hydraulic cam cars (pre-'86) more expensive to service. Need cambelt changes every 36,000–40,000 miles or every 4 years, preferably tensioner too. Sump pan can rust, especially if engine has been 'steam cleaned'. A dirty engine with peeling paint on the cam cover is a good sign. Check spec carefully. Some 1.3 CLs were 4-speed, not 5-speed. Will eventually rust, so check round the edges. Normal for cam covers to lose their paint. Engines should look scruffy, not 'steam cleaned', because steam cleaning washes off rustproofing.

Polo (1994–2000)

What's good: Strong UK image. A bottle green two-door Polo with a sunroof has been described as 'the most middle-class car you can buy'. (Bottle green is the 'right' colour and two rather than four side doors says 'it's a second car'.) All have good, fairly upright driving position, second only to the Fiat Punto. Big car ride (much better than Punto). 3-year dealer warranty, necessitating VW franchise servicing. Comparatively good performance in NCAP crash tests. Cordoba Vario-based estate launched spring '98. Facelifted inside and out for 2000. Very well thought of by independent VW dealers and service agents who regard them as 100% reliable.

What's bad: Gearchange quality varies. Despite VW's best efforts, Spanish build quality in general can vary. PAS not available even as an option on slow 1.0 versions. 1.4 automatic not really powerful enough. Surprisingly old-fashioned dashboard. Sky high used prices. 1.9 diesel not very economical when pushed. Ugly Cordoba-based saloon versions not as comfortable as hatchbacks, but have big, deep boots. 1.9SDi diesel frugal but noisy. Dashboard shows its age compared to much more cheerful Lupo. Did quite badly in 'R' reg JD Power Customer Satisfaction Survey. Was 115th in 'S' and 'T' reg survey, behind the Rover 600 and way behind the Ford Fiesta. Has appetite for front tyres, front brake discs and front pads. Reports of rusting of the doors of 1994–1999 Polos and also rust spots developing on the door frames.

What to watch out for: Paying too much for a two- or three-year-old. Particularly paying too much for a used Polo saloon, which is really nothing more than a SEAT Cordoba. Very variable gearshift quality. Faulty self-adjusting clutch cables may cause premature clutch failure. Electric windows can play up. Check front discs and pads as tend to need replacing every 30,000 miles. If buying a 1994–1999 Polo, check the doors and door frames carefully for rust, especially under the window rubber. Also look for rust spots on the front valence where they could have been caused by stone chips.

Recalls: 1996 (to June 1996 build): faults in steel wheels may lead to loss of tyre pressure.

Polo (2000–2002)

What's good: See above. Still the most status you can buy in a small ordinary hatchback, but silver now the best colour. Apart from attractive new front and interior, the car looks the same as the previous Polo but is actually 75% new with stiffer shell, tighter shut lines, higher specs (PAS and ABS on all models) and a huge range of engines from 1.0 litre 50 bhp to 1.6 litre 16v with 125 bhp. The new three-cylinder pump injector 1.4 TDI is amazing, offering 75 bhp and 144 lb ft torque which makes it quick off the mark as well as very economical, from £11,670 in UK. Four-Star rating in Euro NCAP crash tests. Have seen a year old Polo sell at public auction for 86% of its new list price.

What's bad: Expensive, ranging in price at launch from £8,290 to £14,460. Gearchange quality still varies. GTi feels top heavy on corners and does not inspire confidence. Spanish rather than German build quality. To be replaced by new model on Fabia floorpan in 2002.

What to watch out for: Too soon to say.

Polo (2002 on)

What's good: New Polo on same floorpan as Skoda Fabia to arrive 2002, benefiting from customer development of the Fabia. Will be about 3,900mm long and expected to earn a four star NCAP crash safety rating. Will be new three cylinder 1.2 litre petrol engines with 55bhp and 65bhp, three cylinder 1.4 litre TDI with 75bhp, a 1.4 direct injected petrol engine and a 1.4 litre 85bhp 'fuel stratified injection' petrol engine as well as existing 1.9 litre 64bhp SDi diesel and 100bhp TDIPD. With a sharpened Fabia chassis should handle much better than current Polo.

What's bad: Too soon to say.

What to watch out for: Too soon to say.

Polo Caddy Kombi (1998 on)

What's good: Kombi version of Polo/Ibiza/Cordoba-based Caddy van. 75 bhp 1.6i petrol and 60 bhp 1.9 SDI. Very spacious in the back and surprisingly good fun to drive. 90 bhp TDI on the way, and already in Caddy van.

What's bad: Doesn't ride as well as Citroën Berlingo Multispace. Not as practical as Renault Kangoo Combi.

What to watch out for: Second-hand examples which have led an extremely hard double life as weekday van and weekend transport for the family and its dogs.

Scirocco Mk II 1983–1991

What's good: Like the Mk 1 Scirocco, still based on the original Mk 1 Golf floorpan. Decent handling. Quite spacious inside. Variety of engines from standard 75bhp 1.6 to hot 136bhp 1.8 litre 16v, the first VAG car to get the new 16v engine. This is the one to have, but it's a rare car and only ever had power steering in LHD format. Other engines included a 90bhp carburettor 1.8 and the fuel-injected 112bhp 1.8 from the Golf GTi.

What's bad: Usual Mk1 Golf problems such as a curious across the gate gearchange and spongey brakes due to a complicated linkage from the brake pedal on the right hand side of the car to the master cylinder on the left hand side (obviously not a problem with LHDs). They also rust, but nothing like as badly as Mk 1 Golfs.

What to watch out for: Wear their miles well so are often clocked. But the newest is going to be at least ten years old and less than £750 so the main thing to look for is rust and anything likely to lead to an expensive repair, such as a clutch replacement.

Recalls: Same general cooling system recalls as other VWs: first to fit pressure rlease valve to the tubing, then to replace the heater matrix if it sprung a leak.

Sharan (1995 on)

What's good: VW-badged Galaxy carries the most prestige and holds its value best. Got the 110 bhp TDI engine before Galaxy or Alhambra. Also first to offer 110 bhp TDI with 4-speed autobox. 1.8 20v from spring '98. Falling used values led to price cuts and VW dealers offering 'S' reg TDI 110 'S' specs with aircon for £16,450 at 4–6 months old. Three-Star performer in NCAP crash tests (6 points front impact; 15 points side impact). Y2k revamp includes six-speed TDI 115PD and six-speed 204 bhp MPV-6 (also with 5-speed Tiptronic and/or four wheel drive.

What's bad: VW 2.0 litre 8v petrol engines not as good as Ford's 2.0 and 2.3 litre twin-cams. Began to suffer from over-supply in 1998. Below average 'customer satisfaction'. On early models water can enter car via ventilation, soak the underfloor and get into the ECU which controls the electric windows and alarm system. On later models, this ECU has been moved. Aircon vulnerable to front-end shunts. Also shifted in later models. TDIs can blow turbos and catalytic converters. Have also been manual gearbox problems with TDIs. Came second bottom in 'P' reg JD Power Customer Satisfaction Survey, but by 'R' reg had improved. S and T platers 18th from bottom in 2001 Top Gear/JD Power Customer Satisfaction Survey.

What to watch out for: RHD imports not to UK spec, missing important items such as air conditioning, rear seat heating, etc.

Recalls: 1997: (built Jan '96–Apr '97): problems with optional child seats. 1997 (built Dec '95–July '96): brake pads may overheat. 1998:

(Aug '96–Feb '98 build): loss of power due to wiring loom failure. 13/1/2000: 80,000 Galaxys, Alhambras and Sharans VIN TV000001– YV509825 recalled to check for contamination of brake fluid through master cylinder vent. Brake master cylinders of older cars to be replaced.

T4 Caravelle (to 2002)

What's good: Acres of space for 8 people and their luggage even in SWB versions. 2.5TDI engine by far the best engine, giving 80–90 mph cruising and 35 mpg. Good to drive. Multivan comes with curtains, and seats fold flat into bed.

What's bad: Earlier non-TDI models were awful to drive. Only available from VW commercial vehicle dealers. VR6 is a heavy drinker. TDI's timing belt drives water pump and, if water pump fails, so does belt. Injection distribution pump timing difficult and expensive to re-set when renewing timing belt.

What to watch out for: Van-based, so paint quality of early models was not up to car standards. Much improved after 1996 facelift. Metallics are best.

Vento (1992–1996)

What's good: Like the Jetta, underrated and consequently cheap. Euro Car Parts (0541 506506) supplies cheap parts. TDI is roomy, sensible, economical and quite quick. VR6 (if you can find one) is a performance bargain. More rigid body shell and better protection from rear end impacts than Golf Mk III.

What's bad: UK market treated them just like the Jetta. Otherwise see Golf Mk III. VR6 needs suspension mods to drive well.

What to watch out for: See Golf Mk III.

Recalls: See Recalls for Golf Mk III.

Index

The Good Garage Guide, the Car Clubs Directory, the list of UK Car Auction Sites and the Car by Car Breakdown are compiled alphabetically for easy reference. For these sections, only manufacturers (Car Clubs) and specialists (Good Garage Guide) are indexed here.

Index